National Survey of State Laws

National Survey of State Laws

3rd EDITION

Richard A. Leiter, Editor

GALE GROUP

Detroit
San Francisco
London
Boston
Woodbridge, CT

Richard A. Leiter, *Editor*

The Gale Group Staff

Amy R. Suchowski, *Editor*
Keith Jones, *Managing Editor*

Wendy Blurton, *Production Assistant*
Evi Seoud, *Assistant Production Manager*
Mary Beth Trimper, *Production Director*

Eastword Publications Development, Inc., *Typesetters*

Library of Congress Catalog Card Number KF386.N38 1997

ISBN 0-7876-0068-7

Printed in the United States of America

To R. M. M. (aka Roy Martin Mevsky) my mentor, colleague, and friend.

CONTENTS

TOPIC CROSS REFERENCE TABLE

Additional References:	Found In:	Additional References:	Found In:
Age Limits	Abortion, Adoption, Annulment and Prohibited Marriage, Capital Punishment, Compulsory Education, Legal Ages, Marriage Age Requirements, Right to Die, Wills	Doctors	Abortion, Child Abuse, Medical Records, Right to Die
		Education, Schools	Education Laws, Part III., Gun Control, Illegal Drugs, State Lotteries
AIDS	Medical Records, Prohibited Consensual Sex Oriented Activity	Employee	Legal Holidays, Minimum Wage, Right to Work, Whistleblower
Alcohol	Legal Ages, Drunk Driving	Employer	Minimum Wage, Right to Work, Whistleblower
Apprentice	Right to Work, Minimum Wage	Employment	Civil Rights, Legal Holidays, Minimum Wage, Right to Work, Whistleblower
Assisted Suicide	Right to Die		
Attorney's Fees	Antitrust, Civil Rights, Deceptive Trade Practices	False Advertising	Deceptive Trade Practices
Automobiles	Deceptive Trade Practices, Lemon Laws, Interest Rates, Drunk Driving	Firearms	Gun Control, Capital Punishment, Stalking
Child Support	State Lotteries	Homosexuality	Adoption, Annulment and Prohibited Marriages, Capital Punishment, Prohibited Consensual Sex Oriented Activity
Collection of Debts	Civil Statutes of Limitations, State Lotteries		
Consent	Abortion, Adoption, Legal Ages, Marriage Age Requirements, Medical Records, Right to Die: Durable Power of Attorney, Euthanasia, Living Wills	Immunity	Child Abuse, Right to Die, Whistleblower
		Mandatory Reporting	Child Abuse, Medical Records
		Medical Treatment	Abortion, Legal Ages, Right to Die
Consumer	Consumer Taxes, Deceptive Trade Practices, Interest Rates, Lemon Laws	Parental Consent	Abortion, Marriage Age Requirements
Contracts	Civil Statutes of Limitations, Legal Ages	Physician	Abortion, Child Abuse, Medical Records, Right to Die
Discrimination	Adoption, Annulment and Prohibited Marriage, Civil Rights, Leases & Rental Agreements,	Pregnancy	Abortion, Capital Punishment, Right to Die
		Privilege	Child Abuse, Medical Records

Additional References:	Found In:	Additional References:	Found In:
Records	Medical Records, Privacy of School Records	Spousal Consent	Abortion, Adoption
Residency	Abortion, Adoption, Attorneys, Grounds for Divorce, Personal Income Tax	Statute of Limitations	Adoption, Antitrust, Civil Rights, Civil Statutes of Limitations, Criminal Statute of Limitations
Schools	Compulsory Education, Corporal Punishment in Public Schools, Illegal Drugs, Prayer in Public Schools, Privacy of School Records	Uniform Acts	Adoption, Child Custody, Deceptive Trade Practices, Leases & Rental Agreements, Legal Ages, Marital Property, Negligence, Right to Die, Wills
Sexual Abuse	Capital Punishment, Child Abuse, Protective Orders, Stalking	Venereal Disease	Legal Ages, Medical Records, Prohibited Consensual Sexual Activity
Sexually Transmitted Diseases	Legal Ages, Medical Records, Prohibited Consensual Sexual Activity	Waiting Period	Abortion, Adoption, Gun Control
Sodomy	Criminal Statute of Limitations, Grounds for Divorce, Prohibited Consensual Sex Oriented Activity	Weapons	Capital Punishment, Corporal Punishment in Public Schools, Gun Control, Illegal Drugs
		Witnesses	Capital Punishment, Wills

PREFACE

National Survey of State Laws provides an overall view of some of the most-asked about and controversial legal topics in the United States. Presented in chart format, this reference allows users to make basic state-by-state comparisons of current state laws. The subjects featured fall into eight general legal categories:

    Business and Consumer Laws
    Criminal Laws
    Education Laws
    Employment Laws
    Family Laws
    General Civil Laws
    Real Estate Laws
    Tax Laws

The types of topics covered range from Abortion to the Right to Die, Gun Control to Prayer in Public Schools, Personal Income Tax to Right to Work, and Lemon Laws to Leases and Rental Agreements.

The information presented is culled from laws on the books as of March 1, 1999.

Arrangement

National Survey of State Laws is divided by legal category into eight sections. Within each section each topic is arranged alphabetically and is presented in its own subsection, which begins with a general overview followed by a table that briefly summarizes each state's and the District of Columbia's statutes on particular aspects of law.

The salient points of each law appear at the top of each column. Beneath, brief statements provide the core points of the state statute. References to each state's statute or code section covering that law are also presented, enabling users who are interested in reading the original text to find it in the state's code of law. The appendix comprises a list of **Statutory Compilations Used in This Book** and provides the abbreviations and full names of each state code.

Selection of Topics

Aside from being controversial and sought-after, the topics presented in *National Survey of State Laws* must meet another criterion: state statutes covering that topic must be available. In many cases, there are no statues; here the common law, or the law of the courts, which is determined by many cases taken together, forms the single rule of law pertaining to that topic.

There are also a few instances where state statutes have been rendered ineffectual by the states' adopting uniform acts or by U.S. Supreme Court decisions. Therefore, comparisons for these types of laws are not included here. However, because two situations in which the Supreme Court has seized jurisdiction over state laws—Prayer in Public School and Abortion—remain so controversial, we've included them in *National Survey of State Laws* for state-by-state comparison.

Topic Cross Reference Table

This edition includes a Topic Cross Reference Table included immediately behind the Table of Contents. This table is designed to help patrons that are looking for information that crosses the content of more than one chapter. For example, if you are interested in the laws dealing with legal age requirements for various activities, you can now find all chapters with information dealing with age limits by turning to the Cross Reference Table first. This will direct you to eight chapters with information regarding age limits in addition to the one titled, "Legal Ages." References have been made only to the *chapters* that contain relevant information, not to page numbers where specific references occur.

Acknowledgments

This book could not have been done without the hard work and support of many people. Thank you to my "team" of research assistants: Demi Antionette Mezingo, Jared Ellison, Clifford Lockett, Abigail Williams, and Tiffany Countryman. Together they made the difficult task of checking every citation in the book look easy. In adition, special thanks go out to Jamie Price for her initial compilation of the new chapter on gambling and again, to Tiffany for updating it and finishing it off. A special note of thanks must be made to Lisa Bruce, my secretary/administrative assistant, who contributed much to the project.

I must also acknowledge Cheryl Rae Nyberg, whose book, *Subject Compilation of State Laws,* was of invaluable assistance to us in the compilation of each edition of this book. Thank you also for your thoughtful suggestions and for your encouragement.

Thank you also to my editor at Gale, Amy Suchowski, for her quiet confidence, patience, and good humor throughout the project. Thanks also must be extended to Tim Gall and staff at Eastword for their excellent job typesetting the corrections and all the new text.

Finally, thanks all around to my family: my wonderful wife Wendy (I love you), my fantastic kids Maddie, Anne, and Becky and the Leiter Boys Club, Rascal, Sammy, and Ed. I also wish to acknowledge our Creator and Only Hope without whom none of this would have even mattered. He not only gave us life, but gave it to us abundantly.

Editor's Note

Always consult an attorney before making decisions of any legal consequence. Never use a reference such as this, which is not meant to be an exposition of the law but a source for comparisons, as a definitive statement of the law.

Comments and suggestions regarding future editions of *National Survey of State Laws* are welcome and should be addressed to:

Editor, *National Survey of State Laws*
The Gale Group
27500 Drake Road
Farmington Hills, MI 48331-3535
Phone: 248-699-GALE
Toll-free: 1-800-877-GALE

I. BUSINESS AND CONSUMER LAWS

1. ANTITRUST

Antitrust violations are "crimes" committed by business entities that injure both competing businesses and the consumer by artificially inflating or fixing prices.

Antitrust laws came into national prominence in the late nineteenth century with the rise of the giant industrial monopolies. Two types of monopolies, horizontal and vertical, were felt to be particularly harmful to competition. In a horizontal monopoly, a single entity owns all or an unreasonable percentage of the firms competing in the same business, such as all the telephone or oil companies. In a vertical monopoly, a single entity owns all or an unreasonable percentage of all levels of business within a single industry, for example, all the forests, logging firms, mills, printing plants, and newspapers.

Through the exercise of its power to regulate interstate commerce, Congress has enacted the most sweeping of antitrust regulations in the Sherman Antitrust Act. Because of the great size of the businesses engaged in antitrust or anti-competitive practices as well, the federal government has taken the lead in enforcing against these types of unfair business practices.

Most antitrust statutes are enforced in two ways: the state attorney general can sue on behalf of the state in order to correct the unfair practice, either by obtaining an injunction prohibiting the offensive practice or by ordering fines or other redress to be paid or otherwise addressed to the consumers; the other way is by a private right of action, whereby consumers themselves or competing businesses sue to recover for damages or injuries suffered as a result of the offending behavior.

Table 1: Antitrust

State	Code Section	Private Action	Statutes of Limitation	Attorney's Fees
FEDERAL	Tit. 15 §§4, 15(a-b), 21	Yes; a person who is a foreign state may not recover an amount in excess of damages, the cost of the suit, including a reasonable attorney's fee	4 yrs.	Yes; a person who is a foreign state may not recover an amount in excess of damages, the cost of the suit, including a reasonable attorney's fee
ALABAMA	6-5-60	Yes	Not specified	No
ALASKA	45.50.562 to 596	Yes; attorney general power to enforce	4 yrs.	Yes; restoration, injunction, treble damages, costs of suit; misdemeanor, civil penalty not more than $20,000 or 12 mths prison
ARIZONA	44-1401 to 1416	Yes	4 yrs.	Yes
ARKANSAS	4-75-301, *et seq.*	No prerequisite; it is the duty of the attorney general to enforce the status	Not specified	Attorney general receives costs
CALIFORNIA	Bus. & Prof. §16700, *et seq.*	Yes; attorney general may bring action on behalf of state	4 yrs.	Yes
COLORADO	6-2-101, *et seq.*; 6-4-101, *et seq.*; 13-80-101	Yes; attorney general may bring action on behalf of state	6 yrs. for actions brought by attorney general; 4 yrs. for other actions	No
CONNECTICUT	Connecticut Anti-Trust Act: 35-24, *et seq.*	Yes; attorney general also enforces	4 yrs.	Yes
DELAWARE	Anti-Trust Act: Tit. 6 §§2101, *et seq.*	Yes; attorney general also enforces	3 yrs.	Yes
DISTRICT OF COLUMBIA	28-4501, *et seq.*; 28-4511	Yes; corporation counsel power to enforce	4 yrs.	Yes
FLORIDA	542.15, *et seq.*	Yes; attorney general also enforces	1 yr. (plus period for attorney general action)	Yes
GEORGIA	13-8-31, *et seq.*	Unfair competition, restraint of trade for distributors, dealers, and their representatives doing business in Georgia of farm equipment and/or machinery	Not specified	Not specified
HAWAII	480-13, 20, 24	Yes; attorney general shall enforce criminal and civil provisions	4 yrs.	Yes
IDAHO	48-101, *et seq.*	Yes; attorney general also enforces	Not specified	Yes

Table 1: Antitrust—Continued

State	Code Section	Private Action	Statutes of Limitation	Attorney's Fees
ILLINOIS	Ch. 38 §§60-1 to 60-11	Yes	4 yrs.	Yes
INDIANA	24-1-1-1, *et seq.*; 24-1-2-1, *et seq.*; 24-1-3-1, *et seq.*	Yes; attorney general power to enforce	5 yrs. (24-1-2-4)	Yes; treble damages, cost of suit
IOWA	Iowa Competition Law: 553.1, *et seq.*	Yes; state may also bring suit	4 yrs. 553.16	Yes for individual plaintiff but not for state
KANSAS	50-101, *et seq.*; 50-112, *et seq.*	Yes; attorney general and county attorney power to enforce	Not specified	Yes; misdemeanor penalty not less than $100 or more than $1,000 or not less than 30 days or more than 6 months prison; actual damages
KENTUCKY	365.020, *et seq.* (Unfair Trade Practices)	Yes	Not specified	No
LOUISIANA	51.121, *et seq.*	Yes; attorney general also enforces	Not specified	Yes
MAINE	Tit. 10 §§1101, *et seq.*	Yes; attorney general power to enforce	Not specified	No
MARYLAND	Maryland Antitrust Act: Com. Law II §§11-201, *et seq.*	Yes; attorney general power to enforce	4 yrs.	Yes
MASSACHUSETTS	Massachusetts Antitrust Act: Ch. 93 §§1, *et seq.*	Yes; attorney general also enforces	4 yrs.	Yes
MICHIGAN	Michigan Antitrust Reform Act: 445.772, *et seq.*	Yes; attorney general also enforces	4 yrs.	Yes
MINNESOTA	Minnesota Antitrust Law of 1971: 325D.49, *et seq.*	Yes; attorney general also enforces	4 yrs.	Yes
MISSISSIPPI	75-21-1, *et seq.*	Yes; attorney general and district attorney per attorney general also enforce civil and criminal features of antitrust statutes	Not specified	No; $500 penalty
MISSOURI	Missouri Antitrust Act: 416.011, *et seq.*	Yes; attorney general also enforces	4 yrs.	Yes
MONTANA	30-14-201, *et seq.*	Yes; injured person or the attorney general; Dept. of Commerce power to enforce	Not specified	Not specified
NEBRASKA	59-801, *et seq.*	Yes; attorney general power to enforce	Not specified	Yes
NEVADA	598A.010, *et seq.*	Yes; attorney general power to enforce	4 yrs.	Yes
NEW HAMPSHIRE	Nevada Unfair Trade Practice Act: 356:1, *et seq.*	Yes; Dept. of Justice power to enforce	4 yrs.	Yes

Table 1: Antitrust—Continued

State	Code Section	Private Action	Statutes of Limitation	Attorney's Fees
NEW JERSEY	New Jersey Antitrust Act: 56:9-1, *et seq.*	Yes; attorney general power to institute proceedings	4 yrs.	Yes
NEW MEXICO	New Mexico Antitrust Act: 57-1-1, *et seq.*	Yes; attorney general power to enforce	4 yrs.	Yes
NEW YORK	Gen. Bus. §§340, *et seq.*	Yes; no prerequisite for administrative action but private party plaintiff must notify the attorney general	4 yrs. (suspended during pendency of federal action based in whole or in part on same matter)	Yes
NORTH CAROLINA	75-1, *et seq.*	Yes	4 yrs.	Yes
NORTH DAKOTA	51-08.1-01, *et seq.*	Yes; attorney general power to enforce	4 yrs. or 1 yr. after conclusion of action by state	Yes
OHIO	1331:01, *et seq.*	Yes; attorney general power to enforce	None	No
OKLAHOMA	Tit. 79 §§1, *et seq.*	Yes; attorney general power to enforce	4 yrs.	Yes
OREGON	646.705, *et seq.*	Yes; attorney general power to enforce	4 yrs. or within 1 yr. after conclusion of any proceeding based on the same matter	Yes; individual and state win reasonable attorney's fees and expert's fees
PENNSYLVANIA	Unfair Trade Practices & Consumer Protection Law: Tit. 73 §§201, *et seq.*	Yes; attorney general power to enforce	Not specified	No
RHODE ISLAND	Rhode Island Antitrust Act: 6-36-1, *et seq.*	Yes, but private party plaintiff must notify attorney general of his complaint and file proof of service	4 yrs.	Yes; treble damages, reasonable costs and attorney's fees
SOUTH CAROLINA	South Carolina Unfair Trade Practices Act: 39-5-10, *et seq.*	Yes; attorney general power to enforce; however, 3 days before instituting legal proceedings, must give person chance to present reason why action should not be instituted	3 yrs.	Yes
SOUTH DAKOTA	37-1-3.1, *et seq.*	Yes; state's attorney power to enforce and must immediately notify the attorney general; the attorney general shall aid in prosecution	4 yrs.	Yes
TENNESSEE	47-25-101, *et seq.*	Yes; attorney general and reporter power to institute criminal proceedings	Not specified	No

Table 1: Antitrust—Continued

State	Code Section	Private Action	Statutes of Limitation	Attorney's Fees
TEXAS	Texas Fair Enterprise & Antitrust Act of 1983: Bus. & Com. §§15.01, *et seq.*	Yes; attorney general power to enforce	4 yrs. or 1 yr. after conclusion of action based on the same act	Yes; actual damages, interest on damages, and cost of suit
UTAH	76-10-911, *et seq.*	Yes attorney general power to enforce	4 yrs. or 1 yr. after conclusion of action	Yes; treble damages and cost of suit
VERMONT	No statutory provisions			
VIRGINIA	Virginia Antitrust Act: 59.1-9.1, *et seq.*	Yes; attorney general power to enforce	4 yrs.	Yes
WASHINGTON	19.86.010, *et seq.*	Yes; attorney general power to enforce and may recover cost of action and attorney's fees on behalf of state	4 yrs., except when attorney general brings action in whole or in part; in matter of private action, the private action's statute of limitations is suspended	Yes; recover actual damages, cost of suit, and attorney's fees; cost may increase damages to amount not to exceed three times actual damages sustained
WEST VIRGINIA	West Virginia Antitrust Act: 47-18-1, *et seq.*	Yes; attorney general power to enforce	4 yrs., unless one civil action is brought, then any other is suspended during the first's pendency and one year after	Yes; treble damages, attorney's fees, filing fees, and reasonable expenses of discovery and document reproduction
WISCONSIN	133.01, *et seq.*	Yes; dept. of justice or district attorney power to enforce	6 yrs. Statute begins running upon discovery of a cause of action by an aggrieved party. Other actions have suspended statute of limitations during pendency of any civil or criminal action and for one year afterward	Yes; treble damages sustained, cost of suit
WYOMING	40-4-101, *et seq.*	Yes; attorney general and county attorney power to enforce	Not specified	No

2. ATTORNEYS

Legal Education and Admission to the Bar

When the American Bar Association (ABA) was founded a little more than one hundred years ago, its first priority was to set standards for legal education. Its Section on Legal Education and Admission to the Bar immediately set out to accredit law schools and monitor the quality of the legal education each school provided. The purpose was to guard against widely varying levels of preparedness and education and, thus, professionalism, among attorneys.

What has become a near-universal requirement for becoming a lawyer is possession of a diploma from an ABA-accredited law school, which allows a law school graduate to take the bar examination in any state. Few states permit graduates of non-ABA accredited law schools to sit for their own bar exams, though California allows individuals who have not attended law school but have diligently and in good faith studied law for at least four years to sit for its bar exam. New York, Vermont, Washington, and Wyoming also have conditions under which individuals who have not graduated from law school may sit for the bar exam. But by and large a law degree is necessary to take the bar exam, and in most cases it must be from an ABA-accredited school.

Many states allow reciprocity to attorneys already admitted to the bar in other states, while some place various restrictions upon attorneys admitted outside their jurisdictions, such as requiring attorneys admitted elsewhere to have actively been in practice for a certain number of years before s/he can be admitted without an examination. States that do not permit attorneys from other jurisdictions to be admitted without examination require them to take a special or abbreviated exam. These states have a large number of attorneys and maintain that the requirement of the bar exam limits the numbers of attorneys coming into the state.

Many states have responded to the lack of practical skills among some members of the bar by requiring every attorney to take a required number of continuing legal education courses each year. Mandatory Continuing Legal Education (MCLE) generally focuses on areas of the law that are undergoing rapid, dramatic changes or on areas that strengthen practical skills. Though only about two-thirds of the states have MCLE requirements to date, the trend is clearly to require such ongoing education and MCLE is likely to be a universal requirement in the future.

Table 2: Attorneys

State/Code Section	Education	Age	Exam	Reciprocity	MCLE	Admitting Body	Residency
ALABAMA S.Ct. Rule for Mandatory C.L.E. 1, *et seq.;* 34-3-1, *et seq.*; S.Ct. Rules governing admission to bar	Law school: graduation after at least 3 yrs. of 30 wks. each from ABA or AALS approved school or graduation after 4 yrs. of 30 wks. each from Birmingham School of Law, Jones Law Inst. or Miles College School of Law; Undergraduate: graduation from any accredited college or university	19	MBE, including MPRE, and essay exam; multistate score from another jurisdiction accepted for 20 mos. if equal or better than national median; 3 days	Professors who have taught for 3 yrs. at accredited Alabama law schools and who are admitted in another state may apply for admission without exam. Examination is required for all other applicants	12 hrs. each calendar year	Board of Bar Examiners	None
ALASKA 08.08.010, *et seq.* Alaska Bar Rules	Law school: ABA or AALS accredited law school or graduate of non-accredited school who has practiced in another jurisdiction for at least 5 yrs; one may register as law clerk to qualify as applicant without completing law school by presenting proof of bachelor's degree and completion of first year of law school; must have regular full-time employment with Alaska judge or attorney, tutor, and meet other specified study requirements	18	2 ½ days, includes MBE and essay on Alaska law and Alaska practicum; MPRE administered separately also required; MBE scores from other jurisdictions not transferable	May be admitted without exam if practiced 5 out of 7 years and passed exam in reciprocal state	No	Board of Governors	None required
ARIZONA Sup. Ct. Rules 31-80	Law school: ABA accredited or actively practiced 5 of last 7 yrs. in another state	21	MBE and MPRE and essay; 3 tries	Exam required by all applicants	15 hrs. per year	Supreme Court	None
ARKANSAS 16-22-2-1; Ark. Rule for CLE 3; Rules Governing Adm. to Bar	Law school: approved by ABA	21 unless graduate of accredited, recognized, or Class A law school	MBE and essay MPRE unlimited number	Exam required by all applicants	Resident: 12 hrs. annually; Nonresident: must comply to requirements of their state and file annual certificate of completion	Courts of state	None

Table 2: Attorneys—Continued

State/Code Section	Education	Age	Exam	Reciprocity	MCLE	Admitting Body	Residency
CALIFORNIA Bus. & Prof. §§6060, *et seq.;* §§6070, *et seq.*	Law school: Graduate from law school accredited by examination committee full-time for 3 yrs. or part time for 4 yrs. or proof applicant has otherwise diligently and in good faith studied law for at least 4 yrs; students at unaccredited law school must take preliminary bar exam at end of first year of law school; undergraduate: 2 yrs. or apparent intellectual ability equivalent to 2 yrs. of college work	18	MBE, essay, and MPRE	Must: (1) meet age and moral character requirements; (2) be admitted before highest court in sister state or foreign country; (3) have actively engaged in practice of law 4 of last 6 yrs.; (4) may have to take attorney exam	36 hrs. every 36 months, 8 hrs. of which must be law practice management or legal ethics, of which 4 hrs. must be legal ethics	Supreme Court	None
COLORADO CRCP Rules 201, 260; 12-5-101	Law school: Class A: First professional degree from ABA-approved law school; Class B: ABA-approved or state-approved or common law English speaking nation, if portion of legal education from foreign jurisdiction, must graduate from ABA-approved school or, if graduate of state accredited school, then applicant must be admitted in state and have practiced law 5 of 7 yrs.		Class A: MPRE; Class B: MBE and additional subjects, MPRE	Class A applicant: admitted in another jurisdiction and actively practiced for 5 of last 7 yrs. or scored 152 (scaled) on MBE within last 2 yrs.; Class B applicant: all others, must take written exam, MBE, MPRE, essay	45 units every 3 yrs., 7 units must be ethics	Supreme Court	

Table 2: Attorneys—Continued

State/Code Section	Education	Age	Exam	Reciprocity	MCLE	Admitting Body	Residency
CONNECTICUT Rules of Prac. for Sup. Ct. §§12, *et seq.*	Law school: graduate of school accredited by committee or Master of Laws from accredited school; must have passed professional responsibility exam or course	18	2 day exam, MBE, and essay; MBE scores not transferable; no limit to number of times	(1) Practiced court of original jurisdiction (10 yrs. if ever failed Conn. Bar Exam); (2) meets other requirements; (3) passed course or exam in professional responsibility; (4) intends that major portion of practice shall be in Connecticut shall be given temporary license for 1 year; if after 1 year s/he intends to continue practice in Conn., temporary license may be made permanent	None	Superior Court	Must show intent to practice in state
DELAWARE Sup. Ct. Rules 52, 70; Rules for Mandatory CLE 4; Board of Bar Examiners Rules 13	Law school: baccalaureate law degree or equivalent from ABA approved law school; Undergraduate: baccalaureate degree or equivalent or pass exam determined by board	21	MBE, essay, and Delaware Professional Conduct Examination	None; exam required of all applicants	30 hrs. every 2 yrs.	Supreme Court on recommendation of board of 12 examiners	5 mos. clerkship in Delaware required for admission
DISTRICT OF COLUMBIA D.C. Ct. App. Rule 46	Law school: ABA approved law school or if not, 26 semester hrs. at accredited school		MBE, essay, and MPRE; MBE scores from other jurisdictions may be transferred	(1) Active member in good standing of other jurisdiction immediately preceding, or (2) J.D. or LL.B. from accredited school, admitted to any state or territory with at least 133 scaled score on MBE, and passed MPRE; must apply within 25 mos. of MBE	None	D.C. Court of Appeals	

Table 2: Attorneys—Continued

State/Code Section	Education	Age	Exam	Reciprocity	MCLE	Admitting Body	Residency
FLORIDA Rules Re Fla. Bar 6-10.3; Rules of S.Ct. relating to admission to the bar Art. III, VI	Law school: graduate of ABA approved law school; Undergraduate: bachelor degree from regionally accredited school	18	MBE, essay, and MPRE; MBE scores not transferable	None; exam required of all applicants	30 credit hrs. every 3 yrs., 2 in ethics	Supreme Court	
GEORGIA 15-19-30, *et seq.;* State Bar Rules & (2-101) Regs R.8-104; Rules Governing Adm. to Prac. of Law part B §4	Law school: must complete requirements approved by ABA, AALS, or GA Board of Examiners, requiring 3 yrs. of classroom attendance at 400 hrs./yr.; Undergraduate: degree from accredited school or passed CLEP test		MBE, essay, MPRE; MBE scores not transferable; can take prior to graduation; MPT as of 1/1/99	None; exam required of all applicants	12 hrs. minimum per year	Superior Court	
HAWAII Sup. Ct. Rules 1	Law school: graduate of ABA approved school or unaccredited and 5 of last 6 yrs. practice; LL.M. not satisfactory substitute for J.D. or LL.B.		MBE, essay, including legal ethics; MBE scores not transferable; MPRE	Exam required of all. Full-time faculty of U. of Hawaii Law School who meet citizenship and education requirements and admitted in another jurisdiction admitted for 3 yrs.; after 3 yrs. may be given permanent license	None	Supreme Court	None
IDAHO 3-408, 3-101	Law school: graduate of ABA approved school; attorney applicants must be admitted to highest court of another state and practiced 5 of last 7 yrs.	Age of majority	MBE, essay; attorney applicants licensed for more than 5 yrs. need not take MBE, MPRE	Exam required of all applicants	30 credit hrs. every 3 yrs.	Board of Commissioners of State Bar	

Table 2: Attorneys—Continued

State/Code Section	Education	Age	Exam	Reciprocity	MCLE	Admitting Body	Residency
ILLINOIS ILCS S. Ct. Rule 701	Law school: First law degree from ABA approved school; Undergraduate: must be graduate of 4 yr. high school or prep school and successfully completed at least 90 semester hrs. at college or university approved by Board of Law Examiners; in lieu of college or preliminary work, Board may accept satisfactory completion of program or curriculum of particular college or university	21	Professional responsibility and academic exam; after fifth exam failure, permission of board or Supreme Court is required before admission to another exam; MPRE, MBE	Practiced in another jurisdiction 5 of last 7 yrs.; passed MPRE	None	Board of Law Examiners	
INDIANA Rules for Admission to the Bar & the Discipline of Attys. Rule 13	Law school: graduation from ABA approved school or approved list of Indiana Supreme Court or agency thereof	21	Conducted by Board of Law Examiners usually in Indianapolis; does not use MBE; four times must pass MPRE	1 yr. conditional admission to members in good standing of another bar who are 21, residents of Indiana, of good moral character, and practiced for 5 of last 7 yrs.; may be received for 5 one-year periods after which admission shall be permanent	No less than 6 hrs. each calendar year and no less than 36 hrs. each 3-year educational period	Supreme Court	
IOWA 602.10101, *et seq.*; Sup. Ct. Rules 101, *et seq.*, Rule 123	Law school: LL.B. or J.D. from reputable law school		IA essay test; MBE; MPRE; MPT	Member of any other U.S. bar who is resident may be admitted without exam if practiced 5 of last 7 yrs. with bona fide intent to practice in Iowa	Minimum 15 hrs. during each calendar year and 2 ethics credits during every 2-year period	Supreme Court	Required for admission

Table 2: Attorneys—Continued

State/Code Section	Education	Age	Exam	Reciprocity	MCLE	Admitting Body	Residency
KANSAS Rules 7-101, *et seq.* Sup.Ct. Rules 701	Law school: degree from ABA accredited law school; Undergraduate: bachelor's degree from accredited college		Essay questions on local law, MBE, MPRE; MBE scores may be transferred from another jurisdiction if within 13 mos. of current exam and if applicant passed entire bar exam of other jurisdiction	Exam required of all. Temporary license granted if: (1) attorney passed written bar exam in some other jurisdiction more than 5 yrs. ago; (2) has or intends to become Kansas resident to accept employment other than practice of law; (3) will perform legal services only for single employer; (4) of good moral character	36 hrs. every 3 yrs. including at least 12 hrs. per year (at least 2 hrs. in professional responsibility) except: (1) during first year of practice; (2) retired or inactive; (3) federal and state judges; (4) others exempted for good cause	Supreme Court	
KENTUCKY Supreme Ct. Rules 2.070; 3.661; 3.665[1]; 3.666	Law school: graduate of ABA or AALS approved law school		MBE; written exam on 14 topics; must receive 75% or more; may take exam 3 times; must first pass MPRE before can sit for MBE; MPRE	Citizen of U.S. admitted in D.C. or state and has practiced 5 of last 7 yrs. provided qualifications were equal or higher than those required for admission in Kentucky	12.5 hrs./ yr.; at least 2 hrs. of legal ethics	Supreme Court	
LOUISIANA Supreme Ct. Rules 30, *et seq.*; CLE Rule 1, *et seq.*; State Bar Art. of Inc. Art. 14 §7; Art. 15 §10	Law school: ABA approved law school	18	MBE not used, but all applicants must pass MPRE, essay	None; exam required of all applicants	15 hrs. per year, including not less than 1 hr. legal ethics, professional responsibility, and rules of conduct	Supreme Court	Citizen of U.S. or resident alien

Table 2: Attorneys—Continued

State/Code Section	Education	Age	Exam	Reciprocity	MCLE	Admitting Body	Residency
MAINE Tit. 4 §§801, *et seq.* Maine Bar Admission Rules, Rule 10	Law school: ABA accredited; Undergraduate: at least 2 yrs. at accredited school if successfully completed 2/3 of ABA law school requirements plus 1 year in attorney's office in the state		MBE; MPRE and general examination; essay	None; exam required of all applicants	None	Supreme Court	
MARYLAND Bus. Occ. §§10-101, *et seq.*; Bd. of Law Examiners Rule 4, *et seq.* Rules Governing Admission to the Bar Rule 4	Law school: J.D. or equivalent at school recognized by Board of Law Examiners; Undergraduate: 90 semester hrs. college work and adequate academic work to enter ABA approved school	18 to be admitted to bar but not to take exam	MBE, essay test; MBE scores transferable from another jurisdiction if score of 140 or better; MPRE not required	If practiced 5 of last 7 yrs. and proof of good, moral character and intent to practice or teach	None	Court of Appeals and State Board of Law Examiners	
MASSACHUSETTS Ch. 221 §§37, *et seq.*; Supreme Judicial Court Rule 3:01, *et seq.*	Law school: ABA approved or authorized foreign law school; Undergraduate: bachelor's degree	Over 18	State law and MBE; must pass MPRE	Admitted elsewhere and satisfactory moral character and legal ability	None	Supreme Judicial Court and Superior Court	
MICHIGAN 600.901, 600.934, 600.937, 600.946; Rules Concerning the State Bar 17 §1 Rules for the Board of Law Examiners Rule 1	Law school: reputable and qualified law school in U.S. or its territories; Undergraduate: at least 2 yrs. of study	18	MBE, no additional local bar examination requirements; out-of-state MBE scores accepted if within preceding 3 yrs. and person meets all other requirements for admission and other state grants reciprocal right to elect to use score on MBE administered in Michigan	Practiced or taught 3 of last 5 yrs.	12 hrs. in first year; 12 in second and 12 in third year of practice	Supreme Court or any circuit court	

Table 2: Attorneys—Continued

State/Code Section	Education	Age	Exam	Reciprocity	MCLE	Admitting Body	Residency
MINNESOTA 481.01, *et seq.;* S. Ct. Admis. Rules 2, *et seq.*	Law school: J.D. or LL.B. from ABA approved school	18	MBE, MPRE, additional questions	Engaged in law 5 of last 7 years; passed exam in other state within last 2 yrs. and scored at least 145 on MBE; good moral character	45 hrs. every 3 yrs.	Supreme Court	Must be resident or designate Clerk of Appellate Courts as agent for service of process or maintain office in state
MISSISSIPPI 73-3-2, *et seq.* Supreme Ct. Rules Governing Admission to the Miss. Bar Rule I, *et seq.*	Law school: 3 yr. law course at ABA approved school; Undergraduate: bachelor's degree or 3 yrs. of college work	21	MBE, additional subjects; MPRE	Must have practiced at least 5 yrs.; other state must reciprocate with Mississippi; must meet other requirements for admission	15 hrs. per year	Supreme Court	
MISSOURI Supreme Ct. Rules 8.03, *et seq.;* 484.010, *et seq.*	Law school: J.D. or LL.B. from ABA approved school; Undergraduate: ¾ of bachelor's work	18	MBE, MPRE, essay questions on local law; MBE scores may be transferred from another jurisdiction if taken within last 19 mos., score was at least 128 and applicant passed bar in other state	Member of bar of another state and has practiced or taught for 5 of preceding 10 yrs.	15 hrs. per yr.	Supreme Court	
MONTANA 37-61-101, *et seq.,* Montana S. Ct. Rule 4	Law school: ABA accredited law school approved by Montana Supreme Court	21	MBE, MPRE, and essay; MBE scores from another jurisdiction admissible if taken within 2 yrs. of examination date	Certain attorney applicants may be admitted without examination or by abbreviated examination	15 hrs./yr.	Supreme Court	Must be resident of state

Table 2: Attorneys—Continued

State/Code Section	Education	Age	Exam	Reciprocity	MCLE	Admitting Body	Residency
NEBRASKA 7-101, *et seq.,* Rules of the Supreme Ct. Admission of Attys. Rule 1, *et seq.*	Law school: LL.B. or J.D. from reputable law school, law school with similar entrance requirements and course of study at U. of Neb. Law School and AALS member; Undergraduate: at least equivalent to 3 yrs. of high school course; Professional degree from ABA law school	21	MBE, Nebraska law. MPRE	Admission upon showing that admission in another state required equal qualification and has practiced 5 of last 7 years	None; except county attorneys must complete continuing education hours established by the NE County Attorney Standards Advisory Council, not to exceed 36 hours annually (§23-1216); and public defender shall take at least 10 hrs. of continuing education annually (§23-3406)	Supreme Court	
NEVADA S. Ct. Rules 48, 51, 64-66, 77, 98, 210, 72	Law school: Bachelor of Laws or equivalent from ABA approved school	Age of majority	MBE 4 times, additional exam; MBE scores from other jurisdictions not admissible, MPRE (no limit to number of times)	Exam required of all. Law faculty members may be admitted if practiced for at least 5 yrs. and faculty for at least 2 years	12 hrs. per year	Supreme Court	

Table 2: Attorneys—Continued

State/Code Section	Education	Age	Exam	Reciprocity	MCLE	Admitting Body	Residency
NEW HAMPSHIRE Ch. 311 §§2, 8; S. Ct. Rule 42, *et seq.*; S. Ct. Rule 53.1	Law school: graduate of 3-year full-time or 4-year part-time program from ABA approved school or foreign law school of common law country Undergraduate; 3 yrs. of work required for bachelor's degree	18	MBE, additional essay questions; MBE scores from other jurisdictions not admissible; MPRE	None. Exam required of all.	12 hrs./yr. at least two hrs. must be in legal ethics, professional responsibility, substance abuse, or attorney-client disputes	Supreme Court	
NEW JERSEY Rules of General Application Rule 1:27	Law school: bachelor's degree or equivalent from ABA approved law school	18	MBE, additional subjects, MPRE, essay	In certain instances teachers at New Jersey law schools may be admitted without examination	None	Supreme Court	
NEW MEXICO Supreme Ct. Rules; Rules Governing Admission to the Bar, Rule 15-103; Rules Governing the Practice of Law, 18-201	Law school: graduate of law school fully accredited by ABA	21	MBE, MPRE, additional subjects; no provision for transfer of MBE scores from other jurisdictions; essay	None; all applicants must take exam	15 hrs., at least 1 hr. ethics; newly admitted members must take 10 hrs. practice skills in first 2 yrs. of practice	Supreme Court	
NEW YORK 6 NY Jus 2d §3 *et seq.*	Law school: graduation from approved law school or 4 years of study in office of practicing attorney and at least one year in approved law school or approved study of law in foreign country	21	MBE, additional subjects, MPRE, essay	May be admitted without exam from reciprocal states. Must have practiced 5 of last 7 yrs.	None	Appellate Division of Supreme Court	

Table 2: Attorneys—Continued

State/Code Section	Education	Age	Exam	Reciprocity	MCLE	Admitting Body	Residency
NORTH CAROLINA 84-24; Rules Governing Admission to the Practice of Law §0501, *et seq.* Continuing Legal Education Rules of the NC Bar Rule 18	Law school: degree from law school approved by Council of the North Carolina State Bar	18	MBE, state examination; MBE scores not transferable from another jurisdiction; MPRE, essay	Must be in good standing, practiced or taught for 4 of last 6 yrs., and state from which s/he comes must grant reciprocity to N.C.	12 hrs. per year, at least 2 on professional responsibility and during first 3 yrs. of admission, 9-12 hrs. in practical skills courses	General Court of Justice upon recommendation from Board of Law Examiners	
NORTH DAKOTA 27-11-02; Admin. Rule 1, 4; USDC Rule 2; CLE Rule 3	Law school: J.D. or equivalent from law school approved or provisionally approved by ABA	18	MBE, MPRE, additional subjects; scores from other jurisdictions accepted if taken same year as N.D. exam, essay	Meets educational requirements, is admitted to bar in another state, has practiced or taught for at least 5 yrs. and 4 of immediate last 5 yrs.	45 hrs. in each 3-year period	Supreme Court	Non-resident eligible for admission but must designate clerk of court as agent for service of process
OHIO Supreme Court Rules for Government of Bar of Ohio Rule I, *et seq.*	Law school: degree from ABA approved law school; bachelor's degree from accredited institution	21	MBE, additional subjects; MBE scores from other jurisdictions not accepted	Must have passed bar and been admitted in another state; engaged in practice of law for last 5 out of 10 yrs.; intend to practice in Ohio and have not failed Ohio bar exam.	24 hrs. every 2 yrs. of which at least 2 hrs. must relate to legal ethics	Supreme Court	Must be resident of Ohio or intent to establish permanent Ohio residence
OKLAHOMA Tit. 5 §1, *et seq.;* Appendix 5; Appendix 1-B	Law school: graduate of law school accredited by ABA or Board of Bar Examiners	18	MPRE, essay, MBE	Ex-judges of other states and attorneys who have practiced for at least 5 yrs. immediately preceding	12 hrs. per calendar yr., 1 hr. must be professional responsibility or legal ethics or legal malpractice	Supreme Court	Resident of Oklahoma

Table 2: Attorneys—Continued

State/Code Section	Education	Age	Exam	Reciprocity	MCLE	Admitting Body	Residency
OREGON 9.005-9.755; 9.990; Rules for Adm. of Attorneys Rule 1.05 *et seq.* Min CLE Rule 3	Law school: degree from ABA approved law school	18	MBE, MPRE, additional subjects; MBE scores from other jurisdictions not accepted; essay	All applicants must pass exam	45 hrs. over 3-year period including 6 hrs. of legal ethics. New admittees: 15 hrs., inc. 10 hrs. of practical skills and 2 hrs. of ethics	Supreme Court	
PENNSYLVANIA Pa. Bar Admis. Rules 103, 203, *et seq.*; Rules for CLE Rule 105	Law school: LL.B. or J.D.; Undergraduate: degree from accredited school or equivalent education		MBE, additional subjects; MBE scores from other jurisdictions not accepted; MPRE not required	Member in good standing of bar of reciprocal state; must have practiced or taught 5 of past 7 yrs.; if ever failed Pa. bar, must take exam	5 hrs. each fiscal year on Rules of Professional Conduct and on subject of professionalism generally	Court Administrator of Pennsylvania	
RHODE ISLAND Sup. Ct. Rules Art. IV, Rule 3, Art. II, Rule 1 *et seq.*	Law school: graduate of school approved and accredited by ABA and Board of Bar Examiners	21	MBE, additional subjects; no person may take exam more than 3 times except by court order; MPRE	If in practice or teaching 5 of last 10 years, applicant must take only essay portion of exam	10 hrs. each yr.	Supreme court	
SOUTH CAROLINA SC App. Ct. Rules Rule 402, 408	Law school: graduate of law school approved by ABA or S.C. Supreme Court	21	MBE, additional subjects; MBE scores from other jurisdiction accepted only if taken immediately before essay portion of this exam and for this exam only; MPRE	Exam required of all applicants	14 hrs. per year	Supreme Court	

Table 2: Attorneys—Continued

State/Code Section	Education	Age	Exam	Reciprocity	MCLE	Admitting Body	Residency
SOUTH DAKOTA 16-16-1, *et seq.*; 16-17-1, *et seq.*; 16-18-1, *et seq.*	Law school: graduation from ABA accredited law school	18	MBE, MPRE, additional subjects; MBE scores from other jurisdictions accepted	None; exam required of all applicants	None	Supreme Court	Must be resident, maintain office in state or designate clerk of Supreme Court as agent for service of process
TENNESSEE 23-1-101, *et seq.*; 23-2, *et seq.*; 23-3, *et seq.*; Rules of Sup. Ct. Rule 6, Rule 7 §1.01, *et seq.*; Rule 21 §3.01, *et seq.*	Law school: graduate of ABA accredited law school; Undergraduate: bachelor's degree from regionally accredited school	18	MBE, other subjects; MBE scores from other jurisdictions not accepted; MPRE	Meets educational requirements; admitted in another state; has practiced at least 5 yrs; has passed equivalent exam	12 hrs. each calendar year and 3 additional hrs. per year ethics and professionalism	State Board of Law Examiners supervised by Supreme Court	Citizen of Tennessee
TEXAS Gov. §§2.024; 81.061, *et seq.*, Art. 12 §6; Rules Gov. Adm. to Bar. Rule 1, *et seq.*	Law school: graduate of approved law school	18	MBE, MPRE, additional subjects; MBE scores from other jurisdictions not accepted; essay	Must have practiced 5 of 7 preceding years	15 hrs. per reporting period, at least 1 hr. of which is devoted to legal ethics and professional responsibility	Supreme Court	
UTAH 78-51-10	Law school: graduate of ABA accredited law school	21	MBE, MPRE, other subjects; MBE scores from other states not accepted; essay	None; exam required of all	27 hrs. during each 2-year period, at least 3 hrs. legal ethics	Supreme Court	U.S. citizen or intends to become one

Table 2: Attorneys—Continued

State/Code Section	Education	Age	Exam	Reciprocity	MCLE	Admit-ting Body	Resi-dency
VERMONT Tit. 12, App. I, Pt. II; CLE Rules §3; Adm. to Bar §§5, *et seq.*	Law school: degree from ABA approved law school, 6 mos. internship with Vt. attorney or study under supervision of Vt. attorney who has been admitted for at least 3 yrs.; Undergraduate: at least ¾ of bachelor's work	18	MBE, additional subjects; MBE scores of 137 or greater may be transferred from another jurisdiction; MPRE, essay	Must have practiced 5 of preceding 10 yrs.	20 hrs. during each 2-year period, at least 2 hrs. legal ethics	Supreme Court	
VIRGINIA 54.1-3925, *et seq.*; Rules of S. Ct. of Va. 1A:1, *et seq.*	Law school: graduate of ABA approved law school or 3 yrs. study under conditions prescribed by Board of Bar Examiners. Received Bachelor's degree from 4 yr. accredited college or university	18	MBE, MPRE, other subjects; essay; MPRE not required	Any lawyer entitled to practice before highest court of any other state or territory for not less than 5 yrs. may be admitted without exam	12 hrs. per year, at least 2 hrs. legal ethics or professionalism	Supreme Court	
WASHINGTON 2.48; Admissions to Practice Rules 1, *et seq.*	Law school: graduate of approved law school or completion of law clerk program; Undergraduate: not specified if law school graduate; if law office study, must have bachelor's degree from approved college or university		MBE not used; MPRE not required; essay	Exam required for all	15 hrs. per year except year of admission and following year; 45 hrs. per 3 yrs.	Board of Governors	
WEST VIRGINIA Ch. 30, Art. 2; Admission to Practice of Law Rule 3.0 *et seq.*, State Bar Const. Chp. VII	Law school: graduate of ABA and AALS accredited law school or equivalent; Undergraduate: degree from accredited college or university	18	MBE, MPRE, additional subjects; MBE scores from other jurisdictions admitted if passing score within last 13 mos.	Applicant's state of bar membership must be reciprocal with W. Va.; must have practiced for preceding 5 yrs.	24 hrs. every 2 fiscal years, at least 3 hrs. in legal ethics or office management	Supreme Court of Appeals	

Table 2: Attorneys—Continued

State/Code Section	Education	Age	Exam	Reciprocity	MCLE	Admitting Body	Residency
WISCONSIN SCR 40.02, *et seq.*; 31.02	Law school: graduate of ABA accredited law school	Age of majority	MBE, other subjects; MBE scores from other jurisdictions may be transferred; graduates of ABA approved law schools in Wisconsin may be admitted without exam upon production of diploma and certificate showing satisfactory completion of requirements relating to Wisconsin law; MPRE not required	Must have actively practiced for 3 of last 5 yrs. May be admitted without exam from reciprocal states	30 hrs. every 2 years	Supreme Court	
WYOMING 5-2-118; 33-5-100, *et seq.*	Law school: 3 yrs. in law school approved by state board of examiners or 1 yr. in law school and 2 yrs. in office of judge or member of bar, or 2 yrs. law school and 1 yr. in law office or judge	21	MBE, other subjects; MBE scores from other jurisdictions accepted; MPRE, essay	Attorneys from other states may be admitted without examination upon showing they are still in good standing in other state and of good moral character. Practiced 5 of 7 preceding years	15 hrs. per year	Supreme Court	

Note: ABA = American Bar Association; AALS = American Association of Law Schools; MBE = Multistate Bar Examination; MCLE = Mandatory Continuing Legal Education; MPRE = Multistate Professional Responsibility Examination.

3. DECEPTIVE TRADE PRACTICES

A deceptive trade practice is an activity in which an individual or business engages that is calculated to mislead or lure the public into purchasing a product or service. False advertising and odometer tampering are two of the most blatant examples of this commercial lying. Such activities are given special status as offenses against the citizenry in general and are therefore accorded by law special enforcement status.

Deceptive trade practices result in criminal prosecution in some states; in others, statutes provide for private enforcement, whereby a citizen is entitled to sue a business for violating deceptive trade practice laws and may be able to recover punitive damages and/or statutory fines. The attorney general of the state may also bring a lawsuit against an offending business enterprise.

Because a deceptive trade practice may affect individuals or businesses from more than one state, a number of states have adopted the standardized Uniform Deceptive Trade Practices Act. The Uniform Act does not add or detract from the law of any one state; rather, it is inclusive and tends to cover, in general terms, all the prohibitions and issues addressed in state law in this area. For example, the Uniform Act prohibits making deceptive representations in connection with commercial goods. This obviously covers odometer tampering, but it also addresses all forms of deception in the markcting or advertising of goods and services.

There is little controversy among the states over what activity amounts to a deceptive trade practice. However, there is a great deal of variety concerning the remedies available for the violations and who may sue for those violations. There are two main purposes of the statutes providing for remedies for businesses engaging in unlawful activity: (1) injunctions or restraining orders forbidding the continued deceptive trade practice and (2) punishment via fines, damages, and imprisonment. But because businesses are generally in violation of deceptive trade practice laws, and because it is difficult to determine whom to punish in the violating business, fines are generally the most effective method of extracting restitution.

Table 3: Deceptive Trade Practices

State	Uniform Deceptive Trade Practices Act Adopted	Auto Odometer Tampering Forbidden	False Advertising Forbidden	Who May Bring Suit	Remedies Available
ALABAMA	Similar act	Yes (§8-19-5; 15)	Yes, but won't apply if advertiser didn't know it was false, cooperates with attorney general, and discontinues the ad (§13A-9-42)	Private parties, attorney general, district attorney (§8-19-8)	Restraining orders (§8-19-8); actual damages or $100, whichever is greater, or in court's discretion up to three times actual damages (§8-19-10); willful violation is Class A misdemeanor (§8-19-12); civil penalty up to $2,000 per violation (§8-19-11)
ALASKA	No	Yes (§45.50.471; 18)	Yes (§45.50.471)	Attorney general (§45.50.501); private or class action suites (§45.50.531)	Injunction; $200 or actual damages, whichever is greater; treble damages or equitable relief (§45.50.531)
ARIZONA	No	Yes; Class 1 misdemeanor (§44-1223)	Yes (§44-1522); unlawful practice (§13-2203); Class 1 misdemeanor	Attorney general; consumer (§44-1524)	Subpoena; injunction, civil damages (§44-1526-1528); if willfully violated: $10,000 civil penalty (§44-1531); violating injunction: $25,000 penalty (§44-1532).
ARKANSAS	No	Yes; license may be denied or revoked for violation (§23-112-308, 13)	Yes (exception for those falsely advertising unknowingly) (§4-88-107)	Petition consumer protection (§4-88-110 to 111); attorney general	Injunction and return any money for purchased good to consumer; suspend corporate charter or business permit; possible $10,000 fine per violation if violation willful (§4-88-113)
CALIFORNIA	No	Yes (Veh. C. §28050.5, 28051); misdemeanor (Veh. §40000.15)	Yes (Bus. & Prof. §17500 et seq.)	Class action suits; attorney general; district attorney or other prosecuting attorney may bring suit for injunctive and civil penalties (Bus & Prof. §17535); any individual may bring suit for injunction or restitution (Bus. & Prof. §17203)	Violation of provision misdemeanor punishable by imprisonment in county jail not exceeding 6 months or a fine not exceeding $2500/both. (Bus. & Prof. §17500)

Table 3: Deceptive Trade Practices—Continued

State	Uniform Deceptive Trade Practices Act Adopted	Auto Odometer Tampering Forbidden	False Advertising Forbidden	Who May Bring Suit	Remedies Available
COLORADO	Adopted with modifications; Colorado Consumer Protection Act 6-1-101	Yes (§42-6-206)	Yes (§6-1-105)	Class action; attorney general; private citizens; district attorney (§6-1-113)	Enjoin practice and sue for civil penalty; individuals may receive damages and attorneys fees; treble damages or $250, whichever is greater (§6-1-113)
CONNECTICUT	Fed. Trade Comm. Act (§§42-110a to 42-110q; 42-144 to 42-149)	Yes (§14-106b)	None generally but §42-110b describes "unfair or deceptive acts" in trade, defined as including advertising by §42-110a4	Private parties; attorney general; class action; Commissioner of Consumer Protection (§§42-110d, g)	Willful violation: $2,000 for each offense; costs; attorney's fees; injunctive or equitable relief §42-110d
DELAWARE	Yes (Tit. 6 §§2531, *et seq.*) Uniform Deceptive Trade Practices Act (6 §2536)	Yes (Tit. 21 §§6401, 6404)	Unlawful (Tit. 6 §2513)	Attorney general and victims of deceptive trade practices (6 §2522) Service in accordance with 6 §2514	Violation of Tit.6 §2501 is $100 (Tit. 6 §2503); enjoin practice or other appropriate relief (Tit. 6 §§2522 to 2524); actual damages (Tit. 6 §2524); treble damages (Tit. 6 §2533[c]); injunction, attorney's fees (Tit. 6 §2533)
DISTRICT OF COLUMBIA	Yes (§28-3904)	No	Unlawful (§28-3904)	Director of Department of Consumer and Regulatory Affairs; consumer (§28-3905)	Appropriate civil penalties: injunction, actual and treble damages, attorney's fees; consumer redress remedies; punitive damages (§28-3905)
FLORIDA	No (§§501.201, *et seq.*) Florida Deceptive & Unfair Trade Practices Act	Yes; guilty of felony in third degree if violated (§319.35)	Yes; insurance health clinics (§641.441); fairs, public expositions (§616.241); food (§500.04); "deceptive acts" (§501.204); false, misleading, deceptive advertising and sales (§817.40; §817.41; §817.411)	Department of Insurance and Victims (§641.443 *et seq.*); Department of Agriculture & Consumer Services (§616.242); Department of Agriculture & Consumer Services (§500.121); state attorney, Department of Legal Affairs, consumer (§501.207; §501.211)	False advertising: 2nd degree misdemeanor §817.45; food: 2nd degree misdemeanor §500.177

Table 3: Deceptive Trade Practices—Continued

State	Uniform Deceptive Trade Practices Act Adopted	Auto Odometer Tampering Forbidden	False Advertising Forbidden	Who May Bring Suit	Remedies Available
GEORGIA	Yes (§10-1-370 to 375; 390 to 407) Uniform Deceptive Trade Practices Act	Yes (§40-8-5); violator liable for three times actual damages or $1,500, whichever is greater, costs and attorney's fees	Yes (§§10-1-420, 421)	Administrator; private party (§§10-1-397, 398)	Misdemeanor (§10-1-420); civil penalty $25,000 (10-1-405); enjoining practices (§10-1-423); exemplary damages for intentional violation, limited to actual damages if bona fide error (§10-1-399, 400); fine over $100 but less than $1,000 or prison for up to 20 days or both (§10-1-421); exception for ignorance (§10-1-396)
HAWAII	Yes (§481A) Uniform Deceptive Trade Practice Act	Yes (§486-77)(1) and (4)	Yes (§481A-3; 708.871 Criminal Code) false advertising misdemeanor	Consumer Protection Agency (§487); private parties (§481A-4)	Injunction; costs to prevailing party; attorney's fees (481A-4)
IDAHO	Yes, with modifications (§48-601) Idaho Consumer Protection Act	Yes (§49-1629); purchaser of vehicle could bring action and recover court costs and attorney's fees (49-1630)	Yes (48-603); Insurance policies (§41-1303); generally (§41-1235); food, drugs, and cosmetics (§37-131)	State (48-606); private party (48-608); odometer tampering—purchaser of vehicle (49-1630)	Declaratory judgment, enjoining practices, specific performance, civil penalties up to $5,000, recover reasonable costs, investigative expenses, and attorney's fees (48-606 and 607); in private action recover actual damages or $1,000 whichever is greater, costs, and attorney's fees (48-608). Odometer tampering: court costs and attorney's fees (49-1630)
ILLINOIS	Yes (§815 ILCS 510/1 *et seq.*)	Class A misdemeanor (§720 ILCS 5/17-11)	Yes; (§815 ILCS 510/2)	State attorney or attorney general may enjoin; private party (815 ILCS 510/3	Injunctive relief, costs or attorney's fees (815 ILCS 510/3)
INDIANA	No (§24-5-0.5-1 to 10)	Yes (§9-19-9-2)	Yes; (§35-43-5-3) Class A misdemeanor	Consumer or consumer class; attorney general (§24-5-0.5-4)	Actual damages; attorney's fees; attorney general may seek injunction, costs and up to $15,000 for violating injunction (IC §24-5-0.5-4); penalty up to $500 for incurable deceptive act (§24-5-0.5-8)

Table 3: Deceptive Trade Practices—Continued

State	Uniform Deceptive Trade Practices Act Adopted	Auto Odometer Tampering Forbidden	False Advertising Forbidden	Who May Bring Suit	Remedies Available
IOWA	No. Consumer fraud (§714.16)	Yes (§321.71)	Yes §714.16 food, drug, and cosmetics (126.16) criminal (714.16)	Attorney general (714.16; 126.7) city attorney; county attorney (126.7)	Temporary restraining order; preliminary injunction; permanent injunction; civil penalty not to exceed $40,000; costs of court, investigation, reasonable attorney's fees (714.16)
KANSAS	No (§§50-623, *et seq.*) 15 §198	Yes §21-3757 injured customer may void sale and recover penalties and attorney's fees based on 15 U.S.C. §§1981, *et seq.*	Yes (§50-626)	Attorney general investigates and enforces (§§50-628, 631); consumer may bring individual or class action (§50-634)	Obtain declaratory or injunctive relief and actual damages (§50-632); individuals may get attorney's fees (§50-634); reasonable expenses and investigation fees (50-632); civil penalty not more than $5,000 (50-636); restraining order (§50-634)
KENTUCKY	No. Consumer Protection Act (§367.120)	Yes; license may be revoked and civil penalties of $5,000 per violation (§367.990; 190.270)	Yes (§367.170)	Attorney general, consumer (§§367.190, 367.220)	Injunction, $2,000 to city per violation (§367.990(2)); any order necessary to restore a person in interest (§367.200); actual damages, punitive damages if appropriate, reasonable attorney's fees and costs (367.220)
LOUISIANA	Yes (51:1401-1418) Unfair Trade Practices and Consumer Protection Law	Yes; misdemeanor with fine up to $500 and/or up to 90 days prison (32 §726.1)	Yes (§1405) advertisements, untrue or misleading, prohibited. (51:411)	Attorney general (§1404); individual who has suffered ascertainable loss (§1409)	Actual damages, and if willful, violator must pay treble damages plus attorneys fees and costs; injunctive relief (§1407); additional relief as necessary to compensate (§§1408, 1409)
MAINE	Yes (Tit. 10 §§1211 to 1216; Tit. 5 §§206 to 214)	Yes (Tit. 29 §365)	Unlawful (Tit. 10 §1212)	Attorney general, person likely to be damaged by practice may get an injunction (Tit. 10 §1213) and (Tit. 5 §209 & 5 §213)	Injunction, possible to get attorney's fees and costs; also available are common law and other statutory remedies (Tit. 10 §1213) (Tit. 5 §213)
MARYLAND	No (Com. Law §§13-301, *et seq.*)	Yes (Transp. 22 §415)	Yes (Com. Law §13-301)	Consumer Protection Division; attorney general; consumer (Com. Law §13-401)	Fine up to $1,000; injunction; actual damages; possibly attorney's fees (Com. Law §§13-401, *et seq.*) misdemeanor $1,000 and/or up to 12 months in jail (Com. Law §13-411)

Table 3: Deceptive Trade Practices—Continued

State	Uniform Deceptive Trade Practices Act Adopted	Auto Odometer Tampering Forbidden	False Advertising Forbidden	Who May Bring Suit	Remedies Available
MASSACHUSETTS	Yes (Ch. 93A §21(a))	Yes, liable for three times actual damages or $1,500, whichever is greater (Ch. 266 §141); attorney's fees	Unlawful (Ch. 93A §2); (Ch. 266 §91, *et seq.*)	Attorney general; private parties (Ch. 93A §9)	Injunction, double or treble damages, attorney's fees and costs (Ch. 93A §11)
MICHIGAN	No (MCL §§445.901 to 922) Michigan Consumer Protection Act	Yes (§257.233a) three times amount of actual damages or $1,500 whichever is greater, cost of action and attorney's fees. (§257.233a)	Yes (MCL 445.903)	Attorney general, prosecuting attorney, or private citizen; class action by attorney general (MCL 445.910)	Injunction; actual damages or $250.00 whichever is greater, plus attorney's fees; persistent and knowing violation $25,000
MINNESOTA	Yes (§§325D.43-48)	Yes (§325 E.14); Gross misdemeanor, actual damages, costs and disbursements, attorney's fees; court has discretion to award an amount for damages not to exceed three times active damages or $1,500, whichever is greater. (§325 E.16)	Yes (§325 D.44)	Attorney general, county attorney (§325 F.70); any person likely to be damaged (§325 D.46)	Injunction (§325 F.70); court costs, attorney's fees (§325 D.45)
MISSISSIPPI	Yes; (§§75-24-1, *et seq.*)	Yes (§63-7-203); violation is misdemeanor and punishable by fine up to $500 and/or prison up to 6 months (§63-7-209)	Yes (§75-24-5)	Attorney general, district attorney, county attorneys; injured consumers; no class actions (§75-24-15)	Restoration of money or property (§75-24-11): civil penalty up to $10,000 for willful violations; individual may recovery attorney's fees; injunction (§75-24-9); misdemeanor: fined up to $1,000 (§75-24-20)

Table 3: Deceptive Trade Practices—Continued

State	Uniform Deceptive Trade Practices Act Adopted	Auto Odometer Tampering Forbidden	False Advertising Forbidden	Who May Bring Suit	Remedies Available
MISSOURI	No (§407.010 to 407.130)	Yes; liable in civil damages (§407.546); injunction (§407.551); odometer fraud in the first degree is a Class A misdemeanor (§407.516); in the second degree, Class D felony (§407.521); in the third degree is a Class C misdemeanor (§407.526)	Yes (§407.020); misdemeanor penalty (§570.160, 170)	Consumer, class action (§407.025) attorney general (§407.100)	For odometer tampering: civil, criminal, and injunctive remedies available; for false advertising: court may award punitives, attorney's fees, injunction (§407.025) restitution civil penalty not more than $1,000 (§407.100) treble damages or $25,000 whichever is greater (§407.546)
MONTANA	Montana Unfair Trade Practices and Consumer Protection Act of 1973 (§§30-14-101 to 224)	Yes (§61-3-607); fine up to $5,000 and/or prison up to 10 years; motor vehicle dealer revocation of license	Yes (§30-14-103)	County attorney; attorney general; individuals but not class actions (§30-14-121) dept. of commerce (§30-14-111)	Recovery of out-of-pocket losses (§30-14-132); the greater of $200 or actual damages, treble damages; injunction (§30-14-133)
NEBRASKA	Yes with modifications (§§87-301 to 306) (Sections 2(a)(12) and 7 not adopted)	Yes (§60-2301)	Yes (§87-302)	Person likely to be damaged (§87-303); attorney general	Criminal penalties for violating Act; costs, perhaps attorney's fees, plus other common law and statutory remedies (§87-303); injunction; civil penalty up to $2,000 (§87-303.11)
NEVADA	Revised Uniform Act adopted with significant variations (§§598.0903 to 598.0925)	Yes (§484.6062); tamperer is guilty of misdemeanor; person selling a tampered-with vehicle guilty of gross misdemeanor (484.6067)	Yes (§598.0915, 207.171) Criminal Code (§207.175)	Attorney General; consumer advocate; consumer if he is victim of deceptive trade practice (§§41.600; 598.0963) district attorney (§207.174)	Injunctions; return of money or property; penalties up to $10,000 for each violation possible and willful violation is misdemeanor, second is gross misdemeanor, third is a felony (§598.0999); suspension of right to conduct business or dissolution of corporation possible (§598.0999); criminal and civil penalties (§§207.174 and 175)

Table 3: Deceptive Trade Practices—Continued

State	Uniform Deceptive Trade Practices Act Adopted	Auto Odometer Tampering Forbidden	False Advertising Forbidden	Who May Bring Suit	Remedies Available
NEW HAMPSHIRE	Yes (§358A:2)	Yes (§262.17) first offense misdemeanor, 2nd offense Class B felony	Yes (§358A:2)	Attorney General, consumer protection (§358A:4); private actions (§358A:10), class actions (§358A:10a)	Misdemeanor penalty (§358A:6); injunctive; equitable relief; attorney's fees; actual damages or $200 whichever is greater; willful violation up to treble damages not less than double damages (§358A:10)
NEW JERSEY	No (§§56:8-1, *et seq.*)	Yes (§2C:21-8)	Yes (§56:8-2)	Attorney general, private party (§56.8-10)	Penalty as Attorney General deems proper (§56.8-3.1); injunction; penalty up to $7,500 for first offense and $15,000 for second (§56:8-13) attorney general may recover costs of suit in an action maintained by the state (§56:8-11)
NEW MEXICO	Yes (§§57-12-1, *et seq.*)	No specific statute against tampering, although provisions for auto sellers, etc. to include odometer statement with car (§66-3-10, 101) (§66-3-107)	Yes (§§57-15-1,2)	Attorney general (§§57-15-6, 8) and any private person likely to be damaged may seek injunctive relief or damages (§57-12-10); (§57-12-8) attorney general (§57-15-5); district attorney	Injunctive relief, actual damages or $100 whichever is greater, $300 or treble damages whichever is greater, attorney's fees and costs (§57-12-10); civil penalty not exceeding $5,000 per violation (§57-12-11) false advertising civil penalty not to exceed $500 (§57-15-4); restitution; prevailing party may also receive costs and attorney's fee; civil penalties up to $500
NEW YORK	No; Consumer Protection From Deceptive Acts and Practices (§349-350-e)	Yes (Gen. Bus. §392-e)	Yes (Gen. Bus. §350)	Attorney general (Gen. Bus. §350-c); private litigation (Gen. Bus. §350-e) for party injured	Civil penalty up to $500; actual damages or $50, whichever is greater (Gen. Bus. § 350-c); possibly treble damages; possibly attorney's fees
NORTH CAROLINA	No	Yes (§20-343)	Yes (§§75-1.1; 75-29)	Attorney general; consumer (§§75-15.2, 16)	Civil penalties: up to (§75-15.2) $5,000; treble damages for one injured (§75-16); attorney's fees (§75-16.1)
NORTH DAKOTA	No; Unfair Trade Practices Law (§51-10)	Yes; violation is a Class C felony if prior conviction; otherwise Class B misdemeanor (§39-21-51)	Yes (§§51-12-01; 15-12-08)	Attorney general, state's attorney (§51-12-14)	False advertising is a misdemeanor (Class B); injunction (§51-12-14); (§51-12-13)

Table 3: Deceptive Trade Practices—Continued

State	Uniform Deceptive Trade Practices Act Adopted	Auto Odometer Tampering Forbidden	False Advertising Forbidden	Who May Bring Suit	Remedies Available
OHIO	Adopted with modifications (Ch. 4165); (overlaps with Uniform Consumer Sales Practice Act (§1345.01-13)	Yes (§§4549.42, 46, 49)	Yes (§4165.02)	Attorney general; class actions; person likely to be damaged (§4165.03) (§1345.07) (§1345.09)	Civil penalty of not more than $25,000 if practice found to be unfair, deceptive, etc. (§1345.07); injunction; other remedies as available at common law and other statutes (§1345.09)
OKLAHOMA	Yes (Tit. 15 §§751 to 765) Oklahoma Consumer Protection Act	Yes (Tit. 47 §12-501) Odometer Setting Act (47 §12-503) misdemeanor fine not more than $1,000 or imprisonment for not more than 1 year or both fine and imprisonment (47 §12-506)	Yes (Tit. 15 §753)	Attorney general; district attorney (Tit. 15 §756.1); consumer (Tit. 15 §761.1)	Declaratory judgment, enjoin, restrain, actual damages (Tit. 15 §756.1); violator liable to aggrieved consumer for actual damages and litigation costs, including attorney's fees (Tit. 15 §761.1); civil penalty: if violation is unconscionable, penalty of up to $2,000 (Tit. 15 §761.1)
OREGON	Main provisions adopted with significant variations (§§646.605 to 656)	Yes; Class C felony (§815.410); $1,500 or treble the actual damage, whichever is greater, plus costs and reasonable attorney's fees	Yes (§646.608)	State, consumers (§646.618) (§646.638)	Civil actions may be brought to recover actual damages or $200, whichever is greater; punitive and equitable relief also (§646.638); injunction; attorney's fees
PENNSYLVANIA	No (Tit. 73 §§201(1) to (9)) Unfair Trade Practices and Consumer Protection Law	Yes; license denied or revoked; constitutes deceptive practices (Tit. 75 §7132); three times actual damages or $1,500, whichever is greater, and attorney's fees (Tit. 75 §7138); criminal penalties (Tit. 75 §7139)	Yes (Tit. 73§201 (2) and (3))	Private actions, attorney general, district attorney (73 §201-4), consumer-purchaser suffering ascertainable loss (Tit. 73 §201-9.2)	Private actions for actual damages or $100 whichever is greater; court may award treble damages but not less than $100 (Tit. 73 §201-9.2); civil penalty up to $1,000 (Tit. 73 §201-8); suspend right to do business (Tit. 73 §201.9)
RHODE ISLAND	No (§§6-13.1-1 to 12)	Yes (§§31-23.2-4; 31-23.2-3); prison up to 5 years or fine up to $10,000 or $1.00 per mile mileage fraud; revocation of license (31-23.2-7)	Yes (§6.13.1-1)	Attorney general (§6-13.1-5); consumer with ascertainable loss (§6-13.1-5.2) Class actions allowed (§6-13.1-5.2)	The greater of actual damages or $200; punitives or equitable damages; injunction; attorney's fees, costs (§6-13.1-5.2)

Table 3: Deceptive Trade Practices—Continued

State	Uniform Deceptive Trade Practices Act Adopted	Auto Odometer Tampering Forbidden	False Advertising Forbidden	Who May Bring Suit	Remedies Available
SOUTH CAROLINA	No (§§39-5-10, *et seq.*) South Carolina Unfair Trade Practice Act	Yes (§§56-15-350, 180)	Yes (§39-5-10) (§39-5-20)	Attorney general (§39-5-50); any person suffering ascertainable loss (§39-5-140); solicitor, county attorney or city attorney with prior approval by the attorney general (§39-5-130)	Treble damages, actual damages, costs, and attorney's fees (§39-5-140); civil penalty up to $5,000 (§39-5-110)
SOUTH DAKOTA	No (§37-24)	Yes (§32-15-33); violator is guilty of Class 1 misdemeanor	Yes (§37-24-6); class 2 misdemeanor	Attorney general; (§37-24-23) any individual (§37-24-31)	False advertising Class I misdemeanor punishable criminally (§§22-41-10, 11, 12); injunction; civil penalty up to $2,000 (§37-24-27); actual damages (§37-24-31)
TENNESSEE	No (§47-18-101 *et seq.*) Tennessee Consumer Protection Act of 1977	Yes (§47-18-104, (16)) Class A misdemeanor (§39-14-132)	Yes (§47-18-104); Class B misdemeanor (§39-14-127)	Attorney general; individual for damages and injunction (§47-18-106; §47-18-107; §47-18-108; §47-18-109); Div. of consumer affairs in the Dept. of Commerce and Insurance	Injunctive relief, damages for injured customers; revocation of violator's license; willful violators fined up to $1,000 (§§47-18-106, 108, amended 1991, Ch. 468); also possibly treble damages for willful violator (§47-18-109)
TEXAS	No (Bus. & Com. §§17.41 to 505) Deceptive Trade Practices and Consumer Protection Act	Yes (Bus. & Com. §17.46(16))	Yes (Bus. & Com. §17.46)	Attorney general; consumers; consumer protection division, district attorney (Bus. & Com. §§17.47, 17.48, 17.56)	Actual and treble damages (Bus. & Com. §17.50); injunctive relief, restitution, attorney's fees and costs, plus remedies available in other laws (Bus. & Com. §17.43, §17.50); restraining order (Bus. & Com. §17.47) civil penalty not more than $2,000 (Bus. & Com. §17.47)

Table 3: Deceptive Trade Practices—Continued

State	Uniform Deceptive Trade Practices Act Adopted	Auto Odometer Tampering Forbidden	False Advertising Forbidden	Who May Bring Suit	Remedies Available
UTAH	No (§13-11a-1, *et seq.*)	Yes third degree felony (§41-1a-1319); Class B misdemeanor to offer for sale, sell, use, or install a device that causes the odometer to register miles other than true miles (§41-1a-1310)	Yes (§13-11a-3); unfair methods of competition in commerce and unfair or deceptive acts or practices in commerce are unlawful	Enforcing authority; consumer; class action (§13-11a-4)	Declaratory judgment, enjoin, greater of $2,000 or actual damages; actual damages (§§13-11a-4); costs and attorney's fees; no injunction without a correction notice to defendant and 10 day wait for defendant to comply (§13-11a-4); remedies are in addition to remedies available for same conduct under state or local law
VERMONT	No (Tit. 9 §2453)	Yes (Tit. 23 §1704a); fined not more than $175.00	Yes (Tit. 9 §2453)	Attorney general, state attorney (Tit. 9 §2458); damaged consumer (Tit. 9 §2461)	Injunction; civil penalty up to $10,000 (Tit. 9 §2458); equitable relief, actual damages, attorneys fees, exemplary damages (Tit. 9 §2461) restitution of cash or goods (Tit. 9 §2458)
VIRGINIA	No (§§59.1-196, *et seq.*) Virginia Consumer Protection Act of 1977	Yes (§46.2-112)	Yes (§§59.1-200; 59.1-196)	Attorney general; commonwealth attorney (§59.1-203); harmed individual (§59.1-204)	Enjoin violations, actual damages or $100, whichever is greater (§59.1-204); penalty for willful violation is fine up to $1,000; attorney's fees and costs (§59.1-206)
WASHINGTON	No (§19.86)	Yes (§46.37.540); civil suit may recover costs and attorney's fees (§46.37.590)	Yes (§19.86.020)	Any injured person, attorney general (§§19.86.090, 095)	Civil penalties; injunctive degrees; treble damages, including costs and attorney's fees (§19.86.090); (treble damages may not exceed $10,000); actual damages; injunctive relief
WEST VIRGINIA	No	Unlawful practices generally (§46A-6); odometer disclosure requirements (§174-3-12a); no specific provision against tampering	Yes (§46A-6-102) (§46A-6-104)	Consumer with ascertainable loss (§46A-6-106)	The greater of actual damages or $200; injunction (§46A-6-106); equitable relief

Table 3: Deceptive Trade Practices—Continued

State	Uniform Deceptive Trade Practices Act Adopted	Auto Odometer Tampering Forbidden	False Advertising Forbidden	Who May Bring Suit	Remedies Available
WISCONSIN	No (§423.301); Wisconsin Consumer Act (§§421 to 427)	Yes (§347.415) up to $5,000 fine and/or up to 12 months in county jail (§347.50)	Yes (§423.301) remedies—customer entitled to retain goods received without obligation to pay and recover any sums paid to merchant (§425.305)	Class actions; individuals (§426.110); administrator	Monetary awards (§425.305); actual damages; unenforced obligations; attorney's fees; fine up to $2,000 (§425.401); injunction (§426.110)
WYOMING	Yes (§§40-12-101 to 112) Wyoming Consumer Protection Act	Yes (§31-16-119) purchaser may recover costs and reasonable attorney's fees (§31-16-123)	Yes (§40-12-105)	Attorney general (§40-12-102; §40-12-106); class actions, actual damages, consumers (§40-12-108)	Restraining order; injunction; actual damages for consumer; costs and fees (§40-12-108); other common law remedies not barred

4. INTEREST RATES

Every state has very specific limits on the amount of interest that may be charged on consumer contracts, ranging anywhere from 5 to 15 percent. But because parties may always agree to interest rates that are above the legal limit, most consumer contracts include interest rates that are above that limit.

Thus few states have limits on what can be expressly agreed to in a contract. For example, Alaska limits express contract terms to 5 percent over the legal rate, while the District of Columbia has the highest stated ceiling, at 24 percent. A number of states allow the limit to be pegged to the rate set by the Federal Reserve Board; most of these states have limits of 5 percent above the Federal Reserve. Potentially, these may be much higher than the District of Columbia's 24 percent. Overall, it appears that the more rural the state, the lower the limits. Presumably, farmers are protected and are more secure with lower interest rates than citizens of generally urban states with larger economies.

Usury is an unconscionable and exorbitant rate or amount of interest which exceeds those permitted by law. There is a great variety of statutory remedies for usury. A few states class usury as a crime and prescribe prison for violations of its usury laws. The majority of states provide for economic remedies such as forfeiture of all interest paid, recovery of double the usurious amount, payment of a fine, or making the contract unenforceable. Some states even specify that banks or savings and loans pay penalties. North Dakota has one of the more extreme usury penalties: it requires payment of all interest plus 25 percent of the principal.

For the most part there are myriad exceptions to the legal interest rate, which may be tied to the character of the lender, borrower, loan amount, the nature of the contract, or the matter that is the subject of the contract. Effectively, legal interest rates are no more than general guidelines for all transactions rather than the specific limits placed on them. There are so many exceptions in many states that it is often necessary to find a different rate for every conceivable situation.

Table 4: Interest Rates

State	Legal Maximum Rate of Interest	Usury Penalty	Judgments	Exceptions
ALABAMA	If agreed upon in writing, up to 8% per year, otherwise 6% per year (§8-8-1)	Forfeiture of all interest and interest paid deducted from principal (§8-8-12)	Other than costs, dollar judgments bear interest from date of entry at 12%; judgment on contract action bears interest at rate in contract (§8-8-10)	Loans over $2000 (§8-8-5); debts under National Housing Act. Veterans' Benefits acts (§8-8-6); industrial development boards and medical clinic boards (§11-54-97, 11-58-15); bonds issued by public or non-profit organizations (§8-8-7); public housing bonds, State Board of Education Securities (§§24-1-32; 16-3-28); public hospital corporations (§22-21-6)
ALASKA	Absent contract: 10.5%; express contract agreement: 5% over legal rate (§45.45.010)(a)	One paying usurious interest may recover double amount thereof within 2 years (§45.45.030)	10.5% interest unless contract action, then use contract rate (§09.30.070)	Contract where principal amount exceeds $25,000 (§45.45.010)(a)
ARIZONA	10% per year; any rate may be agreed and contracted upon (§44-1201)	Forfeit all interest (§44-1202); usurious payments deemed to be made toward principal; if payments exceed principal, judgment may be given in favor of debtor with interest at rate of 10% (§§44-1203, 1204)	At allowable rate or as agreed upon as long as not in excess of that permitted by law (§44-1201)	Loans under $1,000 (§6-652)
ARKANSAS	Consumer and nonconsumer rate is 5% above Federal Reserve discount rate (consumer rate is capped at 17%) (Const. Art. XIX §13)	Contracts calling for more than lawful rate are void as to unpaid interest and debtor may recover twice amount of interest paid (Const. Art. XIX §13)	Rate of interest for contracts in which no rate of interest is agreed upon shall be 6% per annum. (Const. Art. XIX §13)	

Table 4: Interest Rates—Continued

State	Legal Maximum Rate of Interest	Usury Penalty	Judgments	Exceptions
CALIFORNIA	Loan/forbearance of any money, goods, or things in action, or accounts after demand—7% or contract rate (Const. XV §1) contract rate shall not exceed 12% (Civil Code §1916-1)	Contract or agreement for greater than 12% shall be null and void as to any agreement to pay interest (Civil Code §1916-2); debtor may recover treble amount paid; willful violation—guilty of loan-sharking, a felony and punishable by imprisonment in state prison for not more than 5 yrs. or county jail for not more than 1 yr. (Civil Code §1916-3)	Set by legislature at not over 10% rate (Const. Art. XV §1); in absence of setting of such rate, rate of interest is 7% (Const. Art. XV §1)	Incorporated insurer (Ins. §1100.1); licensed broker-deals (Corp. §25211.5); indebtedness issued pursuant to corporate securities law (Corp. §25116); licensed business and industrial development corporation (Fin. §31410); state and national banks acting as trustees (Fin. §1504); foreign banks (Fin. §1716); bank holding companies (Fin. §3707); state and federal savings and loans (Fin. §7675)
COLORADO	8% (§5-12-101); maximum rate that may be contracted for is 45% (§5-12-103); interest on consumer loan may not exceed 12% unless made by supervised lender (§§5-3-201, 508)	Criminal penalty for knowingly exceeding 45% (§18-15-104) Class 6 felony	8% if none specified in contract; if contract rate is variable, then at rate on day of judgment (§5-12-102[4])	Savings and loans (§11-41-115); mortgages (§5-13-101); business and agricultural loans (§5-13-102); small business loans (§5-13-103); loans governed by certain federal acts (§5-13-104); all others generally (§5-13-105)
CONNECTICUT	12% (§37-4)	Loan is not enforceable (§36-243)	Absent agreement to contrary, 8% (§37-1)	Loans before September 12, 1911 (§37-9); bank; savings and loan; credit union; certain mortgages; loan for motor vehicle; boat; loan for higher education; loan under $5,000 (§36a-563); pawnbroker and loan broker (§21-44)
DELAWARE	5% over Federal Reserve discount rate; same maximum rate even if agreed upon in writing (Tit. 6 §2301)	Debtor not required to pay excess over legal rate; if whole debt is paid with interest over legal rate, debtor may recover 3 times amount of excess interest or $500, whichever is greater, if action brought within 1 year (Tit. 6 §2304[b]	5% over Federal Reserve discount rate; same maximum rate even if agreed upon in writing (Tit. 6 §2301)	No limit where loan exceeds $100,000 and is not secured by mortgage on borrower's personal residence (Tit.6§2301(c))

Table 4: Interest Rates—Continued

State	Legal Maximum Rate of Interest	Usury Penalty	Judgments	Exceptions
DISTRICT OF COLUMBIA	In absence of agreement: 6%/yr. (§28-3302); by contract in writing: Up to 24% (§28-3301)	Small loans: Loss of interest and ¼ of principal: $300 fine and prison 30-90 days and restitution of property illegally obtained; in other cases: forfeiture of interest; usurious interest paid may be recovered (§26-705, 707; 28-3303; 3304)	4% allowed on judgments against the District of Columbia, its officers, employees acting within scope of employment (26 USC §6621; see also §28-3302)	Federally insured bank or savings and loan and on direct motor vehicle installment loans (§§28-3308; 28-3601 to 3602)
FLORIDA	12% without contract; parties may contract for a greater or lesser rate (§687.01)	All interest forfeited and repaid double (§687.04); criminal usury: credit at rate of 25-45% is misdemeanor with penalty of up to 60 days in prison and/or $500 fine; over 45% is 3rd degree felony; keeping the books/ records for loan at 25% is 3rd degree misdemeanor, and if loan or forbearance is criminal, debt is not enforceable (§687.071)	Set yearly by the state comptroller by averaging discount rate of Fed. Reserve Bank of N.Y. for the preceding year and adding 500 basis pts. to the averaged discount rate (55.03)	If specifically licensed in business and making loan (§516.031); on sale of motor vehicles (§§520.01, *et seq.*)
GEORGIA	7% per year when rate not specified; higher than 7% must be in writing; maximum 16% where principal is $3000 or less; no limit on rate if loan is between $3000 and $250,000 and must be in simple interest in written contract (§7-4-2)	Forfeiture of entire interest (§7-4-10); criminal penalty (§7-4-18)	12% unless contract specifies rate (§7-4-12)	Small industrial loans (§7-3-14)
HAWAII	10% (§478-2)	Creditor may recover principal only; debtor recovers costs; creditor fined up to $250 and/or prison up to 1 year (§478-6)	10% on judgment for any civil suit (§478-3)	

Table 4: Interest Rates—Continued

State	Legal Maximum Rate of Interest	Usury Penalty	Judgments	Exceptions
IDAHO	12% unless express contract (§28-22-104; see also §28-42-201)	Forfeiture of entire interest plus twice the amount of such interest (§22-22-107)	5% plus annual average yield on U.S. Treasury securities as determined by Idaho state treasurer (§28-22-104)	
ILLINOIS	5% unless contract (394 N.E.2d 380)	Recipient subject to suit for twice total of all interest, charges, and attorney's fees and court costs (815 ILCS 205/6)	9% or 6% when judgment debtor is unit of local government, school district, or community college (735 ILCS 5/2-1302; 735 ILCS 5/12-109)	Under Consumer Installment Loan Act (205 ILCS 670/1); short-term loans (815 ILCS 205/4.1a); installment loans (815 ILCS 205/4a; 205 ILCS 670/15); pawnbrokers (§205 ILCS 510/2); farm development loan (205 ILCS 3605/5 to 3605/12); reverse mortgage loan (205 ILCS 305/46)
INDIANA	21% for unsupervised consumer loan (24-4.5-3-201)	Most business loans not subject to limit; Class B misdemeanor for supervised lender to knowingly charge in excess of 24-4.5-3-508 for consumer loan (24-4.5-5-301); consumer has right to refund of amount paid in excess of statute and up to 3 times the amount in its discretion (24-4.5-5-202)	At contract rate up to 10% and 10% if no contract (24-4.6-1-101); government entities liable for 8% from date of judgment or settlement if not paid within 180 days (34-4-16.5-17)	Supervised loan is a consumer loan in which rate of loan finance charge exceeds 21% (24-4.5-3-501)
IOWA	5% unless agreed upon in writing then not to exceed amount specified in §535.2(3)	Plaintiff may have judgment only for principal debt without interest or costs; forfeiture of 8% by the year of principal remaining unpaid at time of judgment (§535.5)	10% unless rate (up to §535.2 amount) expressed in contract (§535.3)	Automobile installment contract; mobile/modular home sales contract; semi-tractor and travel trailer installment sales (§321)
KANSAS	10% (§16-201); maximum rate at which parties may contract: 15% (§16-207)	Forfeit all interest; lose a sum of money to pay borrower's attorney fees (§16-207)	4% above federal discount rate as of July 1 preceding judgment (§16-204); where judgment on contract, contract rate controls (§16-205)	Business and agricultural loans; note secured by real estate mortgage; qualified plan loans (§16-207)

Table 4: Interest Rates—Continued

State	Legal Maximum Rate of Interest	Usury Penalty	Judgments	Exceptions
KENTUCKY	8% absent agreement otherwise (KRS §360.010); parties may agree to a rate not to exceed 4% above discount rate of Fed. Reserve Bank or 19% whichever is less for principal amount of $15,000 (360.010)	Borrower may recover twice amount paid (KRS §360.020)	12% unless contract, then contract rate (KRS §360.040)	Banks (§360.010(2)); credit union (§290.425); small loans (§288.530)
LOUISIANA	One point over average prime subject always to cap of 14% and floor of 7% (Civ. Code Ann. Art. 2924)	Entire interest forfeited (§9:3501)	Legal interest (§13:4203); state agencies: 6% (§13:5112)	Secured by mortgage (§9:3504); borrowing for commercial/business purposes (§9:3509); obligation secured by a mortgage (§9:3504)
MAINE	6% unless otherwise agreed (Tit. 9-B §432)		15% for damages not exceeding $30,000 (Tit. 14 §1602-A); civil actions Dist. Ct. juris. 8%	
MARYLAND	6% (Const. Art. III §57); up to 8% in written agreement (Com. Law §12-103)	Forfeit 3 times excess of interest and charges collected or $500, whichever is greater (Com. Law §12-114)	10%; money judgment may carry contract rate until originally scheduled maturity date (Cts. & Jud. Proc. §11-106, 107, 301)	Mortgage secured loans (Com. Law §12-103); unsecured loans secured by other than savings (Com. Law §12-103); installment loans not secured by real property (Com. Law §12-103); open-end retail accounts (Com. Law §12-506); installment sales contract for motor vehicles and other consumer goods (Com. Law §12-609, 610)
MASSACHUSETTS	6% unless contract (Ch. 107 §3)	Over 20%: criminal usury; usurious loan may be voided by Supreme (Ch. 271 §49) Judicial or Supreme Court in equity	12% (Ch. 231 §6B); at contract rate if contract up to 12% (Ch. 231 §6C); sanctions defenses/counterclaims for frivolous or not in good faith actions (Ch. 231 §6F)	Small loans (Ch. 140 §96); open-end credit transaction (Ch 140 §114B); life insurance policy loans (Ch. 175 §142)
MICHIGAN	5% (MCL§438.31, *et seq.*); maximum rate with written agreement: 7%	Loss of all interest, official fees, delinquency or collection charge, attorney's fees or court costs (MCL§438.32)	13% (MCL§600.6013, 600.6301)	Small loans (MCL§493.1); credit union loans (MCL§490.14)

Table 4: Interest Rates—Continued

State	Legal Maximum Rate of Interest	Usury Penalty	Judgments	Exceptions
MINNESOTA	6% legal rate (§334.01); written contract up to 8%	Contract for greater interest void (§§47.20; 334.03); payor may recover full interest and premiums paid with costs (§334.02); usurious interest by banks, savings and loans and credit unions results in forfeitures of all interest and payor may recover twice interest paid (§48.196)	Determined on or before December 20 of prior year by state court, administrator based on secondary market yield (§549.09)	State banks/savings associations (§48.195); state credit union (§52.14); dealers under Securities Exchange Act (§334.19); mortgage loans (§47.204); business and agricultural loans (§334.011). Plans subject to provisions of Employee Retirement Income Security Act of 1974 (§334.01); loans secured by savings accounts (331.012)
MISSISSIPPI	8% (§75-17-1[1]); contract rate not to exceed greater of 10% or 5% above discount rate (§75-17-1[2])	Forfeit all interest and finance charge; if rate exceeds maximum by 100%, any amount paid (principal or interest) may be recovered (§75-67-119); person willfully charging usurious rates guilty of misdemeanor and fine up to $1000 (§75-67-119)	Judgments at contract rate if contract exists; otherwise at per annum rate set by judge (§75-17-7)	Residential real property loan (§75-17-1); small loans (§75-67-101); mobile homes (§75-17-23); partnership, joint venture, religious society, unincorporated assoc. or domestic or foreign corp. (75-17-1 [3])
MISSOURI	Absent agreement, 9% (§408.020); otherwise, 10% (§408.030); contract rate not to exceed 10% except when market rate is higher (408.030)	If usury collected, excess over legal rate applied to principal or debtor may recover (§408.060) (408.050); debtor may recover twice amount of interest paid, costs of suit, and attorney's fees (408.030)	9% or higher rate lawfully stipulated (§408.040)	Loans to corporations, business loans, some real estate loans, agricultural (§408.035); business loan over $5000 (§408.035)
MONTANA	10% (§31-1-106); 15% maximum rate by written agreement, up to 6 percentage points above prime rate of major New York banks (§31-1-107)	Forfeiture of double interest received (§31-1-108)	10% or contract rate (§25-9-205)	Regulated lenders exempt (§§31-1-111, 112)

Table 4: Interest Rates—Continued

State	Legal Maximum Rate of Interest	Usury Penalty	Judgments	Exceptions
NEBRASKA	Up to 15% for contract (§45-101.03); otherwise legal rate, 6% (§45-102)	Only principal recoverable (§§45-105, 110); principal plus interest not exceeding legal contract rate (45-110)	1% above bond equivalent yield; rate of contract (§45-103); or specifically provided by law (§45-103)	Loans by Department of Banking, loan to any corporation; principal over $25,000; loan guaranteed by state/federal government on securities, open credit accounts; savings and loans; business or agricultural purpose loans; installment contract for goods and services (§45-101.04); loan to any partnership or trust (45-101.04)
NEVADA	No limit for what parties may contract; otherwise prime rate of Nevada's largest bank plus 2% (§§99.040, 050)	Parties may agree for any rate on any contract (§99.050)	Contract rate or prime rate at largest bank in Nevada plus 2% (§17.130)	Licensee may lend at any interest rate (§677.730)
NEW HAMPSHIRE	10% unless differently stipulated in writing (§336:1)	No usury provisions	10% unless otherwise agreed upon in writing (§336:1)	Educational institutions (§195-F:15); public utility (§374-C:14); pawnbrokers (§399-A:3); small loans (§399-A:3); home mortgage loan (§398-A:2)
NEW JERSEY	6% or up to 16% for contract (§31:1-1); loans in excess of 30% or 50% to corporations are not permitted (§2C:21-19)	Only amount lent may be recovered (§31:1-3)		Loan for over $50,000; savings and loans; banks; Department of Housing and Urban Affairs and other organizations authorized by the Emergency Home Finance Act of 1970; state or federal government or quasi-governmental organizations (§31:1-1)
NEW MEXICO	6% in absence of contract fixed rate (§56-8-3)	Forfeiture of all interest and if paid, borrower may recover twice amount (§56-8-13)	8¾% unless judgment is on a contract, in which case interest on recovery will be the contract rate, but if the money judgment is for tortious conduct, interest on judgment will be 15%	
NEW YORK	16% (Gen. Oblig. §5-501(1)); Banking §14-a)	Usurious notes void (Gen. Oblig. (§5-511(1)); borrower may recover any amount in excess over legal rate (Gen. Oblig. §5-513); if bank, savings and loan, or trust company, interest forfeited and recovery of twice interest paid (Gen. Oblig. §5-511(1))	9% (Civ. Prac. L. & R. §§5003, 5004)	See Gen. Oblig. §§5-501, *et seq.*; debit balance on customer accounts with a broker or dealer (Gen. Oblig. §5-525)

Table 4: Interest Rates—Continued

State	Legal Maximum Rate of Interest	Usury Penalty	Judgments	Exceptions
NORTH CAROLINA	8% (§24-1); may contract for higher rate (§24-1.1)	Forfeiture of all interest; party paying may recover double interest paid (§24-2)	8% (§24-1) or at contract rate (§24-5)	Home loans secured by mortgage or first deed of trust (§24-1.1A); installment (§24-1.2); savings and loans (§24-1.4); loans to corporations (§24-9)
NORTH DAKOTA	6% (§47-14-05); if contract in writing, up to 5.5% higher than average interest on treasury bills (§47-14-09)	Forfeit all interest and 25% of principal (§47-14-10); Class B misdemeanor (§47-14-11); if interest paid, twice amount paid may be recovered (§47-14-10)	Contract rate, otherwise 12% (§28-20-34)	Loans to corporations; agency funded by state/federal government; amount over $35,000 (§47-14-09); loans to partnerships/limited partnerships (§47-14-09)
OHIO	8% (§1343.01)	Excess interest applied to principal (§1343.04)	In accordance with §1343.01, §1343.02; rate specified in instrument (§1343.02)	Amount exceeds $100,000; broker/dealer registered; secured by mortgage or deed of trust; business loan (§1343.01)
OKLAHOMA	6%, or by contract (Tit. 15 §266)	Forfeiture of entire interest; if amount over legal interest is paid, it may be recovered double (Const. Art. XIV §3); if a bank is guilty of loaning at usurious rate, cancellation of bank charter and liquidation of assets of bank (15 §272)	At contract rate or 4 percentage points above average treasury bill rate for preceding year, not to exceed 10% in action against state/political subdivision (Tit. 12 §727)	Pawnshops (Tit. 59 §1510); small loans and retail installment (Uniform Consumer Credit Code) (Tit. 14A §3-201)
OREGON	Unless otherwise agreed, 9% (§82.010)	Forfeit interest on loan but borrower must repay the principal (§82.010)	9% unless contract, then contract rate (§82.010)	Business or agricultural loan; loan under $50,000 (§82.010)
PENNSYLVANIA	6% (Tit. 41 §§201, 202)	Borrower not required to pay amount over legal rate and may recover triple the amount in excess; attorney's fees may be awarded and an intentional violation is 3rd degree misdemeanor (Tit. 41 §§501, *et seq.*)	Interest at lawful rate (Tit. 42 §8101)	Federal Housing Administration, Veteran's Administration or other department/agency of U.S. government (Tit. 41 §§301, 302); business loans in excess of $10,000; unsecured; noncollateralized loan in excess of $35,000; obligation to pay a sum of money in an original bona fide principal amount more than $50,000 (41 §301)

Table 4: Interest Rates—Continued

State	Legal Maximum Rate of Interest	Usury Penalty	Judgments	Exceptions
RHODE ISLAND	12% absent agreement otherwise (§6-26-1); otherwise, 21% (§6-26-2)	Contract shall be void; knowing violation is criminal usury with imprisonment up to 5 years (§6-26-3); borrower may recover twice amount of usurious interest paid (§6-26-4)	12% unless otherwise already agreed upon rate (§9-21-10)	Corporation; pawnbroker (§19-26-18); persons licensed (§6-26-2); revolving or open-end credit plan (§6-27-4); finance charge for retail sales (§6-27-4)
SOUTH CAROLINA	8 ¾ % (§34-31-20)	Usury penalty laws repealed June 25, 1982, but old law may apply to transactions before then (formerly §34-31-50)	14% (§34-31-20)	See South Carolina Consumer Protection Code (§37-1-101 *et seq.*)
SOUTH DAKOTA	Absent agreement, 15% (§54-3-4); various official state interest rates: Category A-9%; Category B-12%; Category C-15%; Category D-1% per month or fraction thereof; Category E-6% (54-3-16)	Penalties repealed July 1982	12% (§54-3-5.1)	Real estate mortgages; Uniform Credit Code security agreements; revolving charge accounts (§54-11-5); regulated lenders §(54-3-13)
TENNESSEE	10% (§47-14-103)	Contract unenforceable; if found unconscionable, lender must refund charges, fees, and commission fees and successful plaintiff may recover reasonable attorney's fees (§47-14-117); willful collection shall be a misdemeanor punishable by a fine not less than $100 or more than amount of usury received or at court's discretion imprisonment in county jail or workhouse for less than 1 yr. (47-14-112)	10% or at contract rate (§47-14-121)	Installment loans (§§45-2-1106, 1107); loans under $1000; (§47-14-104); savings and loans (§45-3-705); single payment loans §(47-14-104)

Table 4: Interest Rates—Continued

State	Legal Maximum Rate of Interest	Usury Penalty	Judgments	Exceptions
TEXAS	When not specified, 6% (Tex. Rev. Civ. Stat. Ann. Art. 5069-1.03)	Forfeits 3 times amount of usurious interest contracted for and unreasonable attorney's fees (§5069-1.06[1]); contract for interest in excess of twice allowed interest shall forfeit all principal plus above penalties; any usury is a misdemeanor with fine of up to $1000 (§5069-1.06[1], [2])	If contract rate, then lesser of the contract rate or 18% (§5069-1.05[1])	Loans over $250,000 (§5069-1.04(b)(2))
UTAH	10% absent contract (§15-1-1)	Fed. postjudgment interest rate as of Jan. 1 of each year plus 2%	Judgment on contract shall conform to contract and shall bear interest agreed to by parties	Pawnbroker (§11-6-4)
VERMONT	12% (Tit. 9 §41(a)	Lender knowingly charging in excess of legal rate may forfeit all interest, all expenses of collection, and reasonable attorney's fee (§9-50); contract void; criminal penalties up to $500 fine and/or 2 years in prison (Tit. 8 §2233)	12% (Tit. 12 §2903)	Retail installment contract (Tit. 9 §41(a), 2405); municipal bonds (Tit. 24 §1761); loan secured for recreational vehicle, aircraft, water craft, and farm equipment (Tit. 9 §41(a))
VIRGINIA	8% unless contract specifies (§6.1-330.53)	Borrower may recover twice interest paid, court costs, and unreasonable attorney's fees (§6.1-330.56, 57)	9% (§6.1-330.54) or at contract rate, whichever is higher	Revolving credit accounts (§6.1-330.64); private college/university (§6.1-330.66); state or national banks; savings and loans; credit unions (§6.1-330.48); secured by mortgage or deed of trust (§6.1-330.71); installment credit plan (6.1-330.77)
WASHINGTON	12% absent written contract rate (§19.52.010[1])	Debtor entitled to costs, attorney's fees, and amount paid in excess of what lender is entitled to (§19.52.030[1])	Contract rate as long as within statutory limit or maximum rate (§4.56.110); child support, 12%	

Table 4: Interest Rates—Continued

State	Legal Maximum Rate of Interest	Usury Penalty	Judgments	Exceptions
WEST VIRGINIA	6% absent written agreement otherwise (§47-6-5); 8% maximum contract rate (§47-6-5(b))	Void as to all interest and debtor may recover 4 times all interest agreed to be paid with $100 minimum (§47-6-6); if supervised lender willfully makes excess charge it is guilty of misdemeanor (§46A-5-103)	10% (§§56-6-31; 46A-3-111)	Life insurer (§33-13-8); consumer credit sales (§46a-3-101); installment sale for business purposes; loans for business purposes (§47-6-11)
WISCONSIN	5% unless otherwise agreed in writing (§138.04)	Lender intentionally violating fined $25 to $500 and prison up to 6 months (§138.06(2))	12% (§815.05(8)7)	State-chartered banks, credit unions, savings and loans, etc. (§138.041); residential mortgage loans (§138.052(7));loans to corporations (§138.05(5)); installment contract on auto (§218.01)
WYOMING	7% absent agreement otherwise or provision of law (§40-14-106)		10% unless agreement (§1-16-102(a))	Uniform Credit Code adopted (§§40-14-101 to 702)

5. LEMON LAWS

Everyone has heard of someone who has bought a new car that was a "lemon." The car had either one major defect that could not be repaired or numerous minor defects that were always in need of repair.

Prior to the 1970s, when consumer advocacy hit its peak and numerous laws were enacted to protect the buyers of lemons, the only recourse the purchaser had was his or her warranty. As long as the manufacturer and dealer exercised their best efforts to fix the car while it was under warranty, the owner was stuck with the lemon. After the warranty period expired, the owner paid for the repairs.

"Lemon laws," or new car warranty laws, were enacted to place limits on what the consumer must endure should he or she purchase a lemon. Under the terms of the lemon laws, if the car cannot be fixed, the consumer must be compensated, either with a new car or with a cash refund. States are split among those that leave the decision of the specific remedy up to the consumer, manufacturer, or seller. All states now have lemon laws. In many states, the consumer has at least one year from the date of purchase to make a claim under the law. Most states allow the consumer two years or 24,000 miles, whichever comes first, to make a claim.

Table 5: Lemon Laws

State	Code Section	Title of Act	Definition of Defects	Time Limit for Manufacturer Repair	Remedies
ALABAMA	8-20A-2	Motor Vehicle Lemon Law Rights	Nonconformity to any applicable express warranties	24 months following delivery of vehicle or 24,000 miles, whichever comes first	Consumer's option: replace with comparable new car or accept return of car and refund consumer full contract price and nonrefundable portions of extended warranties and services, all collateral charges, all finance charges incurred after first reported nonconformity and incidental damages; all this minus allowance for consumer's use of nonconforming vehicle
ALASKA	45.45.300, *et seq.*		Nonconformity to applicable express warranties	Term of express warranty or within 1 year from date of delivery to original owner, whichever is first	Replacement of vehicle with new, comparable one or refund full purchase price less a reasonable allowance for use of motor vehicle
ARIZONA	44-1262, *et seq.*		Nonconformity to applicable express warranties of any defect/condition which substantially impairs use and value of motor vehicle	Time period of express warranty or during one year period following date of original delivery to consumer, whichever is earlier	Replacement with new motor vehicle or refund to consumer of full purchase price including all collateral charges, less a reasonable allowance for consumer's use of vehicle
ARKANSAS	4-90-401, *et seq.*	New Motor Vehicle Quality Assurance Act	Nonconformity to applicable manufacturer's express warranty or implied warranty of any defect/condition that substantially impairs use, value, or safety of motor vehicle	24 months following delivery of vehicle or 24,000 miles, whichever comes later	Consumer's option: replace with new motor vehicle acceptable to consumer or repurchase motor vehicle and return full purchase plus collateral and reasonably incurred incidental charges; less reasonable offset for use and physical damage
CALIFORNIA	Civ. §1793.22	Tanner Consumer Protection Act	Nonconformity to applicable express warranties which substantially impairs the use, value, or safety of motor vehicle	1 yr. from date of delivery to buyer or 12,000 miles, whichever occurs first	Replace the goods or reimburse buyer in an amount equal to the purchase price paid by the buyer, less the amount directly attributable to the use by the buyer prior to the discovery of the nonconformity

Table 5: Lemon Laws—Continued

State	Code Section	Title of Act	Definition of Defects	Time Limit for Manufacturer Repair	Remedies
COLORADO	42-12-101, *et seq.*		Nonconformity to express warranties which substantially impairs use and market value of motor vehicle	Warranty period or within 1 year following date of original delivery of vehicle to consumer, whichever is the earlier date	Manufacturer's option: (1) replace with comparable vehicle or (2) accept return of vehicle from consumer and refund full purchase price, including sales tax, fees and similar governmental charges, less a reasonable allowance for consumer's use
CONNECTICUT	42-179	New Automobile Warranties	Nonconformity to applicable express warranties which substantially impairs the use, safety, or value of motor vehicle	Repair defects covered by written warranties within 2 years following original delivery or first 18,000 miles, whichever is first	Replace vehicle with new vehicle acceptable to consumer or refund (upon accepting return of vehicle) the (1) full contract price including but not limited to charges for undercoating, dealer prep, transportation, and installed options; (2) all collateral charges, including but not limited to sales tax, license and regulation fees, and similar government charges; (3) all finance charges after he first reports conformity and during any subsequent period vehicle is out of service due to repair; (4) all incidental damages, less a reasonable allowance for consumer's use
DELAWARE	Tit. 6 §5001		Nonconformity to any applicable express warranty which substantially impairs the use, value, or safety of motor vehicle	Term of warranty or during period of 1 year following date of original delivery to consumer, whichever is earlier	Consumer's option: replace with comparable new automobile acceptable to consumer or repurchase and refund full purchase, including all credits and allowances for any trade-in vehicle
DISTRICT OF COLUMBIA	40-1301, *et seq.*	Automobile Consumer Protection Act of 1984	Nonconformity to all warranties which results in significant impairment of vehicle	First 18,000 miles of operation or during period of 2 years following date of delivery to original purchaser, whichever is earlier	Consumer's option: replace with comparable vehicle or accept return and refund full purchase price, including all sales tax, license fees, registration fees, and any similar governmental charges; less reasonable allowance for use

Table 5: Lemon Laws—Continued

State	Code Section	Title of Act	Definition of Defects	Time Limit for Manufacturer Repair	Remedies
FLORIDA	681.10, *et seq.*	Motor Vehicle Warranty Enforcement Act	Nonconformity to warranties which significantly impair the use, value, or safety of motor vehicle	1 year after date of original delivery to consumer or 12,000 miles of operation, whichever is earlier	Consumer's unconditional option: Replace with vehicle acceptable to consumer or repurchase vehicle and refund to consumer full purchase price, including all reasonably incurred collateral and incidental charges, less reasonable offset for use
GEORGIA	10-1-780, *et seq.*	Motor Vehicle Warranty Rights Act	Nonconformity to applicable express warranties which significantly impair the use, value, or safety of motor vehicle	Within 12 months following purchase of vehicle or 12,000 miles following purchase of vehicle, whichever occurs first	Consumer's option: replace with identical or reasonably equivalent vehicle including payment of all collateral charges which consumer/lessor will incur a second time, less reasonable offset for use or repurchase and refund purchase price plus all collateral charges and incidental costs, less reasonable offset for use
HAWAII	490:2-313.1	Not specified	Nonconformity to all applicable express warranties that substantially impairs the use and market value of vehicle	Within express warranty term	Replace with comparable vehicle or accept return and refund the full purchase price including all collateral charges, excluding interest, and less a reasonable allowance for consumer's use of vehicle
IDAHO	48-901, *et seq.*	Not specified	Nonconformity to applicable express warranties which significantly impairs use, value, or safety of vehicle	1 year period following date of original delivery of vehicle to buyer or first 12,000 miles, whichever is earlier	Consumer's option: replace with comparable new vehicle or accept return and refund full purchase price including all collateral charges, less a reasonable allowance for buyer's use of vehicle
ILLINOIS	815 ILCS 380/1, *et seq.*	New Vehicle Buyer Protection Act 815 ILCS	Nonconformity to applicable express warranties which significantly impair the use, value, or safety of motor vehicle	Within statutory warranty period: the period of one year or 12,000 miles, whichever occurs first after date of delivery of a new vehicle to consumer	Replace with new vehicle of like model line, if available, or otherwise a comparable motor vehicle or accept return and refund consumer full purchase price of new vehicle, including all collateral charges, less a reasonable allowance for consumer use of vehicle

Table 5: Lemon Laws—Continued

State	Code Section	Title of Act	Definition of Defects	Time Limit for Manufacturer Repair	Remedies
INDIANA	24-5-13-1, *et seq.*	Indiana Motor Vehicle Protection Act of 1988	Nonconformity to applicable express warranties which significantly impairs the use, market value or safety of motor vehicle or renders vehicle nonconforming to terms of applicable manufacturer's warranty	If reported within term of protection: 18 months after date of delivery to buyer or 18,000 miles whichever occurs first	Consumer's option: Replace with vehicle of comparable value, including reimbursement to buyer of any fees of transferring registration or sales tax incurred as result of replacement or refund full contract price of vehicle, including all credits and allowances for any trade-in vehicle and less reasonable allowance for use.
IOWA	322G.1, *et seq.*	Not specified	Nonconformity to all applicable express warranties	Term of manufacturer's written warranty or during period of 2 years following date of original delivery of a motor vehicle to consumer or first 24,000 miles, whichever is first	Replace with identical or reasonably equivalent vehicle, including collateral and incidental charges less reasonable offset for use, or refund full purchase or lease price including all collateral and reasonably incurred incidental charges, less a reasonable offset for consumer's use
KANSAS	50-645, *et seq.*	Lemon Law	Nonconformity to applicable warranties which significantly impairs the use or value of motor vehicle	1 year from date of original delivery of vehicle to consumer or term of any warranties, whichever is earlier	Replace with comparable vehicle under warranty or accept return and refund full purchase price including all collateral charges, less a reasonable allowance for consumer's use
KENTUCKY	367.840, *et seq.*	Not specified	Nonconformity to applicable express warranties which significantly impairs the use, value, or safety of the motor vehicle	First 12 months following date of delivery or first 12,000 miles, whichever is first	Consumer's option: replace vehicle with comparable motor vehicle or accept return and refund full purchase price including amount paid for vehicle, finance charge, all sales tax, license fee, registration fee, any similar governmental charges, plus all collateral charges, less reasonable offset for use
LOUISIANA	51:1941, *et seq.*	Louisiana Lemon Law	Nonconformity to applicable express warranties	Term of warranty or during period of 1 year following date of original delivery, whichever is earlier	Manufacturer's option: Replace with comparable new motor vehicle or accept return and refund full purchase price plus any amounts paid by the consumer at the timet of sale and all collateral costs, less a reasonable allowance for use

Table 5: Lemon Laws—Continued

State	Code Section	Title of Act	Definition of Defects	Time Limit for Manufacturer Repair	Remedies
MAINE	10-1161	Not specified	Nonconformity to all express warranties which significantly impairs use, safety, or value of vehicle	Term of express warranties within a period of 2 years following date of original delivery to consumer, or during first 18,000 miles, whichever is earlier date	Buyer's option: replace with comparable new vehicle or accept return of vehicle and refund full purchase price (or in case of lease, payments made so far) including any paid financing charges, all collateral charges, and incidentals, less reasonable allowance for use
MARYLAND	Com. Law §§14-1501, *et seq.*	Automotive Warranty Enforcement Act	Nonconformity to all applicable express warranties which significantly affects use or market value of vehicle	Warranty period equal to or greater than first 15,000 miles or first 15 months following date of original delivery of vehicle to consumer	Consumer's option: replace with comparable motor vehicle acceptable to customer or accept return and refund full purchase price including all excise tax license fees, registration fees, and any similar governmental charges, less reasonable allowance for consumer's use (not to exceed 15% of purchase price) and for damage not attributable to normal wear
MASSACHUSETTS	Ch. 90§7N½	Not specified	Nonconformity to applicable express warranties or implied warranty which significantly affects use, market value, or safety of vehicle	Term of protection: one year or 15,000 miles of use from date of original delivery	Manufacturer's option: replace with vehicle acceptable to consumer or accept return and refund full contract price including all credits and allowances for any trade-in vehicle, less a reasonable allowance for use
MICHIGAN	257.1401, *et. seq.*	Warranties on New Motor Vehicles Act	Nonconformity to manufacturer's express warranties that significantly affects use or value of vehicle	Term of manufacturer's express warranty or 1 year from date of delivery of new motor vehicle to original consumer, whichever is earlier	Manufacturer's option: replace with a comparable replacement vehicle currently in production and acceptable to consumer or accept return of vehicle and refund full purchase price including cost of any options or other modifications installed or made by or for the manufacturer, less a reasonable allowance for consumer's use of vehicle, not to exceed 10¢ per mile driven at time of initial report of same defect or conditions or 10% of purchase price, whichever is less, and less an amount equal to any appraised damage that is not attributable to normal wear and tear

Table 5: Lemon Laws—Continued

State	Code Section	Title of Act	Definition of Defects	Time Limit for Manufacturer Repair	Remedies
MINNESOTA	325F.665	Not specified	Nonconformity to all applicable express warranties which significantly affects the use or market value of vehicle	During term of applicable express warranty or during period of 2 years following date of original delivery of vehicle to consumer, whichever is earlier	Buyer's option: Replace with comparable vehicle or accept return and refund to consumer full purchase price including cost of any options or other modifications made/installed/ arranged by manufacturer (or agents or dealer) within 30 days of original delivery, and all other charges, less a reasonable allowance for consumer use of vehicle
MISSISSIPPI	63-17-151, *et seq.*	Motor Vehicle Warranty Enforcement Act	Nonconformity to all applicable express warranties which significantly affects the use, market value, or safety of vehicle	Term of express warranties or during period of 1 year following date of original delivery of motor vehicle to consumer, whichever period expires earlier	Consumer's option: replace with comparable vehicle acceptable to consumer or accept return and refund full purchase price, including all reasonably incurred collateral charges, less a reasonable allowance for consumer's use
MISSOURI	407.560, *et seq.*	Not specified	Nonconformity to all applicable express warranties which significantly affects the use, market value, or safety of vehicle	Term of express warranties or during 1 year following date of original delivery to consumer, whichever expires earlier	Manufacturer's option: replace with comparable new vehicle acceptable to consumer or take title from consumer and refund full purchase price, including all reasonably incurred collateral charges, less reasonable allowance for use
MONTANA	61-4-501, *et seq.*	Not specified	Nonconformity to all applicable express warranties which significantly affects the use, market value, or safety of vehicle	Warranty period within 2 years after date of original delivery to consumer or during first 18,000 miles of operation, whichever is earlier; however, if consumer notifies manufacturer in writing of nonconformity within warranty, manufacturer must fix regardless of expiration of warranty	Manufacturer's option: replace with new vehicle of same model and style and of equal value unless for reasons of lack of availability such replacement is impossible, in which case it shall be replaced with vehicle of comparable market value or accept return and refund full purchase price plus reasonable collateral and incidental damages, less a reasonable allowance for consumer's use of vehicle

Table 5: Lemon Laws—Continued

State	Code Section	Title of Act	Definition of Defects	Time Limit for Manufacturer Repair	Remedies
NEBRASKA	60-2701, *et seq.*	Not specified	Nonconformity to all applicable express warranties which significantly affects the use or market value of vehicle	Term of such express warranties or during period of 1 year following date of original delivery of new vehicle to consumer, whichever is earlier	Replace with comparable vehicle or accept return and refund full purchase price including all sales tax, license fees, registration fees, and any similar government charges, less a reasonable allowance for consumer's use
NEVADA	597.600, *et seq.*		Nonconformity to all applicable express warranties which significantly affects the use or market value of vehicle	Before expiration of manufacturer's express warranties or no later than 1 year after date of delivery to original buyer, whichever is earlier 597.610	Replace with comparable vehicle of same model having same features; if vehicle cannot be delivered within reasonable time, then a comparable vehicle substantially similar to replaced vehicle or accept return and refund full purchase price including all sales tax, license fees, registration fees, and other similar governmental charges, less a reasonable allowance for consumer's use 597.630
NEW HAMPSHIRE	357-D:1, *et seq.*	Not specified	Nonconformity to all applicable express warranties or implied warranties which significantly affects the use or market value of vehicle	Term of express/ implied warranty or within 1 year following date of original delivery, whichever is earlier	Within 30 days after an order by the New Hampshire new motor vehicle arbitration board, the manufacturer shall at consumer's option replace the motor vehicle with a new motor vehicle or accept return and refund full purchase price and all credits and allowances for trade-in/down payment, license fees, finance charges, credit charges, registration fees and other similar charges and incidental and consequential damages less a reasonable allowance for use.

Table 5: Lemon Laws—Continued

State	Code Section	Title of Act	Definition of Defects	Time Limit for Manufacturer Repair	Remedies
NEW JERSEY	56:12-30, *et seq.*	Not specified "Lemon Law"	Nonconformity to express warranties which significantly affects the use, market value, or safety of vehicle	Term of warranty or during period of 1 year following date of original delivery to consumer, or 12,000 miles of operation, whichever is earlier	Option of consumer: accept return and refund full purchase price including any stated credit/allowance for consumer's used motor vehicle, cost of any options/ other modifications arranged, installed/ made by manufacturer within 30 days after date of original delivery and sales tax, license and registration fees, finance charges and other incidental fees less a reasonable allowance for use
NEW MEXICO	57-16A-1, *et seq.*	Motor Vehicle Quality Assurance Act	Nonconformity to all applicable express warranties which significantly affects the use or market value of vehicle	Term of express warranties or 1 year following date of original delivery, whichever is earlier	Replace with comparable vehicle or accept return and refund full purchase price including all collateral charges, less a reasonable allowance for consumer's use of vehicle
NEW YORK	Gen. Bus. §198-a	New Car Lemon Law	Nonconformity to all express warranties	First 18,000 miles or during period of 2 years following date of original delivery, whichever is earlier reporting of nonconformity by consumers	Consumer's option: replace vehicle with comparable motor vehicle or accept return and refund full purchase price, or if applicable, the lease price and any trade-in allowance plus fees and charges less reasonable allowance for consumer's use in excess of first 12,000 miles pursuant to mileage deduction formula and a reasonable allowance for any damage not attributable to normal wear and improvements; vehicle must be sold and registered in New York
NORTH CAROLINA	20-351, *et seq.*	New Motor Vehicles Warranties Act	Nonconformity to all applicable express warranties which significantly affects the value of vehicle	For period of 1 year or term of express warranties, whichever is greater, following date of original delivery of vehicle to consumer; can occur no later than 24 months or 24,000 miles following original delivery	Consumer's option: replace with comparable new vehicle or accept return and refund full contract price, all collateral charges, all finance charges incurred since reporting nonconformity, and any incidental damages and monetary consequential damages, less reasonable allowance for consumer's use

Table 5: Lemon Laws—Continued

State	Code Section	Title of Act	Definition of Defects	Time Limit for Manufacturer Repair	Remedies
NORTH DAKOTA	51-07-16, *et seq.*	Not specified	Nonconformity to all applicable express warranties which significantly affects the use or market value of vehicle	Term of express warranties or during period of 1 year following date of original delivery to consumer, whichever is earlier 51-07-17	Replace with comparable vehicle or accept return and refund full purchase price, including all collateral charges, less reasonable allowance for consumer's use 51-07-18
OHIO	1345.71, *et seq.*	Not specified	Nonconformity to express warranty of the manufacturer or distributor which substantially impairs the use, value, or safety of a motor vehicle	1 year following date of original delivery or during first 18,000 miles, whichever is earlier	Consumer's option: replace with new vehicle acceptable to consumer or accept return of vehicle from consumer and refund full purchase price, all collateral charges, all finance charges, and all incidental damages
OKLAHOMA	15-901	Not specified	Nonconformity to any applicable express warranties which significantly affects the use or market value of vehicle	Term of express warranties or during 1 year following date of original delivery to consumer, whichever is earlier	Replace with new vehicle or accept return and refund full purchase price including all taxes, license, registration fees, and all similar governmental fees, excluding interest, less a reasonable allowance for consumer's use
OREGON	646.315, *et seq.*	Not specified	Nonconformity to applicable manufacturer's express warranties which significantly affects the use or market value of vehicle	During period of 1 year following date of original delivery of motor vehicle to consumer or during period ending on date on which mileage reaches 12,000 miles, whichever is earlier	Replace with new motor vehicle or accept return and refund full purchase/lease price paid, including taxes, license and registration fees, and any similar collateral charges, excluding interest, less a reasonable allowance for consumer's use of vehicle
PENNSYLVANIA	Tit. 73 §§1951, *et seq.*	Automobile Lemon Law	Nonconformity to warranties which significantly affects the use, market value, or safety of vehicle	1 year following date of actual delivery to consumer, within first 12,000 miles of use or during time of the warranty, whichever may first occur	Purchaser's option: replace with comparable vehicle of equal value or accept return and refund full purchase price, including all collateral charges, less a reasonable allowance for purchaser's use not exceeding 10¢ per mile or 10% of purchase price, whichever is less

Table 5: Lemon Laws—Continued

State	Code Section	Title of Act	Definition of Defects	Time Limit for Manufacturer Repair	Remedies
RHODE ISLAND	31-5.2-1, *et seq.*	Not specified	Nonconformity to applicable express warranties or implied warranties	Term of protection equals 1 year or 15,000 miles from date of original delivery, whichever comes first	Consumer's option: replace with comparable new vehicle in good working condition or accept return and refund full contract price of vehicle including all credits and allowances for any trade-in vehicle, less a reasonable allowance for use
SOUTH CAROLINA	56-28-30, *et seq.*	Not specified	Nonconformity to all applicable express warranties which significantly affects the use, safety, or market value of vehicle	Within 1 year of purchase or first 12,000 miles of operation, whichever occurs first and if it is reported during terms of express warranty	Manufacturer's option: replace with comparable vehicle or accept return and refund full purchase price as delivered including applicable finance charges, sales taxes, license fees, registration fees, and any other similar governmental charges, less a reasonable allowance for consumer's use of vehicle
SOUTH DAKOTA	32-6D-1, *et seq.*	Not specified	Nonconformity to any express warranty which significantly impairs the use, value, or safety of vehicle	Reported within lemon law rights pd.—one year after date of original delivery of vehicle or first 12,000 miles whichever occurs earlier; however, obligation to repair does not extend beyond period of two years following delivery or 24,000 miles whichever occurs first	Consumer's option: replace with comparable vehicle or accept return and refund full contract price including all incidental charges and fees
TENNESSEE	55-24-201, *et seq.*	Not specified	Nonconformity to all applicable express warranties	Term of applicable warranties or 1 year following date of original delivery of vehicle to consumer, whichever comes first	Replace with comparable vehicle or accept return and refund full purchase price (cost paid by consumer including all collateral charges, less a reasonable allowance for use)
TEXAS	Tex. Rev. Civ. Stat. Ann. Art. 4413(36) §6.07	Texas Motor Vehicle Commission Code	Nonconformity to all applicable express warranties which significantly affects the use or market value of vehicle	Term of such express warranties within one year of purchase or first 12,000 miles whichever occurs first	Replace with comparable motor vehicle or accept return and refund full purchase price less a reasonable allowance for owner's use and any other allowances or refunds payable to owner

Table 5: Lemon Laws—Continued

State	Code Section	Title of Act	Definition of Defects	Time Limit for Manufacturer Repair	Remedies
UTAH	13-20-1, *et seq.*	New Motor Vehicles Warranties Act	Nonconformity to all applicable express warranties which significantly affects the use, safety, or market value of vehicle	Term of express warranties or 1 year following date of original delivery of vehicle to consumer, whichever is earlier	Replace with comparable new vehicle or accept return and refund full purchase price, including all collateral charges, less a reasonable allowance for consumer's use
VERMONT	Tit. 9 §4172	Not specified	Nonconformity to applicable manufacturer's express warranties which significantly affects the use, safety, or market value of vehicle	Term of warranty	Consumer's option: replace with new vehicle from same manufacturer of comparable worth to the same make and model with all the options and accessories and with appropriate adjustments being allowed for any model year differences or accept return and refund full purchase price as indicated in purchase contract and all credits and allowances for any trade-in or downpayment, licensing fees, finance charges, credit charges, registration fees and any similar charges, and incidental and consequential damages, less reasonable allowance for use
VIRGINIA	59.1-207.9, *et seq.*	Virginia Motor Vehicle Warranty Enforcement Act	Nonconformity to all warranties which significantly affects the use, safety, or market value of vehicle	Manufacturer's warranty period or lemon law rights period ending 18 months after date of original delivery to consumer of new motor vehicle	Replace with comparable vehicle acceptable to consumer or accept return and refund full purchase price, including all collateral charges, and incidental damages, less a reasonable allowance for consumer's use of vehicle up to first notice of nonconformity given

Table 5: Lemon Laws—Continued

State	Code Section	Title of Act	Definition of Defects	Time Limit for Manufacturer Repair	Remedies
WASHINGTON	19.118.021, *et seq.*	Not specified	Nonconformity to the Warranty which significantly affects the use, value, or safety of the vehicle	Term of the warranty period (period ending 2 years after date of original delivery or first 24,000 miles, whichever is first) or period of coverage of applicable manufacturer's written warranty, whichever is less	Consumer's option: replace with identical or reasonably equivalent vehicle including any service contract, undercoating, rustproofing, and factory or dealer installed options. Manufacturer responsible for sales tax, license and registration fees. Compensation for reasonable offset for use to be paid by consumer to manufacturer; or repurchase vehicle, manufacturer shall refund to consumer the purchase price, all collateral charges and incidental costs, less a reasonable offset for use
WEST VIRGINIA	46A-6A-3	Not specified	Nonconformity to all applicable express warranties which significantly affects the use or market value of vehicle	Term of express warranties or during 1 year following date of original delivery of vehicle to consumer, whichever is later date	Repair or replace with comparable new vehicle which does conform to the warranties
WISCONSIN	218.015	Not specified	Nonconformity to applicable express warranties which significantly affects the use, safety, or market value of vehicle	Term of warranty or 1 year after first delivery of motor vehicle to consumer, whichever is sooner	Consumer's option: accept return and replace with comparable new vehicle and refund any collateral costs or accept return and refund full purchase price plus any sales tax, finance charge, amount paid by the consumer at point of sale, and collateral costs, less a reasonable allowance for use
WYOMING	40-17-101	Not specified	Nonconformity to applicable express warranties which significantly affects the use or market value of vehicle	1 year following original delivery of vehicle to consumer	Replace with new or comparable vehicle of same type and similarly equipped or accept return and refund full purchase price including all collateral charges less a reasonable allowance for consumer's use

II. CRIMINAL LAWS

6. CAPITAL PUNISHMENT

The acceptance of capital punishment, or the death penalty, as a sentence for heinous criminal acts has been hotly debated across the nation over the last few decades. On the books in most states, the death penalty has been challenged by many, originally on grounds that it violated the Constitutional prohibition against cruel and unusual punishment, and later on the procedural grounds that there were not enough due process protections for defendants accused of capital crimes. In general, it was held that since the sentence was so severe, the law must impose the strictest standards of proof to sentence a defendant to death. Consequently, many states have gone through periods in which the death penalty was held as legal, then illegal, then revised and held as legal, then illegal again, and then further revised and held as legal once more. This shifting status often brought unbalanced—unjust—sentencing. For instance, in many of these states one of two defendants accused of identical unrelated crimes committed within weeks of each other drew the death sentence while the other did not, merely because the statute under which they were sentenced was ruled unconstitutional in the intervening time.

The Supreme Court has since handed down explicit guidelines defining the legal imposition of the death penalty, allowing states a new opportunity to legislate a legal death penalty statute that is less likely to be ruled unconstitutional in the future. This does not mean that the process is not still open to attack. As of this writing, new cases on the death penalty are currently wending their way through the courts to the Supreme Court.

Thirty-seven states currently have death penalty statutes on the books. In a few states, the statute remains on the books though it has been declared unconstitutional. In some of these cases, the state legislature can either revise or rewrite the death penalty statute if it chooses to make it the law.

There are thirteen states that authorize the death penalty for non-homicide crimes. Of note is California, often known for its radical politics, which lists treason as a capital crime. Other common non-homicide capital offenses are kidnapping, hijacking, and other serious crimes that involve hostage-taking or placing a victim in extreme danger.

Some states have very complicated criminal statutes; therefore, the following tables may contain less information on some states if nothing explicit can be determined from the state statute alone. Occasionally it is necessary to consult lists or sentencing guidelines that are not part of the code to determine these rules.

Table 6: Capital Punishment

State/Code Section	Allowed	Effect of Incapacity	Minimum Age	Non-homicidal	Capital Homicide	Method of Execution
ALABAMA 13A-5-39, *et seq.*	Yes	Mitigating circumstance if defendant under influence of extreme mental or emotional disturbance; forbid execution of "insane" person	No minimum age	None	Homicide during the commission of kidnapping; robbery; rape/sodomy; burglary; sexual abuse; arson; hijacking; murder of police officer or public official while on duty or when related to or caused by or is related to his official position, act, or capacity; murder for pecuniary or other valuable consideration; two or more persons murdered in same act/ course of conduct; victim less than 14 years old; murder under life sentence; murder during arson or by means of explosives; murder by defendant who has previously been convicted of murder within 20 years; murder of witness in civil or criminal trial when murder is caused by or related to the testimony	Electrocution
ALASKA 12.55.015	Not authorized					
ARIZONA 13-703	Yes, for 1st degree murder with mitigating factors	Considered mitigating circumstance	15	None	Previous capital convictions or homicides; previous conviction of a "serious offense"; previous felonies with use or threat of violence; knowingly created grave risk of death to persons in addition to victim; procured commission of offense by payment; especially heinous, cruel or depraved manner; adult person and victim under 15 or over 70; victim on duty peace officer and defendant knew or should have known; in custody of state dept. of corrections, law enforcement agency or jail at time of homicide	Lethal injection. If defendant is convicted for crime committed prior to November 23, 1992, s/he shall choose between lethal gas or lethal injection.

Table 6: Capital Punishment—Continued

State/Code Section	Allowed	Effect of Incapacity	Minimum Age	Non-homicidal	Capital Homicide	Method of Execution
ARKANSAS 5-4-601, *et seq.*; 5-51-201	Yes, capital murder	If no aggravating circumstances are found or if mitigating circumstances outweigh aggravating circumstances, the court shall impose life in prison without parole	Chronological age does not necessarily control jury's determination (*Giles v. Statz* 549 S.W. 2d 479 (1977))	Treason	Homicide committed by a person incarcerated for felony conviction; committed by person unlawfully at liberty after being imprisoned for felony conviction; use of threat or violence in commission of felony; knowingly created grave risk of death to person other than victim or caused the death of more than one person in the same criminal episode; committed in order to prevent arrest or escape custody; committed for pecuniary gain; committed for purposes of disrupting/hindering lawful exercise of any government or political function; especially cruel or depraved manner by use of torture or methods evidencing the defendant's pleasure in committing the murder; committed by means of destructive explosive, bomb, similar device	Lethal injection or electrocution if lethal injection held unconstitutional

Table 6: Capital Punishment—Continued

State/Code Section	Allowed	Effect of Incapacity	Minimum Age	Non-homicidal	Capital Homicide	Method of Execution
CALIFORNIA Pen. Code §§37; 190, *et seq.*;§§3604, *et seq.*; §§3700, *et seq.*	Yes, if crime is 1st degree murder with enumerated special circumstances	If defendant found insane at any time prior to execution, the execution is suspended. Upon recovery, execution is rescheduled	18	Treason	Murder committed for financial gain; previously convicted of first/second degree murder; multiple murders in same proceeding; bomb, explosives, grave risk; for purposes of avoiding lawful arrest or attempt to escape lawful custody; murder intentional and involved the infliction of torture; intentional killing of peace officer, federal law officer/ agent, fireman in performance of duties, and defendant should have known or knew official status of victim; victim was a juror in any court of record in local, state, or federal system in any state and the murder was intentionally carried out in retaliation or prevention of the victim's official duties; the murder was intentional and perpetrated by means of a firearm being discharged from a motor vehicle intentionally at another outside the vehicle with intent to kill; witness of crime intentionally killed to prevent retaliatory testimony at criminal proceeding; retaliation against judge or former judge of this state or any other state, prosecutor, etc.; state officials or officials of any local government of this state or any other state for reasons relating to their office; lying in wait; especially cruel, atrocious, heinous; racial; committed along with robbery, kidnapping, rape, sodomy, oral copulation, burglary, performance of a lewd act upon a child under the age of 14; arson, train wrecking; carjacking; intentionally poisoned; mayhem; rape by instrument	Lethal gas or lethal injection, but if defendant fails to choose, lethal gas

Table 6: Capital Punishment—Continued

State/Code Section	Allowed	Effect of Incapacity	Minimum Age	Non-homicidal	Capital Homicide	Method of Execution
COLORADO 16-11-101, *et seq.*; 18-3-101, *et seq*; 18-3-301, *et seq.*	Yes for Class 1 felonies	Mitigating factor; suspend sentence	Age is mitigating factor; no one under 18 (*Sullivan v. People,* 111 Colo. 205, 139 P.2d 876 (1943))	First degree kidnapping if victim has been injured, but defendant will not be sentenced to death if victim is liberated alive prior to the conviction of kidnapper. Treason.	Murder committed by person imprisoned for Class 1, 2 or 3 felony; previous crime of violence; intentionally killed peace officer/former peace officer, judge, firefighter, elected official, federal officer he knew or should have known to be engaged in official duties or retaliation for past official duties; kidnapped person intentionally killed; agreement to kill; explosives or incendiary device; pecuniary gain	Lethal injection
CONNECTICUT 53a-46a; 53a-54b; 54-100, *et seq.*	Yes, capital felony	Suspend sentence	18		Murder committed in commission of felony; 2 or more prior felonies involving infliction of serious bodily injury; knowingly created grave risk of death to other persons; murder of a police officer, chief inspector in criminal justice, constable performing criminal law duties, special police; especially heinous, cruel, depraved manner; committed for pecuniary gain; murder committed by a kidnapper of kidnap victim either during abduction or before victim can be returned to safety; seller of illegal narcotic if purchaser dies as a result of use of narcotic; murder of person under 16; during commission of 1st degree sex assault	Lethal injection by a continuous intravenous injection of a substance or substances sufficient to cause death

Table 6: Capital Punishment—Continued

State/Code Section	Allowed	Effect of Incapacity	Minimum Age	Non-homicidal	Capital Homicide	Method of Execution
DELAWARE Tit. 11, §§636, 4209; §406	Yes	Exempt from execution while incapacitated	No minimum age	None	Murder committed while in or escaped from custody/confinement; committed for purposes of avoiding/preventing arrest or for effecting escape from custody; committed against law enforcement officer, corrections employee, fireman engaged in duties; committed against judge, attorney general, other state officer (former or present) during or because of exercise of official duty; hostage/ransom; witness to crime to avoid testimony; paid for it/pecuniary gain; convicted of prior felony using or threat of violence; rape, sodomy, unlawful sexual intercourse, arson, kidnapping, burglary; multiple victims; outrageously or wantonly vile, horrible or inhumane treatment involving torture, depravity of mind or use of explosive device or poison; agent or employee of another person; defendant serving life sentence; victim was pregnant, handicapped, severely disabled or 62 years of age or older; child 14 years or younger and murderer was 4 years older; present or past nongovernment informant or provided information and killed in retaliation; murder was premeditated and result of substantial planning; or murder committed for purpose of interfering with victim's exercise of a constitutional right protected by the first amendment or because of the victim's race, religion, national origin, or disability	Lethal injection
DISTRICT OF COLUMBIA 22-2404	No					

70

Table 6: Capital Punishment—Continued

State/Code Section	Allowed	Effect of Incapacity	Minimum Age	Non-homicidal	Capital Homicide	Method of Execution
FLORIDA 775.082, 782.04(1); 921.141; 922.07; 922.10; 921.142; 922.08	Yes	Exempt from execution if insane or pregnant for duration of condition	No minimum age	May apply to capital drug trafficking	Capital felony committed by person serving sentence of imprisonment or under community control; previous capital felony or felony using or threat of violence; knowingly created great risk of death to many persons; the capital felony was committed while defendant was engaged in, was an accomplice, in commission of or attempt to commit or flight after committing or attempt to commit any robbery, sexual battery, aggravated child abuse, arson, burglary, kidnapping, aircraft piracy, unlawful throwing, placing, or discharging of a destructive device or bombings; capital felony for purposes of avoiding lawful arrest or effecting escape from custody; capital felony for pecuniary gain; capital felony to hinder lawful exercise of governmental function or enforcement of laws; capital felony especially heinous, atrocious or cruel; premeditated homicide; victim of capital felony was public official or law enforcement officer engaged in official duties; victim of capital murder was less than 12 years old	Electrocution

Table 6: Capital Punishment—Continued

State/Code Section	Allowed	Effect of Incapacity	Minimum Age	Non-homicidal	Capital Homicide	Method of Execution
GEORGIA 17-10-30, *et seq.*	Yes	Suspend sentence; shall not be executed	17	Aircraft hijacking or treason	Murder, rape, armed robbery, kidnapping committed by person with prior record of conviction for capital felony; murder, rape, armed robbery, kidnapping committed while engaged in commission of other capital felony; knowingly created grave risk of death to multiple persons in public place by use of weapon/device; murder committed for financial gain; judicial officer, district attorney or solicitor (or formers) because of exercise of duties; committed as agent of another; outrageously or wantonly vile, horrible or inhuman; against peace officer, corrections officer, fireman while performing duties; offender escaped from lawful custody/confinement; avoiding lawful arrest	Electrocution
HAWAII 706-656	No					

Table 6: Capital Punishment—Continued

State/Code Section	Allowed	Effect of Incapacity	Minimum Age	Non-homicidal	Capital Homicide	Method of Execution
IDAHO 18-4001, *et seq.*; 19-2515, *et seq.*; 19-2700, *et seq.*	Yes	If as result of mortal disease or defect a person lacks capacity to understand proceedings against him, he cannot be tried, convicted, sentenced or punished so long as incapacity endures	No minimum age	Kidnapping in the 1st degree unless prior to imposition of sentence victim is liberated unharmed	Murder committed by person guilty of a previous conviction of another murder; knowingly created great risk of death; committed for remuneration; especially heinous, atrocious or cruel; circumstances show utter disregard for human life; murder of 1st degree with specific intent to cause death; propensity to commit murder, i.e., a continuing threat to society; murder of former/present peace officer, judicial officer, executive officer, officer of the court, fireman, prosecuting attorney for reasons relating to the performance of their official duties; murder of witness in criminal or civil proceeding; murder committed during perpetration of arson, rape, robbery, burglary, kidnapping or mayhem and defendant killed, intended to kill, or acted with reckless indifference to human life; murder while escaping or attempting to escape from a penal institution	Lethal injection; firing squad if lethal injection not possible

Table 6: Capital Punishment—Continued

State/Code Section	Allowed	Effect of Incapacity	Minimum Age	Non-homicidal	Capital Homicide	Method of Execution
ILLINOIS 720 ILCS 5/9-1, *et seq*; 720 ILCS 5/10-2; 720 ILCS 5/30-1; 725 ILCS 5/119-5; 730 ILCS 5/5-5-3	Yes		18	Treason; aggravated kidnapping for ransom	First degree murder committed upon a peace officer or fireman in the performance of his duties; an employee of the Department of Corrections in the performance of his duties; an inmate in a correctional facility or otherwise was present in the facility with the approval of the prison administration; murder involves more than one victim; committed during hijacking of airplane, train, ship, bus, or other public conveyance; committed for financial gain; committed during robbery, arson, kidnapping, drug conspiracy, sexual assault; victim is under 12; murder of witness in order to prevent victim from testifying against defendant; while defendant was incarcerated and was committing any other offense punishable under IL law as a felony	Lethal injection or, if lethal injection held illegal or unconstitutional, electrocution
INDIANA 35-50-2-3; 35-50-2-9; 35-38-6-1, *et seq*.	Yes	Hearing to determine whether defendant has ability to understand proceedings. If ability lacking, court can delay or continue trial	16	None	Intentional murder while committing/attempting to commit arson, burglary, child molesting, criminal deviate conduct, kidnapping, rape, robbery, carjacking, criminal gang activity dealing in cocaine or narcotic drug; unlawful detonation of explosive with intent to injure; lying in wait; hiring or hired to kill; victim was law enforcement officer, etc.; defendant committed crime by discharging firearm into house or from vehicle; another conviction of murder; under sentence of life imprisonment and time; victim dismembered; victim less than 12 years old; victim was witness against defendant	Lethal injection
IOWA 902.1	No					

Table 6: Capital Punishment—Continued

State/Code Section	Allowed	Effect of Incapacity	Minimum Age	Non-homicidal	Capital Homicide	Method of Execution
KANSAS 21-3401; 21-3436; 21-3439, 21-4624; 22-4001	Yes	Suspend sentence	18	None	Murder committed in the commission of, attempt to commit, or in flight from an inherently dangerous felony, including: kidnapping, robbery, rape, burglary, theft, child abuse, sodomy, arson, treason; murder committed for hire or hiring one to commit murder; murder committed while defendant is in custody of correctional institution; murder of law enforcement officer; of multiple persons; of child under 14 in commission of kidnapping	Lethal injection
KENTUCKY 431.220; 431.240; 532.025; 640.040	Yes	Execution suspended if person is insane or pregnant with child until restored to sanity or delivered of child	16	None	Prior capital offense conviction; substantial history of serious assaultive criminal convictions while committing arson, robbery, burglary, rape, sodomy; knowingly created great risk of death to more than 1 person in a public place; for remuneration; intentional and resulted in multiple deaths; intentional and victim state or local official or police officer in performance of duties	Electrocution
LOUISIANA 14:30, *et seq.*; 14:113; 15:567, *et seq.*	Yes	If woman defendant is found to be pregnant, execution is stayed until 90-120 days from end of pregnancy. A person may not be executed while suffering from mental illness	No minimum age	Treason	Murder committed during commission of aggravated rape, forcible rape; aggravated kidnapping; aggravated burglary; aggravated arson; aggravated escape; armed robbery or simple robbery or first degree robbery victim was fireman or police officer engaged in lawful duties; previous conviction of murder and other serious crimes; knowingly created a risk of death or great bodily harm to more than 1 person; for remuneration; especially heinous, atrocious or cruel; victim under age of 12 years; distribution, etc. of a controlled dangerous substance; victim was witness against defendant	Lethal injection
MAINE Tit. 17A §§1251, 1152	No					

Table 6: Capital Punishment—Continued

State/Code Section	Allowed	Effect of Incapacity	Minimum Age	Non-homicidal	Capital Homicide	Method of Execution
MARYLAND Art. 27 §§71, 75, 412, 413, 627	Yes	Execution of incompetent prohibited	18	None	Victim was law enforcement officer on duty; defendant was confined to correctional institution; escaped/attempted to escape lawful custody, evade arrest, or detention; kidnapping; child abduction; for remuneration; while under death or life sentence; more than one murder in first degree arising from same incident; while committing/attempting to commit robbery, arson, rape, sexual offense	Lethal ultrashort-acting barbiturate gas injection
MASSACHUSETTS Ch. 279 §§57-71	No; statutes still on books but *Commonwealth v. Colon-Cruz*, 393 Mass. 150, 470 N.E.2d 116 (1984) said state statute violates state constitution	Suspend sentence if insane or pregnant	No minimum age		Victim was police officer, special police officer, state or federal law enforcement officer, officer or employee of the department of corrections, sheriff's department, fireman, etc. acting in official duty; while defendant incarcerated; victim was judge, prosecuting attorney, juror or witness in official duty; previous murder conviction or of an offense in any federal state or territorial jurisdiction of the U.S. which is the same or necessarily includes the elements of an offense of murder in 1st degree; for hire; to avoid arrest, while escaping; involved torture or infliction of extreme pain; course of conduct-killing or serious injury to more than one person; explosive device; while rape, rape of a child, assault on a child, indecent assault and battery on a child under 14 years old, assault with intent to rape, assault on a 16-year-old with intent to rape; assault and battery, kidnapping, kidnapping for ransom; breaking and entering with intent to commit a felony, armed assault in a dwelling, confining or putting in fear or harming for purpose of stealing from depositories; murder occurred while in defendant in possession of a sawed-off shotgun or machine gun; robbery, arson, etc.	Electrocution or at election of prisoner, lethal injection

Table 6: Capital Punishment—Continued

State/Code Section	Allowed	Effect of Incapacity	Minimum Age	Non-homicidal	Capital Homicide	Method of Execution
MICHIGAN Const. Art. 4 §46; §750.316	No					
MINNESOTA 609.10; 609.185; 1911 Minn. Laws Ch. 387	No					
MISSISSIPPI 97-3-21; 97-7-67; 97-25-55; 99-19-49, *et seq.*; 99-19-101	Yes	Suspend sentence if insane or pregnant	No minimum age	Treason; aircraft piracy	Murder committed while under sentence of imprisonment; previous conviction of another capital offense or felony involving violence; knowingly created great risk of death to many persons; while committing/attempting to commit robbery, rape, arson, burglary, kidnapping, aircraft piracy; sexual battery, unnatural intercourse with child under 12 years, nonconsensual unnatural intercourse with mankind, battery of child, unlawful detonation of explosives; avoiding/preventing arrest or escape from custody; for pecuniary gain; disrupt/hinder lawful exercise or enforcement of laws; heinous, atrocious or cruelty	Lethal injection; lethal gas if lethal injection held unconstitutional

Table 6: Capital Punishment—Continued

State/Code Section	Allowed	Effect of Incapacity	Minimum Age	Non-homicidal	Capital Homicide	Method of Execution
MISSOURI 546.720; 552.060; 565.020; 565.032; 562.051; 576.07; 195.214	Yes	Sentence is suspended until certified as free of mental disease or defect	16	All class 4 felonies including treason, kidnapping, distribution of controlled substance near schools, public or other government assisted housing; placing bombs near/in buses or terminals	Murder committed by one with prior conviction for murder in 1st degree or multiple assaultive convictions; while committing or attempting to commit another homicide; knowingly created great risk of death to more than 1 person; for monetary value; victim was judicial or former judicial officer, present or former prosecuting attorney or assistant prosecuting attorney, assistant circuit attorney, peace officer, elected official during or because of the exercise of official business/ duty; for hire; outrageously or wantonly vile, horrible or inhuman; while escaping, avoiding, or awaiting arrest; engaged in rape, sodomy, burglary, robbery, kidnapping or any felony offense; victim was witness or potential witness; victim was employee of correctional system in course of duty; victim was an inmate of correctional facility/ institution; hijacking; to conceal or prevent prosecution of a felony offense; to prevent victim from initiating/aiding prosecution; murder was commission of a crime which is part of a pattern of criminal street gang activity	Lethal gas or lethal injection

Table 6: Capital Punishment—Continued

State/Code Section	Allowed	Effect of Incapacity	Minimum Age	Non-homicidal	Capital Homicide	Method of Execution
MONTANA 45-5-102; 46-18-220; 46-18-301, *et seq.*; 46-19-101,*et seq.*; 46-19-201, *et seq.*	Yes	If defendant is found to be mentally unfit, sentence is suspended, but if fitness is regained, execution must be carried out unless so much time has elapsed that it would be unjust	No minimum age, however, if defendant is less than 18 years old this is a mitigating circum-stance	Aggravated assault or aggravated kidnapping while incarcerated at state prison by person previously convicted for murder or persistent felony offender	Murder committed while currently serving sentence of imprisonment; previous murder conviction; committed by torture; lying in wait or ambush; part of scheme or operation which would result in death of more than 1 person; victim was peace officer performing duty; aggravated kidnapping; while incarcerated at state prison by person previously convicted of murder or persistent felony offender; while committing sexual assault, sexual intercourse without consent, deviate sexual conduct or incest and victim less than 18 years	Hanging by the neck or lethal injection, at election of defendant
NEBRASKA 28-105, *et seq.*; 28-303; 29-2519, *et seq.*	Yes	If woman convict is found to be pregnant, execution is suspended until she is no longer pregnant; if convict is determined to be mentally incompetent, execution is suspended until competency is restored	18	None	Previous felony conviction involving of violence; multiple victims; for hire, pecuniary gain; defendant hired another to commit murder for defendant; law enforcement official or public servant with custody of defendant; committed to hinder lawful exercise of governmental function or enforcement of laws; to conceal crime or identity of person committing crime; offender should have known victim was public servant; especially heinous, atrocious, cruel; created great risk of death to at least several persons	Electrocution

Table 6: Capital Punishment—Continued

State/Code Section	Allowed	Effect of Incapacity	Minimum Age	Non-homicidal	Capital Homicide	Method of Execution
NEVADA 176.025; 176.345, *et seq.*; 176.415, *et seq.*; 200.030, *et seq.*	Yes	Suspend sentence when defendant is found insane or pregnant	16	None	First degree murder and murder of multiple victims (random, no motive); involved torture; peace officer or fireman engaged in official duties; for remuneration; avoid lawful arrest or effect escape from custody; connection with robbery, sexual assault, arson, burglary, kidnapping; knowingly created great risk of death to more than one person other than the victim; previous murder/felony convictions involving use/threat of violence; offender serving sentence; victim was less than 14 years old; murder committed because of victim's race, religion, or ethnic background	Lethal injection
NEW HAMPSHIRE 630:1, *et seq.*	Yes	Exempt from execution if pregnant	17	None	Intentional murder or infliction of serious bodily injury leading to death; committed by a person already in prison; already convicted of murder; defendant previously been convicted of 2 or more state or federal crimes punishable by terms of imprisonment of more than one year on different occasions involving crimes upon a person or distribution of controlled substances; defendant created grave risk of death to one or more persons during commission of capita murder; murder committed with premeditation and planning; especially heinous, cruel or depraved manner; for pecuniary gain; committed for purpose of escape from lawful custody	Lethal injection, or hanging if lethal injection becomes impractical to carry out

Table 6: Capital Punishment—Continued

State/Code Section	Allowed	Effect of Incapacity	Minimum Age	Non-homicidal	Capital Homicide	Method of Execution
NEW JERSEY 30:4-82; §§2A:4A-22; 2C:11-3; 2C:49-2	Yes	Exempt from execution if mentally ill/ retarded	18		Previous murder conviction; purposely knowingly created grave risk of death to another other than victim; outrageously or wantonly vile, horrible or inhuman; for pecuniary value; defendant paid for it; purpose was to escape detection, apprehension, trial, punishment or confinement for another offense committed by defendant or another; in connection with murder, robbery, sexual assault, arson, burglary, kidnapping; victim was public servant, relating to official duties; was leader of narcotics trafficking network and committed or committed with leader's direction in furtherance of conspiracy; homicidal act caused or risked widespread injury or damage; victim less than 14 years	Lethal injection after sedation
NEW MEXICO 31-14-4, *et seq.*; 28-6-1; 31-18-14(A); 31-20A-5; 20-12-42	Yes	Suspend sentence if insane or pregnant	18	Espionage	Peace officer engaged in duties; connection with kidnapping, criminal sexual contact of a minor or criminal sexual penetration; attempt to escape penal institution of New Mexico; victim was employee of corrections and criminal rehabilitation, while incarcerated; incarcerated at time of offense; for hire; witness to a crime to prevent testimony, reporting of crime or in retaliation	Lethal injection
NEW YORK Penal §60.06; 125.27; Crim. Pro. §400.27	No; declared unconstitutional except murder in 1st degree	Suspend sentence if insane	18 at time of crime		Victim was public officer in official duty; victim was employee of state correctional institution in official duty; defendant was under sentence for a minimum of 15 year or had escaped from confinement or custody; committed an act of terrorism	Current of electricity

Table 6: Capital Punishment—Continued

State/Code Section	Allowed	Effect of Incapacity	Minimum Age	Non-homicidal	Capital Homicide	Method of Execution
NORTH CAROLINA 14-17; 15A-1001, *et seq.*; 15A-2000; 122C-313; 15-187	Yes	Exempt from execution if insane	17; no minimum age for first degree murder while serving prison sentence for prior murder or which work on escape from such sentence.		Capital felony committed by person lawfully incarcerated; previous capital felony convictions; previous felony conviction involving use/threat of violence; avoid lawful arrest or escape from custody; in connection with homicide, rape or sex offense, robbery, arson, burglary, kidnapping or aircraft piracy or bombing; for pecuniary gain; hinder lawful exercise of governmental function or enforcement of laws; victim was law enforcement officer, employee of Corrections Department jailer, fireman, judge or justice, prosecutor, juror or witness while engaged in duties or former; especially heinous, atrocious, or cruel; great risk of death to more than one person; in connection with other crimes of violence against other person(s)	Lethal gas or at convict's request, lethal injection
NORTH DAKOTA Ch. 12-50 repealed by N.D. Laws Ch. 116 §41	No					
OHIO 2929.02, *et seq.*; 2949.22, *et seq.*	Yes	Suspend sentence if insane or pregnant	18		Assassination of public official; for hire; escape detection, apprehension, trial or punishment for another offense; committed while a prisoner in detention facility; prior murder convictions or multiple victims now; victim was peace officer; rape, kidnapping, aggravated arson, aggravated robbery, aggravated burglary; witness of crime to prevent testimony or retaliation for testimony	Electrocution or at convict's request, lethal injection

Table 6: Capital Punishment—Continued

State/Code Section	Allowed	Effect of Incapacity	Minimum Age	Non-homicidal	Capital Homicide	Method of Execution
OKLAHOMA Tit. 21 §§701.10, *et seq.*; Tit. 22 §§1005, *et seq.*	Yes	Suspend sentence if insane or pregnant	No minimum age		Previous felony conviction involving use/threat of violence; knowingly created great risk of death to more than one person; for remuneration or employed another for remuneration; especially heinous, atrocious or cruel; avoiding lawful arrest or prosecution; committed while serving sentence for felony; probability of defendant being continuing threat to society; victim was a peace officer or guard	Lethal injection or electrocution if lethal injection held to be unconstitutional or firing squad if both of above found to be unconstitutional
OREGON 137.080, *et seq.*; 137.473; 161.295, *et seq.;* 163.105, 163.150	Yes	Prohibits death penalty	14		In determining aggravating circumstances, court shall consider any evidence received during proceeding; presentence report; any other relevant evidence court deems trustworthy and reliable	Lethal injection

Table 6: Capital Punishment—Continued

State/Code Section	Allowed	Effect of Incapacity	Minimum Age	Non-homicidal	Capital Homicide	Method of Execution
PENNSYLVANIA Tit. 18 §1102; Tit. 42 §9711; Tit. 61 §2121.1	Yes		No minimum age	None	Murder of fireman, peace officer, public servant killed in performance of duties; victim was a judge of any court in unified judicial system, attorney general of Pennsylvania, deputy attorney general, district attorney/ assistant district attorney, member of a general assembly, governor, lieutenant governor, auditor general, state treasurer, state law enforcement official, local law enforcement official, federal law enforcement official or person employed to assist or assisting any law enforcement official in performance of his/her duties; in defendant paid or was paid to perform the murder; the victim was a hostage being held for ransom; during an aircraft hijacking; victim was prosecution witness to prevent testimony; during perpetration of a felony; knowingly created grave risk of death to another in addition to victim; torture; significant history of felony convictions involving use/ threat of violence; previous life sentence or death; defendant convicted of voluntary manslaughter either before or at time of killing; defendant committed the killing or was accomplice in killing; committed during perpetration of a felony under the Controlled Substance, Drug, Device & Cosmetic Act; victim was or had been in competition with defendant in the sale, manufacture, distribution or delivery of any controlled substance, counterfeit controlled substance, etc.; victim was under 12; victim was known to defendant to be in her third trimester of pregnancy; at the time of killing, victim was or had been a non-governmental informant; defendant was under court order restricting defendant's behavior toward the victim	Lethal injection

Table 6: Capital Punishment—Continued

State/Code Section	Allowed	Effect of Incapacity	Minimum Age	Non-homicidal	Capital Homicide	Method of Execution
RHODE ISLAND 11-23-2	No					
SOUTH CAROLINA 16-3-10, *et seq.*; 24-3-530; 44-23-210, *et seq.*	Yes	A female who is pregnant may not be executed until 9 months after she is no longer pregnant	No minimum age	None	Murder in connection with any criminal sexual conduct, kidnapping, burglary, armed robbery, larceny with use of deadly weapon, poison, drug trafficking, physical torture during commission of a drug trafficking felony; prior murder conviction; dismemberment of a person; knowingly created great risk of death to multiple persons in public place; for money or monetary value; judicial officer, solicitor, or other officer of the court (or formers) because of exercise of duties; agent/employee of another; law enforcement officer, peace officer, correction employees, fireman (or formers) related to duty; family members of above-mentioned; multiple victims; victim is a child 11 or under; killing of a witness; killing by mob, lynching; killing during a duel	Electrocution or lethal injection, at the election of the defendant, but if lethal injection is held unconstitutional, then electrocution

Table 6: Capital Punishment—Continued

State/Code Section	Allowed	Effect of Incapacity	Minimum Age	Non-homicidal	Capital Homicide	Method of Execution
SOUTH DAKOTA 22-16-4; 23A-27A-1, *et seq.*	Yes	Sentence suspended during period of mental incompetency or while defendant is pregnant. In event of pregnancy, execution may be carried out not less than 30 days nor more than 90 days from end of pregnancy	No minimum age		Prior felony convictions, class A/B felony/serious assaultive criminal convictions; knowingly created great risk of death to others; for the benefit of the defendant or another; for the purpose of receiving money or any other thing of monetary value; for remuneration or as agent/employee of another; members of criminal justice system (judge, attorneys) related to their exercise of duties; outrageously or wantonly vile, horrible or inhuman; law officer, corrections employee, fireman while engaged in performance of official duties; offender escaped from lawful custody/confinement; avoiding lawful arrest of himself or another; in connection with distributing, manufacturing or dispensing illegal substances; testimony regarding impact of crime on victim's family; if victim is less than 13 years old	Lethal injection
TENNESSEE 39-13-201, *et seq.*; 37-1-102; 40-23-114	Yes	Prohibited for mentally retarded	18		Offender over 18, victim under 12; previous felony convictions; great risk of death to multiple persons other than victim; employed or done for remuneration; especially heinous, atrocious or cruel; avoiding lawful arrest of defendant or another; in connection with any first degree murder, arson, rape, robbery, burglary, theft, kidnapping, aircraft piracy, bombing; committed while in lawful custody/confinement or escape from; committed against law enforcement officer, corrections person, firefighter engaged in duties, also judge, attorney general, district attorney, etc. (and formers) due to performance of duties; against elected official; "mass" murderer; mutilation of victim's body	Electrocution

Table 6: Capital Punishment—Continued

State/Code Section	Allowed	Effect of Incapacity	Minimum Age	Non-homicidal	Capital Homicide	Method of Execution
TEXAS Crim. Proc. §§8.07; 12.31; 19.03; 43.14; Pen. 12.31, 19.03, 8.07; CCrP 37.071, 43.14	Yes	Exempt from execution	17		Victim is peace officer or fireman in official duty; while committing/attempting to commit kidnapping, burglary, robbery, aggravated sexual assault or arson; obstruction; retaliation; for remuneration or employs another; while escaping; incarcerated and victim is employee or inmate; murder more than one person during same criminal transaction or scheme or course of conduct; victim under 6 years	Lethal injection
UTAH 77-15-1; 77-19-13; 77-18-5.5; 76-3-206, *et seq.*; 76-5-202	Yes	If defendant is found incompetent or pregnant, sentence is suspended until competency returns or person is no longer pregnant, at which time sentence is reimposed and to be carried out within 30-60 days	No minimum age		Offender confined in jail or other correctional facility; multiple murders; knowingly creates great risk of death to person other than victim; in connection with aggravated robbery, robbery, rape, rape of child, object rape, object rape of child, forcible sodomy, sodomy upon child, sexual abuse of child, child abuse of child under 14, aggravated sex assault, aggravated arson, arson, burglary, kidnapping; avoiding lawful arrest; pecuniary or other personal gain; contracted; previously convicted of murder or felony involving use/threat of violence; purpose of preventing witness from testifying in criminal procedure or person from offering evidence or hindering lawful governmental function or enforcement of laws; official or candidate for public office, homicide based on/related to official position; firefighter, peace officer, law officer or anyone involved in criminal justice system; bombs; in connection with unlawful control of aircraft, train, other public conveyance; poison; hostage/ransom	Defendant at time of execution may select either firing squad or lethal injection. If s/he does not select, then lethal injection

Table 6: Capital Punishment—Continued

State/Code Section	Allowed	Effect of Incapacity	Minimum Age	Non-homicidal	Capital Homicide	Method of Execution
VERMONT Tit. 13 §§7101, *et seq.*	No. Vermont has death penalty statute but it has never been amended to conform to Supreme Court's decision in *Furman v. Georgia,* 408 U.S. 238 (1972); hence constitution-ally invalid.					Electrocution
VIRGINIA 18.2-10; 18.2-17, 31; 19.2-167, *et seq.*; 53.1-233, 19.2-264.2, *et seq.*	Yes	Cannot stand trial for criminal offense if insane	No minimum age		Capital offenses include willful, deliberate, premeditated killing: In connection with abduction for extortion of money or pecuniary benefit; for hire; committed while confined to state correctional facility; armed robbery; rape, sodomy; law officer for purposes of interfering with official duties; multiple murders; victim under 12 in commission of abduction, intended to extort money or for pecuniary benefit; controlled substance; outrageously or wantonly vile, horrible or inhuman; continuing serious threat to society	Electrocution or by lethal injection

Table 6: Capital Punishment—Continued

State/Code Section	Allowed	Effect of Incapacity	Minimum Age	Non-homicidal	Capital Homicide	Method of Execution
WASHINGTON 10.95.010, *et seq.*; 10.95.180; 9.82.01	Yes	Mitigating factor; exempt from execution of mentally retarded	No minimum age	Treason	Law enforcement officer, corrections officer or firefighter in performance of official duties; offender escaped from confinement; offender in custody as consequence of felony conviction; agreement for money or value; contracted; obtain, maintain or advance position in organization; during course of or as a result of shooting from or near a motor vehicle used as a transport; victim was member or former member of criminal justice system (judge, attorney, juror, parole officer, etc.) related to their official duties; committed to conceal crime or identity of person committing crime; multiple victims; in connection with robbery, rape, burglary, kidnapping, arson; victim was news reporter and committed to obstruct investigation, research or reporting activities	Hanging or lethal injection
WEST VIRGINIA 61-11-2 (1984)	No					
WISCONSIN 939.50(3)(a); 940.01	No					

Table 6: Capital Punishment—Continued

State/Code Section	Allowed	Effect of Incapacity	Minimum Age	Non-homicidal	Capital Homicide	Method of Execution
WYOMING 6-2-101, *et seq.*; 7-13-901, *et seq.*	Yes	Suspend sentence if mentally incapacitated or pregnant	16	None	While under sentence, on parole/probation, after escaping detention or released on bail; previous conviction for murder in first degree or felony using violence; knowingly created great risk of death to 2 or more persons; while committing/attempting to commit aircraft piracy or unlawful discharge of bomb; while escaping or avoiding arrest; for pecuniary gain; was especially atrocious or cruel; court official in exercise of official duty; victim is less than 17 years or older than 65 years; victim especially vulnerable due to significant mental or physical disability; poses substantial and continuing threat or likely to commit acts again; while committing/attempting to commit robbery, sexual assault, arson, burglary, kidnapping	Lethal injection or lethal gas if injection ruled unconstitutional

7. COMPUTER CRIMES

The body of laws governing crimes on the Internet are some of the most rapidly changing of all state laws. Controversy surrounding issues such as pornography on the Internet and the World Wide Web, the copying and posting of copyrighted information from an authorized site on the Internet to another site, and privacy of communication and access to materials on the Internet are still being hotly debated and no clear method for dealing with them has yet been devised. In addition, recent efforts to regulate the world of the Internet have taken place largely in the federal level. As of this writing, major federal legislation has just been enacted that covers many activities on the Internet, but the regulations have not yet been written enforcing its various provisions and much of the act is not yet effective. Accordingly, there is still much speculation about what the law means.

On the state level, the one thing upon which there is much unanimity is that theft of information or money in electronic form is much the same as theft in any other form. State laws on computer crime, therefore, focus on theft of information or money through the use of a computer or an on-line computer service.

Virtually every state requires that one have the requisite mental state before they may be convicted of a computer crime. One must willfully, knowingly or purposely access computer-based data and intend to steal, destroy or alter computer-based information, steal services, passwords, or otherwise interfere with hardware or software, etc. It is not enough for purposes of these laws to accidently or unintentionally wander into areas on the internet where valuable or secure information may reside. If one enters such an area using computers or computer technology, his/her intent must be to steal, destroy or defraud to be found guilty of a crime.

Only a handful of states don't explicitly ban access to certain computer files. In most states mere access can be prosecuted as a crime. In addition, many states have the additional requirement that damage sustained by the victim of the crime be of a certain amount before the crime becomes a felony. For example, in New Jersey, if damage is more than $200, it is a felony. If it is less, it is a misdemeanor. The limit is $1,000 in North Carolina, $5,000 in West Virginia. In very few states, there is either no misdemeanor provision at all, or no money amount distinguishing the one from the other.

As the technology becomes ubiquitous, the law in this controversial area is sure to be subject to tremendous change and development over the next few years. In the meantime, this chapter can be used at least as a guidepost to identify the specific laws in question even if the specific provisions change in the details.

Table 7: Computer Crimes

State	Code Section	Mental State Required for Prosecution	Misdemeanor	Felony	Attempt Proscribed	Civil Action
ALABAMA	13A-8-100, *et seq.*	Willfully, knowingly, w/o authorization or w/o reasonable grounds	Access; alter, damage, or destroy hard/software valued under $2,500 Class A Misdemeanor	Access plus scheme to defraud. Alter, damage, or destroy hard/software valued over $2500 or cause interruption of public/government services Class C felony if purpose of offense is to scheme, defraud or obtain property. Class B felony if damage = or > $2,500; interruption of government operation or public/ utility service. Class A felony if action causes physical injury to person not involved in said act.	No	No
ALASKA	11.46.740	Knowingly, intentionally	None	Obtain or change information about a person, Class C felony	No	No
ARIZONA	13-2316	Intentionally	None	Access; access plus scheme to defraud; computer fraud in the 1st degree = class 3 felony, computer fraud in the 2nd degree = class 5 felony	No	No
ARKANSAS	5.41-101, *et seq.*	Intentionally, purposefully	Access with damage under $2500	Access with damage over $2500	No	Yes

Table 7: Computer Crimes—Continued

State	Code Section	Mental State Required for Prosecution	Misdemeanor	Felony	Attempt Proscribed	Civil Action
CALIFORNIA	Penal Code 502 Note:Section does not specifically classify crimes listed as either felony or misdemeanor. Offenses listed in misdemeanor or felony columns are based on the levels of punishments imposed rather than by explicit classification	Knowingly	Access; introduce virus; traffic in providing access; theft of services valued under $400	Access plus scheme to defraud; alter, damage or destroy hard/software valued over $5000; theft of services valued over $400	No	Yes
COLORADO	18.5.5-101 to 18.5.5-102	Knowingly	Class 3 misdemeanor of loss or damage is less than one hundred dollars Class 2 if between 100 and 500 dollars	Class 5 felony if between $500 and $15,000 Class 3 felony if $15,000 or more	No	No
CONNECTICUT	53a-250, *et seq.*	Knowingly	Class A misdemeanor: when unauthorized access to computer systems or theft computer services or interruption of computer services or misuse of computer system info or destruction of computer equipment and total damage exceeds $500. Class B misdemeanor: same computer crimes and damages $500 or less	Class B felony: when he/she commits same offenses listed above and damage exceeds $10,000. Class C felony: ditto and damage exceeds $5,000. Class D felony: ditto and damage exceeds $1,000 or reckless conduct creates risk of physical injury.	No	Yes

Table 7: Computer Crimes—Continued

State	Code Section	Mental State Required for Prosecution	Misdemeanor	Felony	Attempt Proscribed	Civil Action
DELAWARE	11 §§931, *et seq.*	Knowingly, intentionally, recklessly	Class A misdemeanor: when unauthorized access, theft of computer services, interruption of computer services, misuse of computer system info or destruction of computer equipment and damages $500 or less.	Class G felony: same offenses and damages >$500. Class F felony: same offenses and damages exceeds $1,000 or risk of injury to another person. Class E felony: same offenses and damages exceed $5,000. Class D felony: same and damages exceed $10,000.	No	Yes
DISTRICT OF COLUMBIA	None					
FLORIDA	815.01, *et seq.*	Willfully, knowingly, and w/o authorization	Misdemeanor of the 1st degree: For offenses against computer equipment and supplies: if damage between $200 and $1,000	For offenses against intellectual property: felony of the 3rd degree: if offense is committed; felony of the 2nd degree: w/ purpose to scheme, defraud, or obtain property. For offenses against computer equipment and supplies: felony if the 3rd degree: if damage between $200 and $1,000; felony of the 2nd degree: if damage is $1,000 or greater or there is interruption of govt service or public service/utility. For offenses against computer users: felony of the 3rd degree: if offense is committed; felony 2nd degree: w/ purpose to scheme, defraud or obtain property.	No	No

Table 7: Computer Crimes—Continued

State	Code Section	Mental State Required for Prosecution	Misdemeanor	Felony	Attempt Proscribed	Civil Action
GEORGIA	16-9-91, *et seq.* Note:Section does not specifically classify crimes listed as either felony or misdemeanor. Offenses listed in misdemeanor or felony columns are based on the levels of punishments imposed rather than by explicit classification.	Knowingly, intentional	Traffic in passwords	Computer theft, trespass (including modify, destroy, interfere with use), invasion of privacy, forgery	No	Yes
HAWAII	708-890, *et seq.*	Intentionally		Class C felony: access plus scheme to defraud; obtain/change credit information	No	No
IDAHO	18-2201 to 18-2202	Knowingly	Use, accesses, or attempts to access.	Access or attempt to access w/ purpose to scheme, defraud or obtain property/ money/ services; or you alter/ damage/ destroy computer, computer system, computer network or software/ data/ documentation.	Yes	No

Table 7: Computer Crimes—Continued

State	Code Section	Mental State Required for Prosecution	Misdemeanor	Felony	Attempt Proscribed	Civil Action
ILLINOIS	720 1LCS 5/ 16D-1, *et seq*	Knowingly		Class 4 felony: access w/ purpose to scheme, defraud or deceive. Class 3 felony: damages computer or alter/ delete/ destroy program or data in connection w/ scheme, defraud or deceive. If offender accesses computer and obtains money or control of money in connection w/ his/ her scheme, defraud or deception, guilty of: Class 4 felony: if value of money, property, or services is $1,000 or less; Class 3 felony: if value between $1,000 and $50,000; Class 2 felony: if valur$50,000 or more.	Yes	No
INDIANA	35-43-1-4; 35-43-2-3	Knowingly; intentionally	Class A Misdemeanor: access	Class D felony: computer tampering.	No	No
KANSAS	21-3755	Intentionally	Computer crime which causes loss of value less than $500 is a class A nonperson misdemeanor. Criminal computer access is a class A nonperson misdemeanor.	Computer crime causing loss of value b/t $500 and $25,000 is a severity level 9, nonperson felony. Computer crime causing $25,000 or more is severity level 7, nonperson felony.	Yes	No
KENTUCKY	434.840, *et seq.*	Knowingly; intentionally	Unlawful access to a computer in 2nd degree is Class A.	Unlawful access to computer in 1st degree is Class C felony. Misuse of computer info is a Class C felony.	Yes	No

Table 7: Computer Crimes—Continued

State	Code Section	Mental State Required for Prosecution	Misdemeanor	Felony	Attempt Proscribed	Civil Action
LOUISIANA	14.73.1, *et seq.* Note:Section does not specifically classify crimes listed as either felony or misdemeanor. Offenses listed in misdemeanor or felony columns are based on the levels of punishments imposed rather than by explicit classification.	Intentionally	Alter, damage or destroy hard/ software valued under $500; interfere with use of another valued under $500	Alter, damage or destroy hard/ software valued over $500; interfere with use of another valued over $500	No	No
MAINE	Tit. 17-A §§431, *et seq.*	Intentionally	Access	Copying; alter, damage or destroy hard/software; introduce virus	No	No
MARYLAND	Art. 27 §146	Intentionally; willfully	A person who illegally accesses computer is guilty of a misdemeanor		Yes	No
MASSACHUSETTS	Ch. 266 §33A	Intentionally	none	none	Yes	No
MICHIGAN	752.791, *et seq.*	Intentionally	If violation involves $100 or less.	If violation involves more than $100.	No	No
MINNESOTA	609.87, *et seq.*	Intentionally	Misdemeanor: Commission of unauthorized computer access. Gross Misdemeanors: commission in a manner that creates risk to public health/ safety, commission in a manner that compromises the security of data, conviction of second or subsequent misdemeanors w/i 5 years.	Commission of unauthorized computer access in a manner that creates a grave risk of causing death of a person, conviction of second or subsequent gross misdemeanor.	No	No

Table 7: Computer Crimes—Continued

State	Code Section	Mental State Required for Prosecution	Misdemeanor	Felony	Attempt Proscribed	Civil Action
MISSISSIPPI	97-45-1, *et seq.* Note:Section does not specifically classify crimes listed as either felony or misdemeanor. Offenses listed in misdemeanor or felony columns are based on the levels of punishments imposed rather than by explicit classification.	Intentionally	Access; any of the following, causing damages less than $100: interfere with use; alter, damage or destroy hard/software; traffic in passwords	Access plus scheme to defraud; any of the following, causing damages greater than $100: interfere with use; alter, damage or destroy hard/ software; traffic in passwords	No	No
MISSOURI	537.525, 569.093, *et seq.*	Knowingly	Class A misdemeanor: tampering w/ computer equipment, tampering w/ computer users.	Tampering w/ computer equipment w/ purpose to scheme, defraud, or obtain property the value of wh/ is $150 or more is Class D felony. If damage to computer or related parts is b/t $150 and $1,000, then Class D felony. If damage is $1,000 or more, then Class C felony. Tampering w/ computer users w/ purpose to scheme, defraud, or obtain property the value of wh/ is $150 or more is a Class D felony.	No	Yes

Table 7: Computer Crimes—Continued

State	Code Section	Mental State Required for Prosecution	Misdemeanor	Felony	Attempt Proscribed	Civil Action
MONTANA	45-2-101, 45-6-310 to 45-6-311	Knowingly, purposefully	Any of the following, causing damages less than $500: access; access plus scheme to defraud; alter, damage or destroy hard/ software	Any of the following, causing damages greater than $500: access; access plus scheme to defraud; alter, damage or destroy hard/ software	No	No
NEBRASKA	28.1343, *et seq.*	Intentionally	Commission of unauthorized computer access in a manner that creates risk to public health/ safety is class I misdemeanor. Commission of unauthorized computer access in a manner that compromises the security of data is class II misdemeanor. Unlawfully accessing computer to obtain confidential public info is class II misdemeanor. Second or Subsequent offense is a class I misdemeanor. Accessing w/o authorization or exceeding authorization is class V misdemeanor. Second or subsequent offense is class II.	Access w/ intent to deprive or obtain property/ services is a class IV felony. If you do and the value of property/ services is $1,000 or more, then class III felony. Access and damage, disruption, or distribution of destructive computer program, then class IV felony. If you do so and cause losses w/ a value of $1,000 or more, then class III felony.	No	No

Table 7: Computer Crimes—Continued

State	Code Section	Mental State Required for Prosecution	Misdemeanor	Felony	Attempt Proscribed	Civil Action
NEVADA	205.473, *et seq.*	Knowingly, willfully	Unlawful access is a misdemeanor as well as unlawful interference w/ or denial if access or use	Unlawful access done to defraud or obtain property or causing damages excess of $500 or interrupts/ impairs public service/ utility is a class c felony; unlawful interference w/ or denial of access of use done to defraud or obtain property is a class C felony.	No	No
NEW HAMPSHIRE	638:16, *et seq.*	Knowingly	Computer crime is a misdemeanor if damage is $500 or less.	Computer crime w/ damages exceeding $1,000 is a class A felony. Computer crime w/ damages exceeding $500 or offender's conduct creates risk of physical injury	No	No
NEW JERSEY	2C:20-23, *et seq.* Note:Section does not specifically classify crimes listed as either felony or misdemeanor. Offenses listed in misdemeanor or felony columns are based on the levels of punishments imposed rather than by explicit classification.	Purposefully, knowingly	Access; any of the following, causing damages less than $200: access plus scheme to defraud; alter, damage or destroy hard/ software	Access; any of the following, causing damages greater than $200: access plus scheme to defraud; alter, damage or destroy hard/software	No	No

Table 7: Computer Crimes—Continued

State	Code Section	Mental State Required for Prosecution	Misdemeanor	Felony	Attempt Proscribed	Civil Action
NEW MEXICO	30-45-1, *et seq.*	Knowingly, willfully	Any of the following, causing damages less than $250: access; access plus scheme to defraud; alter, damage or destroy hard/ software; disclosure, copy or display of computer information	Any of the following, causing damages greater than $250: access; access plus scheme to defraud; alter, damage or destroy hard/ software; disclosure, copy or display of computer information	No	No
NEW YORK	Penal Code 156.00, *et seq.*	Knowingly	Unauthorized use of computer is a class A misdemeanor. Computer tampering in fourth degree is a class A misdemeanor.	Computer tampering in third degree is a class E felony. Computer tampering in second degree is a class D felony. Computer tampering in first degree is a class C felony. Unlawful duplication of computer related material is a class E felony. Criminal possession of computer related material is a class E felony.	No	No
NORTH CAROLINA	14-453, *et seq.*	Willfully	Class 1 misdemeanors: unlawful access of computers for purposes other than to scheme, defraud, or obtain property, Altering/ damaging/ destroying computer software, programs or data.	Class H felony: to access computer w/ purpose to scheme, defraud, obtain property. Also class H felony: to damage computer, computer system, computer network, or parts thereof	No	No
NORTH DAKOTA	12.1-06.1-08	Intentionally	Computer crime is a class A misdemeanor	Computer fraud = Class C felony.	Yes	No
OHIO	2913.01, *et seq.*	Knowingly	None	Unauthorized use of computer property is felony of the 5th degree	Yes	No

Table 7: Computer Crimes—Continued

State	Code Section	Mental State Required for Prosecution	Misdemeanor	Felony	Attempt Proscribed	Civil Action
OKLAHOMA	Tit. 21, §§1951, *et seq.*	Willfully	Access or use of cause to be used computer services	Access plus scheme to defraud; alter, damage or destroy hard/software; denial of access; traffic in passwords. There are several prohibited acts under the Computer Crimes Act classified as a felony.	Yes	Yes
OREGON	164.125; 164.377	Knowingly	Access Class A misdemeanor	Class C felony: access plus scheme to defraud; alter, damage or destroy hard/software; theft of data or services	Yes	No
PENNSYLVANIA	3933	Intentionally and knowingly	Offenses under §1911(a)(1) or(3) is a misdemeanor of the first degree	Offenses under §3933(a)(1) is felony of third degree	No	No
RHODE ISLAND	11-52-1, *et seq.*	Purposefully	Theft of data or services valued under $500	Access of computer for fraudulent purposes; intentional access, alteration, damage, or destruction; computer theft w/ a value over $500; use if false information and tampering w/ computer source documents.	No	Yes
SOUTH CAROLINA	16-16-19, *et seq.*	Willfully, knowingly, and maliciously	Computer crime in the second degree = class A misdemeanor; Computer crime in the third degree = class B misdemeanor	Computer crime in the first degree = class E felony; Second or subsequent convictions of computer crimes in the second degree = class F felony	No	No

Table 7: Computer Crimes—Continued

State	Code Section	Mental State Required for Prosecution	Misdemeanor	Felony	Attempt Proscribed	Civil Action
SOUTH DAKOTA	43-43B-1, *et seq.*	Knowingly	Obtaining use, altering or destroying system, access and disclosure w/o consent where value one thousand dollars or less - class 1 misdemeanor; Also obtaining use, altering or destroying system as part of deception where value involved is $1,000 or less - class 1 misdemeanor.	Obtaining use, altering or destroying system, access and disclosure w/o consent where value involved is more than $1,000 - class 6 felony; Obtaining use, altering or destroying system as part of deception - value is more than $1,000 - class 4 felony.	Yes	No
TENNESSEE	39-14-601, *et seq.;* 39-14-105	Knowingly, directly or indirectly	Access is class C misdemeanor; introducing virus is class B. Hacking into any computer system is class A.	Access for purpose of fraudulently obtaining money, property or services.	Yes	No
TEXAS	Penal Code 33.01, *et seq.*	Knowingly, intentionally	Break of computer security is class B misdemeanor; Class A if the amount involved is < $1,500	Break of computer security is a state of jail felony if amount involved is b/t $1,500 and $20,000 or amount is less than $1,500 and defendant has previous conviction; felony of third degree is amount b/t $20,000 and 100k; felony of second degree if amount b/t 100k and 200k; felony of first degree if amount is or exceeds 200k	No	No
UTAH	76-6-702, *et seq.*	Intentionally, knowingly	When damage < $300 or info is not confidential then class B misdemeanor; when damage b/t $300 and $1,000, then class A	When damage b/t $1,000 and $5,000, third degree felony; when damage is or exceeds $5,000 then second degree, there is also a third degree felony	Yes	No

Table 7: Computer Crimes—Continued

State	Code Section	Mental State Required for Prosecution	Misdemeanor	Felony	Attempt Proscribed	Civil Action
VERMONT	None					
VIRGINIA	18.2-152.1, *et seq.*	Intentionally	Computer fraud w/ value of property or services less than $200, class 1 misdemeanor; Computer trespass is class 3 misdemeanor; if damages $2,500 or more, then class 1; computer invasion of privacy is class 3; theft of computer services is class 1; personal trespass by computer done unlawfully but not maliciously is class 1	Computer fraud w/ value of property or services obtained $200 or more, class 5 felony; computer trespass w/ damages $2,500 or more caused by malicious act, class 6; Personal trespass by computer done maliciously is class 3	No	Yes
WASHINGTON	9A.52.110, *et seq.*	Intentionally	Computer tresspass in second degree is a gross misdemeanor	Computer tresspass in first degree is class C felony	No	No
WEST VIRGINIA	61-3C-1, *et seq.*	Knowingly, willfully	Unauthorized access to computer services; unauthorized possession of computer data or programs having value of < $5,000; dissruption or denial of computer services; unauthorized possession of computer information; disclosure of computer security info; obtaining confidential public info.; computer invasion of privacy	Computer fraud and access to legislature computer; unauthorized possession of computer data or programs having value of $5,000 or more; alteration, destruction, etc. of computer equipment	Yes	Yes

Table 7: Computer Crimes—Continued

State	Code Section	Mental State Required for Prosecution	Misdemeanor	Felony	Attempt Proscribed	Civil Action
WISCONSIN	943.70	Willfully, knowingly	Offenses against computer data and programs class A misdemeanor; offenses against computers, computer equipment and supplies is class A misdemeanor	Offenses against computer data and programs is if offense is to defraud or obtain property, class E; if damage greater than $2,500 or act causes interruption/ impairment of govt operations or public utility/ service, class D; if offense creates risk of death or bodily harm to another, class E. Offense against computer, computer equipment or supplies is class E if offense is done to defraud or obtain property; class D if damage > $2,500; and class C if act creates risk of death or bodily harm to another	No	Aggrieved party may sue for injunctive relief
WYOMING	6-3-501, *et seq.*	Knowingly	Crime against computer equipment and supplies	Crimes against intellectual property (means data including programs); crimes against computer equipment and suppplies if done w/ intent to scheme, defraud, or obtain property; crimes against computer users	No	No

8. CRIMINAL STATUTES OF LIMITATION

A statute of limitation is a law allowing criminals to go free if they are not apprehended by authorities within a prescribed number of years after the crime in question is committed.

Statutes of limitation generally require the criminal to remain in the state, gainfully employed and visible, seeming to necessitate that the criminal remain "catchable." If the authorities fail to discover a criminal living in the open within a specified amount of time, society has determined that at that point the criminal should be able to live free from the possibility of prosecution. It appears that this notion is born out of a sense of mercy more than pragmatics: if the criminal is a fugitive, out of the state in which the crime was committed or otherwise living in hiding, this tolls, or suspends, the statute. (Once the criminal reenters the state the statute resumes running.) However, if the criminal were living an open, public, so-called "reformed" life, after a reasonable period of time he is allowed to be free from capture.

Not all crimes are governed by statutes of limitation. Murder, for example, has none. Sex offenses with minors, crimes of violence, kidnapping, arson, and forgery have no statutes of limitation in a number of states. In Arizona, California, Oklahoma, and Utah, crimes involving public money or public records have no statutes of limitation. While in Colorado, treason has none.

Many states have adopted systems that classify felonies by category. Therefore, in order to effectively compare statutes of limitation provisions, it is necessary to determine which crimes in that state fit into particular classes. For example, Missouri lists murder or Class A felonies as crimes with no statutes of limitation. Each crime must then be looked up in that state's statutes to determine its classification.

Table 8: Criminal Statutes Of Limitation

State	Code Section	Felonies	Misdemeanors	Acts During Which Statute Does Not Run
ALABAMA	15-3-1, *et seq.*	Arson, forgery, any capital offense, rape, counterfeiting, use, attempted use, or threat of violence, felony with serious physical injury/death, any sex offense with one under 16, drug trafficking: none; other felonies: 3 yrs.; conversion of state or county revenue: 6 yrs.; unlawfully taking or using temporarily the property of another: 30 days	12 mos.	Prosecution commences upon indictment, issuing warrant or binding over of defendant
ALASKA	12.10.010, 020, 040	Murder: none; 10 years for certain violent felonies; other felonies: 5 yrs., unless fraud is element, then extended 1 yr. after discovery of fraud; official misconduct in public office: extension and up to 3 yrs.	5 yrs.	If outside the state hiding, maximum extension 3 yrs.
ARIZONA	13-107	Murder, misuse of public money, falsifying public records: none; other felonies: 7 yrs.	1 yr.; petty offenses: 6 mos.	Absent from state or no reasonably ascertainable residence in state
ARKANSAS	5-1-109	Murder: none; Class Y and A felonies: 6 yrs.; Class B, C, D, or unclassified felonies: 3 yrs.; if offense involves fraud or breach of fiduciary duty: 1 yr.; felonious conduct in public office: 5 yrs. with max. extension to 10 yrs.; if offense is against minor and limitation period has not expired since victim turned 18, statutory period for offense starts at age of majority.	1 yr.	Continually absent from state or has no reasonably ascertainable home or work within the state, max. extension 3 yrs.
CALIFORNIA	Pen. §§799 *et seq.*	Murder, other offenses punishable by death or life imprisonment, embezzlement of public funds: none; offenses punishable by 8 or more years in prison: 6 yrs.; offenses punishable by imprisonment: 3 yrs.; sexual exploitation by physician or therapist: 2 yrs.	1 yr. violations: 1 yr.; misdemeanor violation committed on a minor under 14: 2 yrs.	Not in state, max. extension 3 yrs.; statutory periods do not begin until offense is or should have been discovered

Table 8: Criminal Statutes Of Limitation—Continued

State	Code Section	Felonies	Misdemeanors	Acts During Which Statute Does Not Run
COLORADO	16-5-401	Murder, attempt, conspiracy, or solicitation to commit murder, kidnapping, attempt, conspiracy or solicitation to commit kidnapping, treason, attempt, conspiracy, or solicitation to commit treason, any forgery regardless of penalty provided, attempt, conspiracy or solicitation to commit any forgery regardless of penalty provided: none; sexual assault, aggravated incest, trafficking in or sexual exploitation of children, soliciting for child prostitution, pandering or procurement of a child: 10 yrs.; other felonies: 3 yrs. (bribery and abuse of public office: 3 yr. extension; sexual offenses on children under 15 yrs. of age: 7 yr. extension)	18 mos.; Class I and II and traffic offenses: 1 yr.; petty offenses: 6 mos.; 3rd degree sexual assault: additional 5yrs.	Absent from state: 5 yrs. maximum extension
CONNECTICUT	54-193 *et seq.*	Murder or capital, Class A felony: none; if imprisonment is more than 1 yr.: 5 yrs.; any other: 1 yr.; sexual abuse, exploitation, or assault: 2 yrs. after victim reaches majority or 5 yrs. from date of notification by victim, whichever is earlier (5 yrs. max.)	1 yr.	Fleeing or residing outside state
DELAWARE	Tit. 11 §205(a), (b), (g)	Murder: none; others: 5 yrs.; any offense which includes forgery, fraud, breach of fiduciary duty, theft or misapplication of property, misconduct in public office: additional 3 yrs.; any sexual offense where victim was under 18 yrs. of age: within 2 yrs. of initial disclosure	Class A: 3 yrs.; others: 2 yrs.	Fleeing or hiding from justice
DISTRICT OF COLUMBIA	23-113	1st or 2nd degree murder: none; other felonies in 1st and 2nd degree: 6 yrs.; all other crimes: 3 yrs.; except if offense included official misconduct, fraud or breach of fiduciary trust: max. 9 yrs. felony, 6 yrs. misdemeanor	3 yrs.	Fleeing or action commenced

Table 8: Criminal Statutes Of Limitation—Continued

State	Code Section	Felonies	Misdemeanors	Acts During Which Statute Does Not Run
FLORIDA	775.15	Capital or life felony: none; 1st degree felony and 2nd degree felony for abuse or neglect of aged or disabled adult: 4 yrs.; others: 3 yrs.; other felonviolation of securities transaction: 5 yrs.; violation of environmental control: 5 yrs. of date of discovery; any offense which fraud or breach of fiduciary obligation is a material element: 3 yrs.; misconduct in public office: within 2 yrs. of leaving office or any above limit, whichever is greater; sexual offenses (battery, assault, intercourse under age 18): begins running at age 16 or when violation is reported, whichever is earlier.	1st degree misdemeanor of for abuse or neglect of aged or disabled adult: 3 yrs.; other 1st degree misdemeanors: 2 yrs.; 2nd degree and noncriminal violations: 1 yr.	Continually absent from state, no reasonably ascertainable work or abode in state: maximum extension 3 yrs.
GEORGIA	17-3-1, 2, 2.1	Murder: none; crimes punishable by death or life imprisonment: 7 yrs.; others: 4 yrs.; crimes against victims under 14: 7 yrs.; for victims under 16 yrs. of age of offenses such as rape, sodomy, incest, and child molestation (occurring after 7/1/92), the statute will run upon the victim turning 16 or when the violation is reported, whichever occurs earlier.	2 yrs.	6 nonresident; when person or crime is unknown
HAWAII	701-108	1st or 2nd degree murder or 1st or 2nd degree attempted murder: none; manslaughter where death was not caused by operating a motor vehicle: 10 yrs.; Class A felony: 6 yrs.; others: 3 yrs.; if fraud or breach of fiduciary obligation is element: 2-6 yrs. extension after discovery; if based on misconduct in public office: 2-3 yrs. extension upon discovery	Misdemeanor or parking violation: 2 yrs.; petty misdemeanors: 1 yr.	Continuously absent from state or no reasonably ascertainable residence or work within the state, while prosecution is pending: maximum extension 3 yrs.
IDAHO	19-401, *et seq.*	Murder: none; other felonies and felonies committed upon or against a minor child: 5 yrs.; sexual abuse of or lewd conduct with a child under 16 yrs. of age: 5 yrs. after the child reaches the age of 18; ritualized abuse of child: 3 yrs. after initial disclosure by victim	1 yr.	Absent from state
ILLINOIS	720 ILCS 5/3-5; 5/3-7; 5/3-6	1st or 2nd degree murder, involuntary manslaughter, reckless homicide, treason, arson, forgery: none; others: 3 yrs.	18 mos.	Nonresident

Table 8: Criminal Statutes Of Limitation—Continued

State	Code Section	Felonies	Misdemeanors	Acts During Which Statute Does Not Run
INDIANA	35-41-4-2	Murder, Class A felony: none; others, Class B, C, D felony, forgery of an instrument for payment: 5 yrs.; child molesting (if person is at least 16 and victim is not more than 2 yrs. younger: 5 yrs.), vicarious sexual gratification, child solicitation or seduction, incest: when alleged victim turns 31 yrs. of age	2 yrs.; infraction or violation of pending ordinance: 1 yr.	Nonresident, absent state, conceals self or evidence of crime; prosecution is considered timely if defendant pleads guilty at any time
IOWA	802.1, *et seq.*	1st and 2nd degree murder: none; others: 3 yrs.; sexual abuse of child under 12: no later than 6 mos. after child turns 18; sexual exploitation by counselor or the rapist: 5 yrs. of date of last treatment; fraud or breach of fiduciary duty: extension up to 3 yrs.	Serious misdemeanor: 3 yrs.; simple misdemeanor or violation of ordinances: 1 yr.	Outside state or nonresident
KANSAS	21-3106	Murder: none; if victim is the Kansas public employees retirement system: 10 yrs.; victim under 16, indecent liberties with child, solicitation of child, incest or sexual exploitation of child and all rape and aggravated criminal sodomy: 5 yrs.; others: 2 yrs.	2 yrs.	Absent state or concealed within state; concealed crime
KENTUCKY	500.050	Felony: none; offense involving sexual intercourse other than by spouse must be reported (and signed by the victim) within 1 yr. of commission to be prosecuted	1 yr.	
LOUISIANA	Crim. Proc. Art. 571 *et seq.*, 572, 575	Crimes with punishment of death or life imprisonment: none; felony punishable by hard labor: 6 yrs.; felony not necessarily punishable by hard labor: 4 yrs.; forcible rape, sexual battery (aggravated), carnal knowledge, indecent behavior or molestation of juvenile, crime against nature involving victim under 17 yrs. of age: 10 yrs. beginning when victim turns 17 yrs. old	Punishment of fine or forfeiture: 6 mos.; fine and/or prison: 2 yrs.	Avoiding detection, fleeing, outside state, absent residence in state; lacks mental capacity to proceed at trial
MAINE	Tit. 17-A §8	Murder, 1st or 2nd degree criminal homicide, incest, rape, or gross sexual assault if victim is under 16 yrs. of age: none; Class A, B, C crime: 6 yrs.; Class D, E crime: 3 yrs.; if breach of fiduciary obligation: 1 yr., max. extension: 5 yrs.; official misconduct: 2 yrs., max. extension: 5 yrs.		Absent state or prosecution pending in state: maximum 5 yrs. extension

Table 8: Criminal Statutes Of Limitation—Continued

State	Code Section	Felonies	Misdemeanors	Acts During Which Statute Does Not Run
MARYLAND	Annotated Cts. & Jud. Proc. §§5-106, 107	Murder: none; manslaughter or homicide by vehicle, welfare or Medicare fraud, tax-related offense, sex discrimination in paying wages, compensation in connection with adoption, unauthorized practice of medicine: 3 yrs.; criminal offense under state election laws, conflict of interest laws, or criminal misfeasance by officer of the state (or conspiracy thereof): 2 yrs.; assault, libel, or slander: 1 yr.	Misdemeanor punishable by imprisonment: none; other misdemeanors: 1 yr.; vehicle violations of unlawfully using a driver's license or fraudulently using false name when applying for driver's license: 2 yrs.; Sabbath breaking, drunkenness, or selling alcoholic beverages after hours or to a minor in Allegany County: 30 days	
MASSACHUSETTS	Ch. 277§63	Murder: none; robbery, intent to rob or murder, dangerous weapon, rape, assault with intent to rape, rape/abuse/assault of child, incestuous marriage/intercourse: 10 yrs.; others: 6 yrs.; indecent assault on child, on mentally retarded person, rape/abuse/assault of child, kidnapping of minor, sexual offenses such as drugging for sex, enticing for marriage, inducing minor into prostitution, lewd and lascivious behavior or acts, dissemination of harmful matter to minors, exhibiting nudity, or crime against nature: when victim reaches 16 yrs. old or violation is reported, whichever is earlier	6 yrs.	Tolled when defendant is not usually and publicly resident
MICHIGAN	767.24	Murder: none; kidnapping, extortion, assault with intent or conspiracy to murder: 10 yrs.; others: 6 yrs.; if victim was under age 18 for any degree of sexual conduct or assault with intent to commit sexual conduct or any sexually abusive activity or material to minor: 6 yrs. or when the victim turns 21 yrs. old, whichever is later	6 yrs.	Not resident, did not usually and publicly reside

Table 8: Criminal Statutes Of Limitation—Continued

State	Code Section	Felonies	Misdemeanors	Acts During Which Statute Does Not Run
MINNESOTA	628.26	Murder: none; bribery, medical assistance fraud, theft: 6 yrs. (if value of property/services in theft is over $35,000: 5 yrs.); familial sexual abuse, criminal sexual conduct: 7 yrs. or if victim under 18 yrs. of age, within 3 yrs. after offense is reported; arson, environmental offenses: 5 yrs.; all others: 3 yrs.	3 yrs.	Not inhabitant of or usually resident within state
MISSISSIPPI	99-1-5	Murder, manslaughter, arson, burglary, forgery, counterfeiting, robbery, larceny, rape, embezzlement, obtaining money under false pretenses of property: none; felonious abuse or battery of child, sexual battery of a child, exploitation of children, touching child for lustful purposes: on or before child's 21st birthday; all others: 2 yrs.	2 yrs.	Absent state, fleeing, hiding
MISSOURI	556.036	Murder or Class A felony: none; others: 3 yrs.; unlawful sexual offenses involving person under 17 yrs. old: 10 yrs.; if fraud or breach of fiduciary duty is material element of offense: 1-3 yrs. after discovery; official misconduct: 2-3 yrs. after offense or public employment	1 yr.; infractions: 6 mos.	Absent state, hiding: maximum 3 yr. extension
MONTANA	45-1-205	Deliberate, mitigated, or negligent homicide: none; others: 5 yrs.; sexual assault, sexual intercourse without consent, indecent exposure, deviate sexual conduct, incest, sexual or ritual abuse of child if victim is under 18 yrs. old at time of offense: within 5 yrs. of victim turning 18 yrs. old; theft involving breach of fiduciary obligation: within 1 yr. of discovery or if involving a minor, within 1 yr. of termination of minority; unlawful use of computer: within 1 yr. of discovery of offense	1 yr.; misdemeanor of fish, wildlife, or outfitter activity laws: within 3 yrs. after offense committed	When offender is not usually and publicly resident of state, or beyond jurisdiction of state
NEBRASKA	29-110	Murder, treason, arson, forgery: none; others: 3 yrs.; if victim is less than 16 yrs. old at time of offense, sexual assault (1, 2, or 3 degree), kidnapping, false imprisonment, child abuse, pandering, debauching a minor: 7 yrs. from offense or victim's 16th birthday, whichever is later	18 mos.; if fine less than $100 or jail time less than 3 mos.: 1 yr.	Fleeing justice

Table 8: Criminal Statutes Of Limitation—Continued

State	Code Section	Felonies	Misdemeanors	Acts During Which Statute Does Not Run
NEVADA	171.080, 085, 090, 095, 100	Murder: none; theft, robbery, arson, burglary, forgery, sexual assault: 4 yrs.; others: 3 yrs.; sexual abuse of a child: by time victim reaches 21 yrs. old or 28 yrs. old if "does not discover or reasonably should not have discovered" he was a victim	Gross misdemeanor: 2 yrs.; others: 1 yr.	Prosecution commences when indictment is presented
NEW HAMPSHIRE	625:8	Murder: none; Class A or B felony or unemployment compensation offense: 6 yrs.; offense of hunting game or fur-bearing animals or violation of off highway recreational vehicles: 3 yrs.; breach of fiduciary duty: within 1 yr. of offense; official misconduct: within 2 yrs. of offense; sexual assault and related offenses when victim is under 18 yrs. old: within 22 yrs. of victim's 18th birthday	1 yr.; violations: 3 mos.	Absent state, no residence or work in state
NEW JERSEY	2C:1-6; 2C:11-3	Murder, manslaughter: none; official misconduct, bribery and related offenses: 7 yrs.; others: 5 yrs.; if victim under 18, prosecution must begin within 5 yrs. after victim attains 18 for sexual assault, criminal sexual contact and endangering welfare of children	Petty offense or disorderly persons offense: 1 yr.	Fleeing justice
NEW MEXICO	30-1-8, 30-1-9 *et seq.*	Capital or 1st degree felony: 15 yrs.; 2nd degree: 6 yrs.; 3rd and 4th degree: 5 yrs.; others: 3 yrs.; child abuse, criminal sexual penetration, or criminal sexual contact of minor: until victim turns 18 yrs. old or the offense is reported, whichever occurs first	2 yrs.; petty: 1 yr.	Fleeing justice or not usually or publicly resident of state; enumerated procedural defects
NEW YORK	Crim. Proc. §30.10	Murder, Class A felony: none; others: 5 yrs.; violation of collection, treatment, disposal of refuse and solid waste: 4 yrs.; breach of fiduciary duty: within 1 yr. of discovery of offense; official misconduct: 5 yrs. of offense	2 yrs.; petty offenses: 1 yr.; tax law misdemeanor: 3 yrs. (NY City adm. code)	Absent state or whereabouts unknown: up to 5 yrs.
NORTH CAROLINA	15-1	None	Malicious misdemeanor: none; others: 2 yrs.	
NORTH DAKOTA	29-04-01 to 04	Murder: none; sexual abuse of children: 7 yrs. or within 3 yrs. of reporting of offense; others: 3 yrs.; if victim is under 15 yrs. old, period of limitation begins when he turns 15 yrs. old	2 yrs.	Absent state

Table 8: Criminal Statutes Of Limitation—Continued

State	Code Section	Felonies	Misdemeanors	Acts During Which Statute Does Not Run
OHIO	2901.13	Murder or aggravated murder: none; others: 6 yrs.; fraud or breach of fiduciary duty: within 1 yr. of discovery of offense; official misconduct: within 2 yrs.	2 yrs.; minor misdemeanor: 6 mos.	Absent state or conceals identity or whereabouts or undiscovered corpus delicti
OKLAHOMA	Tit. 22 §151-153	Murder: none; bribery, embezzlement or misappropriation of public money or other assets, falsification of public records, conspiracy to defraud state or other subdivision, rape or forcible sodomy: 7 yrs.; lewd or indecent proposals or acts against children crimes involving minors in pornography, sodomy, criminal conspiracy, embezzlement, criminal state income tax violations: 5 yrs.; all others: 3 yrs.	3 yrs.	Absent state or not a resident of the state
OREGON	131.125, 145, 155	Murder, manslaughter: none; sexual felonies including criminal mistreatment sexual abuse in 1st and 2nd degree, rape, sodomy, incest, promoting or compelling prostitution: 6 yrs. or if victim was under 18 yrs. old at time of offense, anytime before victim turns 24 yrs. old, whichever occurs first; others: 3 yrs.	Sexual misdemeanors: sexual abuse in the 3rd degree or sending, furnishing, exhibiting or displaying obscene materials to minors: 4 yrs. after the offense is reported or if victim is under 18 yrs. old, upon turning 22 yrs. old, whichever occurs first	Absent state, hides within state, not resident of state; max. extension 3 yrs.
PENNSYLVANIA	Tit. 42 §5551-5554	Murder, manslaughter, voluntary manslaughter, conspiracy to murder, soliciting to commit murder and murder results, felony connected with 1st or 2nd degree murder, vehicular homicide: none; major offenses or conspiracy or solicitation to commit major offense: 5 yrs.; others: 2 yrs.; fraud or breach of fiduciary duty: 3 yrs.; official misconduct: 8 yrs.; sexual offense committed against a minor: period of limitation starts when minor reaches age 18	2 yrs.; summary offenses: 30 days	Absent from state; no ascertainable residence or place of work within state

Table 8: Criminal Statutes Of Limitation—Continued

State	Code Section	Felonies	Misdemeanors	Acts During Which Statute Does Not Run
RHODE ISLAND	12-12-17	Treason against state; homicide, arson, burglary, counterfeiting, forgery, robbery, rape, sexual assault, child molestation, bigamy, manufacturing, selling, distributing or possession of controlled substance, or conspiracy to any of the above: none; larceny, embezzlement, bribery, extortion, racketeering, antitrust violation, or conspiracy to any of the above: 10 yrs.; violations of refuse or hazardous waste disposal or water pollution: 7 yrs.; others: 3 yrs.	3 yrs.	Stolen, lost, destroyed information: extends limitation period one year
SOUTH CAROLINA	No statute of limitation for any criminal prosecution			
SOUTH DAKOTA	23A-42-1, *et seq.*	Murder, Class A, B, or 1 felony: none; all other public offenses: 7 yrs.	7 yrs.	Absent state
TENNESSEE	40-2-101, *et seq.*	Any crime punishable by death or life imprisonment: none; Class A felony: 15 yrs.; Class B felony: 8 yrs.; defrauding state, evading or defeating any tax, fraudulent return: 6 yrs.; Class C or D felony: 4 yrs.; Class E felony: 2 yrs.; others: 3 yrs.; offense committed against a child: 4 yrs. after offense is committed, or when child reaches majority, whichever occurs later	Gaming: 6 mos.; others: 12 mos.	Concealing fact of crime, absent state
TEXAS	Crim. Proc. §12.01	Murder, manslaughter: none; thefts involving fiduciaries or officials forgery, sexual assault, indecency with a child: 10 yrs.; misapplication of fiduciary property: 7 yrs.; other theft, burglary, robbery, arson, and certain sexual assaults: 5 yrs.; others: 3 yrs.	2 yrs.	Absent state
UTAH	76-1-301, 304	Capital felony, murder, manslaughter, embezzlement of public monies or falsification of public records: none; other felony or negligent homicide: 4 yrs.; fraud or breach of fiduciary obligation, official misconduct: 3 yrs. max.; rape, sodomy, or sexual abuse of a child: within 4 yrs. of reporting offense	2 yrs.; infractions: 1 yr.	Absent state

Table 8: Criminal Statutes Of Limitation—Continued

State	Code Section	Felonies	Misdemeanors	Acts During Which Statute Does Not Run
VERMONT	Tit. 13 §§4501, *et seq.*	Arson causing death, kidnapping, murder, aggravated sexual assault: none; arson: 11 yrs.; sexual assault, lewd and lascivious conduct, sexual exploitation of children, grand larceny, robbery, burglary, embezzlement, forgery, bribery, false claims, fraud, felony tax offenses: 6 yrs.; sexual assault or lewd and lascivious conduct of child under 16 yrs. old: 6 yrs. or when the victim turns 24 yrs. old, whichever is earlier; others: 3 yrs.	3 yrs.	Prosecution commences when arrest is made, citation issued, indictment or information presented
VIRGINIA	19.2.8	Murder: none; cruelty to animals: 5 yrs. (except for agricultural animals: 1 yr.); making false presentation under VA Unemployment Compensation Act to receive benefits, attempt to evade or failure to pay taxes, violation of laws re: discharge, dumping, or emission of toxic substance, violation of rules of VA Real Estate Board, illegal sales of wild birds, animals, or freshwater fish: 3 yrs.; malfeasance in office, Building Code violations: 2 yrs.	Petit larceny: 5 yrs.; attempt to produce abortion: 2 yrs.; others: 1 yr.	Fleeing justice or concealing himself to avoid arrest
WASHINGTON	9A.04.080	Murder, arson causing death: none; public official misconduct, arson: 10 yrs.; rape if reported 1 yr. of commission: 10 yrs., or if victim is under 14 yrs. old, 3 yrs. after victim turns 18, whichever is later; rape if not reported within 1 yr.: 3 yrs. or if victim is under 14 yrs. old, 3 yrs. after victim turns 18 yrs. old, but not more than 7 yrs. after rape; child molestation, indecent liberties, incest: if victim is under 14 yrs. old, 3 yrs. after victim turns 18 yrs. old, but not more than 7 yrs. of offense; leading organized crime or criminal profiteering: 6 yrs.; Class C felony: 5 yrs.; bigamy and all other felonies: 3 yrs.	Gross misdemeanors: 2 yrs.; other offenses: 1 yr.	Not publicly a resident
WEST VIRGINIA	61-11-9	None	Petty larceny or perjury: 3 yrs.; others: 1 yr.	Stolen, lost, destroyed indictment

Table 8: Criminal Statutes Of Limitation—Continued

State	Code Section	Felonies	Misdemeanors	Acts During Which Statute Does Not Run
WISCONSIN	939.74	Homicide: none; others: 6 yrs.; sexual assault, physical abuse causing mental harm, sexual exploitation, incest, enticement of, or solicitation for prostitution of a child: before victim turns 26 yrs. old; repeated sexual assault of same child: before victim turns 25 yrs. old	Misdemeanors or adultery: 3 yrs.	Not publicly resident; if victim is unable to seek issuance of a complaint, that time period excluded due to threats, etc.
WYOMING	No statute of limitation for any criminal prosecution			

9. DRUNK DRIVING

Penalties for drunk driving have become tougher over the years as the cost of this dangerous behavior rises. Reckless alcohol consumption among young people has also risen markedly, and it has been met with sharp intolerance. There are often lower legal limits for minor drivers and longer driver's license suspensions.

Drunk driving, driving while intoxicated (DWI), or driving under the influence (DUI), is typically determined by the alcohol content found in the driver's blood. Blood alcohol content (BAC) may be determined in two ways: through breath analysis or urinalysis. Most states have set the legal limit of blood alcohol content at 0.10 percent. Recently, however, fifteen states have lowered the legal limit to 0.08 percent; five passed their laws since the last revision of this book. Also since the last edition of this book three more states have passed laws lowering the BAC to .02% for drivers under 21, bringing to six the total number of states recognizing a special BAC for underage drivers.

Penalties for drunk driving are severe in most states. Virtually every state suspends the driver's license on a first offense, and the length of suspension increases sharply with each successive offense. There is, however, a great deal of variation in the lengths of suspension of driving privileges among the states. Several states include revocation on the third or fourth offense.

The newest development in the laws of drunk driving concern court-ordered attendance at an alcohol abuse rehabilitation program upon conviction for driving while intoxicated. Most have some sort of rehabilitation requirement for problem drinkers and drivers.

Table 9: Drunk Driving

State	Code Section	BAC Legal Limit	Rehabilitation Required?	Driver's License Suspension?	Other Penalties
ALABAMA	32-5A-191	.08% BAC	Yes on first offense; DUI court referral program approved by state	1st offense: 90 days; 2nd: 1 yr.; 3rd: 3 yrs.; 4th or subsequent: 5 yrs.	1st: imprisonment up to 1 yr. and/or $600-$2100; 2nd within 5 yrs.: up to 1 yr. including mandatory min. sentence of 48 hrs. and min. 20 days community service $1100-$5100; 3rd within 5 yrs.: min. 60 days, max. 1 yr. and $2100-$10,100; 4th or subsequent within 5 yrs.: felony conviction, min. 1 yr., max. 10 yrs. and $4100-$10,000
ALASKA	28.35.030; 28.15.181	.10% BAC as determined by test taken within 4 hours of offense	Yes, must satisfy screening, evaluation, referral, and program requirements of agency authorized by state to provide rehabilitative treatment	1st: 90 days min.; 2nd: 1 yr. min.; 3rd: 3 yrs. min., 4th or subsequent: 5 yrs. min.	1st: min. 72 hrs. and min. $250; 2nd: min. 20 days and min. $500; 3rd: min. 60 days and min. $1000; 4th min. 120 days and min. $2000; 5th min. 240 days and min. $3000; 6th and subsequent: min. 360 days and min. $4000
ARIZONA	28-1381, *et seq.*	.10% BAC within 2 hrs. of driving or being in actual physical control of vehicle	Yes, alcohol abuse screening session by screening or treatment facility approved by health services; alcohol abuse classes or approved treatment facility if necessary	1st: 90 days; 2nd within 5 yrs. or within 1 yr. of similar conviction in another state: revocation	1st: min. 10 days or 24 hrs. (if court ordered program completed) and min. $250 and max. 40 hrs. community service; 2nd within 60 months or 1 yr. of similar conviction in another state: min. 90 days or 30 days if court ordered program completed and min. $500
ARKANSAS	5-65-103, *et seq.*	.10% BAC as determined by test	Alcohol education program prescribed and approved of by Arkansas Highway Safety Program or alcoholism treatment program approved by Division of Alcohol and Drug Abuse Prevention	1st: 120 days; 2nd within 3 yrs.: 16 mos.; 3rd within 3 yrs.: 30 mos.; 4th within 3 yrs.: 4 yrs.	1st: 1 day to 1 yr. prison, court can order public service in lieu of jail and $150-1000; 2nd within 3 yrs.: 7 days to 1 yr. and $400-3000; 3rd within 3 yrs.: 90 days to 1 yr. and $900-5000; 4th within 3 yrs.: felony, 1-6 yrs. and $900-5000

Table 9: Drunk Driving—Continued

State	Code Section	BAC Legal Limit	Rehabilitation Required?	Driver's License Suspension?	Other Penalties
CALIFORNIA	Veh. §§23152, *et seq.*	.08% BAC at time of driving as determined by chemical test within 3 hrs. of driving (rebuttably presumed that percentage at time of driving was more than at time of test); if test is less than .05% BAC, BAC presumed not .08% when driving; if test is .05-.08%, not presumption but evidence of .08%; .08% at time of test equals .08% at time of driving	Yes: if probation, must participate in an alcohol and other drug education and counseling program in driver's county of residence or employment	1st: 6 mos., or if probation granted, could be 90 days with exception of traveling to work and rehab program; 2nd: 18 mos.; 3rd: 3 yrs., after 24 mos. a restricted license may be granted upon completion of an 18 or 30 month authorized program; 4th: 4 yrs., after 24 mos. a restricted license may be granted upon completion of an 18 or 30 month authorized program	1st: 96 hrs. to 6 mos. prison (48 hrs. continuous) and $390-1000; 2nd within 7 yrs.: 90 days to 1 yr. (48 hrs. continuous or 10 days min. community service) and $390-1000; 3rd within 7 yrs.: 120 days to 1 yr. and $390-$1000 and designation as habitual traffic offender for 3 yrs.; 4th within 7 yrs.: 180 days to 1 yr. and $390-1000 and designation as habitual traffic offender for 3 yrs. Note: penalties increase if violations include bodily injury.
COLORADO	42-4-1301; 42-2-129; 42-2-132	.10% BAC at the time of driving or within 2 hrs. after driving (if there was between .05% and .10% BAC, presumption is that driver was impaired)	Yes, alcohol and drug driving safety programs in each judicial district provide presentence alcohol and drug evaluations and recommend treatment	1 yr.	1st: 5 days to 1 yr. and court may fine $300-1000 and 48-96 hrs. useful public service; 2nd within 5 yrs.: 90 days to 1 yr. and court may fine $500-1500 and 60-120 hrs. useful public service; 3rd within 5 yrs.: 70 days to 1 yr. and court may fine $400-1000 and 56-112 hrs. of useful public service and designation as habitual offender
CONNECTICUT	14-227a	.10% BAC at time of offense	Court may order participation in alcohol education and treatment program in addition to any fine or sentence	1st: 1 yr.; 2nd: 2 yrs.; 3rd: 3 yrs.; 4th: permanently	1st: $500-1000 and jail up to 6 mos. (48 consecutive hrs.) or 100 hrs. community service; 2nd within 5 yrs.: $500-2000 and jail up to 1 yr. (10 days consecutive); 3rd within 5 yrs.: $1000-4000 and jail up to 2 yrs. (120 days consecutive); 4th within 5 yrs.: $2000-8000 and jail up to 3 yrs. (1 yr. non-suspendable)

Table 9: Drunk Driving—Continued

State	Code Section	BAC Legal Limit	Rehabilitation Required?	Driver's License Suspension?	Other Penalties
DELAWARE	21 §4177	.10% BAC as shown by test taken within 4 hours of offense (evidence of .05-.10% BAC raises no presumption of intoxication but may be used as factor in intoxication determination)	Yes, may include course of instruction and/or program of rehabilitation (1st offense may include max. of 6 mos. confinement)	1st or 2nd: 1 yr.; 3rd or more: 18 mos.	1st: $230-1150 and/or 60 days-6 mos.; each subsequent offense (including those in other states): $575-2300 and 60 days-18 mos.
DISTRICT OF COLUMBIA	40-716; 40-717.1	.08% BAC; .13% alcohol in urine (less than .05% BAC or .06% in urine is evidence of intoxication but no presumption of intoxication; greater than .05% BAC or .06% in urine constitutes prima facie case of intoxication)	Yes, can request person enter diversion program	Yes for unspecified time	1st: up to $300 and/or 90 days; 2nd within 15 yrs.: $1000 to $5000 and/or up to 1 yr.; 3rd within 15 yrs.: $2000 to $10,000 and/or up to 1 yr. Note: vehicle may be impounded.
FLORIDA	316.193	.08% BAC	Yes, required attendance at licensed substance abuse course	Revocation/suspension upon conviction and vehicle impounded; 1st: 10 days; 2nd within 3 yrs.: 30 days; 3rd within 5 yrs.: 90 days	1st: $250-500 and jail up to 6 mos. and probation up to 1 yr. and community service of 50 hrs. minimum or $10 fine per hour not worked; 2nd within 3 yrs.: $500-1000 and jail up to 9 mos., min. 10 days; 3rd within 5 yrs.: $1000-2500 and jail up to 12 mos., min. 30 days; 4th: 3rd degree felony and min. $1000; if BAC exceeds .20%: 1st: $500-100 and jail up to 9 mos.; 2nd: $1000-2000 and jail up to 12 mos.; 3rd: $2000-5000 and jail up to 12 mos.

Table 9: Drunk Driving—Continued

State	Code Section	BAC Legal Limit	Rehabilitation Required?	Driver's License Suspension?	Other Penalties
GEORGIA	40-5-63; 40-6-391	.10% BAC within 3 hrs. of driving or being in actual physical control	License reinstated upon completion of DUI Alcohol or Drug Use Risk Reduction Program approved by Department of Human Resources and pays fee of $210 or $200.	1st: 1 yr. (person may apply for reinstatement after 120 days if completed DUI Alcohol or Drug Use Risk Reduction Program and pays restoration fee); 2nd within 5 yrs.: 3 yrs. (can apply for reinstatement as noted under 1st offense); 3rd within 5 yrs.: 5 yrs. and considered habitual violator	1st: $300-1000 and 10 days to 12 mos. and min. 40 hrs. of community service; 2nd within 5 yrs.: $600-1000 and 90 days to 12 mos. and min. 80 hrs. of community service; 3rd: $1000-5000 and 120 days to 12 mos. (mandatory 10 days) and min. 20 days community service. For third or subsequent conviction, judge may suspend up to half of fine if defendant attends an alcohol or drug treatment program
HAWAII	291-4, 5	.08% BAC within 3 hrs. after the time of the alleged violation (no presumption for .05-.10% BAC, but may be used in intoxication determination)	1st: 14 hrs. minimum alcohol abuse rehab program including education and counseling or comparable program approved by court; subsequent: may be required pending evaluation by substance abuse counselor	1st: 90 days (court can make it 30 days total prohibition and 60 days only for work and rehab); 2nd: 1 yr. absolute prohibition; 3rd: 1-5 yrs.	1st: $150-1000 and/or min. 48 hrs.-5 days jail and/or 72 hrs. community service; 2nd within 5 yrs.: $500-1000 and/or min. 48 hrs.-60 days (48 hrs. consecutively) jail and/or min. 80 hrs. community service; 3rd within 5 yrs.: $500-1000 and 10-180 days jail (48 hrs. consecutively)
IDAHO	18-8004, *et seq.*	.08% BAC; under age 21, .02-.08% BAC; .20% BAC is considered excessive	Alcoholic evaluation (own expense) at approved facility; if necessary, an appropriate alcoholic treatment must be completed in addition to the rest of the sentence	1st: 30 days absolute, 60-150 days restricted privileges; 2nd within 5 yrs.: 1 yr. absolute suspension after release from confinement; 3rd within 5 yrs.: absolute suspension 1-5 yrs.	1st: up to $1000 and/or up to 6 mos.; 2nd within 5 yrs.: up to $2000 and jail 10 days (1st 48 hrs. consecutive) to 1 yr.; 3rd within 5 yrs.: mandatory 30 days up to 5 yrs. and may be fined up to $5000 and felony conviction. Note: other states' prior convictions count. Also note: separate penalties are listed for minors (under 21 yrs. of age) with BAC less than .01%, and those convicted with excessive BAC (over .20%)

Table 9: Drunk Driving—Continued

State	Code Section	BAC Legal Limit	Rehabilitation Required?	Driver's License Suspension?	Other Penalties
ILLINOIS	625 ILCS 5/ 11-501, *et seq.*	.08% BAC; less than .05% at test: presumed not to be under the influence of alcohol; .05%-.08% at test: no presumption of guilt but take it with other evidence; .10% at test: guilty	Professional evaluation to determine if there is abuse problem and extent; defendant pays cost; program must be approved/ licensed by Dept. of Alcohol and Substance Abuse	Driving privileges revoked for indefinite period.	1st: Class A misdemeanor (if transporting someone under 16 yrs. of age: min. $500 and 5 days of community service in a program benefitting children); 2nd within 5 yrs.: mandatory min. 48 hrs. jail or min. 100 hrs. community service (if transporting someone under 16 yrs. of age: min. $500 and 10 days of community service in a program benefitting children); 3rd or subsequent: Class 4 felony, 1-3 yrs. prison (mandatory min. 48 hrs. and 30 hrs. community service if given probation)
INDIANA	9-30-5-1, *et seq.*	.10% BAC; under age 21, .02-.10%	No	1st: (or 2nd in more than 10 yrs.) 90 days to 2 yrs.; 2nd 5-10 yrs. ago: 180 days to 2 yrs.; 2nd within 5 yrs.: 1-2 yrs. if offense included bodily injury or death: 2-5 yrs. Note: any probationary periods include equipping motor vehicle with functioning certified ignition interlock device	1st: Class A misdemeanor; 2nd within 5 yrs.: min. 5 days jail or min. 80 hrs. community service in addition to Class D felony; 3rd within 10 yrs.: considered habitual violator

Table 9: Drunk Driving—Continued

State	Code Section	BAC Legal Limit	Rehabilitation Required?	Driver's License Suspension?	Other Penalties
IOWA	321J.2, *et seq.*	.10% BAC	1st: may be ordered to attend a course for drinking drivers; 1st if BAC is over .20% or 2nd: must undergo substance abuse evaluation prior to sentencing; 3rd offense or if evaluation recommends treatment: may be assigned to facility by director of corrections dept. Note that any portion of sentence for 2nd, 3rd, or subsequent offense may be served as inpatient treatment for alcoholism or drug addiction or dependency	1st: 180 days (if deferred or suspended sentence: 30-90 days); 2nd within 6 yrs.: 1 yr.; 3rd or subsequent: 6 yrs. (can apply for restoration after 2 yrs.)	1st: serious misdemeanor, $500-1000 and min. 48 hrs. jail, may perform up to 200 hrs. community service in lieu of fine if court allows; 2nd: aggravated misdemeanor, min. $750 and min. 7 days jail; 3rd and subsequent: Class D felony, min. $750 and 30 days to 1 yr. jail
KANSAS	8-1008, 1014, 1567	.08% BAC within 2 hrs. of operating vehicle (if BAC is less than .08%, this may be considered with other evidence of intoxication)	1st: person must enroll in alcohol and drug safety action education or treatment program; 2nd: must complete a treatment program for alcohol and drug abuse plus 60 days of restricted driving privileges (to and from work and alcohol program)	1st: 30 days; 2nd and subsequent: 1 yr.; for 4th and subsequent: license plate may be revoked for 1 yr. Note: all revocations are reinstated at the above time periods only upon completion of alcohol and drug safety program	1st: Class B, nonperson misdemeanor, $200-500 and 48 hrs.-6 mos. jail (within ct's discretion, up to 100 hrs. in public service); 2nd: Class A, nonperson misdemeanor, $500-1000 and 90 days-1 yr. jail (may be sentenced to work release program after 5 days or house arrest after 48 hrs.); 3rd or subsequent: severity level 9, nonperson felony, $1000-2500 and 90 days-12 mos. jail (Note that in lieu of fines, $5 per community hour will be credited.)

Table 9: Drunk Driving—Continued

State	Code Section	BAC Legal Limit	Rehabilitation Required?	Driver's License Suspension?	Other Penalties
KENTUCKY	189A.010, *et seq.*	.10% BAC (.05-.10% not considered a presumption of intoxication but considered with other evidence of intoxication)	1st offense: 90 day alcohol or substance abuse education or treatment program with assessment, defendant pay cost; 2nd within 5 yrs.: 1 yr.; 3rd or subsequent: 1 yr. (possible inpatient). Note that failure to complete program may constitute contempt	1st: 90 days; 2nd within 5 yrs.: 1 yr.; 3rd within 5 yrs.: 2 yrs.; 4th or subsequent: 5 yrs. (if person is under 18 yrs. of age: license revoked until he reaches 18 or the above relevant penalty, whichever is the longer revocation)	1st: $200-500 or 48 hrs. to 30 days jail or 2-30 days community labor; 2nd within 5 yrs.: $350-500 and 7 days to 6 mos. jail and may get 10 days to 6 mos. community labor in addition to jail term; 3rd within 5 yrs.: $500-1000 and 30 days to 12 mos. jail and may get 10 days to 1 yr. community labor in addition to jail term; 4th and subsequent within 5 yrs.: Class D felony. Note: all prior convictions include other states.
LOUISIANA	14:98; 32:414	.10% BAC; under age 21 .02% or more	Court approved substance abuse program and court approved driver improvement program is a min. condition for all probation, parole, or suspension of sentence	1st: 90 days (can be restricted if necessary)-$100 reinstatement fee; 2nd: 1 yr.-$200 reinstatement fee; 3rd or subsequent: 2 yrs.-$300 reinstatement fee	1st: $125-500 and 10 days to 6 mos. jail (possible suspension by attending program with minimal jail time or community service); 2nd: $300-1000 and 30 days to 6 mos. jail (possible suspension by attending program with minimal jail time or community service); 3rd: up to $2000 and 1-5 yrs. jail; 4th: hard labor 10-30 yrs. and up to $5000. Note that prior convictions include other states.
MAINE	Tit. 29 §1310 *et seq.*	.08% BAC (.05-.08% BAC maybe considered with other relevant evidence of intoxication)	Yes, for 2nd and 3rd offense, defendant may be required to participate in a Weekend Intervention Program (or residential treatment program) administered by the Office of Stbstance Abuse	1st (with no previous drunk driving convictions): 90 days; 2nd within 6 yrs.: 1 yr.; 3rd within 6 yrs.: 2 yrs.	All convictions are Class D crimes. 1st (with no previous drunk driving convictions): no less than $300 (if BAC was greater than .15%, was driving in excess of 30 mph over the speed limit, eluded officer, failed to take chemical test requested by police, or had a passenger under 16 yrs. of age: add 48 hrs. of jail); 2nd within 6 yrs.: no less than $500 and 7 days jail; 3rd within 6 years.: no less than $750 and 30 days. Note that penalties are more severe if they caused bodily injury.

Table 9: Drunk Driving—Continued

State	Code Section	BAC Legal Limit	Rehabilitation Required?	Driver's License Suspension?	Other Penalties
MARYLAND	Annotated code of MD. Transp. 16-205; 16-212; 21-902; 27-101	.10% BAC	Driver Improvement Program and Alcohol Education Program required	1st: 45 days; 2nd: 90 days	If "Under the influence": 1st: up to $500, 2 mos. in jail; 2nd: up to $500 and 1 yr. in jail; "While intoxicated": 1st: up to $1000 and/or 1 yr. in jail; 2nd: up to $2000 and/or no more than 2 yrs. in jail; 3rd and subsequent: min. $3000 and/or min. 3 yrs. Note: offenses including bodily injury or death or fleeing/evading police involve stiffer penalties.
MASSACHUSETTS	Ch. 90 §24	.10% BAC (<.05%, presumption is not under the influence; .05-.10% BAC, no presumption)	1st offense: appropriate to defendant with his/her consent as a condition of probation upon written finding that appropriate and adequate treatment is available to defendant and defendant would benefit and safety of public would not be endangered; minimum 14 days in residential alcohol treatment program (defendant pays cost)	1st: 1 yr.; 2nd: 2 yrs.; 3rd: 5 yrs.; 4th or subsequent: 10 yrs. (can apply for new license on grounds of hardship and registrar's discretion: 2nd: within 1 yr.; 3rd: within 2 yrs.; 4th: within 5 yrs.)	1st: $100-1000 or up to 2 yrs. jail (can be just weekends, evenings, and holidays); 2nd within 6 yrs.: $300-1000 and 14 days to 2 yrs. jail; 3rd within 6 yrs.: $500-1000 and 90 days to 2 yrs. jail; 4th or more times within 6 yrs.: $500-1000 and 6 mos. to 2 yrs. jail
MICHIGAN	MCLA 257.625 *et seq.*	.10% BAC	Screening and assessment to determine the likely benefit from rehabilitation. court may order person to participate and successfully complete one or more alcohol or drug education or treatment programs	1st: 6 mos. to 2 yrs. (can get restricted license after 30 days); 2nd and subsequent: 6 mos. to 2 yrs. (can get restricted license after 60 days) or revoked (injuries or death-causing accidents heighten restrictions)	1st: $100-500 and/or up to 90 days jail and costs of prosecution and community service up to 45 days; 2nd within 7 yrs.: $200-1000 and either 10-90 days community service and up to 1 yr. jail or up to 90 days community service and 48 hrs. to 1 yr. jail; 3rd within 10 yrs., felony: $500-5000 and/or 1-5 yrs. jail; Injuries or death-causing accident heightens penalties of all offenses

Table 9: Drunk Driving—Continued

State	Code Section	BAC Legal Limit	Rehabilitation Required?	Driver's License Suspension?	Other Penalties
MINNESOTA	169.121, *et seq.*	.10% BAC within 2 hrs. of time of driving	After 2nd offense within 5 yrs. (including reports of driving with BAC of .07%) must submit to level of care recommended in mandatory chemical use assessment, at driver's expense.	1st: min. 30 days; 2nd within 5 yrs.: min. 180 days and until court has certified treatment/rehabilitation has been successfully completed; 3rd within 5 yrs.: min. 1 yr. and until rehab completed; 4th within 5 yrs.: min. 2 yrs. and until rehab completed	1st: misdemeanor; 2nd within 5 yrs.: gross misdemeanor, min. 30 days jail or 8 hrs. community service for each jail day served less than 30; 3rd within 10 yrs.: gross misdemeanor, min. 30 days jail or 8 hrs. community service for each jail day served less than 30
MISSISSIPPI	63-11-30	.10% BAC; under age 21 .02% or more	Required alcohol safety education program	1st: 90 days and successful completion of program—max. 1 yr. (may petition for hardship after 30 days); 2nd: 2 yrs. (after 1 yr., can be reduced for successful completion of program); 3rd and subsequent: 5 yrs. (eligible for reinstatement after 3 yrs. and successful completion of program)	1st: $250-1000 and/or up to 48 hrs. jail; 2nd within 5 yrs.: $600-1500 and 10 days to 1 yr. jail and 10 days to 1 yr. community service; 3rd or subsequent within 5 yrs.: possible forfeiture of vehicle, $2000-5000, and 1-5 yrs. jail
MISSOURI	577.010, 577.012, 020-041	Intoxicated; (Class B misdemeanor); "Driving with excessive BAC" of .10% or more (Class C misdemeanor)	Yes, court may order participation and successful completion of alcohol or drug-related traffic offender education or rehab program which meets standards established by Dept. of Public Safety and Dept. of Mental Health and professional assessment	Upon failure to submit to breath test (given a 15 day temporary permit) for 1 yr.	1st: Class C misdemeanor; 2nd within 5 yrs. ("prior offender"): Class A misdemeanor; 3rd within 5 yrs. ("persistent offender"): Class D felony, (min. 48 consecutive hrs. in jail or 10 days community service before sentence or parole); After 10 yrs. with no other alcohol-related offenses on record, can apply for expungement

Table 9: Drunk Driving—Continued

State	Code Section	BAC Legal Limit	Rehabilitation Required?	Driver's License Suspension?	Other Penalties
MONTANA	61-5- 205, 208; 61-8-406, 722	.10% BAC	Defendant shall complete alcohol information course at alcohol treatment program approved by Dept. of Corrections & Human Services which may include alcohol or drug treatment or both if considered necessary by counselor conducting program	1st: 6 mos.; subsequent: 1 yr. (completion of alcohol information course or treatment must be completed before revocation ends)	1st: $100-500 and up to 10 days jail; 2nd: $300-500 and 48 hrs. to 30 days jail; 3rd: $500-1000 and 48 hrs. to 6 mos. jail and motor vehicle seized (except for initial 24 or 48 hrs. in jail, rest of jail time can be home arrest)
NEBRASKA	28-106; 39-60-6, .196, *et seq.*	.10% BAC	Presentence evaluation in alcohol assessment, paid for by person convicted; judge may order program based on results of assessment	1st: 6 mos. (if judge orders suspension of sentence or probation, 60 days from time of order); 2nd within 8 yrs.: 1 yr. (if judge orders suspension of sentence or probation, 6 mos. from time of order); 3rd or subsequent within 8 yrs.: 15 yrs. (if judge orders suspension of sentence or probation, 1 yr. from time of order)	1st: $200-500 and 7-60 days jail; 2nd within 8 yrs.: $500 and 30-90 days jail; 3rd within 8 yrs.: $500 and 3 mos.-1 yr. jail; 4th and subsequent: 1-5 yrs. jail and $500-10,000 fine
NEVADA	484.379, *et seq.*	.10% BAC within 2 hrs. after driving or being in actual physical control of vehicle	1st: must pay for and complete educational course on alcohol and substance abuse; 2nd within 7 yrs.: may order to undergo program of treatment for alcoholism or drug abuse (for 1st and 2nd violation: person may apply to undergo 1 yr. program for alcoholism and drug abuse if he's classified by counselor or physician as drug abuser or alcoholic)	Revoked if BAC is greater than .10%	1st: $200-1000 and 2 days to 6 mos. jail or 48 hrs. community service (dressed in "distinctive garb"); 2nd within 7 yrs.: $500-1000 and 10 days to 6 mos. jail; 3rd or subsequent within 7 yrs.: $2000-5000 and 1-6 yrs. jail; in addition to any penalty, civil penalty of $35 paid to court

Table 9: Drunk Driving—Continued

State	Code Section	BAC Legal Limit	Rehabilitation Required?	Driver's License Suspension?	Other Penalties
NEW HAMPSHIRE	263:65-a; 265.82 *et seq.*	.08% BAC	Yes, Impaired Driver Intervention Program; must successfully complete to get license back; must be approved by director of Office of Alcohol and Drug Abuse Prevention and the commissioner	1st: 90 days to 2 yrs.; 2nd within 7 yrs.: 3 yrs.; 3rd within 7 yrs.: indefinite, min. 3 yrs.	1st: $350-1000; 2nd within 7 yrs.: $500-1000 and 10 days (3 in city jail and 7 in DWI offender intervention detention center); 3rd within 7 yrs.: $500-1000 and 30 days jail and 28 day treatment program. (Stiffer penalties for transporting person under 16 yrs. old, speeding 30 mph over limit, or accident resulting in serious bodily injury.)
NEW JERSEY	39:4-50	.10% BAC	Screening, evaluation, referral program, and fee requirements of Div. of Alcoholism's Intoxicated Driving Programs Unit and 12-48 hrs. in two consecutive days in Intoxicated Driver Resource Center and a program of alcohol education and highway safety as proscribed by director of Div. of Motor Vehicles	6 mos. to 1 yr.; 2nd: 2 yrs.; 3rd: 10 yrs. (if driver is under 17 yrs. old, period of revocation begins at 17th birthday)	1st: $250-400 and up to 30 days jail and 12-48 hrs. in Intoxicated Driver Resource Center; 2nd within 10 yrs.: $500-1000, 30 days community service, and 48 hrs. to 90 days jail; 3rd within 10 yrs.: $1000 and min. 180 days jail; up to 90 days of jail can be exchanged for community service (those who are underage for drinking and found DWI are subject to stiffer penalties)
NEW MEXICO	66-5-29; 66-8-102	.08% BAC	May be required by court to enroll in screening program to determine level of abuse and recommendation of treatment, if necessary; must complete any recommended treatment program required by court; 1st offense: must attend driver rehab program for alcohol or drugs, a "DWI school," and any other rehab programs the court finds necessary	1 yr. (on 1st offense suspension can be avoided by attending driver rehab program)	1st: $300-500 and/or up to 90 days jail and min. 48 hrs. of community service; 2nd: $500 and/or up to 1 yr. jail and min. 48 hrs. of community service; 3rd: $750 and min. 30 days-1 yr. jail; 4th: 4th degree felony—min. 6 mos. jail (penalties more severe for BAC over .16% and accident causing bodily injury)

Table 9: Drunk Driving—Continued

State	Code Section	BAC Legal Limit	Rehabilitation Required?	Driver's License Suspension?	Other Penalties
NEW YORK	Veh. & Traf. 1192, 1193	.10% BAC	Court may require attendance at single session of "victims impact program"	1st: 90 days; 2nd within 5yrs.: 6 mos.; 3rd within 10 yrs: 1 yr.	1st: $300-500 and/or up to 15 days jail; 2nd within 5 yrs.: $500-750 and/or 30 days jail; 3rd or more within 10 yrs.: misdemeanor, $750-1500 fine, and/or up to 180 days jail
NORTH CAROLINA	20-138.1, *et seq.*, 179	.08% BAC at any relevant time after the driving	Assessment may be required for alcoholism and substance abuse and appropriate treatment if necessary in program approved by Dept. of Human Res.	Level 5: 30 days; level 4: 60 days; level 3: 90 days	Court assesses the following levels of penalties based upon a list of grossly aggravating, aggravating and mitigating factors: level 5: 24 hrs. jail, 24 hrs. community service, and $100 fine; level 4: 48 hrs. jail, 48 hrs. community service, and $250 fine; level 3: 72 hrs. jail, 72 hrs. community service, and $500; level 2: up to $1000 fine, 7 days-12 mos. jail (after 2 days, can be house arrest for double the time remaining); level 1: up to $2000 fine, 14 days-24 mos. jail (after 4 days, can be house arrest for double the time remaining). Level 1 and 2 reserved for grossly aggravating factors only (such as prior convictions, serious injury, driving with child under 16 yrs. old)
NORTH DAKOTA	39-06.1-10; 39-08-01	.10% BAC at time of test given within 2 hrs. of driving	Order for addiction evaluation by appropriate licensed addiction treatment program with appropriate treatment if necessary	1st: 90 days; 2nd within 5 yrs.: 1 yr.; 3rd within 5 yrs.: 2 yrs.	1st: Class B misdemeanor, min. $250; 2nd within 5 yrs.: Class B misdemeanor, min. $500 and min. 4 days jail or 10 days community service; 3rd within 5 yrs.: Class A misdemeanor, $1000 and min. 60 days jail; 4th within 7 yrs.: Class A misdemeanor, $1000 and 180 days jail

Table 9: Drunk Driving—Continued

State	Code Section	BAC Legal Limit	Rehabilitation Required?	Driver's License Suspension?	Other Penalties
OHIO	Tit. 44 3793.10; 4507.16; 4511.19; 4511.99	.10% BAC (.02% BAC if under 21 yrs. old)	1st: Driver's Intervention Program (as 1 yr. alternative to jail sentence); rehab may be required in sentences; 4th or more: required attendance at alcohol and drug addiction program	1st: 6 mos. to 3 yrs.; 2nd within 5 yrs.: 1-5 yrs.; 3rd within 5 yrs.: 1-10 yrs.; 4th within 5 yrs.: min. 3 yrs.-permanent.	1st: 1st degree misdemeanor, $200-1000 and 3 days or longer jail; 2nd within 5 yrs.: 1st degree misdemeanor, $300-1500, 10 days or longer jail (part of term may be on house arrest or allow work release); 3rd within 5 yrs.: $500-2500 and 30 days to 1 yr. jail (part of term may be on house arrest or allow work release); 4th or more: 60 days-1yr. jail, $750-10,000 fine
OKLAHOMA	Tit. 47 §§6-205.1, 11-902	.10% BAC at time of test given within 2 hrs. after arrest	Referred to Dept. of Mental Health and Substance Abuse Services' alcoholism evaluation facility for evaluation	1st: 180 days; 2nd within 5 yrs.: 1 yr.; 3rd within 5 yrs.: 3 yrs.	1st: up to $1000 and 10 days to 1 yr. jail; subsequent within 10 yrs.: up to $2500 and 1-5 yrs. jail, felony conviction
OREGON	161.615, *et seq.*; 813.010, *et seq.*; 809.420	.08% BAC (any amount for persons under 21 yrs. of age)	Mandatory complete exam by court approved agency/ organization to determine whether individual has a problem condition involving alcohol or controlled substances; complete a treatment program if exam shows it necessary; if none necessary, then complete alcohol and drug information program.	1st: 1 yr.; 2nd or subsequent within 5 yrs.: 3 yrs.	1st: Class A misdemeanor, up to $5000, up to 1 yr. jail, fees for programs; 2nd: impound vehicle in addition to above
PENNSYLVANIA	Tit. 75 1548; 1532; 3731	.10% BAC within 3 hrs. of driving or actual physical control of vehicle	Evaluation to determine extent of person's involvement with alcohol or controlled substances using Court Reporting Network instruments (may order treatment if necessary) and mandatory attendance in approved alcohol highway safety school	1 month (of part of Accelerated Rehabilitation Disposition) to 12 mos.	1st.: misdemeanor in 2nd degree, min. $300, and min. 48 hrs. jail; 2nd within 7 yrs.: min. 30 days; 3rd within 7 yrs.: min. 90 days; 4th within 7 yrs.: min. 1 yr.

Table 9: Drunk Driving—Continued

State	Code Section	BAC Legal Limit	Rehabilitation Required?	Driver's License Suspension?	Other Penalties
RHODE ISLAND	31-27-2	.10% BAC	1st: attendance required at special course on DWI or under the influence of controlled substance and/or alcoholic or drug treatment for individual; 2nd and subsequent: drug and alcohol treatment	1st: 3-6 mos.; 2nd: 1-2 yrs.; 3rd within 5 yrs.: 2-3 yrs.	1st: $100-300 and 10-60 hrs. community service and/or up to 1 yr. jail; 2nd within 5 yrs.: $400 and 10 days to 1 yr. jail; 3rd within 5 yrs.: $400, 6 mos.-1yr. jail, may have car seized and sold by State of Rhode Island and proceeds going to general fund. Note: anyone convicted under this section pays highway assessment fine of $500. Different penalties for those under 18 yrs. of age.
SOUTH CAROLINA	56-5-2930, *et seq.*	"Under influence of intoxicating substances—liquor or drugs"	Evaluation and successful completion of Alcohol and Drug Safety Action Program certified by South Carolina Commission on Alcohol and Drug Abuse prior to reinstatement of license	1st: 6 mos.; 2nd within 10 yrs.: 1 yr.; 3rd within 10 yrs.: 2 yrs.; 4th within 10 yrs.: 3 yrs.; 5th within 10 yrs.: permanent	1st: $300 and 48 hrs. to 30 days jail or 48 hrs. public service; 2nd within 10 yrs.: $2000-5000 and 48 hrs. to 1 yr. jail or min. 10 days public service; 3rd within 10 yrs.: $3500-6000 and 60 days to 3 yrs. jail; 4th within 10 yrs.: 1-5 yrs. jail
SOUTH DAKOTA	32-23-1, *et seq.*; 22-6-1; 22-6-2	.10% BAC or "under the influence"	1st: required if .17% BAC; court-ordered evaluation to determine if addicted to alcohol	1st: min. 30 days to 1 yr.; 2nd: min. 1 yr.; 3rd: min. 1 yr.; 4th: min. 2 yrs.	1st: Class 1 misdemeanor, $1000 and/or 1 yr. jail; 2nd within 5 yrs.: $1000 and/or 1 yr. jail; 3rd within 5 yrs.: Class 6 felony, $2000 and/or 1-2 yrs. jail; 4th: Class 5 felony, 1-5 yrs. jail and may impose fine of $5000
TENNESSEE	55-10-401, 403	"Under the influence" .10% BAC	2nd offense: may be required to participate in court-approved inpatient alcohol and drug treatment program, up to 28 days	1st: 1 yr.; 2nd: 2 yrs.; 3rd: 3-10 yrs.	1st: $350-1500 and 48 hrs. to 11 mos. 29 days jail or 200 hrs. of public service; 2nd within 10 yrs.: $600-3500 and 45 days to 11 mos. 29 days jail; 3rd and subsequent: $1100-10,000 and 120 days to 11 mos. 29 days jail. Note: there are more serious penalties for multiple offenders (within 10 yrs.), serious bodily injury, or minor offenders.

Table 9: Drunk Driving—Continued

State	Code Section	BAC Legal Limit	Rehabilitation Required?	Driver's License Suspension?	Other Penalties
TEXAS	Tex. Codes Ann.-Penal 49-04, 49-09, 12.21, 12.22, 12.34; Tex. Stat. Ann. Art. 42.12	.10% BAC			1st: Class B misdemeanor, $2000 and/or 72 hrs.-180 days jail; 2nd within 10 yrs.: Class A misdemeanor, $4000 and/or 15 days-1 yr. jail; 3rd within 10 yrs.: 3rd degree felony, 2-10 yrs. jail, and max. $10,000 fine; court may order community supervision
UTAH	41-6-44	.08% BAC within 2 hrs. of operation or physical control	1st: assessment and educational series at a licensed alcohol dependency rehab facility (court may order treatment if person has problem); 2nd: same as above (treatment at court's discretion); 3rd and subsequent: same as above (treatment at alcohol rehab facility is mandatory)	1st: 90 days; subsequent within 6 yrs. of prior conviction: 1 yr.	1st: Class B misdemeanor (Class A if bodily injury involved or child under 16 yrs. old is passenger), up to $1000 and 48-240 hrs. jail or 24-50 hrs. community service; 2nd within 6 yrs.: up to $1000 and 240-720 hrs. jail or 80-240 hrs. community service; 3rd within 6 yrs.: up to $1000 and 720-2160 hrs. jail or 240-720 hrs. community service; if prior two convictions were both after 4/23/90, then: min. $1000 and 720-2160 hrs. jail or 240-720 hrs. community service; 4th within 6 yrs.; if at least 3 after 4/23/90, min. $1000 and 720-2160 hrs. jail or 240-720 hrs. community service
VERMONT	Title 23 1201, *et seq.*	.08% BAC	1st: alcohol assessment screening-therapy program or driver rehab if necessary at court's discretion; 2nd: completion or substantial progress in completing therapy program	1st: 90 days; 2nd: 18 months; 3rd: 3 yrs.; 4th: life	1st: max. $750 and/or up to 2 yrs. jail; 2nd: up to $1500 and/or 48 hrs. to 2 yrs. jail; 3rd: up to $2500 and/or up to 5 yrs. jail. Note that serious injury or death carries harsher penalties.
VIRGINIA	18.2-266, *et seq.*	.08% BAC	Alcohol Safety Action Program certified by commission on the VA Alcohol Safety Action Program (VASP) for 1st or 2nd offense at court's discretion	1st: 1 yr.; 2nd within 10 yrs.: 3 yrs.; 3rd within 10 yrs.: 3 yrs.	Class 1 misdemeanor: 2nd within 10 yrs.: $200-2500 and 1 mo. to 1 yr. jail; 3rd: $500-2500 and 2 mos. to 1 yr. jail. Note: harsher penalties for minors with BAC .02-.10% or those transporting minor under 17 yrs. old.

Table 9: Drunk Driving—Continued

State	Code Section	BAC Legal Limit	Rehabilitation Required?	Driver's License Suspension?	Other Penalties
WASHINGTON	46.61.502 et seq.	.10% BAC within 7 hrs. of driving	A diagnostic evaluation and treatment recommendation by alcoholism agency approved by Dept. of Social & Health Services and completion of alcohol information course	1st: 90 days; 2nd within 5 yrs.: 2 yrs. and subject to vehicle seizure and forfeiture	1st: Gross misdemeanor, $350-500 and 24 hrs. to 1 yr. jail; 2nd within 5 yrs.: $750-5000 and 90 days to 1 yr. jail. Higher BAC (above .15%) or refusal to take test results in harsher penalties
WEST VIRGINIA	17C-5-2	.10% BAC	Yes, an approved educational and treatment program	1st: min. 6 mos.; 2nd: 10 yrs.; 3rd within 10 yrs.: life	1st: $100-500 and 1 day to 6 mos. jail; 2nd: $1000-3000 and/or 6 mos. to 1 yr. jail; 3rd: $3000-5000 and/or 1-3 yrs. jail, felony. Bodily injury, death, or .02-.10% BAC for minors results in harsher penalties
WISCONSIN	343.30 et seq.; 346.63 et seq.	.10% BAC	Assessment by approved public treatment facility for examining person's use of alcohol or drugs and for developing a driver safety plan for the person	1st: 6-9 mos.; 2nd within 5 yrs.: 1 yr. to 18 mos., court may order motor vehicle to be seized; 3rd or more within 10 yrs.: 2-3 yrs.	1st: $150-300; 2nd within 5 yrs.: $300-1000 and 5 days to 6 mos. jail; 3rd within 10 yrs.: $600-2000 and 30 days to 1 yr. jail; 4th within 10 yrs.: $600-2000 and 60 days to 1 yr. jail; 5th within 10 yrs.: $600-2000 and 6 mos. to 1 yr. jail. May do community service in lieu of all or part of fine
WYOMING	31-5-233; 31-7-127, 128	.10% BAC (.05-.10% no presumption but may be used as evidence)	Suspension of imprisonment or parole based on pursuit of alcohol education and treatment program prescribed by judge	1st: 90 days; 2nd within 5 yrs.: 1 yr. (vehicle registration also suspended by the state) 3rd conviction within 5 yrs.: 3 yrs.	1st: misdemeanor, up to $750 and/or up to 6 mos. jail; 2nd within 5 yrs.: $200-750 and 7 days to 6 mos. jail. Harsher penalties for serious bodily injury

10. GUN CONTROL

The state laws controlling the purchase of firearms are varied and constantly changing. The laws reviewed here are current as of January 1, 1996, but there is still a great amount of legislation pending before state governments designed primarily to make the legal purchase of guns more difficult. Each state has some form of restriction on the buying of guns, though rural states tend to be less restrictive in controlling guns than highly urban states due to the greater numbers of hunters and sportsmen in their populations. Nonetheless, in most states convicted felons and minors cannot purchase guns; in some, aliens and individuals with mental disabilities cannot. Machine guns, automatic weapons, sawed-off shotguns, and guns with silencers are banned in many.

One of the more controversial restrictions applied to the purchase of guns is a waiting period, in which a certain amount of time must pass between the time an individual applies for a gun license and purchases that gun. With the rise in gun-related crimes, a number of states already have instituted waiting periods to discourage rash actions.

A recent controversial restriction on gun ownership surrounds possession of guns in schools. The controversy arose when the Supreme Court struck down, in 1995, the Federal Gun-Free School Zone Act as an unlawful federal interference with states' abilities to govern themselves. Forty-two states have legislation directly or indirectly affecting possession of guns in and around schools. Some of the states have enacted their legislation since the federal act was overturned, some have had such laws on their books for some time. In any case all but nine states now specifically ban possession of firearms on school grounds.

Table 10: Gun Control

State	Code Section	Illegal Arms	Waiting Period	Who May Not Own	Law Prohibiting Firearms On or Near School Grounds
ALABAMA	13A-11-63, *et seq.*	Short-barreled rifle or Short-barreled shotgun	Delivery 48 hrs. from time of application	1. Convicted of committing or attempting to commit crime of violence; 2. Drug addicts or habitual drunkard; shall not deliver to: a minor or an unsound minor; 3. Reasonable belief applicant has been convicted of crime; 4. Drug addict/habitual drunkard	16-1-24.3 Expulsion of students for one year, who are determined to have brought to schooll or have in their possession a firearm in a school building, on school grounds, or school buses, or at other school-sponsored function.
ALASKA	11.61.200	Device made or adapted to muffle the report of firearm; firearm capable of shooting one or more shots automatically without manual reloading, by a single function of trigger; rifle with barrel less than 16 inches; shotgun with barrel less than 18 inches or firearm made from a rifle or shotgun which, as modified, has an overall length of less than 26 inches; possession, sale, transfer, or manufacture of above firearms is illegal	None	Convicted felon or adjudicated a delinquent minor for conduct constituting a felony if committed by an adult	Felony. 11.61.195(a)(2)(A); 11.61.220(a)(4)(A); 11.61.210(a)(7)-(8)
ARIZONA	13-3101, 3102	Automatic weapons, rifle with barrel less than 16 inches or shotgun barrel less than 18 inches, or any firearm made from rifle/shotgun which as modified has overall length of less than 26 inches, device made or adapted to muffle the report of firearm; firearm capable of shooting one or more shots automatically without manual reloading, by a single function of trigger	None	1. Anyone found to constitute a danger to himself or others pursuant to court order and whose court-ordered treatment has not been terminated by court order; 2. Convicted felon involving violence or possession and use of deadly weapon or dangerous instrument and whose civil rights have not been restored; 3. Imprisoned or in correctional/detention facility	Misdemeanor or Felony. 13-3102(A)(12)

Table 10: Gun Control—Continued

State	Code Section	Illegal Arms	Waiting Period	Who May Not Own	Law Prohibiting Firearms On or Near School Grounds
ARKANSAS	5-73-103, 104	Machine gun, sawed-off shotgun or rifle, firearm specially made or adapted for silent discharge, removing or altering serial mark or ID # on firearm	None	1. Convicted felon; 2. Adjudicatcd mentally ill; 3. Committed involuntarily to any mental institution	Felony. 5-73-119
CALIFORNIA	Penal §§12020, 12021, 12071, 12072	Cane gun; wallet gun; any firearm not immediately recognized as such; short-barreled shotgun or rifle, i.e., barrel of less than 18 inches for shotgun, less than 16 inches for rifle, or less than 26 inches designed to fire a fixed shotgun shell or cartridge; zip gun; any bullet with explosive agent; multi-burst trigger activator; any unconventional pistol; any undetectable firearm.	10 days	1. Concealed weapons, under 21 yrs.; other fircarms, under 18 yrs.; 2. Convicted felon, including those certified by juvenile court for prosecution as adult; 3. Addicted to use of any narcotic drug; 4. Anyone whose express condition of probation is not to own firearm; 5. Persons convicted of certain misdemeanors	Felony.
COLORADO	18-12-102, *et seq.*	"Dangerous weapons": firearm silencer, machine gun, short rifle/shotgun, ballistic knife, those with ID or serial number altered or removed	None	Minor (under 18), previous conviction of felony attempt or conspiracy to commit such offenses	Misdemeanor. 18-12-105.5
CONNECTICUT	29-33, 35; 53a-211, *et seq.*	Sawed-off shotgun with barrel less than 18 inches or overall length of less than 26 inches; silencer; pistol/revolver without permit outside house or business	2 weeks from mailing of written application	1. Minors (pistol/revolver); 2. Conviction of felony; 3. Aliens (pistol/revolver)	Felony. 53a-217

Table 10: Gun Control—Continued

State	Code Section	Illegal Arms	Waiting Period	Who May Not Own	Law Prohibiting Firearms On or Near School Grounds
DELAWARE	Title 11 §1444 & §1445, §1448	Destructive weapons: firearm silencer, sawed-off shotgun, machine gun or any other firearm which is adaptable for use as a machine gun. Dangerous weapons: weapon compressed by air or spring which discharges pellet, slug, or bullet (except B.B. or airgun)	None	1. Convicted of felony or crime of violence involving physical injury to another, whether or not having in his possession any weapon during commission of such crime; 2. Anyone ever committed for mental disorder to hospital, sanitarium, or mental institution; 3. Convicted of unlawful use, possession, or sale of narcotic or dangerous drug; 4. Juvenile adjudicated as delinquent if conduct as adult would constitute a felony until 25th birthday; 5. Minor (under 18)	Felony. Title 11 §1457
DISTRICT OF COLUMBIA	22-3203, 3214, 3204	Machine gun, sawed-off shotgun, or weapon/instrument of kind commonly known as a blackjack, slingshot, sand club; silencers; imitation pistol with unlawful intent; unlicensed pistol concealed	None	Pistols: 1. Drug addict; 2. Convicted felon; 3. Convicted of soliciting prostitution, keeping bawdy or disorderly house; 4. Vagrants	Felony. 22.3202.1
FLORIDA	790.001, *et seq.*	Short-barreled rifle or shotgun, machine gun	3 days excluding weekends and legal holidays	1. Minors (under 21); 2. Convicted felon (or 3 yrs. after sentence or probation fulfilled); 3. Has been convicted or committed for abuse of a controlled substance within last 3 yrs. 4. Anyone who chronically or habitually abuses alcohol or other substances; 5. Has been adjudicated incapacitated (or 5 yrs. after restoration of capacity) 6. Been committed to mental institution (unless free from disability for 5 yrs.) 7. Person subject to injunction against committing acts of domestic violence	Felony. 790.115, 810.095

Table 10: Gun Control—Continued

State	Code Section	Illegal Arms	Waiting Period	Who May Not Own	Law Prohibiting Firearms On or Near School Grounds
GEORGIA	16-11-121, *et seq.*	Sawed-off shotgun or rifle; machine gun; dangerous weapon ("rocket launcher," "bazooka" or "recoilless rifle," "mortar," "hand grenade") or silencer	None, but 60 days for license to carry pistol	1. Convicted felon; convicted of offense arising out of possession, manufacture, or use of a controlled substance; fugitive from justice; pending proceedings for felony, forcible misdemeanor, for carrying deadly weapon within school safety zone or at public gathering; 2. Under 21 yrs. old; 3. Anyone hospitalized as inpatient at any mental hospital or drug or alcohol treatment center within 5 yrs. of applying for gun license.	Felony. 16-11-127.1
HAWAII	134-1, *et seq.*	Automatic firearms; rifles with barrel length less than 16 inches; shotguns with barrels less than 18 inches; cannons; mufflers/silencers; hand grenades; assault pistol; any ammunition coated with teflon or designed to explode/ segment upon impact	14 days generally	1. Fugitive from justice; 2. Under indictment or convicted of felony or crime of violence or illegal sale of drug; 3. Under treatment for addiction to dangerous, harmful, or detrimental drug; or intoxicating liquor; 4. Diagnosed with significant behavioral, emotional, or mental disorder or acquitted of a crime on grounds of mental disease/ disorder or committed to institution for persons with developmental disorder or mental retardation; 5. Anyone under 25 yrs. and has been adjudicated by family court to have committed a felony, two or more crimes of violence or illegal sale of drugs; 6. Minors who are under treatment for addiction to drugs/alcohol, fugitives from justice or determined not to be responsible for a criminal act or who has been committed to an institution on account of mental disease/defect/ disorder	None

Table 10: Gun Control—Continued

State	Code Section	Illegal Arms	Waiting Period	Who May Not Own	Law Prohibiting Firearms On or Near School Grounds
IDAHO	18-3302 *et seq.*		None	1. Convicted felon; 2. Person in penal institution; 3. Under 18 without consent or accompaniment of parent or guardian (except sawed-off gun/rifle or automatic weapon)	Misdemeanor. 18-3302C; 18-33025D
ILLINOIS	720 ILCS 5/ 24-1, 5/24-3, 5/24-3.1	Machine gun; rifle with barrel less than 16 inches; shotgun with barrel less than 18 inches or any weapon made from rifle or shotgun and as modified has overall length less than 26 inches; stun gun or taser; explosive or metal-piercing bullet	72 hrs.	1. Concealed weapon: under 18 yrs.; 2. Under 21 yrs. if convicted of misdemeanor other than traffic offense or adjudged delinquent; 3. Narcotic addict; 4. Patient in mental hospital within past 5 yrs.; 5. Mentally retarded	Felony. 720, ILCS 5/24-1
INDIANA	35-47-1-7; 35-47-2-7, 8; 35-47-5-4.1, 8, 11	Machine gun; sawed-off shotgun; armor-piercing handgun ammunition	7 days	1. Convicted felon; 2. Drug abuser; 3. Alcohol abuser; 4. Mentally incompetent; 5. Under 18 (except if parent or guardian)	Felony. 35-47-9-2
IOWA	724.1, *et seq.*	Offensive weapons: machine guns, short-barreled rifle or shotgun; any weapon other than shotgun or muzzle-loading rifle, cannon, pistol, revolver, or musket, which fires or can be made to fire a projectile by the explosion of a propellant charge; any bullet containing any explosive mixture capable of exploding upon impact	None	1. Convicted felon; 2. under 18 yrs. old; 3. addicted to the use of alcohol ar any controlled substance; 4. history of repeated acts of violence; 5. issuing officer reasonably determines applicant constitutes a danger to any person; 6. convicted of a crime defined in chapter 708	Felony. 724.4B; 714.4A
KANSAS	21-4201, *et seq.*	Shotgun with barrel less than 18 inches; automatic weapons; cartridges which can be fired by handgun and have plastic-coated bullets with core of less than 60% lead by weight; any device for use in silencing firearm	Certain cities and counties have waiting period but not state-wide	1. Both addicted to and an unlawful user of a controlled substance; 2. Person convicted of felonies specified under 21-4204(a)(3) and (4) may be denied gun ownership if they have been convicted within either the last 5 years or the last 10 years, depending on the crime	Misdemeanor. 21-4202

Table 10: Gun Control—Continued

State	Code Section	Illegal Arms	Waiting Period	Who May Not Own	Law Prohibiting Firearms On or Near School Grounds
KENTUCKY	527.010, *et seq.*; 237.060 *et seq.*	Armor-piercing or "black talon" ammunition	None	Convicted felon not granted full pardon/relief (including youthful offender convicted of felony offense); minor under 18 yrs. old (except when hunting or with permission of parent)	Felony. 527.070
LOUISIANA	14:95.1; 40:1751, *et seq.*	Machine and sub-machine guns; those with serial or ID # removed or altered	None	Convicted of certain felonies (murder, manslaughter, aggravated battery, violating uniform controlled substances law, etc.)	Misdemeanor or Felony. 14:95.6; 114:95.2
MAINE	Tit. 15§393; Tit. 17A §§1051, *et seq.*	Machine gun; armor-piercing ammunition	None	A person who has been convicted of a crime punishable by imprisonment for one year or more and including juveniles convicted of crimes which would have disqualified an adult. Five years from the date person is discharged from the sentences imposed s/he may apply for a permit to carry a firearm. However, that person may not be given a permit for a concealed weapon	Misdemeanor. Tit. 20-A, 6552
MARYLAND	Art. 27 §§291A, 442, 481A, *et seq.*	Short-barreled rifle or shotgun	7 days	1. Fugitive from justice; 2. Convicted felon; convicted of crime of violence; 3. Habitual drunkard; 4. Addict/habitual user of narcotics/amphetamines/ barbiturates; 5. If spent more than 30 consecutive days in mental institution for treatment; 6. Under 21 yrs.	Misdemeanor. 27, 36A
MASSACHUSETTS	Ch. 269 §§10, *et seq.*; Ch. 140 §§121, *et seq.*	Machine guns or sawed-off shotgun, etc. legal in appropriate circumstances (i.e., place of business, home, etc.—with license)	None	1. Alien; 2. Convicted felon; 3. Convicted of unlawful use, possession, or sale of drugs or habitual drunkenness; 4. Under 18 yrs. (15-18 with parents' permission); 5. Confined in mental hospital or institution for mental illness; 6. Currently under order to surrender firearms license or ID card	Misdemeanor. 269,10(j)

Table 10: Gun Control—Continued

State	Code Section	Illegal Arms	Waiting Period	Who May Not Own	Law Prohibiting Firearms On or Near School Grounds
MICHIGAN	MCL 750.223-229, 28.422, 28.92	Machine gun; automatic or semi-automatic weapons; silencers; mufflers; armor-piercing ammunition	None	1. Under 18 yrs.; 2. Committed felony; 3. Insane and not restored to sanity by court order or under order for commitment due to mental illness; 4. Must answer 70% of answers correctly on Basic Pistol Safety Questionnaire in order to purchase gun	Misdemeanor. 750.243d
MINNESOTA	609.66, 67; 624.713; 624.7132	Silencer; machine gun or machine gun conversion kit; short-barreled shotgun; spring gun	5 days	1. Minor under 18: Pistol or semi-automatic military-style assault weapon, except under supervision of parent/guardian, military instruction, firing range, successful completion of training course; 2. Convicted of crime of violence unless 10 yrs. has elapsed or civil rights have been restored, including juveniles; 3. Mentally ill; 4. Convicted for unlawful use, possession, sale of controlled substance other than small amount of marijuana or person who's been hospitalized or committed for treatment for habitual use of controlled substance or marijuana unless proof that they haven't abused in 2 yrs.; 5. Chemically dependent; 6. Peace officer who is informally admitted to treatment facility for chemical dependency unless he receives certificate for discharge; 7. Pistol or semi-automatic military-style assault weapon: aliens, fugitives from justice, those dishonorably discharged from armed forces	Felony. 609.66

Table 10: Gun Control—Continued

State	Code Section	Illegal Arms	Waiting Period	Who May Not Own	Law Prohibiting Firearms On or Near School Grounds
MISSISSIPPI	97-37-1, *et seq.*	Carrying machine gun or fully automatic firearm, short-barreled rifle less than 16 inches, or shotgun less than 18 inches; silencer or muffler; toy pistols that can fire or make an explosion (cap pistols are expressly excepted)	None	1. Students on campus/ education property; 2. Minors under 18; 3. Convicted felons (unless they have certificates of rehabilitation); 4. intoxicated persons	Misdemeanor. 97-37-17
MISSOURI	571.020, *et seq.*	Machine gun; short-barreled rifle/ shotgun; silencer; gas gun; explosive weapon; bullet which explodes upon impact	7 days	Concealable weapon: 1. Convicted of dangerous felony; 2. Fugitive from justice, habitually intoxicated or drugged condition, or mentally incompetent; 3. Under 21 yrs. old; 4. Dishonorably discharged from armed services; 5. MO resident for less than 6 mos.; 6. Not citizen of U.S.	Misdemeanor. 571.030.1
MONTANA	45-8-301, *et seq.*	Sawed-off rifle or shotgun; machine guns except registered and on own property; silencer	None	1. Convicted felon; 2. Adjudicated mental incompetents; 3. Illegal aliens; 4. Minors	Felony. 45-8-334; 45-8-361
NEBRASKA	28-1201, *et seq.*	Machine gun; short rifle or short shotgun; defaced firearm; stolen firearm	None	1. Under 18: revolver, pistol, or any short-barreled hand firearm; 2. Convicted felon/fugitive from justice: barrel less than 18 inches	Misdemeanor. 28-1204.04
NEVADA	202.253, *et seq.*	Metal penetrating bullets; short-barreled rifle or shotgun; machine gun or silencer	Certain cities and counties may impose waiting period	1. Minor under 14 unless supervised; 2. Ex-felon unless pardoned or civil rights restored	Misdemeanor. 202.265
NEW HAMPSHIRE	159:1, *et seq.*	Teflon coated or armor piercing bullet	After approval number received from telephone call-in check	1. Career criminals; 2. Convicted felons; 3. Minors	193-D:1

Table 10: Gun Control—Continued

State	Code Section	Illegal Arms	Waiting Period	Who May Not Own	Law Prohibiting Firearms On or Near School Grounds
NEW JERSEY	2C:39-1, *et seq.*; 2C:58-1, *et seq.*	Sawed-off shotgun, silencer; imitation firearm (intended for unlawful use); defaced firearms; armor penetrating bullets; stun guns; machine guns or assault firearms if unlicensed	30 days resident; 45 days nonresident	1. Convicted of aggravated assault, arson, burglary, escape, extortion, homicide, kidnapping, robbery, aggravated sexual assault, or sexual assault or any order prohibiting possession of firearms; 2. Committed for mental disorder unless satisfactory proof he no longer suffers from a disorder which interferes or handicaps him in handling a firearm; 3. Convicted of unlawful use, possession, or sale of controlled dangerous substance; 4. Minors under 18; 5. Drug dependent; 6. Physical defect which makes it unsafe for him to handle firearms	Misdemeanor. 2C:39-5e
NEW MEXICO	30-7-1 *et seq.*		None	Convicted felon	Felony. 30-7-2.1
NEW YORK	Penal §§265, *et seq.*	Machine gun, silencer, stun gun, electronic dart gun, bullet with explosive substance on impact, armor piercing ammunition, 20 or more firearms	None	1. Convicted felon; 2. Alien; 3. Minor under 16: possession of air gun, spring gun, weapon where loaded or blank cartridges can be used	Misdemeanor. Penal 265.01(3); 265.06
NORTH CAROLINA	14-402, *et seq.*	Machine gun, submachine gun, or other like weapons, unlicensed pistol or crossbow	30 days	1. Convicted felon cannot own handgun or gun with barrel less than 18 inches or overall length less than 26 inches or any weapon of mass death and destruction within 5 yrs. of conviction or termination of sentence, whichever is later; 2. Fugitive from justice; 3. Unlawful user of drugs; 4. Adjudicated incompetent on grounds of mental illness	Misdemeanor or Felony. 14-269.2(b)

Table 10: Gun Control—Continued

State	Code Section	Illegal Arms	Waiting Period	Who May Not Own	Law Prohibiting Firearms On or Near School Grounds
NORTH DAKOTA	62.1-02-01, *et seq.*	Machine gun; fully automatic rifle; silencer; federally licensed firearm or dangerous weapon not in compliance with National Firearms Act	None	1. Convicted of felony involving violence or intimidation from date of conviction or release from incarceration for 10 yrs. (whichever is later); 2. Convicted of other felonies not mentioned above or Class A misdemeanors for 5 yrs.; 3. Diagnosed and confined/committed to hospital or other institution as mentally ill or mentally deficient person (does not apply if more than 3 yrs. have passed); 4. Under 18 unless supervised and for purposes of safety training, hunting, target shooting	Misdemeanor. 62.1-02-05
OHIO	2923.11, *et seq.*	Sawed-off automatic firearm; zip gun; firearm or ammunition manufactured and designed for military purposes; silencer or muffler (unless qualified and licensed)	None	1. Fugitive from justice; 2. Under indictment or convicted of felony of violence or adjudged juvenile delinquent for commission of such felony; 3. Under indictment or convicted of illegal possession, use, sale of drugs; 4. Drug dependent or chronic alcoholic; 5. Mentally incompetent; 6. Under 18 except for hunting or marksmanship and under adult supervision	Felony. 2923.122
OKLAHOMA	Tit. 21 §§1272, *et seq.*	Sawed-off shotgun or rifle; slung shot	None	1. Minors (except for hunting, etc. and under adult supervision); 2. Convicted felon, unless pardoned (includes those adjudicated as delinquent child—within 10 yrs.); 3. Mentally incompetent or insane	Misdemeanor. Tit. 21, 1277; Felony. 1280.1

Table 10: Gun Control—Continued

State	Code Section	Illegal Arms	Waiting Period	Who May Not Own	Law Prohibiting Firearms On or Near School Grounds
OREGON	166.250, *et seq.*	Machine gun; short-barreled rifle/ shotgun; silencer; armor piercing ammunition	15 days	1. Under 18 yrs., except for hunting or with parent's consent; 2. Convicted felon or juvenile felony offender (within 4 yrs.); 3. Committed to Mental Health and Developmental Disability Services Division or mentally ill; 4. Subj. to order prohibiting purchase or possession of firearms	Felony. 166.170
PENNSYLVANIA	Tit. 18 §§908, 6105, 6110, 6111	Machine gun; sawed-off shotgun; firearm specially made or adopted for concealment or silent discharge	48 hrs.	1. Former convict of crime of violence; 2. No delivery to persons under 18 yrs.; 3. If you have reason to believe convicted of crime of violence; drug addict; habitual drunkard; unsound mind	Misdemeanor. 912
RHODE ISLAND	11-47-2, *et seq.*	Sawed-off shotgun or rifle; machine gun; silencer; armor piercing bullets; defaced firearm	7 days	1. Aliens (less than 10 yrs.); 2. Mentally incompetent under treatment/confinement; 3. Drug addict adjudicated or in treatment; 4. Habitual drunkard adjudicated or in treatment; 5. Convicted of crime of violence; 6. Fugitive frnm justice	Felony. 11-47-60; 11.-47-60.2
SOUTH CAROLINA	16-23-30, 230, 520	Machine gun; sawed-off shotgun/rifle, military firearm; teflon-coated ammunition, defaced firearm	None	1. Convicted of crime of violence; 2.: Member of subversive organization; 3. Under 21 with military exception; 4. Anyone court has adjudged to be unfit to possess pistol	Misdemeanor or Felony. 16-23-420
SOUTH DAKOTA	22-1-2; 22-14-6, 16; 23-7-9, 46	Controlled weapon-silencer; machine gun; short shotgun or rifle	48 hrs.	1. Convicted of crime of violence in last 15 yrs.; 2. Minor (under 18 yrs. old)	Misdemeanor. 13-32-7
TENNESSEE	39-17-1301, *et seq.*	Machine gun; short-barreled rifle or shotgun; silencer; explosive weapon; device designed, made or adapted for delivering or shooting an explosive weapon	15 days	1. Convicted of felony (imprisonment exceeding 1 yr.) unless pardoned or conviction expunged; 2. Fugitives from justice; 3. Unsound mind; 4. Minors; 5. Addicted to alcohol; 6. Drug addict; 7. Convicted of illegal sale of alcoholic beverages	Misdemeanor or Felony. 39-17-1309

Table 10: Gun Control—Continued

State	Code Section	Illegal Arms	Waiting Period	Who May Not Own	Law Prohibiting Firearms On or Near School Grounds
TEXAS	Penal §§46.05, *et seq.*	Machine gun; short-barreled firearm; silencer; armor-piercing ammunition; zip gun; explosive weapon	None	1. Convicted felon within 5 yrs. of release or parole; 2. Sale, rental, lease, or gift to minor under 18 without parental consent	Felony. Penal 46.04
UTAH	76-10-501, *et seq.*	None listed	None	1. Convicted of crime of violence or on parole or under indictment; 2. Addicted to use of narcotic drugs; 3. Mentally incompetent or defective; 4. Illegal alien; 5. Dishonorably discharged from Armed Forces	Misdemeanor. 76-10-505.5; Felony. 76-3-203
VERMONT	Tit. 13 §§4001, *et seq.*	Silencer; "zip" gun	None	Child under 16 without permission of parents	Misdemeanor. Tit. 13, 4004
VIRGINIA	18.2-290, *et seq.*	Sawed-off shotgun/rifle; machine gun	State Police have until end of next business day after inquiry for possible criminal record by telephone	1. Convicted felons or those subject to protective order; 2. Minors: handguns; 3. Aliens; 4. Legally incompetent, mentally incapacitated, involuntary committed, insanity-acquitted	Felony. 18.2-308.1
WASHINGTON	9.41.040, *et seq.*	Machine gun, short-barreled shotgun or rifle	5 days (up to 60 days for non-residents)	1. Aliens; 2. Convicted of serious offense or domestic violence/harassment offense or felony in which firearm was used or displayed (unless charge dismissed or received probation); 3. Minors under 18, except as provided (hunter's safety course, hunting, trapping, etc.); 4. Felony conviction for violation of Uniform Controlled Substances Act (or equivalent); 5. Convicted 3 times within 5 yrs. of driving under the influence; 6. Committed by court for treatment of mental illness	Misdemeanor. 9.41.280

Table 10: Gun Control—Continued

State	Code Section	Illegal Arms	Waiting Period	Who May Not Own	Law Prohibiting Firearms On or Near School Grounds
WEST VIRGINIA	61-7-7, 9	Machine gun; submachine gun or other fully automatic weapon	None	1. Convicted of felony; 2. Discharged from armed forces (U.S.) less than honorably; 3. Mentally incompetent; 4. Alien; 5. Addicted to drugs/alcohol or unlawful user; 6. Minors (under 18) without parental permission	Misdemeanor. 61-7-11a
WISCONSIN	175.35; 941.26, *et seq.*	Machine gun or other fully-automatic weapon; short-barreled rifle/shotgun; silencer	48 hrs.	1. Convicted of felony in this state or what would have been a felony if committed in this state or adjudicated delinquent for act considered felony for adult; 2. Mental disease or defect reason for not guilty or insanity	Misdemeanor. 948.605
WYOMING	6-8-102, *et seq.*	Not listed	None	Convicted of violent felony or attempt to commit violent felony	None

11. ILLEGAL DRUGS

Although the 1960s and 1970s seemed to hail a new level of legal tolerance toward recreational drug use, the movement became mired in reality in the 1980s when society as a whole grew intolerant of drug use of any kind, largely due to the destructive nature and violent criminal character of the drug trafficking and distribution business.

As a result, what little ground gained toward the legalization of recreational drugs was either lost or frozen, and drug traffickers and dealers now face increasingly stiffer penalties. Notwithstanding the religious use of peyote, virtually no state recognizes legal possession or use of any "recreational drug." Alaska is apparently the most liberal state, with no prescribed penalty for the personal use or possession of marijuana. (Many states have made possession of small amounts of marijuana a misdemeanor. In most of these states, there are also stiff penalties for possession near school grounds or sale to minors—even an offense called "reckless" possession near school grounds.)

Drug laws are among the most complex criminal laws on the books. Often certain offenses are given class designations whereby any number of specific criminal offenses are grouped into various classes and sentences prescribed according to mandated terms, called "sentencing guidelines." Sentencing guidelines set absolute minimum and maximum sentences for specific crimes and take much of the discretion for setting sentences away from judges. Sentencing guidelines have become very controversial lately as legislatures attempt to assert more control over punishments imposed on criminals. From year to year, punishments, it seems, vary often enough not to put them on the books.

One recent trend in drug legislation is the growing incorporation of special enhancements directed at selling to or from minors. About six states have recently amended these particular laws by incorporating mandatory sentencing to adults selling to minors. While such laws have been common, some of the new amendments are becoming more specific by including language such as that found in California. That states new laws note particularly that enhancements attach when the seller is over 18 and the buyer is a minor 4 years younger. The intent of the legislation to protect minors from influence by corrupt adults is easy to see. The specific age and number of years difference between the parties is less clear.

In most cases in the following tables, reference to the code sections give a picture of the potential punishments for the violation of a specific crime. Since the class schedules among illegal drugs overlap and because the penalties are often extremely involved and difficult to summarize, reference is often made only to the class designation. In these cases, however, it is still possible to draw comparisons among states by studying the degrees assigned to the violation. In addition, quick reference to the individual state code listed should provide easy access to more detailed information.

Table 11a: Illegal Drugs: Cocaine

State	Code Section	Possession	Sale	Trafficking
ALABAMA	20-2-1.; 13A-12-210 to 215, 231 (2)	Class C felony	28-500 g.: mandatory 3 yrs. and $50,000; 500 g. to 1 kg.: mandatory 5 yrs. and $100,000; 1-10 kg.: mandatory 15 yrs. and $250,000; Over 10 kg.: mandatory life without parole; Sale to minor: Class A felony; Subsequent offense: offenses subject to the Habitual Felony Offender Act; Unlawful distribution of controlled substance: Class B felony	Class A felony; 28-500 g.: minimum 3 yrs. and $50,000 fine; 500 g. -1 kilo: min. 5 yrs and $100,000 fine; 1-10 kilos: min. 15 yrs. and $250,000 fine; Over 10 kilos: life without parole
ALASKA	11.71.010, *et seq.*	Possessing any amount: Class C felony	Delivering to one under 19 and at least 3 yrs. younger: unclassified felony; Manufactures or delivers any amount: Class B felony	"Continuing criminal enterprise": unclassified felony
ARIZONA	13-3401, *et seq.*; 36-2501, *et seq.*	Class 4 felony, but for one not previously convicted of felony, court can make it Class 1 misdemeanor; Fine of not less than $1000 or 3 times the value of substance, whichever is greater	Class 3 felony; Fine of greater of 3 times value of drugs or $1000; Selling to minors: Class 2 felony and fine of $2000 or 3 times value, whatever is greater. In drug-free school zone: add 1 yr. to sentence and fine for selling to minors	Class 2 felony (transport/import); Class 3 felony (manufacture)
ARKANSAS	5-64-401, *et seq.*	Class C felony	Class Y felony: depending on amount, prison from 10 to 40 yrs. or life and fines between $25,000 and $250,000; Subsequent offense: double penalties; increased penalties within 1000 ft. of school	1 g. of cocaine in possession creates a rebuttable presumption of intent to deliver

Table 11a: Illegal Drugs: Cocaine—Continued

State	Code Section	Possession	Sale	Trafficking
CALIFORNIA	Health & Safety §11000, *et seq.* §11350, *et seq.*	State prison and fine up to $70; if probation granted, there are additional requirements	State prison 2-4 yrs.; Possession for sale of "cocaine base": state prison 3-5 yrs.; Sale to minors: state prison 3, 5, or 7 yrs.; Sale to school children: 5, 7, or 9 yrs.; Anyone over 18 who sells to a minor or uses a minor in the sale process is punishable in state prison for 3, 6, or 9 yrs.; Sale within 1000 ft. of school: additional 3, 4, or 5 yrs.; Anyone over 18 yrs who sells to a minor at least 4 years younger as a full and separate enhancement shall be punished by imprisonment in state prison for 3, 4 or 5 yrs. Sale on many public areas punishable by state prison for 5, 7, or 9 yrs. if seller 5 yrs. older than minor	Transport/import 3-5 yrs.; County to noncontiguous county: 3, 6, or 9 yrs.
COLORADO	18-18-101, *et seq.*	Class 4 felony; Subsequent Offense: twice or more within 6 months and amount greater than 28.5 g.: Defendant shall be sentenced to the Dept. of Corrections for at least the minimum and fined no less than $1000 but not over $500,000 with no probation or suspension	Class 3 felony; Sale to minor within 1000 ft. of school or public property-Dept. of Corrections for minimum 5 yrs.; Subsequent offense near school: 20 yrs.	
CONNECTICUT	21a 240; 243, 278	7 yrs. and/or $50,000; Subsequent offense: 15 yrs. and/or $100,000; Third offense: 25 yrs. and/or $250,000	15 yrs. and $50,000; 1 oz. (or ½ g. in free-base form) or more: 5-20 yrs. minimum, to life maximum (by a non-drug dependent person); Subsequent offense: 10-25 yrs.; Within 1000 ft. of school: additional mandatory 3 yrs.	

Table 11a: Illegal Drugs: Cocaine—Continued

State	Code Section	Possession	Sale	Trafficking
DELAWARE	Tit. 16 §4701, *et seq.* 4751, 4753A	Possession, use, consumption: Class A misdemeanor. If applicable, can be subject to First Offenders Controlled Substances Diversion Program (§4764)	Class C felony: $5000-$50,000; If not addicted: felony, mandatory 6 yrs.; To a minor: Class C felony; if under 16, mandatory 1 yr. prison; On school property: up to 15 yrs. and $250,000; Subsequent offense: if not addicted: mandatory 12 yrs.; Where death as a result involved: Class B felony-$10,000-$100,000 fine; If person knowingly purchases from a minor: Class C felony; (More severe penalties if near school §4767-68); If the seller is under the age of 16 there is a mandatory sentence of 1 year. not subject to suspension/ probation/ pardon; If seller is under the age of 14 mandatory sentence of 2 years	If on any single occasion one has: 5-50 g.: 3 yrs. minimum and $5000; 50-100 g.: 5 yrs. minimum and $100,000; More than 100 g.: 15 yrs. minimum and $400,000
DISTRICT OF COLUMBIA	33-501, *et seq.;* 33-541	Possession: up to 30 yrs.,up to $500,000; Subsequent offense: double penalties	Sale, manufacture, distribute: not over 30 yrs. and/or $500,000; Subsequent offense: double penalties; Within drug-free zone or to minors: up to twice the punishment.	
FLORIDA	775.082 to .084; 893.01, *et seq.*	3rd degree felony; Possession of 28 g. is trafficking	2nd degree felony (penalties more severe near school)	All sentencing is to be done pursuant to sentencing guidelines: 28-200 g.: $50,000; 200-400 g.: $100,000; 400 g.-150 kg.: 15 yrs. and $250,000; Over 150 kg.: 1st degree felony with life imprisonment
GEORGIA	16-13-20, *et seq.*	Over 28 g. is trafficking; Possession of any amount is a felony punishable with minimum 2-15 yrs.; Subsequent offense: minimum 5-30 yrs.	Felony: 5-30 yrs.; Subsequent offense: mandatory life	28-200 g.: mandatory 10 yrs. and $200,000; 200-400 g.: mandatory 15 yrs. and $300,000; Over 400 g.: mandatory 25 yrs. and $1,000,000
HAWAII	329-14, *et seq.;* 712-1240, *et seq.*	1/8- 1 oz.: Class B felony; 1 oz. or more: Class A felony; Subsequent offense: Class A or B felony based on quantity	Any amount: Class B felony; 1/8 oz. or more, or any amount to a minor: Class A felony	

Table 11a: Illegal Drugs: Cocaine—Continued

State	Code Section	Possession	Sale	Trafficking
IDAHO	37-2701, *et seq.*	Felony, up to 7 yrs. and/or $15,000; Subsequent offense: double penalties; Possession of 28 g. or more is trafficking	Felony, up to life and $25,000; Subsequent offense: double penalties	28-200 g.: Mandatory 3 yrs. and minimum $10,000; 200-400 g.: Mandatory 5 yrs. and minimum $15,000; Over 400 g.: mandatory 10 yrs. and minimum $25,000; Maximum sentence life; maximum fine $100,000
ILLINOIS	720 ILCS 570/ 200, *et seq.*; Uniform Controlled Substances Act	1-15 g.: Class 1 felony, $250,000 15-100 g.: Class 1 felony, mandatory 4-15 yrs.; 100-400 g.: mandatory 6-30 yrs.; 400-900 g.: mandatory 8-40 yrs.; Over 900 g.: mandatory 10-50 yrs.; Fines for any offense involving 100 g. or more: greater of $200,000 or street value	15-100 g.: 6-30 yrs.; 100-400 g.: 9-40 yrs.; 400-900 g.: 12-50 yrs.; Over 900 g.: 15-60 yrs.; Sale to minors: double penalties; Within 1000 ft. of truck stop or safety rest: double penalties; Within 1000 ft. of school: Class Y felony	Trafficking: double penalties
INDIANA	35-48-2-1 *et seq.*; 35-48-4-1, *et seq.*	Possession of any amount: at least Class D felony Under 3 g. but within 1000 feet of school property: Class B felony; Over 3 g.: Class C felony; Possession of 3 g. or more within 1000 feet of school property: Class A felony	Class B felony unless amount is over 3 grams or delivery to minor 3 yrs. younger or delivery on/in school property or within 1000 feet of property or on school bus, then Class A felony	

Table 11a: Illegal Drugs: Cocaine—Continued

State	Code Section	Possession	Sale	Trafficking
IOWA	124.101, *et seq.*		500 g. or less: Class C felony, $1000 to $50,000 500g. to 5 kg.: Class B felony, $5000 to $100,000 Over 5 kg.: Class B felony, up to 50 yrs. and $1,000,000 Subsequent offense: triple penalties; More severe penalties for distribution to minors or person 3 yrs. younger; An adult who distributes to a minor: Class B felony, min. confinement 5 yrs. within 1,000 ft. of public/ private school grounds, or recreational area, on a school bus, min. confinement 10 yrs.	
KANSAS	65-4101, *et seq.*	Level 4 felony; Subsequent offense: Level 2 felony; Third offense: Level 1 felony and life in prison	Level 3 felony; Subsequent offense: Level 2 felony; Third offense: Level 1 felony and life in prison; Sell within 1000 ft. of school or to minors: Level 2 felony	
KENTUCKY	218A.010, *et seq.*	Class D felony Subsequent offense: Class C felony	Class C felony; Subsequent offense: Class B felony; Selling to minor: Class C felony 1st offense, Class B felony subsequent offenses.	First offense: Class C felony; Subsequent offense: Class B felony; Within 1000 yds. of school: higher penalties
LOUISIANA	§§40:961, *et seq.*	Under 28 g.: 5 yrs. with or without hard labor and $5,000; 28-200 g.: 10-60 yrs. hard labor and $50,000 to $150,000; 200-400 g.: 20-60 yrs. hard labor and $100,000 to $350,000; Over 400 g.: 30-60 yrs. hard labor and $250,000 to $600,000	5-30 yrs. hard labor and/or up to $50,000; Sale to minors by persons over 25: life imprisonment; Sale to minors by those at least 3 yrs. his junior: double penalties	Production or manufacturing cocaine base: 40-99 yrs. hard labor without parole or suspension and up to $500,000 fine
MAINE	Tit. 17A §§1101, *et seq.*	Class D crime; Over 14 g.: Class B crime and creates presumption of trafficking	Class B crime; 7 g. or more creates presumption of furnishing; Sale to minor or within 1000 ft. of school: more serious penalties	Possession of 14 g. or more is trafficking

Table 11a: Illegal Drugs: Cocaine—Continued

State	Code Section	Possession	Sale	Trafficking
MARYLAND	Art. 27 §§276, *et seq.*	Misdemeanor with penalty of up to 4 yrs. and/or $25,000; Bringing 28 g. into state: felony with penalty of up to $50,000 and/or 25 yrs.; Subsequent offense: double penalties	Felony with penalty of 20 yrs. and/or $25,000; Sale of more than 448 g. or 50 g. of crack: not less than 40 yrs.; Subsequent offense: double penalties; 2 yrs. mandatory, not less than 10 yr. sentence; Third offense: not less than 40 yrs. Sale to minors or near school property: stricter penalties	If "drug kingpin" 20-40 yrs. and/or $1,000,000 fine
MASSACHUSETTS	Ch. 94c §§1, *et seq.*	1 yr. and/or $1,000 Subsequent offense: 2 yrs. and/or $2000; Over 14 g. is trafficking	2½-10 yrs. and/or $1000 to $10,000; Subsequent offense: 5-15 yrs. and/or $2500 to $25,000	14-28 g.: 3-15 yrs. and/or $2500 to $25,000; 28-100 g.: 5-20 yrs. and/or $5000 to $50,000; 100-200 g.: 10-20 yrs. and/or $10,000 to $100,000; Over 200 g.: 15-20 yrs. and/or $50,000 to $500,000
MICHIGAN	333.7214; 333.7401, *et seq.*	Under 25 g.: Up to 4 yrs. and/or $25,000; 25-50 g.: 1-4 yrs. and/or up to $25,000 or probation for life; 50-225 g.: 10-20 yrs.; 225-650 g.: 20-30 yrs.; Over 650 g.: life imprisonment	Felony: Under 50 g.: 1-20 yrs. and/or $25,000 or probation for life; 50-225 g.: 10-20 yrs.; 225-650 g.: 20-30 yrs.; Over 650 g.: life imprisonment; Sale to minor or near school property: up to double penalties	
MINNESOTA	152.01, *et seq.*	Any possession: 15 yrs. and/or $100,000; 3-6 g.:up to 20 yrs. and/or $250,000; 6-25 g.: up to 25 yrs. and/or $500,000; Over 25 g.: up to 30 yrs. and/or $1,000,000; Subsequent offense: depends on level of prior offenses, 4-40 yrs. and/or up to $1,000,000	Any amount: up to 20 yrs. and/or $250,000; 3-10 g.: up to 25 yrs. and/or $500,000; Over 10 g.: up to 30 yrs. and/or $1,000,000; Subsequent offense: depends on level of prior offense, 4-40 yrs. and/or up to $1,000,000; Sale to minor -any amount: up to 25 yrs. and/or $500,000	
MISSISSIPPI	41-29-101, *et seq.*	Felony: up to 3 yrs. and/or $1000 to $30,000 Subsequent offense: double penalty	No specified term up to 30 yrs. and/or $5000 to $1,000,000 Subsequent offense: double penalty; Mandatory 30 yrs. without parole for 3 or more offenses within 12 month period	Any one over 21 who sells 2 or more oz. of cocaine in a 12 month period shall have life in prison without suspension or parole

Table 11a: Illegal Drugs: Cocaine—Continued

State	Code Section	Possession	Sale	Trafficking
MISSOURI	195.010, *et seq.*	Class C felony; Subsequent offense: subject to prior & persistent offenders statute §195.295	Class B felony; Subsequent offense: subject to prior & persistent offenders statute §195.295; Distribution to minor under 17 or 2 yrs. junior: Class B felony; Within 1000 ft. of school: Class A felony	Trafficking drugs in 2nd degree; Delivery associated/attempt to deliver: 150-450 g.: Class B felony: More than 450 g.: Class A felony term without parole; 2-6 g: cocaine base (crack): Class B felony; Over 6 g.:Class A felony, term without parole; Buying/attempting to buy: 150-450 g.: Class B felony; More than 450 g.: Class A felony; 2-6 g. cocaine base (crack): Class B felony; Over 6 g.: Class A felony
MONTANA	45-9-101, *et seq.*; 50-32-101, *et seq.*	Up to 5 yrs. and/or $50,000; Criminal possession with intent to sell: up to 20 yrs. and/or $50,000	Two yrs. to life and/or $50,000 (4 yrs. if sale to minor); Subsequent offense: 10 yrs. to life and/or $50,000 (20 yrs. if sale to minor); Third offense: not less than 20 yrs. and/or $50,000 (40 yrs. if sale to minor); Offense of criminal sale of dangerous drugs on or near school property: 3 yrs. to life and/or $50,000	Criminal production/ manufacture: 5 yrs. to life and/or $50,000; Subsequent offense: 20 yrs. to life and/or $50,000; Third offense: 40 yrs. to life and/or $50,000
NEBRASKA	28-401, *et seq.*	Class 4 felony	10-28 g.: Class1 D felony; 28-40 g.: Class 1C felony; Over 140 g.: Class 1B felony (Crack or cocaine); Class III felony anyone 18 or older who knowingly sells to a minor in, on, or within 1,000 ft. of the real property of a private/ public school. From elementary through university or youth centers: Shall be punished by the next higher penalty classification greater than Class B felony	

Table 11a: Illegal Drugs: Cocaine—Continued

State	Code Section	Possession	Sale	Trafficking
NEVADA	453.011; 453.510	1-6 yrs. and $5000; Subsequent offense: 1-10 yrs. and $10,000; Third offense: 1-20 yrs. and $20,000	1-20 yrs. and $20,000; Subsequent offense: 5-20 yrs. and $20,000; Third offense: life or 15 yrs. mandatory and $20,000	4-14 g.: 3-20 yrs. and $50,000; 14-28 g.: 10 yrs. and $100,000; Over 28 g.: 25 yrs.and $500,000; Double penalties for sale near school
NEW HAMPSHIRE	318-B:1, *et seq.*	Class B felony with fine up to $25,000; Subsequent offense: Class A felony with fine up to $50,000	Under .5 oz. (less than 1 oz.of crack): up to 7 yrs. and/or $100,000; .5 to 5 oz. (1 oz.-5 oz. of crack): up to 20 yrs. and/or $300,000; 5 oz. and over: up to 30 yrs. and/or $500,000; Subsequent offense: Under .5 oz. (less than 1 oz. of crack): up to 15 yrs. and/or $200,000; .5 to 5 oz. (1 oz. -5 oz. of crack): up to 40 yrs. and/or $500,000; 5 oz. and over: maximum life and/or $500,000	
NEW JERSEY	24:21 1, *et seq.*; 2C:35-2, *et seq.*	Crime of 3rd degree, $25,000	.5 oz. or less: crime of 3rd degree, $50,000; .5 oz. to 5 oz.: crime of 2nd degree; Over 5 oz.: crime of 1st degree, fixed prison term and $300,000; Selling within 1000 feet of school: fixed prison term and up to $100,000; Selling to minor or pregnant female: double penalties	Leader of narcotics trafficking network: life (25 yr. minimum before parole) and/or $500,000
NEW MEXICO	30-31-1, *et seq.*	4th degree felony	2nd degree felony; Subsequent offense: 1st degree felony; Within drug-free school zone: 1st degree felony	
NEW YORK	Penal §§220, *et seq.*; Pub. Health §§3306, 3307	Knowingly possessing: Any amount: Class A misdemeanor; Criminal possession in the fifth (5th) degree Over 500 mg.: Class D felony; Over 1/8 oz.: Class C felony; Over 1/2 oz.: Class B felony; Over 2 oz.: Class A-II felony; Over 4 oz.: class A-I felony; Any amount with intent to sell: Class D felony; Any amount of narcotic drug with intent to sell: Class B felony	Class D felony in general, then: Over 1/2 oz.: Class A-II felony; Over 2 oz.: Class A-I felony; On school grounds or narcotic preparation to someone under 21: Class B felony	

Table 11a: Illegal Drugs: Cocaine—Continued

State	Code Section	Possession	Sale	Trafficking
NORTH CAROLINA	90-86, *et seq.*	Class I felony	Class H felony; Selling of controlled substance to person under 16 or pregnant female or within 300 ft. of school property: Class E felony	28-200 g.: Class G felony, 35-42 mos. and $50,000; 200-400 g.: Class F felony, 70-84 mos. and $100,000; 400 g. and over: Class D felony, 175-219 mos. and $250,000
NORTH DAKOTA	19-03.1-01, *et seq.*	Class C felony; Within 1000 ft. of school: Class B felony	Class A felony: at least 1 yr.; 2nd offense: at least 5 yrs.; 3rd offense: 20 yrs.; If over 500 g. of cocaine or over 5 g. of crack: Class B felony; Sale within 1000 ft. of school or to a minor: at least 4 yrs.; Selling to a minor by an 18 year old; Subsequent offense: 8 yrs	
OHIO	2925.01, *et seq.*; 3719.01, *et seq.*	4th degree felony, $1500; Subsequent offense: 3rd degree felony, $2500; but 10-30 g.: 3rd degree felony with 18 mos. mandatory; 30-100 g.: 2nd degree with 18 mos.-3 yrs. mandatory: Over 100 g.: 1st degree felony with 15 yrs.-life; Subsequent offense: one degree higher	Under 10 g.: 3rd degree felony; 10-30 g.: 2nd degree felony, 3 yrs. mandatory; 30-100 g.: 1st degree felony, 5 yrs. mandatory; Over 100 g.: 1st degree felony, 15 yrs.-life; Within 1000 ft. of school or 100 ft. of juvenile: more severe penalties; Subsequent offense: one degree higher	Ship, transport, manufacture, produce: 2nd or 3rd degree felony; Subsequent offense: one degree higher
OKLAHOMA	Tit. 63 §§2-101, *et seq.*	Felony, 2-10 yrs.; Subsequent offense: felony, 4-20 yrs.; Within 1000 ft. of school or in presence of child under 12: up to double penalties; Subsequent offense: up to triple penalties	Felony, 5 yrs.-life, up to $100,000; Subsequent offense: double penalties with at least 10 yrs; Within 1000 ft. of school or in presence of child under 12: up to double penalties; Subsequent offense: up to triple penalties	
OREGON	Chapter 475	Class B or C felony	8-10 g.: Commercial drug offense if over $300 cash, firearm or packaging materials; stolen property; using public lands or customer lists; Over 10 g.: Category 6 crime	Class A or B felony; Delivery and manufacture of over 10 g.: Category 8 crime
PENNSYLVANIA	Tit. 35 §§780-101, *et seq.*	Misdemeanor, 1 yr. and/or $5000; Subsequent offense: 3 yrs. and/or $25,000	Felony, 15 yrs. and/or $250,00 or higher fine if necessary to recover drug profit; Subsequent offense or sale to minor: double penalties	

Table 11a: Illegal Drugs: Cocaine—Continued

State	Code Section	Possession	Sale	Trafficking
RHODE ISLAND	21-28-4.01, *et seq.*	*Nolo contendere* pleas: 100 hrs. community service and drug education program; Up to 1 oz.: 3 yrs. and/or $500 to $5000; 1 oz.-1 kg.: 10-50 yrs. and/or $10,000-$50,000; Over 1 kg.: 20 yrs. to life and $25,000 to $1,000,000	Person not drug dependent: life and/or $10,000 to $500,000; Drug dependent: 30 yrs. and or $3000 to $100,000; 1 kg.: minimum 10-50 yrs. and/or $10,000 to $500,000; Over 1 kg.: 20 yrs.-life and/or $25,000-$1,000,000; Sale to minor or 3 yrs. junior: minimum 15 yrs. and up to $500,000; Within 300 yds. of school: double penalties	
SOUTH CAROLINA	44-53-110	Misdemeanor, up to 2 yrs. and/or $5000; Possession of 10 g. of cocaine *prima facie* evidence of violation of intent to sell; Subsequent offense: felony, 5 yrs. and/or $5000; Third offense: felony, 4 yrs. and/or $10,000 For crack: less than 1 g.: felony, 5 yrs. and $5000; 2nd offense: 10 yrs. and $10,000; Subsequent offense: 10-115 yrs. and $15,000; Possession of over 10 grains is *prima facie* evidence of intent to sell/distribute	Any amount: felony, up to 5 yrs. and/or $5,000; 10-28 g.: 3-10 yrs. and/or $10,000; 28-200 g.: 7-25 yrs. and/or $50,000; 200-400 g.: 10-25 yrs. and/or $100,000; Over 400 g.: 15-30 yrs. and/or $200,000; Subsequent offense: felony, 10 yrs. and/or $10,000; Third offense: 15-20 yrs. and/or $20,000; For crack: felony, up to 15 yrs. and $25,000; 2nd offense: up to 25 yrs. and $50,000; Subsequent offense: up to 30 yrs.and $100,000 Sale to minor: up to 20 yrs. and/or $30,000; Sale within ½-mile radius of school: $10,000 and up to 10 yrs. (10-15 for crack)	10-28 g.: 3-10 yrs. without probation and $25,000; 2nd offense: 5-30 yrs. and $50,000; Subsequent offense: 25-30 yrs. and $50,000; 28-100 g.: 7-25 yrs. without probation and $50,000; 2nd offense: 7-30 yrs. and $50,000; Subsequent offense: 25-30 yrs. and $50,000; 100-200 g.: mandatory 25 yrs. without probation and $50,000; 200-400 g.: mandatory 25 yrs. without probation and $100,000; 400 g. and over: mandatory 25-30 yrs. without probation and $200,000
SOUTH DAKOTA	22-42-1, *et seq.* 34-20B-1, *et. seq.*	Class 5 felony	Fine up to $10,000 for any conviction: Class 4 felony, mandatory 1 yr. without suspension; Sale to minor: Class 2 felony, mandatory 5 yrs.; Subsequent offense: mandatory 10 yrs. without suspension; To minor: mandatory 15 yrs. without suspension Sale in drug-free zone: Class 4 felony, min. 5 yrs.	

Table 11a: Illegal Drugs: Cocaine—Continued

State	Code Section	Possession	Sale	Trafficking
TENNESSEE	39-17-408, *et seq.*	Possession or casual exchange: Class A misdemeanor unless adult to minor and adult is 2 yrs. the minor's senior, then felony; Subsequent offense: if 2 or more prior convictions: Class E felony; Less than .5 grams is a class C felony, may be fined up to $100,000.; Class B .5 grams or less and at commission of crime, death occurred, defendant concealed a deadly weapon.	Less than .5 g.: Class C felony and up to 100,000; Over .5 g.: Class B felony and up to $100,000; Over 26 g.: Class B felony and up to $200,000; Over 300 g.: Class A felony and up to $500,000; Sale to minor under 18 or in drug-free school zone: one class higher than amount required; Minimum penalty amounts: 1st drug felony: $2000; 2nd: $2500; 3rd: $3000	
TEXAS	Health & Safety §§481.032, *et seq.*	4-200 g.: 2nd degree felony; 200-400 g.: 1st degree felony; 400 g. and over: 10-99 yrs. or life at Texas Dept. of Criminal Justice institution and/or $100,000	Less than 1 g.: state jail felony; 1-4 g.: 2nd degree felony; 4-200 g.: 1st degree felony; 200-400 g.: Texas Dept. of Criminal Justice institution for life or 10-99 yrs. and/or $100,000; 400 g. and over: Texas Dept. of Criminal Justice institution for life or 15-99 yrs. and/or $250,000; Delivery to minor under 17 who is enrolled in school: 2nd degree felony; Within drug-free zone: penalties doubled	
UTAH	58-37, et. seq.	3rd degree felony; Subsequent offense: one degree greater penalty than provided	2nd degree felony; Subsequent offense: 1st degree felony; Within 1000 ft. of school or to minor: one degree more than provided except 1st degree is mandatory 5 yrs.	
VERMONT	Tit. 18 §4231	Up to 2.5 g.: 1 yr. and/or $2000; 2.5 g. to 1 oz.: up to 5 yrs. and/or $100,000; 1 oz. to 1 lb: up to 10 yrs. and/or $250,000; 1 lb. and over: up to 20 yrs. and/or $1,000,000; Subsequent offense: double penalties	Delivery: 3 yrs. and/or $75,000; Sale: 5 yrs. and/or $100,000; Sale or delivery of: 2.5 g.-1 oz.: 10 yrs. and/or $250,000; Over 1 oz.: 20 yrs. and/or $1,000,000; Subsequent offense: double penalties; Sale to minor or on school grounds: up to 5-10 yrs. and/or $25,000	

Table 11a: Illegal Drugs: Cocaine—Continued

State	Code Section	Possession	Sale	Trafficking
VIRGINIA	18.2-247; 54.1-3448	Class 5 felony	5-40 yrs. and up to $500,000 If defendant proves he gave drug (1) not for profit; (2) not to an inmate, or (3) not for recipient to become addicted, then Class 5 felony; "Drug kingpin" if over 500 kg.: up to $1,000,000 and 20 yrs. to life with 20 yrs. mandatory; Subsequent offense: at court or jury's discretion, life or not less than 5 yrs. and up to $500,000; Sale to minor or within 1000 ft. of school: stricter penalties	
WASHINGTON	69.50.101, *et seq.*	Up to 5 yrs. and/or $10,000; Less than 2 kg.: up to 10 yrs. and/or $25,000; Over 2 kg.: up to 10 yrs. and/or up to $100,000 for first 2 kg. and $50 for each gram in excess of 2 kg.; Subsequent offense: double penalties	Up to 5 yrs., $10,000; Subsequent offense: up to double penalties; Sale within 1000 ft. of school: double penalties; Sale to minor: Class 6 felony	
WEST VIRGINIA	60A-1-101 to 60A-8-13	Misdemeanor, 90 days to 6 months and/or $1000; Subsequent offense: double penalties	Felony, 1-15 yrs. and/or $25,000; Subsequent offense: double penalties; Sale to minor or within 1000 ft. of school: mandatory 2 yrs.	Transport into the state with intent to deliver: felony, 1-15 yrs. and/or $25,000
WISCONSIN	§961.51 *et seq.*	Possession or attempt to possess: 1 yr. and/or up to $5000; Subsequent offense: 2 yrs. and/or $10,000	Under 5g.: up to 10 yrs. and $500,000; 5-15 g.: 1-15 yrs. and up to $500,000; 15-40 g.: 3-20 yrs. and up to $500,000; 40-100 g. 5-30 yrs. and up to $500,000; Over 100 g.: 10-30 yrs. and up to $500,000; Sale within 1000 ft. of school: mandatory 3 yrs. without parole	
WYOMING	35-7-1001 to 1057	Less than 3 g. of cocaine or less than .5 g. of crack: misdemeanor, up to 1 yr. and/or $1000; Greater than 3 g. of cocaine or .5 g. of crack: felony, 7 yrs. and/or $15,000; Subsequent offense: up to 5 yrs. and/or $5000 or double penalties	Up to 20 yrs. and/or $25,000; Subsequent offense or sale to minor or within drug-free zone: double penalties	

Table 11b: Illegal Drugs: Heroin

State	Code Section	Possession	Sale	Trafficking
ALABAMA	20-2-1; 20-2-23(2)(j); 13A-12-210 to 215, 231(3)	Class C felony	4-14 g.: mandatory 3 yrs. and $50,000; 14-28 g.: 10 yrs. and $100,000; 28-56 g.: 25 yrs. and $500,000; 56 g. or more: life without parole; Sale to minor: Class A felony; Unlawful distribution of controlled substance: Class B felony; Subsequent offense: subject to Habitual Felony Offender Act	Class A felony: 4-14 g.: minimum 3 yrs. and $50,000 fine; 14-28 g.: minimum10 yrs. and $100,000 fine; 28-56 g.: minimum 25 yrs. and $500,000 fine; Over 56 g.: life without parole
ALASKA	11.71.010, *et seq.*	Possession of any amount: Class C felony	Sale to anyone under 19 at least 3 yrs. younger than seller: unclassified felony; Sale of heroin in general: Class A felony	Participation in "continuing criminal enterprise": unclassified felony
ARIZONA	13-3401, *et seq.*; 36-2501, *et seq.*	Class 4 felony, but for one not previously convicted of felony, court can make it Class 1 misdemeanor; fine of not less than $1000 or 3 times the value of substance, whichever is greater	Class 3 felony and fine of greater of 3 times value of drugs or $1000; Sale to minor: Class 2 felony and $2000 fine or 3 times value, whichever is greater; In drug-free school zone: add 1 yr. to sentence and fine for selling to minors	Class 2 felony (transport/import); Class 3 felony (manufacture)
ARKANSAS	5-64-101, *et seq.*	Class C felony	Class Y felony; Depending on amount, prison from 10-40 yrs. or life and fines between $25,000 and $250,000; Increased penalty within 1000 ft. of school	Rebuttable presumption of intent to deliver if person has 100 mg. or more

Table 11b: Illegal Drugs: Heroin—Continued

State	Code Section	Possession	Sale	Trafficking
CALIFORNIA	Health & Safety §11000, *et seq.;* §11350, *et seq.*	State prison and fine up to $70; if probation granted, there are additional requirements	State prison 2-4 yrs.; Possession/purchasing for sale: State prison 3-5 yrs.; Sale to minors: state prison 3, 5, or 7 yrs.; Sale to school children: 5, 7, or 9 yrs.; Anyone over 18 who sells to a minor or uses a minor in the sale process is punishable in state prison for 3, 6, or 9 yrs.; Sale within 1000 ft. of school: additional 3, 4, or 5 yrs.; If sale occurred upon the grounds of a school, church, synagogue or youth center, punishment is automatically enhanced by one year; if seller is over 18 and buyer is a minor at least four years younger, then punishment is enhanced by one, two, or three years at the discretion of the court. Sale on many public areas punishable by state prison for 5, 7, or 9 yrs. if seller is 5 yrs. older than minor; in addition, maximum fine of $50,000	Transport/import: 3-5 yrs.; County to noncontiguous county: 3, 6, or 9 yrs.
COLORADO	18-18-101, *et seq.*	Class 3 felony; Subsequent Offense: twice or more within 6 months and amount greater than 28.5 g.: Defendant shall be sentenced to the Dept. of Corrections for at least the minimum and fined no less than $1000 but not over $500,000 with no probation or suspension	Class 3 felony; Sale to minor within 1000 ft. of school or on public property: Dept. of Corrections for minimum 5 yrs.; Subsequent offense near school: 20 yrs.	
CONNECTICUT	21a-240, 243, 278	7 yrs.and/or $50,000; Subsequent offense: 15 yrs. and/or $100,000; Third offense: 25 yrs. and/or $250,000	15 yrs. and $50,000; 1 oz. or more: 5-20 yrs. minimum to life maximum (by a non-drug dependent person); Subsequent offense: 10-25 yrs.; Within 1500 ft. of school: additional mandatory 5 yrs.	

Table 11b: Illegal Drugs: Heroin—Continued

State	Code Section	Possession	Sale	Trafficking
DELAWARE	Tit. 16 §4701, *et seq.;* 4751, 4753A	Possession, use, consumption: Class A misdemeanor: (if applicable, can be subject to First Offenders Controlled Substances Diversion Program §4764)	Class C felony: $5000-$50,000; If not addicted: felony, mandatory 6 yrs.; To a minor: Class C felony, if under 16, mandatory 1 yr. prison; On school property: up to 15 yrs. and $250,000; Subsequent offense: if not addicted, mandatory 6 yrs.; otherwise 12 yrs.; Where death involved as a result: Class B felony, $10,000-$100,000 fine; If seller is under 16 mandatory sentence of 1 year. no parole, probation, or suspension; If seller is under 14 mandatory sentence of 2 yrs.; More severe penalties if near school §4767-68; Knowingly purchasing from a minor, Class C felony	If on any occasion, one knowingly sells, delivers, brings: 5-15 g.: minimum 3 yrs. and $75,000; 15-50 g.: minimum 10 yrs. and $150,000; 50 g. and over: minimum 25 yrs. and $750,000
DISTRICT OF COLUMBIA	33-501, *et seq.;* 33-541	Possess: crime with up to 30 yrs. and/or up to $500,000; Subsequent offense: double penalties	Sale, manufacture, distribution: crime with up to 30 yrs. and/or $500,000; Subsequent offense: double penalties; Within drug-free zone or sale to minors: up to twice the punishment	
FLORIDA	775.082, *et seq.;* 893.01, *et seq.*	3rd degree felony; Possession of 4 g. is trafficking	2nd degree felony; Sales of over 10 g.: 1st degree felony (penalties more severe near school)	All sentencing to be done pursuant to sentencing guidelines: 4-14 g.: $5000; 14-28 g.: $100,000; 28 g.-30 kg.: 25 yrs. and $500,000; Over 30 kg.: 1st degree felony, life imprisonment
GEORGIA	16-13-20, *et seq.*	4 g. or more is trafficking: Possession of any amount is a felony punishable with minimum 2-15 yrs.; Subsequent offense: minimum 5-30 yrs.	Felony: 5-30 yrs.; Subsequent offense: life imprisonment	4-14 g.: mandatory 5 yrs. and $50,000; 14-28 g.: mandatory 10 yrs. and $100,000; Over 28 g.: mandatory 25 yrs. and $500,000
HAWAII	329-14, *et seq.;* 712-1240, *et seq.*	1/8-1 oz.: Class B felony; 1 oz. or more: Class A felony; Subsequent offense: Class A or B felony based on quantity	Any amount: Class B felony; 1/8 oz. or more, or any amount to a minor: Class A felony	

Table 11b: Illegal Drugs: Heroin—Continued

State	Code Section	Possession	Sale	Trafficking
IDAHO	37-2701, *et seq.*	Felony, up to 7 yrs. and/or $15,000; Subsequent offense: double penalties; Possession of 2 g. or more is trafficking	Felony, up to life and $25,000; Subsequent offense: double penalties	2-7 g.: mandatory 3 yrs. and minimum $10,000; 7-28 g.: mandatory 10 yrs. and minimum $15,000; 28 g. and over: mandatory 15 yrs. and minimum $25,000; Maximum sentence is $100,000 and life; Second trafficking conviction: double penalties
ILLINOIS	720 ILCS 570/ 200, *et seq.*; Uniform Controlled Substances Act	10-15 g.: Class 1 felony, $250,000; 15-100 g.: Class 1 felony, mandatory 4-15 yrs.; 100-400 g.: mandatory 6-30 yrs.; 400-900 g.: mandatory 8-40 yrs.; Over 900 g.: mandatory 10-50 yrs.; Fines for any offense involving 100 g. or more: greater of $200,000 or street value	15-100 g.: 6-30 yrs.; 100-400 g.: 9-40 yrs.; 400-900 g.: 12-50 yrs.; Over 900 g.: 15-60 yrs.; Within 1000 ft. of truck stop or safety rest: double penalties; Within 1000 ft. of school: Class X felony	Trafficking: double penalties
INDIANA	35-48-4-1, *et seq.*; 35-48-21, *et seq.*	Possession of any amount: At least Class D felony; Under 3 g. but within 1000 feet of school property: Class B felony; Over 3 g.: Class C felony; Possession of 3 g. or more within 1000 feet of school property: Class A felony	Class B felony unless amount is over 3 g. or delivery to a minor 3 yrs. younger or delivery in/on school property or within 1000 ft. of school property or on school bus, then Class A felony	

Table 11b: Illegal Drugs: Heroin—Continued

State	Code Section	Possession	Sale	Trafficking
IOWA	124.101, *et seq.*		Less than 100 g.: Class C felony, $1000 to $50,000; 100g. to 1 kg.: Class B felony, $5000 to $100,000; Over 1 kg.: Class B felony, up to 50 yrs. and $1,000,000; Subsequent offense: triple penalties; More severe penalties for distribution to minors or 3 yrs. younger; An adult distributing to a minor: Class B felony, min. confinement of five ("5") years, if within 1,000 ft. of public/ private school property or recreation area, school bus, min. confinement of 10 yrs.	
KANSAS	65-4101, *et seq.*	Level 4 felony; Subsequent offense: Level 3 felony; Third offense: Level 1 felony and life in prison	Level 3 felony; Subsequent offense: Level 2 felony; Third offense: Level 1 felony and life in prison; Sell within 1000 ft. of school or to minor: Level 2 felony	
KENTUCKY	218A.010, *et seq.*	Class D felony; Subsequent offense: Class C felony	Class C felony; Subsequent offense: Class B felony; Selling to minor: Class C felony 1st offense: Class B subsequent offense	First offense: Class C felony; Subsequent offense: Class B felony; Within 1000 yds. of school: higher penalty
LOUISIANA	§40:961, *et seq.*	Minimum of 4 yrs. at hard labor up to 10 yrs. without probation or suspension and/ or fine to $5000	Life imprisonment at hard labor without probation or suspension and perhaps fine up to $50,000; Sale to minors by those over 25 yrs. old: life imprisonment; Sale to minor or someone 3 yrs. junior: double penalties	
MAINE	Tit. 17A §§1101, *et seq.*	Class C crime; 4 g. creates presumption of trafficking	Class B crime; 2 g. or more creates presumption of furnishing; More serious penalties for sale to minor or within 1000 ft. of school	Possession of 4 g. or more is trafficking
MARYLAND	Art. 27 §276, *et seq.*	Misdemeanor with penalty of up to 4 yrs. and/or $25,000; Bringing 4 g. into state: felony with penalty of up to $50,000 and/or up to 25 yrs.; Subsequent offense: double penalties	Felony with penalty of 20 yrs. and/or $25,000; Sale of more than 28 g.: not less than 40 yrs.; Subsequent offense: double penalties, 2 yrs. mandatory, not less than 10 yrs. sentence; 3rd offense: not less than 40 yrs. Sale to minors or near school property: stricter penalties	If "drug kingpin": 20-40 yrs. and/or $1,000,000

Table 11b: Illegal Drugs: Heroin—Continued

State	Code Section	Possession	Sale	Trafficking
MASSACHUSETTS	Ch. 94c §1, *et seq.*	2 yrs. and/or $2000; Subsequent offense: 2.5-5 yrs. and/or $5000; Greater than 14 grams is trafficking	1-10 yrs. and/or $1000 to $10,000; Subsequent offense: 5-15 yrs. and/or $2500 to $25,000; 3rd offense: not less than 40 yrs.; Sale to minors or near school property: stricter penalties	14-28 g.: 5-20 yrs. and/or $5000 to $50,000; 28-100 g.: 7-20 yrs. and/or $5000 to $50,000; 100-200 g.: 10-20 yrs. and/or $10,000 to $100,000; Over 200 g.: 15-20 yrs. and/or $50,000 to $500,000
MICHIGAN	333.7212; 333.7401, *et seq.*	Under 25 g.: Up to 4 yrs. and/or $25,000; 25-50 g.: 1-4 yrs. and/or up to $25,000 or probation for life; 50-225 g.: 10-20 yrs.; 225-650 g.: 20-30 yrs.; Over 650 g.: life imprisonment	Felony; Under 50 g.: 1-20 yrs. and/or $25,000 or probation for life; 50-225 g.: 10-20 yrs.; 225-650 g.: 20-30 yrs.; Over 650 g.: life imprisonment; Sale to minor or near school property: up to double penalties	
MINNESOTA	152.01, *et seq.*	Any possession: 15 yrs. and/or $100,000; 10-50 g.: Up to 20 yrs. and/or $250,000; 50-500 g.: Up to 25 yrs. and/or $500,000; Over 500 g.: Up to 30 yrs. and/or $1,000,000; Subsequent offense: Depends on level of prior offenses; 4-40 yrs. and/or up to $1,000,000	Any amount: up to 20 yrs. and/or $250,000; 10-50 g.: up to 25 yrs. and/or $500,000; Over 50 g.: up to 30 yrs. and $1,000,000; Subsequent offense: depends on level of prior offense; 4-40 yrs. and/or up to $1,000,000; Sale to minor, any amount: up to 25 yrs. and/or $500,000	
MISSISSIPPI	41-29-101, *et seq.*	Felony, up to 3 yrs. and/or $1000 to $30,000; Subsequent offense: double penalty; 3 or more offenses within 12 month period: 30 yrs. without parole	No specified term up to 30 yrs. and/or $5000 to $1,000,000; Subsequent offense: double penalty	Anyone over 21 yrs. old who sells 2 oz. or more of heroin in a 12 month period shall have life in prison without suspension or parole

Table 11b: Illegal Drugs: Heroin—Continued

State	Code Section	Possession	Sale	Trafficking
MISSOURI	195.010, *et seq.*	Class C felony; Subsequent offense: subject to prior & persistent offenders §195.295	Class B felony; Subsequent offense: subject to prior & persistent offenders §195.295; Distribution to minor under 17 or 2 yrs. junior: Class B felony; Within 1000 ft. of school: Class A felony	Trafficking in 2nd degree: Delivering, attempting to distribute or produce: 30-90 g.: Class A felony; Over 90 g.: Class B felony, term without parole; Possessing, buying, attempting to buy: 30-90 g.: Class B felony; Over 90 g.: Class A felony
MONTANA	45-9-101, *et seq.*; 50-32-101, *et seq.*	2 to 5 yrs. and/or $50,000; Criminal possession with intent to sell: 2 to 20 yrs. and/or $50,000	2 yrs. to life and/or $50,000 (4 yrs. if sale to minor); Subsequent offense: 10 yrs. to life and/or $50,000 (20 yrs. if sale to minor); Third offense: not less than 20 yrs. and/or $50,000 (40 yrs. if sale to minor); Offense of criminal sale of dangerous drugs on or near school property: 3 yrs. to life and/or $50,000	Criminal production/manufacture: 5 yrs. to life and/or $50,000; 2nd offense: 20 yrs. to life and/or $50,000; 3rd offense: 40 yrs. to life and/or $50,000
NEBRASKA	28-401, *et seq.*	Class IV felony	28-100 g.: Class 1D felony; 100-500 g.: Class 1C felony; Over 500 g.: Class 1B felony; Class felony: anyone 18 yrs. or older who knowingly sells to a minor in on or within 1,000 ft. of the real property of a private/public school from elementary level to university or a youth center shall be punished by the best higher penalty classification greater then class B felony	
NEVADA	453.011, 510	1-6 yrs. and $5000; Subsequent offense: 1-10 yrs. and $10,000; Third offense: 1-20 yrs. and $20,000	1-20 yrs., and $20,000; Subsequent offense: 5-20 yrs. and $20,000; Third offense: life or 15 yrs. mandatory and $20,000	4-14 g.: 3-20 yrs. and $50,000; 14-28 g.: 10 yrs. and $100,000; Over 28 g.: 25 yrs. and $500,000; Double penalties for sale near school

Table 11b: Illegal Drugs: Heroin—Continued

State	Code Section	Possession	Sale	Trafficking
NEW HAMPSHIRE	318-B:1, *et seq.*	Class B felony with fine up to $25,000; Subsequent offense: Class A felony with fine up to $50,000	Class A felony; Under 1 g.: up to 7 yrs. and/or $200,000; 1-5 g.: up to 20 yrs. and/or $300,000; 5 g. and over: up to 30 yrs. and/or $500,000; Subsequent offense: under 1 g.: Up to 15 yrs. and/or $200,000; 1-5 g.: up to 40 yrs. and/or $500,000; 5 g. and over: maximum life and/or $500,000	
NEW JERSEY	24:21-1, *et seq.*; 2C:35-2, *et seq.*	Crime of 3rd degree, $25,000	.5 oz. or less: crime of 3rd degree, $50,000; .5 oz. to 5 oz.: crime of 2nd degree; Over 5 oz.: crime of 1st degree, fixed prison term and $300,000; Selling within 1000 feet of school: fixed prison term and up to $100,000; Selling to minor or pregnant female: double penalties	Leader of narcotics trafficking network: life (25 yr. minimum before parole) and/or $500,000
NEW MEXICO	30-31-1, *et seq.*	4th degree felony	2nd degree felony; Subsequent offense: 1st degree felony; Within drug-free school zone: 1st degree felony	
NEW YORK	Penal §220, *et seq.*; Pub. Health §3306-3307	Knowingly possessing any amount: Class A misdemeanor; Over 500 mg.: Class D felony; Over ⅛ oz.: Class C felony; Over ½ oz.: Class B felony; Over 2 oz.: Class A-II felony; Over 4 oz.: Class A-I felony; Any amount with intent to sell: Class D felony; Any amount of narcotic drug with intent to sell: Class B felony	Class D felony in general, then: Over ½ oz.: Class A-II felony; Over 2 oz.: Class A-I felony; On school grounds or sale to someone under 21: Class B felony	
NORTH CAROLINA	90-86, *et seq.*	Class I felony	Class H felony; Sale of controlled substance to person under 16 or to pregnant female or within 300 ft. of school property: Class E felony	4-14 g.: Class F felony, 70-84 mos. and $50,000; 14-28 g.: Class E felony, 90-117 mos. and $100,000; 28 g. and over: Class C felony, 225-279 mos. and $500,000

Table 11b: Illegal Drugs: Heroin—Continued

State	Code Section	Possession	Sale	Trafficking
NORTH DAKOTA	19-03.1-01, *et seq.*	Class C felony; Within 1000 ft. of school: Class B felony	Class A felony: at least 1 yr.; 2nd offense: at least 5 yrs.; 3rd offense: 20 yrs.; If over 100 g.: Class B felony; Within 1000 ft. of school or to minor or delivery to a minor by an 18 year old: at least 4 yrs.; Subsequent offense: 8 yrs.	
OHIO	2925.01, *et seq.*; 3719.01, *et seq.*	4th degree felony, $1500; Subsequent offense: 3rd degree felony, $2500; Unless 10-30 g.: 3rd degree felony with 18 mos. mandatory; 30-100 g.: 2nd degree felony with 3 yrs.; Over 100 g.: 1st degree felony, 15 yrs. to life; Subsequent offense: one degree higher	Under 10 g.: 3rd degree felony; 10-30 g.: 2nd degree felony, 3 yrs. mandatory; 30-100 g.: 1st degree felony, 5 yrs. mandatory; Over 100 g.: 1st degree felony, 15 yrs.-life; Within 1000 ft. of school or within 100 ft. of juvenile: more severe penalties	Ship, transport, manufacture, produce: 2nd or 3rd degree felony; Subsequent offense: one degree higher
OKLAHOMA	Tit. 63 §2-101, *et seq.*	Felony, 2-10 yrs.; Subsequent offense: felony, 4-20 yrs.; Within 1000 ft. of school or in presence of child under 12: up to double penalties; Subsequent offense: up to triple penalties	Felony, 5 yrs.-life and up to $100,000; Subsequent offense: double penalties with at least 10 yrs.; Within 1000 ft. of school or in presence of child under 12: up to double penalties; Subsequent offense: up to triple penalties	
OREGON	Chapter 475	Class B felony	3-5 g.: Commercial drug offense if greater than $300 cash, firearm, packaging materials, customer list, stolen property, or using public lands; Over 5 g.: Category 6 crime	Class A felony; Delivery and manufacture of over 5 g.: Category 8 crime
PENNSYLVANIA	Tit. 35 §780-101, *et seq.*	Misdemeanor, 1 yr. and/or $5000; Subsequent offense: 3 yrs. and/or $25,000	Felony, 15 yrs. and/or $250,00 or higher fine if necessary to recover drug profit; Subsequent offense or sale to minor: double penalties	
RHODE ISLAND	21-28-4.01, *et seq.*	3 yrs. and/or $500 to $5000; *Nolo contendere* plea: 100 hrs. of community service and drug education program; 1 oz.-1 kg.: 10-50 years and/or $10,000-$500,000 Over 1 kg.: 20 yrs. to life and $25,000 to $1,000,000	Person not drug dependent: life and/or $10,000 to $500,000; Drug dependent: 30 yrs. and/or $3000 to $100,000; Over 1 oz.-1 kg.: minimum 10-50 yrs. and/or $10,000 to $500,000; Over 1 kg.:20 yrs.-life and/or $25,000-$1,000,000 Within 300 yds. of school: double penalties; Sale to minor or 3 yrs. junior: minimum 15 yrs. and up to $500,000	

Table 11b: Illegal Drugs: Heroin—Continued

State	Code Section	Possession	Sale	Trafficking
SOUTH CAROLINA	44-53-110, 370	Misdemeanor, up to 2 yrs. and/or $5000; Subsequent offense: felony, 5 yrs. and/or $5000; Third offense: felony, 5 yrs. and/or $10,000; Possession of more than 2 grains of heroin is *prima facie* evidence of intent to sell/distribute	Any amount: felony, 15 yrs. and/or $25,000; Subsequent offense: felony, 5-30 yrs. and $15,000; Third offense: 15-30 yrs. and $50,000; Sale within ½-mile radius of school: up to 10 yrs. and $10,000; Sale to minor: up to 20 yrs. without parole or suspension and $30,000	Trafficking in illegal drugs: 4-14 g.: 7-25 yrs. without parole or suspension and $50,000; Subsequent offense: 25 yrs. and $100,000; 14-28 g.: mandatory 25 yrs. without parole or suspension and $200,000; Over 28 g.: mandatory 25-40 yrs. without parole or suspension and $200,000
SOUTH DAKOTA	22-42-1, *et seq.;* 34-20B-1, *et seq.*	Class 5 felony	Class 4 felony, mandatory 1 yr. without suspension, fine up to $10,000 for any conviction: Sale to minor: Class 2 felony, mandatory 5 yrs.; Subsequent offense: mandatory 10 yrs. without suspension; Sale to minor: mandatory 15 yrs. without suspension; Sale within drug-free zone: class 4 felony, minimum 5 yrs.	
TENNESSEE	39-17-408, *et seq.*	Possession or casual exchange of less than .5 oz.: Class A misdemeanor unless adult to minor and adult is 2 yrs. the minor's senior, then felony; Subsequent offense: If two or more prior convictions: Class E felony; Less than .5 grams is a Class C felony, may be fined up to $100,000; Class B:.5 grams or less if injury or death occurrence or defendant was in possession of deadly weapon.	Class B felony and/or $100,000; Over 15 g.: Class B felony and/or $200,000; Over 150 g.: Class A felony and/or $500,000; Sale to minor under 18 or in drug-free school zone: one class higher than amount required; Minimum penalty amounts: 1st drug felony: $2000; 2nd: $2500; 3rd: $3000	

Table 11b: Illegal Drugs: Heroin—Continued

State	Code Section	Possession	Sale	Trafficking
TEXAS	Health & Safety §481.032, *et seq.*	Less than 1 g.: state jail felony; 1-4 g.: 3rd degree felony; 4-200 g.: 2nd degree felony; 200-400 g.: 1st degree felony; 400 g. and over: 10-99 yrs. or life in Texas Department of Criminal Justice institution and/or $100,000	Less than 1 g.: state jail felony; 1-4 g.: 2nd degree felony; 4-200 g.: 1st degree felony; 200-400 g.: Texas Dept. of Criminal Justice institution for life or 10-99 yrs. and/or $100,000; 400 g. and over: Texas Dept. of Criminal Justice institution for life or 15-99 yrs. and/or $250,000; Delivery to minor under 17 who is enrolled in school: 2nd degree felony; Within drug-free zone: stricter penalties	
UTAH	58-37, *et seq.*	3rd degree felony; Subsequent offense: one degree greater penalty than provided	2nd degree felony; Subsequent offense: 1st degree felony; Within 1000 ft. of school or sale to a minor: one degree higher than provided except 1st degree felony is 5 yrs. mandatory	
VERMONT	Tit. 18 §4233	Up to 200 mg.: up to 1 yr. and/or $2000; 200 mg.-1 g.: up to 5 yrs. and/or $100,000; 1-2 g.: up to 10 yrs. and/or $250,000; 2 g. and over: up to 20 yrs. and/or $1,000,000; Subsequent offense: up to double penalties	Delivery: up to 3 yrs. and/or $75,000; Sale: up to 5 yrs. and/or $100,000; Sale or delivery of: over 200 mg.: 10 yrs. and/or $250,000; over 1 g.: 20 yrs. and/or $1,000,000; Subsequent offense: double penalties; Sale to minors or on school grounds: up to 5 or 10 yrs. and/or $250,000	
VIRGINIA	54.1-3445; 18.2-250	Class 5 felony	5-40 yrs. and up to $500,000; If defendant proves he gave drug (1) not for profit, (2) not to an inmate, or (3) not for recipient to become addicted, then Class 5 felony; "Drug kingpin" if over 100 kg.: up to $1,000,000 and 20 yrs.-life (20 mandatory) Subsequent offense: at court or jury's discretion, subsequent offense 5 yrs. to life and/or $500,000; Sale to minor or within 1000 ft. of school: stricter penalties	

Table 11b: Illegal Drugs: Heroin—Continued

State	Code Section	Possession	Sale	Trafficking
WASHINGTON	69.50.401, *et seq.*	Up to 5 yrs. and/or $10,000; Less than 2 kg.: up to 10 yrs. and/or $25,000; Over 2 kg.:$100,000 and $50 for each g. in excess; Subsequent offense: double penalties	Mandatory 2 yrs. without suspension and fine in amount to eliminate all profits gained up to $500,000 for each count; Subsequent offense: mandatory 10 yrs. without suspension and fine in amount to eliminate all profits gained up to $500,000 for each count; Sale to minors: Class C felony; Sale within 1000 ft. of school: double penalties	
WEST VIRGINIA	60A-1-101 to 60A-8-13	Misdemeanor, 90 days-6 months and/or $1000; Subsequent offense: double penalties	Felony, 1-15 yrs. and/or $25,000; Subsequent offense: double penalties; Sale to minor or within 1000 ft. of school: mandatory 2 yrs.	Transport into state with intent to deliver: felony, 1-15 yrs. and/or $25,000
WISCONSIN	§961.51 *et seq.*	1 yr. and/or $5000; Subsequent offense: double penalties	Under 3 g.: up to 15 yrs. and/or $1000 to $200,000; 3-10 g.: 6 months-15 yrs. and/or $1000 to $250,000; 10-50 g.: 1-15 yrs. and/or $1000 to $500,000; 50-200 g.: 3-15 yrs. and/or $1000 to $500,000; 200-400 g.: 5-15 yrs. and/or $1000 to $500,000; Over 400 g.: 10-30 yrs. and $1000 to $1,000,000; Sale to minor: double penalties; Sale within 1000 ft. of school: mandatory 3 yrs. without parole	
WYOMING	35-7-1001 to 1057	Less than 3 g.: misdemeanor, up to 1 yr. and/or $1000; Over 3 g.: felony, 7 yrs. and/or $15,000; Subsequent offense: up to 5 yrs. and/or $5000 or double penalties	Up to 20 yrs. and/or $25,000; Subsequent offense or sale to minor or within drug-free zone: double penalties	

Table 11c: Illegal Drugs: Marijuana

State	Code Section	Possession	Sale	Trafficking
ALABAMA	20-2-1, *et seq.*; 20-2-23 3 (j); 13A-12-210 to 215, 231	Personal use: Class A misdemeanor; Subsequent offense or possession of marijuana for other than personal use: Class C felony	Class B felony; Class A for sale to minor; Sale on school campus or within 3 mile radius: 5 yrs.	1 kilo-100 lbs: minimum 3 yrs. and mandatory $25,000; 100-500 lbs.: minimum 5 yrs. and mandatory $50,000; 500-1000 lbs.: minimum. 15 yrs. and mandatory $200,000; Over 1000 lbs.: life without parole
ALASKA	11.71.010, *et seq.*	To possess marijuana with reckless disregard that possession occurs within 500 feet of a school or recreation/ youth center or on a school bus or to knowingly maintain storage or transportation facilities for keeping/ distributing or to render a drug counterfeit or to possess 25 or more plants: Class C felony		
ARIZONA	13-3401, 3405; 36-2501, *et seq.*	Under 2 lb.: Class 6 felony; 2-4 lbs.: Class 5 felony; 4 lbs. and over: Class 4 felony; fine of not less than $750 or 3 times the value of the controlled substance, whichever is greater	Under 2 lbs.: Class 4 felony; 2-4 lbs.: Class 3 felony; over 4 lbs.: Class 2 felony: fine of the greater of $750 or 3 times value of substance; Sale within drug-free school zone: add 1 yr. to sentence and fine of $2000	Producing marijuana: less than 2 lbs.: Class 5 felony; 2-4 lbs.: Class 4 felony; Over 4 lbs.: Class 3 felony; Transporting/ importing: less than 2 lbs.: Class 3 felony; Over 2 lbs.: Class 2 felony
ARKANSAS	5-64-101, *et seq.*	1st offense: Class A misdemeanor; 2nd offense: Class D felony; 3rd offense: Class C felony	Delivery or intent to deliver marijuana is a Class C felony, 4-30 yrs., depending on the amount sold, and/or fine of $25,000 to $100,000; increased penalty within 1000 ft. of school	1 oz. possession of marijuana creates rebuttable presumption or intent to deliver

Table 11c: Illegal Drugs: Marijuana—Continued

State	Code Section	Possession	Sale	Trafficking
CALIFORNIA	Health & Safety §11000, *et seq.*; 11357, *et seq.*	Possession of any concentrated cannabis: prison in county jail up to 1 yr. or fine up to $500 or both; Up to 28.5 grams: misdemeanor and fine of up to $100; Over 28.5 grams: prison up to 6 months or fine up to $500 or both; If over 18 and possession under 28.5 grams on grounds of school: misdemeanor and fine up to $500; Under 18 and possession under 28.5 grams on grounds of school: misdemeanor and fine up to $250; Subsequent offense: subject to treatment or rehabilitation program	Possession for sale: imprisonment in state prison 2-4 yrs. for transporting, selling, etc. If under 28.5 grams: misdemeanor and fine up to $100	
COLORADO	18-18-101, *et seq.*, 18-18-406	Under 1 oz.: Class 2 petty offense, $100 fine; 1-8 oz.: Class 1 misdemeanor or Class 5 felony with prior conviction; Over 8 oz.: Class 5 felony or Class 4 felony with prior conviction; Public use: Class 2 petty offense, $100 fine and 15 days	Class 4 felony (transferring under 1 oz. for no consideration is possession, not a dispensing offense); Subsequent offense: Class 3 felony, fine up to $10,000; Over 18 yrs. old selling to minor under 15: Class 4 felony, fine up to $5,000	
CONNECTICUT	21a-278, 279	Under 4 oz.: 1 yr. and/or $1000; Over 4 oz.: 5 yrs. and/or $2000; Over 1 kilo: 5-20 yrs. to life; Subsequent offense: Under 4 oz.: 5 yrs. and/or $3000; Over 4 oz.: 10 yrs. and/or $5000; add 2 yrs. if within 1500 ft. of school or child day care center	Over 1 kilo: 5-20 yrs.; Subsequent offense: 10-25 yrs.; If sale within 1500 ft. of school or child day care center: additional mandatory 3 yrs.; Sale to minor or person 2 yrs. junior: additional mandatory 2 yrs.	

Table 11c: Illegal Drugs: Marijuana—Continued

State	Code Section	Possession	Sale	Trafficking
DELAWARE	Tit. 16 §4701, *et seq.*	Class A misdemeanor (If applicable, can be subject to First Offenders Controlled Substances Diversion Program §4764); Knowingly making a purchase from a minor under 18: Class E felony. Purchasing from a minor under 16, 6 months no suspension, probation, parole. Seller is under 14 yrs. 1 year mandatory sentence	Class E felony: 5 yrs. and $1000 to $10,000 (more severe if near school §4767-68)	5-100 lbs.: $25,000 and minimum 3 yrs.; 100-500 lbs.: $50,000 and minimum 5 yrs.; Over 500 lbs.: $100,000 and minimum 15 yrs.
DISTRICT OF COLUMBIA	33-501, *et seq.*; 33-541	Misdemeanor, up to 1 yr. and/or $1000; Subsequent offense: double penalties	Crime with penalty of 1 yr. and/or $10,000; Subsequent offense: double penalties; Within drug-free zone or sale to minor: up to twice the punishment	
FLORIDA	893.13, *et seq.*	3rd degree felony; Under 20 g.: 1st degree misdemeanor; In excess of 100 lbs. is trafficking (1st degree felony)	3rd degree felony, unless less than 20 g. for no consideration, then 1st degree misdemeanor: penalty as in §§775.082, 083, 084; Subsequent offense: 10 yrs.	All sentencing done pursuant to sentencing guidelines: 100-2000 lbs.: mandatory $25,000; 2000-10,000 lbs.: mandatory $50,000; Over 10,000 lbs.: 15 yrs. and mandatory $200,000
GEORGIA	16-13-30, *et seq.*	Over 50 lbs. is trafficking; possession at all is a felony with penalty of 1-10 yrs.	Felony: 5-30 yrs.	50-2000 lbs.: 5 yrs. and mandatory $100,000; 2000-10,000 lbs.: 7 yrs. and mandatory $250,000; Over 10,000 lbs.: 15 yrs. and mandatory $1,000,000

Table 11c: Illegal Drugs: Marijuana—Continued

State	Code Section	Possession	Sale	Trafficking
HAWAII	329-14, *et seq.*; 712-1240, *et seq.*	Possession of 25 or more marijuana plants or possession of 1 lb. or more of anything containing marijuana: Class C felony; 2 lbs. or more: Class B felony; 25 lbs. or more: Class A felony; Possession of over 100 plants: Class A felony; Distribution of any small amount or possession of any small amount: misdemeanor	Sale of any amount: Class C felony; 1 lb. or more: Class B felony; 5 lbs. or more: Class A felony	
IDAHO	37-2701, *et seq.*	Under 3 oz.: misdemeanor with penalty of up to 1 yr. or $1,000 or both; Over 3 oz.: felony, 5 yrs. and $10,000; Subsequent offense: double penalty	Felony: 5 yrs. and $15,000; Subsequent offense: double penalty	1 lb. or more or 25 plants or more: felony; 1-5 lbs. or 25-50 plants: mandatory 1 yr. and $5,000; 5-25 lbs. or 50-100 plants: mandatory 3 yrs. and $10,000; 25-100 lbs. or over 100 plants: mandatory 5 yrs. and $15,000; Maximum number of yrs. 15 and maximum fine $50,000
ILLINOIS	720 ILCS 570/ 100, *et seq.,* Uniform Controlled Substances Act; 720 ILCS 550/1, *et seq.*	Under 2.5 g.: Class C misdemeanor; 2.5-10 g.: Class B misdemeanor; 10-30 g.: Class A misdemeanor; 30-500 g: Class 4 felony; Over 500 g.: Class 3 felony; Subsequent offense: 10-30 g.: Class 4 felony; 30-500 g.: Class 3 felony; Producing plants: 1-5: Class A misdemeanor; 5-20: Class 4 felony; 20-50: Class 3 felony; Over 50: Class 2 felony with fine up to $100,000	Under 2.5 g.: Class B misdemeanor; 2.5-10 g.: Class A misdemeanor; 10-30 g.: Class 4 felony; 30-500 g.: Class 3 felony and up to $50,000 fine; Over 500 g.: Class 2 felony for which a fine not to exceed $100,000 may be imposed; Enhanced penalties for sale to person 3 yrs. junior or on school grounds	Over 2500 g. is trafficking: penalty is double that of sale

Table 11c: Illegal Drugs: Marijuana—Continued

State	Code Section	Possession	Sale	Trafficking
INDIANA	35-48-2-1, *et seq.*	Under 30 g.: Class A misdemeanor; Over 30 g.: Class D felony; Subsequent offense: Class D felony	Class A misdemeanor; 10 lbs. or more or delivered on school property or bus or within 1000 feet of either: Class C felony; Class C felony: 10 lbs or more on a school bus; Sale of 30 g. to 10 lbs. and recipient a minor and person has prior conviction involving marijuana: Class D felony	
IOWA	124.101, *et seq.*		Under 50 kg.: Class D felony, fine $1000 to $5000; 50 to 100 kg.: Class C felony, fine $1000 to $50,000; 100 to 1000 kg.: Class B felony, $5000 to $100,000; Over 1000 kg.: Class B felony with penalty of up to 50 yrs. and $1,000,000; Subsequent offense: triple penalties; more severe penalties for distribution to minor or to person 3 yrs. younger	
KANSAS	65-4101, *et seq.*	Class A nonperson misdemeanor; Subsequent offense: Level 4 felony	Level 3 felony; Sell within 1000 ft. of school or to minor: Level 2 felony	
KENTUCKY	218A.010, *et seq.*	Class A misdemeanor (includes less than 5 plants); over 5 plants: Class D felony	Under 8 oz.: Class A misdemeanor; Subsequent offense: Class D felony; 8 oz. to 5 lbs.: Class D felony; Subsequent offense: Class C felony Over 5 lbs.: Class C felony; Subsequent offense: Class B felony; Possession of over 8 oz. is *prima facie* evidence of intent to sell	
LOUISIANA	§40:961, *et seq.*	Up to 6 mos. in parish jail and/or up to $500; Second conviction of this amount: up to 5 yrs. and/or up to $2000; Subsequent convictions: up to 20 yrs; 60-2000 lbs.: 10-60 yrs. hard labor and $50,000 to $100,000; 2000-10,000 lbs.: 20-80 yrs. hard labor and $100,000 to $400,000; Over 10,000 lbs.: 50-80 yrs. hard labor and $400,000 to $1,000,000		

Table 11c: Illegal Drugs: Marijuana—Continued

State	Code Section	Possession	Sale	Trafficking
MAINE	Tit. 174A §1101, *et seq.*	Over 2 lbs. creates presumption of trafficking: Class E crime	Over 1.25 oz. creates presumption of furnishing: Class D crime	Class D crime; Possession of over 2 lbs. or over 100 plants: Class C crime; Over 20 lbs. or over 500 plants: Class B crime
MARYLAND	Art. 27 §276, *et seq.*	1 yr. and/or $1,000; Bringing 100 or more lbs. into state is felony with penalty of up to 25 yrs. and/or fine up to $50,000; Subsequent offense: double penalties	Felony with penalty of 5 yrs. and/or fine of $15,000; 50 lbs. or more: felony with not less than 40 yrs.; Subsequent offense: double penalties, mandatory 2 yrs.	If "drug kingpin": 20-40 yrs. and/or $1,000,000 fine
MASSACHUSETTS	Ch. 94c §1, *et seq.*	6 months and/or $500; Subsequent offense: 2 yrs. and/or $2000; Over 50 lbs. is trafficking	1-2 yrs. and/or $500 to $5000; Subsequent offense: 1-2.5 yrs. and/or $1000 to $10,000	50-100 lbs.: 2.5-15 yrs and $500 to $10,000; 100-2000 lbs.: 3-15 yrs. and $2500 to $25,000; 2000-10,000 lbs.: 5-15 yrs. and $5000 to $50,000; Over 10,000 lbs.: 10-15 yrs. and $20,000 to $200,000
MICHIGAN	333.7401, *et seq.*	Misdemeanor with penalty of 1 yr. and/or $2000	Felony: less than 5 kg. or 20 plants: up to 4 yrs. and/or $20,000; 5-45 kg. or 20-200 plants: up to 7 yrs. and/or $500,000; Over 45 kg. or over 200 plants: up to 15 yrs. and/or $10,000,000; Sale to minor or near school property: up to double penalties	
MINNESOTA	152.01, *et seq.*	Small amount: petty misdemeanor $200 and maybe drug education program; 10+ kg.: up to 20 yrs. and/or $250,000; 50-100 kg.: up to 25 yrs. and/or $500,000; 100+ kg.: up to 30 yrs. and/or $1,000,000; Subsequent offense: depends on level of prior offense; if misdemeanor, may be required to participate in chemical dependency evaluation and treatment	Any small amount for sale: up to 5 yrs. and/or $10,000; Small amount without remuneration: petty misdemeanor with fine of up to $200 and maybe drug education program; 5+ kg.: up to 20 yrs. and/or $250,000; 25+ kg.: up to 25 yrs. and/or $500,000; 50+ kg.: up to 30 yrs. and/or $1,000,000; 5 kg. or more in school or park or public housing zone: up to 25 yrs. and/or $500,000	

Table 11c: Illegal Drugs: Marijuana—Continued

State	Code Section	Possession	Sale	Trafficking
MISSISSIPPI	41-29-101, *et seq.*	Under 1 oz.: $100 to $250; 1 g. to 1 oz. in motor vehicle: misdemeanor, $1000 and 90 days in county jail; 1 oz. to 1 kg.: $1000 and 1 yr. county jail or $3000 and 3 yrs. penitentiary; Over 1 kg.: 20 yrs. and/or $1000 to $1,000,000; Subsequent offense within 2 yrs.: misdemeanor, 5-60 days and $250 fine and mandatory participation in drug education program; Third offense in 2 yrs.: misdemeanor, 5 days-6 months and $250 to $500 fine	Under 1 oz.: up to 3 yrs. and/or $3000; First-time offender with over 1 oz. but less than 1 kg.: up to 20 yrs. and/or $30,000; Over 1 oz.: up to 30 yrs. and/or $5,000 to $1,000,000; Subsequent offense: double penalties	Anyone over 21 selling 10 lbs. or more of marijuana during any 12 month period shall have life in prison without suspension/parole
MISSOURI	195.010, *et seq.*	Under 35 g.: Class A misdemeanor; Over 35 g.: Class C felony; Subsequent offense: subject to prior & persistent offenders statute §195.295	Less than 5 g.: Class C felony; More than 5 g.: Class B felony; Subsequent offense: subject to prior & persistent offenders statute §195.295; Distribution to minor 17 years old or 2 yrs. junior: Class B felony; Within 1000 ft. of school or public housing: Class A felony	Trafficking drugs 2nd degree: Distribution / attempt to deliver: 30-100 kg.: Class B felony; 100+ kg.: term of prison for Class A felony without parole; Buying/attempt to purchase: 30-100 kg.: Class B felony; 100+ kg. or over 500 plants: Class A felony
MONTANA	45-9-101, *et seq.*; 50-32-101, *et seq.*	Under 60 g.: misdemeanor with penalty of 6 months in county jail and fine of $100 to $500; Subsequent offense: $1000 fine and 1 yr. in county jail or up to 3 yrs. in state penitentiary	1 yr. to life and $50,000; Subsequent offense: 2 yrs. to life and $50,000; Offense of criminal sale of dangerous drugs on or near school property: 3 years to life and/or $50,000 fine	Criminal production/ manufacture: Less than 1 lb. or 30 plants: up to 10 yrs. and $50,000; Over 1 lb. or 30 plants: 2 yrs. to life and/or $50,000; Subsequent offense: up to double penalties

Table 11c: Illegal Drugs: Marijuana—Continued

State	Code Section	Possession	Sale	Trafficking
NEBRASKA	28-401, *et seq.*	Under 1 oz.(if first offense): Citation, $100, and attend a course; 2nd offense: Citation, $200, up to 5 days in jail, and Class IV misdemeanor; 3rd offense: Class IIIA misdemeanor, $300, and up to 7 days jail Over 1 oz.: Class IIIA misdemeanor; Over 1 lb.: Class IV felony	1 oz.-1 lb.: Class IIIA misdemeanor; Over 1 lb.: Class IV felony	
NEVADA	453.011, *et seq.*	For someone under 21: 1-6 yrs. and $2000 or 1 yr. in county jail; $1000 and 6 mos. driver's license suspension (same for 2nd and 3rd offenses); For someone over 21: up to 1 yr. and up to $1000; Subsequent offense: 1-6 yrs. and $5000	1-10 yrs. and up to $10,000; 2nd offense: 2-15 yrs. and up to $15,000; 3rd offense: 5-20 yrs. and up to $20,000	100-2000 lbs.: 3-20 yrs. and minimum $25,000; 2000-10,000 lbs.: 5-20 yrs. and minimum$50,000; Over 10,000 lbs.: 15 yrs. to life and minimum $200,000
NEW HAMPSHIRE	318-B:1, *et seq.*	Misdemeanor	Under 1 oz.: up to 3 yrs. and/or $25,000; 1 oz. to 5 lbs.: up to 7 yrs. and/or $100,000; Over 5 lbs.: up to 20 yrs. and/or $300,000; Subsequent offense: Under 1 oz.: up to 6 yrs. and/or $50,000; 1 oz. to 5 lbs.: up to 15 yrs. and/or $200,000; Over 5 lbs.: up to 40 yrs. and/or $500,000	
NEW JERSEY	24:21-1, *et seq.*; 2C:35-2, *et seq.*	Under 50 g.: disorderly person and 100 hrs. of community service (if within 1000 ft. of school); Over 50g.: 4th degree crime, $15,000	Less than 1 oz.: 4th degree crime; 1 oz. to 5 lbs.: 3rd degree crime, up to $15,000; Over 5 lbs.: 2nd degree crime	Leader of narcotics trafficking network: life (25 year minimum before parole) and/ or $500,000
NEW MEXICO	30-31-1, *et seq.*	Under 1 oz.: petty misdemeanor, 15 days and $50-$100; 1-8 oz.: misdemeanor, 1 yr. and $100-$1000; Over 8 oz.: 4th degree felony; Subsequent offense: Under 1 oz.: misdemeanor, 1 yr., $100-$1000	4th degree felony; If over 100 lbs., 3rd degree felony; Subsequent offense: 3rd degree felony; If over 100 lbs.: 2nd degree felony; Higher penalties if in drug-free school zone	

Table 11c: Illegal Drugs: Marijuana—Continued

State	Code Section	Possession	Sale	Trafficking
NEW YORK	Penal §220, *et seq.*; Pub. Health §3306, 3307	Under 25g: $100; Over 25 g. or public use: Class B misdemeanor; Over 2 oz.: Class A misdemeanor; Over 8 oz.: Class E felony; Over 16 oz.: Class D felony; Over 10 lbs.: Class C felony; Subsequent offense: Under 25 g.: $200; Third offense: $250 and 15 days	Under 2 g. or 1 cigarette: Class B misdemeanor; Under 25 g.: Class A misdemeanor; Over 25 g.: Class E felony; Over 4 oz. or sale to a minor: Class D felony; Over 16 oz.: Class C felony	
NORTH CAROLINA	90-86, *et seq.*	Class 3 misdemeanor; Over .5 oz.: Class 1 misdemeanor, $100 fine; Subsequent offense over .5 oz.: Class I felony Over 1.5 oz.: Class I felony;	Class I felony but not when under 5 g. for no consideration	50-100 lbs.: Class H felony, 25-30 mos. and/or $5000; 100-2000 lbs.: Class G felony, 35-42 mos. and/or $25,000; 2000-10,000 lbs.: Class F felony, 70-84 mos. and/or $50,000; Over 10,000 lbs.: Class D felony, 175-219 mos. and/or $200,000
NORTH DAKOTA	19-03.1-01, *et seq.*	Under .5 oz.: Class B misdemeanor; Under 1 oz.: Class A misdemeanor (may be expunged from record if no further conviction for 2 yrs.); Under .5 oz. while operating a motor vehicle: Class A misdemeanor	Class B felony; 100 lbs. or more: Class A felony; Delivery to a minor by an 18 year old.	
OHIO	2925.01, *et seq.*; 3719.01, *et seq.*	Under 20 g. and gift: minor misdemeanor; Subsequent offense: misdemeanor of 3rd degree; Under 100 g.: minor misdemeanor and $100; 100-200 g.: 4th degree misdemeanor and $250; 200-600 g.: 4th degree felony; Over 600 g.: 3rd degree felony; Subsequent offense: 200-600 g.: 3rd degree felony; Over 600 g.: 2nd degree felony	Under 200 g.: 4th degree felony; 200-600 g.: 3rd degree felony; Over 600 g.: 2nd degree felony, 6 mos. mandatory; Subsequent offense: Under 200 g.: 3rd degree felony; 200-600 g.: 2nd degree felony; Over 600 g.: 1 yr. mandatory; Stricter penalties if sale within 1000 ft. of school or 100 ft. of juvenile	2nd degree felony, 1 yr. and $1000; Subsequent offense: 2 yrs. and $2000

Table 11c: Illegal Drugs: Marijuana—Continued

State	Code Section	Possession	Sale	Trafficking
OKLAHOMA	Tit. 63 §2-101, *et seq.*	Misdemeanor with penalty of up to 1 yr. or fined $10,000; Subsequent offense: felony, 2-10 yrs. Fine not to exceed $25,000	Felony, 2-10 yrs. and/or up to $5000; Subsequent offense: double penalties	Between 25-1000 lbs.: $25,000 to $100,000; Over 1000 lbs.: $100,000 to $500,000
OREGON	Chapter 475	Less than 1 oz.: $500-$1000	110-150 g.: commercial drug offense if over $300 cash, firearm, packaging materials, customer list, stolen property, or using public lands; Over 150 g.: Category 6 crime	Class B felony (Category 8 if over 150 g.); 5 g.-1 oz.: Class A misdemeanor; less than 5 g.: $500-$1000 fine; Within 1000 ft. of school: Class C misdemeanor
PENNSYLVANIA	Tit. 35 §780-101, *et seq.*	Under 30 g.: misdemeanor, 30 days and/or $500; Over 30 g.: misdemeanor, 1 yr. and/or $5000 Subsequent offense over 30g.: double penalties	Over 1000 lbs.: felony, up to 10 yrs. and/or $100,000 or enough to recoup drug profit; Subsequent offense or sale to minor: double penalties	
RHODE ISLAND	21-28-1.01, *et seq.*	Misdemeanor, up to 1 yr. and/or $200 to $500; 1-5 kg.: 10-50 yrs. and/or $10,000-$500,000 Over 5 kg.: 20 yrs. to life and $25,000 to $1,000,000	1-5 kg.: 10-50 yrs. and/or $10,000-$500,000 Over 5 kg.: 20 yrs. to life and $25,000 to $1,000,000; Sale within 300 yds. of school: double penalties; Sale to minor or person 3 yrs. junior: minimum 2-5 yrs. and $10,000	
SOUTH CAROLINA	44-53-110	Misdemeanor: up to 6 mos. and/or $1000; Subsequent offense: misdemeanor, 1 yr. and/or $2000 Under 1 oz.: 30 days and/or $100 to $200; Over 1 oz.: *Prima facie* guilty of sale; Subsequent offense under 1 oz.: 1 yr. and/or $200 to $1000	Misdemeanor: up to 5 yrs. and/or $5,000; Subsequent offense: felony, up to 10 yrs. and/or $10,000; Third offense: felony, 5-20 yrs. and/or $20,000; Sale to minor: misdemeanor, up to 10 yrs. and $10,000	10-100 lbs.: 1-10 yrs. and $10,000; 2nd offense: 5-20 yrs and $15,000; Subsequent offense: mandatory 25 yrs. and $25,000; 100-2000 lbs. or 100-1000 plants: mandatory 25 yrs. and $25,000; 2000-10,000 lbs. or 1000-10,000 plants: mandatory 25 yrs. and $50,000; Over 10,000 lbs. or over 10,000 plants: 25-30 yrs. and $200,000

Table 11c: Illegal Drugs: Marijuana—Continued

State	Code Section	Possession	Sale	Trafficking
SOUTH DAKOTA	22-42-6, *et seq.*; 34-20B-1 to 114	Under .5 lb.: Class 1 misdemeanor; .5 to 1 lb.: Class 6 felony; 1-10 lbs.: Class 5 felony; Over 10 lbs.: Class 4 felony; May be civil penalty for violation up to $10,000 in any of the above cases	Under .5 oz. or without consideration: Class 2 misdemeanor; Under 1 oz.: Class 1 misdemeanor, mandatory 15 days without suspension; 1 oz.-.5 lb.: Class 6 felony; .5-1 lb.: Class 5 felony; Over 1 lb.: Class 4 felony; Sale to a minor: Class 5 felony; Sale in drug-free zone: Class 4 felony, minimum 5 yrs. Also may be civil penalty up to $10,000 in any of above cases; All felonies: mandatory 30 days without suspension; Subsequent offense: mandatory 1 yr.	
TENNESSEE	39-17-408, *et seq.*	Possession or casual exchange of: Less than .5 oz.: Class A misdemeanor and attendance at drug offender school and minimum $250 fine; Casual exchange to a minor from an adult 2 yrs. his senior and adult knows minor is a minor: felony; Subsequent offense: $500 minimum; Third: $750 minimum; Two or more prior convictions, then Class E felony; 20 plants to 99 plants: Class C felony, fined up to $100,000.	.5 oz. to 10 lbs.: Class E felony and/or $5000; 10 lbs. + 1 g. to 70 lbs.: Class D felony and/or $50,000; 70 lbs. + 1 g.: Class B felony and/ or $200,000; Over 700 lbs.: Class A felony and/or $500,000; Sale to minor under 18 or in drug-free zone: one class higher than amount required; Minimum penalty amounts: 1st drug felony offense: $2000; 2nd: $2500; 3rd: $3000	
TEXAS	Health & Safety §481.032, *et seq.*	Under 2 oz.: Class B misdemeanor; 2-4 oz.: Class A misdemeanor; 4 oz. to 5 lbs.: State jail felony; 5-50 lbs.: 3rd degree felony; 50-2000 lbs.: 2nd degree felony; Over 2000 lbs.: Texas Dept. of Criminal Justice institution for life or 5-99 yrs. and $50,000	.25 oz. or less: Class B misdemeanor (if no remuneration); .25 oz. or less: Class A misdemeanor (with remuneration); .25 oz. to 5 lbs.: state jail felony; 5 lbs. to 50 lbs.: 2nd degree felony; 50-2000 lbs.: 1st degree felony; Over 2000 lbs.: Texas Dept. of Criminal Justice institution for life or 10-99 yrs. and/or $100.000; Delivery to minor under 17 who is enrolled in school and over .25 oz.: 2nd degree felony; Within drug-free zone: penalties doubled	

Table 11c: Illegal Drugs: Marijuana—Continued

State	Code Section	Possession	Sale	Trafficking
UTAH	58-37-1, *et seq.*	Under 1 oz.: Class B misdemeanor; 1-16 oz. not yet extracted from plant: Class A misdemeanor; Over 1 lb.-100 lbs.: 3rd degree felony; Over 100 lbs.: 2nd degree felony; Subsequent offense: one degree greater penalty than provided for	3rd degree felony; subsequent offense: 2nd degree felony; Within 1000 ft. of school or sale to a minor: one degree more than provided except 1st degree felony is 5 yrs. mandatory	
VERMONT	Tit. 18§4230	Under 2 oz. and/or less than 3 plants: up to 6 months and/or $500; More than 2 oz. and/or more than 3 plants: up to 3 yrs. and/or $10,000; More than 1 lb. or more than 10 plants: up to 5 yrs. and/or $100,000; More than 10 lbs. or more than 25 plants: up to 15 yrs. and/or $500,000; Subsequent offense: Under 2 oz.: up to 2 yrs. and/or $2000	Under .5 oz.: 2 yrs. and/or $10,000; .5 oz.-1 lb.: up to 5 yrs. and/or $100,000; More than 1 lb.: up to 15 yrs. and/or $500,000; Subsequent offense: double penalties	
VIRGINIA	54.1-3445, 18.2-247	Misdemeanor, jail up to 30 days and/or $500; Subsequent offense: Class 1 misdemeanor	Up to .5 oz.: Class 1 misdemeanor; .5 oz.-5 lbs.: Class 5 felony; Over 5 lbs.: 5-30 yrs.; Proof that person gave drug only as an accommodation not for remuneration or to induce him to become addicted shall be guilty of Class 1 misdemeanor; Sale to minor or within 1000 ft. of school: stricter penalties	
WASHINGTON	69.50.101, *et seq.*	Up to 5 yrs. and/or $10,000; 40 g. or less is misdemeanor; Subsequent offense: double penalties	Less than 40 g.: misdemeanor, up to 5 yrs. in correctional facility and $10,000; Subsequent offense: up to double penalties; Unlawful delivery of controlled substance used by person delivered to and resulting in user's death: deliverer guilty of controlled substance homicide: Class B felony	
WEST VIRGINIA	60A-1-101 to 8-13	Misdemeanor, 90 days-6 mos. and/or $1000; Court may mitigate first offense of under 15 g.; Subsequent offense: double penalties	Felony, 1-3 yrs. and/or $10,000; Subsequent offense: double penalties; Sale to minor or within 1000 ft. of school: mandatory 2 yrs.	Transport into state with intent to deliver: felony, 1-5 yrs. and/or $15,000

Table 11c: Illegal Drugs: Marijuana—Continued

State	Code Section	Possession	Sale	Trafficking
WISCONSIN	§961.51 *et seq.*	Misdemeanor, up to 6 mos. and/or fine up to $1000; Subsequent offense: double penalties	Less than 500 g. or 10 plants: up to 3 yrs. and $500 to $25,000; 500 to 2500 g. or 10-50 plants: 3 mos. to 5 yrs. and $1000 to $50,000; Over 2500 g. or more than 50 plants: 1 to 10 yrs. and $1000 to $100,000; Subsequent offense or sale to minor: double penalties; Sale within 1000 ft. of school of less than 25 g. or 5 plants: mandatory 1 yr. without probation	
WYOMING	35-7-1001 to 1057	Less than 3 oz.: misdemeanor, up to 1 yr. and/or $1000; Over 3 oz.: felony, up to 5 yrs. and/or $10,000; Subsequent offense: up to 5 yrs. and/or $5000 or double penalties	Up to 10 yrs. and/or $10,000; Subsequent offense or sale to minor or sale in drug-free zone: double penalties	

12. PROHIBITED CONSENSUAL SEXUAL ACTIVITY

The laws covered by this chapter concern state legislation intended to control the private sexual practices of citizens. A related issue, that of exposure of a sexual partner to AIDS is also covered here, therefore, it covers situations where the sex act is not fully consensual, such as whether the victim of a sexual crime can compel testing of the perpetrator. In any case, knowingly exposing another to the AIDS virus may be a crime whether the sexual activity is a crime or not.

For centuries, public norms in western culture generated virtually no controversy with respect to the laws governing sexual conduct. This does not mean that there was no "illegal" sexual conduct. It only means that there was general disapproval of it, even while such practices were being engaged in on a regular basis by certain segments of society. However, as gay men and women have become more visible and vocal about their lifestyles and practices, and more demanding that their contact be accepted as "normal" in the "general" conscience of society, the old laws are beginning to be called into question. The boldest challenge to these laws has been a Supreme Court case decided in the mid 1980's in which a person was arrested for violating Georgia's statute prohibiting sodomy. The challenge was based on the principle that consensual sex between two adults was a private matter which the state had no authority to regulate. In that case, the defendant lost, and the Supreme Court held that the state has sufficient interest in preventing sodomy to warrant the enactment of laws banning the behavior. These laws are continuously subject to court challenges and the reader is advised that the courts may hold a statute unconstitutional and the statute would remain in the books. Therefore, even though a statute is listed in this chapter, it does not mean that the law is still "good."

Since that decision, various state sodomy statutes have been challenged around the country. Many have been struck down as violations of an individual's right to privacy. Some states have amended their statutes to make the ban apply specifically to juveniles. A few states only ban sodomy between persons of the same sex, while most states apply the ban to both sexes.

An interesting feature about these statutes concerns the terms used in various states. Crime against "nature" is the most commonly (twelve times) used term for sodomy (which is used only seven times), but perusal of the following chart will reveal some states using the terms "buggery," "unnatural" or "perverted sexual practices," "unnatural intercourse," "deviate sexual conduct," and "homosexual acts," to describe prohibited sexual conduct. As an aside, the state of Utah uses the term "the infamous crime against nature" to describe the act in their capital punishment statute where it is considered an aggravating factor making the defendant subject to the death penalty.

This chapter also includes references to statutes in which exposure of another to the AIDS virus has been made a crime. Intentional exposure of another to AIDS is a felony in many states. In addition, many states give the victim of a sexual offense the right to require a convicted perpetrator to submit to a test for AIDS. Mandatory testing is always been controversial and resisted by libertarians, but in criminal cases involving sex offenses, there is less resistance to the idea of forcing people to be tested.

The final area covered in this chapter involves categories of crimes that are used to prohibit various kinds of sexual activity. The statutes listed in the column headed "Other Crimes Relating to Consensual Sexual Acts" range from explicit bans on prostitution, lewd public acts, and indecent exposure, to loitering and disorderly conduct. Although some of the offenses listed, such as loitering, can be applied to activity that is non-sexual in nature, statutes which are used to disrupt or prohibit sexual activity. These laws illustrate the difficulties which law enforcement officers and officials have in trying to regulate intimate, private behavior. The laws are very general and often vague and may be applied to numerous activities deemed offensive by the person charged with enforcing public order.

Table 12: Prohibited Consensual Sexual Activity

State	Sodomy: Applicability to:	Sodomy: Penalty	Exposing Another to/ Compelled Testing for AIDS/HIV Virus	Other Crimes Relating to Consensual Sex Acts
ALABAMA	Same sex	13A-6-65 (a)(3) Sexual misconduct: Class A misdemeanor (consent is not defense)		13A-11-9 Loitering: violation 13A-6-68 Indecent exposure: Class A misdemeanor 13A-12-30 Public lewdness: Class C misdemeanor
ALASKA				11.41.460 Indecent exposure: Class B misdemeanor 11.61.110 (a)(7) Disorderly conduct: Class B misdemeanor
ARIZONA	Both sexes	13-1411 Crime against nature: Class 3 misdemeanor	13-1415 Allows for order for HIV test if defendant charged with sexual offense	13-1402 Indecent exposure: Class 1 misdemeanor 13-1403 Public sexual indecency: Class 1 misdemeanor 13-1408 Adultery: Class 3 misdemeanor 13-1412 Lewd and lascivious acts: Class 3 misdemeanor 13-2905 Loitering: Class 3 misdemeanor
ARKANSAS	Same sex	5-14-122 Sodomy: Class A misdemeanor	5-14-123 Exposing another person to HIV: Class A felony 16-82-101 Testing for HIV-Sexual offenses: if victim request it is mandatory defendant be tested if convicted of sexual assault	5-14-111 Public sexual indecency: Class A misdemeanor 5-14-112 Indecent exposure: Class A misdemeanor 5-71-213 Loitering: Class C misdemeanor
CALIFORNIA	Both sexes	Pen. §286 Sodomy under 18 years of age or incompetent: misdemeanor	Pen. §1202.1 Testing for HIV required if convicted of sexual offense in §§261, 261.5, 262, 286, 288a, 288	Pen. §314 Lewd or obscene conduct; indecent exposure; obscene exhibitions: misdemeanor Pen. §372 Public nuisance: misdemeanor Pen. §647 Disorderly conduct: misdemeanor
COLORADO			18-3-415 Any defendant bound over for trial for any sexual offense involving penetration shall be ordered by court to submit to HIV testing	18-9-106 Disorderly conduct: Class 1 petty offense 18-7-301 Public indecency: Class 1 petty offense 18-7-302 Indecent exposure: Class 3 misdemeanor 18-9-112 (2)(c) Loitering: Class 1 petty offense

Table 12: Prohibited Consensual Sexual Activity—Continued

State	Sodomy: Applicability to:	Sodomy: Penalty	Exposing Another to/ Compelled Testing for AIDS/HIV Virus	Other Crimes Relating to Consensual Sex Acts
CONNECTICUT				53a-82 Prostitution: Class A misdemeanor 53a-181 Breach of peace: Class B misdemeanor 53a-181a Public disturbance: infraction 53a-182 Disorderly conduct: Class A misdemeanor 53a-182a Obstructing free passage: Class C misdemeanor 53a-186 Public indecency: Class B misdemeanor
DELAWARE				11,§1301 Disorderly conduct: unclassified misdemeanor 11,§764 Indecent exposure in 2nd degree: unclassified misdemeanor 11,§1321 Loitering: violation 11,§1341 Lewdness: Class B misdemeanor 11,§765 Sexual harassment: unclassified misdemeanor
DISTRICT OF COLUMBIA				22-301 Adultery 22-1002 Fornication 22-1107 Disorderly conduct: misdemeanor 22-1112 Lewd, indecent, or obscene acts: misdemeanor 22-2701 Inviting for purposes of prostitution: misdemeanor 22-2701.1 Prostitution
FLORIDA	Both sexes	800.02 Unnatural and lascivious act: misdemeanor of the 2nd degree	775.0877 Criminal transmission of HIV: felony, 3rd degree; only applies to list of enumerated sexual offenses, only if positive test for HIV and only if defendant commits a 2nd or subsequent offense of enumerated list 384.24 Unlawful for person with sexually transmitted disease to have sexual intercourse with another unless other person told of disease and consents: misdemeanor of 1st degree	877.03 Breach of peace: misdemeanor of the 2nd degree 800.03 Exposure of sex organs: misdemeanor of the 1st degree 798.02 Lewd and lascivious behavior: misdemeanor 2nd degree 796.07 Prostitution, lewd, indecent act: misdemeanor in 2nd degree

Table 12: Prohibited Consensual Sexual Activity—Continued

State	Sodomy: Applicability to:	Sodomy: Penalty	Exposing Another to/ Compelled Testing for AIDS/HIV Virus	Other Crimes Relating to Consensual Sex Acts
GEORGIA	Both sexes	16-6-2 Sodomy: not less than 1 nor more than 20 years Aggravated sodomy: life *or* not less than 10 nor more than 20 years	15-6-60 Reckless conduct by HIV infected person: felony 17-10-15 HIV test required for AIDS-transmitting crimes (sodomy; aggravated sodomy; solicitation of sodomy)	16-6-8 Public indecency: misdemeanor 16-6-15 Solicitation of sodomy: misdemeanor; if solicited person under 17 years old: felony 16-6-16 Masturbation for hire: misdemeanor 16-11-39 Disorderly conduct: misdemeanor
HAWAII				707-734 Indecent exposure: petty misdemeanor 712-1217 Open lewdness: petty misdemeanor
IDAHO	Both sexes	18-6605 Crime against nature: felony not less than 5 years	39-608 Transfer of body fluid which may contain the HIV virus: felony	18-4104 Participation in, or production or presentation of, obscene live conduct in public place: misdemeanor 18-4105 Public display/exhibit of offensive sexual material: misdemeanor
ILLINOIS			720 ILCS 5/12-16.2 Criminal transmission of HIV: Class 2 felony 720 ILCS 5/12-18 HIV testing may be requested by victim of sexual assault crime upon preliminary hearing or indictment	720 ILCS 5/11-9 Public indecency: Class A misdemeanor
INDIANA			35-38-1-9.5 HIV testing required if convicted of sex crime or offense related to controlled substances	35-45-4-1 Public indecency-indecent exposure: Class A misdemeanor
IOWA			709B.2 Victim may request HIV testing of defendant convicted of sexual assault	709.9 Indecent exposure: serious misdemeanor
KANSAS	Same sex	21-3505 Criminal sodomy: Class B nonperson misdemeanor	22-2913 HIV test of convicted person requested by victim of sexual activity crime mandatory	21-3508 Lewd and lascivious behavior: Class B nonperson misdemeanor
KENTUCKY	Same sex	510.100 Sodomy in the 4th degree: Class A misdemeanor	510.320 Upon conviction of sexual activity crime, court shall order HIV testing of defendant	510.150 Indecent exposure: Class B misdemeanor
LOUISIANA	Both sexes	14§89 Crime against nature: fined not more than $2,000, or imprisoned with or without hard labor for not more than 5 years, or both	14§43.5 Intentional exposure to AIDS virus: fined not more than $5,000, imprisoned with or without hard labor for not more than 10 years, or both 15§535 Court shall order HIV test of person convicted of sexual offense	14§106 Obscenity (indecent exposure): not less than $1,000 nor more than $2,500, or imprisoned with or without hard labor for not less than 6 months not more than 3 years, or both

Table 12: Prohibited Consensual Sexual Activity—Continued

State	Sodomy: Applicability to:	Sodomy: Penalty	Exposing Another to/ Compelled Testing for AIDS/HIV Virus	Other Crimes Relating to Consensual Sex Acts
MAINE			5§19203-F Victim may petition court to order HIV test of convicted sexual offender	17-A-854 Public indecency: Class E crime
MARYLAND	Both sexes	Crim. Law 27§554 Unnatural or perverted sexual practices: felony; fined not more than $1,000 or imprisoned for not more than 10 years, or both	Health-Gen. §18-601.1 Exposure of other individuals by individual with HIV virus: misdemeanor Crimes & Punish. 27§765 Victim may request HIV testing upon conviction of crime involving sexual activity	Crim. Law 27§335A Indecent exposure: misdemeanor Crim. Law 27§15 Lewdness: misdemeanor
MASSACHUSETTS	Both sexes	272§34 Crime against nature: felony		272§16 Open and gross lewdness and lascivious behavior: felony; 2 to 3 years 272§26 Resorting to restaurants or taverns for immoral purposes: misdemeanor 272§29 Dissemination or possession of obscene matter: felony 272§35 Unnatural and lascivious acts: felony 272§43 Disorderliness in public conveyances; disturbance of travelers: misdemeanor 272§53 Indecent exposure: misdemeanor
MICHIGAN	Both sexes	750.158 Crime against nature or sodomy: felony; not more than 15 years		750.168 Disorderly conduct: misdemeanor 750.335 Lewd and lascivious cohabitation and gross lewdness: misdemeanor 750.335a Indecent exposure: misdemeanor 750.338 Gross indecency between male persons: felony 750.338a Gross indecency between female persons: felony 750.448 Soliciting and accosting: misdemeanor

Table 12: Prohibited Consensual Sexual Activity—Continued

State	Sodomy: Applicability to:	Sodomy: Penalty	Exposing Another to/ Compelled Testing for AIDS/HIV Virus	Other Crimes Relating to Consensual Sex Acts
MINNESOTA	Both sexes	609.293 Sodomy: misdemeanor	609.2241 Knowing transfer of communicable disease: if crime involved sexual penetration with another person without having first informed the other person that the person has a communicable disease; if crime involved transfer of blood, sperm ... except for medical research; if crime involved sharing of nonsterile needles; penalty is as provided under attempt, assault, and murder statutes 611A.19 Victim may request HIV test of convicted sexual offender	617.23 Indecent exposure: misdemeanor
MISSISSIPPI	Both sexes	97-29-59 Unnatural intercourse: felony	99-19-203 Any person convicted of sex offense after 7/1/94 shall be tested for HIV	97-29-31 Indecent exposure (public): misdemeanor- Fine not exceeding $500 or imprisonment up to 6 months or both 97-35-3 Disorderly conduct: misdemeanor 97-35-11 Indecent exposure (private property): misdemeanor 97-35-15 Disturbance of public peace: misdemeanor
MISSOURI			191.677 Knowingly infected with HIV-prohibited acts, create risk of transmittal: felony 191.663 Any person convicted of or who pleads guilty to sex offense in Chap. 556 shall be ordered by court to undergo HIV test	§566-093 Sexual misconduct in 2nd degree: Class B misdemeanor §566-095 Sexual misconduct in 3rd degree: Class C misdemeanor §566-130 Indecent exposure: Class A misdemeanor
MONTANA	Both sexes	45-5-505 Deviate sexual conduct: felony; not more than 10 years or up to $50,000 or both	50-18-112 Exposure of another to sexually transmitted disease: misdemeanor 46-18-256 Any person convicted of sexual offense must be tested for HIV if victim requests	45-5-504 Indecent exposure: misdemeanor 45-8-201 Obscenity: misdemeanor
NEBRASKA			29-2290 If victim of sexual assault or sex offense involving penetration requests, the court shall order HIV testing of convicted	28-806 Public indecency: Class II misdemeanor

Table 12: Prohibited Consensual Sexual Activity—Continued

State	Sodomy: Applicability to:	Sodomy: Penalty	Exposing Another to/ Compelled Testing for AIDS/HIV Virus	Other Crimes Relating to Consensual Sex Acts
NEVADA	Both sexes	201.190 Crime against nature: Category D felony Imprisonment 1-4 years	201.205 Intentional transmission of HIV: Category B felony 441A.320 As soon as practical after a person is arrested for a crime in which the victim alleges involved sexual penetration, the arrestee will be tested for HIV	201.210 Open or gross lewdness: gross misdemeanor 1st offense; subsequent offense category D felony 201.220 Indecent exposure: gross misdemeanor 1st offense; subsequent offense category D felony 207.030 Engage in lewdness in public: misdemeanor
NEW HAMPSHIRE			632-A:10-6 Any person convicted of offense under this chapter shall be administered an HIV test	645:1 Indecent exposure: misdemeanor Class B felony if previously convicted
NEW JERSEY			2C:43-2.2 Upon request of victim, any person convicted of sexual assault or aggravated sexual assault shall be HIV tested	2C:14-4 Lewdness: misdemeanor 2C:34-4 Public communication of obscenity: crime of 4th degree; not more than 18 months
NEW MEXICO			24.28.5.1 Victim of sexual offense may petition court for HIV testing of convicted sexual offender	30-9-14 Indecent exposure: misdemeanor 30-9-14.1 Indecent dancing: petty misdemeanor 30-9-14.2 Indecent waitering: petty misdemeanor
NEW YORK	Both sexes	Pen. 130.38 Consensual sodomy: Class B misdemeanor	Crim. Proc. 390.15 Upon request of victim of felony offense enumerated in any section of Pen. 130, the court must order the convicted person to be tested for HIV	Pen. 240.20 Disorderly conduct: violation Pen. 240.35 Loitering: violation Pen. 245.00 Public lewdness: Class B misdemeanor Pen. 245.01 Exposure of a person: violation
NORTH CAROLINA	Both sexes	14-177 Crime against nature: Class I felony		14-190.9 Indecent exposure: Class 2 misdemeanor
NORTH DAKOTA			12.1-20-17 HIV transfer of body fluid: Class A felony (affirmative defense-transferred by consensual sex) 23-07.7-02 If victim petitions court may order defendant charged with sex offense under Chap. 12.1-20 to be HIV tested	12.1-20-12.1 Indecent exposure: Class B misdemeanor 12.1-31-01 Disorderly conduct: Class B misdemeanor
OHIO			2907.27 If person charged with violation of sections 2907.02, .03, or .04, the court shall order the accused to submit to HIV testing	2917.11 Disorderly conduct: misdemeanor 2907.09 Public indecency: 4th degree misdemeanor 2907.07 Importuning: 1st degree misdemeanor

Table 12: Prohibited Consensual Sexual Activity—Continued

State	Sodomy: Applicability to:	Sodomy: Penalty	Exposing Another to/ Compelled Testing for AIDS/HIV Virus	Other Crimes Relating to Consensual Sex Acts
OKLAHOMA	Both sexes	21§886 Crime against nature: felony; 10 years	21§1192.1 Knowingly engaging in conduct reasonably likely to transfer HIV virus: felony; not more than 5 years	21§22 Public indecency: misdemeanor 21§1021 Indecent exposure: felony; not more than 10 years 21§1029 Prostitution, lewdness, or assignation: misdemeanor
OREGON			135.139 Upon request of victim of sex crime, court may order HIV testing of convicted offender	163.465 Public indecency: Class A misdemeanor
PENNSYLVANIA				18§5503 Disorderly conduct: summary offense 18§3127 Indecent exposure: misdemeanor 2nd degree 18§5901 Open lewdness: misdemeanor 3rd degree
RHODE ISLAND	Both sexes	11-10-1 Sodomy: felony; not more than 20 nor less than 7 years	23-11-1 Exposing another person to infection: misdemeanor; fined $100 or imprisoned not more than 3 months	11-45-1 Disorderly conduct: misdemeanor 11-34-8 Loitering for indecent purposes: misdemeanor 11-3-4-8.1 Soliciting from motor vehicles for indecent purposes: misdemeanor
SOUTH CAROLINA	Both sexes	16-15-120 Buggery or sodomy: Class F felony; 5 years	44-29-145 Knowingly exposing others to AIDS virus: felony; not more than 10 years 16-3-740 Court shall order HIV testing of convicted person for sexual battery or sexual conduct defined in 16-3-800 within 15 days of conviction	16-15-90 Lewdness: misdemeanor 16-15-130 Indecent exposure: misdemeanor 16-15-365 Exposure of private parts: misdemeanor
SOUTH DAKOTA			23A-35B-3 Victim where exchange of body fluids has occurred may petition court to order HIV testing of defendant	22-24-1 Indecent exposure: Class 1 misdemeanor
TENNESSEE	Same sex	39-13-510 Homosexual acts: Class C misdemeanor	68-10-107 Exposure of others by infected person: Class C misdemeanor (sexually transmitted disease) 39-13-521 When a person is initially arrested for allegedly violating §§39-13-502, 39-13-503, 39-13-506, 39-13-522, that person shall undergo HIV testing immediately	39-13-511 Indecent exposure: Class B misdemeanor 39-13-512 Prostitution for hire, includes loitering for hire; expresses (includes both hetero- and homosexual activities): Class B misdemeanor

Table 12: Prohibited Consensual Sexual Activity—Continued

State	Sodomy: Applicability to:	Sodomy: Penalty	Exposing Another to/ Compelled Testing for AIDS/HIV Virus	Other Crimes Relating to Consensual Sex Acts
TEXAS	Same sex	Pen. 21.06 Homosexual conduct: Class C misdemeanor	Crim. Proc. §21.31 Upon indictment for felony sex offense or upon request of victim of alleged sex offense, court may order HIV testing of offender	Pen. 21.07 Public lewdness: Class A misdemeanor Pen. 21.08 Indecent exposure: Class B misdemeanor Pen. 42.01 Disorderly conduct: Class C misdemeanor
UTAH	Both sexes	76-5-403 Sodomy: Class B misdemeanor	76-5-502 At victim's request, person convicted of sex offense or attempted sex offense must be HIV tested	76-9-102 Disorderly conduct: Class C misdemeanor 76-9-702 Lewdness: Class B misdemeanor
VERMONT			18§1096 Exposure of sexually transmitted disease: misdemeanor	13§2601 Lewd and lascivious conduct: felony; not more than 5 years 13§2632 Not engage or occupy a building for purpose of lewdness: misdemeanor
VIRGINIA	Both sexes	18.2-361 Crime against nature: Class 6 felony	18.2-62 Testing for HIV may be requested following arrest for crime involving sexual assault or §§18.2-361, 18.2-366, 18.2-370, and 18.2-370.1	18.2-345 Lewd and lascivious cohabitation: Class 3 misdemeanor 18.2-387 Indecent exposure: Class 1 misdemeanor
WASHINGTON			70.24.340 All persons convicted of sexual offense under 9A.44 shall be HIV tested as soon as possible after sentencing	9A.88.010 Indecent exposure: misdemeanor
WEST VIRGINIA			16-3C-2 Upon conviction of sexual offense, HIV testing of convicted mandatorily ordered by the court	61-8-4 Lewd and lascivious cohabitation or conduct: misdemeanor 61-8-9 Indecent exposure: misdemeanor
WISCONSIN			968.38 In a criminal action for sex assault, the district attorney or victim may request the court order the defendant to be HIV tested	944.17 Sexual gratification: Class A misdemeanor 944.20 Lewd and lascivious behavior: Class A misdemeanor 947.01 Disorderly conduct: Class B misdemeanor 947.02 Vagrancy: Class C misdemeanor
WYOMING				6-4-201 Public indecency: misdemeanor

III.   EDUCATION LAWS

13. COMPULSORY EDUCATION

Public schools are a relatively new concept in Western culture. Not until the nineteenth century did states officially begin to take responsibility for educating children. Before that time education was a private matter, either handled by parents, churches, or communities that joined together and paid a teacher to educate their children.

Some early state constitutions and territory charters specifically stated that the government was responsible for the training of children in morals and the overall knowledge necessary for them to become responsible citizens. Often this responsibility was acted upon merely by subsidizing the building of schools; minimum requirements for the type of education or the number of years of education that were required of students were not set.

Today education is a responsibility that local, state, and federal governments take seriously. The teaching of morality has given way to standard academic focuses, and compulsory education laws, requiring public school attendance of all children generally between the ages of seven and sixteen, have been enacted. However, these rules frequently exempt children with permanent or temporary mental or physical disabilities, and a few states exempt student who live more than two miles from a public transportation route. Alternatives to state-run schools, including private and parochial schools and home schools, are also available.

Table 13: Compulsory Education

State	Code Section	Age Requirements	Exceptions	Home School Provisions	Penalties on Parents for Noncompliance
ALABAMA	16-28-1, *et seq.*	Between 7 and 16	Church school students; child privately tutored by certified instructor; child whose physical/mental condition prevents attendance; child would be compelled to walk over 2 miles to attend public school; child legally and regularly employed; children over 16 who have completed public school course of study	Exempted from Chapter 46 regulating certain schools and courses of instruction (§§16-46-1, *et seq.*)	Misdemeanor: Fine up to $100 and possibly up to 90 days hard labor for the county
ALASKA	14.30.010, *et seq.*	Between 7 and 16	Comparable education provided through religious or private school or tutoring; attends school operated by federal government; child has physical/mental condition making attendance impractical; child is in custody of court or law enforcement officer; child is temporarily ill or injured, resides over 2 miles from a route for public transportation, or has completed the 12th grade or is suspended or denied admittance under 14.30.045; child is enrolled in an approved correspondence study or is well-served by an educational experience of another kind that is approved	Tutoring by personnel certified according to §14.20.020 who holds bachelor's degree from accredited institution among other requirements	Knowing noncompliance is violation with fine up to $300; every 5 days of noncompliance is separate violation
ARIZONA	15-802	Between 6 and 16	Child receives home instruction and takes a standardized achievement test; child attends a private school full time (at least 175 days per year); physical/mental condition makes attendance impractical; child has completed 10th grade; child is over 14 and employed at a lawful wage-earning occupation with consent of custodian/parent; child enrolled in vocational education; child enrolled in another state-provided education program; waiver may be granted for good cause; child was suspended	Instruction must be in reading, grammar, mathematics, social studies, and science by a person passing a reading, grammar, and mathematics proficiency exam; home schooled child must be allowed to participate in interscholastic athletics for school district in which he/she resides	Class 3 misdemeanor; petty offense for failure to provide attendant for home-schooled child

Table 13: Compulsory Education—Continued

State	Code Section	Age Requirements	Exceptions	Home School Provisions	Penalties on Parents for Noncompliance
ARKANSAS	6-18-201	Between 5 and 17	Child has received a high school diploma; parent may elect to withhold child from kindergarten; any child over 16 enrolled in post-secondary vocational institution or college or specific adult education programs upon certain conditions	Parents must give written notice of intent to home school; with curriculum, schedules, and qualifications of teacher presented to superintendent for each semester; child must submit to standardized achievement tests annually and at 8, if test results are unsatisfactory, child shall be enrolled in a public, private, or parochial school (§6-15-501) et. seq.	Misdemeanor; each day is separate offense and fine of $10 to $50
CALIFORNIA	Educ. §§48200, *et seq.*; 48400; 48293	Between 6 and 18; unless otherwise exempted, persons 16 to 18 must attend special continuation education classes	Children attending private schools; child being tutored by person with state credential for grade being taught; children holding work permits (subject to compulsory part-time classes); child of 15 may take a leave of absence for supervised travel, study, training, or work not available to the student under another education option if certain conditions are met; illegal aliens (under Proposition 187 under judicial attack)		Guilty of an infraction; 1st conviction: fine up to $100; 2nd conviction: fine up to $250, 3rd or subsequent convictions: fine up to $500; in lieu of any fines, court may order person placed in parent education and counseling program
COLORADO	22-33-104, *et seq.*	Between 7 and 16	Child ill or injured temporarily; child attends an independent or parochial school that provides a "basic academic education"; child absent due to a physical/mental/emotional disability; child is lawfully employed; child is in custody of court or law enforcement authority; child graduated 12th grade; child is instructed at home; child is suspended or expelled	Parents not subject to "Teacher Certification Act of 1975"; must provide 4 hours of instruction on average a day; must include reading, writing, speaking, math, history, civics, literature, science, and the Constitution; parents must give written notice every year and children shall be evaluated at grades 3, 5, 7, 9 and 11	Attendance officer designated for enforcement of compulsory education; board of education of each school district shall adopt policies and procedures for habitually truant child

Table 13: Compulsory Education—Continued

State	Code Section	Age Requirements	Exceptions	Home School Provisions	Penalties on Parents for Noncompliance
CONNECTICUT	10-184; 185	Between 7 and 16	Child receiving equivalent instruction elsewhere	Must include: reading, writing, spelling, English grammar, geography, arithmetic, U.S. history and citizenship; child must be receiving an equivalent instruction	Fine maximum $25 per day: each day is distinct offense; exception for parents of child destitute of clothing
DELAWARE	Tit. 14 §§2702, *et seq.*	Between 5 and 16	Private school attendance; mentally or physically handicapped; by parents' request with written documentation of physician or psychiatrist		1st offense: $5 minimum; subsequent offenses: fine of $25 to $50; default of payment: 1st offense: 2 days; subsequent: 5 days
DISTRICT OF COLUMBIA	31-401, *et seq.*	Between 5 and 18	Child obtained diploma; if 17 and lawfully employed, school hours may be flexible	Regular attendance in an independent school; private or parochial instruction	Misdemeanor; at least $100 fine or prison up to 5 days or both per offense or community service in the alternate; One offense is the equivalent of missing 2 full-day sessions or 4 half-day sessions in one month; failure to enroll child is also offense
FLORIDA	232.01, *et seq.*	Between 6 and 16	Enrolled in parochial school or home education program; child whose physical, mental, or emotional condition prevents successful participation; child 14 or over who is employed under child labor laws; certificate of exemption has been granted from a circuit judge; parent does not have access to childcare	Parent must either hold a valid Florida certificate or notify superintendent of schools, maintain a portfolio of records and materials, and evaluate education annually, including a national student achievement test or other method of evaluation	Non-enrollment: superintendent shall begin criminal prosecution; refusing to have child attend regularly is second degree misdemeanor

Table 13: Compulsory Education—Continued

State	Code Section	Age Requirements	Exceptions	Home School Provisions	Penalties on Parents for Noncompliance
GEORGIA	20-2-690.1	Between 7 and 16	Private school or home study	Must teach at least reading, language arts, math, social studies, and science; parents must give annual notice; parent must have at least a high school diploma or may employ a tutor with a baccalaureate college degree; subject to standardized testing; must provide annual progress assessment report	Misdemeanor; fine up to $100 and/or prison up to 30 days; each day's absence is separate offense
HAWAII	298-9	Between 6 and 18	Child is physically or mentally unable to attend; child is at least 15 and suitably employed and excused by school representative or judge; permission after investigation by the family court; child has graduated high school; child is enrolled in an appropriate alternative educational program		Petty misdemeanor
IDAHO	33-202, *et seq.*	Between 7 and 16	Child is otherwise comparably instructed; child's physical/ mental/emotional condition does not permit attendance	Comparably instructed	Proceedings brought under provisions of the Youth Rehabilitation Act
ILLINOIS	105 ILCS 5/ 26-1	Between 7 and 16	Child attending private or parochial school; child is physically/mentally unable to attend school; child is excused by county superintendent; child 12 to 14 attending confirmation classes; pregnant female with complications to pregnancy; child is necessarily and lawfully employed; excused for temporary cause by principal or teacher	*People v. Levisen*, 90 N.E.2d 213 (1950). Home instruction may constitute a private school.	Conviction is Class C misdemeanor subject to up to 30 days imprisonment and/or fine up to $500
INDIANA	20-8.1-3-17, *et seq.*	Between 7 and 16 if an exit interview requirement is met; otherwise 18	Child attends another school taught in the English language; child provided with instruction equivalent to public education or in nonaccredited, nonpublic school; child is physically/ mentally unfit for attendance	Notice to superintendent of school and must provide an "equivalent education" (*See Mazanec v. North Judson-San Pierre Sch. Corp.*, 614 F. Supp. 1152 (N.D.Ind. 1875), affirmed. 798 F. 2d 230 (7th Cir. 1986))	Class B misdemeanor

Table 13: Compulsory Education—Continued

State	Code Section	Age Requirements	Exceptions	Home School Provisions	Penalties on Parents for Noncompliance
IOWA	299.1, *et seq.;* 299A.1, *et seq.*	Between 6 and 16	Accredited nonpublic school, private college preparatory school or competent private instruction; completed requirements for graduation from accredited school or GED; sufficient reason by court of record or judge; while attending religious services or receiving religious instruction; physical/mental conditions do not permit attendance	Competent private instruction; minimum 148 days; annual achievement evaluation reported to school	School officers will use means available to school; if persists, referred to county attorney for mediation or prosecution; violations of agreement (mediation): 1st offense: up to 10 days jail or up to $100 fine or 40 hours of community service; 2nd offense: up to 20 days jail and/or up to $500 fine or community service; 3rd or more: up to 30 days jail and/or up to $1000 fine or community service
KANSAS	72-1111, *et seq.*	Between 7 and 16	Private, denominational, or parochial school taught by competent instructor; exceptional students may have different requirements	Home school held not to be equivalent of "private, denominational or parochial school," *State v. Lowry,* 191 K. 701-704; 383 P. 2d 962. Home school does not meet requirements of compulsory school attendance law. (See *State v. Garber,* 197 K. 567-569, 419 P.2d 896. and *In Re Sawyer,* 234 K.436, 439, 442, 672 P.2d 1093 (1983))	Secretary of Social & Rehabilitative Services investigates matter; determination made as to criminal prosecution or county attorney can make petition alleging child in need of care
KENTUCKY	159.010, *et seq.*	Between 6 and 16	Graduate from approved 4 year high school; enrolled in private, parochial, or church school; child less than 7 years old and in regular attendance in a private kindergarten-nursery school; physical/mental condition prevents it; enrolled in state supported school for exceptional children		1st offense: $100 fine; 2nd offense: $250 fine; subsequent: Class B misdemeanor

Table 13: Compulsory Education—Continued

State	Code Section	Age Requirements	Exceptions	Home School Provisions	Penalties on Parents for Noncompliance
LOUISIANA	17:221, *et seq.*	Between 7 and 17	Mentally/physically/emotionally incapacitated to perform school duties; children living outside boundaries of city, town, or municipality; children temporarily excused from school (personal or relative's illness, death, religion); withdrawal by student with written consent of parent, guardian, or tutor	Parent must apply to Board of Elementary and Secondary Education for approval of home study; must make renewal application each year; must sustain curriculum of quality at least equal to that offered by public schools; competency-based education exams may be administered by local school board upon parental request	Fine up to $15 for each offense; each day violated is separate offense
MAINE	Tit. 20-A §5001A	Between 7 and 17	Graduates early; 15 years old or finished 9th grade; permission from parent; approved by principal for suitable program of work and study; permission from school board and written agreement that parent and board will annually meet until 17th birthday to review educational needs; habitual truant; matriculated and attending post-secondary, degree-granting institution full-time; equivalent instruction from private school or other approved manner	"Equivalent instruction" approved by commissioner; local boards not required to play any role in application, review and approval, or oversight of program	Civil violation; district court may order injunctive relief or counseling
MARYLAND	Educ. 7-301	Between 5 and 16	Receiving other regular, thorough instruction in studies usually taught in public schools to children of same age group; mental/emotional/physical condition which makes his instruction detrimental to his progress or whose presence presents danger of serious physical harm to others	Receiving otherwise regular, thorough instruction in studies usually taught in public schools to children of same age group	Guilty of misdemeanor; first conviction: subject to fine up to $50 and/or up to 10 days jail; subsequent conviction: fine of $100 and/or up to 30 days jail
MASSACHUSETTS	76 §1, *et seq.*	Established by Board of Education; pending such establishment :7 & 16 (St. 1965, c. 741); 7 minimum (*Alvord v. Chester*, 180 Mass. 20, 61 N.E. 263 (1901));	14 to 16 years old, completed 6th grade, holds permit for employment in domestic service or farm, and is regularly employed there 6 hours per day minimum; 14 to 16 years old, meets requirements and has written permission of superintendent to engage in non-wage earning employment at home; physical/mental condition does not permit	Approval falls to superintendent or school committee; may review curriculum, method of evaluation, nature of textbooks and other factors (*Care & Protection of Charles*, 504 N.E. 2d 592 (1987))	Up to $20 fine for any absence over 7 days (or 14½ days) in a period of 6 months

Table 13: Compulsory Education—Continued

State	Code Section	Age Requirements	Exceptions	Home School Provisions	Penalties on Parents for Noncompliance
MICHIGAN	MCL 380.1561	Between 6 and 16	Enrolled in approved non-public school which teaches subjects comparable to those in public schools to children of same age; child regularly employed as page or messenger in either house of the legislature; under 9 years old and doesn't reside within 2.5 miles of nearest traveled road of public school and transportation not provided; age 12 to 14 while in attendance of confirmation classes not to exceed 5 months	To be valid, school must meet requirements of private and parochial schools act; parents entitled to administrative hearing to this matter (*People v. Bennett,* 501 N.W. 2d 106 (1993))	Warrant issued, hearing and determination made; misdemeanor: fine of $5 to $50 and/or 2 to 90 days jail
MINNESOTA	120.101, *et seq.;* 127.2	Between 7 and 16	"Good cause" determined by school board including: physical/ mental condition prevents it; complete graduation requirements	Writing, reading, literature and fine arts, math, science, social studies including history, geography, and government, and health and physical education; instruction, textbooks, and materials must be in English; teacher must hold B.A. degree, pass competency exam, be supervised by person with teaching license or have teaching license; child must be assessed each year with standardized achievement test; superintendent can make on-site visits to evaluate	Misdemeanor
MISSISSIPPI	37-13-91	Between 6 and 17	Child is physically/mentally/ emotionally incapable of attendance; child enrolled in special or remedial type education; educated in legitimate home instruction program	Parent must file a "certificate of enrollment" and education must be a "legitimate home instruction program."	Guilty of "contributing to the neglect of a child" and punished according to §97-5-39: misdemeanor with fine up to $1000 and/or up to 1 year in jail

Table 13: Compulsory Education—Continued

State	Code Section	Age Requirements	Exceptions	Home School Provisions	Penalties on Parents for Noncompliance
MISSOURI	167.031, *et seq.*	Between 7 and 16	Determined mentally/physically incapable of attendance; child is 14 to 16 and legally and desirably employed	Primary purpose is provision of private or religious-based instruction; no more than 4 pupils may be unrelated by consanguinity to the 3rd degree; no tuition charged; parents must keep written records, samples of child's work, evaluation of progress; minimum hours of instruction in reading, language arts, math, social studies, science	Class C misdemeanor; upon conviction each successive school day is separate violation
MONTANA	20-5-102, *et seq.*	Between 7 and the later of attaining 16 or finishing 8th grade	Enrolled in another district or state; supervised correspondence or home study; excused by district judge or board of trustees; enrolled in nonpublic or home school	Give notice to county superintendent; maintain records; give 180 days of instruction; building complies with health and safety regulations; provide organized course of study in subjects required by public schools	Fine of $5 to $20; if parent refuses to pay he shall be imprisoned in county jail 10 to 30 days
NEBRASKA	79-201, *et seq.*; 43-2007	Between 7 and 16	Child has graduated high school; child 14 is employed and has completed 8th grade and earnings are necessary for his support or dependents; child is physically/mentally incapacitated; illness or severe weather conditions make attendance impossible	Home school valid if complies with §§79-1701 through 79-1707; subject to and governed by the provisions of the general school laws of the state so far as the same apply to grades, qualifications, and certification of teachers and promotion of pupils; adequate supplies and equipment, course of study substantially same as given in the public schools where children would have attended	Attendance officer gives warning and subsequently files a complaint with judge in county court; another violation and no notice is given parent and complaint may be filed immediately; Class III misdemeanor

Table 13: Compulsory Education—Continued

State	Code Section	Age Requirements	Exceptions	Home School Provisions	Penalties on Parents for Noncompliance
NEVADA	392.040, *et seq.*	Between 7 and 17	Private school; physical/mental condition preventing attendance; completion of 12 grades; receiving equivalent, approved instruction; residence too far from nearest school; with written evidence, child over 14 must work for his or parents' support or with board's authority	Equivalent instruction of the kind and amount approved by the state board of education	Misdemeanor
NEW HAMPSHIRE	193.1, *et seq.*, 193-A, *et seq.*	Between 6 and 16	If in the best welfare of the child; approved private school; physical/mental condition prevents or makes attendance undesirable; receiving home education	Planned and supervised instructional and related educational activities including curriculum and instruction in science, math, language, government, history, health, reading, writing and spelling, history of U.S. and New Hampshire constitution and exposure to and appreciation of art and music; notification and evaluation required	Guilty of violation and fines levied
NEW JERSEY	18A:38-25, *et seq.*	Between 6 and 16	Mental condition such that student cannot benefit; physical condition prevents attendance; day school where instruction is equivalent to that provided in public schools for children of similar grades and attainments	Academically equivalent instruction other than at school (*State v. Massa,* 231 A.2d 252 (1967))	Convicted as disorderly persons; 1st offense: up to $25 fine; subsequent: up to $100 fine
NEW MEXICO	22-12-1, *et seq.*	5 years to age of majority	Private school, home school, or state institution; graduated from high school; 16 years old and employed in gainful trade or occupation or engaged in alternative form of education sufficient for the person's educational needs and the parent/guardian consents; consent of parent/guardian if resident and under 8 years old; unable to benefit because of learning disabilities, mental/physical/emotional condition	Means of meeting requirement of compulsory education	1st offense: petty misdemeanor, $25 to $100 fine or community service; 2nd and subsequent: petty misdemeanor, up to $500 fine or up to 6 months jail

Table 13: Compulsory Education—Continued

State	Code Section	Age Requirements	Exceptions	Home School Provisions	Penalties on Parents for Noncompliance
NEW YORK	Educ. §§3201, *et seq.*	Between 6 and 16	Non-public or home instruction; mental/physical condition endangers him or others; completed 4 year high school program; full-time employment certificate; may also be allowed to attend part-time with employment	Must be evaluated by school superintendent to determine if education is substantially equivalent to that provided in local public schools; parent does not have to be certified to be considered competent (*In Re Blackwelder,* 139 Misc. 2d 776, 528 N.Y.S.2d 759 (1988); *In Re Franz,* 55 A.D.2d 424, 390 N.Y.S.2d 940 (1977))	1st offense: fine not exceeding $10 or 10 days jail; subsequent offense: up to $50 and/or 30 days jail
NORTH CAROLINA	115C-378	Between 7 and 16	Approved by state board of education (mental or physical inability to attend, immediate demands of the farm or home, etc.)	Maintain such minimum curriculum standards as are required of public schools; must be recognized by Office of Non-Public Schools and meet requirements of Article 39 of Chapter 115C (115C-547, *et seq.* standardized testing, high school competency, health and safety standards notice)	Class 3 misdemeanor
NORTH DAKOTA	15-34.1-01, *et seq.*	Between 7 and 16	Enrolled in approved private/ parochial school; has completed high school; child needed to support family; child has handicap rendering participation impracticable; child receiving home-based instruction	Home instructors must be certified to teach in N.D., have a B.A., or scored appropriately on national teacher exam given in N.D.; must include certain subjects; at least 4 hours per day, 175 days per year; records kept; notice given; standardized achievement test given	

Table 13: Compulsory Education—Continued

State	Code Section	Age Requirements	Exceptions	Home School Provisions	Penalties on Parents for Noncompliance
OHIO	3321.01, *et seq.*	Between 6 and 18	Child received high school diploma; lawfully employed (if over 14 for necessary work); physical/mental condition does not permit attendance; child being instructed at home	Instructed by person qualified to teach in required branches; approval necessary by district superintendent; if challenged, a religious-based exemption must pass 3-pronged test: (1) Are religious beliefs sincere? (2) Will application of compulsory education law infringe on right to free exercise of religion? (3) Does the state have an overriding interest? *Wisconsin v. Yoder,* 406 U.S. 205 (1972) (adopted in Ohio in *State v. Whisner* 470 S.2d 181 (1976))	File complaint; required to give $100 bond conditioned that child will attend school; violation: $5 to $20 fine; upon refusal to pay fine, imprisonment 10 to 30 days
OKLAHOMA	Tit. 70 §10-105;§1744	Between 5 and 18; deaf children between 7 and 21	Mental/physical disability prevents attendance; child is 16 and has permission of school and parents; emergency	Instruction must be in good faith and equivalent to that given by the state; Op. Atty. Gen. 73-129 (Feb. 13, 1973)	Misdemeanor; 1st offense: $5 to $25; 2nd offense: $10 to $50; subsequent: $25 to $100
OREGON	339.005, *et seq.*	Between 7 and 18	Child has completed 12th grade; attending private school; proof of equivalent knowledge of subjects through 12th grade; children taught by parent or private teacher; over 16 and lawfully employed	Give notice to superintendent and notice must be acknowledged by him; annual examination given and results submitted to superintendent; if insufficient score, student may be ordered to attend public school	Written notice to parent given; upon noncompliance, district superintendent notified

Table 13: Compulsory Education—Continued

State	Code Section	Age Requirements	Exceptions	Home School Provisions	Penalties on Parents for Noncompliance
PENNSYLVANIA	Tit. 24 §§13-1326, *et seq.*	Between 8 and 17	Graduated high school; 15 and with approval, child may enroll in private trade school; enrolled in home education program pursuant to Tit. 24 §13-1327.1 or private school; physical/mental defects rendering education impracticable; 16 and lawfully employed; 15 and engaged in farming or domestic service or 14 if engaged in same having achieved highest elementary grade; resides over 2 miles from nearest public highway, school or free public transportation is not furnished	File annual notice with a notarized affidavit of various information including proposed education objectives and immunization record; evaluation by teacher or administrator; minimum course requirements at each educational level; portfolio of records and materials	$2 for first offense and up to $5 for each subsequent offense together with costs and upon default of payment subjected to county jail up to 5 days
RHODE ISLAND	16-19-1, *et seq.*	Between 6 and 16	Child attends private school or is home-instructed by approval of school committee; physical/mental condition of child renders attendance impracticable	Period of attendance is same as public schools; register kept and reading, writing, geography, arithmetic, history of Rhode Island and U.S., and principles of American government are taught	$50 for each absent day and if days exceed 30 during a school year parent shall be imprisoned up to 6 months and/or fined up to $500
SOUTH CAROLINA	59-65-10, *et seq.*	Between 5 and 17	Enrolled in private, parochial, or other approved program; child graduated; physical/mental disability; 8th grade completed and gainfully and lawfully employed; disruptive to educational program and enters into gainful employment until 17	Instruction given under auspices of South Carolina Association of Independent Home Schools and its requirements exempts home school from further requirements; otherwise, instruction must be approved; parent has at least a high school diploma or GED; include 180 days of instruction per year; curriculum includes reading, writing, math, science, social studies; composition and literature (in grades 7–12)	$50 fine or prison up to 30 days; each absence is separate offense; court may suspend any conviction in its discretion

Table 13: Compulsory Education—Continued

State	Code Section	Age Requirements	Exceptions	Home School Provisions	Penalties on Parents for Noncompliance
SOUTH DAKOTA	13-27-1, *et seq.*	Between 6 and 16	Child achieved 8th grade and fits into a religious exemption; competent instruction received from another source; illness in the family	Parent need not be certified but Department of Education may ensure instruction is being provided and inspect records; may not instruct over 22 children; must take national standardized test provided by school district; must be for equivalent period of time as public school; must include basic skills of language arts and math	Class 2 misdemeanor; each subsequent offense is Class 1 misdemeanor
TENNESSEE	49-6-3001, *et seq.*	Between 7 and 17 inclusive	Child has graduated high school or has GED; physical/mental incapacity; mentally or physically incapacitated to perform school duties; child is 17 and conduct is detrimental to good order and benefit of other children; home school or nonpublic school instruction	Approved by local education agency; teacher/parent must have at least GED for teaching K-8, baccalaureate degree for 9-12; give notice; maintain records; at least 4 hours per day; standardized tests taken; parents associated with church-related school organizations exempt from requirements	After written notice to parents, superintendent turns over to juvenile judge who may, in his discretion, fine parent/guardian up to $50 and/or 5 hours community service
TEXAS	Educ. §25.085, *et seq.*	Between 6 and 17	Child is 16, and in a course of instruction as recommended by a public agency with custody of child; child is 17 and has a high school certificate; enrolled in private or parochial school which includes a course in good citizenship; handicapped child or child with mental condition making attendance infeasible; child enrolled in Texas Academy of Leadership in Humanities or Texas Academy of Math and Sciences; is expelled	Allowed	Warn parent in writing; on noncompliance, file complaint against parents for offense of Class C misdemeanor; each day constitutes separate offense

Table 13: Compulsory Education—Continued

State	Code Section	Age Requirements	Exceptions	Home School Provisions	Penalties on Parents for Noncompliance
UTAH	53A-11-101, *et seq.*	Between 6 and 18	Child 16 may be partially released if completed 8th grade; completed work for graduation; home-schooled; physical/mental condition making attendance impracticable; employment provides proper influences and adequate educational opportunities; child is 16 and determined unable to profit from school because of inability or negative attitude toward discipline	Subjects proscribed by state board of education; same length of time required as in district's schools	Misdemeanor; report to appropriate juvenile court
VERMONT	Tit. 16 §§1121, *et seq.;* Tit. 16, §166b	Between 7 and 16	Child physically/mentally unable to attend; child has completed 10th grade; child is excused by superintendent	Written notice must be given; enrollment reports; progress assessments through standardized tests or licensed teacher	Truant officer gives notice and upon noncompliance without a legal excuse fine of up to $1000; also complaint entered to town grand juror
VIRGINIA	22.1-254, *et seq.*	Between 5 and 18	Enrolled in private, parochial, or home instruction or taught by qualified tutor; children suffering infectious diseases; children under 10 living over 2.5 miles from school unless transportation provided within 1 mile; children 10 to 17 living over 2.5 miles from school unless transportation within 1.5 miles; achieved high school diploma; upon recommendation of court; expulsion or other offense	Parent must hold baccalaureate degree or be certified teacher or use approved correspondence course or other approved program including standards of board of education for language arts and mathematics; parent must give notice; approved achievement tests or evaluation required	Class 4 misdemeanor
WASHINGTON	28A.225.010	Between 8 and 18	Enrolled in private school; home-based instruction; physically/mentally incapable of attending; child is 15 or older and legally employed or proficient through 9th grade or has met graduation requirements or has received certificate of educational competence	Instruction in occupational education, science, math, language, social studies, history, health, writing, reading, spelling, and appreciation for art and music; must be supervised by certified person or by a parent with 45 college level credit hours	$25 for each day of unexcused absence and/or community service; attendance officer may, through school district's attorney, petition juvenile court to assume jurisdiction

Table 13: Compulsory Education—Continued

State	Code Section	Age Requirements	Exceptions	Home School Provisions	Penalties on Parents for Noncompliance
WEST VIRGINIA	18-8-1	Between 6 and 16	Enrolled in private, parochial, or other approved school; instruction in home; physical/mental incapacity; residence over 2 miles from school or school bus route; conditions rendering attendance impossible or hazardous; child has graduated; work permit granted for students who have completed 8th grade; serious illness or death in family; destitution in the home	Notice given; records kept; if child's education is suffering or for another compelling reason, superintendent may seek court order denying home instruction; instructor must have graduated high school or had formal education 4 hours higher than the most advanced student; child must take standardized test	First offense: $50 to $100 and cost of prosecution; subsequent offense: $50–100 fine plus 5 to 20 days jail; each absent day is separate offense
WISCONSIN	118.15, *et seq.*	Between 6 and 18	Child has graduated; physical/mental condition renders incapable; child is home-schooled or attends private school; at 16 child may attend technical school leading to high school graduation	Must meet requirements for a private school such as at least 875 hours of instruction each year; instruction in reading, language arts, math, social studies, science, and health; performance monitored on regular basis	Fine up to $500 and/or prison up to 30 days; if child's disobedience can be shown, action shall be dismissed
WYOMING	21-4-101, *et seq.*	Between 7 and 16 (or completion of 8th grade)	Board believes attendance detrimental to mental/physical health of child or other children; attendance would be undue hardship; home-schooled or private school; student is suspended or expelled	Meets requirements of basic academic educational program including reading, writing, math, civics, history, literature, and science; parent must submit curriculum to local board	Misdemeanor: at least $5 to $25 fine and/or prison up to 10 days

14. CORPORAL PUNISHMENT IN PUBLIC SCHOOLS

In 1977, the U.S. Supreme Court ruled in *Ingraham* v. *Wright,* that schools may use corporal punishment despite parental objection. Prior to that ruling, there were few, if any, state statutes regulating the use of physical means of discipline in schools. After the decision, states began to address the issue. At present, twenty-five states have statutes covering corporal punishment.

The following chart covers only state statutes regarding corporal punishment. It should be noted that there are also local rules that authorize the use of corporal punishment or that require parental consent before corporal punishment can be imposed upon a child. Local school districts, and even individual schools, often have their own policies and procedures for handling disciplinary problems.

This issue has become very controversial lately. With heightened public awareness of child abuse and increased sensitivity to the emotional well-being of children, many schools and teachers, unfortunately, are loath to impose any discipline whatsoever upon students for fear of emotionally scarring them or being accused of child abuse themselves.

Table 14: Corporal Punishment In Public Schools

State	Code Section	Punishment Allowed	Circumstances Allowable
ALABAMA	16-1-24.1	Local school boards to adopt code for conduct and discipline of students.	
ALASKA	11.81.430		When use of force is consistent with the welfare of the students and if authorized by school regulations adopted by the school board
ARIZONA	15-843	Procedures for disciplining pupils, including the use of corporal punishment, are decided and allowed by governing board; use of corporal punishment is to be consistent with state board of education guidelines.	
ARKANSAS	6-18-505	Use of corporal punishment only in specifically authorized school district and administered in accord with district's written student discipline policy.	"In order to maintain discipline and order within public schools."
CALIFORNIA	Educ. §§49000, 49001	Corporal punishment prohibited.	
COLORADO	No statutory provisions		
CONNECTICUT	No statutory provisions		
DELAWARE	Tit. 14, §701	Teachers may exercise same authority as parents, including the administration of corporal punishment where deemed necessary in accordance with district board of education policy.	
DISTRICT OF COLUMBIA	No statutory provisions		
FLORIDA	232.27	Corporal punishment allowed, subject to prescribed procedures.	Must have approval in principle by the principal before it is used; presence of another informed adult; and that an explanation is provided to parents.
GEORGIA	20-2-730, 732	Corporal punishment allowed, subject to various restrictions.	It may not be excessive or unduly severe or be used as a first line of punishment; it must be administered in the presence of a school official; a written explanation must be provided on request; and it may not be administered if a physician certifies that the child's mental or emotional stability could be affected.

Table 14: Corporal Punishment In Public Schools—Continued

State	Code Section	Punishment Allowed	Circumstances Allowable
HAWAII	298-16	Physical punishment may not be used, but a teacher may use reasonable force to restrain a student in attendance from hurting himself or any other person or property with other teacher present and out of other students' presence.	
IDAHO	No statutory provisions		
ILLINOIS	No statutory provisions		
INDIANA	20-8.1-5.1-3	Teachers can take disciplinary action necessary to promote orderly student conduct.	
IOWA	280.21	Infliction of corporal punishment not allowed. Physical contact not considered corporal punishment if "reasonable and necessary under the circumstances."	
KANSAS	No statutory provisions		
KENTUCKY	161.180	Hold pupils to a "strict account for their conduct on school premises."	
LOUISIANA	17:223, 17:416.1	Each city school board shall have discretion in the use of corporal punishment; corporal punishment allowed in a reasonable manner; corporal punishment discretionary, but rules to implement and control any form of corporal punishment to be adopted by each city school board or parish.	"Good cause."
MAINE	No statutory provisions		
MARYLAND	Educ. 7-305	Corporal punishment may not be administered to discipline student.	Disciplinary measures deemed appropriate to maintain "atmosphere of order" may be permitted by county school boards
MASSACHUSETTS	Ch. 71 §37G	Prohibits corporal punishment, but any member of school committee, teacher, or agent of school may use reasonable force to protect themselves, pupils, or other persons from an assault by a pupil.	
MICHIGAN	380.1312	Corporal punishment or threats of corporal punishment not to be inflicted "under any circumstances"; reasonable physical force may be used in self-defense or in defense of others, to obtain possession of weapon or other dangerous object or to protect property or to restrain or to remove noncomplying child from interfering with order of school.	
MINNESOTA	127.45	Corporal punishment prohibited.	
MISSISSIPPI	15.41312	Corporal punishment prohibited.	Reasonable physical force as necessary to maintain order.

Table 14: Corporal Punishment In Public Schools—Continued

State	Code Section	Punishment Allowed	Circumstances Allowable
MISSOURI	160.261	"Spanking" approved and not considered child abuse when administered in reasonable manner and in accordance with written policy of discipline approved by board; where unreasonableness is alleged, initial investigation to be by school and not division of family services.	
MONTANA	20-4-302	No school district employee may inflict corporal punishment on a pupil.	Physical pain resulting from a physical restraint which is reasonable and necessary is not corporal punishment (to quell a disturbance, provide self-protection, protect others from physical injury, obtain possession of a weapon, protect property from serious harm, maintain orderly conduct.
NEBRASKA	79-4, 140	Corporal punishment prohibited.	
NEVADA	392.465	Corporal punishment prohibited.	Reasonable and necessary force for: quell disturbance; obtain possession of weapon; self-defense; to escort disruptive student.
NEW HAMPSHIRE	627.6 (11)		Teachers justified in using necessary force to maintain discipline.
NEW JERSEY	18A:6-1	Corporal punishment prohibited.	Reasonable force may be used to quell a disturbance, obtain possession of weapons, etc., for self-defense or for protection of person or property and not considered corporal punishment.
NEW MEXICO	22-5-4.3	Each school district creates rules of conduct which may include corporal punishment.	
NEW YORK	No statutory provisions		
NORTH CAROLINA	115C-288; 115C-390, 391	Principals, teachers, and others may use reasonable force in the exercise of lawful authority to restrain or correct pupils and maintain order; local boards may not prohibit use of such force but are to adopt policies governing administration of corporal punishment, including at a minimum: notice to students and parents; teacher and no other students present.	

Table 14: Corporal Punishment In Public Schools—Continued

State	Code Section	Punishment Allowed	Circumstances Allowable
NORTH DAKOTA	12.1-05-05	Use of force in disciplining students permitted provided it does not create substantial risk of death, serious bodily injury, disfigurement, or gross degradation.	
OHIO	3319.41	Corporal punishment prohibited.	Board may not prohibit use of reasonable force to quell a disturbance, threatening physical injury; gain possession of weapon; or protect property.
OKLAHOMA	Tit. 70, §6-114	Boards to adopt policy for the control and discipline of students.	
OREGON	339.250	Infliction of corporal punishment is not authorized.	
PENNSYLVANIA	No statutory provisions		
RHODE ISLAND	No statutory provisions		
SOUTH CAROLINA	59-63-260	Boards may provide corporal punishment for any pupil that it deems just and proper.	
SOUTH DAKOTA	13-32-2	Use of physical force that is reasonable and necessary for supervisory control over students.	
TENNESSEE	49-6-4103; 4104	Corporal punishment allowed if imposed in reasonable manner; local board of education shall adopt rules and regulations to implement and control corporal punishment in its schools.	"Good cause"; in order to maintain discipline and order.
TEXAS	No statutory provisions		
UTAH	53A-11-802	Corporal punishment prohibited.	Use of reasonable and necessary physical restraint or force for self-defense or other appropriate circumstances listed in statute.
VERMONT	Tit. 16, §1161a	Corporal punishment prohibited, but reasonable and necessary force may be used to quell a disturbance, obtain possession of weapon, in self-defense, or protection of persons or property.	
VIRGINIA	22.1-279.1	Corporal punishment prohibited, but "incidental, minor or reasonable physical contact or other actions" permitted to maintain order and control; reasonable and necessary force permitted to quell a disturbance or remove a child to prevent harm, in self-defense, to obtain possession of weapon, etc.	
WASHINGTON	28A-150-300	Use of corporal punishment is prohibited.	
WEST VIRGINIA	18A-5-1 (d)	Corporal punishment is prohibited.	

Table 14: Corporal Punishment In Public Schools—Continued

State	Code Section	Punishment Allowed	Circumstances Allowable
WISCONSIN	118.31	Corporal punishment generally prohibited; reasonable and necessary force allowed in self-defense, to protect others, etc., and as proscribed by school board policy.	
WYOMING	21-4-308	Boards may adopt rules for reasonable forms of punishment and disciplinary measures that teachers are authorized to impose.	

15. PRAYER IN PUBLIC SCHOOLS

Although the United States Supreme Court ruled prayer in public schools unconstitutional in 1962, many individual states have not taken action to conform with the Court's edict. Until the early 1960s, there were no laws on the subject of prayer in schools. After the Supreme Court struck down the practice—without reference to any legal precedent or established legal theory—many states responded by drafting laws *authorizing* prayers and moments of silence designed to avoid the Supreme Court's definition of impermissible activity. Twenty-nine states have enacted such laws. For example, Delaware authorizes a brief period of silence up to two minutes of silence "to be used according to the dictates of the individual conscience of each student"; other states' statutes authorize "brief times" or one, two, or five minutes of "silent prayer," "silent reflection," or "silent meditation."

The law in this area, though settled, is still controversial. There are strong efforts afoot to reintroduce prayer in public schools, particularly by individuals who maintain that the current crisis in public education (low test scores, violence in the classrooms, drug and alcohol abuse) began when prayer was made illegal, and, conversely, strong efforts to fight the reintroduction, particularly by proponents of the theory of the separation of church and state.

The prevailing theme in the proposals to reintroduce prayer in public schools is one of voluntariness. Such efforts, however, are doomed as long as peer pressure in the classroom is equated with state action; that is, as states cannot encourage a particular religious practice, peer pressure exerted upon nonparticipants in a "voluntary" program is considered coercive.

Table 15: Prayer In Public Schools

State	Code Section	Provisions
ALABAMA	16-1-20.1 & 16-1-20.3.	Period of silence not to exceed one minute in duration, shall be observed for meditation or voluntary prayer, and during any such period no other activities shall be engaged in; student-initiated voluntary prayer permitted
ALASKA	No statutory provisions	
ARIZONA	No statutory provisions	
ARKANSAS	No statutory provisions	
CALIFORNIA	No statutory provisions	
COLORADO	No statutory provisions	
CONNECTICUT	10-16a	Silent meditation
DELAWARE	Tit. 14 §4101	A brief period of silence not to exceed two minutes to be used according to dictates of individual student's conscience. First Amendment read to students on first day.
DISTRICT OF COLUMBIA	No statutory provisions	
FLORIDA	233.062	Brief period not to exceed two minutes, for the purpose of silent prayer or meditation
GEORGIA	20-2-1050	Brief period of quiet reflection for up to 60 seconds
HAWAII	No statutory provisions	
IDAHO	No statutory provisions	
ILLINOIS	105 ILCS 20/1	Brief period of silence which shall not be conducted as a religious exercise but shall be an opportunity for silent prayer or for silent reflection
INDIANA	20-10.1-7-11	Brief period of silent prayer or meditation
IOWA	No statutory provisions	
KANSAS	72-5308a	Brief period of silence to be used as opportunity for silent prayer or for silent reflection
KENTUCKY	158.175	Recitation of Lord's prayer to teach our country's history and as an affirmation of the freedom of religion in this country, if authorized by local school district; pupil's participation is voluntary
LOUISIANA	17:2115(A)	Brief time of silent meditation or prayer
MAINE	Tit. 20-A, §4805	Period of silence shall be observed for reflection or meditation
MARYLAND	Educ. §7-104	Meditate silently for approximately one minute; student or teacher may read the holy scriptures or pray
MASSACHUSETTS	Ch. 71 §1A & 1B	Period of silence not to exceed one minute in duration shall be observed for personal thoughts; voiluntary prayer with approval of child's parents
MICHIGAN	§380.1565	Opportunity to observe time in silent meditation
MINNESOTA	No statutory provisions	
MISSISSIPPI	37-13-4.1	Student-initiated voluntary prayer permitted on school property
MISSOURI	No statutory provisions	

Table 15: Prayer In Public Schools—Continued

State	Code Section	Provisions
MONTANA	20-7-112	Any teacher, principal, or superintendent may open the school day with a prayer
NEBRASKA	No statutory provisions	
NEVADA	388075	Silent period for voluntary individual meditation, prayer, or reflection
NEW HAMPSHIRE	189:1-b	Period of not more than five minutes shall be available to those who wish to exercise their right to freedom of assembly and participate voluntarily in the free exercise of religion; no teacher supervision
NEW JERSEY	18A:36-4	Observe a one minute period of silence to be used solely at the discretion of the individual student for quiet and private contemplation or introspection
NEW MEXICO	No statutory provisions	
NEW YORK	Educ. §3029-a	Brief period of silent meditation which may be opportunity for silent meditation on a religious theme or silent reflection
NORTH CAROLINA	No statutory provisions	
NORTH DAKOTA	15-47-30.1	Period of silence not to exceed one minute for meditation or prayer
OHIO	3313.601	Reasonable periods of time for programs or meditation upon a moral, philosophical, or patriotic theme
OKLAHOMA	11-101.1	Shall permit those students and teachers who wish to do so to participate in voluntary prayer
OREGON	No statutory provisions	
PENNSYLVANIA	Tit. 24 §15-1516.1	Brief period of silent prayer or meditation which is not a religious exercise but an opportunity for prayer or reflection as child is disposed
RHODE ISLAND	16-12-3.1	Period of silence not to exceed one minute in duration shall be observed for meditation and silence maintained
SOUTH CAROLINA	No statutory provisions	
SOUTH DAKOTA	No statutory provisions	
TENNESSEE	49-6-1004	Mandatory period of silence of approximately one minute; voluntary student participation in or initiation of prayer permitted
TEXAS	Educ. 25.401	Student has absolute right to individually, voluntarily, and silently pray or meditate in a nondisruptive manner
UTAH	No statutory provisions	
VERMONT	No statutory provisions	
VIRGINIA	22.1-203 & .1	School may establish the daily observance of one minute of silence; students may engage in voluntary student-initiated prayer
WASHINGTON	No statutory provisions	
WEST VIRGINIA	Const. Art. III, §15A	Designated brief time for students to exercise their right to personal and private contemplation, meditation, or prayer

Table 15: Prayer In Public Schools—Continued

State	Code Section	Provisions
WISCONSIN	No statutory provisions	
WYOMING	No statutory provisions	

16. PRIVACY OF SCHOOL RECORDS

The question of the right of privacy and, specifically, who should have access to student records has divided parents and students from school teachers and administrators. There are strong arguments on both sides. School teachers and administrators believe, traditionally, that they should be able to deal with the children they teach in utter confidence—especially when it comes to evaluation of ability, behavior, and psychological factors. School administrators may have critical opinions and evaluations to make and pass on to colleagues in order to effectively deal with a particular student's potential for success or failure in school. Release of these opinions to the family or the student may actually have a detrimental effect on the student and/or the teacher or the school's ability to help the student.

On the other hand, students and parents have a deep interest in knowing how they or their child is evaluated—to know what school administrators are saying about the child and what impact those opinions are having on his or her progress in school. Parents may worry that negative evaluations or assessments may be off-base, inaccurate, or the result of an objective evaluation that misses personal situations and emotions. In addition, negative evaluations may be the result of physical or psychological handicaps or deficiencies in ability that need special attention and may be helped if parents or students are made aware of them. Parents have a responsibility for the quality of education that their children receive as well as a right to participate in decisions that affect class placement and particular courses and subjects taught.

This dynamic between the parents' right to have input into their child's education and the school's responsibility to professionally teach and discipline their students is what has driven the development of certain privacy rules. There is also a new dynamic that is becoming a factor in education and, specifically, access to records: over the last thirty years, the growing disillusionment with our traditional education system, which insisted on certain standards of performance for all students, has given way to the belief that each child has different learning curves

and behavioral norms that need to be respected. As a result, standards of education and behavior are no longer standard and regular but adjust to the needs, wants, and potential of each student and his or her family. In order to monitor the attention that individual children are getting, laws have guaranteed parents access to student records.

Another area concerning school records that is becoming an issue encompasses child abuse, neglect, and personal health. With today's broader definition of abuse, a family's religious convictions or practices, cultural heritage, social orientation, or lack of awareness may qualify. In an extreme example, state authorities took custody of minor children because their parents failed to keep their children's dental appointments! There may be a need for parents to monitor school records in order to see that educators are not misinterpreting and misconstruing various family customs, practices, and behavior or undermining certain training being done at home.

FERPA

The Family Educational Records Protection Act (FERPA) was originally passed in 1976 and has been amended many times since. Its purpose is to guarantee parents free access to student school records. Under provisions of the Act, the Secretary of Education has the authority to withhold all federal funding to institutions that do not make school records available to a student's parents. There are exceptions to this rule, such as authorizing the transfer of transcripts when a student changes schools or applies for admission elsewhere, for researchers doing studies of educational techniques and practices when such research can be conducted confidentially and anonymously, for state or federal officials conducting audits of public assistance programs, or in the course of normal business. Many states now rely on FERPA to protect student privacy and insure parental access. A few states have gone beyond the protections of the federal act.

Table 16: Privacy of School Records

State	Code Section	Who Has Access	Penalties
FEDERAL	20 U.S.C. §1232g Family Educational Records Protection Act	Parents, specifically authorized state or federal officials for purposes of auditing public assistance programs; when student reaches 18 years old, right belongs to student only; researchers for purposes of gathering data to improve educational testing or educational curriculum (provided privacy is protected), authorized school administrators or other educational institutions as authorized by student or parents for purposes of application for admission to an educational institution or for employment.	Withdrawal of all federal funding
ALABAMA	36-12-40	Parent of minor child may inspect regulation and circulation records of any school that pertain to his child.	
ALASKA	25.20.130	Both custodial and non-custodial parent	
ARIZONA	15-141 & 15-142	Governed by FERPA; if school district permits release of directory information, it must provide it also for recruiting representatives of militia. Department of Juvenile Corrections has access to any pupil referred.	Injunctive or special relief by Superior Court
ARKANSAS	6-20-510	Records regarding handicapped students or foster children are to be kept confidential by respective school districts and Department of Education.	
CALIFORNIA	Educ. §§49060, *et seq.*	Implements FERPA and eliminates conflicts with it.	
COLORADO	22-2-111; 24-72-204	Unless contrary to federal, state or judicial law, law enforcement officers have access without parental consent. Student records are confidential except when requested by the governor or a committee of the general assembly.	
CONNECTICUT	10-154a	Parents generally assured access. Communication relating to alcohol or drugs between the nurse and student need not be disclosed to parent.	
DELAWARE	Tit. 14 §4111	Confidential with stated exceptions: duly authorized government agency; authorized school personnel by request of pupil aged 14 or older; parent/guardian.	Unless malice can be proven, no cause of action for participation in formulation or disclosure of records
DISTRICT OF COLUMBIA	No known provisions		
FLORIDA	228-093, *et seq.*	FERPA mostly implemented. Parents and pupils have access; after pupil is 18 or attending post-secondary educational institution, the right belongs to the student only.	Injunctive relief and attorney's fees available
GEORGIA	20-2-720	Both parents (includes noncustodial parent unless court order removed right or terminated parental rights)	

Table 16: Privacy of School Records—Continued

State	Code Section	Who Has Access	Penalties
HAWAII	298-19, 298-13.5	§298-19 provides for the keeping of records but mentions nothing about access; authorized police officers have access to attendance records or student.	
IDAHO	32-717A	Custodial and non-custodial parent	
ILLINOIS	105 ILCS 10/1, *et seq.*	Inspection allowed by students and parents but restricted to third parties. Exceptions listed in 105 ILCS 10/6 (9). Information communicated in confidence by a student or parents to school personnel is not available. All rights and privileges become student's exclusively at age 18.	Damages and other remedies available
INDIANA	20-10.1-22.4-1 & 2	Custodial and noncustodial parent, unless court order limiting noncustodial parent	
IOWA	22.7	Student's personal information in records is confidential.	
KANSAS	72-6214	Governed by FERPA.	
KENTUCKY	164.283; KY Rules of Evid. R. 506	Parents of any student under age 21. Counselor-student communications are privileged. All student academic records are confidential with exemptions cited in 164.283 (3)-(19).	
LOUISIANA	L.S.A R.S. 9-351	Custodial and non-custodial parent has right to inspect child's records.	
MAINE	Tit. 20-1 §6001	Governed by FERPA.	
MARYLAND	Educ. 7-410; State Gov't. 10-616 (k)	Teacher's, principal's, or counselor's observations during consultations are not admissible as evidence against student. Only "persons in interest" or "an elected or appointed official who supervises the student" may inspect student's records.	
MASSACHUSETTS	Ch. 71 §34A, G	Student (transcript), parent, guardian, student over 18 may inspect.	
MICHIGAN	600.2165	In legal proceedings, counselors, teachers, and school employees may not disclose information or records of student's behavior received in confidence without consent.	
MINNESOTA	13.02, *et seq.*	Records are private except for directory information and shall be released only pursuant to valid court order. Minor may request information to be withheld from parent or guardian if in best interest of minor.	
MISSISSIPPI	37-15-3	Governed by FERPA; records not available to the general public.	
MISSOURI	No known provisions		
MONTANA	7-1-4144	Public records private unless person they concern requests them to be public.	
NEBRASKA	84-712.05, *et seq.*	Records withheld from public unless disclosed in court or administrative proceeding or for routine directory information.	

Table 16: Privacy of School Records—Continued

State	Code Section	Who Has Access	Penalties
NEVADA	49.290, 291; 125.520	Both custodial and non-custodial parent; privilege for counselor-pupil and teacher-pupil communication.	
NEW HAMPSHIRE	91-A:5	Exempted from public access.	
NEW JERSEY	18A:36-19	Parent/guardian or pupil with reasonable protection of privacy rights. State board of education establishes rules.	
NEW MEXICO	40-4-9.1 (J) (4) (C)	Both custodial and non-custodial parent	
NEW YORK	Pub. O. §87; Educ §3222	Parent applies for schooling record for complying minor. Access according to §87 Pub. O.	
NORTH CAROLINA	8-53.4; 115C-3; 115C-174.13; 115C-402	Not subject to public inspection; minimum competency test scores of students available consistent with FERPA; counselor communication privileged.	
NORTH DAKOTA	15-21.1-06	Any record of student's medical treatment is confidential and may not be released without written consent of student; if student is under 14, written consent of student's parent/guardian is required.	
OHIO	149.41; 3319.321	No release without student's consent if over 18; if 18 or under, consent of parent or guardian is necessary. Directory information may be released. Rights of school district to renew or select student records are restricted.	
OKLAHOMA	Tit. 51 §24A.16; Tit. 70 §6-115	Confidential except for directory information; teacher may not reveal student-obtained information unless required by contract or released to a parent or guardian of such child on request.	Misdemeanor for teacher to reveal information regarding any child except as required in performance of contractual duties or requested by parents.
OREGON	336.187; 326.565	Consistent with state and federal law regarding record custody and disclosure; disclosure allowed to law enforcement and/or child protective services and/or health professionals in "health or safety emergency."	
PENNSYLVANIA	Tit. 23 §5309; Tit. 24§1409	Both parents; child's school health record transferred to other PA school or to parent/guardian.	
RHODE ISLAND	16-38-5	No specific provisions.	Misdemeanor to circulate a questionnaire "so framed as to ask intimate questions about themselves or families, thus trespassing upon the pupils' constitutional rights and invading the privacy of the home" without approval of local school commissioner and department of education

Table 16: Privacy of School Records—Continued

State	Code Section	Who Has Access	Penalties
SOUTH CAROLINA	30-1-10, *et seq.*	Records of school district considered public records and dealt with according to Title 30.	Failure to deliver to requesting party: misdemeanor, up to $500 fine
SOUTH DAKOTA	19-13-21.1; 25-5-7.3; 27B-6-2	Access may not be denied parent who is not child's primary residential parent. County board of mental retardation has access to the school records of any case under investigation. School counselors' communications are privileged except in cases of child abuse or if waived.	
TENNESSEE	10-7-504	School records are confidential except when compelled under legal process or released for safety of person or property. Outsiders are authorized access to pupil records for research and statistical purposes and pupil may give consent for others to have access.	
TEXAS	Educ. 26.004	Parent has access to all written records concerning the parent's child.	
UTAH	30-3-29	Both custodial and non-custodial parent	
VERMONT	Tit. 1 §317(11)	Confidential; limits on release of school records except as required by FERPA.	
VIRGINIA	12.1-287; 22.1-380.1	Limits on access; equal access to student directory information must be given to representatives of armed forces.	
WASHINGTON	42.17.310	Personal information in school records exempt from public inspection and copying.	
WEST VIRGINIA	No known provisions		
WISCONSIN	118.125, 126	All records confidential. Pupil, parents, courts and school officials (under certain circumstances), and persons designated by parents or pupil; behavioral records must be destroyed one year after graduation unless graduate requests otherwise. Student's records as they relate to health are treated as health records: school psychologist, counselor, social worker and nurse, teacher, or administrator working in alcohol or drug abuse program activities shall keep student communications regarding such confidential unless pupil consents to disclosure or if there is serious and imminent danger to anyone's health or safety or if required to be disclosed by law.	
WYOMING	No known provisions		

IV. EMPLOYMENT LAWS

17. LEGAL HOLIDAYS

The diversity of our country is reflected in the various holidays recognized by the individual states. While many holidays, including New Year's Day, Memorial Day, and Labor Day, are considered legal holidays in all states, others, such as Good Friday and Robert E. Lee's Birthday, are recognized in only a handful, while a few are particular to only one state, for example Alaska Day and Pioneer Day.

The recognition of civil rights leader Martin Luther King, Jr.'s birthday has sparked a great deal of controversy. It is not recognized in every state, and in some of the states where it is recognized, it is not a paid holiday for state employees. And in a few states, though it is an official day of recognition, it is not a legal holiday. The most interesting variation on the celebration of Martin Luther King, Jr. Day is in Louisiana, where it is one of six other days that are interchangeably recognized. Each year the governor is authorized to declare any two of these days as an official state holiday, except that every two years Martin Luther King, Jr.'s birthday must be one of the two days selected.

Due to the myriad local holidays in the states, only the major holidays are featured below for comparison.

Table 17: Legal Holidays

State	Code Section	Holidays
ALABAMA	1-3-8	New Year's Day; Martin Luther King, Jr.'s Birthday; Mardi Gras (Mobile & Baldwin Counties only); Washington's and Jefferson's Birthday; Memorial Day; Independence Day; Labor Day; Columbus Day; Fraternal Day; Veterans Day; Thanksgiving; Christmas; Jefferson Davis Birthday; Confederate Memorial Day; Robert E. Lee's Birthday
ALASKA	44.12.010	New Year's Day; Martin Luther King, Jr.'s Birthday; President's Day; Memorial Day; Independence Day; Labor Day; Veterans Day; Thanksgiving; Christmas; Alaska Day; Seward's Day
ARIZONA	1-301	New Year's Day; President's Day; Memorial Day; Independence Day; Labor Day; Columbus Day; Veterans Day; Thanksgiving; Christmas; Martin Luther King, Jr.'s Birthday
ARKANSAS	1-5-101; 69-101	New Year's Day; Martin Luther King, Jr.'s and Robert E. Lee's Birthday; Washington's Birthday; Memorial Day; Independence Day; Labor Day; Veterans Day; Thanksgiving; Christmas Eve; Christmas; employee's birthday
CALIFORNIA	Gov. Code §6700	New Year's Day; Martin Luther King, Jr.'s Birthday; Washington's Birthday; Lincoln's Birthday; Good Friday; Admission Day; Memorial Day; Independence Day; Labor Day; Columbus Day; Veterans Day; Thanksgiving; Christmas; Cesar Chavez Day
COLORADO	24-11-101	New Year's Day; Martin Luther King, Jr.'s Birthday; Washington-Lincoln Day; Memorial Day; Independence Day; Columbus Day; Veterans Day; Thanksgiving; Christmas
CONNECTICUT	§1-4	New Year's Day; Martin Luther King, Jr.'s Birthday; Lincoln's B-day; Washington's Birthday; Memorial Day; Independence Day; Labor Day; Columbus Day; Veterans Day; Thanksgiving; Christmas;
DELAWARE	Tit. 1 §501	New Year's Day; Martin Luther King, Jr.'s Birthday; President's Day; Good Friday; Memorial Day; Independence Day; Labor Day; Columbus Day; Veterans Day; Thanksgiving; Christmas; Day of biennial general elections; Friday following Thanksgiving
DISTRICT OF COLUMBIA	§28-2701	New Year's Day; Martin Luther King, Jr.'s Birthday; Washington's Birthday; Memorial Day; Independence Day; Labor Day; Columbus Day; Veterans Day; Thanksgiving; Christmas
FLORIDA	110.117; 683.01; legal holidays-public holidays	New Year's Day; Martin Luther King, Jr.'s Birthday; Memorial Day; Independence Day; Labor Day; Veterans Day; Thanksgiving; friday after Thanksgiving; Christmas. Following are not official holidays but paid days off for state employees: Robert E. Lee's Birthday; Lincoln's Birthday; Susan B. Anthony's Birthday; Washington's Birthday; Shrove Tuesday; Good Friday; Pascua Florida Day; Confederate Memorial Day; Jefferson Davis's Birthday; Columbus Day
GEORGIA	1-4-1; Ga. Gov. Memos dated 10/18/90 and 10/16/91	New Year's Day; Martin Luther King, Jr.'s Birthday; Memorial Day; Independence Day; Labor Day; Columbus Day; Veterans Day; Thanksgiving; Friday after Thanksgiving; Christmas Eve; Christmas; Confederate Memorial Day; Washington's Birthday is holiday but paid day off is taken by state employees at Christmastime; Friday after Thanksgiving is designated as paid day off in honor of Robert E. Lee's Birthday
HAWAII	8-1	New Year's Day; Martin Luther King, Jr.'s Birthday; President's Day; Good Friday; Memorial Day; Independence Day; Labor Day; Veterans Day; Thanksgiving; Christmas; Prince Jonah Kuhio Kalanianaole Day; King Kamehameha Day; Admission Day; Election Day except primary election

Table 17: Legal Holidays—Continued

State	Code Section	Holidays
IDAHO	73-108	New Year's Day; Martin Luther King, Jr.'s Birthday and Idaho Human Rights Day; Washington's Birthday; Memorial Day; Independence Day; Labor Day; Columbus Day; Veterans Day; Thanksgiving; Christmas
ILLINOIS	205 ILCS 630/17	New Year's Day; Martin Luther King, Jr.'s Birthday; President's Day; Lincoln's Birthday; Casimir Pulaski's Birthday; Good Friday; Memorial Day; Independence Day; Labor Day; Columbus Day; Veterans Day; Thanksgiving; Christmas
INDIANA	1-1-9-1, 2	New Year's Day; Martin Luther King, Jr.'s Birthday; Washington's Birthday; Lincoln's Birthday; Good Friday; Memorial Day; Independence Day; Labor Day; Columbus Day; Veterans Day; Thanksgiving; Christmas; day of any primary or general election for national, state, or city officials (Election Day)
IOWA	1C.1, 1C.2	New Year's Day; Martin Luther King, Jr.'s Birthday; Washington's Birthday (public holiday but not paid day off for state employees); Memorial Day; Independence Day; Labor Day; Columbus Day (not paid day off for state empl.); Veterans Day; Thanksgiving; Friday after Thanksgiving; Christmas
KANSAS	SA §35-107	New Year's Day; Martin Luther King, Jr.'s Birthday; Washington's Birthday; Lincoln's Birthday; Memorial Day; Independence Day; Labor Day; Columbus Day; Veterans Day; Thanksgiving; Christmas
KENTUCKY	2.110	New Year's Day; Martin Luther King, Jr.'s Birthday; Washington's Birthday; Lincoln's Birthday; Memorial Day; Independence Day; Labor Day; Columbus Day; Veterans Day; Thanksgiving; Christmas; Jefferson Davis's Birthday; Robert E. Lee's Birthday; Confederate Memorial Day; Franklin D. Roosevelt's Birthday
LOUISIANA	1:55	New Year's Day; Mardi Gras; Memorial Day; Independence Day; Labor Day; Veterans Day; Thanksgiving; Christmas; Good Friday; general election day in even numbered years; Also, governor has authority to declare following paid holidays: Martin Luther King, Jr.'s Birthday; Robert E. Lee's Birthday; Washington's Birthday; Memorial Day; Confederate Memorial Day; Acadian Day; s/he must declare 2, including national Memorial Day every year and Martin Luther King, Jr.'s Birthday every other year; Battle of New Orleans; Huey P. Long Day; All Saints Day
MAINE	Tit. 4, §1051; 20-A, §4802	New Year's Day; Martin Luther King, Jr.'s Birthday; Washington's Birthday; Memorial Day; Independence Day; Labor Day; Columbus Day; Veterans Day; Thanksgiving; Christmas; Patriot's Day
MARYLAND	Art. 1 §27	New Year's Day; Martin Luther King, Jr.'s Birthday; Washington's Birthday; Lincoln's Birthday; Good Friday; Memorial Day; Independence Day; Labor Day; Columbus Day; Veterans Day; Thanksgiving; Christmas; Maryland Day; Defender's Day; any day of general or congressional election
MASSACHUSETTS	Ch. 4 §7, cl. Eighteenth Eighteenth A	New Year's Day; Martin Luther King, Jr.'s Birthday; Washington's Birthday; Memorial Day; Independence Day; Labor Day; Columbus Day; Veterans Day; Thanksgiving; Christmas; Patriot's Day
MICHIGAN	435.101	New Year's Day; Martin Luther King, Jr.'s Birthday; President's Day; Washington's Birthday (not paid day off for state employees); Lincoln's Birthday (not paid day off for state employees); Memorial Day; Independence Day; Labor Day; Veterans Day; Thanksgiving; Friday after Thanksgiving; Christmas Eve; Christmas; New Year's Eve; Columbus Day

Table 17: Legal Holidays—Continued

State	Code Section	Holidays
MINNESOTA	645.44 subd. 5	New Year's Day; Martin Luther King, Jr.'s Birthday; Washington's and Lincoln's Birthday; Memorial Day; Independence Day; Labor Day; Columbus Day (not a holiday for executive branch); Veterans Day; Thanksgiving; Friday after Thanksgiving (for executive branch); Christmas
MISSISSIPPI	3-3-7	New Year's Day; Martin Luther King, Jr.'s and Robert E. Lee's Birthday; Washington's Birthday; Memorial Day and Jefferson Davis's Birthday; Independence Day; Labor Day; Veterans Day; Thanksgiving; Christmas; Confederate Memorial Day
MISSOURI	9.010	New Year's Day; Martin Luther King, Jr.'s Birthday; Washington's Birthday; Lincoln's Birthday; Truman Day; Memorial Day; Independence Day; Labor Day; Columbus Day; Veterans Day; Thanksgiving; Christmas
MONTANA	1-1-216	New Year's Day; Martin Luther King, Jr.'s Birthday; Lincoln's and Washington's Birthday; Labor Day; Columbus Day; Veteran's Day; Thanksgiving Day; Christmas Day; state general election day
NEBRASKA	25-2221	New Year's Day; Martin Luther King, Jr.'s Birthday; President's Day; Arbor Day; Memorial Day; Independence Day; Labor Day; Columbus Day; Veterans Day; Thanksgiving; day after Thanksgiving; Christmas
NEVADA	236.015	New Year's Day; Martin Luther King, Jr.'s Birthday; Washington's Birthday; Memorial Day; Independence Day; Labor Day; Veterans Day; Thanksgiving; Friday after Thanksgiving (Family Day); Christmas; Nevada Day
NEW HAMPSHIRE	288:1, 2	New Year's Day; Washington's Birthday; Memorial Day; Independence Day; Labor Day; Columbus Day (not paid day off for state employees); Veterans Day; Thanksgiving; Civil Rights Day (not paid day off for state employees); Christmas Day
NEW JERSEY	36:1-1, 1.2	New Year's Day; Martin Luther King, Jr.'s Birthday; Washington's Birthday; Lincoln's Birthday; Good Friday; Memorial Day; Independence Day; Labor Day; Columbus Day; Veterans Day; Thanksgiving; Christmas; any general election day
NEW MEXICO	12-5-2	New Year's Day; Martin Luther King, Jr.'s Birthday; President's Day; Washington's and Lincoln's Birthday; Memorial Day; Independence Day; Labor Day; Columbus Day; Veterans Day; Thanksgiving; Christmas
NEW YORK	Gen. Constr. Law §24, 25	New Year's Day; Martin Luther King, Jr.'s Birthday; Washington's Birthday; Lincoln's Birthday; Memorial Day; Independence Day; Labor Day; Columbus Day; Veterans Day; Thanksgiving; Christmas Flag Day; any general election day
NORTH CAROLINA	103-4	New Year's Day; Martin Luther King, Jr.'s Birthday; Good Friday; Independence Day; Labor Day; Veterans Day; Thanksgiving; Christmas; Memorial Day; Robert E. Lee's Birthday; Washington's Birthday; Greek Independence Day; Anniversary of signing of Halifax Resolves; Confederate Memorial Day; Anniversary of Mecklenburg Declaration of Independence; Yom Kippur; Columbus Day; and the Tuesday after the first Monday in November in election years
NORTH DAKOTA	1-03-01, 2 and 2.1	New Year's Day; Martin Luther King, Jr.'s Birthday; Washington's Birthday; Good Friday; Memorial Day; Independence Day; Labor Day; Veterans Day; Thanksgiving; Christmas; state offices close at noon on Christmas Eve

Table 17: Legal Holidays—Continued

State	Code Section	Holidays
OHIO	1.14	New Year's Day; Martin Luther King, Jr.'s Birthday; Washington's and Lincoln's Birthday; Memorial Day; Independence Day; Labor Day; Columbus Day; Veterans Day; Thanksgiving; Christmas
OKLAHOMA	Tit. 25 §§82.1, 82.2	New Year's Day; Martin Luther King, Jr.'s Birthday; Washington's Birthday; Memorial Day; Independence Day; Labor Day; Veterans Day; Thanksgiving; Friday after Thanksgiving; Christmas; Senior Citizen's Day
OREGON	187.010, 020	New Year's Day; Martin Luther King, Jr.'s Birthday; President's Day; Memorial Day; Independence Day; Labor Day; Columbus Day; Veterans Day; Thanksgiving; Christmas
PENNSYLVANIA	Tit. 44, §11	New Year's Day; Martin Luther King, Jr.'s Birthday; President's Day; Good Friday; Memorial Day; Independence Day; Labor Day; Columbus Day; Veterans Day; Thanksgiving; Christmas; Flag Day (not paid day off for state employees); Election Day
RHODE ISLAND	25-1-1	New Year's Day; Martin Luther King, Jr.'s Birthday; Washington's Birthday (legal holiday but not paid day off for state employees); Lincoln's Birthday; Good Friday; Memorial Day; Independence Day; Labor Day; Columbus Day; Veterans Day; Thanksgiving; Christmas; Rhode Island Independence Day (legal holiday but not paid day off for state employees)
SOUTH CAROLINA	53-5-10	New Year's Day; Washington's Birthday; Memorial Day; Independence Day; Labor Day; Veterans Day; Thanksgiving; Friday after Thanksgiving; Christmas; Day after Christmas; general election days in even numbered years; state employees have the option of one of the following nonnational holidays: Martin Luther King, Jr.'s Birthday, Robert E. Lee Birthday, Confederate Memorial Day, Jefferson Davis' Birthday
SOUTH DAKOTA	1-5-1	New Year's Day; Martin Luther King, Jr.'s Birthday; Washington's and Lincoln's Birthday; Memorial Day; Independence Day; Labor Day; Veterans Day; Thanksgiving; Christmas; Native American Day
TENNESSEE	15-1-101	New Year's Day; Martin Luther King, Jr.'s Birthday; Washington's Birthday; Good Friday; Memorial Day; Independence Day; Labor Day; Columbus Day; Veterans Day; Thanksgiving; Christmas; any day set apart for county, state, or national elections throughout the state
TEXAS	U.T.C.A. Government Code §662.003	New Year's Day; Martin Luther King, Jr.'s Birthday; President's Day; Memorial Day; Independence Day; Labor Day; Veterans Day; Thanksgiving; Friday after Thanksgiving; Christmas Eve; Christmas; day after Christmas; (Confederate Heroes Day; Texas Independence Day; San Jacinto Day; Emancipation Day in Texas; Lyndon Baines Johnson Day; Election Day: state holidays)
UTAH	63-13-2	New Year's Day; Martin Luther King, Jr.'s Birthday; President's Day; Memorial Day; Independence Day; Labor Day; Columbus Day; Veterans Day; Thanksgiving; Christmas; Pioneer Day
VERMONT	Tit. 1 §371	New Year's Day; Martin Luther King, Jr.'s Birthday (legal holiday but not paid day off for state employees); Washington's Birthday; Lincoln's Birthday (legal holiday but not paid day off for state employees); Memorial Day; Independence Day; Labor Day; Columbus Day; Veterans Day; Thanksgiving; Christmas; Town Meeting Day; Bennington Battle Day

Table 17: Legal Holidays—Continued

State	Code Section	Holidays
VIRGINIA	2.1-21	New Year's Day; Lee-Jackson-King Day; Washington's Birthday; Memorial Day; Independence Day; Labor Day; Columbus and Yorktown Day; Election Day; Veterans Day; Thanksgiving; Friday after Thanksgiving; Christmas
WASHINGTON	1.16.050	New Year's Day; Martin Luther King, Jr.'s Birthday; President's Day; Memorial Day; Independence Day; Labor Day; Veterans Day; Thanksgiving; Friday after Thanksgiving; Christmas
WEST VIRGINIA	2-2-1	New Year's Day; Martin Luther King, Jr.'s Birthday; Washington's Birthday; Lincoln's Birthday; Memorial Day; Independence Day; Labor Day; Columbus Day; Veterans Day; Thanksgiving; Christmas; West Virginia Day; any national, state, or other election day throughout any district or municipality
WISCONSIN	895.20	New Year's Day; Martin Luther King, Jr.'s Birthday; President's Day; Good Friday (11am-3pm observed for purpose of worship); Memorial Day; Independence Day; Labor Day; any primary election day in September; Columbus Day; any general election day in November; Veterans Day; Thanksgiving; Christmas Eve; Christmas
WYOMING	8-4-101	New Year's Day; *Martin Luther King, Jr.'s Birthday; *Washington's and Lincoln's Birthday; Memorial Day; Independence Day; Labor Day; *Veterans Day; Thanksgiving; Christmas; *Wyoming Equality Day; *public school not dismissed except by order of board of trustees of the district

18. MINIMUM WAGE

The federal government has established a minimum wage, or the least dollar amount that may be paid hourly workers, that applies to all workers in all fifty states who are engaged in interstate commerce or the production of goods for interstate commerce (and closely allied enterprises) or are employed by an enterprise engaged in interstate commerce or the production of goods for commerce. Businesses engaged in "interstate commerce" are defined as those with potential to come in contact with interstate travelers or consumers in other states.

Thus the federal minimum wage does not apply to all occupations. Domestic workers are not covered in many situations; fishermen, employees of certain small newspapers, babysitters, and agricultural seasonal workers in small family farms are some of the common exemptions from the federal minimum wage law. Others who are exempt include those in seasonal employment, such as at amusement parks or seasonal recreation centers, and in "exempt" occupations, such as managers, salesmen, or administrators who are not paid on an hourly basis. Further, if a local business does not qualify as participating in interstate commerce, it, too, would be exempt. These exempt occupations are covered by state minimum wage laws that can be higher or lower than the federal minimum wage which is now $5.15 per hour. However, if the state minimum wage is higher than the federal minimum wage and the employee is subject to both state and federal law, the higher rate will apply.

Subminimum wages are hourly rates below the established minimum wage that may be paid for a limited time to learners, apprentices, messengers, student workers, and those employed in occupations not ordinarily given to full-time workers. The subminimum wage permits businesses to be able to continue to hire certain types of workers in certain nontraditional, "convenience" occupations.

Overall, there is little variation among states in regard to the minimum wage. Since the federal government has established a national minimum wage covering virtually all occupations, most states have simply adopted that wage as their standard, though a few have established higher rates and a few lower. The only surprise is in the number of states that have simply taken no action at all, perhaps determining that the market is the best regulator of wages. That is, if the wage is too low, the employer will either get no applicants or ones with no experience and no skills. Generally, the higher the wage, the better the applicant pool. However, there are circumstances in which workers may be taken advantage of either out of desperation or ignorance. This is precisely why the minimum wage exists.

Table 18: Minimum Wage

State	Code Section	Minimum Wage Per Hour	Subminimum Wage Per Hour
FEDERAL 29 USC §206	Federal Labor Standards Act	$5.15 (eff. 9/1/99); applies to all employees covered by FLSA in 50 states, territories, and possessions except for American Samoa; standard applies to employees, not specifically exempt, who are: (1) engaged in interstate commerce; (2) engaged in production of goods for commerce; or (3) employed in an enterprise engaged in commerce or production of goods for commerce	At least 85% of federal minimum wage for up to 90 days of training for individuals under 20 years of age
ALABAMA	No statutory provisions		
ALASKA	23.10.065; 23.10.070; Rules & Regs 8AAL 15.125, eff. 12/9/78	$5.65 Public school bus drivers shall be paid double the minimum wage (23.10.065) Employer must pay employees wages @ a rate not less than 50¢ an hour greater than/to prevailing Federal Min-wages	Department of Labor Commissioner to set percentage rate of statutory minimum for learners and/or apprentices
ARIZONA	§23-362	Can't exceed fed. min. wage	None
ARKANSAS	11-4-201 to11-4-219	(11-4-210) $5.15 as 10/1/97	85% min wage for any full time student
CALIFORNIA	Labor Code §1182.11	$5.75 3-1-98 for all industries	85% of minimum wage rate for first 160 hours of employment, by state wage board order
COLORADO	8-6-109, *et seq.*	The Director of the Division of Labor shall set the minimum wage rate appropriate for each occupation	85% of minimum wage to unemancipated minors or to persons with a physical disability
CONNECTICUT	31-58j	$4.25	85% of minimum wage for first 200 hours of employment
DELAWARE	Tit. 19 §902(a)	$5.15	None
DISTRICT OF COLUMBIA	36-220.1(10), .220.2(a) and (b), effective 10/93	$1.00 over federal minimum wage ($6.15)	Specific rates established by wage orders for various categories of employees
FLORIDA	No statutory provisions		
GEORGIA	34-4-3, -4	$3.25	Rate set by Commissioner (34-4-4)
HAWAII	387-2	$5.25	Rate set by Director
IDAHO	44-1502	$5.15 9/1/97	Rate set by Director (apprentices) 44-1506
ILLINOIS	820 §105/4, 105/6	$5.15	70% of minimum wage for up to six months
INDIANA	22-2-2-4	$3.35 untill 10/98	None
IOWA	91D.1(1)(a)	$4.65	$4.25 if under 90 calendar days of employment

Table 18: Minimum Wage—Continued

State	Code Section	Minimum Wage Per Hour	Subminimum Wage Per Hour
KANSAS	44-1203(a) and (b)	$2.65	The Secretary of Human Resources may set special lower wage rates for learners and workers with handicaps or in state institutions
KENTUCKY	337.275(1)	$4.25	None
LOUISIANA	No statutory provisions		
MAINE	Tit. 26 §664	$5.15	None
MARYLAND	Labor & Employment 3-413	$5.15	Not less than 80% of the minimum wage for learners and apprentices (3-410)
MASSACHUSETTS	Ch. 151 §§1, *et seq.*	$5.25 6/11/98	Scale of rates for specified occupations
MICHIGAN	408.384	$5.15	less 20 yrs. $4.25 1st 90 days
MINNESOTA	177.21-35	$5.15; $4.90 for employer whose annual gross income is less than $500,000 (177.24)	$4.25 1st 90 days if less than 20 yrs
MISSISSIPPI	No statutory provisions		
MISSOURI	290.502; 290.517	$5.15	85% of federal minimum wage
MONTANA	39-3-404(1), 39-3-409	Must be equal to federal minimum wage, except if gross sales of employer are $110,000 or less, the minimum wage is $4.00	None
NEBRASKA	48-1203(1), (3)	$5.15 9/1/97	$4.25 1st days
NEVADA	Notice of Labor Commission dated 4/1/91 and §608.250(1)	$5.15; $4.38 for employees below age 18	85% for minors
NEW HAMPSHIRE	279:21	$5.15	75% of the statutory minimum for learners and apprentices
NEW JERSEY	34:11-56a4; 34:11-56a17	$5.05	85% of minimum wage
NEW MEXICO	50-4-22(A)	$4.25	None
NEW YORK	Labor Law §652(1)	$4.25	None
NORTH CAROLINA	95-25.3(a) and (b)	$5.15	90% of the statutory minimum for learners and apprentices
NORTH DAKOTA	34-06-03, *et seq.*	$5.15; the Commissioner of Labor may adopt standards for rates of minimum wage for each occupation in the state	The Commissioner may issue permits to individuals to earn less than the minimum wage set for that ocupation if the person is impaired physically or mentally or if s/he is a learner or an apprentice in that occupation
OHIO	4111.02	$4.25	80% for period not exceeding 180 days

Table 18: Minimum Wage—Continued

State	Code Section	Minimum Wage Per Hour	Subminimum Wage Per Hour
OKLAHOMA	Tit. 40 §197.2	$5.15	Commissioner of Labor shall set amount for learners and apprentices 197.11
OREGON	653.025	1998 - $6.00 after Dec. 98, $6.50	Commissioner may determine for student-learners
PENNSYLVANIA	Tit. 43 §333.104	$5.15	85% of the statutory minimum for learners and/or apprentices
RHODE ISLAND	28-12-3, 10	$5.15	At rate determined by director of labor, for up to 90 days
SOUTH CAROLINA	No statutory provisions	Only for state employees	
SOUTH DAKOTA	60-11-3; 60-12-3; 60-11-4.1	$5.15	$4.25 for employees age 18 or 19 for up to 90 days; 75% for minor under 18
TENNESSEE	No statutory provisions		
TEXAS	Tex. Codes Ann. Labor 62.061, *et seq.*	$3.35	60% minimum wage
UTAH	34-40-103	$5.15	Set by the Commission for first 160 hours of employment; 85% for minors
VERMONT	Tit. 21 §384(a)	$5.25 9/30/97	Determined by wage board for learners, apprentices, or handicapped persons
VIRGINIA	40.1-28.10	$5.15	$4.25
WASHINGTON	49.46.020	$4.90	$4.25 for 90 days to any employee under 20 years of age.
WEST VIRGINIA	21-5C-2(a)	$5.15	85% or $4.25, whichever is greater, for first 90 days if under age 19
WISCONSIN	Ch. 104.01, *et seq.*	$5.15 = fed min wage	The Department may make rules and grant licenses to any employer employing learner employees or handicapped employees
WYOMING	27-4-202	$1.60	None

19. RIGHT TO WORK

As labor unions began to organize and to bargain with employers on behalf of its members, many troublesome issues began to arise. For instance, if a union negotiated a contract with a company, did the contract cover only union members or those employees who refused to join the union too? Could the union insist that the employer refuse to hire nonunion members? If a member violated some union policy, could the union insist that the employer fire the employee?

To say that the union had the power to decide who worked and who did not meant that the employer was deprived of a fundamental right in running his business. Conversely, if an employer who hired and fired whom he pleased, it meant that, potentially, the union contract could be undermined simply by hiring nonunion employees.

Over the years an intricate system of rules, regulations, and laws has evolved to manage the many thorny issues that have arisen in the context of union contracts, including the protection of the rights of nonunion employees to work for unionized employers. These "right to work" laws generally forbid both unions and employers from denying a nonunion employee a job solely on account of his union status. Twenty-two states are currently "right to work" states. Twenty-eight and the District of Columbia have no statutory provision, apparently allowing the union to bargain with the employer for the right to insist upon union membership as a condition for employment.

Table 19: Right to Work

State	Code Section	Policy	Prohibited Activity	Penalties
ALABAMA	25-7-30, *et seq.*	The right of persons to work shall not be denied or abridged on account of membership or nonmembership in any labor union or labor organization.	Any agreement/combination between employer and labor union or organization denying nonmembers right to work is prohibited; labor organizations cannot require membership, abstention, or payment of union dues.	Harmed person may recover such damages sustained by reason of denial or deprivation of employment.
ALASKA	No statutory provisions			
ARIZONA	23-1302, *et seq.*; Ariz. Const. Art. XXV	No person shall be denied opportunity to work because of nonmembership in a union.	Threatened or actual interference with person, his family, or property to force him to join union, strike against his will, or leave job; conspiracy to induce persons to refuse to work with nonmembers; agreements which exclude person from employment because of nonmembership in union.	Any act/agreement in violation of article is illegal and void; damages; injunctive relief.
ARKANSAS	Ark. Const. Amend. XXXIV; 11-3-301, *et seq.*	Freedom of organized labor to bargain collectively and unorganized labor to bargain individually.	Union affiliation or non-affiliation not to be condition of employment; contracts to exclude persons from employment.	Persons violating chapter guilty of a misdemeanor; fined not less than $100 nor more than $5,000.
CALIFORNIA	No statutory provisions			
COLORADO	No statutory provisions			
CONNECTICUT	No statutory provisions			
DELAWARE	No statutory provisions			
DISTRICT OF COLUMBIA	No statutory provisions			
FLORIDA	Fla. Const. Art. I §6	The right of persons to work shall not be denied or abridged by membership or nonmembership in any labor union or organization.	Public employees do not have right to strike; right of employees to bargain collectively through a labor union shall not be denied or abridged.	
GEORGIA	34-6-21, *et seq.*	No person shall be required as a condition of employment to be or remain a member of a labor organization or to resign or to refrain from membership with a labor organization.	Membership in or payment to labor organization as condition of employment; contracts requiring membership in or payment to labor organization as contrary to public policy; deduction from wages of fees for labor organization without individual's order or request.	Injunctive relief; costs and reasonable attorney's fees; actual damages ; misdemeanor punished as provided in §17-10-3

Table 19: Right to Work—Continued

State	Code Section	Policy	Prohibited Activity	Penalties
HAWAII	No statutory provisions			
IDAHO	44-2001, *et seq.*	The right to work shall not be subject to undue restraint or coercion, infringed upon or restrained in any way based on membership, affiliation, or financial support of a labor organization.	Freedom of choice guaranteed, discrimination prohibited; deductions from wages unless signed written authorization by employee; coercion and intimidation of employee, his family, or property.	Any agreement null and void and of no legal effect; misdemeanor and fined not more than $1,000 or imprisonment not more than 90 days or both; injunctive relief; may recover any and all damages including costs & attorney's fees.
ILLINOIS	No statutory provisions			
INDIANA	No statutory provisions			
IOWA	731.1, *et seq.*	No person shall be deprived of the right to work at a chosen occupation because of membership, affiliation, withdrawal/expulsion, or refusal to join any labor union	Refusal to employ because of membership in a labor organization; contracts to exclude; union dues as prerequisite to employment; deducting dues from pay unless signed written authorization from employee.	Any contract contravening policy is illegal and void; guilty of a serious misdemeanor; injunction.
KANSAS	44-831; Kan. Const. Art. XV §12	There is a cause of action if there is a constitutional violation. No person shall be denied opportunity to obtain or retain employment because of membership or nonmembership in any labor organization.	Agreements to exclude persons from employment or continuance of employment based on membership or nonmembership in any labor organization.	Damages; attorney's fees.
KENTUCKY	No statutory provisions			
LOUISIANA	23:981 to 23:987	All persons shall have the right to form, join, and assist labor organizations or to refrain from such activities without fear of penalty or reprisals.	Cannot be required to become or remain member of labor organization or pay dues or fees as condition of employment; agreements between labor organization and employer.	Such agreements are unlawful, null and void, and of no legal effect; misdemeanor; fined not more than $1,000 and imprisoned for not more than 90 days; injunctive relief; recover any and all damages.
MAINE	No statutory provisions			
MARYLAND	No statutory provisions			
MASSACHUSETTS	No statutory provisions			
MICHIGAN	No statutory provisions			
MINNESOTA	No statutory provisions			

Table 19: Right to Work—Continued

State	Code Section	Policy	Prohibited Activity	Penalties
MISSISSIPPI	71-1-47; Miss. Const. Art VII §198-A	The right to work shall not be denied or abridged because of membership or nonmembership in a labor union or organization.	Agreement or combination between employer and labor organization to make membership condition of employment or where union or organization acquires an employment monopoly; requirement to become or remain member; requirement to abstain or refrain from membership; requirement to pay dues.	Misdemeanor; fined not less than $25.00 nor more than $250.
MISSOURI	No statutory provisions			
MONTANA	No statutory provisions			
NEBRASKA	48-217, 911; Neb. Const. Art. XV §13	No person shall be denied employment because of membership, affiliation, resignation, or expulsion in or from a labor organization or because of refusal to join or pay fees.	Contracts between employer and labor organization to exclude because of membership or nonmembership; right to strike and right to work.	Guilty of a class IV misdemeanor; fined not less than $100 or more than $500. (28-106)
NEVADA	613.230, *et seq.*	No person shall be denied the opportunity to obtain or retain employment because of nonmembership in a labor organization.	Agreements prohibiting employment because of nonmembership in labor organization; strike or picketing to force or induce employer to make agreement; compelling person to join labor organization, strike, or leave employment; conspiracy to cause discharge or denial of employment or to induce refusal of work on basis of membership.	Any act in violation shall be illegal and void; liable for damages; injunctive relief.
NEW HAMPSHIRE	No statutory provisions			
NEW JERSEY	No statute deals with union-security contracts but the state courts have upheld closed-shop and union-shop agreements. F. F. East Co. v. United Oysterman's Union 21 A.2d. 799			
NEW MEXICO	No statutory provisions			

Table 19: Right to Work—Continued

State	Code Section	Policy	Prohibited Activity	Penalties
NEW YORK	No statutory provisions			
NORTH CAROLINA	95-78, *et seq.*	The right to live includes the right to work. The right to work shall not be denied or abridged on account of membership or nonmembership in any labor union or organization.	Agreement or combination between employer and labor organization where nonmembers are denied right to work or where membership is made condition of employment or where organization acquires employment monopoly; membership status as condition of employment; payment of dues as condition of employment.	Any damages sustained.
NORTH DAKOTA	34-01-14	The right of a person to work shall not be abridged or denied on account of membership or nonmembership in any labor union or organization.	All contracts in negation or abrogation of right to work are invalid; "agency shop" dues "check off" of nonmember of union as condition of employment or continuance.	None.
OHIO	§4113.02	None stated.	Any agreement between employer and employee in which either party agrees to join, quit, or remain a part of a labor organization as a condition of employment is "contrary to public policy and void."	Contract void.
OKLAHOMA	No statutory provisions			
OREGON	No statutory provisions			
PENNSYLVANIA	No statutory provisions			
RHODE ISLAND	No statutory provisions			
SOUTH CAROLINA	41-7-10, *et seq.*	The denial of the right to work because of membership or nonmembership in a labor organization is against public policy.	Agreements between employer and labor organization denying nonmembers right to work or requiring union membership; requirement of membership or to refrain from membership or payment of dues as condition of employment; deduction of dues from wages without authorization; contracts declared to be unlawful by §41-7-20 or 41-7-30; 41-7-40.	Misdemeanor; imprisoned for not less than 10 nor more than 30 days; or fined not less than 10 nor more than $1,000 or both; damages, costs, and attorney's fees.

Table 19: Right to Work—Continued

State	Code Section	Policy	Prohibited Activity	Penalties
SOUTH DAKOTA	60-8-3, *et seq.*; 60-10-10; Art. VI §2 South Dakota Constitution	The right of persons to work shall not be denied or abridged on account of membership or nonmembership in a labor union or organization.	Any agreement relating to employment denying free exercise of right to work; any coercion to enter into such agreement; coercion of employee to join union; interference with right to work by use of force or violence.	Class 2 misdemeanor; thirty days imprisonment in county jail or $100 fine or both. (22-6-2)
TENNESSEE	50-1-201, *et seq.*	It is unlawful to deny employment because of affiliation or nonaffiliation with a labor union.	Contracts for exclusion from employment because of affiliation or nonaffiliation with labor union; exclusion from employment for payment or failure to pay union dues.	Class A misdemeanor; imprisoned for not greater than 11 months and 29 days or fine not to exceed ($2,500) or both. (40-35-111)
TEXAS	Labor Code §101.003, *et seq.*	No person shall be denied employment on account of membership or nonmembership in a labor union.	Any contract which requires membership or nonmembership; denial of right to work and bargain freely with employer, individually or collectively.	
UTAH	34-34-2, *et seq.*	The right of persons to work shall not be denied or abridged on account of membership or nonmembership in a labor union, labor organization, or any other type of association.	Agreement, understanding, or practice denying right to work based on membership in labor organization; compelling person to join or not join organization; employer cannot require union membership, abstinence from membership, or payment of dues or fees.	Injunctive relief; any and all damages; injunction ; misdemeanor.
VERMONT	No statutory provisions			
VIRGINIA	40.1-58, *et seq.*	The right to work shall not be abridged or denied on account of membership or nonmembership in a labor union or organization.	Agreements between labor organization to deny nonmembers right to work or where membership is made condition of employment or where union acquires monopoly; requirement of membership, nonmembership, or payment of dues as condition of employment.	Damages sustained; agreements in violation are illegal and contrary to public policy; illegal conduct contrary to public policy; misdemeanor; injunctive relief.
WASHINGTON	No statutory provisions			
WEST VIRGINIA	No statutory provisions			
WISCONSIN	No statutory provisions			

Table 19: Right to Work—Continued

State	Code Section	Policy	Prohibited Activity	Penalties
WYOMING	27-7-109, *et seq.*	No person is required to become a member of a labor organization or abstain therefrom as a condition of employment.	Requirement of membership or nonmembership or payment of dues as a condition of employment; requirement of connection with or approval from labor union.	Misdemeanor; damages sustained; injunctive relief; fine not to exceed $1,000 or imprisonment in county jail not to exceed 6 months or both.

20. WHISTLEBLOWER STATUTES

Whistleblower statutes protect employees when they find themselves in the difficult position of discovering their employer violating a law or in some way breaching the public trust. If the employer is warned of the problem but takes no action, or asks the employee to keep the situation confidential, the employee may be personally participating in a crime and may be exposed to a certain amount of personal liability. Sometimes, the right thing to do is to report the employer to the authorities (or, "blow the whistle"), but the employee may risk losing his job or position within the company. In this situation, the employee may be torn between a legal or ethical duty and perceived loyalty to his employer. "Whistleblower" issues arise in various circumstances, such as when an employee discovers that his employer that is a government contractor is overbilling the government, or when a public or private employer is discovered cutting corners on safety matters in violation of rules and regulations under state occupational health and safety acts. Other situations may involve employer practices of job discrimination, abuse of adult or juvenile patients in a health care facility, or medical malpractice.

In these situations, if an employee exposes an unsafe, illegal or unethical practice to the authorities, the employee may be the subject of punitive or retaliatory action, such as, dismissal, transfer to an undesirable job assignment, demotion, etc. Whistleblower statutes may prohibit dismissal or other retaliatory action against the employee. They may also provide for enhanced monetary awards to employees who blow the "whistle" on an unscrupulous employer.

State whistleblower statutes vary in a number of respects. Some states only provide explicit protection of public employees or those working for government contractors. Statutes also vary with respect to whom is protected or on whom the whistle may be blown. Some states extend protection to other co-workers who assist the whistleblower, some explicitly protect an employee who blows the whistle on fellow employees or another person or business entity with a business relationship with the employer.

Most states limit remedies that an employee may recover to actual damages, such as back pay or fringe benefits. In some cases, however, the employee is given a money award tied to the illegal or unethical activity exposed. In South Carolina, if the employee's report or complaint results in a savings of public funds, s/he may recover 25% of the estimated net savings in the first year after corrective action is undertaken, up to $2,000.

It should be noted that in addition to state statutes, there are a number of federal whistleblower provisions which protect employees in much the same way. However, many federal laws include much harsher penalties for employers and greater rewards for employees who risk careers and livelihoods by reporting activity that is damaging to the public trust.

Table 20: Whistleblowing

State	Code Section	Prohibited Activity	Public or Private Employees	Opportunity for Employer to Correct?	Remedies	Penalties
ALABAMA	25-5-11.1 25-8-57	Terminating for filing a written notice of violation of safety rule under §25-5-11 (c)(4)	Both	Ala §25-8-57 regarding children workers	Can not discharge, discipline, threaten, harass, blacklist, or in any other manner discriminate if employee disclosed information, refused to obey an illegal order, or revealed any violation of this chapter	
	36-26A-1, *et. seq.*	Can not discharge, demote, transfer, or otherwise discipline regarding compensation, terms, conditions, or privileges	Public		Can bring civil action within 2 years of violation; court can award back pay, front pay, and compensatory damages	
ALASKA	39.90.100 to .150	Discharge, threaten, disqualify or otherwise discriminate for actual or expected reports to a public body or for participating in court action, investigation, hearing or inquiry held by public body on matter of public concern	Public		Civil action for punitive damages as well as other appropriately found relief; a municipality isn't liable if it adopts an ordinance that provides similar protections	Civil fine, maximum $10,000
	18.60 .088 & .089	Can not discharge or discriminate if employee or representative files a complaint, institutes proceeding or testifies regarding a violation of safety or health standard that threatens physical harm or imminent danger	Private	Yes	May file complaint with commissioner of health and safety within 30 days of the violation to get reinstatement, back pay, and other appropriate relief	

Table 20: Whistleblowing—Continued

State	Code Section	Prohibited Activity	Public or Private Employees	Opportunity for Employer to Correct?	Remedies	Penalties
ARIZONA	38-531; 38-534	An employee who has control over personnel actions can not take reprisal against an employee for disclosure of information to public body on violation of any law or mismanagement, waste of funds, or abuse of authority	Public		May recover, under civil action, attorney's fees, costs, back pay, general and special damages and full reinstatement or injunctive relief; may make a complaint to appropriate independent personnel board, school district governing board, or community college governing board of discharged for disclosing; excludes state university or boards of regents which have a rule or provision for protecting employees at time personnel action is taken; employee can appeal final administrative decision or get trial de novo in superior court	Civil penalty, maximum $5,000
	23-425 & 23-418	Can not discharge or discriminate if employee files a complaint, institutes a proceeding, or testifies regarding a violation of health or safety statutes	Both		May file a complaint with commissioner within 30 days of violation for reinstatement, back pay, and other appropriate relief	If willful or repeated violating: maximum $10,000 for each violation; minimum $5,000 for each violation
ARKANSAS	16-123-108	Can not discriminate if employee in good faith opposed an act or practice made unlawful, or testified or participated in a proceeding regarding a violation of Arkansas Civil Rights Act	Both		Can file civil action within 1 year of violation to enjoin further violations, recover compensatory and punitive damages and court and attorney's fees	
CALIFORNIA	Labor §1102.5-1105	Can not prevent or retaliate against employee for disclosing to government or law enforcement agency when employee has reasonable cause to believe there's a violation	Both		Can recover damages for injury suffered	Misdemeanor: individual, up to 1 year in county jail and/or $1,000 fine; corporate, maximum $5,000 fine

Table 20: Whistleblowing—Continued

State	Code Section	Prohibited Activity	Public or Private Employees	Opportunity for Employer to Correct?	Remedies	Penalties
COLORADO	24-50.5-101 to 107	Can not initiate or administer any disciplinary action if employee disclosed information on actions of state agencies that are not in the public interest, unless employee knows information is false or discloses with disregard for truth, or disclosed information on records closed to public inspection or discloses information which is confidential under any other law	Public		If employee in state personnel system: may file a written complaint within 30 days with state personnel board to get reinstatement, back pay, restore lost service credit, records expunged, and any other additional relief as found appropriate by the board. If not or have already filed a complaint, but complaint denied: can bring civil suit to recover damages, court costs and other relief	
	§24-114-101, *et. seq.*	Can not initiate or administer any disciplinary action if employee discloses information unless employee knows information is false, or information confidential under laws	Private	Employee must make good faith effort to provide supervisor or appointing authority or member of general assembly with information to be disclosed before disclosing	Can bring civil action; court can give damages, court costs and other appropriate relief	
CONNECTICUT	31-51m, 4-61dd	Can not discharge, discipline, or otherwise penalize because employee or their representative reports a violation or suspected violation or requested an investigation, hearing, or inquiry or if public employee reports to a public body concerning unethical practices, mismanagement, or abuse of authority, <u>unless</u> employee knows such report is false	Both		If employer violates statute, employee may, after exhausting all available administrative remedies, bring civil action within 90 days of final administrative decision or the violation for reinstatement, back pay, to reestablish benefits, court and attorney's fees. If public, transmit facts and information to auditors of public accounts; if discriminate against can file claim within 30 days of incident with employee review board or in accordance with collective bargaining contract	

Table 20: Whistleblowing—Continued

State	Code Section	Prohibited Activity	Public or Private Employees	Opportunity for Employer to Correct?	Remedies	Penalties
DELAWARE	Tit. 29 §5115	Can not discharge, threaten, or otherwise discriminate because employee reported to an elected official a violation or suspected violation of law or regulation unless employee knows report is false	Public		Civil action: for injunctive relief, actual damages, or both within 90 days of alleged violation	
DISTRICT OF COLUMBIA	1-616.3; 1-619.1	Can not discharge, suspend, demote, or other retaliatory action if employee discloses or threatens to disclose, provide information or testify or object or refuse to participate in violation of a law or rule or misuse of government resources or funds under control of government official	Public		Can file civil action within 1 year for injunction, recission, reinstatement, full fringe benefits and seniority rights, back pay and benefits, and attorney and court fees	

Table 20: Whistleblowing—Continued

State	Code Section	Prohibited Activity	Public or Private Employees	Opportunity for Employer to Correct?	Remedies	Penalties
FLORIDA	112.3187	Can not dismiss, discipline, or other adverse personnel action against employee for disclosing information of any violation or suspected violation of law or regulation or act by independent contractor which creates a substantial and specific danger to the public's health, safety, and welfare or act of gross management malfeasance, gross public waste of funds or gross neglect of duty unless information known by employee to be false	Both		If employee of state agency: file complaint after pursuing administrative remedy or civil action within 180 days after receipt of notice of investigation termination. If local public employee: have 60 days after violation to file complaint with appropriate local government authority. Then can bring civil action within 180 days after final decision of local governmental authority, or 180 days after violation if authority hasn't an administrative procedure by ordinance or contract. Any other person: after exhausting all available contractual or administrative remedies may bring civil action within 180 days after violation. Relief: reinstatement, back and full benefits, lost wages, reasonable costs, injunction, temporary reinstatement	
GEORGIA	45-1-4	No action may be taken or threatened by any public employer with authority to take, direct others to take, recommend or approve as a reprisal for making a complaint or disclosing information to the public employer unless information disclosed with knowledge that it was false or with willful disregard for its truth or falsity	Public		Can have any prohibited action taken by employer set aside in a proceeding in court	

Table 20: Whistleblowing—Continued

State	Code Section	Prohibited Activity	Public or Private Employees	Opportunity for Employer to Correct?	Remedies	Penalties
HAWAII	378.61, *et seq.*	Can not discharge, threaten, or otherwise discriminate because employee or their representative reports or is about to report to public body a violation or suspected violation of law or rule or is requested by public body to participate in a hearing, investigation, inquiry, or court action <u>unless</u> employee knows report is false	Both		Civil action: injunction, actual damages or both within 90 days after violation. Court remedies: reinstatement, back pay, full reinstatement of benefits and seniority rights, actual damages and any other appropriate relief as well as court costs and attorney's fees	Person: fine, maximum $500 for each violation
IDAHO	6-2101, *et. seq.*	Can not take adverse action against an employee because employee or its representative communicates in good faith the existence of any waste of public funds, property or manpower or violation or suspected violation of a law, rule, or regulation including participating in an investigation, hearing, court proceeding, legislative or other inquiry or other form of administrative review, or where employee refused or objected to directive they reasonably believe violates law, rule, or regulation and employer cannot implement rules or policies that unreasonably restrict employee's ability to document a violation	Public		Civil action: for injunction and/or actual damages within 180 days of violation. Court remedies: injunction, reinstatement, reinstate full benefits and seniority rights, back pay, reasonable court costs and attorney's fees	Civil fine: maximum $500
ILLINOIS	5 ILCS 395/.01, *et seq.*	Can not reprimand, suspend, discharge, demote, deny promotion or transfer because employee of a constitutional officer reports violation of any law, rule, regulation, mismanagement, gross waste of funds, abuse of authority, or substantial and specific danger to public health and safety unless disclosure is prohibited by law	Public			

Table 20: Whistleblowing—Continued

State	Code Section	Prohibited Activity	Public or Private Employees	Opportunity for Employer to Correct?	Remedies	Penalties
INDIANA	4-15-10-4 & 36-1-8-8 (public); 22-5-3-3 (private)	Can not dismiss, withhold salary increases or employment-related benefits, transfer or reassign, deny promotion or demote if employee reports violation of federal law or regulation, state law or rule, violates ordinance of a political subdivision or misuse of public funds	Both		Report to supervisor or appointing authority or state ethics commission if supervisor or appointing authority involved with violation. If no good faith effort made by reportee, submit a written report to any concerned person, agency, or organization; can also seek a legal remedy	Class A infraction
IOWA	70A.28 & 29	Can not discharge, deny appointment or promotion, if employee discloses information they reasonably believe evidences a violation of law or rule, mismanagement, gross abuse of funds, abuse of authority, or a substantial and specific danger to public health or safety, unless disclosure prohibited by statute	Public		If employer is not head of a state department/ agency or serves in a supervisory capacity within the executive branch of state government, employee can enforce through civil action, and employer is liable for affirmative relief including reinstatement, back pay, or any other equitable relief including attorney's fees and costs. If employee permanent, classified.	Simple misdemeanor
KANSAS	75-2973	Can not prohibit employee from discussing the agency's operation with member of legislature, reporting violation of state or federal law, rules or regulations or require prior notice to making report	Public		If employee is permanent, classified, can appeal to state civil service board, any court of law or administrative hearing, if filed within 30 days of alleged disciplinary action. If employee is unclassified, can bring civil action, for injunction and/or actual damage, within 90 days of alleged violation. Court can grant reinstatement, back wages, full reinstatement of benefits and seniority rights, actual damages, and reasonable attorney fees and witness fees	If officer or employee is permanent, classified, suspension on leave without pay for maximum of 30 days; if willful or repeated violation, may require resignation.or disqualificatio n for appointment to or employment as a state officer or employee for maximum of 2 years

Table 20: Whistleblowing—Continued

State	Code Section	Prohibited Activity	Public or Private Employees	Opportunity for Employer to Correct?	Remedies	Penalties
KENTUCKY	61.101, *et seq.*	Can not subject to reprisal, threat to use authority, or influence in any manner, against any person who supports, aids, or substantiates a report or an employee who in good faith reports, discloses, divulges any facts, or information relative to an actual or suspected violation of any law, statute, executive order, administrative regulation, mandate, rule or ordinance, mismanagement, fraud, waste, abuse of authority or substantial and specific danger to public health or safety	Public		Civil action for injuries or punitive damages within 90 days after violation	
KENTUCKY (cont.)	338.121 & 338.991	Can not discharge or discriminate if employee or representative files a complaint, institutes a proceeding or testifies regarding a violation of any occupational safety or health statute that threatens physical harm and imminent danger	Both		File a complaint with commissioner for reinstatement, back pay, and other appropriate relief	If willfully or repeatedly violates, minimum $5,000 and maximum $70,000 per violation; otherwise civil penalty, maximum $10,000 per violation
LOUISIANA	30:2026	Can not act in a retaliatory manner against an employee who discloses or threatens to disclose a violation of environmental law, rule or regulation or provides information to or testifies before an investigation hearing	Both		Civil action for triple damages and all court costs and attorney's fees and all other civil and criminal remedies	
	42:1169	Can not discipline or reprise an employee who reports a violation of any rule, order, or regulation, or any acts of impropriety within a government entity or related to the scope and/or duties of public employment or public office within state government	Public		If employee is suspended, demoted, or dismissed, then report to board of ethics for elected officials or the commission on ethics for public employees. Remedies: reinstatement, back pay and benefits	

Table 20: Whistleblowing—Continued

State	Code Section	Prohibited Activity	Public or Private Employees	Opportunity for Employer to Correct?	Remedies	Penalties
MAINE	26§831	Can not discharge, threaten, or otherwise discriminate if employee reports a violation of a law or rule of the state, political subdivision or US, a condition or practice that would put at risk the health or safety of that employee or is requested to participate in an investigation, hearing, or inquiry or refuses to carry out a directive that violates the act	Both	Yes	Employee must first report violation to a supervisor and give the employer a reasonable opportunity to correct unless employee has specific reason to believe that reports to employer won't result in correction	
MARYLAND	3-301, *et seq.*	Can not take or refuse to take any personnel action as reprisal if applicant or employee discloses abuse of authority, gross mismanagement or waste of money, violation of law or substantial and specific danger to public health or safety and seeks a remedy	Public		Can submit a complaint to the secretary within 1 year of first knowledge of violation; if violation found, secretary can remove detrimental information from complainant's personnel record, reinstatement, promotion or end of suspension, back pay, leave or seniority and attorney's and court fees	
MASSACHUSETTS	149§185	Can not discharge, suspend, demote, or other retaliatory action if employee discloses or threatens to disclose; provides information or testifies; or objects or refuses to participate in violation of law, rule or risk to public health, safety, or environment	Public	Employee must bring violation to attention of his/her supervisor and afford them with the opportunity to correct unless employee a) was certain supervisors know of violation and situation is an emergency, b) reasonably fears physical harm resulting from disclosure or c) unless disclosure is evidence of a crime	Can file civil action within 2 years of incident, court can give all civil law tort remedies including: temporary restraining order, preliminary/ permanent injunction, reinstatement, reinstate full benefits and seniority rights, back pay, benefits, court and attorney's fees	

Table 20: Whistleblowing—Continued

State	Code Section	Prohibited Activity	Public or Private Employees	Opportunity for Employer to Correct?	Remedies	Penalties
MICHIGAN	15§361, *et seq.*; 257 §2035 vehicle inspection	Can not discharge, threaten, or otherwise discriminate if employee or representative of employee reports or is about to report violation of law, regulation, or rule or because employee testifies in hearing or a court action unless employee knows disclosure is false	Both		Can file civil action within 90 days if violation for injunction and/or actual damages, including attorney's fees. Court may award: reinstatement, back pay, reinstate benefits and seniority rights, and court costs	Civil fine, maximum $500
MINNESOTA	181.931, *et seq.*	Can not discharge, discipline, threaten, or otherwise discriminate or penalize if employee reports violation of federal or state law or rule or is requested to testify or refuses to perform an action that he/she reasonably believes is in violation unless its disclosure of confidential communication provided by civil law	Both		Can file civil action to recover all damages and attorney's fees as well as injunctive relief	Civil penalty; $25 per day per injured employee, maximum $750 per injured employee
MISSISSIPPI	25-9-171, *et seq.*	Can not dismiss or otherwise adversely affect the compensation or employment status if employee testifies or provides information to an investigative body	Public		Can file civil action (without exhausting administrative remedies) for back pay and reinstatement	Each member of any agency's governing board or authority or executive director may be individually liable for civil fine; maximum $10,000 per violation

Table 20: Whistleblowing—Continued

State	Code Section	Prohibited Activity	Public or Private Employees	Opportunity for Employer to Correct?	Remedies	Penalties
MISSOURI	105.055	Can not take or prohibit disciplinary action if employee discusses operations of agency, with any member of legislature or state auditor, any violation of law, rule or regulation, mismanagement, gross waste of public funds, abuse of authority, or substantial and specific danger to public health or safety, as long as disclosure not specifically prohibited by law	Public	No prior notice required	Can file an administrative appeal, if disciplinary action taken, with state personnel advisory board within 30 days of action; board can modify and/or reverse disciplinary action and order appropriate relief	State personnel advisory board can recommend that violator be suspended without pay for maximum 30 days; if willful or repeated violation, recommend forfeiture and disqualification of appointment or state employment for a maximum of 2 years
MONTANA	39-2-901, *et seq.*	Can not discharge or otherwise terminate employee in retaliation if employee refused to violate constitutional provision, statute or administrative rule regarding public health, safety, or welfare or reports a violation of the same	Both		Must first exhaust internal procedures for appealing discharge, but after 90 days or exhaustion, whichever comes first, can file an action (within 1 year of discharge) to get back pay and fringe benefits (for a maximum 4 years, less interim earnings) and punitive damages if employer engaged in fraud or malice in discharging	

Table 20: Whistleblowing—Continued

State	Code Section	Prohibited Activity	Public or Private Employees	Opportunity for Employer to Correct?	Remedies	Penalties
NEBRASKA	81-2701, *et seq.*	Person with authority to recommend, approve, direct, or take other personnel action can not dismiss, demote, transfer, reassign, suspend, or other personnel action if employee discloses information or testifies before public counsel or other officials	Public		If incident occurs or is about to occur, employee contacts public counsel who sends finding to personnel appeals board or director/chief operations officer of agency, who, after a hearing, can stay or reverse personnel action, grant back pay or other appropriate relief and reasonable attorney's fees, or employee can maintain an action under Administrative Procedures Act for damages, reinstatement, back pay or other relief including attorney's fees	
	71-6035	Can not discriminate or retaliate if resident or employee initiates or participates in proceeding under Nebraska Nursing Home Act or presents a grievance or information to home administration, ombudsman, or public officials	Private		Can file a private action for any relief permitted by law	Civil fine, minimum $250, maximum $5,000 or immediate revocation of nursing home's license to operate
NEVADA	281.611, *et seq.*	Can not directly or indirectly intimidate, threaten, coerce, command, or influence another state officer or employee or prevent disclosure of violation of state law/regulation, abuse of authority, substantial and specific danger to public health or safety or gross waste of public money	Public		Can file a written appeal with department of personnel within 2 years of disclosing; hearing officer can order person to desist and refrain from such action	
	618.445	Can not discharge or discriminate if employee files a complaint, institutes a proceeding or testifies regarding a violation of health and safety statutes	Both		Can file a complaint after first notifying employer and division, within 30 days of the violation for a reinstatement, back pay and lost work benefits	

Table 20: Whistleblowing—Continued

State	Code Section	Prohibited Activity	Public or Private Employees	Opportunity for Employer to Correct?	Remedies	Penalties
NEW HAMPSHIRE	98-E:1, *et seq.*	Can not interfere in any way with employee's right to publicly discuss and give opinions as an individual on all matters concerning the state and its policies, unless its disclosure on confidential and privileged records or communication	Public			If willfully and knowingly violates any provision is guilty of a violation
	275-E:1, *et seq.*	Can not discharge, threaten, or otherwise discriminate if employee reports violation of any state, federal or political subdivision law or rule, or testifies as to a violation or refuses to execute a directive which would result in a violation	Both	Must first bring allegation to supervisor and allow for a reasonable opportunity to correct unless employee has specific reason to believe notice wouldn't result in prompt remedy of violation	Employee must first make a reasonable effort to remedy incident though in-house grievance procedure, then can get hearing with labor commissioner or his/her designee who can reinstate, order back pay, fringe benefits, and seniority rights as well as injunctive relief	Failure to comply with rules shall be a violation for each day of non-compliance
NEW JERSEY	34:19-1, *et seq.*	Can not discharge, suspend, demote, or take other retaliatory action if employee discloses or threatens to disclose an activity, policy, or practice of employer or other, with whom there's a business relationship, testify or object to or refuse to participate if action violates law, rule is fraudulent or criminal or incompatible with clear mandate concerning public health, safety, welfare, or protection of the environment	Both	Must bring violation to attention of a supervisor and afford a reasonable opportunity to correct, unless violation is known to supervisor or employee reasonably fears physical harm as a result of disclosure and situation is an emergency in nature	Can file civil action within one year of incident and receive all remedies available in civil law torts including injunction, reinstatement, reinstate full benefits and seniority rights, back pay and benefits, reasonable court and attorney's fees, punitive damages	Civil fine, maximum $1,000 for first violation and maximum of $5,000 for each subsequent violation
NEW MEXICO	50-9-25	Can not discharge or discriminate if employee files complaint, testifies, exercises a right or institutes a proceeding related to OHSA	Both		Can file complaint with secretary within 30 days of incident and get reinstatement or rehiring with back pay	

Table 20: Whistleblowing—Continued

State	Code Section	Prohibited Activity	Public or Private Employees	Opportunity for Employer to Correct?	Remedies	Penalties
NEW YORK	Labor §740	Can not discharge, suspend, demote or take other adverse employment action if employee discloses or threatens to, provides information or testifies, or objects to or refuses to participate in an action that violates law, rule, or regulation or presents a substantial and specific danger to public health or safety	Both	Must first report violation to supervisor and allow a reasonable opportunity to correct	Can file a civil action within one year of incident to get an injunction, reinstatement, full fringe benefits and seniority rights, back pay, and reasonable attorney's and court costs	
NORTH CAROLINA	126-84, *et seq.*	Can not discharge, threaten or otherwise discriminate if employee or their representative reports or is about to report a violation of state or federal law, rule, or regulation, fraud, misappropriation of state resources or substantial and specific danger to public health and safety	Public		Can file in superior court for damages, an injunction or other appropriate relief within one year of incident. Remedies include reinstatement, back pay, full fringe benefits and seniority rights and reasonable attorney's fees. If court finds willful violation, damages 3 times the amount of actual costs and reasonable attorney's fees	
	95-240, *et seq.*	Can not discriminate, discharge, suspend, demote or take other adverse action if employee or representative files claim, initiates an action or testifies on worker's compensation, OHSA, and wages or hours	Both		Can file complaint with Commission of Labor within 180 days of the incident; after 180 days, employee can request a right-to-sue letter, then can file civil action within 90 days of issuance of the right to sue and get injunction, reinstatement, full fringe benefits and seniority rights, back pay and benefits and reasonable attorney's fees. If court finds willful violation, can get treble damages	

Table 20: Whistleblowing—Continued

State	Code Section	Prohibited Activity	Public or Private Employees	Opportunity for Employer to Correct?	Remedies	Penalties
NORTH DAKOTA	34-11.1-04, -07,-08	Can not dismiss, withhold salary increase or benefits, transfer, reassign, deny promotion or demote or otherwise discriminate if employee reports in writing a violation of federal or state laws, agency rules or misuse of public resources	Public		All available legal remedies	Violation is a class B misdemeanor
OHIO	124.34; 4113.51	Can not take any disciplinary or retaliatory action including withholding pay, benefits, transfer/reassigning, removing/suspending, reducing pay/position or denying a promotion; if employee reports a violation of state or federal statute, ordinance, or regulation of a political subdivision	Both	Must notify and file a report; employer has 24 hours to correct	Can file a civil action for injunction, reinstatement, back pay, full fringe benefits and seniority rights, court and attorney's fees. If employer deliberately violates statute, court can award interest on back pay	
OKLAHOMA	74§840-2.5	No officer or employee of any state agency shall prohibit or take disciplinary action if employee disclosed public information, reports a violation of state or federal law, rule, or policy, mismanagement, gross waste of public funds, abuse of authority, or substantial and specific danger to public health and safety	Public		Can file an appeal with Oklahoma Merit Protection Commission within 30 days of disciplinary action to get corrective action	Violator can be suspended without pay, demoted or discharged, probation for 6 months. If they knowingly or willfully violate, court will forfeit their position and hold them ineligible for appointment or employment for a minimum of 1 year and maximum of 5 years
	40§402, *et seq.*	Can not discharge, discriminate, or take adverse personnel action if employee files a complaint, institutes a proceeding, or testifies regarding a violation of Occupational Safety and Health Act which causes or is likely to cause death or serious physical harm	Public	Yes	File complaint with commissioner	Misdemeanor

Table 20: Whistleblowing—Continued

State	Code Section	Prohibited Activity	Public or Private Employees	Opportunity for Employer to Correct?	Remedies	Penalties
OREGON	659.505, *et seq.*	A public employer can not discriminate, dismiss, demote, transfer, reassign, or take other disciplinary action if employee responds to official request to disclose or threatens to disclose a violation of federal or state law, rule or regulation, mismanagement, gross waste of funds, abuse of authority, or substantial and specific danger to public health and safety or the fact that a recipient of state funds is subject to a felony or misdemeanor or warrant for arrest	Public		Can file civil action within 90 days of disciplinary action for injunction or monetary damages	
	654.062	Can not bar, discharge, or otherwise discriminate if employee or prospective employee or representative of employee opposes, makes a complaint, institutes a proceeding or testifies about a violation of law, regulation or standard pertaining to safety and health	Both		Can file complaint with commissioner of the Bureau of Labor & Industries within 30 days of violation for reinstatement and back pay as well as other appropriate relief. Can also file civil action	
PENNSYLVANIA	43 §1421, *et seq.*	Can not discharge, threaten, retaliate, or otherwise discriminate if employee responds to official request or because employee or representative reports or is about to report a violation or waste	Both		Can file a civil action for injunction and/or damage within 180 days after disciplinary action. Court can award reinstatement, back pay, full fringe benefits and seniority rights, actual damages and reasonable attorney's fees	Civil fine maximum $500. If violation with intent to discourage disclosure of criminal activity, court can suspend person from public service for a maximum 6 months unless person holds an elected public office

Table 20: Whistleblowing—Continued

State	Code Section	Prohibited Activity	Public or Private Employees	Opportunity for Employer to Correct?	Remedies	Penalties
RHODE ISLAND	28-50-1	Can not discharge, threaten, or otherwise discriminate if employee or representative reports to a public body or is about to regarding a violation of state or federal law, regulation or rule or because employee responds to an official request	Both		Can file a civil action within 3 years of the violation for an injunction and/or actual damages including reinstatement, back pay, full fringe benefits and seniority rights, and attorney's fees	
SOUTH CAROLINA	8-27-10, *et seq.*	Can not dismiss, suspend, demote, or decrease compensation if employee files a report for violation of federal or state statute, laws, regulations, ordinances, substantial abuse, misuse, or loss of substantial public funds or resources	Public		If employee report results in saving of public funds, 25% of estimated net savings from first year implementation or a maximum of $2,000 will be rewarded employee; once employee exhausted all available grievance or other administrative remedies, can file a nonjury civil action within 1 year of reporting or exhaustion of all available grievance, judicial or administrative remedies to get reinstatement, back pay, actual damages (maximum $15,000), reasonable attorney's fees (maximum $10,000 for trial and $5,000 for appeal)	
	41-15-510	Can not discharge or discriminate if employee files complaint, institutes a proceeding or testifies regarding statutes, rules, or regulations regarding occupational safety and health	Both		Can file complaint with commission of labor within 30 days of the violation for reinstatement, back pay and other appropriate relief	
SOUTH DAKOTA	3-6-26 & 27; 3-6A-52.	Can not deprive of freedom of speech to report violation of state law or file a suggestion.	Public		Can file a grievance with the career service commission	

Table 20: Whistleblowing—Continued

State	Code Section	Prohibited Activity	Public or Private Employees	Opportunity for Employer to Correct?	Remedies	Penalties
SOUTH DAKOTA (cont.)	60-11:17.1; 60-12-21	Can not discharge, discriminate, or engage in any economic or otherwise reprisal if employee makes a complaint about violation of wage rules or any other complaint or testimony; can not threaten to terminate of take other retaliatory action if employee reports or is about to report sex discrimination in wages	Private			
TENNESSEE	50-1-304; 49-50-1401	Can not discharge or terminate if employee refuses to participate in or refuses to remain silent about violation of criminal or civil code, US laws, or neglect to protect public health, safety or welfare	Public		Can sue employer for retaliatory discharge and get damages	
	50-3-106; 50-3-409	Can not discharge or discriminate if employee files a complaint, institutes a proceeding, or testifies regarding a violation of any statute or regarding occupational safety and health	Both		Can file a complaint with Commission of Labor within 30 days of the violation for reinstatement, back pay, and other appropriate relief	
TEXAS	554.001	Can not suspend, terminate or take other adverse personnel action if employee reports a violation of law by employer or other employee	Public		Must report to appropriate law enforcement authority, then exhaust grievance or appeal process before suing no later than 90th day after violation, for injunction, actual damages, court costs and reasonable attorney fees. May also get reinstatement, back pay, full fringe benefits, seniority rights, and set maximum on compensatory damages	Supervisor, maximum $1,000 fine

Table 20: Whistleblowing—Continued

State	Code Section	Prohibited Activity	Public or Private Employees	Opportunity for Employer to Correct?	Remedies	Penalties
UTAH	67-21-1, *et seq.*	Can not discharge, threaten, or otherwise discriminate if employee reports, testifies or objects/ refuses to carry out directive that violates law, rule, or regulation of state, US or political subdivision or shows waste of public funds, property or manpower	Public		Can file civil action within 180 days of violation for injunction or actual damages and court and attorney's fees. In addition court can award reinstatement, back pay, full fringe benefits and seniority rights	Violator subject to civil fine, maximum $500
VERMONT	21 §231	Can not discharge or discriminate if employee files a complaint, institutes a proceeding or testifies regarding a violation of occupational, health and safety code	Both		Can file a complaint with commission within 30 days of violation to get reinstatement with back pay as well as other relief	
VIRGINIA	40.1-51.2:1 & 51.2:2	Can not discharge or discriminate if employee files, testifies, or otherwise acts to exercise rights under safety and health statute	Private	Yes in conciliation after complaint filed and investigation indicates a violation	Can file complaint with commissioner within 30 days of violation for reinstatement and back pay. If commissioner refuses to issue a charge, employee can file in circuit court for appropriate relief	
WASHINGTON	42.40.01, *et seq.* 49.60.21; 42.41.01, *et seq.*	Can not intimidate, threaten, coerce, command, influence, or attempt the above if employee discloses to auditor information of improper government action or identifies rules warranting review or provides information unless disclosing is prohibited by law	Public		File complaint with governing body of the local government within 30 days of violation, then can request a hearing to get reinstatement, back pay, injunctive relief, and costs and attorney's fees	Retaliator subject to maximum $3,000 penalty and suspension or dismissal

Table 20: Whistleblowing—Continued

State	Code Section	Prohibited Activity	Public or Private Employees	Opportunity for Employer to Correct?	Remedies	Penalties
WEST VIRGINIA	6C-1-1, *et seq.*	Can not discharge, threaten, or otherwise discriminate or retaliate if employee or representative reports or testifies as to a violation of state or federal statute or regulation, or ordinance of political subdivision or regulation or code of conduct or ethics designed to protect public from employer waste	Public		Can file civil action within 180 days of violation for reinstatement, back pay, full fringe benefits and seniority rights, actual damages, court and attorney's fees	Civil fine maximum $500 and if violator holds a public office by election or appointment and committed violation with intent to discourage disclosure: suspension maximum 6 months
	21-3A-13	Can not discharge or discriminate if employee files a complaint, institutes a proceeding or testifies regarding a violation of the occupational safety and health act	Public		Can file complaint with commissioner within 30 days for reinstatement, back pay, and other appropriate relief	
WISCONSIN	230.80, *et seq.*	Can not initiate, administer, or threaten to take retaliatory action if employee discloses violation of state or federal law, rule, or regulation, mismanagement or abuse of authority, substantial waste of public funds or a danger to public health or safety	Public	Commission will conduct conciliation after complaint filed and investigation indicates a violation	Can file complaint with state employment relation commission within 60 days of retaliation. The commission can award reinstatement, back pay, expungement of adverse material on employee's file, and attorney's fees	If respondent fails to comply with commission order, minimum $10, maximum $100 for every day of failure
WYOMING	27-11-109(e)	Can not discharge or discriminate if employee files a notice of complaint or institutes a proceeding or testifies as to a violation of the occupational health and safety statutes	Both			

V. FAMILY LAWS

21. ABORTION

The laws governing abortion are the most controversial in the United States today. The disunity among states regarding these laws, particularly those that define a legal abortion, reflects society's conflicting views toward abortion.

Abortion laws, as treated here, contain three main parts: a definition of an illegal abortion, a definition of a legal abortion, and a section dealing with consent and/or notice. There are also sections dealing with the penalties for violating the laws, residency requirements, waiting periods, and abortionists' licensing requirements. These sections are impossible to compare. Because the Supreme Court through inconsistent rulings has caused the laws regulating abortion to be so unsettled, many state legislatures are not enacting any legislation pending the outcome of various lawsuits and federal legislation. Therefore, waiting periods, spousal notification, and other particulars mentioned below are *not* separately treated because the Court has virtually preempted the states' power to legislate in these areas. However, these sections are ancillary to those questions regarding the legality of the act itself.

Illegal Abortion

In no state is unrestricted abortion legal; indeed, virtually all states begin with the presumption that abortion is a crime, though all state statutes do have definitions of legal abortions. About twenty states define an illegal abortion in terms of the definition of a legal abortion; for example, Hawaii defines an illegal abortion as failure to meet the criterion of a legal abortion. (The definition of a legal abortion, in Hawaii, is simply the destruction of a nonviable fetus.) About fifteen states, however, predominately in the East and the South, do define illegal abortions without reference to legal instances of abortion. A few of these, interestingly, include in their definitions the provision that if the mother dies, *then* the abortion is illegal. Of these states, only some have specific statutes defining an illegal abortion; others merely define a legal abortion and impose penalties for their violation. The remaining states have definitions that specifically mention the limits of when an abortion is acceptable. For example, West Virginia defines an illegal abortion as any activity "with intent to destroy an unborn child or produce abortion [or] if mother dies unless to save the mother."

Legal Abortion

Legal abortion is universally defined in terms of the mother's convenience or health. Though few definitions mention the life or health of the fetus, many refer to its "viability" as a standard for when an abortion may be performed with impunity, and without further attempt to define the term. These definitions are objective in that specific time parameters are set, outside of which an abortion cannot legally be done, absent exigent circumstances. The most unrestrictive of all definitions occur in Hawaii and Alaska, where a legal abortion is an abortion on "any nonviable fetus." Interestingly, the definition of an illegal abortion in these two states is equally open; they say essentially that any act knowingly found to be contrary to the legal definition is illegal. After viability has been established, most states give additional instances when abortion may be legal: to save the life of the mother or if there are severe defects present in the fetus.

Partial Birth Abortion

The procedure called "partial birth abortion" has lately become the subject of numerous state statutes in the wake of the controversial vetoing by President Clinton of a federal bill that would have banned the procedure. The term means an abortion in which the person performing the abortion deliberately and intentionally delivers a living fetus or a substantial portion thereof into the vagina for the purpose of performing a procedure the person knows will kill the fetus, performs the procedure, kills the fetus and completes the delivery. In the last two years, twenty-one states have enacted legislation banning or limiting the practice of this procedure.

State of the Statutes

Prior to 1973 and the *Roe* v. *Wade* decision by the Supreme Court (410 U.S. 113 (1973)), the regulation of abortion was left to the states. In *Roe* v. *Wade,* the Supreme Court decided that the Constitution protected a woman's right to abortion, a novel right said to be found in the unstated right to privacy, from state regulation during the first trimester of pregnancy. However, the Court also held that the states have an "important and legitimate interest in protecting the potentiality of human life." The abortion controversy has revolved around the states' consequent attempts to protect unborn life. The Supreme Court's patchwork of opinions following *Roe* has left abortion a highly unsettled area of law. Many statutes reflect state attempts at balancing a woman's right to choose an abortion with the state's compelling interest in protecting fetal life.

The statutes in this chapter are as they currently appear in the state codes. Interestingly enough, some of the statutes may be unconstitutional if challenged, based on prior Supreme Court rulings. Following are the general areas of abortion legislation and the Supreme Court's treatment of each:

- *Parental Consent.* States may require a minor seeking an abortion to obtain the consent of a parent or guardian as long as there is an adequate judicial bypass procedure.

- *Informed Consent.* A state may require a physician to provide a woman with such information such as alternatives to abortion, sources of financial aid, development of the child, and the gestational age of the child. Prior to 1992, informed consent provisions were unconstitutional.

- *Spousal Consent.* A state may not require a married woman to obtain her husband's consent before undergoing an abortion.

- *Abortion Method.* A state may not require the physician performing the abortion to use the technique providing for the best opportunity for the unborn child to survive the abortion.

- *Second Physician.* A state may not require that a second physician attend the abortion to take immediate control of the care of a child born alive in an abortion unless the provision has an exception for a situation when the health of the mother was endangered.

- *Waiting Period.* A twenty-four hour waiting period does not constitute an undue burden on a woman's decision to abort and, therefore, is constitutional. Prior to 1992, waiting period requirements were unconstitutional.

- *Parental Notice.* A state may require that one parent be notified of a minor's abortion, but not two.

- *Fetal Remains.* States may not require that the remains of the unborn child are disposed of in a "human and sane" manner as it may suggest a mandate for some sort of "decent burial."

Table 21: Abortion

State/Code Section	Statutory Definition of		Penalty	Consent	Residency	License
	Illegal Abortion	Legal Abortion				
ALABAMA 13A-13-7; 26-21-1 to 26-22-5	Willfully administers by drug, substance, instrument which induces abortion or miscarriage. <u>Partial Birth Abortion</u> (26-23-1 to 26-23-6): Any physician who performs a partial birth abortion within this state and thereby kills a human fetus shall be guilty of a Class C felony and upon conviction shall be punished as prescribed by law. (except to save life of mother.)	Necessary purpose to preserve life, health of mother	Fine of $100 to $1,000 and imprisonment to 12 months	Written consent of parent or guardian to perform abortion on unemancipated minor or judicial waiver of consent		
ALASKA 18.16.010–18.16.090	Knowingly doesn't meet standards for legal abortion. <u>Partial Birth Abortion</u> (§18.16.050): Partial birth abortion unlawful unless to save life of mother when no other medical procedure would suffice	Terminate pregnancy of nonviable fetus	Fine to $1,000 and/or imprisonment up to 5 years	Of patient or one parent or guardian if unmarried, unemancipated patient less than 18, except in medical emergency or judicial waiver of consent	30 days before procedure	Licensed M.D., by State Medical Board hospital or facility approved by Dept. of Health & Social Services
ARIZONA 13-3603; 36-2152; 36-2153	By drug, instrument with intent to procure miscarriage (unless necessary to save mother's life). <u>Partial Birth Abortion:</u> Felony unless to save the life of the mother if no other medical procedure would save the mother's life	Necessary to preserve life of mother	Imprisonment 2 to 5 years	Written consent of one parent or legal guardian if unmarried or unemancipated patient is under 18, except by court order or medical emergency		

Table 21: Abortion—Continued

State/Code Section	Statutory Definition of		Penalty	Consent	Residency	License
	Illegal Abortion	Legal Abortion				
ARKANSAS 5-61-101 to 102; 20-9-302; 20-16-601; 20-16-701 to 707; 20-16-801, *et seq.*	Intentional termination of pregnancy with intent other than to increase probability of live birth or to remove dead or dying fetus. Viable fetus defined as one which can live outside the womb; fetus is presumed nonviable prior to end of 25th week of pregnancy. <u>Partial Birth Abortion</u> (§§51-61-201 to 51-61-204): Felony unless to save the woman's life when no other form of abortion would suffice for that purpose	No abortion of viable fetus other than as necessary to preserve life of mother, or where pregnancy is result of rape or of incest of minor; written certification by licensed physician required	Fine to $1,000 and imprisonment 1 to 5 years (Class A misdemeanor)	If minor or incompetent, written notice to parent or guardian required at least 48 hours before procedure, except by court order, medical emergency, upon declaration of child abuse, neglect, incest, parents' whereabouts unknown, or parent and minor have not been in contact for at least 1 yr.		Physicians must be licensed to practice medicine in state
CALIFORNIA Health & Safety §§123400 to 123450; Pen. §§274 to 276	By drugs, medicine, or instrument with intent to procure miscarriage	Continuation of pregnancy would greatly impair life or health of mother, or pregnancy result of rape or incest	Imprisonment in the state prison	In case of unemancipated minor, written consent of minor and one parent or legal guardian, or by order of petition to Juvenile Court or in a medical emergency requiring immediate medical attention		Approved hospital and unanimous approval of medical committee of hospital (unless the health of mother impaired or rape or incest); certified physician/ surgeon

Table 21: Abortion—Continued

State/Code Section	Statutory Definition of		Penalty	Consent	Residency	License
	Illegal Abortion	Legal Abortion				
COLORADO 18-6-101 to 105 (portions declared unconstitutional by *People* v. *Norton*, 181 Co. 47, 507 P.2d 862 [1973] although they have not been repealed)	Ends or causes pregnancy to be ended by any means other than justified medical termination or birth	Intentional ending of pregnancy by licensed physician using accepted medical procedures and as required, with appropriate consent. Continuation of pregnancy likely to result in death or permanent physical or mental impairment of mother, or child born with grave mental or physical retardation, or within first 16 weeks of pregnancy and pregnancy result of sexual assault or incest. Court declared unconstitutional, but not repealed	Class 4 felony but if woman dies class 2 felony	Mother; mother and father, if married; mother and parent/guardian if under 18 years; if married, mother and her husband (although similar parental consent declared unconstitutional under *Planned Parenthood of Missouri v. Danforth*, 428 U.S. 52 (1976).		Licensed physician using accepted medical procedures in a hospital licensed by Dept. of Public Health and Environment
CONNECTICUT 19a-600, *et seq.*		Pregnant woman's decision to terminate pregnancy before viability—after viability, only to preserve life or health of pregnant woman		Minors (persons less than 16 years) must be provided with information and counseling and then sign and date standard form (unless medical emergency)		
DELAWARE Tit. 11 §654, Tit. 24 §1766; Tit. 24 §§1780-1795	By drugs or act done with intent to cause termination of pregnancy	Continuation of pregnancy would result in death or injury to mother; mental and/or physical retardation of child or pregnancy result of rape or incest or unlawful sexual intercourse, but must be performed within first 20 weeks	Felony; maximum fine of $5,000 and imprisonment 2 to 10 years	24 hour waiting period following written consent and full explanation of procedure; if unmarried and under 18 or mentally ill or incompetent, consent of parent	120 days before procedure unless employed in state or patient of state-licensed M.D. or medical emergency	Licensed M.D., national accredited hospital; approval of hospital abortion review board

Table 21: Abortion—Continued

State/Code Section	Statutory Definition of		Penalty	Consent	Residency	License
	Illegal Abortion	Legal Abortion				
DISTRICT OF COLUMBIA 22-201	By means of instrument, drugs, or whatever attempts to or procures abortion unless necessary for preservation of mother's life or health	When necessary to preserve life or health of mother	Imprisonment 1 to 10 years; if mother dies (second degree murder), imprisonment 20 years to life			Under direction of competent licensed practitioner of medicine
FLORIDA 390.001, *et seq.*; 797.02; 797.03	Termination of pregnancy during last trimester which does not meet requirements of legal abortion. Partial Birth Abortion: Prohibited except when necessary to save the life of the mother when her life is physically endangered and no other medical procedure would suffice for that purpose	Regulated only in last trimester, necessary to save life or preserve health of mother and requires 2 physicians' certifications of medical necessity	Third degree felony; imprisonment to 5 yrs. or 2nd degree misdemeanor; up to 60 days imprisonment	Voluntary written consent of mother or of the court-appointed guardian of a mentally incompetent woman, except in a medical emergency		Validly licensed hospital, or medical facility; third trimester only in hospital
GEORGIA 16-12-140 *et seq.*; 15-11-110 *et seq.*	By administering medicine, drugs, or substance or using instrument with intent to procure miscarriage or abortion. Partial Birth Abortion: Unlawful except to save the mother's life when that life is physically endangered and no other medical procedure will suffice to save her life	Preserve life or health of mother	Imprisonment 1 to 10 years	Except in medical emergency, written, informed consent of parent or guardian of unemancipated minor under the age of 18; parent must have 24-hour notice before scheduled abortion, unless waived or unless minor obtains judicial approval that minor is either mature enough to decide without parents' consent or parents' consent is not in best interests of the minor		First trimester: licensed M.D.; second trimester: licensed M.D. and licensed hospital or health facility; third trimester: licensed M.D. and 2 consulting M.D.s certifying necessity of abortion to preserve life or health of mother

Table 21: Abortion—Continued

State/Code Section	Statutory Definition of		Penalty	Consent	Residency	License
	Illegal Abortion	Legal Abortion				
HAWAII 453-16	Failure to meet standards for legal abortion	Terminate pregnancy of nonviable fetus	Fine to $1,000 and/or imprisonment to 5 years		90 days immediately preceding abortion	Licensed M.D., licensed hospital
IDAHO 18-603 *et seq.*	Provides, supplies, administers drugs or substances to woman, or uses instrument with intent to produce abortion. <u>Partial Birth Abortion:</u> Unlawful except when necessary to save the life of the mother when it is physically endangered	In first and second trimesters: consultation between licensed M.D. and mother and determination by M.D. that abortion is appropriate considering various mental, physical, family factors including circumstances of pregnancy (such as rape or incest). Third trimester: must be necessary to preserve life of mother or fetus and M.D. must consult another corroborating physician.	Felony; fine to $5,000 and/or imprisonment 2 to 5 years; mother, fine to $5,000, and/ or imprisonment 1 to 5 years	Mother must give "informed consent" after information about development of fetus, adoption and other services, risks, etc.; parents or guardian of unmarried woman under 18 or unemancipated woman shall be notified 24 hours prior to performance of abortion, if possible		First trimester: in hospital or properly staffed clinic or physician's office with arrangements with nearby acute care hospital for complications or emergencies; second trimester: same as first except that procedure must be performed in licensed hospital and in the "best medical interest" of pregnant woman; third trimester: same as second except requires corroboration of consulting M.D. and procedure must be necessary to preserve life of mother or fetus

Table 21: Abortion—Continued

State/Code Section	Statutory Definition of		Penalty	Consent	Residency	License
	Illegal Abortion	Legal Abortion				
ILLINOIS 720 ILCS 510/1 to 520/10	Use of any instrument, drug, or any other device to terminate pregnancy of a woman known to be pregnant with an intention other than to increase the probability of a live birth, to preserve the life or health of the child after live birth, or to remove a dead fetus	If fetus nonviable and abortion not necessary to preserve mother's health, M.D. must certify nonviability; if fetus is viable, abortion must be medically necessary to preserve life, health of mother; M.D. must certify this necessity	Fine to $1,000 and/or imprisonment 3 to 7 years for M.D. (Class 2 felony); if fetus could have survived with or without support and M.D. does not use method to keep it alive: Class 3 felony	48 hours prior to abortion procedure on an unmarried woman less than 18, actual or constructive notice must be given to an adult family member; exceptions for medical emergency or judicial notice		Licensed M.D.
INDIANA 16.34 *et seq.*	Any abortion not as provided for in 1st or 2nd trimester. <u>Partial Birth Abortion</u>: A person may not lawfully or knowingly perform a partial birth abortion unless a physician reasonably believes it is necessary to save the life of the mother and that no other medical procedure is sufficient	During first trimester with mother's consent and based on physician's professional and medical judgement; after first trimester but before viability, permissible with mother's consent and if performed in hospital or surgical center; after viability, procedure necessary to prevent impairment of life, health of mother and performed in hospital with premature birth care unit and with 2nd physician present	Class C felony; Statute, Class A misdemeanor for not meeting proper consent requirements	Written consent of mother, not applicable in emergency; if unemancipated minor under 18 yrs. old, performing abortion not in accordance with written consent of one parent or legal guardian; court can waive parental consent requirement; not applicable in emergency		First trimester: professional judgment of attending licensed M.D.; second trimester, before viability: same as first and licensed hospital; after viability: same as second and reasons for procedure regarding mother certified by M.D. to hospital.

Table 21: Abortion—Continued

State/Code Section	Statutory Definition of		Penalty	Consent	Residency	License
	Illegal Abortion	Legal Abortion				
IOWA 707.7; *et seq.*	"Feticide": Intentional termination of human pregnancy after end of second trimester. "Abortion": Termination of a human pregnancy with the intent other than to produce a live birth or remove a dead fetus. "Partial Birth Equivalent": A person who intentionally kills a viable fetus aborted alive shall be guilty of a Class B felony.	Necessary to preserve life or health of mother or fetus; after end of second trimester with every reasonable effort made to preserve life of viable fetus	Class C felony (attempted feticide—Class D felony)	Knowledge and voluntary consent of pregnant mother. Unmarried woman less than 18 must have parental notification 48 hours before the abortion; judicial waiver possible		Licensed M.D.
KANSAS 65-6701 *et seq.*	To perform or induce abortion when fetus is viable, that is, in attending physician's best medical judgement, fetus is capable of sustained survival outside the uterus without extraordinary medical means	As long as fetus is not viable (and mother's informed consent obtained); unless 2nd M.D. certifies that abortion is necessary to preserve life of mother or fetus has severe, life-threatening deformity or abnormality	Class A person misdemeanor	Informed consent of all women before abortion (not applicable in emergency); notice must be given to one of unemancipated minor's parents or guardian (court can waive notice requirement on finding minor sufficiently mature or notice not in minor's best interest)		Licensed M.D.; 2nd M.D. (not financially associated with 1st M.D.) to certify abortion of viable fetus to preserve life of mother

Table 21: Abortion—Continued

State/Code Section	Statutory Definition of		Penalty	Consent	Residency	License
	Illegal Abortion	Legal Abortion				
KENTUCKY 311.710 to 830; 311.990	Abortion after viability unlawful except to preserve life or health of woman, but abortionist shall take all reasonable steps to preserve the life and health of the child	M.D. determines abortion is necessary in his clinical judgement and with second opinion of M.D. and mother supplies informed consent. Permissible during first trimester; after viability of fetus, necessary to preserve life or health of mother	Aborting when M.D. did not believe it necessary or did not receive a written referral or violating notice to spouse provisions or violating any regulations on abortions after viability or use of saline method of abortion after first trimester is Class D felony; non-licensed physician performing abortion is Class B felony; performing abortion on viable fetus except to preserve life and health of mother: Class C felony; violating woman's consent provisions or aborting with reckless disregard of whether mother is minor is Class A misdemeanor	Written informed consent with two-hour waiting period of mother; of one parent or guardian if mother under 18 and unemancipated, except when medical emergency or by judicial proceedings for court to waive parental consent; doctor must notify spouse if possible prior to abortion, if not possible, within 30 days of abortion		First trimester: by a woman upon herself with advice of licensed M.D.; after first trimester, advice of a licensed M.D. except must be in licensed hospital, except in medical emergency

Table 21: Abortion—Continued

State/Code Section	Statutory Definition of		Penalty	Consent	Residency	License
	Illegal Abortion	Legal Abortion				
LOUISIANA 14:87, *et seq.* 40:1299.31 to 40.1299.35.18	Administration of drug or substance or use of instrument with intent of procuring premature delivery of the embryo or fetus by any person, even the woman herself. A person who kills a viable child during labor shall be sentenced to life imprisonment at hard labor, except when the death of the child results from an express act to save the life of the child or the mother. Partial Birth Abortion: Unlawful except when necessary to save life of a woman endangered by physical disorder, physical illness, or physical injury when no other medical procedure would suffice	After viability or third trimester, any termination of pregnancy necessary to preserve life, health of mother and/or fetus or when pregnancy resulted from rape or incest and fetus is not viable	Crime of abortion: 1-10 yrs., imprisoned at hard labor and $1000–10,000 fine	Written informed consent of woman 24 hours prior to abortion; if unemancipated minor, signed consent of parent or guardian or court, except in medical emergency or if judicial consent		After first trimester, licensed M.D. must make judgment of advisability or necessity of abortion, shall certify medical reasons for viability abortion, and procedure must be performed in licensed hospital
MAINE Tit. 22 §§1591 to 1599	Intentional interruption of a pregnancy by the application of external agents, whether chemical or physical, or the ingestion of chemical agents with an intention other than to produce a live birth or to remove a dead fetus	Before viability by physician; after viability, only when necessary to preserve life or health of mother	Class D Crime: M.D. failing to perform any action required: fine up to $1000 for each violation, not taking reasonable steps to preserve life of live born child: subject to homicide, manslaughter and/or malpractice liability	Informed written consent by minor and consent of one parent/guardian required for persons under 18 yrs. old except in emergencies or if judicial consent is obtained; informed written consent of all women required		Licensed M.D.

Table 21: Abortion—Continued

State/Code Section	Statutory Definition of		Penalty	Consent	Residency	License
	Illegal Abortion	Legal Abortion				
MARYLAND Health & Gen. §§20-207 to 214; 20-103	Viability is defined as when, in M.D.'s best medical judgement, there is a reasonable likelihood of the fetus' sustained survival outside the womb	Performed before fetus is viable or at anytime where termination procedure is necessary to protect life, health of woman or fetus is affected by serious genetic defect/abnormality (procedure must be least intrusive and not inconsistent with established medical practice)	M.D. not liable if decision to abort made in good faith and in best medical judgement	M.D. may not perform an abortion on an unmarried minor unless M.D. first gives notice to parent or guardian, unless minor does not live with parent/guardian and reasonable efforts to give notice are unsuccessful or if in M.D.'s judgment notice to parent/guardian may lead to physical or emotional abuse, or the minor is mature and capable of informed consent or notice would not be in the best interest of minor		Licensed M.D.

Table 21: Abortion—Continued

State/Code Section	Statutory Definition of		Penalty	Consent	Residency	License
	Illegal Abortion	Legal Abortion				
MASSACHUSETTS Ch. 112§§12K to 12U	Failure to meet standards for legal abortion; violation of procedural standards such as informed consent, medical procedure required, etc. Knowing destruction of the life of an unborn child or the intentional expulsion or removal of an unborn child from the womb other than for the principal purpose of live birth or removing a dead fetus	Under 24 weeks, abortion may be performed only by M.D. and only if in M.D.'s best judgment the abortion is necessary under the circumstances; after 24 weeks M.D. must provide written statement that: 1) necessary to save life of mother; 2) continuation will impose substantial risk of grave physical or mental impairment; no procedure can be used which destroys or injures fetus unless in M.D.'s opinion other available procedures would be greater risk to mother or future pregnancies and all reasonable steps must be taken to preserve life, health of aborted child	Violation of standards of performing legal abortion: fine of $500 to $2,000 and/or imprisonment 3 months to 5 years	Written informed consent within 24 hours before procedure except in emergencies; if mother less than 18 years and unmarried, consent of both parents or guardians or court, except in medical emergency, or if convinced of mother's maturity and that procedure is in mother's best interest.		Licensed M.D. except in medical emergency; after 13th week, must be performed in licensed hospital

Table 21: Abortion—Continued

State/Code Section	Statutory Definition of		Penalty	Consent	Residency	License
	Illegal Abortion	Legal Abortion				
MICHIGAN MCL 750.14; MCL 722.901 *et seq.;* MCL 333.17016	Drug, substance, instrument, or device employed with intent to terminate pregnancy for a purpose other than to increase probability of a live birth, to preserve the health of the child, or to remove a dead fetus. <u>Partial Birth Abortion:</u> Unlawful except to save the life of a mother endangered by physical illness, physical injury, or physical disorder when no other medical procedure will suffice	After viability, when necessary to preserve life of mother	Felony: fine to $2,000 and/or imprisonment to 4 years; if mother dies, manslaughter, fine to $7,500 and/or imprisonment to 15 years; violation of parental consent requirement is a misdemeanor	No abortion may be performed on minor without her consent and that of one parent or guardian except in medical emergency; court may waive parental consent if minor is mature and well-informed so as to be able to make the decision, or waiver is in minor's best interest	Require-ments apply even if minor is not resident	
MINNESOTA 145.411 to 424 and 617.20 to 22	Failure to meet standards of legal abortion; sale or manufacture of drug, substance, or instrument intended for unlawful use in miscarriage or abortion procedure; act, procedure, or use of any instrument, medicine, or drug which is supplied, prescribed for, or administered to a pregnant woman which results in the termination of pregnancy	Before viability, by a trained M.D. After viability (second half of gestation), must be performed in hospital and necessary to preserve life, health of mother and procedure used will reasonably assure live birth. After 20th week, 2nd M.D. must be immediately accessible for any resulting live birth	Felony	Informed consent of mother		Licensed M.D., and licensed abortion facility or hospital

Table 21: Abortion—Continued

State/Code Section	Statutory Definition of		Penalty	Consent	Residency	License
	Illegal Abortion	Legal Abortion				
MISSISSIPPI 97-3-3, 5; 41-75-1, *et. seq.*	Willfully or knowingly by means of instrument, medicine, drug, or any other substance causing any pregnant woman to abort or miscarry	Necessary to preserve mother's life; pregnancy result of rape	Felony: imprisonment 1 to 10 years; if mother dies, murder; if M.D. or nurse convicted, license will be revoked; misdemeanor: $25-200 and imprisonment up to 3 mos. if selling, giving away, possessing or in any manner anything causing unlawful abortion.	Written informed consent of the mother at least 24 hours before the abortion, except in emergency; unmarried woman under 18 must have written consent of both parents, with exceptions for medical emergency or judicial waiver		Licensed M.D.; prior advice of two licensed M.D.s required in writing
MISSOURI 188.010 to 230	Intentional destruction of the life of an embryo or fetus in the womb or intentional termination of pregnancy with intention other than live birth or removal of dead unborn child. Also, illegal to perform abortion for purpose of providing fetal organs/tissue for transplant or other purpose. Also, illegal to use public facilities, employees or funds for abortion, except where necessary to save mother's life	After viability, necessary to preserve life, health of mother; (method used must be one most likely to preserve life, health of fetus unless greater risk to mother)	Fine to $1,000 and imprisonment to 1 year; second degree murder to take the life of a child aborted alive; anyone not a physician attempting to perform an abortion or without privileges at hospital offering OB/Gyn care is guilty of Class B felony; Class A misdemeanor and revocation of M.D. or health practitioner's license for committing or assisting in unlawful abortion; failure to maintain confidentiality: misdemeanor	Prior, informed, written consent of mother; if mother is less than 18 and unemancipated, informed written consent of one parent/guardian or court order		Licensed M.D. only. After 16 wks., must be performed in hospital; after viability, licensed M.D. must certify abortion necessary including medical indicators and method to be utilized with reasoning for decision; second M.D. must be in attendance to aid fetus; at 20 weeks, M.D. required to determine whether fetus is viable, using ordinary skill and care and testing

291

Table 21: Abortion—Continued

State/Code Section	Statutory Definition of		Penalty	Consent	Residency	License
	Illegal Abortion	Legal Abortion				
MONTANA 50-20-101 to 112; 50-20-401	Use or prescription of any instrument, medicine, drug, or other substance or device to intentionally terminate the pregnancy of a woman known to be pregnant, with an intention other than to increase the probability of a live birth, to preserve the life or health of the child, or to remove a dead fetus. Partial Birth Abortion: Unlawful except to save the life of mother when endangered by physical disorder, illness, or injury when no other medical procedure would save the woman's life	After viability, if necessary according to M.D. to preserve life or health of mother; procedure utilized must not negligently or intentionally endanger life of fetus unless to preserve mother's life	Violation of infant protection; violation of abortion practices by M.D.: felony, fine to $1,000 and/or imprisonment to 5 years; violation of consent provisions or of inducing woman to have abortion: misdemeanor, fine to $500 and/or imprisonment to 6 months; no penalties may be placed on the mother	Informed consent of mother 24 hours prior to procedure, signed by mother and her M.D. except when M.D. certifies necessary to preserve mother's life; if married, written notice of spouse unless voluntarily separated from her; if under 18 years and unmarried, written notice of a parent/guardian		Licensed M.D., after first 3 months in licensed hospital; after viability, M.D. must certify in writing necessity of procedure including grounds for decision plus two other M.D.s must confirm decision except when necessary to preserve mother's life
NEBRASKA 71-6901, *et seq.*; 28-325-347	Act, procedure, device, or prescription administered to a woman to produce premature expulsion, removal, or termination of the human life within the womb of the pregnant woman unless the child's viability is threatened by continuation of the pregnancy	Before viability or if woman is victim of abuse or neglect or if the M.D. has certification in writing that the continued pregnancy is a threat to woman's life, health	Class III misdemeanor: M.D. who performs abortion in violation of any standards	Unemancipated woman under 18 yrs. old or incompetent requires at least 48 hr. written notice to a parent or guardian by delivery or certified mail; court may waive requirements if find woman is mature; parent may authorize abortion in writing; voluntary and informed consent of woman 24 hours before abortion, except in emergency		Licensed M.D.

Table 21: Abortion—Continued

State/Code Section	Statutory Definition of		Penalty	Consent	Residency	License
	Illegal Abortion	Legal Abortion				
NEVADA §§442.240 to 270	Termination of a human pregnancy with an intention other than to produce the birth of an infant capable of sustained survival by natural or artificial support or to remove a dead fetus	Only within first 24 weeks unless necessary to preserve life, health of mother	Violation of notice or consent statutes: misdemeanor; failure to take steps to preserve life of infant: M.D. liable for malpractice and wrongful death	Informed consent of mother, certified by M.D.; if mother under 18, unemancipated and unmarried, actual notice to parent/ guardian required before procedure unless immediately necessary to protect life, health of minor; if actual notice is unsuccessful, then M.D. must delay abortion until s/he has notified parent by certified mail; court may authorize abortion if mature or in minor's best interest		Licensed M.D. who must exercise "best clinical judgment"; licensed hospital after 24th week and records of mother must contain facts upon which M.D. based decision that continued pregnancy would endanger life, health of mother
NEW HAMPSHIRE 585:12, 585:13 and 585:14 are repealed.		Death of fetus specifically not homicide. 630:1				
NEW JERSEY (Abortion) repealed effective September 1, 1979. No replacement statute enacted						
NEW MEXICO 30-5-1 to 3	Failure to meet standards of justified termination; or by administering medical drug or other substance or means whereby an untimely termination of pregnancy is produced with intent to destroy fetus and not a justified medical termination	Continuation likely to result in death or impairment of mother's mental or physical health or fetus likely to have grave physical or mental defect; or pregnancy result of rape or incest	Criminal abortion: fourth degree felony; abortion resulting in woman's death: second degree felony	Mother must "request" procedure; if under 18 the procedure must be requested by her and parent/ guardian		Licensed M.D., licensed hospital, written certification of hospital board required (a committee of 2 licensed M.D.s and alternates who decide questions of medical justification of specific case)

293

Table 21: Abortion—Continued

State/Code Section	Statutory Definition of		Penalty	Consent	Residency	License
	Illegal Abortion	Legal Abortion				
NEW YORK Penal §125.05, §125.20, §125.40-60; Pub. Health §4164	(1) Failure to meet standards for legal abortion; (2) if causes mother to die; (3) if not within first 24 weeks; (4) administering or taking drugs or any other manner with intent to cause a miscarriage	Within first 24 weeks or necessary to preserve mother's life; if mother performs abortion it must be on the advice of M.D. within the first 24 weeks or to preserve her own life	If not justifiable abortional act and after 24 wks., Class E or D felony; if woman dies from act, Class B felony; self-abortion or issuing abortion articles, Class B or A misdemeanor			Licensed M.D.; after 12th wk., must be in hospital on in-patient basis. After 20th wk., 2nd M.D. must be present to handle medical care of any live birth
NORTH CAROLINA 14-44 to 46; 90-21.6 to 90-21.10	Willfully administer to mother, prescribe, advise, procure substance or instrument with intent to destroy child or procure miscarriage	First 20 weeks of pregnancy no medical requirements regarding mother or fetus; after 20 weeks, must be substantial risk that would threaten life, health of mother	Class H felony: Fine and/or imprisonment up to 10 years; Class I felony: Fine and/or imprisonment up to 5 years; Class I misdemeanor for failing to attain parental consent	Unemancipated minor needs written consent plus written consent of parent/guardian, exception for medical emergency or judicial waiver		Licensed M.D., licensed hospital or clinic

Table 21: Abortion—Continued

State/Code Section	Statutory Definition of		Penalty	Consent	Residency	License
	Illegal Abortion	Legal Abortion				
NORTH DAKOTA 14-02.1-01 to 12	(1) Non-licensed person performs abortion; (2) if licensed M.D. but doesn't conform to standards for legal abortion; termination of human pregnancy with an intention other than to produce a live birth or to remove a dead embryo or fetus	During 1st 12 wks., no restrictions. After viability, necessary to preserve life of mother or continuance would impair her physical or mental health and must be in a hospital	M.D.: Class A misdemeanor; anyone not M.D. who performs abortion: Class B felony; if M.D. does not take proper care to preserve life of unborn or born viable fetus: Class C felony; all other violations of N.D. Abortion Control Act: Class A misdemeanor	Informed consent of mother as certified by M.D. at least 24 hours before procedure; before viability, if mother is unemancipated minor M.D. must inform both parents or guardian at least 24 hours before minor's consent; or emergency or judicial waiver; after viability, husband's written consent, unless separated, or consent of a parent/guardian if mother is less than 18 years and unmarried, unless procedure is necessary to preserve life, health of mother; court can authorize abortion on minor without parental consent		Licensed M.D. using medical standards applicable; licensed hospital required after first 12 weeks of pregnancy as well as M.D. must certify facts and have 2 M.D.s concur with his medical judgement for abortion, unless medical emergency

Table 21: Abortion—Continued

State/Code Section	Statutory Definition of		Penalty	Consent	Residency	License
	Illegal Abortion	Legal Abortion				
OHIO 2919.11 to 18	(1) Failure to obtain informed consent; (2) taking life of fetus born alive or failing to provide reasonable medical attention to same; purposeful termination of a human pregnancy by any person, including the mother herself, with the intention other than to produce a live birth or remove a dead fetus	Performed or induced by a physician who determines in good faith that the fetus is not viable or to prevent the death or serious bodily injury of the pregnant woman	Violators guilty of unlawful abortion: first degree misdemeanor; second violation: fourth degree felony	Informed consent of mother; if mother is unemancipated minor, parental informed consent also required with 24 hrs. "actual notice"; court may authorize minor to consent without parental notification; other family members over 21 may issue consent if minor in danger of physical, sexual, or emotional abuse from parent; constructive notice (of at least 48 hrs.) by both certified and ordinary mail allowed if parents or family members cannot be reached with reasonable effort		Licensed physician

Table 21: Abortion—Continued

State/Code Section	Statutory Definition of		Penalty	Consent	Residency	License
	Illegal Abortion	Legal Abortion				
OKLAHOMA Tit. 63§§1-730 to 741; 21§§713 to 714; 21§861; 21§684	(1)Non-licensed person performs abortion; (2) failure to meet standards for legal abortion; (3) taking life of viable fetus unless necessary to preserve life, health of mother or failure to provide medical aid to fetus; purposeful termination of a human pregnancy with intent other than to produce a live birth or remove a dead fetus. Partial Birth Abortion: Physicians shall be fined $10,000 and/or imprisoned for not more than 2 years for performing a partial birth abortion except when necessary to save the mother when her life is endangered by a physical disorder, illness, or injury	After viability, necessary to preserve life, health of mother (viability presumed after 24th week). If abortion is self-induced, must be under supervision of M.D.	Person who administers or uses drugs or any other instrument to procure miscarriage unless to save life of mother: 2-5 yrs. imprisonment; person not M.D. performing abortion: 1 to 3 years in state penitentiary; anyone aborting viable fetus not to prevent mother's death or health impairment: homicide; willful killing of unborn quick child by injuring mother or any other means (drugs, medicines, instruments): manslaughter			Licensed M.D.; approved hospital required after first trimester; M.D. must certify necessity of procedure after viability, including factors considered; after viability M.D. required to aid fetus, except in medical emergency

Table 21: Abortion—Continued

State/Code Section	Statutory Definition of		Penalty	Consent	Residency	License
	Illegal Abortion	Legal Abortion				
OREGON 435.435 to 990						No M.D. is required to give advice with respect to or participate in any abortion if refusal is based on election not to do so and M.D. so advises patient; no hospital employee or member of medical staff is required to participate in abortions if individual notifies hospital of such election

Table 21: Abortion—Continued

State/Code Section	Statutory Definition of		Penalty	Consent	Residency	License
	Illegal Abortion	Legal Abortion				
PENNSYLVANIA Tit. 18§§3201 to 3220	(1) Failure to obtain informed consent of woman; (2) failure to meet standards for legal abortion; (3) using any means to cause the death of an unborn child but not meaning use of intrauterine device or the birth control pill; (4) solely for the reason of the child's sex; (5) without making diagnosis of gestational age; (6) use of public funds, facilities, or officials	M.D. must find, in his clinical judgement, that abortion must be necessary or that a "referring M.D." has sent a written signed statement saying so; after viability, 24 wks., necessary to preserve life of mother or prevent serious risk of substantial and irreversible impairment of bodily function. Viability defined as when M.D., based on facts of particular case, finds reasonable likelihood of fetus' sustained survival outside the mother's body.	Failing to adequately care for viable fetus, M.D. violating medical consultation provisions, finding abortion necessary, violation of 2nd M.D. requirement: Felony in 3rd degree and license may be revoked; person inducing abortion in violation of legal standards: 1st offense: summary offense; 2nd and subsequent offenses: 3rd degree misdemeanor; violation of informed consent or spousal notification provisions (spousal consent found unconstitutional in *Planned Parenthood of Southeastern Pennsylvania v. Casey*, but remain in Pennsylvania's statue nontheless): guilty of "unprofessional conduct" and license may be revoked; violation of gestational age determination requirement: 3 mos. suspension of license and if falsification of records, misdemeanor in the 3rd degree	Except for medical emergency, physician must give information to mother at least 24 hours before abortion; if mother under 18 years and not emancipated, both mother's and one parent/ guardian's informed consent required—court may authorize M.D. to perform abortion. If the woman is married, she must provide signed statement that she has notified her spouse of the abortion (Spousal consent found unconstitutional in Planned Parenthood of Southeastern Pennsylvania V. Casey, but remain in DA's statute nonetheless)		Licensed M.D., licensed hospital or facility (hospital after 24 wks. with 2nd M.D. to aid fetus

Table 21: Abortion—Continued

State/Code Section	Statutory Definition of		Penalty	Consent	Residency	License
	Illegal Abortion	Legal Abortion				
RHODE ISLAND 23-4.7-1 to 8; 11-9-18; 23-4.8-1 to 5; 23-4.12	(1) Failure to obtain informed consent; (2) failure to provide for any fetus born alive (unless necessary to preserve life of mother); administering to pregnant woman medicine, drug, instrument, etc. with intent to terminate pregnancy. Partial Birth Abortion is unlawful except to save the life of a woman endangered by physical injury when no other medical procedure would suffice, felony for abortionist, mother may not be charged.		Physician who violates consent provisions guilty of "unprofessional conduct;" failure to provide medical care for infant born alive: fine up to $5000 and/or imprisonment 5 years; charge of manslaughter if baby dies	Informed written consent after required disclosures unless emergency; if mother under 18 years and unemancipated, parental consent of at least one parent required; court can consent; if married, husband must be notified if reasonably possible by physician or in written statement by woman unless separated or emergency		

Table 21: Abortion—Continued

State/Code Section	Statutory Definition of		Penalty	Consent	Residency	License
	Illegal Abortion	Legal Abortion				
SOUTH CAROLINA 44-41-10 to 85	(1) Failure to meet standards for legal abortion; (2) self-abortion that does not meet standards for legal abortion; (3) use of instrument, medicine, drug, or other substance or device with intent to terminate pregnancy for reasons other than to increase probability of a live birth, preserve child's life or health, or to remove a dead fetus. Partial Birth abortion: physician performing is guilty of a felony and subject to $5,000 fine and/or no less than 5 years in prison except when performed to save life of mother endangered by physical disorder, illness, or injury when no other medical procedure would suffice.	First trimester, with mother's consent; second trimester with consent in hospital; third trimester, necessary to preserve life or health of mother; if basis is mental health must be so certified by two consulting M.D.s (one a consulting psychiatrist) in writing	Felony, fine to $5,000 and/or imprisonment 2 to 5 years for person unlawfully inducing abortion; fine to $1,000 and/or imprisonment to 2 years for mother soliciting abortion or self-aborting unlawfully; failure to obtain required consent is prima facie evidence of interference with family relations in civil actions; parents have common law rights if abortion is intentionally performed without conforming to consent standards for minors or others: misdemeanor, min. $2,000-10,000 fine and/or up to 3 yrs. imprisonment; third or subsequent offense: 60 days to 3 yrs.	Mother's written consent required; if mother married and in third trimester, husband's consent is required; if mother under 17 years and unmarried, parental/guardian consent of one parent required, except in medical emergency of if pregnancy is result of incest: court may order minor's right to abortion without parental consent. Spousal or parental consent for incompetent woman.		First trimester on advice of licensed M.D.; second trimester must be performed by licensed M.D. in licensed hospital; third trimester, second M.D.'s written recommendation required, facts and reasons supporting recommendations must be certified by both M.D.s

Table 21: Abortion—Continued

State/Code Section	Statutory Definition of		Penalty	Consent	Residency	License
	Illegal Abortion	Legal Abortion				
SOUTH DAKOTA 22-17-5, 6; 34-23A-1 to 45. termination of pregnancy of female known to be pregnant with knowledge that the termination with those means will cause the death of the fetus.	(1) Failure to meet standards for legal abortion; (2) failure of M.D. to obtain informed consent; (3)Partial Birth abortion is unlawful except in order to save the life of the mother when it is endangered by physical disorder, illness, or injury and no other medical procedure would suffice.	1-24th wk.—in M.D.'s medical judgement; after 24th week, necessary to preserve life, health of mother	Violating informed consent statutes: Class 2 misdemeanor, fine of $100 and/or imprisonment 30 days; any unauthorized abortion: Class 6 felony, fine to $2000 and/or imprisonment 2 years; intentional killing of fetus by causing injury to mother: Class 4 felony	Voluntary written informed consent of mother 24 hours before procedure; if mother unmarried minor, 48-hr. notice to parent/guardian also required; if mother is married minor, husband's consent is required. Parental consent exempted with medical emergency, judicial waiver.		First 12 weeks, licensed M.D., solely medical judgment; after 24 wks., licensed M.D. and hospital. After 12 wks., only for medical necessity
TENNESSEE 39-15-201 to 209; 37-10-301 to 307	(1) Failure to meet standards for legal abortion including residency requirement; (2) attempted criminal abortion; (3) coerced or compelled abortion; (4) administering to pregnant woman medicine, drug, or any substance or instrument with intent to destroy such child(5) Partial Birth abortion: no person shall knowingly perform a partial birth abortion except when necessary to save the life of the mother if endangered by a physical disorder, illness, or injury.	First trimester w/ woman's consent upon advice of her M.D., after first trimester and b/f viability w/ same, but in a hospital. After viability, necessary to preserve life, health of mother	Impermissible abortion: Class C felony; mother attempting to procure a miscarriage: Class E felony; M.D. fails to use due care to preserve life of baby born alive or violation of 48-hour waiting period: Class E felony; abortion on non-Tenn. resident: Class C felony; coercion to obtain abortion: Class A misdemeanor; M.D. performs abortion on minor violating consent statute: misdemeanor	Informed, written consent of mother, 48-hour waiting period between M.D. giving mother information and consent; after viability, same as first trimester except M.D. must certify in writing to the hospital that procedure was necessary; by at least one parent must consent to abortion to be performed on minor; no parental consent necessary if emergency; minor may petition court for waiver	Mother must produce to M.D. evidence she is bona fide resident prior to procedure except in medical emergency, (but M.D. must still give information to mother)	First trimester, licensed M.D. upon his medical advice and woman's consent; after first trimester to viability, licensed M.D., licensed hospital; after viability, only to preserve life of mother

Table 21: Abortion—Continued

State/Code Section	Statutory Definition of		Penalty	Consent	Residency	License
	Illegal Abortion	Legal Abortion				
TEXAS Civ. Stat. §§4512.5,.7, H&S 245.001 *et seq.*; 4495b subchap. D	(1) Destroys the vitality or life of child in birth or before (which otherwise would have been born alive); (2) operating a facility without license, failure to meet Board of Health standards, or failure to make reports to Department of Health; (3) act performed after pregnancy with intent to cause termination of pregnancy other than for purpose of birth of live fetus or removal of dead fetus; (4) with public funds unless mother's life is in danger; (5) in third trimester (viability) unless for benefit of woman's or fetus' health	Abortion during third trimester of viable child permissible only if necessary to prevent death or substantial risk of serious impairment to woman's physical or mental health, or if fetus has severe and irreversible abnormality	Abortion of viable fetus: imprisonment 5 years to life; operating facility without license: fine $100 to $500 per day, Class C misdemeanor; failure to report as legally required: Class A misdemeanor			Licensed physician; at separately licensed facility (unless necessary to protect life, health of mother). Third trimester: must certify in writing medical indications supporting M.D.'s judgement. Private hospital or facility is not required to make their facilities available for an abortion unless M.D. determines mother's life is immediately endangered

Table 21: Abortion—Continued

State/Code Section	Statutory Definition of		Penalty	Consent	Residency	License
	Illegal Abortion	Legal Abortion				
UTAH 76-7-301 to 324	(1) Failure to meet standards for legal abortion; (2) coercing someone to have abortion (3) intentional termination of human pregnancy including all procedures undertaken to kill alive, unborn child or produce a miscarriage(4) <u>Partial Birth Abortion</u> after viability has been determined, no person may knowingly perform a partial birth abortion, or dilation and extraction procedure, or a Saline abortion procedure, unless all other available abortion procedures would pose a risk a risk to the life or health of the pregnant woman, or, when due to a serious medical emergency, time does not permit.	Before 20 weeks, abortion is necessary to save mother's life or health, if woman was raped or incest committed, or child has grave defects; after 20 weeks, necessary to preserve health, life of mother or if child would be born with grave defects	Failure to meet standards, coercion, person performing unauthorized abortion not using medical skills to save unborn child, experimentation or buying or selling unborn child: third degree felony. M.D. not giving informed consent: "unprofessional conduct," license may be revoked/ suspended	Notice, if possible, to parents/guardian if minor unmarried (mandatory if public funds used), mother or husband if married; informed consent of mother required. M.D. must provide mother with information regarding abortion at least 24 hours before procedure except in medical emergency		Licensed M.D.; after first 90 days, in licensed hospital; must have concurrence of attending M.D.

Table 21: Abortion—Continued

State/Code Section	Statutory Definition of		Penalty	Consent	Residency	License
	Illegal Abortion	Legal Abortion				
VERMONT Tit.13 §§101 to 104	Willfully administers, advises any thing or any means with intent to procure miscarriage; whether mother dies or mother does not die (mother not liable)	Necessary to preserve mother's life	If mother dies: imprisonment 5 to 20 years; if mother does not die: imprisonment 3 to 10 years; advertising/ dealing in information about procuring miscarriages: imprisonment 3 to 10 years; person selling or giving anything to produce miscarriage: imprisonment 1 to 3 years and/or fine of $200 to $500			
VIRGINIA 18.2-71 to 76.2	Failure to meet standards for legal abortion; cause or administer drug or other means to woman with intent to destroy unborn child or produce abortion or miscarriage; Partial Birth Abortion: a physician shall not knowingly perform a partial birth abortion that is not necessary to save the life of a mother.	First trimester, no restrictions; second trimester, in licensed hospital; third trimester, continuation of pregnancy likely to result in death, physical or mental impairment of mother	Class 4 felony: imprisonment 2 to 10 years and/ or fine to $100,000; Class 3 misdemeanor: encourage or promote performance of abortion	Informed, written consent of mother (if incompetent, written permission from parent or guardian must be obtained)		Anytime, licensed M.D.; second and third trimesters, licensed hospital; third trimester, attending M.D. and two consulting M.D.s certify medical necessity; if necessary to save mother's life, or substantial and irremediable impairment of mental or physical health of the mother. No condition applies except licensed M.D. Life support for the child must on hand and used if necessary.

Table 21: Abortion—Continued

State/Code Section	Statutory Definition of		Penalty	Consent	Residency	License
	Illegal Abortion	Legal Abortion				
WASHINGTON 9.02 *et seq.*	Any medical treatment intended to induce the termination of a pregnancy except for the purpose of producing a live birth. <u>Partial Birth Infanticide:</u> Regulating partial-birth infanticide is not regulating abortion, but rather is proscribing infanticide by restricting the killing of a live infant who is in the process of birth. Partial birth infanticide is unlawful, but does not apply when the procedure was used to prevent the death of the mother when no other medical procedure would suffice, including the induction of labour or cesarean section.	Reproductive Privacy Act: "The state may not deny or interfere with a woman's right to choose to have an abortion prior to viability of the fetus or to protect her life or health." State may regulate as is medically necessary to protect the life, health of mother and consistent with established medical practice and in keeping with the least restrictive on the woman's right to have an abortion	Unauthorized abortion performed: Class C felony			Licensed M.D., and licensed hospital, except when medical emergency, licensed health care provider may assist

Table 21: Abortion—Continued

State/Code Section	Statutory Definition of		Penalty	Consent	Residency	License
	Illegal Abortion	Legal Abortion				
WEST VIRGINIA 61-2-8; 16-2F-1, *et seq.*, 33-43-8	Administer substance or use means with intent to destroy unborn child or produce abortion; unless in good faith to save woman or child. <u>Partial Birth abortion:</u> any person knowingly performing a partial birth abortion other than to save the life of mother endangered by a physical disorder, illness, or injury is guilty of a felony and shall be fined $10,000 to $50,000 and/or imprisoned not more than two years.	Necessary to save life of mother or fetus. performed by an M.D.	Performing illegal abortion: felony: imprisonment 3 to 10 years; if mother dies: murder; violation of minor notification requirements: misdemeanor, $500-1,000 fine and/or up to 30 days in county jail	24 hours actual notice or 48 hours constructive notice to parent/guardian of minor under 18 who has not graduated from high school, minor can petition court for waiver of notification or it may be waived by another M.D. not associated with attending M.D., unless emergency		
WISCONSIN 940.04; 48.375	(1) Intentionally destroys life of unborn child; (2) causes death of mother during procedure; (3) mother intentionally destroys unborn child or consents to same; (4) mother intentionally destroys life of unborn quick child or consents to same	Necessary to save life of mother or advised by two other M.D.s as necessary	Person other than mother performs abortion: imprisonment up to 3 years and/or fine to $5,000; mother dies or intentionally destroys life of unborn quick child: imprisonment to 15 years; mother performs or consents to abortion: imprisonment to 6 months and fine to $200; mother performs or consents to abortion on quick child: imprisonment to 2 years	Informed written consent of unemancipated minor as well as informed, written consent of 1 of her parents, or an adult family member, or her guardian, unless the pregnancy is a result of sexual assault, or incest, or a physician believes the minor to be suicidal, or medical emergency, or subject to a judicial waiver		Licensed M.D., licensed maternity hospital except in medical emergency

Table 21: Abortion—Continued

State/Code Section	Statutory Definition of		Penalty	Consent	Residency	License
	Illegal Abortion	Legal Abortion				
WYOMING 35-6-101 to 118	(1)Any procedure after viability that is not "necessary," (2) M.D. who intentionally terminates viability of unborn fetus during legal abortion; (3) use of other than accepted medical procedures, other than licensed M.D. (including pregnant woman) performs act, procedure, prescription administered to produce premature expulsion, removal, or termination of fetus except when continuation of pregnancy threatens fetus's viability; (4) using public funds for abortion other than those resulting from incest or sexual assault	After viability, necessary to preserve health, life of mother according to appropriate medical judgement	M.D. aborting viable fetus, use of other than accepted medical procedures, person other than M.D. performing abortion: felony, imprisonment up to 14 years	Unemancipated Minor's written consent and one of minor's parents must have written notification 48 hours before abortion; M.D. must have minor's and one parent's consent or court order; minor can petition court to waive parental consent. Consent not required for an emergency.		Licensed M.D.

22. ADOPTION

There is great variety among states regarding adoption laws, perhaps due to the very personal nature of these laws. A long legal tradition did not surround family law, and as state governments began to take responsibility for regulating family relationships, they tended to develop very unique and regional variations on aspects of family law, including adoption. These variations spawned difficult legal conflicts as modern families grew more mobile, and these conflicts gave rise to the desire to standardize laws among the states into Model Acts and Uniform Laws. Although the need for adoption standardization is strong to date, only eight states have adopted the Uniform Adoption Act.

Any adult may adopt any other person with only minor logical restrictions. A married person must apply for adoption jointly with his or her spouse, for example, and, if the child in certain states is over the age of ten, twelve, or fourteen, the state will require his or her consent as well (except in Louisiana and Wisconsin, where the child's consent is not required). "Objective" standards, like Hawaii's requirement of a "proper" adopter, or Illinois's "reputable" one, and Virginia's "natural" one, also are present, as are specific requirements, for example, that the adopter be at least ten years older than the adoptee. Sometimes the adoptee must be a minor, sometimes not. In Florida homosexuals are, from the face of the statute, specifically excluded from adopting; it is unclear whether terms such as "proper," "reputable," or "natural" refer to a prospective parent's sexual orientation.

The laws of adoption, as are the laws of the family in general, are changing as society's traditional values are increasingly scrutinized. There is a growing trend to recognize the rights and opinions of children at younger ages, and to recognize the rights of non-traditional individuals. Indeed, same-sex couples are recognized as adoptive parents in a number of states. Also, some states appear headed in the direction of "open" adoption, whereby any individual may adopt any other individual for any reason.

Federal Law

Federal law has preempted the entire scope of the laws of adoption regarding Native Americans, provoking no small amount of controversy over a non-Native American family's ability to adopt a Native American. When a member of the Aleut tribe had a baby out of wedlock, a non-Native couple living in Vancouver, British Columbia, adopted the child. The tribe sued and won the right to intervene in the adoption after claiming that they had a vital interest in preserving the child's Indian heritage. A California court, in this 1991 case, upheld the tribe's right to intervene, but in the child's interest let her remain with her adoptive parents because she had been living with them for nearly two years.

Table 22: Adoption

State/Code Section; Uniform Act	Who May Be Adopted	Child's Consent	Who May Adopt	Adoptive Home Residency Prior to Decree	State Agency/ Court	Statute of Limitation to Challenge
FEDERAL 25 U.S.C. §§1901-1023 Indian Child Welfare Act				Placement preferences	Indian Tribe exclusive jurisdiction/Tribal	2 years
ALABAMA 26-10A-1 to 26-10A-38; No	(1) Any minor (2) Any adult under following conditions: (a) He or she is permanently disabled (b) He or she is determined to be mentally retarded	14 years and older	Any adult person or husband and wife jointly; no rule or regulation of Department of Human Resources shall prevent adoption by single parent, regardless of age; or by a person because he works outside the home.	60 days	Dept. of Human Resources/Probate	1 year
ALASKA 25.23.010 to 25.23.240; Yes	Any person	10 years and older unless court dispenses with minor's consent in minor's best interest	Husband and wife together; unmarried adult, including father or mother of person to be adopted; married person without other spouse joining, if other spouse is not person to be adopted, and other person is parent of adoptee and consents to adoption or consent is excused by court or spouses are legally separated.	Yes	Health & Social Services/Superior	1 year
ARIZONA 8-101 to 8-145; No	Any child under 18 years of age or foreign born person under age 21 who is not illegal alien	12 years and older in open court	Any adult resident of the state is eligible to adopt; husband and wife may jointly adopt children. Adults may adopt adult relatives.	No	Economic Security/Superior	1 year
ARKANSAS 9-9-201 to 224; 9-9-301 to 303; 9-9-402 to 412; 9-9-501 to 508; Yes	Any person	10 years and older unless court dispenses with minor's consent in minor's best interest	Husband and wife together, unmarried adult, unmarried parent of child, single married parent of child if other parent consents or they are legally separated	6 months	Human Services/ Probate	1 year

Table 22: Adoption—Continued

State/Code Section; Uniform Act	Who May Be Adopted	Child's Consent	Who May Adopt	Adoptive Home Residency Prior to Decree	State Agency/ Court	Statute of Limitation to Challenge
CALIFORNIA Family §8600 *et seq.*; No	Any unmarried minor child at least 10 years younger than prospective adoptive parent or parents	12 years and older	Any adult 10 years older than child	No	Social Services/ Superior	Procedural: 3 years; other: 5 years
COLORADO 14-1-101; 19-5-201 to 304; No	Any person (age 18–21 upon court approval may be adopted as a child)	12 years and older (through counselling)	Minor with court approval or any person over 21. Married person must petition jointly with spouse unless such spouse is natural parent of or has previously adopted child or is legally separated.	No	Social Services/ Juvenile	Jurisdic- tional or procedural defect: 90 days
CONNECTICUT 45a-724 to 765; No	Any person (except between persons over age of majority, there must be written consent of spouses if any of adopted person)	12 years and older	Married persons must join in adoption unless court finds sufficient reason for nonjoinder.	No	Children and Youth Services/ Probate	Not specified
DELAWARE Tit. 13-901 to 965; No	Any person	14 years and older	Unmarried person; divorced or legally separated person; husband and wife who are living together. Must be legal resident in Delaware and over 21.	6 mos.–1 year	Dept. of Services for Children, Youth & Families/ Family	2 years
DISTRICT OF COLUMBIA 16-301 to 315; No	Any person	14 years and older	Any person, provided spouse (if any) joins in petition unless spouse is natural parent of adoptee and consents thereto.	No	Mayor or licensed agency/Superior	1 year

Table 22: Adoption—Continued

State/Code Section; Uniform Act	Who May Be Adopted	Child's Consent	Who May Adopt	Adoptive Home Residency Prior to Decree	State Agency/ Court	Statute of Limitation to Challenge
FLORIDA Ch. 63; No	Any person	12 years and older	Any adult or unmarried natural parent except homosexuals. Married person must be joined by spouse unless such spouse is parent and consents, or failure to join or consent, is excused.	Yes, within 90 days, final home investigation (2 visits) to assess suitability (unless adoption is by relation, i.e., stepparent)	Dept. of Health & Rehabilitative Services/Circuit	1 year
GEORGIA 19-8-1 to 26; No	Any child 10 years younger than petitioner; any adult who gives written consent.	14 years and older	Any adult at least 25 years of age or married and living with spouse and bona fide resident for 6 mos. prior to filing petition.	No	Dept. of Human Resources/ Superior	Not specified
HAWAII 578-1 to 17; No	Any person	10 years and older; if married adult, consent of spouse also	Any proper adult person, not married, or married to legal parent of minor, or husband and wife jointly.	No	Human Services/ Family	1 year
IDAHO 16-1501 *et seq.*; No	Any child; with consent of parents, if living; any adult where the person adopting has sustained relation of parent.	12 years and older	Any adult resident of Idaho for at least 6 consecutive mos. prior to filing who is either 15 years older than child or 25 years of age or older; except spouse of natural parent or person adopting adult who has shown a substantial relationship as a parent has been maintained in excess of 1 yr. may adopt without above age restriction. No married person can adopt without consent of spouse.	No	Dept. of Health & Welfare/District	Not specified

Table 22: Adoption—Continued

State/Code Section; Uniform Act	Who May Be Adopted	Child's Consent	Who May Adopt	Adoptive Home Residency Prior to Decree	State Agency/ Court	Statute of Limitation to Challenge
ILLINOIS 750 ILCS 50/1 to 50/24; No	Any child; any adult residing in home 2 years, or a relative.	14 years and older	Any reputable person of legal age who has resided continually in Illinois for at least 6 months. Residency requirement waived in adoption of relative. If petitioner is married, husband or wife must join in petition. Minor may also petition by leave of court upon good cause shown.	6 months	Department of Children and Family Services/ Circuit	30 days–1 year after entry of order
INDIANA 31-3-1-1; No	Any person	14 years and older	Any resident of state. If married, spouse must join. Spouse must consent if such spouse is natural or adoptive parent. Nonresidents of state may adopt hard to place child as defined in §31-3-3-1.	Period of supervision within sole discretion of court hearing adoption petition	Public Welfare/ Probate	6 mos. after entry or decree or 1 yr. after adoptive parents obtain custody, whichever is greater— after that time, no challenge even for defective proceedings
IOWA 600.1, *et seq.*; No	Any person	14 years and older	Unmarried adult; husband and wife together; husband or wife separately under certain circumstances.	180 days	Human Services/ District	Not specified
KANSAS 59-2111, *et seq.*; No	Any person; adult with consent (if married, spouse's consent also)	14 years and older and of sound intellect	Any adult, or husband and wife jointly, except one spouse cannot adopt without consent of other.	Not required	Social & Rehabilitative Services/District	Not specified
KENTUCKY 199.470; No	Any person	12 years and older	Any person over 18 who is a resident of or who has resided in Kentucky for 12 months immediately preceding filing. Husband and wife must petition jointly (except in certain circumstances).	In some adoptions, 90 days prior to filing adoption petition; temporary custody pending decision in some cases.	Cabinet for Human Resources/ Circuit	1 yr.; ethnological ancestry difference: 5 years

Table 22: Adoption—Continued

State/Code Section; Uniform Act	Who May Be Adopted	Child's Consent	Who May Adopt	Adoptive Home Residency Prior to Decree	State Agency/ Court	Statute of Limitation to Challenge
LOUISIANA Ch. C. Art. 1167-1270; No	Any child or adult	Not required	Any single person 18 years of age or older, or married couple jointly. Special procedures exist to adopt adult.	1 year	Dept. of Social Services/Juvenile	30 days–6 mos. for fraud or duress
MAINE Tit. 19 §1101 *et seq.*; No	Any person, minor or adult; only a minor can be placed under guardianship	14 years and older		1 year may be required at discretion of court	Human Services/ Probate	Not specified
MARYLAND Fam. Law §5-301, *et seq.*; No	Any person	10 years and older	Any adult, even though single or unmarried. Court cannot deny petition just because petitioner is single. Married persons must act jointly unless legally separated or if one spouse is natural parent of adoptee or spouse is incompetent.	Not required	Social Services Administration/ Circuit or Equity	1 year
MASSACHUSETTS Ch. 210; No	Any person younger than adopter; Department of Social Services must verify that child under 14 not registered as missing person.	12 years and older	Any person of full age, his spouse joining, may, subject to certain exceptions, petition to adopt any person younger than himself (other than petitioner's spouse, brother, sister, aunt, or uncle of whole or half blood).	6 months if adoptee is under 14 unless requirement waived	Social Services/ Probate	1 year for appeal
MICHIGAN MCLA §710 *et seq.*; No	Any person	14 years and older	Any person; if married, spouse must join. Cannot have been convicted of child solicitation or criminal sexual conduct.	Not required, but child may be placed in adoption home during rehearing or appeal period or for temporary placement	Social Services/ Probate	21 days from entry of order or denial of petition for rehearing

Table 22: Adoption—Continued

State/Code Section; Uniform Act	Who May Be Adopted	Child's Consent	Who May Adopt	Adoptive Home Residency Prior to Decree	State Agency/ Court	Statute of Limitation to Challenge
MINNESOTA 259.21; No	Any person	14 years and older	Any person who has resided in the state for more than one year, unless length of residence is reduced to 30 days in child's best interest or waive it altogether.	3 months; may be waived by court	Human Services/ Juvenile	Not specified
MISSISSIPPI 93-17-1, *et seq.*; No	Any person	14 years and older	Any unmarried adult, or husband and wife jointly. Must be Mississippi resident for 90 days preceding filing except under certain circumstances.	6 months; waiting period may be shortened if child resided in adoptive home prior to entry of interlocutory decree or is stepchild of petitioner.	Dept. of Human Services/Public Welfare/Chancery	6 months to challenge interlocutory decree; or final decree
MISSOURI 453.010 to 170; No	Any person	14 years and older	Court may order joinder for spouse of petitioner.	No (preference given to home where child has lived for at least 18 mos.	Social Services, Family Services Division/Juvenile Div. of Circuit Court	1 year
MONTANA 40-8-101, *et seq.;* Yes	Any person	12 years and older	Unmarried person who is at least 18 yrs. old. Husband and wife jointly, unless one spouse is parent of the child.	6 months may be recommended by the court	Department of Family Services/ District or Tribal	Not specified
NEBRASKA 43-101 to 43-160; No	Any child. Adoption of American Indian children is governed by the Nebraska Indian Child Welfare Act (§43-1501).	14 years and older	Any adult person may adopt minor child; adult child may be adopted by spouse of such child's parent. Husband and wife must jointly adopt child, unless he or she is parent of child.	6 months (except in adoptions of adults)	Department of Social Services/ County	2 years

Table 22: Adoption—Continued

State/Code Section; Uniform Act	Who May Be Adopted	Child's Consent	Who May Adopt	Adoptive Home Residency Prior to Decree	State Agency/ Court	Statute of Limitation to Challenge
NEVADA 127 *et seq.*; No	Any person (consent of spouse required for adult persons)	14 years and older	Minor: Any adult who is 10 years older than adoptee. If petitioner is married, spouse must join. Must have resided in state during 6 months preceding adoption. Adult: Any adult may adopt younger adult except spouse.	6 months	Human Resources, Division of Child and Family Services/District	Any amendments or annulments by petitioner must be made by 10th day of next month after decree entered.
NEW HAMPSHIRE 170-B *et seq.*; No	Any person	12 years and older	Any person age 18 or older and not homosexual may petition to adopt any other individual except his or her spouse. Failure to join spouse to petition must be excused (unless other spouse is parent of person to be adopted and consents to adoption).	6 months	Division for Children, Youth and Families, Dept. of Health and Human Services/Probate	1 year
NEW JERSEY 9:3 *et seq.* (minor); 2A:22-1 *et seq.* (adult); No	Any person. If adult adoption, must be 10 years younger than petitioner	10 years and older	Any person of at least 18 yrs. If petitioner is married, spouse must consent or application may be made jointly. Court may waive any of these requirements for good cause.	6 months	Human Services/ Superior, Chancery Division, Family Part.	Not specified.
NEW MEXICO 32A-5-1 *et seq.*(minor); 40-14-1 thru 15 (adult); Yes	Any person; any adult with his consent	10 years and older.	Any individual approved by the court as a suitable adoptive parent. If petitioner is married, spouse must join unless natural parent of adoptee or legally separated or excused from joining by court. Must live in state 6 mos. before filing petition.	90 days if less than one year old when placed; 180 days if more than one year old when placed (unless waived).	Human Services, Social Services Division/District	1 year (except where Indian Child Welfare Act of 1978 prevails)

Table 22: Adoption—Continued

State/Code Section; Uniform Act	Who May Be Adopted	Child's Consent	Who May Adopt	Adoptive Home Residency Prior to Decree	State Agency/ Court	Statute of Limitation to Challenge
NEW YORK DOM. REL. §109-117; No	Any person	14 years and older.	Adult unmarried person or adult husband and wife together unless legally separated pursuant to decree or for at least 3 yrs. prior to filing. Adult or minor husband and wife, together or separately, may adopt child either born in or out of wedlock.	6 months	As defined by social services law/Family	Not specified.
NORTH CAROLINA 48; No	Any person; any adult with his consent	12 years and older	Any proper adult person over 18 yrs. old (unless biological parent of spouse of biological parent), or husband and wife jointly or one spouse gives consent. Must have resided in North Carolina for six months next preceding filing of petition. Residency requirement waived under certain circumstances.	At least 1 yr.; provisional period decreed by court	Human Resources/ Superior	Final order must be within 3 yrs. of filing. any appeal must be completed in no more than 2 yrs.
NORTH DAKOTA Ch. 14-15; Yes	Any person	10 years and older	Unmarried adult or parent of child to be adopted. Husband and wife jointly unless legally separated or excused.	6 months	Human Services or County Social Services Board/ District	1 year
OHIO 3107; Yes	Any child; certain adults only.	12 years and older	Unmarried adult; unmarried minor parent of adoptee; husband and wife (at least one of whom is adult) together, unless legally separated or under certain other circumstances.	6 months	Human Services/ Probate	1 year
OKLAHOMA Tit.10 §60.1 *et seq.*; Yes	Any person; any adult with his consent	12 years and older.	Husband and wife, or either if other spouse is parent of child; unmarried person 21 years or older; married person 21 years or older who is legally separated from spouse; unmarried father or mother of illegitimate child.	6 months, discretionary	Department of Human Services/ District	Not specified

Table 22: Adoption—Continued

State/Code Section; Uniform Act	Who May Be Adopted	Child's Consent	Who May Adopt	Adoptive Home Residency Prior to Decree	State Agency/ Court	Statute of Limitation to Challenge
OREGON 109.305, *et seq.*; No	Any person; any adult who consents	14 years and older	Any person. Who is a resident of Oregon. If petitioner is married, spouse must join. Compliance with Indian Child Welfare Act required if applicable.	Not required	Children's Services Division/ Probate or Circuit	1 year
PENNSYLVANIA Tit. 23 §§2101 to 2910; No	Any person	12 years and older	Any person	Not required, but may do temporary placement	Pennsylvania Adoption Cooperative Exchange (PACE) in Dept. of Public Welfare/Common Pleas	Not specified
RHODE ISLAND 15-7 *et seq.*; No	Any person	14 years and older	Any person residing in state may adopt any person younger than himself. If petitioner is married, spouse must join; however, requirement may be waived if it can be shown adoption would be in child's best interest. Nonresident may petition under certain circumstances.	6 months, but court may waive for good cause	Child Welfare Services Dept. for Children and their Families/Family (adults-Probate)	1 yr. for parent who has not had notice.
SOUTH CAROLINA 20-7-1646 to 1890; No	Any person	14 years and older	Any South Carolina resident may petition court to adopt child except in exceptional circumstances. Any adult person may adopt any other adult person.	6 months	State Dept. of Social Services/ Family	1 year

Table 22: Adoption—Continued

State/Code Section; Uniform Act	Who May Be Adopted	Child's Consent	Who May Adopt	Adoptive Home Residency Prior to Decree	State Agency/ Court	Statute of Limitation to Challenge
SOUTH DAKOTA 25-6 *et seq.*; No	Any person	12 years and older	Any adult person may adopt any child at least 10 years younger. Any adult may adopt another adult with the latter's consent. And other requirements.	6 months	Social Services/ Circuit	None specified; Except in cases of fraud, adoptions finalized under chapter 25-6 prior to July 1, 1993 are legalized, cured and valid. But any claims arising from such adoptions must be initiated prior to July 1, 1995.
TENNESSEE 36-1 *et seq.*; No	Any person	14 years and older	Any person over 18 years of age who has been Tennessee resident for one year. Residency requirement may be waived under certain circumstances. Spouse shall join in petition if competent (unless natural parent of child to be adopted)	1 year	Human Services/ Chancery or Circuit	1 year
TEXAS Fam. Ch. 11, 16; No	Any person	12 years and older	Any adult. If petitioner is married, spouse must join. (unless one is parent of child)	6 months (may be waived)	Human Services/ District	2 years (not for lack of required document though)
UTAH 78-30 *et seq.*; No	Any person 10 years younger than petitioner	12 years and older	Any adult. Must have consent of spouse if married.	6 mos.; in some cases, 1 yr.	Family Services/ District or Juvenile	Not specified.
VERMONT Tit.15 §§431, *et seq.*; No	Any person; if adult, must have his and any spouse's consent	14 years and older	Any proper person of age and sound mind. If petitioner is married, spouse must consent.	6 months	Social & Rehabilitation Services/Probate	1 year for child's dissent after reaching majority

Table 22: Adoption—Continued

State/Code Section; Uniform Act	Who May Be Adopted	Child's Consent	Who May Adopt	Adoptive Home Residency Prior to Decree	State Agency/ Court	Statute of Limitation to Challenge
VIRGINIA 63.1-220, *et seq.*; No	Any child; adult under certain conditions	14 years and older	Any natural person may petition to adopt minor child. If petitioner is married, spouse must join. Any natural person may adopt another adult under certain conditions.	6 months	Public Welfare or Social Services/ Circuit	6 months
WASHINGTON 26.33; No	Any person	14 years and older	Any legally competent person, 18 years of age or over.	Not required	Social & Health Services/Superior	1 year
WEST VIRGINIA 48-4	Any person	12 years and older	Any person not married or any person with his or her spouse's consent or husband and wife jointly.	6 months	Department of Human Services/ Circuit	1 year
WISCONSIN 48.81, *et seq.*; No	Any person minor; adult, 882.04	No child's consent required; however, minors 14 and older must attend hearing unless court orders otherwise.	Unmarried adult, husband and wife jointly, spouse of minor's parent may adopt minor. Must be Wisconsin residents and (if practicable and if requested by birth parent) of same religion as adoptee's natural parents. Any resident adult may adopt any other adult.	6 months	Department of Health & Social Services/Circuit	40 days 808.04(7)
WYOMING 1-22-101; No	Any person	14 years and older	Any adult person who has resided in state during 60 days immediately preceding filing of petition and who is determined by court to be fit and competent to be a parent.	6 months	Department of Family Services/ District	10 years

23. ANNULMENT AND PROHIBITED MARRIAGE

Annulment

Annulment differs from divorce in that it addresses defects in a marital relationship occurring at the time of the formation of that relationship. Thus, if a marriage is illegally formed, when it is annulled the parties regain their legal rights and responsibilities as they existed before the marriage occurred. By contrast, a divorce deals with problems in a marital relationship arising after the marriage is formed. Traditionally, after a divorce the parties have continuing legal status as ex-spouses involving division of property, custody of children, and alimony.

Annulments are becoming similar to divorces in that with annulments courts may now divide marital property, order the payment of spousal support or alimony, or decree nearly anything that would be common upon a decree of divorce. Unlike with divorce, however, certain rights or entitlements such as worker's compensation benefits or alimony from a previous marriage that may have ended upon marriage will be restarted upon annulment, because the decree legally makes the marriage nonexistent.

Grounds for annulments and prohibited marriages are varied. Insanity, fraud, force, duress, impotency, being underage, and polygamy are all leading grounds for annulment. There are also a few more creative grounds. Colorado, for instance, has an annulment provision considering if the act were done as "Jest or Dare." A couple of states will also make a marriage void or voidable if a party is found to have AIDS or venereal disease.

Prohibited Marriage

Many states prohibit marriage between parties more closely related than second cousins, though in some states first cousins may marry. In three states that pro-hibit marriages of first cousins, an exception is made for elderly parties: in Arizona and Indiana if parties are over 65 and one is sterile, or in Wisconsin if the woman is over 55 and one party is sterile. Only in Rhode Island do special exceptions exist for a particular religious group: Jews are permitted to marry according to religious law exclusive of state rules.

An issue which has lately caused a great deal of controversy is same-sex marriages. Until 1993, same sex marriages were specifically banned in only about seven states. However, in that year the Supreme Court of Hawaii ruled that the state's prohibition of same sex marriages was a violation of the equal protection clause of the U.S. Constitution because it discriminated on the basis of sex. The court then sent the case back to the trial court to gather additional evidence regarding the state's "compelling interest" in banning same sex marriages. Immediately, fearful that they would be compelled under the constitutional principles of full faith and credit, to honor Hawaiian same sex marriages, many states reacted by passing legislation specifically banning the practice. However, voters in Hawaii have approved a constitutional amendment giving the legislature the authority to limit marriage to persons of the opposite sex. (This is passed pending the ultimate decision of the Hawaiian court. It is still undecided.)

To date, at least fifteen states, including Hawaii, have passed laws prohibiting same sex marriages. There are nearly as many states that currently have similar legislation pending. Nebraska, has introduced a bill that would legalize same sex marriages. One state, Colorado, has passed a law making same sex marriage illegal, only to have it vetoed by their governor. The law in this area remains unsettled, and the lower court in Hawaii is not expected to rule on the case underlying the supreme court's decision until late 1996 or early 1997.

Table 23: Annulment and Prohibited Marriage

State	Code Section	Grounds	Time Limitation	Legitimacy of Children	Prohibited Marriages
ALABAMA	13A-13-1; 30-1-3; 30-1-19	Bigamy; incest; under age of 14		Children of incestuous marriage before annulment is legitimate	Bigamous; incestuous; same sex
ALASKA	25.05.01, *et seq.*; 25.20.050, 25.24.030	Underage; insufficient understanding for consent; consent was obtained by force or fraud; party fails to consummate; either party of unsound mind	Cannot be brought after party freely cohabits with the other after age of consent if underage or coming to reason if of unsound mind or knowledge of fraud if fraud is involved.	Children legitimate if parents subsequently marry	Either party has living spouse at time; parties related closer than fourth degree of consanguinity; same sex
ARIZONA	25-101, 125, 301; 25-301 et seq.	Superior courts may dissolve and adjudge marriage null and void when cause alleged constitutes impediment rendering it void	Common law rules apply		Between parents and children, grandparents and grandchildren, brothers and sisters, (half and whole), aunt and nephew, uncle and niece, first cousins unless both are over 65 or one is not able to reproduce; same sex
ARKANSAS	9-111-104-9-11-109 and 9-12-101-9-12-202	Incapable of consent due to age or understanding; incapable for physical causes; if consent obtained by fraud or force; underage; incest	Parents or guardians can annul marriage where consent was not provided or age misrepresented		Between parents and child, grand-dparents and grand-children, brother and sister (half-blood included), uncle and niece, aunt and nephew, first cousins, includes illegiti-mate children and relations; biga-mous; same sex

Table 23: Annulment and Prohibited Marriage—Continued

State	Code Section	Grounds	Time Limitation	Legitimacy of Children	Prohibited Marriages
CALIFORNIA	Family 2200, 2201, 2210, 2211;Civil 4100	Party did not have capability to consent; another living spouse; unsound mind; consent obtained by force or fraud; physically incapable of entering marriage state	Age of consent: Underage party within 4 yrs. of reaching age of consent or by parent before party has reached age; Fraud: Within 4 yrs. of discovery of fraud by injured party; Husband/Wife living: Either party during life or by former spouse; Unsound mind: Any time before death; Consent by force: Within 4 yrs. of marriage by injured party; Physical incapability: Within 4 yrs. by injured party		Ancestor and descendant of any degree, brother and sister (half-blood included), uncle and niece, aunt and nephew; bigamy and polygamy; same sex
COLORADO	14-10-111; 14-2-110	Consent lacking due to mental incapacity, alcohol, drugs; underage; jest or dare; duress; fraudulent act; physical incapacity to consummate	Lacking capacity due to mental infirmity, influence of alcohol, drugs, or fraud duress, jest or dare: six months after knowledge of described condition; lack of physical capacity to consummate the marriage: one year after the knowledge of condition; underage and lacked consent of parents or guardian: 24 months from date of marriage Prohibited marriages: Declaration of invalidity must be brought prior to death of either party	Children of invalid marriage are legitimate	Prior marriage still valid; between (ancestor and descendant, brother and sister, whole or half-blood uncle and niece, aunt and nephew; also whole or half blood) Marriage void by law of the place where marriage was contracted

Table 23: Annulment and Prohibited Marriage—Continued

State	Code Section	Grounds	Time Limitation	Legitimacy of Children	Prohibited Marriages
CONNECTICUT	46b-40, 60; 46b-21	Lack of mutual consent (460 A.2d 945); physical incapacity to consummate (11 Conn. Sup. 361); bigamous marriage is a nullity (18 Conn. Sup. 472)		Children of void marriage are legitimate	No man may marry his mother, grandmother, daughter, granddaughter, sister, aunt niece, stepmother, or stepdaughter, nor a woman her father, grandfather son, grandson, brother, uncle, nephew, stepfather, or stepson.
DELAWARE	Tit. 13 §1506, 101, 1301	Innocent party may demand for unsoundness of mind, influence of alcohol, drugs, etc.; physical incapacity to consummate; underage without consent of parents; fraud; duress; jest; dare; bigamy; polygamy; incestuous	Lack of capacity, fraud, duress, jest or dare: Within 90 days of obtaining knowledge; Inability to consummate: 1 yr. after knowledge obtained; Underage: Within 1 yr. of marriage; Prohibited: Anytime before death of either party	Children born of annulled marriage or out of wedlock are legitimate	Between person and ancestor, descendant, brother, sister, uncle, aunt, niece, nephew, first cousin; patient in mental hospital; person of any degree of unsoundness of mind, habitual drunkard, confirmed users of narcotics, one party has communicable disease, not divorced, marriage between paupers.
DISTRICT OF COLUMBIA	30-101, 103; 16-907, 908; 16-904	Marriage of an idiot or adjudged lunatic; consent by force or fraud or coercion; physical incapacity; underage; Insanity: unless voluntary cohabitation after discovery of insanity. Nonage: unless voluntary cohabitation after attaining age of legal consent		Children born in or out of wedlock are legitimate children of father and mother and their blood and adopted relatives	Marriage to one whose previous marriage has not been terminated by death or divorce (bigamy); between ancestor and descendant, uncle and niece, aunt and nephew, brother and sister and corresponding in-law relationships, marriage in foreign state to avoid law

Table 23: Annulment and Prohibited Marriage—Continued

State	Code Section	Grounds	Time Limitation	Legitimacy of Children	Prohibited Marriages
FLORIDA	741.21; 826.01	No statutory provisions			No marriage between persons related by lineal consanguinity, sister, aunt, niece, brother, uncle, nephew; common law marriages (after 1967); bigamy (felony: 826.01 *et seq.*)
GEORGIA	19-3-3, *et seq.*; 19-4-1	Unable, unwilling, or fraudulently induced to contract; unsound, under 16 and parental consent	no annulment granted where children are born or are to be born of marriage	Issue of void marriage is legitimate, if legitimate children born before annulment	Related by blood or marriage, father and daughter or stepdaughter, mother and son or stepson, brother and sister (whole- or half-blood), grandparent and grandchild, aunt and nephew, uncle and niece (penalty of prison 1-3 yrs.); same sex; bigamous
HAWAII	580-21-29; 572 *et seq.* Const. Art. 1 §28	Underage; spouse still living; lacking mental capacity; consent obtained by force, duress, fraud and no subsequent cohabitation; party afflicted with loathsome disease and was unknown to party seeking annulment	For spouse still living: Anytime during either party's lifetime; Underage: Until they attain legal age and freely cohabit as man and wife; Physical incapacity: Within 2 yrs. of marriage; Lack of mental capacity: Until mental capacity attained and parties freely cohabit as man and wife	Issue of annulled or prohibited marriages are legitimate.	Between ancestor and descendant any degree, brother and sister half or whole-blood, uncle and niece, aunt and nephew legitimate or illegitimate; bigamous. Note: Hawaii's Supreme Court has now ruled that failure of the state to issue marriage licenses to same sex partners is unconstitutional. Baehr v. Miike, 950 P.20 1234 (Haw. 1997). This ruling has not been overturned, but voters have passed a constitutional amendment that makes it all but ineffective.

Table 23: Annulment and Prohibited Marriage—Continued

State	Code Section	Grounds	Time Limitation	Legitimacy of Children	Prohibited Marriages
IDAHO	32-204-207, 501 to 503	Underage; former spouse living; unsound mind	Underage: Anytime before majority reached; Spouse living: Anytime during life; Unsound mind: Anytime before death; Fraud: Within 4 yrs. of discovery; Force: Within 4 yrs. of marriage; Incapacity to consummate: 4 yrs. from marriage	Not affected by annulment unless grounds is fraud, that woman was pregnant with another man's child, childrend must be born before annulment judgment	Incestuous; between ancestor and descendant, brother and sister, uncle and niece, aunt and nephew, first cousin; polygamous marriages; same sex
ILLINOIS	750 ILCS 5/212, 5/301, 5/302, 5/303	Capacity lacking (infirmity, alcohol, drugs, force, duress, fraud); physically incapable of consummating; underage; prohibited marriage	90 days after knowledge of lack of capaicty (either party), 1 year after knowledge of inability to consummate, any time prior to reaching age of consent	Children born or adopted of prohibited or annulled marriage are legitimate	Former marriage undissolved; between ancestor and descendant, brother and sister half-or whold blood, uncle and niece, aunt and nephew, half-or whole first cousins, (unless no chance of reproduction and both parties over 50 yrs.); common law marriages, same sex
INDIANA	31-11-8, *et seq.* 31-13-1-1 and 31-13-1-2.	Underage or mentally incompetent to consent; obtained by fraud; unsound mind; married in another state with intent to evade marriage laws of Indiana		Children of incestuous marriage are legitimate; child conceived before marriage is annulled is legitimate	More closely related than second cousin unless first cousins married after September 1, 1977, and both 65 at marriage; bigamous marriages
IOWA	595.19; 595.2, 598.29, 31	Prohibited; impotency; prior marriage undissolved; lacking capacity to consent; underage		Children of annulled marriage are legitimate	Undissolved prior marriage; between descendant and ancestor, brother and sister, aunt and nephew, uncle and niece, first cousins
KANSAS	23-102; 60-1602; 23-115	Induced by fraud; mistake of fact; lack of knowledge of a material fact or any other reason justifying rescission of contract of marriage			Between ancestor and descendant, brother and sister, uncle and niece, aunt and nephew, first cousins; incestuous, same sex

Table 23: Annulment and Prohibited Marriage—Continued

State	Code Section	Grounds	Time Limitation	Legitimacy of Children	Prohibited Marriages
KENTUCKY	391.100; 402.010-.030, 070; 403.120;	Capacity lacking (force, fraud); physical capacity for marriage lacking; underage; prohibited	Underage: Must be annulled before cohabitation after eighteenth birthday; No consent; physical incapacity: Within 90 days of knowledge; Prohibited: No later than 1 yr. after discovery	Children born of unlawful or void marriages are legitimate	Any kin closer than second cousin whole or half blood; with person mentally disabled; living spouse; underage; solemnized before one without authority unless parties believed he had authority
LOUISIANA	Civ. §§94 to 96	Null without marriage ceremony by procuration or in violation of an impediment; consent not freely given; purported marriage between same sex has no civil effects		Child of marriage contracted in good faith is legitimate	Same sex
MAINE	19-A§701 and 19-A§§751-753	Mental illness/ retardation of sufficient degree; polygamous marriage			Between ancestor and descendant, brother and sister, aunt and nephew, uncle and niece, first cousins unless cousins obtain physician's certificate of genetic counseling required by §61 prior to marriage. Marriage out of state to evade law, polygamous, same sex
MARYLAND	Md. Rules Tit. 8 Chap. 110 Rule S76; Md. Fam. §2-201, 2-202, 5-202	Bigamy; underage		Children of annulled or void marriages are legitimate.	Those within certain degrees of consanguinity or affinity; same sex

Table 23: Annulment and Prohibited Marriage—Continued

State	Code Section	Grounds	Time Limitation	Legitimacy of Children	Prohibited Marriages
MASSACHUSETTS	§207:1 to 8; 14 to 17	Nonage; insanity		Issue of relationship in consanguinity or affinity is illegitimate; issue of marriage void for prior marriage of insanity, or nonage of parties is legitimate	Former spouse living; polygamous; marriage between ancestors or descendants, brother and sister, aunt and nephew, uncle and niece, first cousins; these provisions continue even after dissolution, by death or divorce, of marriage by which affinity was created unless divorce was given because original marriage was unlawful or void
MICHIGAN	552.34, *et seq.;* 551.5-.6	Underage; insanity; physical incapacity to consummate; force or fraud; marriage of doubtful validity (may be affirmed or annulled)	Underage: Unless they freely cohabit upon reaching majority; Incapacity: 2 years from marriage; Lunatic: Unless upon restoration of reason, they freely cohabit; Force or fraud: Unless there is voluntary cohabitation prior to commencement of suit	Issue of marriage void for nonage or bigamy or insanity are legitimate.	Bigamous; those with syphilis or gonorrhea (felony)
MINNESOTA	518.01-.02, 517.01, 517.03	Lacking capacity to consent (mental, alcohol, drugs, force, fraud); no physical capacity to consummate; underage	Lacking capacity to consent: 90 days after obtaining knowledge of condition; Lacking physical capacity: 1 yr. after obtaining knowledge of condition; Underage: Before reaching proper age		Previously undissolved marriage; between ancestor and descendant, brother and sister, uncle and niece, aunt and nephew, first cousins all family restrictions for half or whole blood, except for those permitted by established custom of aboriginal cultures; bigamous; same sex

Table 23: Annulment and Prohibited Marriage—Continued

State	Code Section	Grounds	Time Limitation	Legitimacy of Children	Prohibited Marriages
MISSISSIPPI	93-1-1; 93-7-1-5	Incurable impotency, insanity, or idiocy; incapable of consent from lack of understanding, force, fraud (unless ratified); pregnant by another man and husband did not know (unless ratified)	Insanity, lack of consent, pregnancy: Within 6 months of marriage	Void or annulled marriage's issue is legitimate, but issue of incestuous marriage is not	Bigamous and incestuous marriages are void (between ancestor and descendant, brother and sister, aunt and nephew, uncle and niece, first cousins by blood, daughter or son-in-law to father or mother-in-law). Marriage between persons of the same sex is prohibited and void.
MISSOURI	451.020, 040; 451.022	Lacking capacity to consummate			Between ancestor and descendant, brother and sister, uncle and niece, aunt and nephew, first cousins; whether legitimate or illigetimate between persons lacking capacity to consummate; bigamous; common law marriages, same sex
MONTANA	40-1-103, 40-1-401, 402	Lacking consent (mental, alcohol, duress, fraud, force); no physical capacity to consummate; underage; prohibited	Mental infirmity, alcohol, drugs: Within 1 yr. after knowledge; Force, duress, fraud: 2 yrs. after knowledge; Physical incapacity: Party must not know at time of marriage and must bring within 4 yrs.; Underage: Until age of majority; Prohibited: Anytime prior to death of parties.	Children born of prohibited marriages legitimate	Previous marriage undissolved; between ancestor and descendant, brother and sister, first cousins, uncle and niece, aunt and nephew; same sex

Table 23: Annulment and Prohibited Marriage—Continued

State	Code Section	Grounds	Time Limitation	Legitimacy of Children	Prohibited Marriages
NEBRASKA	42-103, 118, 374, 377	Underage (if they separate during such nonage and do not cohabitation after); consent obtained by force or fraud and no subsequent cohabitation; impotency; previous marriage undissolved; mental illness or retardation at marriage; force or fraud		Children born to annulled marriages shall be legitimate unless otherwise decreed by court	Marriage void when previous marriage undissolved; either party at marriage is mentally incompetent to enter marriage relation; between ancestor and descendant, brother and sister, first cousins, uncle and niece, aunt and nephew; between persons with venereal disease
NEVADA	125.290 to 350, 410	Underage; lack of understanding to consent; insanity; fraud; where grounds to void the contract in equity	Underage: Within 1 yr. after 18; Fraud: May not annul if after discovery parties voluntarily cohabit; insanity: may not annul if freely cohabit after restored to sound mind	Issue of all marriages deemed null are legitimate	Previous marriage undissolved; not nearer in kin than second cousins; common law marriages
NEW HAMPSHIRE	457:1; 458:1, 23	Underage until confirming marriage upon reaching age; bigamy		Issue of incestuous marriage are treated as children of unwed parents unless while married it was valid in the jurisdiction where contracted, then children are legitimate; legitimacy not affected by decree of nullity	Between ancestor and descendant, brother and sister, uncle and niece, aunt and nephew, cousins; same sex; previous marriage undissolved; proxy marriages
NEW JERSEY	2A:34-1, 20; 37:1-1	Previous marriage undissolved; impotency; lack of consent due to alcohol, understanding capacity, drugs, duress, fraud; underage	Incestuous: During lifetime of parties	Children of annulled marriage are legitimate	Between ancestor and descendant, brother and sister, uncle and niece, aunt and nephew of whole or half blood

Table 23: Annulment and Prohibited Marriage—Continued

State	Code Section	Grounds	Time Limitation	Legitimacy of Children	Prohibited Marriages
NEW MEXICO	40-1-9 40-1-7	Underage	Underage: Anytime until age of majority	Children are legitimate if marriage declared void	Between ancestor and descendant, brother and sister, uncle and niece, aunt and nephew, whether whole or half blood, legitimate or illegitimate
NEW YORK	Dom. Rel. §5-7, 24, 140	Undissolved previous marriage; underage; incurable mental illness (for period of 5 yrs. or more); physical incapacity; consent by force, duress or fraud; incapable of consent for want of understanding	Undissolved: Anytime during lifetime of parties; Underage: Until legal age of consent and cohabitation; Mental: Anytime during which illness continues, if for period of 5 yrs. or more, annulment may be brought; Physical incapacity: Within 5 yrs. of marriage if unknown at marriage; Force, duress, fraud: Within civil statute of limitations unless voluntary cohabitation after discovery	Children of annulled or void marriages are legitimate	Between ancestor and descendant, brother and sister whole or half blood, uncle and niece, aunt and nephew, when previous marriage undissolved
NORTH CAROLINA	51-3, 50-11.1	Underage; previously undissolved marriage; impotent; lack of consent due to lack of will or understanding; belief that female is pregnant	Age: Marriage will not be declared void if girl is pregnant or if cohabitation after 16	Children born of voidable marriage are legitimate	Bigamy; between double first cousins or nearer in kin than first cousin
NORTH DAKOTA	14-04-01, *et seq.*, 14-03-03, 14-03-06; 14-03-01	Underage; previous marriage undissolved; unsound mind; fraud; or force (unless ratified); physically incapable; incestuous	Previous marriage undissolved: Anytime during life of parties; Underage: Within 4 yrs. of age of consent or unless voluntary cohabitation; Unsound mind: Anytime; Fraud, force or physically incapable: 4 yrs. of the marriage; Incestuous: Anytime	Issue of annulled or prohibited marriages are legitimate	Between ancestor and descendant, brother and sister, uncle and niece, aunt and nephew, first cousins; bigamous, same sex

Table 23: Annulment and Prohibited Marriage—Continued

State	Code Section	Grounds	Time Limitation	Legitimacy of Children	Prohibited Marriages
OHIO	3105.31-32	Underage; previous marriage undissolved; mental incompetence; consent obtained by fraud or force; never consummated	Underage: Within 2 yrs. of age of consent unless voluntary cohabitation; Previous marriage undissolved: Anytime during life of parties; Mental: Anytime before death; Fraud: Within 2 yrs. of discovering fraud unless voluntary cohabitation; Force: 2 yrs. after marriage unless voluntary cohabitation; No consummation: 2 yrs. from marriage	Statute assuring legitimacy repealed. (formerly 3105.33)	Between persons nearer in kin than second cousins; previous marriage undissolved
OKLAHOMA	Tit. 43 §§2,3, 128	Incapable of contracting due to lack of age or understanding		Issue of annulled marriage are legitimate	Between ancestor and descendant, stepparent and stepchild, uncle and niece, aunt and nephew, brother and sister, first cousins (but will recognize marriage of first cousins married in state where it is legal); same sex
OREGON	106.020-030, 190; 107.015	Incapable of consent for age or lack of understanding; consent obtained by force or fraud (not otherwise ratified)		Issue of prohibited marriage is legitimate	Previous marriage undissolved; between first cousins or any persons nearer in kin; whole or half blood (unless parties are first cousins by adoption only); same sex
PENNSYLVANIA	Tit. 23 §§1304, 1704, 3304-3305, 5102	Previous marriage undissolved; within consanguinity lines prohibited; lacked capacity by insanity or serious mental disorder or did not intend to consent; underage; one party is weak-minded, unsound mind, or under influence of alcohol or drugs; induced by fraud or duress; impotence	Underage or under the influence: Within 60 days of marriage	Pennsylvania no longer recognizes status of being illegitimate (i.e., "all children legitimate irrespective of marital status of parents")	Between ancestor and descendant, aunt and nephew, brother and sister, uncle and niece, first cousins, bigamous, same sex

Table 23: Annulment and Prohibited Marriage—Continued

State	Code Section	Grounds	Time Limitation	Legitimacy of Children	Prohibited Marriages
RHODE ISLAND	15-1-1, *et. seq.*	No statutory provision for annulment		Issue of idiot or lunatic or bigamous marriage is illegitimate	Bigamous; marriage of idiot or lunatic absolutely void; between ancestor and descendant, stepparent and stepchild, parent-in-law and son- or daughter-in-law; parent or parent-in-law and son- or daughter-in-law, brother and sister, uncle and niece, aunt and nephew; special exceptions for Jewish marriages allowed by Jewish religious law
SOUTH CAROLINA	20-1-10, 80, 90, 530, 550, 20-1-15	Marriage invalid without consummation by cohabitation		Parties entering bigamous marriage in good faith have legitimate children	Mental incompetent; between ancestor and descendant, spouse of ancestor or descendant, uncle and niece, aunt and nephew; bigamous marriages are void unless former spouse absent and unheard of for 5 yrs. Same sex
SOUTH DAKOTA	25-1-1, 25-3-1, *et seq.* 25-1-8	Underage; previous marriage undissolved; either party of unsound mind; consent by fraud or force; physical incapacity	Underage: Until couple cohabits after reaching age of consent unless willful cohabitation; Previous marriage undissolved: Anytime during life of party; Unsound mind: Anytime during life of party; Force or fraud: Within 4 yrs. of discovery unless willful cohabitation; Physical incapacity: 4 yrs. after marriage	Children are legitimate when marriage is annulled for reasons of mental illness or previously undissolved marriage	Between ancestor and descendant, brother and sister, uncle and niece, aunt and nephew, cousins, stepparent and stepchild; same sex; bigamous
TENNESSEE	36-3-101 102; 36-4-125; 36-3-113	Previous marriage (unless absent for 5 yrs. and not known to be living)		Annulment shall not affect the legitimacy of children	Between ancestor and descendant, brother and sister, uncle and niece, aunt and nephew, bigamous, same sex

Table 23: Annulment and Prohibited Marriage—Continued

State	Code Section	Grounds	Time Limitation	Legitimacy of Children	Prohibited Marriages
TEXAS	Fam. §§2.01, *et seq.* Fam. §§6.201, et seq. 6.101, 102	Unless ratified: underage; under influence of alcohol and drugs; impotency (mental or physical); fraud; duress, or force; mental incompetence; concealed divorce which occurred within 30 days preceding marriage; marriage took place within 72 hours after marriage license; previous marriage undissolved (although presumption is that most recent marriage is valid)	Underage: Suit to annul must be brought within 90 days of fourteenth birthday of the underage party or 90 days of when petitioner knew or should have known (but not after 18th birthday); Concealed divorce: Within 30 days		Between ancestor and descendant, brother and sister (by whole, half-blood, or adoption), aunt and nephew, uncle and niece, spouse of ancestor or descendant, descendant of husband or wife; same sex; bigamous
UTAH	30-1-1, through 3, 30-1-17.1	When marriage prohibited and grounds existing at common law		Previous undissolved marriage: if contracted in good faith; issue of later marriages are legitimate	Between ancestor and descendant, brother and sister, uncle and niece, aunt and nephew, first cousins or if both 65 or older, or 55 or older and one found by court to be unable to reproduce, or between relations within but not including fifth degree of consanguinity; person with AIDS, syphilis, gonorrhea; previous marriage undissolved; underage; same sex

Table 23: Annulment and Prohibited Marriage—Continued

State	Code Section	Grounds	Time Limitation	Legitimacy of Children	Prohibited Marriages
VERMONT	Tit. 15 §§511, *et seq.*	Under 16; idiocy or lunacy; physically incapable of marriage state; consent had by force or fraud	Underage: Until parties obtain legal age and cohabit; Idiocy: Anytime during their life (unless restored to reason); Physical incapacity: 2 yrs. from marriage; Consent by force or fraud: Anytime unless parties after commencement of action voluntarily cohabit	Children of annulled marriage are legitimate	Between ancestor and descendant, brother and sister, aunt and nephew, uncle and niece; prohibitions apply even after divorce has dissolved relationship unless marriage was void or unlawful; living husband or wife
VIRGINIA	20-38.1; 20-43; 20-45.1, 2; 20-89.1	Mentally incapacitated; fraud; duress; impotency; if without other's knowledge: either convicted of felony before marriage; if without other's knowledge: wife pregnant by another man, husband fathered another child born within 10 months after marriage; either had been a prostitute; no annulment allowed for fraud, duress, mental incapacity, felony, pregnancy or fathering if parties cohabited after knowledge	All actions must be brought within 2 yrs. of marriage	Children of prohibited marriages are legitimate	Previous marriage undissolved; between ancestor and descendant, brother and sister, uncle and niece, aunt and nephew; same sex; bigamous; parties under 18 and have not complied with consent provisions
WASHINGTON	26.04.010, 26.04.020, 130	Under 17 without waiver of superior court judge		Children born during a marriage later voided are born and remain legitimate.	Previous marriage undissolved; between persons of same sex; between persons closer in kin than second cousins; voidable marriages: underage or without sufficient understanding; consent gained by fraud or duress voidable by party laboring under disability or upon whom force or fraud was imposed

Table 23: Annulment and Prohibited Marriage—Continued

State	Code Section	Grounds	Time Limitation	Legitimacy of Children	Prohibited Marriages
WEST VIRGINIA	42-1-7; 48-1-2, 3	Previous marriage undissolved; within line of prohibited consanguinity; party insane; venereal disease; impotency; underage; convicted of infamous offense prior to marriage; wife with child of another man or had been a prostitute; husband had been a licentious person 48-2-2		Children of annulled or prohibited marriage are legitimate §42-1-7	Between ancestor and descendant, brother and sister, half-brother and half-sister, aunt and nephew, uncle and niece, first cousins, double cousins (unless relationship created solely by adoption) 48-1-2, 3. Out of state marriage entered into to avoid State law
WISCONSIN	767.03, 60; 765.001-.31	Consent lacking; underage; mental infirmity; alcohol; drugs; force; duress; fraud; lack capacity to consummate	Underage: Within 1 yr. of marriage; Mental infirmity, alcohol, drugs, force, duress, fraud, no capacity to consummate: Within 1 yr. of knowledge where marriage prohibited by law, 10 yrs.; bigamy no limit	Issue of void marriage is legitimate 767.60	Previous marriage undissolved; between person of same sex; between persons no closer in kin than second cousins (unless woman is 55 or one party is sterile and they are first cousins); one lacking understanding to consent 765.03
WYOMING	20-2-101, 117	Prohibited marriages; underage; physical incapacity; fraud or duress with no subsequent voluntary cohabitation 20-2-101(c)	Underage: Until couple cohabits upon reaching age of consent; Physical incapacity: Until 2 yrs. after marriage 20-2-101(d),(e),(f)	Legitimacy not affected by dissolution 20-2-117	Previous marriage undissolved; between person of same sex; party mentally incompetent; between ancestor and descendant, brother and sister, uncle and niece, aunt and nephew, first cousins 20-2-101

24. CHILD ABUSE

If child abuse is not the most serious crime facing our society today, it is certainly one of the most heart-wrenching. There are many attempts under way to remedy the underlying causes of child abuse, but, until it is eliminated states have unanimously responded with laws specifically designed to identify and punish child abusers.

Child abuse is an insidious type of crime where the victims are, for many reasons unable to, or are fearful of confronting or reporting the perpetrator to authorities. Therefore, the laws surrounding abusive activity contain an element not found in many other criminal statutes. Under the laws of many states, third parties with knowledge of, and reasonable cause to believe that abuse has occurred, are under a legal obligation to report the situation to the authorities.

The reporting provision is the most controversial and the most problematic of this area of the law. In our society, many relationships are held in particularly high regard and communications in those relationships are given special protection. For example, the law seeks to encourage communication between patient and doctor, client and attorney, and congregant and clergy, and protects the content of any communication between them from discovery by third parties by providing a "privilege," or a rule, that prohibits the doctor, lawyer or clergy from revealing the content of any communications that take place within that particular professional relationship. There are also certain occasions, not covered by the privilege where parties may presume their relationship to be confidential, such as between parent and teacher. Under the child abuse laws for some of these relationships, the professional in such relationships must now report any known or suspected abusive behavior to the proper authorities.

Virtually every state requires doctors, teachers, day care providers and law enforcement officers to report child abuse, but there is less uniformity among the states with regard to lawyers, clergy, therapists, or counselors. A few states require commercial photographic film processors to report to the proper authorities evidence of abusive activity. Some states are very specific in stating exactly who may be protected by the privilege, but some are noticeably vague. This is because the privilege itself is considered so important that a general abrogation of the privilege may be generally detrimental to the important relationships involved. For example, some states require health care professionals to report incidences of abuse, while others list as many as 20-25 professions, including dentists, chiropractors, nurses, hospital personnel and Christian Science practitioners.

The loss or abuse of privilege is not the only controversial or problematic provision of these laws. In many states, the definitions of what constitutes abuse is so broad as to cover a number of different circumstances, including some that may not be abusive at all. Coupled with the fact that in many states one need only have a reasonable suspicion that abuse has occurred in order to report it to the authorities, the laws have left many people fearful that innocent behavior may be misinterpreted by well-meaning, or worse, ill-meaning, private citizens.

The agency to whom suspected abuse is reported is often a state child protection office that is not hindered by the same constitutional restrictions to which traditional law enforcement agencies are subject. These agencies are sometimes allowed to take custody of children prior to actually proving that abuse has occurred. This is done in order to protect the child in question from potential abuse when the agent believes that there is a strong likelihood that the child will be, or continue to be harmed. Some critics of these laws fear the potential of extreme invasions into relationships between parent and child on the basis of very little evidence. Indeed, there have been cases where significant charges of child abuse have been made against individuals and severe action taken against them, such as children taken away from parents, day care centers closed down, only to have the charges later dismissed as lacking any concrete evidence whatsoever. For these reasons most states have passed laws that impose penalties not only for failure to report suspected abuse, but also for false reporting.

Table 24: Child Abuse

State	Code Section	What Constitutes Abuse	Mandatory Reporting Required By	Basis of Report of Abuse/ neglect	To Whom Reported	Penalty for Failure to Report or False Report-ing
ALABAMA	26-14-1, et seq.	Harm or threatened harm to a child's health or welfare through nonaccidental physical or mental injury or sexual abuse/ exploitation	All hospitals, doctors, medical examiners, dentists, chiropractors, nurses, school teachers, pharmacists, law enforcement officers, social workers, day care workers, mental health professionals	When a child is known or suspected to be victim of abuse or neglect	Department of Human Resources	Knowingly fail to report: misdemeanor with up to 6 months jail or $500
ALASKA	47.17.010, et seq.	Physical injury or neglect, mental injury (injury to emotional well-being or intellectual or psychological capacity of child as evidenced by an observable and substantial impairment on child's ability to function); sexual abuse/exploitation, maltreatment	Practitioners of healing arts; school teachers; social workers; peace officers; child care providers; administrative officers of institutions; paid employees of counseling or crisis intervention programs; child fatality review teams	Have reasonable cause to suspect that child has suffered harm as a result of abuse or neglect	Department of Health and Social Services	Class B misdemeanor
ARIZONA	13-3620, 8-201	Infliction or allowing of physical injury, impairment of bodily function or disfigurement, serious emotional damage as evidenced by severe anxiety, depression, withdrawal, or aggressive behavior caused by acts or omissions of individual having care and custody of child	Physician, resident, dentist, chiropractor, medical examiner, nurse, psychologist, social worker, school personnel, peace officer, parent, counselor, clergyman/priest	Observation or examination of child discloses reasonable grounds to believe minor is a victim of injury or abuse	To peace officer or child protective services of the department of economic security	Class 1 misdemeanor
ARKANSAS	12-12-501, et seq.	Specific incidents listed in 12-12-503 include abuse, maltreatment, neglect, sexual abuse/ exploitation, abandonment Extreme and repeated cruelty; intentional, negligent, non-justifiable conduct constituting physical, psychological, or sexual abuse	Any person; physician, dentist, nurse medical personnel, teacher, school counsel, social or family worker, day care center worker, foster care worker, mental health professional, peace officer, law enforcement official, prosecuting attorney or judge	Reasonable cause to suspect maltreatment or observance of conditions or circumstances which would reasonably result in maltreatment	Department of Human Services	Class C misdemeanor; willful failure to report: civilly liable for all damages proximately caused by that failure. Class A misdemeanor: False notification

Table 24: Child Abuse—Continued

State	Code Section	What Constitutes Abuse	Mandatory Reporting Required By	Basis of Report of Abuse/ neglect	To Whom Reported	Penalty for Failure to Report or False Report- ing
CALIFORNIA	Penal Code §11164, *et seq.*	Sexual abuse or exploitation as listed by incident in 11165.1; negligent treatment or maltreatment indicating or threatening harm to child's health or welfare; willful cruelty or unjustifiable punishment; any physical injury inflicted other than by accidental means	Health practitioner, child care custodian (includes teachers); employees of child protective agencies; child visitation monitors; fire fighter; animal control officer; humane society officer	Knows or reasonably suspects or observes child abuse	To a child protective agency (police or sheriff's department, county probation department, or country welfare department)	Misdemeanor; up to 6 months in jail and/or up to $1,000
COLORADO	19-3-301, *et seq.*	Act or omission where child subject to sexual assault, molestation, exploitation, or prostitution; where child is in need of food, clothing, shelter, medical care or supervision because parent or guardian fails to do so; where child exhibits evidence of skin bruising, bleeding, malnutrition, burns, fractures, etc.; or circumstances indicate a condition that may not be the product of an accidental occurrence	Physicians, child health associate, dentist, chiropractor, nurse, hospital personnel, school employee, social worker, mental health professional, Christian Science practitioner, veterinarian, peace officer, pharmacist, psychologist, fireman, victim's advocate, commercial film and photographic print processor	Reasonable cause to know or suspect that a child is subject to circumstances or conditions which would reasonably result in abuse or neglect	Country or district department of social services or local law enforcement agency	Willful violation: Class 3 misdemeanor plus liability for proximately caused damages
CONNECTICUT	§17a-100, *et seq.*	Injuries which are at variance with the history given of them or other than by accidental means; malnutrition, sexual abuse, exploitation, deprivation of necessities, emotional maltreatment, cruel punishment, or school attendance with reasonable cause to suspect abuse	Physician, nurse, medical examiner, dentist, psychologist, school teacher, guidance counselor or principal, social worker, police officer, mental health professional, certified substance abuse counselor, day care center worker, therapist	Reasonable cause to suspect or believe that any child is being abused or in danger of being abused	Commis- sioner of children and families or his repre- sentative	Fined up to $500 for failure to report false report up to $2500 and/or jail up to 1 year

Table 24: Child Abuse—Continued

State	Code Section	What Constitutes Abuse	Mandatory Reporting Required By	Basis of Report of Abuse/ neglect	To Whom Reported	Penalty for Failure to Report or False Report- ing
DELAWARE	16§901, *et seq.*	Physical injury by other than accidental means, injury resulting in mental or emotional condition which is a result of abuse or neglect, sexual abuse, mal- or mistreatment, exploitation or abandonment torture	Persons in healing arts (medicine, dentistry, psychologist), social worker, school employee, medical examiner	Knows or reasonably suspects child abuse or neglect	Division of Child Protective Services of Department of Services for Child, Youth, and their Families	Fined up to $100 and/or jailed up to 15 days
DISTRICT OF COLUMBIA	6-2101, *et seq.*; 2-1351, *et seq.*	The infliction of physical or mental injury upon a child, including excessive corporal punishment, an act of sexual abuse, molestation, exploitation, or injury that results from exposure to drug-related activity	Physician, psychologist, nurse, law enforcement officer, school teacher/official, social service worker, day care worker, mental health professional (any other person <u>may</u> make report), medical examiner, dentist, chiropractor	Suspected or known neglected child or the existence of immediate danger to child; reasonable cause to believe a child is in immediate danger of being mentally or physically abused or neglected	Child Protective Services Division of D.C. Department of Human Services or Metropolitan Police Department	Fined up to $100 and/or jailed up to 30 days
FLORIDA	39.001; 39.201.	Neglect, injury, and harm to include sexual abuse or exploitation, use of or exposure to drugs and mental injury	Physician, mental health professional, spiritual practitioner, school teacher, social worker, law enforcement officer	One who knows or has reasonable cause to suspect neglect, abuse, or abandonment	Department of Health and Rehabilitative Services ("Central Abuse Hotline")	Misdemeanor in 2nd degree; fine of up to $1,000 if knowingly made false report
GEORGIA	19-7-5	Physical injury or death inflicted on a child by other than accidental means including neglect, sexual abuse/ exploitation	Physicians, hospital personnel, dentists psychologists, nurses, social workers, counselors, school teachers/ officials, child welfare agency and child service organization personnel, law enforcement personnel, podiatrists	Reasonable cause to believe a child has been abused	Child welfare agency providing protective services as designated by Department of Human Resources (or in absence of such, to police authority or district attorney)	Misdemeanor

Table 24: Child Abuse—Continued

State	Code Section	What Constitutes Abuse	Mandatory Reporting Required By	Basis of Report of Abuse/neglect	To Whom Reported	Penalty for Failure to Report or False Report-ing
HAWAII	350-1, *et seq.*	Acts or omissions that have resulted in harm to child's physical or psychological health or welfare (or substantial risk of being harmed); specific injuries listed in 350-1	Any licensed, registered professional of the healing arts or any other health-related occupation; school employees; law enforcement employees; child care providers; medical examiners/coroners; employees of public or private social, medical or mental health services agency, recreational\sports employees	Reason to believe that child abuse or neglect has occurred or may occur in reasonably foreseeable future	Department of Human Services or police department	Petty misdemeanor
IDAHO	16-1601, *et seq.*	Sexual misconduct and other injuries not the product of an accidental occurrence including mental injury; Neglect: lacking care necessary for health and well-being; Abandonment: reasonable support or regular personal contact (1 year is prima facie evidence of abandonment)	Physician, nurse, coroner, school teacher, day care personnel, social worker	Reason to believe that a child has been abused, neglected or abandoned, or subject to conditions or circumstances which would reasonably result in abuse, abandonment, or neglect	Department of Health and Welfare	If reported in bad faith, person guilty of a misdemeanor and liable for actual damages or statutory damages of $500, whichever is greater, plus attorney's fees; if acting with malice or oppression, court can award treble actual damages or treble statutory damages, whichever is greater

Table 24: Child Abuse—Continued

State	Code Section	What Constitutes Abuse	Mandatory Reporting Required By	Basis of Report of Abuse/ neglect	To Whom Reported	Penalty for Failure to Report or False Reporting
ILLINOIS	325 ILCS 5/1, *et seq.*	Abused and neglected defined in 5/3 including excessive corporal punishment, torture, sex offenses, injury or substantial risk of injury, and failure to receive proper nourishment, and treatment necessary for child's well-being	Physician, dentist, medical/hospital personnel, substance abuse counselor, Christian Science practitioner, coroner, EMT, crisis/hotline personnel, school personnel, social worker, nurse, day care center worker, psychologist, law enforcement officer, domestic violence program personnel, foster parent, homemaker, child care worker, probation officer, public and private agency personnel	Reasonable cause to believe a child may be abused or neglected	Department of Children and Family Services	Offense of disorderly conduct; second or subsequent offense: Class 4 felony; person who knowingly or willfully transmits false report: Class A misdemeanor if physician, referred to state medical disciplinary board
INDIANA	31-33-1-1, *et seq.*	Mental or physical condition seriously impaired or endangered as a result of neglect or injury; sex offense; child is missing	Health care provider, any member of medical or other private or public institution, school, facility or agency and any other individuals	Reason to believe child is victim of child abuse or neglect, i.e., if presented to individuals of similar background and training, would cause those individuals to believe a child was abused or neglected	Division of Family and Children; child abuse hotline	Intentionally and knowing false report: Class B misdemeanor and liable to person accused for actual damages and possible punitive damages

Table 24: Child Abuse—Continued

State	Code Section	What Constitutes Abuse	Mandatory Reporting Required By	Basis of Report of Abuse/ neglect	To Whom Reported	Penalty for Failure to Report or False Reporting
IOWA	232.68, *et seq.*	Any nonaccidental physical injury or mental injury to child's intellectual or psychological capacity as evidenced by substantial and observable impairment in child's ability to function within normal range; commission of sexual offense; an illegal drug present in child's body; failure in care of child to provide food, shelter, or clothing necessary for child's health and welfare	Any health practitioner, social workers, psychologist, school employee, day care center employees, substance abuse program employee, human services institution employee, peace officer, juvenile detention or shelter care employee, mental health professional, counselor	Reasonably believes a child has suffered abuse	State Department of Human Services (including local, county, and regional offices)	Knowingly and willfully fails to report: simple misdemeanor and civilly liable for proximately caused damages; knowing false report: simple misdemeanor
KANSAS	38-1501, *et seq.*, 21-3609	Infliction of mental, physical, or emotional injury causing deterioration of child including negligent treatment, maltreatment, or exploitation to the extent the child's health or emotional well-being is endangered; includes sexual abuse	Person licensed to practice healing arts or dentistry, law enforcement personnel, psychologists, nurses, family/ marriage therapists, school teachers or administrators, child care workers, social workers, EMS personnel, firefighters, appointed mediators	Reasonably suspects child has been injured as a result of physical, mental, or emotional abuse or neglect or sexual abuse	Department of Social and Reha-bilitation Services or law enforce-ment agency	Willful and knowing failure to report or prevention or interference with reporting: Class B misdemeanor
KENTUCKY	620.010, *et seq.*	Interfering with child's right to adequate food, shelter, clothing and freedom from physical, sexual, or emotional injury or exploitation	Physician, nurse, teacher, school personnel, social worker, coroner, child-caring personnel, dentist, EMT, paramedic, health professional, mental health professional, peace officer, any organization or agency of the above	Knows or has reasonable cause to believe that child is dependent, neglected, or abused	Local law enforce-ment or Kentucky state police, common-wealth's attorney, cabinet or representa-tive	

Table 24: Child Abuse—Continued

State	Code Section	What Constitutes Abuse	Mandatory Reporting Required By	Basis of Report of Abuse/ neglect	To Whom Reported	Penalty for Failure to Report or False Reporting
LOUISIANA	§14:403 Criminal; Art. 609 & 603 Children's Code	Any acts, exploitation, infliction of physical or mental injury or involvement in sexual act which seriously endangers the mental, physical, and emotional health of the child; any neglect-refusal or willful failure to supply necessary food, clothing, shelter, treatment, or counseling to child	Any health practitioner, mental health/social service practitioner, teacher or child care provider, police officer or law enforcement, and commercial film and photographic print processor	Cause to believe that a child's physical or mental health or welfare is endangered as a result of abuse or neglect	Local child protection unit of the Department of Social Services	Knowingly and willfully fails to report or makes a false report: misdemeanor and up to $500 and/or 6 months jail
MAINE	22§4001, 4011, *et seq. 4009*	Threat to child's health or welfare by physical, mental, or emotional injury or impairment, sexual abuse/ exploitation, deprivation of essential needs, abandonment	Medical/osteopathic physician, EMS, medical examiner, dentist, chiropractor, nurse, teacher, guidance counselor, social worker, homemaker, guardian ad litem, social service worker, psychologist, child care worker, mental health professional, law enforcement official, state and municipal fire inspector, municipal code enforcement officer, clergy	Knows or has reasonable cause to suspect a child has been abused or neglected	Department of Human Services	Civil violation with fine of not more than $500
MARYLAND	Family Law §5-701, *et seq.*	Physical or mental injury of a child under circumstances that indicate the child's health or welfare is harmed or at substantial risk of being harmed; sexual abuse	All health practitioners, police officers, educators, human service workers. Any other person, if not notification does not violate privilege or confidentiality	Reason to believe a child has been subjected to abuse or neglect	Social Services Administration of the department or appropriate law enforcement agency	

Table 24: Child Abuse—Continued

State	Code Section	What Constitutes Abuse	Mandatory Reporting Required By	Basis of Report of Abuse/ neglect	To Whom Reported	Penalty for Failure to Report or False Report-ing
MASSACHUSETTS	119§51A	Physical or emotional abuse or injury causing harm to child's health or welfare including sexual abuse/neglect, malnutrition and physical dependence upon addictive drug at birth	Physician, hospital personnel, psychologist, medical examiner, EMT, dentist, nurse, chiropractor, school teacher, educational administrator, counselor, day care worker, probation and parole officers, clerk of the court, social worker, firefighter, policeman, mental health services professional, foster parent	Reasonable cause to believe a child is suffering from physical or emotional injury causing harm or substantial risk of harm to child's health and welfare	Department of Social Services	Fine up to $1,000
MICHIGAN	722.621-623, 633	Harm or threatened harm to child's health or welfare that occurs through nonaccidental physical or mental injury, sexual abuse/ exploitation, or maltreatment or neglect	Physician, coroner, dentist, dental hygienist, EMT, psychologist, therapist/counselor, social worker, school administrator or teacher, law enforcement officer, child care provider, medical examiner	Reasonable cause to suspect child abuse or neglect (pregnancy under 12 or venereal disease in child over 1 month but under 12 years is reasonable cause to suspect abuse)	State Family Independence Agency	Civilly liable for proximately caused damages; guilty of misdemeanor punishable by 93 days in jail and/ or fine of not more than $100
MINNESOTA	626.556	Physical or mental injury inflicted on child other than by accidental means or which can't be reasonably explained; any aversive or deprivation procedures; sexual abuse, neglect-failure to protect a child from conditions which endanger the child's health	Professional and professional's delegate in healing arts, social services, hospital administration, psychological treatment, child care, education, law enforcement, clergy (for information received while engaged in ministerial duties)	Knows or has reason to believe a child is being neglected or physically or sexually abused (or has been in preceding 3 years)	Local welfare agency, police department, or county sheriff	Failure to report: misdemeanor; failure by parent, guardian or caretaker: gross misdemeanor if child suffers harm; if a child dies, felony; knowing or reckless false report: person civilly liable for actual damages suffered and punitive damages and attorney's fees

Table 24: Child Abuse—Continued

State	Code Section	What Constitutes Abuse	Mandatory Reporting Required By	Basis of Report of Abuse/ neglect	To Whom Reported	Penalty for Failure to Report or False Report- ing
MISSISSIPPI	43-21-353; 43-21-105	Sexual abuse or exploitation, emotional abuse, mental injury, nonaccidental physical injury, maltreatment, neglect	Attorney, physician, dentist, nurse, psychologist, social worker, child caregiver, minister, law enforcement officer, school employee	Reasonable cause to suspect that a child is neglected or abused	Department of Human Services	Willful violation: up to $5,000 fine and/ or up to 1 year jail
MISSOURI	210.110, *et seq.*	Any physical injury, sexual abuse, emotional abuse inflicted on child other than by accidental means by caregiver	Physician, medical examiner, dentist, chiropractor, nurse, hospital or clinic personnel, any other health practitioner, psychologist, social worker, mental health professional, day care center worker, juvenile officer, probation or parole officer, teacher, school official, law enforcement officer, Christian Science practitioner	Reasonable cause to suspect that a child has been or may be subjected to abuse or neglect or observes such conditions or circumstances that would reasonably result in abuse or neglect	Missouri Division of Family Services	Class A misdemeanor
MONTANA	41-3-101, 41-3-201, *et seq.*	Harm or threatened harm to child's health and welfare by infliction of physical or mental injury, or sexual abuse or exploitation or neglect or abandonment including acts or omissions of person responsible for child's welfare. Does not include self-defense, defense of others, or action taken to prevent self-harm of child.	Physician, member of hospital staff, coroner, mental health professional, dentist, Christian Science practitioner, religious healers, school teachers and officials, social workers, day care/ child care workers, foster care worker, clergy (unless privileged communication), law enforcement officer, guardian ad litem or court appointed advocate	Know or have reasonable cause to suspect that a child is abused or neglected	Department of Public Health and Human Services or its local affiliate	Guilty of misdemeanor and civilly liable for proximately caused damages

Table 24: Child Abuse—Continued

State	Code Section	What Constitutes Abuse	Mandatory Reporting Required By	Basis of Report of Abuse/ neglect	To Whom Reported	Penalty for Failure to Report or False Report-ing
NEBRASKA	28-710-717	Knowingly, intentionally or negligently causing or permitting a child to be: placed in a situation endangering physical or mental health, cruelly punished, deprived of necessaries, child under 6 years left unattended in vehicle, or sexually abused or exploited	Physician, medical institution, nurse, school employee, social worker, or other person	Reasonable cause to believe that a child has been subjected to abuse or neglect or observes child being subjected to conditions and circumstances which would reasonably result in abuse or neglect	Department of Social Services or law enforcement agency (also a state-wide toll-free number)	Class III misdemeanor
NEVADA	432B.010, *et seq.*	Physical or mental injury of a nonaccidental nature; sexual abuse or exploitation; negligent treatment or maltreatment such that child's health or welfare is harmed	Physician, dentist, coroner, chiropractor, nurse, psychologist, marriage/family therapist, drug/alcohol counselor, EMT, hospital administration and personnel, clergyman, religious healer, Christian Science practitioner, social worker, foster home employees, child care employees, law enforcement officer, probation officer, attorney, volunteer referral abuse service, school employees	Know or have reason to believe a child has been abused or neglected	Law enforcement agency or local office of Division of Child and Family Services of the Department of Human Resources (they also provide a toll-free telephone number for reporting)	Knowing or willful violation: misdemeanor
NEW HAMPSHIRE	1-69g-C:29, *et seq.*	Sexual abuse, intentional physical injury, psychological injury such that child exhibits symptoms of emotional problems generally recognized to result from consistent maltreatment or neglect, or physical injury by other than nonaccidental means	Physician, surgeon, medical examiner, psychiatrist, psychologist, therapist, nurse, dentist, chiropractor, hospital personnel, Christian Science practitioner, school teacher, social worker, day care worker, foster/child care worker, law enforcement official, priest, minister, rabbi	Having reason to suspect that a child has been abused or neglected	Bureau of Children, Division for Children and Youth Services, Department of Health and Human Services	Knowing violation: misdemeanor

Table 24: Child Abuse—Continued

State	Code Section	What Constitutes Abuse	Mandatory Reporting Required By	Basis of Report of Abuse/ neglect	To Whom Reported	Penalty for Failure to Report or False Report- ing
NEW JERSEY	9:6-8.9, *et seq.*	Physical injury by other than nonaccidental means; substantial risk of death; protracted impairment of physical or emotional health; sexual abuse or acts of sexual abuse; willful abandonment; willful isolation of ordinary social contact to indicate emotional or social deprivation; inappropriate placement in institution; neglect by not supplying adequate care, necessaries or supervision	Any person	Having reasonable cause to believe that a child has been subjected to child abuse or acts of child abuse	Division of Youth and Family Services (they also maintain a 24-hour hotline) in Department of Human Services	Knowing violation: disorderly person
NEW MEXICO	32A-4-1, *et seq.*	Physical, emotional or psychological abuse including sexual abuse, exploitation, abandonment, or neglect, torture, confinement, cruel punishment	Physician, law enforcement officer, judge, nurse, school teacher or official, social worker, or any other person suspecting abuse.	Knows or has reasonable suspicion that child is abused or neglected	Law enforcement agency or department office in county where child resides or tribal law enforcement or social services for Indian child	Misdemeanor
NEW YORK	Soc. Services. §411-428	Inflicts injury on child other than by accidental means or with deliberate indifference allows such an injury to be inflicted or creates substantial risk of injury or neglect	Physician, coroner, dentist, chiropractor, psychologist, nurse, school official, hospital personnel, social services worker, day care center worker, mental health professional, Christian Science practitioner, substance abuse/ alcoholism counselor, peace officer, police officer, district attorney, residential care facility worker	Reasonable cause to suspect that a child is abused or maltreated or knows from personal knowledge, facts, conditions, or circumstances which, if correct, would render the child abused or maltreated	Statewide central register of child abuse or local child protective services	Class A misdemeanor

Table 24: Child Abuse—Continued

State	Code Section	What Constitutes Abuse	Mandatory Reporting Required By	Basis of Report of Abuse/ neglect	To Whom Reported	Penalty for Failure to Report or False Report-ing
NORTH CAROLINA	Repealed cff. 7|1|99 7A-516, *et seq. Effective 7|1|99 7B-101, et seq.*	Inflicts or allows to be inflicted or creates a substantial risk of injury other than by accidental means or commits, permits, or encourages any type of sexual abuse or creates or allows serious emotional damage to juvenile or docs not provide proper care or necessary medical care or abandons child uses inappropriate devices or procedures to modify behavior	Any person or institution	Cause to suspect that juvenile is abused, neglected, or dependent, or has died as the result of maltreatment	Director of Department of Social Services in county where juvenile resides	
NORTH DAKOTA	50-25.1-01, *et seq.*	Suffering from serious physical harm or traumatic abuse caused other than by accidental means or deprived child	Physician, nurse, dentist, coroner, mental health professional, religious practitioner, school teacher/ administrator, social worker, day care center worker, police/law enforcement officer, addiction counselor, school counselor, clergy	Having knowledge or reasonable cause to suspect that a child is abused or neglected	Division of Child and Family Services (or other division as determined appropriate by department of human services)	Class B misdemeanor; unless made to law enforcement officer, then Class A misdemeanor; willfully make false report, also liable for all civil damages including exemplary damages
OHIO	2151.01, *et seq.*; 2921.14	Victim of sexual activity offense constituting abuse or exhibits evidence of physical or mental injury inflicted other than by accidental means or threats or harm to child's health and welfare or abandonment or neglect (lack of proper parental care)	Attorney, physician, nurse, other health care professional, coroner, day care worker, school teacher/employer, social worker, professional counselor, speech pathologist, child services agency employee, person rendering spiritual treatment through prayer	Knows or suspects child has suffered or faces threat of suffering any physical or mental wound, injury, disability, or condition that reasonably indicates abuse or neglect	Children Services Board or county department of human services exercising the children services function or municipal or county peace officer in county where child resides	Guilty of making a false report: misdemeanor of the first degree

Table 24: Child Abuse—Continued

State	Code Section	What Constitutes Abuse	Mandatory Reporting Required By	Basis of Report of Abuse/ neglect	To Whom Reported	Penalty for Failure to Report or False Reporting
OKLAHOMA	Tit. 10 7102-7105	Harm or threatened harm to child's health or welfare including but not limited to nonaccidental physical or mental injury sexual abuse/exploitation or negligent treatment (including lack of provision of necessities such as food, shelter, medical care, etc.)	Physician, nurse, teacher, other person who has reason to believe abuse	Having reason to believe that child has had injuries inflicted other than by accidental means where injury appears to have been caused as a result of sexual or physical abuse or neglect	Department of Human Services in county where suspected injury occurred	Any false reporting is reported by Department of Human Services to local law enforcement for criminal investigation and upon conviction, is guilty of misdemeanor and may be fined up to $5,000 plus reasonable attorney's fees incurred in recovering the sanctions
OREGON	419B.005-100	Any assault of a child and any physical injury to a child caused by other than accidental means (including injuries at variance with explanation given for injury), rape, sexual abuse/exploitation, negligent treatment, threatening harm to child's health or welfare, any mental injury which includes observable and substantial impairment to child's ability to function	Peace/law enforcement officers, physician, dentist, nurse, school employee, department of human resources employee, psychologist, clergyman, social worker, chiropractor, optometrist, day car worker, attorney, professional counselor, therapist, EMT, firefighter, naturopathic physician (see right)	Have reasonable cause to believe that child has suffered abuse or has inflicted abuse on child	Children's Services Division	Any public or private official Fine of up to $1,000 (prosecution to commence within 18 months of offense)
PENNSYLVANIA	23§6303, *et seq.*	Act which causes nonaccidental serious physical injury, sexual abuse/exploitation, serious physical neglect constituting prolonged or repeated lack of supervision or failure to provide essentials of life	Physician, coroner, dentist, chiropractor, hospital personnel, Christian Science practitioner, clergy, school teacher/nurse/administrator, social services worker, day care or child center worker, mental health professional, peace officer, law enforcement official	Reasonable cause to suspect (within their respective training) that child is abused	Department of Public Welfare of the Commonwealth	Summary offense for 1st violation; misdemeanor in 3rd degree for 2nd and subsequent offenses

Table 24: Child Abuse—Continued

State	Code Section	What Constitutes Abuse	Mandatory Reporting Required By	Basis of Report of Abuse/ neglect	To Whom Reported	Penalty for Failure to Report or False Reporting
RHODE ISLAND	40-11-1, *et seq.*	Child whose physical or mental health or welfare is harmed or threatened with harm including excessive corporal punishment, sexual abuse/ exploitation, neglect, or abandonment	Physicians, hospitals, health care centers, foster parents, guardians, day care center workers, and any person with reasonable cause	Reasonable cause to know or suspect that a child has been abused or neglected or been the victim of sexual abuse	Department for Children and their Families (department to establish statewide toll-free 24-hour/7-day-a-week telephone number for reporting)	Misdemeanor and up to $500 fine and/or imprisonment for up to 1 year for failure to report; misdemeanor and up to $1000 fine and/or imprisonment for up to 1 year for false report
SOUTH CAROLINA	20-7-490, *et seq.*	Child whose death results from or whose physical or mental health or welfare is harmed or threatened with harm including physical or mental injuries sustained as a result of excessive corporal punishment, sexual abuse/ exploitation, neglect or abandonment	Physician, nurse, dentist, coroner, EMT, mental health or allied health professional, Christian Science practitioner, religious healer, school teacher/counselor, social or public assistance worker, child care or day care center worker, police or law enforcement officer, undertaker, funeral home director/employee, judge	Having reason to believe that a child's physical or mental health or welfare has been or may be adversely affected by abuse or neglect	County Department of Social Services or law enforcement agency in county where child resides	Misdemeanor, and fine up to $500 and/or jail up to 6 months
SOUTH DAKOTA	26-8A-1, *et seq.*	Child who is threatened with substantial harm; sustained emotional harm or mental injury (evidenced by observable and substantial impairment of child's ability to function); subject to sexual abuse/ exploitation; who lacks proper parental care; whose environment is injurious to child's welfare; or who is abandoned	Physician, dentist, chiropractor, optometrist, mental health professional, psychologist, religious healing practitioner, social worker, parole or court services officer, law enforcement officer, teacher, nurse, school counselor/official, child welfare provider, coroner, chemical dependency counselor, domestic abuse shelter worker	Have reasonable cause to suspect a child has been abused or neglected	State's attorney in county where child resides, department of social services or to law enforcement officer	Class 1 misdemeanor

Table 24: Child Abuse—Continued

State	Code Section	What Constitutes Abuse	Mandatory Reporting Required By	Basis of Report of Abuse/ neglect	To Whom Reported	Penalty for Failure to Report or False Reporting
TENNESSEE	37-1-401, *et seq.*	Any wound, injury, disability, or physical or mental condition which is of a nature as to reasonably indicate that it has been caused by brutality, abuse, or neglect; also includes sexual abuse	Physician, chiropractor, hospital personnel, any other health or mental health professional, spiritual healing practitioner, school teacher/personnel, judge, social worker, day care center worker, foster care worker, law enforcement officer, neighbor, relative, friend, or any other person	Having knowledge or being called on to render aid to any child suffering from or sustaining a wound or injury which is of such a nature as to reasonably indicate or which on the basis of available information appears to indicate have been caused by brutality, abuse or neglect	Department of Children's Services	Class A misdemeanor (fine limited to $50): false reporting of child sexual abuse: Class E felony
TEXAS	Family 261.001 et seq.	Child's physical or mental health or welfare has been adversely affected by abuse or neglect; violation of compulsory school attendance on 3 or more occasions; been voluntarily absent from home without consent of parent for substantial length of time without intent to return	"Professionals" including teachers, nurses, doctors, day care employees, employees of state-licensed or certified organizations with direct contact with children, any person	Belief that child has been or will be abused or neglected or child's physical or mental health or welfare has been or may be adversely affected by abuse or neglect	Texas Department of Protective and Regulatory Services	Class B misdemeanor Physical injury resulting in substantial harm; mental or emotional injury; failure to prevent injury;harmful sexual conducto ro pornography; failure to prevent use of controlled substance by child False report: Class A misdemeanor
UTAH	62A-4a-401, *et seq.*	Causing harm or threatened harm to a child's health or welfare through neglect or abuse including nonaccidental physical or mental injury, incest, sexual abuse/ exploitation, molestation, or repeated negligent treatment	Physicians, nurses, other licensed health care professionals, other officials and institutions, any person (except priest/ clergy unless person making confession consents)	Reason to believe that a child has been subjected to abuse or observe a child being subjected to conditions or circumstances which would reasonably result in abuse	Nearest peace officer, law enforcement agency, or office of the division	Class B misdemeanor (must be commenced within 4 years from date of knowledge of offense)

Table 24: Child Abuse—Continued

State	Code Section	What Constitutes Abuse	Mandatory Reporting Required By	Basis of Report of Abuse/ neglect	To Whom Reported	Penalty for Failure to Report or False Report- ing
VERMONT	33§4911, *et seq.*	Child whose physical health, psychological growth and development or welfare is harmed or is at substantial risk of harm by the acts or omissions of persons responsible for child; includes sexual abuse, abandonment, emotional maltreatment, neglect	Physician, chiropractor, nurse, hospital administrator, medical examiner, dentist, psychologist, other health care providers, school teacher/officials, day care worker, social worker, mental health professional, probation officer, camp owner/ administrator/ counselor, police officer, and any other concerned persons	Reasonable cause to believe that a child has been abused or neglected	Commis- sioner of social and rehabilita- tion services or designee	Fined up to $500
VIRGINIA	63.1-248.2, *et seq.*	To create, inflict or threaten to create or inflict or allow to be created or inflicted upon a child a physical or mental injury by other than accidental means or create a substantial risk of death or impairment; neglect; abandonment; sexual abuse/ exploitation	Any person licensed to practice medicine or healing arts, nurses, social worker, probation officer, child care worker, school teacher, Christian Science practitioner, mental health professional, law enforcement officer, mediator, any employee of facility which takes care of children	Have reason to suspect that a child is abused or neglected	Department of Social Services toll-free child abuse or neglect hotline or to department of public welfare or social services in county where child resides	Failure to report within 72 hours of first suspicion of child abuse: fine up to $500; subsequent failures: $100-$1,000 fine False report: Class 4 misdemeanor
WASHINGTON	26.44.010. *et seq.*	The injury, sexual abuse/exploitation or negligent treatment of a child, adult dependent or developmentally disabled person under circumstances which indicate that such child or person's health, welfare, or safety is harmed	All practitioners, coroners, law enforcement officer, school personnel, nurse, social services counselor, psychologist, pharmacist, child care providers, juvenile probation officer, health and social services department employee	Reasonable cause to believe that a child has suffered abuse or neglect	State Department of Social and Health Services or proper law enforcement agency	Gross Misdemeanor

Table 24: Child Abuse—Continued

State	Code Section	What Constitutes Abuse	Mandatory Reporting Required By	Basis of Report of Abuse/ neglect	To Whom Reported	Penalty for Failure to Report or False Report- ing
WEST VIRGINIA	49-6A-1, *et seq.*	Physical, mental, or emotional injury, sexual abuse/ exploitation, negligent treatment, sale or attempted sale of child; any circumstances which harm or threaten the health and welfare of the child	Medical, dental, or mental health professional, religious healer, Christian Science practitioner, school teacher/personnel, social services worker, child care worker, EMT, peace or law enforcement official, circuit court judge, family law master or magistrate, clergy	Reasonable cause to suspect that a child is abused or neglected or observes a child subjected to conditions likely to result in abuse or neglect	State Department of Human Services	Misdemeanor, up to 10 days in county jail and/ or fine of $100
WISCONSIN	48.981	Physical injury inflicted on child other than by accidental means, sexual abuse/ exploitation, emotional damage, (harm to child's psychological or intellectual functioning which is exhibited by anxiety, depression, or other outward behavior) or neglect (failure to provide necessaries of life)	Physician, coroner, nurse, dentist, chiropractor, acupuncturist, or other medical or mental health professional, social worker, marriage or family therapist, counselor, public assistance worker, school teacher/ administrator/ counselor, mediator, child care or day care center worker, physical or occupational therapists, EMT, speech-language pathologists, police or law enforcement officer, attorney, member of treatment staff or alcohol/drug abuse counselor	Reasonable cause to suspect that a child has been abused or neglected or has been threatened with abuse or neglect or that abuse or neglect will occur	The county department (or licensed child welfare agency under contract with the county department) or sheriff or police department	Fine up to $1,000 and/or up to 6 months in jail

Table 24: Child Abuse—Continued

State	Code Section	What Constitutes Abuse	Mandatory Reporting Required By	Basis of Report of Abuse/ neglect	To Whom Reported	Penalty for Failure to Report or False Report- ing
WYOMING	14-3-201, et seq.	The inflicting or causing of physical or mental injury, harm or imminent danger to the physical or mental health or welfare of a child other than by accidental means including abandonment, excessive/ unreasonable corporal punishment, malnutrition, intentional or unintentional neglect or the commission of a sexual offense	Member/staff of medical (public or private) institution, school, or any person	Reasonable cause to believe or suspect that a child has been abused or neglected or who observes any child being subjected to conditions or circumstances which would reasonably result in abuse or neglect	Child protective agency or local law enforcement agency	Misdemeanor, fine up to $500 and/or up to 6 months in jail

25. CHILD CUSTODY

Because of the importance of the laws regarding child custody, all fifty states and the District of Columbia have adopted the Uniform Child Custody Act.

Prior to the twentieth century, it was standard that the father would take sole custody of the children upon divorce. In the twentieth century, however, it became common practice to award custody of children "of tender years" to the mother. It is now most common to award custody to both parents at the same time, in an arrangement known as "joint custody," under which custody of the children is divided into legal and physical custody, with both parents sharing responsibility for the children simultaneously. However, joint custody does not necessarily mean equal custody. Rather, it merely means custody co-exists between parents with the physical arrangements coordinated in the best interests of the children. All but nine states recognize the joint custody arrangement in child custody matters. Nine states, apparently feeling the need to remove the children from the pressures of having to make difficult and emotional decisions, do not consider the wishes of the children when awarding custody. However, it is safe to say that judges will never completely ignore children's wishes in considering custody matters, just as they will not make them bear the brunt of the responsibility for a decision when answering the objections of a parent. In the majority of states listed as not taking into account the child's wishes, the statute also reads that the decision regarding placement of the child must be based on what is in the "best interests" of the child.

Until ten years ago, only a few states recognized a grandparent's desire to visit his or her grandchildren as a *right*. Now, all except the District of Columbia recognize visitation rights of grandparents.

Table 25: Child Custody

State	Code Section	Year Uniform Child Custody Act Adopted	Joint Custody	Grandparent Visitation	Child's Wishes Considered
ALABAMA	30-3-1 to 198	1980	No	Yes, §30-3-4	Yes
ALASKA	25.24.150	1977	Yes, §25-20-060 "shared"	Yes, §25.24.150	Yes
ARIZONA	25-401-25-414, *et seq.*	Uniform Marr. & Div. Act	Yes, §25-403	Yes, §25-409	Yes
ARKANSAS	9-13-101, *et seq.*	1979	No	Yes, §9-13-103	No
CALIFORNIA	Fam. 3400	1973	Yes, Fam. 3080	Yes, Fam. 3100(a), 3102	Yes
COLORADO	14-10-123	1973	No, repealed §14.10.123.5	Yes, §19-1-117	Yes
CONNECTICUT	46b-56 *et seq.*	1978	Yes §46b-56a	Yes, 46b-59	Yes
DELAWARE	Tit. 13 §§721, *et seq.*	1976	Yes, Tit. 13 §§727, 728	Yes, Tit. 13 §728	Yes
DISTRICT OF COLUMBIA	16-911(a)(5); 16-914	1983	Yes, 16-911 (a)(5)	No	Yes
FLORIDA	61.13.351	1977	Yes, §61.13(2)(b)2	Yes, §61.13(2)(c),(6),(7)	Yes
GEORGIA	19-9-1, 19-9-3	1978	Yes, §19-9-3(a)	Yes, §19-9-3(d)	Yes
HAWAII	571-46	1973	Yes, §571-46(1)	Yes, §571-46.3	Yes
IDAHO	32-717	1977	Yes, §32-717B	Yes, §32-719	Yes
ILLINOIS	750 ILCS 5/601, 602, 607	1979	Yes, 750 ILCS 5/602.1	Yes, 750 ILCS 5/607(b)(1)	Yes
INDIANA	31-17-1-1 et seq.	1977	Yes, §31-17-2-13	Yes, §31-17-5-1, *et seq.*	Yes
IOWA	598.41	1977	Yes, §598.41(2)	Yes, §598.35	Yes
KANSAS	60.1610	1978	Yes, §60.1610(4)(A)	Yes, §§38-129; 60.1616(b)	Yes
KENTUCKY	403.270, 405.021	1980	Yes, § 403.270(4)	Yes, §405.021	Yes
LOUISIANA	Civ. Art. 131; Rev. Stat. §9:344	1978	Yes, Civ. Art. 131	Yes, limited, Rev. Stat. 9:344	Yes
MAINE	Tit. 19A-1651-1654	1979	Yes, Tit. 19A 1651	Yes, Tit. 19A- §1801 *et seq.*	Yes
MARYLAND	Fam. §5-203, 9-102	1957	Yes, §5-203(d)(2)	Yes, §9-102	No
MASSACHUSETTS	208:28, 209C §10	1983	Yes, §208: 31; 209C: 10	Yes, Ch. 119 §39D	No
MICHIGAN	722.21 *et seq.*	1976	Yes, §722.26(a)	Yes, §722.27(b)	Yes
MINNESOTA	518.155 *et seq.*	1977	Yes, §518.17 subd. 2	Yes, 518.175 subd. 7, §257.022	Yes
MISSISSIPPI	93-5-23	1982	Yes, §93-5-24	Yes, §93-16-1, *et seq.*	No
MISSOURI	452.375	1978	Yes, §452.375	Yes, §452.402	Yes
MONTANA	40-4-211 *et seq.*	1977	Yes, §40-4-212	Yes, §40-4-217(2); 40-9-102	Yes
NEBRASKA	42-364	1979	Yes, §42-364(5)	Yes, §43-1802, *et seq.*	Yes

Table 25: Child Custody—Continued

State	Code Section	Year Uniform Child Custody Act Adopted	Joint Custody	Grandparent Visitation	Child's Wishes Considered
NEVADA	125.480	1979	Yes, §125.465, 490	Yes, §125A.330, 340	Yes
NEW HAMPSHIRE	458: 17	1979	Yes, §458: 17(II-IV)	Yes, §458.17-d	Yes
NEW JERSEY	§9:2-1 et seq.	1979	Yes, §9: 2-4(a)	Yes, §9-2-7.1	Yes
NEW MEXICO	40-4-9	1981	Yes, §40-4-9.1	Yes, §40-9-2 to 4	Yes
NEW YORK	Dom. Rel. §240	1977	Yes, Dom. Rel. §240	Yes, Dom. Rel. §240(1)	Yes
NORTH CAROLINA	50-11.2	1979	Yes, §50-13.2	Yes, §50-13.2(b1)&2A	Yes
NORTH DAKOTA	14-09-06 et seq.	1969	No	Yes, §14-09-05.1(B1)	Yes
OHIO	3109.04, 3105.21	1977	Yes, §3109.04(A)	Yes, §3109.051	Yes
OKLAHOMA	Tit. 43 §112	1980	Yes, 43§112	Yes, 10§5	Yes
OREGON	107.105	1973	Yes, §§107.105(a), 169	Yes, §109.119, 121, 123	No
PENNSYLVANIA	Tit. 23 §5301	1980	Yes, Tit. 23 §5304	Yes, Tit. 23 §§5311, 5303, 5312	No
RHODE ISLAND	15-5-16	1978	Yes, §15-5-16(g)(1)	Yes, §§15-5-24.1 to 24.3	No
SOUTH CAROLINA	20-3-160	1981	No	Yes, § 20-7-420(33)	No
SOUTH DAKOTA	25-4-45	1978	Yes, §25-5-7 1	Yes, §§25-4-52	Yes
TENNESSEE	36-6-101, 102	1979	Yes, §36-6-101(a)	Yes, §36-6-301	Yes
TEXAS	Fam. 153. 005 et seq.	1983	Yes, Fam. §153.003	Yes, Fam. 153.433	Yes
UTAH	30-3-10, 30-3-5	1980	Yes, §§30-3-10.1, *et seq.*	Yes, §30-5-2	Yes
VERMONT	Tit. 15 §665	1979	Yes, Tit. 15 §665(a)	No	No
VIRGINIA	20-107.2, 20-124.1 *et seq.*	1979	Yes, §§20-124.2(B)	Yes, §20-124.1 & §16.1-241	Yes
WASHINGTON	26.09.050; 26.10.100 *et seq.*	1979	No	Yes, §26.09.240	Yes
WEST VIRGINIA	48-2-15	1981 48-10-1	Yes 48-2-15	Yes, §48-2B-1 to 48-2B-12	Yes
WISCONSIN	767.24	1975	Yes, §767.24(2)(b)	Yes, §767.245	Yes
WYOMING	20-2-113	1973	Yes, 20-2-113(p)	Yes, 20-7-101	Yes

26. GROUNDS FOR DIVORCE

The bond of marriage and the nuclear family unit were thought to be sacred unions to be preserved at all costs. Divorce was a stigma and a "bad" marriage was a thing to be endured for the sake of the family and, in particular, the children. However, the last forty years has seen a remarkable shift in emphasis in the area of divorce.

Originally, in order to obtain a divorce the pleading party had to show fault on the other side of the marriage, proving that the spouse had committed some act or activity believed ruinous to the marital relationship, such as adultery, cruelty, or desertion. The other party could then counter by proving fault in the pleading spouse or that the alleged activity did not occur. Fault was important not only in obtaining the divorce, but also in factoring property divisions and alimony.

No-fault divorce is the relatively recent invention of legislators who deemed it necessary in order to allow women to free themselves from destructive marriages. Under no-fault divorce a party does not need to prove any fault; all that is required is to claim that there exists irretrievable breakdown or irreconcilable differences between the spouses or desertion. The pleading party in a divorce action merely needs to claim that she or he is so unhappy that leaving home (or "constructive desertion") or dissolving the marriage is the only solution.

All states have adopted no-fault divorce, either as the only grounds for divorce or as an additional ground. As a practical matter, however, the other grounds are seldom used owing to the difficulty of proving things like adultery, mental cruelty, and the like. These are only used in situations where proof of fault will affect the court's decisions with regard to the distribution of property, alimony, or child custody. Thus, only about 10 percent of divorces actually go to trial today.

In the accompanying table, the No-Fault column lists the particular type of no-fault statute that exists in the state. If there are no items listed under Grounds, then no-fault is the only ground for divorce in that state. If grounds are listed, no-fault is simply an additional available ground

Table 26: Grounds for Divorce

State	Code Section	Residency	Waiting Period	No Fault	Defenses	Grounds
ALABAMA	30-2-1 to 12	At least one party must be resident and must have resided 6 months prior to filing.		Irretrievable breakdown; separation (2 yrs.).	Condonation, (not if parties connived to commit adultery). Collusion	Adultery; cruelty or violence; drug/alcohol addiction after marriage; insanity (in mental hosp. for 5 successive yrs.); pregnant at time of marriage without husband's knowledge; imprisonment for 2 yrs. if sentence is 7 yrs. or longer; crime against nature with mankind or beast before or after marriage; incompatible temperaments; voluntary abandonment from bed or board for 1 yr.; wife lived apart for 2 years without husband's support while she's residing in state; at time of marriage, incapacitated from entering married state.
ALASKA	25.24.050; 25.24.080; 25.24.120, 130, 200, 210	When marriage solemnized in state and plaintiff is resident, divorce action may be brought		Separation; absence; irremedial breakdown.	For adultery, procurement, connivance, express or implied forgiveness, dual guilt, or waiting over 2 yrs. to bring action; procurement or express forgiveness is defense to any other ground.	Adultery; cruelty or violence; willful desertion for 1 yr.; drug/alcohol addiction; conviction of felony; failure to consummate; incompatible temperament; incurable mental illness (confined to institution for at least 18 mos. prior to divorce action).

Table 26: Grounds for Divorce—Continued

State	Code Section	Residency	Waiting Period	No Fault	Defenses	Grounds
ARIZONA	Uniform Marriage and Divorce Act §§25-311 *et seq.*	One party must be Arizona domiciliary and presence has been maintained 90 days prior to filing for divorce.	If one party denies that marriage is irretrievably broken, court may order conciliation conference and matter is continued for 60 days; at next hearing, court makes finding whether marriage is broken as a result of "no reasonable prospect of reconciliation."	Irretrievable breakdown; separation (both parties must consent and relationship must be irretrievably broken).	Only defense is that marriage is not irretrievably broken.	Only requirement is that relationship is irretrievably broken and the court has made provisions for child custody, support, disposition of property, and support of spouse.
ARKANSAS	9-12-301, 307, 308, 310	One party must be resident at least 60 days before action and a resident 3 months before final decree granted.	30 days from filing for decree (except in willful desertion for 1 year of continuous separation).	Separation:- (lived separate and apart for 18 mos.)	Collusion, consent or equal guilt in adultery.	Impotence; conviction of felony or infamous crime; habitual drunk for one year or cruel and barbarous treatment or offers indignites; adultery; separate for 18 continuous months; and where either spouse legally obligated to support other and having ability to provide common necessities, willfully fails to do so.

Table 26: Grounds for Divorce—Continued

State	Code Section	Residency	Waiting Period	No Fault	Defenses	Grounds
CALIFORNIA	§§4506-4516 Repealed. See Family Code §§2310 *et seq.*	One party must have been resident 6 months and for 3 months in county where action is filed.	If it appears there is a reasonable possibility of reconciliation, proceeding may halt for up to 30 days; no decree is final until 6 months from service or respondent's appearance, whichever is first.	Irreconcilable differences; incurable insanity.		See "No Fault"
COLORADO	Uniform Dissolution of Marriage Act §§14-10-106, 120.3	One spouse domiciliary for 90 days preceding commencement of action.		Irretrievable breakdown.	Lack of jurisdiction and failure to establish a case.	
CONNECTICUT	46b-40, 44, 67	Resident for 12 months before filing or 1 party domiciliary at time of marriage and returned with intent to stay or the cause for dissolution occurred after either moved to the state.	90 days.	Irretrievable breakdown; separation. (lived apart for at least 18 mos. prior to complaint)		Adultery; cruelty or violence; willful desertion for 1 yr.; drug/alcohol addiction; insanity; unexplained absence for at least 7 yrs.; conviction of infamous crime; fraudulent contract; legal confinement for mental illness 5 out of last 6 yrs.
DELAWARE	Tit. 13 §§1503, *et seq.*	Action brought where either party is a resident for 6 months or longer.	Decree final when entered subject to right of appeal within 30 days.	Irretrievable breakdown; voluntary separation.	Defenses of condonation; connivance, recrimination, insanity and lapse of time are preserved only for a marriage that is separated and the separation caused by misconduct; respondent's failure of jurisdictional/ residential requirements.	Separation caused respondent's misconduct, mental illness or incompatibility.

Table 26: Grounds for Divorce—Continued

State	Code Section	Residency	Waiting Period	No Fault	Defenses	Grounds
DISTRICT OF COLUMBIA	16-901, *et seq.*	One party bona fide resident for 6 months.	Divorce not final until time for appeal is up.	Voluntary separation (6 months).		Adultery; cruelty; voluntary separation; marriage contracted while either party had former marriage; marriage contracted during insanity of either party; matrimonially incapacitated; where either party had not attained the Age of legal consent to contract marriage
FLORIDA	61.021, 031, 052, 19	Petitioner must have residence in Florida 6 months before filing suit.	20 days after petition filed.	Irretrievable breakdown; mental incapacity of one or the parties.		Mental incapacity of one party for preceding period of at least 3 yrs.
GEORGIA	19-5-2-19-5-4	One party resident for 6 months before action.	Decree in effect immediately except for irretrievable breakdown, in which case court may not grant divorce in less than 30 days from service on respondent.	Irretrievable breakdown.	For adultery, desertion, cruelty, or intoxication: collusion, both parties guilty, subsequent voluntary condonation and cohabitation, consent.	Adultery; cruelty or violence; willful and continued desertion for at least 1 yr.; drug/alcohol addiction; impotency; mental incapacity or insanity; pregnant at time of marriage by man other than husband; conviction of crime for which the sentence is 2 yrs. or more; force, duress, or fraud in obtaining marriage; irreconcilable differences; intermarriage within prohibited degrees of consanguinity or affinity.

Table 26: Grounds for Divorce—Continued

State	Code Section	Residency	Waiting Period	No Fault	Defenses	Grounds
HAWAII	§§580-41 *et seq.*	One party domiciled or physically present 6 months before filing.	Court fixes time after decree that it is final but not over 1 month.	Irretrievable breakdown; separation (for at least 2 yrs. or under decree of separation).	Recrimination no defense	See "No Fault"
IDAHO	32-601 *et seq.*; 32-901	Plaintiff must be resident for 6 full weeks before commencing action.	Decree entered immediately on determination of issues (for adultery, within 2 yrs., for felony conviction, before the end of sentence or 1 yr. after pardon).	Separation (5 yrs.); irreconcilable differences.	Collusion; condonation; recrimination or limitation and lapse of time.	Adultery; cruelty or violence; willful neglect or desertion; drug/ alcohol addiction; nonsupport; insanity; conviction of felony; separation over 3 yrs.; irreconcilable differences.
ILLINOIS	750 ILCS 5/ 401, *et seq.* and 5/451 *et seq.*	One spouse must be resident of Illinois for 90 days before commencing action.	Final when entered subject to right of appeal.	Irretrievable breakdown; separation (2 yrs.). Note: Under certain conditions, parties may file joint petition for simplified dissolution.	Collusion.	Adultery; cruelty or violence; willful desertion for 1 yr.; drug/alcohol addiction for 2 yrs.; impotency; unexplained absence; conviction of crime; venereal disease; 2 yr. separation by irreconcilable differences; undissolved prior marriage.
INDIANA	31-1-11.5-1 *et seq.*	One party at filing must be resident for 6 months.	Final hearing no sooner than 60 days after filing; continue matter for 45 days if possibility for reconciliation; after 45, judge may enter decree upon request; if no request after 90 days, matter is dismissed.	Irretrievable breakdown.		Impotency; insanity for at least 2 yrs.; conviction of felony.

Table 26: Grounds for Divorce—Continued

State	Code Section	Residency	Waiting Period	No Fault	Defenses	Grounds
IOWA	598.6, 17, 19	Unless respondent is a resident and given personal service, petitioner must have been resident for last year.	90 days after service of original notice.	Irretrievable breakdown.		Irretrievable breakdown.
KANSAS	60-1601, *et seq.*	One party must have been resident for 60 days before filing.	Hearing not for 60 days after filing. (Unless emergency.)	Incompatibility.		Insanity (mental illness/incapacity); incompatibility; failure to perform material marital duty/obligation
KENTUCKY	403 *et seq.*	One party must be resident of state and have been for 180 days before filing.	Final when entered. (Parties have to have lived apart for 60 days prior to decree.)	Irretrievable breakdown.		
LOUISIANA	Civ. Code §§102-104	One spouse must be domiciled in state at time of filing.	Must live separate and apart for 180 days after filing or service of petition	Separation (for at least 6 mos.).	Reconciliation.	Adultery; conviction of felony.
MAINE	Tit. 19 §§661 to 752	Parties must have been married there or resided there when cause of action accrued; plaintiff resides there in good faith in state 6 months prior; plaintiff and/or defendant are residents.	Court may make it final immediately, but otherwise it is subject to an appeal period.	Separation; irreconcilable differences.	Collusion; recrimination is comparative not absolute defense; sometimes condonation in court's discretion.	Adultery; cruelty or violence; utter desertion for 3 consecutive yrs.; drug/alcohol addiction; impotence; nonsupport; insanity (mental illness—confined for at least 7 yrs. prior to action); irreconcilable differences.
MARYLAND	Fam. Law §7-101-103	If grounds occurred outside the state, one party must have resided in state 1 yr. before filing.	Upon meeting requirements, absolute divorce granted.	Separation (2 yrs. or voluntary for 12 months); limited divorce for cruelty, vicious conduct; separation; desertion.	Recrimination or condonation is factor but not absolute bar.	Adultery; desertion for 12 mos. without interruption; insanity (confined for 3 yrs.); conviction of crime (sentenced for at least 3 yrs.); cruelty; voluntary separation grounds for limited divorce.

Table 26: Grounds for Divorce—Continued

State	Code Section	Residency	Waiting Period	No Fault	Defenses	Grounds
MASSACHUSETTS	Ch. 208	Parties must have lived together in the commonwealth unless plaintiff lived there 1 yr. before filing or cause occurred in the commonwealth and plaintiff filed when living there.	90 days unless court orders otherwise.	Irretrievable breakdown.	No defense.	Adultery; cruelty or violence; utter desertion for 1 yr.; drug/alcohol addiction; impotency; nonsupport; conviction of crime (sentenced for at least 5 yrs.); absence (raises presumption of death).
MICHIGAN	MCLA 552.1, *et seq.*	One party must have resided in Michigan for 180 days before filing and defendant resided in county where complaint is filed for 10 days immediately preceding filing except in certain situations.	Final decree entered upon determining plaintiff entitled to divorce.	Irretrievable breakdown.		Breakdown of marriage relationship
MINNESOTA	518	One party must have resided in state or been a domiciliary for 180 days before filing.	Decree entered immediately upon finding irretrievable breakdown, subject to appeal.	Irretrievable breakdown.	All abolished by §518.06.	
MISSISSIPPI	93-5-1, *et seq.*	One party actual, bona fide resident for 6 months before suit.	Final decree entered immediately but may be revoked at any time by granting court upon joint request of parties.	Irreconcilable differences (only if uncontested).	Recrimination not absolute bar; collusion (adultery).	Adultery; cruelty or violence; willful desertion; drug/alcohol addiction; natural impotency; incurable insanity; pregnant at time of marriage; conviction of crime; prior marriage undissolved; in line of consanguinity.

Table 26: Grounds for Divorce—Continued

State	Code Section	Residency	Waiting Period	No Fault	Defenses	Grounds
MISSOURI	452	Either party must be a resident for 90 days.	Final when entered, subject to appeal. Court's order of distribution of marital property is not subject to modification.	Irretrievable breakdown. (Findings of fact to satisfy listed in §452.320 (2).)	Abolished by §452.310.	
MONTANA	40-4-101 to 136	One party must be domiciled in Montana for 90 days.	Decree is final, subject to appeal.	Irretrievable breakdown; separation (180 days) or serious marital discord.	Abolished by §40-4-105.	
NEBRASKA	§§42-341 to 379	Marriage solemnized in the state and one party resides in-state since marriage or one party has resided in-state (making it a permanent home) for 1 yr. before filing.	No suit for divorce heard until 60 days after service of process.	Irretrievable breakdown.		
NEVADA	125.010, 020, 130	Unless grounds accrued in county where action brought, one party must have been a resident at least 6 weeks before filing.	Decree is final when entered.	Separation(1 yr. without cohabitation); incompatibility.		Insanity (for 2 yrs. prior); lived apart without cohabitation for 1 yr; incompatibility.
NEW HAMPSHIRE	458 *et seq.*	Both parties domiciled or plaintiff was domiciled and defendant was personally served or plaintiff domiciled in state at least 1 yr. before action.	No special provision	Irreconcilable differences; separation (absent 2 yrs.)	Condonation and recrimination exist as in common law.	Adultery; cruelty or violence; drug/ alcohol addiction; impotency; nonsupport; unexplained absence (for 2 yrs.); conviction of crime (with imprisonment for more than 1 yr.); joining religious group believing the relation of husband and wife unlawful and refusal to cohabit for 6 mos.; resided outside state for 10 yrs. without returning.

Table 26: Grounds for Divorce—Continued

State	Code Section	Residency	Waiting Period	No Fault	Defenses	Grounds
NEW JERSEY	2A:34 *et seq.*	Either party a bona fide resident of New Jersey at time cause of action arose and until commencement of action (except adultery, 1 yr. before action).	Decree immediately final, pending any appeal.	Separation (18 months).	Abolished by §2A:34-7.	Adultery; cruelty or violence; desertion from 12 mos.; drug/alcohol addiction; insanity/ mental illness (confined for 24 mos.); conviction of crime (imprisonment for at least 18 mos.); deviant sexual behavior without plaintiff's consent.
NEW MEXICO	40-4-1, *et seq.*	New Mexico domicile required plus 6 months residency.	No special provision.	Separation (permanent); incompatibility.		Adultery; cruelty or violence; desertion/ abandonment; incompatibility.
NEW YORK	Dom. Rel. §§170, 171, 202, 230, 231	Were married in state or reside in state as husband and wife and either party has been resident 1 yr. before commencing suit; cause occurred in New York and either or both are 1-yr. residents; either has been resident for 2 yrs.		Separation (1 yr. or more).	Adultery: Offense committed with plaintiff's connivance; offense forgiven (shown affirmatively, by voluntary cohabitation, or by no action commenced within 5 yrs. of discovery of offense); plaintiff also guilty of adultery; defendant may set up misconduct of plaintiff as justification.	Adultery; cruel and inhuman treatment; abandonment (for 1 or more years); imprisonment of defendant for 3 or more consecutive yrs and lived apart for 1 or more yrs.

Table 26: Grounds for Divorce—Continued

State	Code Section	Residency	Waiting Period	No Fault	Defenses	Grounds
NORTH CAROLINA	50	Either party a bona fide resident for 6 months before bringing action.	Decree final immediately.	Separation (one year).		Adultery; cruelty or violence; desertion (abandonment); drug/alcohol addiction; incurable insanity (confined/separated for 3 consecutive yrs.). Offers indignities that renders other spouse's condition/life intolerable/burdensome
NORTH DAKOTA	14-05-03, *et seq.*	Plaintiff resident for 6 months before commencement of action or entry of divorce decree.	Final immediately unless unreasonable lapse of time before commence-ment of action.	Irreconcilable differences.	Connivance; collusion; condonation; lapse of time.	Adultery; cruelty or violence; desertion or neglect; drug/alcohol addiction; nonsupport; insanity for period of 5 yrs.; conviction of felony. Irreconcilable differences.
OHIO	3105 *et seq.*	Plaintiff must have been resident 6 months.	Decree immediately final, but court may order conciliation period for up to 90 days.	Separation (1 yr.); incompatibility.		Adultery; cruelty or violence; desertion; drug/alcohol addiction; nonsupport; imprisonment; prior marriage undissolved; fraudulent contract; other party procures a divorce out of state; gross neglect of duty.

Table 26: Grounds for Divorce—Continued

State	Code Section	Residency	Waiting Period	No Fault	Defenses	Grounds
OKLAHOMA	Tit. 43 §§101, et seq.	One party must have been resident in good faith for 6 months before filing.	Final immediately unless appealed, but neither may marry for 6 months (if so guilty of bigamy) nor cohabit for 30 days (if so guilty of adultery).	Incompatibility.		Adultery; cruelty or violence; abandonment/desertion (1 yr.); drug/alcohol addition; impotency; nonsupport; insanity (for 5 yrs. prior); pregnant at time of marriage (not by husband); conviction of felony; fraudulent contract; procuring divorce out of state not releasing one party; gross neglect of duty.
OREGON	107 et seq.	One party resident for 6 months prior unless marriage solemnized in state and either is resident at time of filing.	Decree final immediately but marital status unaffected for 30 days or determination of any appeal; no trial until 90 days after service (unless emergency).	Irremedial breakdown; separation for 1 yr.	Abolished by §107.036.	When either party was incapable of making Kontract or consenting for want of legal age or sufficient understanding; consent was obtained by force or fraud. Doctrines of fault and in pari delicto abolished by §107.036
PENNSYLVANIA	Tit. 23 §§3101 to 3707; Pa. R. Civ. P. 400; 1920.1-1920.92	Bona fide residency by one party at least 6 months before filing.	Immediately final, subject to appeal. (Can be continued 90–120 days if reasonable prospect of reconciliation)	Irretrievable breakdown; separation (2 yrs.).	Existing common-law defense, to all grounds but irretrievably broken marriage.	Adultery; cruelty or violence; desertion for 1 or more yrs.; insanity (confined for 18 mos.); bigamy; conviction of crime (sentenced to prison for 2 or more yrs. also; indignites makes life intolerable and burdensome; irretrievable breakdown and 90 days passed since action was filed and mutual consent).

Table 26: Grounds for Divorce—Continued

State	Code Section	Residency	Waiting Period	No Fault	Defenses	Grounds
RHODE ISLAND	15-5-1 to 28	One party resident 1 yr.; if based on defendant's residency, he must be personally serviced with process.	Final decree entered anytime within 30 days or 3 months from decision date.	Irretrievable breakdown; separation (for at least 3 yrs.).	Collusion.	Adultery; cruelty or violence; desertion for 5 yrs.; drug/alcohol addiction; impotency; nonsupport; any other gross/ repugnant behavior (refusal and neglect).
SOUTH CAROLINA	20-3-10 to 440	One party resident 1 yr.; if both residents when action commenced, then only 3 month requirement.	Decree cannot be entered until 3 months after filing unless divorce sought on grounds of separation or desertion.	Separation (for 1 yr. continuously).	Collusion.	Adultery; cruelty or violence; desertion for 1 yr.; drug/alcohol addiction; lived apart without cohabitation for 1 year.
SOUTH DAKOTA	25-4-2, *et seq.*	Plaintiff, at time action is commenced, must be a resident.	Action for divorce not heard for 60 days from completed service of plaintiff's summons. (Court can continue for 30 day if reconciliation possible)	Irreconcilable differences.	Connivance; collusion; condonation; limitation or lapse of time.	Adultery; extreme cruelty; wilful desertion or neglect; habitual intemperance; conviction of felony; irreconcilable differences

Table 26: Grounds for Divorce—Continued

State	Code Section	Residency	Waiting Period	No Fault	Defenses	Grounds
TENNESSEE	36-4-101, *et seq.*	No residency required if acts committed while plaintiff was resident; or if grounds arose out of state and plaintiff or defendant has resided in state 6 months preceding filing (1 yr. prior for military personnel or spouse).		Separation of 2 yrs. with no minor children; irreconcilable differences.	For adultery, defense if complainant guilt of like act	Adultery; cruelty or violence including attempted murder of the other; desertion for 1 yr. or absent state for 2 yrs.; drug/ alcohol addiction; impotency; pregnant at time of marriage by another man, without knowledge of husband; conviction of infamous crime or felony; previous marriage unresolved; also irreconcilable differences; lived separately without cohabitation for 2 continuous years and there are no minor children; abandonment or refusing/neglecting to provide when having the ability to do so.
TEXAS	Fam. 3.01, *et seq.*	One party domiciliary for preceding 6 months and resident of county for preceding 90 days.	60 days from when suit was filed.	Separation (3 yrs.); marriage is insupportable due to discord.	Defense of recrimination abolished; condonation is defense only when reasonable expectation of reconciliation; defense of adultery abolished.	Adultery; cruelty or violence; abandonment/ desertion (1 yr.); insanity (confined for at least 3 yrs.); conviction of felony and imprisonment at least 1 yr. (unless spouse testifies against convicted spouse).

Table 26: Grounds for Divorce—Continued

State	Code Section	Residency	Waiting Period	No Fault	Defenses	Grounds
UTAH	30-3 *et seq.*	One party bona fide resident 3 months before commencing action.	Except for good cause, no hearing for 90 days after filing; decree becomes absolute on day signed by court.	Separation (3 yrs.); irreconcilable differences.		Adultery; cruelty or violence; desertion (1 yr.); drug/alcohol addiction; impotency; nonsupport; incurable insanity; conviction of felony; also irreconcilable differences and lived separately under decree of separation for 3 consecutive years.
VERMONT	Tit. 15 §§551, 562, 563, 592, 631	6 months before commencing action and 1 yr. before final hearing. 2 yrs. before commencing action for grounds of insanity.		Separation (6 months).	Recrimination and condonation not defenses.	Adultery; cruelty or violence; severity; desertion (7 years); nonsupport; incurable insanity (confined for 5 yrs.); unexplained absence; conviction of crime with imprisonment over 3 yrs; living apart for 6 consecutive months and resumption of marital relations not reasonably probable.
VIRGINIA	20-91	One party resident and domiciled 6 months before suit. 20-97	Decree immediate on determination of issues.	Separation (1 yr.).		Adultery or sodomy or buggery committed outside the marriage; subsequent conviction of felony; cruelty, caused fear of bodily hurt or willfully deserted 1 yr. from the date of such act; lived separate lives without cohabitation and without interruption for one year.

Table 26: Grounds for Divorce—Continued

State	Code Section	Residency	Waiting Period	No Fault	Defenses	Grounds
WASHINGTON	26.09.030	Plaintiff must be a resident or a member of armed forces stationed in state.	90 days must elapse from point of filing petition; decree is final subject to right of appeal. 26.09.150	Irretrievable breakdown.		
WEST VIRGINIA	48-2-1 et seq.	If cause is adultery, one party must be resident at time action brought; if defendant is nonresident and service cannot be effected within the state, the plaintiff must have been a resident for 1 yr. prior to commencement of action. If ground other than adultery, one party must be resident at time the cause arose or since then has become a resident and lived in state 1 yr. before action; if parties married in West Virginia, then only one must be resident upon filing—no specified length of time.		Irretrievable breakdown; separation (1 yr.). §48-2-4	Condonation; connivance; plaintiff's own misconduct; collusion is not a bar. §48-2-14	Adultery; cruelty or violence; drug/alcohol addiction; nonsupport; insanity; conviction of crime subsequent to the marriage; abuse of child; abandonment or desertion for 6 mos.; irreconcilable differences if other party admits. §48-2-4; also lived apart without cohabitation and without interruption for one year.
WISCONSIN	767.001, *et seq.*	Either party bona fide resident at least 6 months. 767.05 (1)	Judgment effective immediately, except parties cannot remarry for 6 months. 765.03 (2)	Irretrievable breakdown. 767.07 (2)(a)		

Table 26: Grounds for Divorce—Continued

State	Code Section	Residency	Waiting Period	No Fault	Defenses	Grounds
WYOMING	20-2-101, *et seq.*	Plaintiff must have resided 60 days before filing. 20-2-107	Final decree upon issue of determination but never issued less than 20 days from when complaint filed. 20-2-108	Irreconcilable differences. 20-2-104		Insanity; 20-2-105 undissolved prior marriage.

27. MARITAL PROPERTY

Marital property is generally considered to be all property acquired by a couple during their marriage or earned by either spouse during their marriage. It is all property owned by the marital estate. Generally, gifts or inheritances to either spouse along with any money or property earned prior to the marriage are the separate property of that spouse unless it is somehow "converted" into marital property.

There are two general categories that define marital property: community property and not community property. Nine states recognize community property. In these states, all property or income acquired by either spouse during marriage is considered equally owned by both spouses for purposes of the division of the property upon death or divorce or for purposes of business transacted by either spouse. This property ownership scheme has its roots in Spanish Law. Consequently, community property laws are found generally in those states that were originally possessions of or which in some way owe some of their legal heritage to colonial Spain.

If a state is not a community property state, various rules and schemes apply to define the nature of marital property. For example, there are a number of legal options from which a couple may choose when they decide to acquire property together. They may choose joint tenancy, tenancy by the entirety, or tenancy-in-common. In most states, the character of the property in question is determined by the nature of the property itself, the nature of the event giving rise to the need for the particular characterization of property ownership, and the manner, agreement, and instrument by which it was acquired. If the event giving rise to the need for the characterization is divorce, a set of rules will apply to each portion of the marital property, depending on how it was acquired and what kind of property it is: bank account, primary home, automobile, etc.

Upon an individual's death, property will be distributed subject to the individual's legal will or trust, the rules of marital property, and/or intestate succession. A very old common law scheme of division of marital property is known as "dower and curtesy." Dower was a way that a woman, who traditionally was not given the opportunity to own property while married, was given a share of her husband's estate upon his death. Dower generally preserved a percentage share of the value of the estate. Curtesy is essentially the same system in reverse, giving the husband a percentage share of his wife's estate. However, dower and curtesy has generally become obsolete in the modern world. Laws of descent and distribution, divorce and property distribution, and use of joint tenancies, tenancies-in-common, and tenancies by the entirety have largely made it unnecessary to be concerned with the surviving spouse being left with no part of the marital property.

Eleven states have adopted the Uniform Disposition of Community Property Rights at Death Act. This protects couples that move from a community property state into one where community property is not recognized, from drastic changes in the character and disposition of their property upon the death of a spouse. This is an important consideration in today's highly mobile society.

Table 27: Marital Property

State	Community Property	Dower And Curtesy
ALABAMA	No	Dower and curtesy abolished (§43-8-57)
ALASKA	Yes. Community Propery Act 34.77.030	Curtesy: Uniform Probate Code adopted (§13.06-16); dower has been abolished
ARIZONA	Yes (§25-211)	Dower and curtesy abolished (§1-201)
ARKANSAS	No. But Uniform Disposition of Community Property Rights at Death Act (UDCPRDA) adopted. (28-12-101, *et seq.*)	Dower allowed; common law curtesy abolished; statutory allowance called curtesy provided (§28-11-301 *et seq.*)
CALIFORNIA	Yes Fam. C. §751 §770	No estate by dower or curtesy (Prob. C. §6412)
COLORADO	No. But Uniform Disposition of Community Property Rights at Death Act (UDCPRDA) adopted. ((15-20-101, *et seq.*)	Curtesy and dower abolished (§15-11-112)
CONNECTICUT	No. But Uniform Disposition of Community Property Rights at Death Act (UDCPRDA) adopted. (45a-458, *et seq.*)	No dower or curtesy when marriage occurred after April 20, 1877
DELAWARE	No	Dower and curtesy abolished (§12-511)
DISTRICT OF COLUMBIA	No	Curtesy abolished with respect to wife dying on or after November 29, 1957 (§19-102); dower in case of wife intermarried to deceased husband before November 29, 1957, or in case of both husband and wife if spouse dies on or after March 16, 1962 (§19-102)
FLORIDA	No. But Uniform Disposition of Community Property Rights at Death Act (UDCPRDA) adopted. (732.216, *et seq.*)	Dower and curtesy abolished (§732.111); statutory right to elective share of surving spouse recognized (§732.201, *et* seq.)
GEORGIA	No	No tenancy by curtesy (§53-1-2); dower is abolished (§53-1-1)
HAWAII	No. But Uniform Disposition of Community Property Rights at Death Act (UDCPRDA) adopted. (510-21, *et seq.*)	Dower and curtesy: Uniform Probate Code §560:2-112 abolished
IDAHO	Yes (§32-906)	Curtesy and dower abolished (§32-914)
ILLINOIS	No	Dower and curtesy abolished (755 ILCS 5/2-9) as of 1/1/72
INDIANA	No	Dower and curtesy abolished (IC §29-1-2-11)
IOWA	No	Curtesy abolished (§633.238); dower abolished (§633.211)
KANSAS	No	Dower and curtesy abolished (§59-505)
KENTUCKY	No. But Uniform Disposition of Community Property Rights at Death Act (UDCPRDA) adopted. (391.210, *et seq.*)	Dower and curtesy: Yes, with exceptions (KRS §392.010, *et seq.*)
LOUISIANA	Yes, with considerable exceptions (CC Art. 2334, *et seq.*)	Dower and curtesy: Unknown to the law of Louisiana
MAINE	No	Dower and curtesy abolished (T.18-A, §2-113)

Table 27: Marital Property—Continued

State	Community Property	Dower And Curtesy
MARYLAND	No	Dower and curtesy abolished (Est. & Tr. Art.§3-202)
MASSACHUSETTS	No	Curtesy abolished (Ch. 189, §1), but certain dower and curtesy rights (merged and together called "dower") remain
MICHIGAN	No. But Uniform Disposition of Community Property Rights at Death Act (UDCPRDA) adopted. (557.261, *et seq.*)	Dower (§§558.1, *et seq.*); no curtesy or dower allowed in community property (§§557.214)
MINNESOTA	No	Dower and curtesy abolished (§519.09)
MISSISSIPPI	No	Dower and curtesy abolished (§93-3-5)
MISSOURI	No	Dower and curtesy abolished (§474.110)
MONTANA	No. But Uniform Disposition of Community Property Rights at Death Act (UDCPRDA) adopted. (72-9-101, *et seq.*)	Dower and curtesy abolished (§72-2-122)
NEBRASKA	No. unless can prove otherwise§42-603	Dower and curtesy abolished (§30-104)
NEVADA	Yes (§§123.130, 220, 230)	Dower and curtesy abolished (§123.020)
NEW HAMPSHIRE	No	Dower and curtesy abolished (Ch. 560:3)
NEW JERSEY	No	Dower and curtesy abolished as to all property obtained after May 28, 1980 (3B:28-2); some rights exist re property obtained before that date (3B:28-1, *et seq.*)
NEW MEXICO	Yes (§§40-3-6, *et seq.*)	Dower and curtesy abolished (§45-2-112)
NEW YORK	No. But Uniform Disposition of Community Property Rights at Death Act (UDCPRDA) adopted. (Estates, Powers and Trusts Laws §6-6.1, et seq.)	Certain dower rights for widow of marriage before September 1, 1930 (RPL §§190, 190b); curtesy abolished (RPL §189—certain rights remain for widower of woman who died on or before August 31, 1930)
NORTH CAROLINA	No, however Uniform Disposition of Community Property Rights at Death Act adopted (§§31C-1, *et seq.*)	Dower and curtesy abolished (§29-4)
NORTH DAKOTA	No	Dower and curtesy abolished (§14-07-09)
OHIO	No	Dower (§§2103.02; *et seq.*; 3105.10); curtesy abolished (§2103.09), husband has dower interest
OKLAHOMA	Repealed (§43-215)	Dower and curtesy abolished (§§84-214)
OREGON	Repealed effective April 11, 1949 (§108.520). But Uniform Disposition of Community Property Rights at Death Act (UDCPRDA) adopted. (112.705, *et seq.*)	Dower and curtesy abolished for surviving spouse of person who dies after July 1, 1970 (§112.685-695)
PENNSYLVANIA	No. State Supreme Court held community property law (§§48-201, *et seq.*) invalid under state constitution (357 Pa. 581, 55 A.2d 521)	Share of spouse's estate which is allotted to surviving spouse by rules of intestate succession or by election against will is in lieu and full satisfaction of dower or curtesy at common law (§§20-2105)
RHODE ISLAND	No	Dower and curtesy abolished (§33-25-1)

Table 27: Marital Property—Continued

State	Community Property	Dower And Curtesy
SOUTH CAROLINA	No	Dower remains. Wife may renounce §21-5-110; South Carolina Supreme Court declared dower unconstitutional 316 S.E.2d 401, 281 S.C. 516(1984)
SOUTH DAKOTA	No	Dower and curtesy abolished (§§25-2-9; 29-1-3)
TENNESSEE	No	Dower and curtesy, unless vested, abolished as of April 1, 1977 (§31-2-102)
TEXAS	Yes (Fam. C. §§5.01b, 5.02, 5.61; Prob. C. §§38, 45)	Does not exist
UTAH	No	No dower and curtesy rights (§75-2-113)
VERMONT	No	Dower and curtesy rights set forth in §§ 14-461 to 474
VIRGINIA	No. But Uniform Disposition of Community Property Rights at Death Act (UDCPRDA) adopted. (64.1-197, *et seq.*)	Dower and curtesy abolished unless vested before January 1, 1991 (§64.1-19.2)
WASHINGTON	Yes (§26.16.030)	Dower and curtesy abolished (§11.04.060)
WEST VIRGINIA	No	Dower rights set forth at Ch. 43, Art. 1, §§1, *et. seq.*; curtesy abolished but surviving husband has dower rights (Ch. 43, Art. 1 §18)
WISCONSIN	Adopted Uniform Marital Property Act with variations on January 1, 1986 (§§766.31)	No dower or curtesy rights exist
WYOMING	No. But Uniform Disposition of Community Property Rights at Death Act (UDCPRDA) adopted. (2-7-720)	Dower and curtesy abolished (§2-4-101)(b)

28. MARRIAGE AGE REQUIREMENTS

The laws regulating marriage are quite uniform. The right to marry is considered very personal, and once the "age of majority," or when one can marry without the permission of a parent or guardian, is reached, it is the couple's sole decision whether or not to marry. However, below this age, parental consent is required (though states do not require the consent of a parent or guardian who is not present in the country or who has abandoned his or her child). The age of majority is now universally eighteen, except in Mississippi, where the parties need to be twenty-one, and Arkansas, where the female needs only to be sixteen.

While only two states, California and Kentucky, have no statutory minimum age under which marriage licenses will not be issued, many states with a minimum age requirement *do* permit marriages between minors under that age. Virtually all states allowing the marrying of minors require court approval in addition to parental consent. A growing number of states now require counseling for minors seeking to marry. Provisions for under-age marriages exist in order to permit pregnant minor females and/or couples to marry, and prevailing code language still clearly reflects that bias. Ohio has the most explicit rule on this issue. In that state, the juvenile court is authorized to grant official consent to the marriage of underage persons, and the probate court issues the license. According to Ohio statutes, the probate court may delay issuing the license until the court is convinced that the female is pregnant and will carry the child to term or may even delay issuance of the license until the baby is born.

Table 28: Marriage Age Requirements

State	Code Section	Minimum Legal Age With Parental Consent	Minimum Legal Age Without Parental Consent	Comments
ALABAMA	30-1-4, 5	Male: 14; Female: 14	Male: 18; Female: 18	Marriage under 14 is voidable, not void. Marriage between 14 and 18 without parental consent is not grounds for annulment.
ALASKA	25.05.171	Male: 16; Female: 16	Male: 18; Female: 18	Superior court judge may grant permission for person over 14 at hearing with parents and minor.
ARIZONA	25-102	Male: 16; Female: 16	Male: 18; Female: 18	Minors under 16 may be allowed to marry with parental consent and approval of superior court judge.
ARKANSAS	9-11-102 to 105	Male: 17; Female: 16	Male: 18; Female: 18	Minors under minimum age may obtain license in case of pregnancy or birth of child, with parental consent and judicial order.
CALIFORNIA	Family §300-303	Male: No age limit; Female: No age limit	Male: 18; Female: 18	Minors under 18 need parental consent and a court order obtained on the showing the court requires
COLORADO	14-2-106, 108	Male: 16; Female: 16	Male: 18; Female: 18	Minors under 16 may be allowed to marry with parental consent and/ or approval of juvenile court judge (if parents not living together).
CONNECTICUT	46b-30	Male: 16; Female: 16	Male: 18; Female: 18	Minors under 16 may be allowed to marry with parental consent and consent of probate judge.
DELAWARE	Tit. 13 §123	Male: 18; Female: 16	Male: 18; Female: 18	Minors under minimum age may obtain license in case of pregnancy or birth of child with medical certification.
DISTRICT OF COLUMBIA	§30-103, 111	Male: 16; Female: 16	Male: 18; Female: 18	Parental consent not required if minor was previously married.
FLORIDA	741.0405	Male: 16; Female: 16	Male: 18; Female: 18	Parental consent not required if minor was previously married or parents are deceased. Under age 18, a county judge has discretion whether or not to give license if the couple has a child or is expecting one (upon sworn affidavits that they are the parents).
GEORGIA	19-3-2, 19-3-37	Male: 16; Female: 16	Male: 18; Female: 18	Minors under minimum age may obtain license without parental consent in case of pregnancy or birth of child. Parents must appear before judge to consent to marriage.

Table 28: Marriage Age Requirements—Continued

State	Code Section	Minimum Legal Age With Parental Consent	Minimum Legal Age Without Parental Consent	Comments
HAWAII	§572-1 (2), 572-2	Male: 16; Female: 16	Male: 18; Female: 18	In certain circumstances, 15 year olds may obtain license, but never under 15.
IDAHO	32-202	Male: 16; Female: 16	Male: 18; Female: 18	Minors under age 16 may obtain license with parental consent and order of the court.
ILLINOIS	750 ILCS 5/208, 5/203	Male: 16; Female: 16	Male: 18; Female: 18	If no parents to consent, judicial consent with finding that parties are capable of marriage. No provisions for marriage under age 16.
INDIANA	31-11-1-4 to 31-11-1-6	Male: 17; Female: 17	Male: 18; Female: 18	Minors ages 15-17 may obtain license in case of pregnancy, birth of child and with approval of judge of superior or county court.
IOWA	595.2	Male: 16; Female: 16	Male: 18; Female:18	Minors 16-17 may obtain license without parental consent with approval of court if both parents dead or incompetent or marriage in parties' best interest.
KANSAS	23-106	Male: not specified; Female: not specified	Male: 18; Female: 18	No statutory provision for minimum age with consent. Common law prevails. See *State v. Wade,* 766 P. 2d 811 at 815.
KENTUCKY	402.020	Male: 16; Female: 16	Male: 18; Female: 18	Minors under age 18 may obtain license without parental consent in case of pregnancy or birth of child and with permission of district court judge.
LOUISIANA	Children's Code Art. 1545, *et seq.*	Male: 16; Female: 16	Male: 18; Female: 18	Minor under 16 must obtain both parental consent and authorization of court.
MAINE	19-A §652	Male: 16; Female: 16	Male: 18; Female: 18	Minors under 16 may be allowed to marry with parental consent and approval of court.
MARYLAND	Fam. Law 2-301	Male: 16; Female: 16	Male: 18; Female: 18	Minors under 16 may obtain license in case of pregnancy or birth of child.
MASSACHUSETTS	Ch. 207§7, 24, 25	Male: not specified; Female: not specified	Male: 18; Female: 18	No statutory provision for minimum age with consent. Common law prevails. If parent deserted or incapable of consent, not necessary to obtain consent.
MICHIGAN	MCLA §551.51 & 551.103; 551.201	Male: 16; Female: 16; (consent of 1 of the parents required of both sexes)	Male: 18; Female: 18	Minors under 16 may obtain license in case of pregnancy, birth of child, or other special circumstances.
MINNESOTA	517.02	Male: 16; Female: 16	Male: 18; Female: 18	

Table 28: Marriage Age Requirements—Continued

State	Code Section	Minimum Legal Age With Parental Consent	Minimum Legal Age Without Parental Consent	Comments
MISSISSIPPI	93-1-5	Male: 17; Female: 15	Male: 21; Female: 21	Minors under minimum age may obtain license with parental consent and approval of court.
MISSOURI	451.090	Male: 15; Female: 15	Male: 18; Female: 18	Minors under 15 may obtain license under special circumstances and for good cause.
MONTANA	40--1-213; 40-1-202	Male: 16; Female: 16	Male: 18; Female: 18	Minors age 16 or 17 must participate in marriage counseling and must show capable of marriage.
NEBRASKA	42-102	Male: 17; Female: 17	Male: 18; Female: 18	
NEVADA	122.020, 025	Male: 16; Female: 16	Male: 18; Female: 18	Minors under 16 may obtain license by parental consent and approval of court in extraordinary circumstances.
NEW HAMPSHIRE	457:4 to 457:6	Male: 14; Female: 13	Male: 18; Female: 18	Any marriage contracted by persons under 18 may, in discretion of superior court, be annulled at suit of the party who at the time of marriage was under 18. The parent or guardian can also annul, unless the parties confirm marriage upon reaching age of consent (18 years).
NEW JERSEY	37:1-6	Male: 16; Female: 16 (unless parents of unsound mind)	Male: 18; Female: 18	Minors under 16 may obtain license by parental consent and approval of court. If male under 18 yrs. old and has been arrested on charge of sexual intercourse with single female who thereby became pregnant, consent not required.
NEW MEXICO	40-1-5 to 6	Male: 16; Female: 16	Male: 18; Female: 18	Minors under 16 may only obtain license by order of children's court or family division of district court. Courts may authorize marriage in settlement of action to compel support, and establish parentage, or in case of pregnancy.
NEW YORK	Dom. Rel. §§7, C7:1, 15	Male: 14; Female: 14	Male: 18; Female: 18	Minors under 16 must have approval of parents and court. Minors 16 and 17 must have only parental consent.
NORTH CAROLINA	51-2	Male: 16; Female: 16 (One or both parents' consent unless minor has certificate of emancipation)	Male: 18; Female: 18	Female minor 12-18 may obtain license with parental consent in case of pregnancy or birth of child.

Table 28: Marriage Age Requirements—Continued

State	Code Section	Minimum Legal Age With Parental Consent	Minimum Legal Age Without Parental Consent	Comments
NORTH DAKOTA	14-03-02	Male: 16; Female: 16	Male: 18; Female: 18	No license issued to persons under 16.
OHIO	3101.01 to 3101.05	Male: 18; Female: 16	Male: 18; Female: 18	Applicants under 18 must state that they have had marriage counseling. After all conditions are met, the court may delay issuance of consent for minors without parents' or guardians' consent until the female bears the child or the court is convinced she is pregnant and intends to carry the baby to term.
OKLAHOMA	Tit. 43 §3	Male: 16; Female: 16	Male: 18; Female: 18	Minors under 16 may obtain license in case of pregnancy or birth of child with parental consent and court authorization.
OREGON	106.010, 106.060	Male: 17; Female: 17	Male: 18; Female: 18	If parent is out of state and either party is a resident, parental consent not required.
PENNSYLVANIA	Tit. 23 §1304(1) to (2)	Male: 16; Female: 16	Male: 18; Female: 18	Minors under 16 may obtain license with parental consent and approval of court if in best interest of applicant.
RHODE ISLAND	15-2-11	Male: 18; Female: 16	Male: 18; Female: 18	Younger parties may obtain license in special circumstances.
SOUTH CAROLINA	20-1-250, 20-1-300	Male: 16; Female: 14	Male: 18; Female: 18	Younger parties may obtain license in case of pregnancy or birth of child (with proof of pregnancy from doctor).
SOUTH DAKOTA	25-1-9	Male: 16; Female: 16; (consent of 1 parent)	Male: 18; Female: 18	
TENNESSEE	36-3-104 to 107	Male: 16; Female: 16; (3 day waiting period except for certain circumstances where waived)	Male: 18; Female: 18	Minors under 16 may obtain license in special circumstances.
TEXAS	§2.102 §2.101	Male: 14; Female: 14; (consent must be given during 30 day period immediately preceding the date of application for license)	Male: 18; Female: 18	Minors under 18 can petition court in his own name for permission to marry

Table 28: Marriage Age Requirements—Continued

State	Code Section	Minimum Legal Age With Parental Consent	Minimum Legal Age Without Parental Consent	Comments
UTAH	30-1-2; 30-1-9; 30-1-30, 31	Male: 14; Female: 14	Male: 18; Female: 18	Counties are authorized to provide for premarital counseling as a requisite to issuance of license to persons under 19 and persons previously divorced. Parental consent not required if minor was previously married. If minor is under 16 yrs old, she must also receive written authorization from the court
VERMONT	Tit. 18 §5142	Male: 16; Female: 16	Male: 18; Female: 18	Minors under 16 may obtain license with parental consent and court order that "public good" requires them to be married. No persons under 14 may marry.
VIRGINIA	20-48, 49	Male: 16; Female: 16	Male: 18; Female: 18	Parental consent not required if minor was already married. Minors under 16 may obtain license in case of pregnancy or birth of child.
WASHINGTON	26.04.010	Male: 17; Female: 17	Male: 18; Female: 18	Minors under 17 may obtain license in special circumstances.
WEST VIRGINIA	48-1-1	Male: 16; Female: 16	Male: 18; Female: 18	Minors under 16 may obtain license with parental consent and court order.
WISCONSIN	765.02	Male: 16; Female: 16	Male: 18; Female: 18	
WYOMING	20-1-102	Male: 16; Female: 16	Male: 18; Female: 18	Minors under 16 may obtain license in special circumstances.

29. PROTECTIVE ORDERS

Protective orders are typically used in domestic disputes to ban one party from contact with another or from interfering with an order of the court with respect to child visitation or custody rights. They are also frequently used in cases of spousal abuse to keep the violent party from coming into contact with the victim. Protective orders are usually temporary measures that the court uses in order to remedy suspected destructive activity while the parties gather and present evidence showing that a more permanent remedy is required. Protective orders may sometimes be granted *ex parte,* that is without the presence of the party being effected, but only when there is substantial evidence that the party applying for the order is under an imminent threat of injury or when there is good evidence that an order of the court will be violated.

Protective orders have a wide range of temporary duration. Typically, they last for one year with extensions possible under certain particular circumstances.

Five states allow imposition of protective orders for up to three years, and five other states limit them to just 90 days. Ohio has recently enacted a law which sets the duration of a protective order at 5 years, the longest of any state. Violations of protective orders also vary widely. Although most states impose a maximum one year sentence and a $1,000 fine, seven states require mandatory jail time for violating a protective order.

Virtually all states require transmission of protective orders to local law enforcement agencies. Twelve states require transmission within 48 hours. A few states have set up state-wide registries or information systems that keep track of protective orders that are presently in effect. Utilization of technology, such as the internet, and wide area networks, permit easy access to statewide registries. In Iowa, for example, it is required to get certified copies of protective orders into the hands of law enforcement agencies within six hours of issuance.

Table 29: Protective Orders

Code Section	Activity Addressed by Order	Duration	Penalty for a Violation of Order	Who May Apply for Order	Fees Waived?	Transmission to Law Enforcement	Civil Liability
			ALABAMA				
30-5-1, *et al seq.*	Enjoining contacts of abuse; harassing communication; excluding party from dwelling, school or place of employment; regarding minors: award temporary custody and establish visitations as well as temporary support; enjoin defendant from interfering	Up to 1 year, can be amended at any time upon verified petition by either party	Willful violation: Class A misdemeanor, fine not to exceed $2,000 and/or jail up to 1 year; 2nd conviction for violation: minimum of 48 hours unsuspended continuous imprisonment and fine; 3rd or subsequent conviction: minimum sentence of 30 days unsuspended imprisonment and fine	An adult for themselves or another person prevented by physical or mental incapacities or on behalf of minor children	If petitioner can show they have inadequate funds	Copy issued to law enforcement officials with jurisdiction to enforce the order or agreement	Civil contempt
			ALASKA				
repealed 18.66.100-18.66.180	Enjoining contacts of domestic violence, communication or entering a propelled vehicle occupied by or possessed by party; excluding party from dwelling, award temporary custody	Until further order of court for threats and acts of domestic violence 6 months for other acts		Adult or minor through guardian ad litem or attorney	On the basis of indigency. No filing fees	Copy of order transmitted to appropriate local law enforcement agency	
			ARIZONA				
13-3602	Enjoined from committing acts of domestic violence; excluded from dwelling, place of employment, school; participation in domestic violence counseling; prohitbition from possession of a firearm.	6 months after service on defendant unless renewed		Person or other if person is either temporarily or permanently unable to request an order	May be waived under any rule, statute or other law applicable to civil actions; no requirements of community service as a condition of fee waiver.	Within 24 hours after acceptance of service or affidavit has been returned; copies sent to sheriff's office in the county in which party resides	Civil contempt

Table 29: Protective Orders

Code Section	Activity Addressed by Order	Duration	Penalty for a Violation of Order	Who May Apply for Order	Fees Waived?	Transmission to Law Enforcement	Civil Liability
			ARKANSAS				
9-15-201, *et. al seq.*	Exclude from dwelling, place of business or employment, school; award temporary support and custody; establish visitation	Minimum 90 days, maximum 1 year; may be renewed. Temporary order: maximum 30 days	Class A misdemeanor: maximum penalty 1 year imprisonment in county jail or maximum fine of $1,000 or both	Family or household member or on behalf of a family or household member who is a minor or adjudicated incompetent	Yes	Copy issued to law enforcement officer with jurisdiction to accompany petitioner in possession of dwelling or otherwise assist in service of order	Civil contempt
			CALIFORNIA				
Family Code 6240, *et seq.*; 6320, *et seq.*; Penal 273.6	Enjoining contact; excluding from dwelling; enjoining specific behavior; regarding minor child: custody, visitations. Penal code: any person who has domestic abuse perpetrated against him/her as shown by affidavit of reasonable proof	Emergency order: the earlier of the close of the 5th business day after issue or 7 calendar days. Others: 3 year maximum unless extended by office or parties stipulate to permanent order	1 year and/or $1,000; with physical injury: 30 days plus 1 year and/or $2,000	Spouse, cohabitant, fiancé/ fianceé, parent of one's child, blood relations.		By the close of business on day of issuance; local law enforcement agency must notify Department of Justice for domestic violence protective order registry	

Table 29: Protective Orders

Code Section	Activity Addressed by Order	Duration	Penalty for a Violation of Order	Who May Apply for Order	Fees Waived?	Transmission to Law Enforcement	Civil Liability
COLORADO							
14-4-101, *et seq.*	Enjoin contact; exclude party from dwelling or dwelling of another; regarding minor child: temporary custody for maximum of 120 days, visitation. Emergency order: restrain from threatening, molesting, injuring, or contacting another or minor children of either; excluding from dwelling, if minor child, temporary custody	Emergency: maximum close of business on 3rd day following issue, unless continued	Class 2 misdemeanor unless prior conviction under § or other restraining order: Class 1 misdemeanor		No	Law enforcement agency with jurisdiction to enforce the order	Contempt of court
CONNECTICUT							
46b-15	Regarding minor children: temporary custody, visitation; enjoin contact; exclude from dwelling of family or of applicant; threatening, harassing assaulting, molesting sexual assault	6 months unless extended	Criminal trespass: in 1st degree, for entering or remaining in dwelling. Maximum penalty up to 1 year in jail or up to $2000 or both	Family or household member. Subjected to a continuous threat of physical pain or injury		Yes; appropriate law enforcement agency within 48 hours of issuance	Contempt of court

Table 29: Protective Orders

Code Section	Activity Addressed by Order	Duration	Penalty for a Violation of Order	Who May Apply for Order	Fees Waived?	Transmission to Law Enforcement	Civil Liability
			DELAWARE				
Tit. 10 § 1041, *et seq.*	Enjoin contact; exclude from dwelling; regarding minor children: temporary custody, visitations, support; prohibit use/possession of firearms or disposal of property; award monetary compensation to petitioner; counseling	Ex parte order: maximum 30 days. General order: maximum 1 year unless extended	Class A misdemeanor	Member of a protected class on behalf of self and their minor child or an infirm adult		Order entered into Delaware Justice Information system on or before the next business day; copy sent to Delaware law enforcement agency where petitioner resides and/or where abuse received	Contempt
			DISTRICT OF COLUMBIA				
16-1001, *et seq.*	Enjoin contact; order counseling; exclude from dwelling and possession of other personal property; regarding minor children: temporary custody, visitations award court costs and attorney fees to petitioner	Temporary protective order: maximum 14 days. General protective order: maximum 1 year unless extended	Misdemeanor: fine, maximum $1,000 and/or imprisonment: maximum 180 days	Any person or agency		Metropolitan police department	Contempt
			FLORIDA				
741.30 & 31	Exclude from dwelling; enjoin contact; regarding minor children: grant temporary custody visitations, temporary support; counseling	Ex parte temporary: maximum 15 days. General protective order: maximum 1 year, can reapply but maximum an additional year	Misdemeanor in 1st degree	Any family or household member who is a victim of domestic violence or one who has reasonable cause to believe he or she is about to become victim	Yes	Within 24 hours of issuance	Civil contempt

Table 29: Protective Orders

Code Section	Activity Addressed by Order	Duration	Penalty for a Violation of Order	Who May Apply for Order	Fees Waived?	Transmission to Law Enforcement	Civil Liability
GEORGIA							
19-13-1, *et seq.*	Enjoin contact; exclude from dwelling; regarding minor children: grant temporary custody, visitations, support and attorney's fees, counseling; provide suitable alternate housing for petitioner and minor children	Maximum 6 months; temporary order may be converted to permanent order	Misdemeanor	Person who isn't a minor on behalf of self or a minor		Sheriff of the county where order was entered	
HAWAII							
586-1, *et seq.*	Enjoin contact; exclude from dwelling and petitioner's work; regarding minor children: grant temporary visitation, counseling	Temporary restraining order: maximum 90 days. protective order: maximum 3 years	Violation of temporary restraining order: Misdemeanor: required counseling and if 1st conviction, mandatory minimum jail 48 hours and fine of no less than $150 nor more than $500; 2nd conviction mandatory minimum 30 days jail and fine of no less than $250 nor more than $1000, otherwise mandatory minimum 48 hours; court may waive if 2nd was for nondomestic abuse and 1st conviction was for domestic abuse. Violation of protective order: 1st conviction, mandatory minimum jail 48 hours; 2nd conviction domestic, mandatory minimum 30 days. Subsequent violations: after 2nd conviction for violation of same order, mandatory minimum 30 days jail	Any family or household member on behalf of self, a minor member or one who is incapacitated or physically unable to file petition, or any state agency on behalf of minor, incapacitated or unable member		Within 24 hours to county police department	

Table 29: Protective Orders

Code Section	Activity Addressed by Order	Duration	Penalty for a Violation of Order	Who May Apply for Order	Fees Waived?	Transmission to Law Enforcement	Civil Liability
IDAHO							
39-6301, *et seq.*	Enjoin contact; exclude from dwelling; regarding minor children: grant temporary custody; pay court cost's and attorney's fees; counseling	Maximum 3 months unless renewed, maximum 1 year. Ex parte temporary protective order: maximum 14 days, can be reissued	Misdemeanor: maximum 1 year jail and fine, maximum $5,000	Family or household member, even if person has left dwelling to avoid abuse.	Yes	On or before next judicial day	
ILLINOIS							
Ch. 750 §60/201, et seq.	Prohibition of abuse, neglect, or exploitation; exclude from dwelling, counseling; regarding minor children: grant temporary custody, visitations, support	Emergency: minimum 14 to maximum 21 days. Interim: 30 days. Plenary: maximum 2 years. All orders can be extended.	If knowing violation: class A misdemeanor. If violating order concerning minors: Class 4 felony. If willful violation: contempt of court; may include jail, restitution, fines, attorney's fees and costs, or community service. Court encouraged to follow these guidelines: 1st violation: minimum 24 hours jail; 2nd or subsequent violation: minimum 48 hours jail	A person who has been abused by a family or household member, or by any person on behalf of minor child or adult who cannot file due to age, health, disability, or inaccessibility	Yes; no fees for filing petitions or certifying orders.	Certified copy filed with sheriff or other law enforcement official same day order is issued	Contempt of court
INDIANA							
34-26-2-1, *et seq.*	Enjoin contact; exclude from dwelling; regarding minor children: support, custody, maintenance, counseling; refrain from disturbing peace of petitioner; refrain from damaging petitioner's property	Emergency: 60 days maximum. General: maximum 1 year, may be extended, maximum 1 additional year		Person or member of the petitioner's household	Yes, if petitioner demonstrates by affidavit that petitioner is unable to pay due to all relevant circumstances		

Table 29: Protective Orders

Code Section	Activity Addressed by Order	Duration	Penalty for a Violation of Order	Who May Apply for Order	Fees Waived?	Transmission to Law Enforcement	Civil Liability
IOWA							
236.1, *et seq.*	Counseling; enjoin contact; exclude from dwelling, school, or work; regarding minor children: temporary custody, visitations, support	Maximum 1 year. Emergency: maximum 72 hours; may then seek temporary order.	Contempt: required jail sentence; if no contact order: county jail minimum 7 days, a fine may be imposed	Person seeking relief from domestic abuse on behalf of self or unemancipated minor	Yes, if file an affidavit stating insufficient funds	Certified copy to county sheriff within 6 hours of filing of the order	
KANSAS							
60-3101, *et seq.*	Enjoin contact; exclude from dwelling; regarding minors: temporary custody, visitations, support, counseling; provide suitable alternate housing; attorney fees	Emergency: until 5PM on first day that court resumes business. Support order: maximum 1 year, may be extended for 1 year maximum. General: maximum 1 year, may be extended for 1 year maximum	Violation of enjoining contact: assault or battery; violation of exclusion from dwelling: criminal trespass	A person or minor child through a parent or adult residing with the child; cannot apply more than twice a year except in the case of abuse of a minor.	Yes	Copy to police department of petitioner's residential city or to sheriff of the petitioner's residential county if no residential city	Contempt of court
KENTUCKY							
403.715 to .785 (domestic violence) 209.01 to .16 (Kentucky Adult Protective Act)	Enjoin contact; exclude from dwelling; regarding minors: temporary custody, support, counseling; restrain from disposing of or damaging property	Emergency: maximum 14 days, may be extended for 14 days. General: maximum 3 years, may be reissued for a year period, with unlimited reissues	Contempt of court: if intentional violation, Class A misdemeanor	Family member or unmarried couple member who is a resident or has fled to this state to escape domestic violation and abuse	Yes	Copy to appropriate law enforcement agency within 24 hours; copy to appropriate agency for entry of domestic violation records into Law Information Network of Kentucky	Contempt of court

Table 29: Protective Orders

Code Section	Activity Addressed by Order	Duration	Penalty for a Violation of Order	Who May Apply for Order	Fees Waived?	Transmission to Law Enforcement	Civil Liability
			LOUISIANA				
46:2131 to 2142	Enjoin contact; exclude from dwelling; regarding minors: temporary custody, support, visitations, counseling	Maximum 6 months, may be extended	Contempt of court: imprisonment maximum 6 months and/or fine, maximum $500	Any parent; adult household member, parent or district attorney on behalf of minor or incompetent	Paid by perpetrator	Copy of Unifrom Abuse Protection Order to chief law enforcement official of parish where protected persons reside, by end of next business day after filing.	Contempt of court
			MAINE				
15 §321, 19A§4001 et seq.	Enjoin contact; exclude from dwelling, school, or work; support regarding minors: temporary custody, visitations; counseling, court costs and attorney's fee; prohibition from possession of a firearm.	Temporary: remains in effect pending service of final order. General: maximum 2 years, may be extended	Class D crime; if violation of order of support: contempt	Any abused family or household member; if minor, person responsible for the child or represent-ative of Department of Human Services	Yes	For temporary emergency or interim relief; copy to law enforcement agency as soon as possible. General: copy to law enforcement agency most likely to enforce order	
			MARYLAND				
Family Law §4-501, et seq.	Enjoin contact; exclude from dwelling, work, or school; regarding minors: temporary custody, counseling, visitations, maintenance	Temporary: 7 days, may be extended, maximum 30 days. General: maximum 200 days	Contempt, criminal prosecution, imprisonment, or fine. If violate certain clauses: misdemeanor; jail maximum 98 days and/or fine, maximum $500	A household member or minor or vulnerable adult; state's attorney, department of social services, law enforcement officer, blood, marriage or adoptive relative, or adult household member	May be waived	Copy to appropriate law enforcement agency	

397

Table 29: Protective Orders

Code Section	Activity Addressed by Order	Duration	Penalty for a Violation of Order	Who May Apply for Order	Fees Waived?	Transmission to Law Enforcement	Civil Liability
MASSACHUSETTS							
209A §1, *et seq.*; 208 §34C	Enjoin contact; exclude from dwelling (maximum 1 year, may be extended); regarding minors: temporary custody, support; suspend firearms license	Maximum 1 year, may be extended	Fine: maximum $5,000 and/or jail, maximum 2.5 years and order appropriate treatment	A person suffering from abuse from an adult or minor family or household member.	Yes	Copy to appropriate law enforcement agency	Yes
MICHIGAN							
600.2950 personal protection order & 2950a	Enjoin contact; exclude from premise, work; regarding minors: exclude from minor children	Minimum 182 days unless modified	Civil or criminal contempt: jail, maximum 93 days and fined maximum $500	Household member, spouse\ex-spouse, parent of one's child, dating relationship.		Copy entered into law enforcement information network by law enforcement agency designated by court in order	Yes, for false statements made in court
MINNESOTA							
518B.01	Enjoin contact; exclude from dwelling, work; regarding minors: temporary custody, visitation, support; counseling; restitution; continue payment of joint insurance coverage.	General: maximum 1 year, may be extended. Ex parte order: maximum 1 year	Misdemeanor: minimum 3 days jail and counseling. Gross misdemeanor if convicted under certain laws, within 5 years: minimum 10 days and counseling; court may order $10,000 bond if repeat violation likely or if possessing a dangerous weapon	Any family or household member, a guardian, or regarding minors: a reputable adult age 25 or older as determined by the court	Yes	Copy within 24 hours to local law enforcement agency with jurisdiction over the residence of the applicant	Yes, contempt of court

Table 29: Protective Orders

Code Section	Activity Addressed by Order	Duration	Penalty for a Violation of Order	Who May Apply for Order	Fees Waived?	Transmission to Law Enforce-ment	Civil Liability
MISSISSIPPI							
93-21-1, *et seq.*	Enjoin contact; exclude from dwelling; regarding minors: temporary custody, visitations, support; restitution for monetary losses suffered as a result of abuse.	Temporary: maximum 10 days, can be extended another 10 days. General: maximum 1 year, may be extended	Contempt of court: maximum 6 months jail and/or fine, maximum $1,000	Any parent, adult household member, or next friend on behalf of minors or incompetent			Yes, contempt of court
MISSOURI							
455.01, *et seq.*	Temporarily enjoin contact; temporarily exclude from dwelling; regarding minors: temporary custody, visitation, support, counseling; court costs	Full maximum: 180 days, may be renewed for 180 days	Class A misdemeanor unless convicted of same within 5 years: Class D felony	Any adult who has been subject to abuse by present or former family or household member, or who has been the victim of stalking	Yes, court costs assessment determined by the court	Copy to local law enforcement agency in jurisdiction where petitioner resides; copy for entry into Missouri uniform law enforcement system	No
MONTANA							
40-4-121 to 125; 40-15-101, *et seq.* Temporary order during dissolution of marriage only; 45-5-626	Enjoin contact; exclude from dwelling, school, and employment of petitioner; counseling; regarding minors: enjoin contact; prohibition from possession of a firearm; during dissolution, includes temporary maintenance and support	Temporary: maximum 20 days; during dissolution: maximum 1 year, may be modified	Fine: maximum $500 and/or jail maximum 6 months. If 2nd conviction: fine, minimum $200 and maximum $500 and/or jail, minimum 24 hours and maximum 6 months. If 3rd or subsequent offense: fine, minimum $500 and maximum $2,000 and jail, minimum 10 days and maximum 2 years	Victim or regarding minors: parent, guardian ad litem or other representative	May be if inability- to-pay-filing-fees order form submitted	Copy mailed, within 24 hours of receiving proof of service, to the appropriate law enforcement agency	

Table 29: Protective Orders

Code Section	Activity Addressed by Order	Duration	Penalty for a Violation of Order	Who May Apply for Order	Fees Waived?	Transmission to Law Enforcement	Civil Liability
NEBRASKA							
42-901, *et seq.*	Enjoin contact; exclude from dwelling or any other place specified by court	Maximum: 1 year unless modified	Class II misdemeanor if knowingly violated; Class I misdemeanor if violator has prior conviction for violating order; Class IV felony if violator has prior conviction for violating same order	Any victim of domestic abuse	Yes, in good faith	Copy to local police department, local law enforcement agent and local sheriff's office	
NEVADA							
33.017, *et seq.*	Enjoin contact; exclude from dwelling, school, or employment; regarding minors: temporary custody, visitations	Temporary order: maximum 30 days or until hearing. Extended order: 1 year	Misdemeanor or maximum penalty prescribed by law. If violation by violent physical act: fine $1,000 or community service 200 hours; jail, minimum 5 days, maximum 6 months; attorney and medical costs; counseling	Spouse, former spouse, blood or marital relative, parent of one's child, dating relation, minor	Court assesses against respondent at final disposition and can reduce or waive them	Copy by end of next business day to appropriate law enforcement agency with jurisdiction over residence, school, child care facility, or place of employment	Yes, contempt of court
NEW HAMPSHIRE							
173B, *et seq.*	Enjoin contact; exclude from dwelling, school, employment; regarding minors: temporary custody, visitations, support; counseling; court costs and attorney fees	Maximum: 1 year, may be extended	Willful violation: contempt of court; knowingly violation: misdemeanor	Any person; a minor petitioner need not be accompanied by a parent or guardian	Yes	Copy to department of safety and local law enforcement agency having jurisdiction to enforce the order	Yes, contempt of court

Table 29: Protective Orders

Code Section	Activity Addressed by Order	Duration	Penalty for a Violation of Order	Who May Apply for Order	Fees Waived?	Transmission to Law Enforcement	Civil Liability
NEW JERSEY							
2C: 25-17, *et seq.*	Enjoin contact; exclude from dwelling, school, employment; regarding minors: visitation, support, custody, counseling: prohibit from possession or a firearm; reimburse petitioner's related expenses		Contempt: crime in 4th degree. If 2nd or subsequent domestic violation contempt offense: jail minimum 30 days	Any person claiming to be a victim of domestic violence		Copy to appropriate chiefs of police, members of state police, and other law enforcement agencies	Yes, contempt of court
NEW MEXICO							
40-13-2, *et seq.*	Enjoin contact; exclude from dwelling; regarding minors: visitation, support	Maximum: 6 months, may be extended for 6 months	Misdemeanor: jail maximum 1 year and/or fine maximum $1,000. If 2nd or subsequent: jail minimum 72 consecutive hours	Any victim of domestic abuse	Yes	Copy to local law enforcement agency	Yes, contempt of court
NEW YORK							
29A: 1-655 & 656; 153, *et seq.*	Enjoin contact; exclude from dwelling, school, employment; regarding minors: visitation; counseling; reimburse reasonable expenses	Temporary order: 4 calendar days	Contempt	Any person		Copy to sheriff's office or police department in county or city in which petitioner resides	Yes, contempt of court
NORTH CAROLINA							
50B-1, *et seq.*	Enjoin contact; exclude from dwelling; regarding minors: temporary custody, visitations, support, counseling; prohibit purchase of a firearm; court costs and attorney fees	1 year; may be renewed for an additional year	Class A1 misdemeanor	Any aggrieved party; a minor may be represented by a person who resides with or has custody		Copy to police department of city of victim's residence or sheriff of county police department where victim resides	Yes, contempt of court

Table 29: Protective Orders

Code Section	Activity Addressed by Order	Duration	Penalty for a Violation of Order	Who May Apply for Order	Fees Waived?	Transmission to Law Enforcement	Civil Liability
			NORTH DAKOTA				
14.07.1, *et seq.*	Enjoin contact; exclude from dwelling; regarding minors: temporary custody, visitations, support, counseling; surrendder of firearm; court costs and atorney fees	Temporary: maximum 30 days	Class A misdemeanor and contempt of court. If 2nd or subsequent: Class C felony	Any family or household member or any other person where court finds relationship is sufficient to warrant issuance of domestic violation protective order	Yes	Copy transmitted by close of business to local law enforcement agency with jurisdiction over victim's residence	Yes, contempt of court
			OHIO				
3113.31	Enjoin contact; exclude from dwelling, school, employment; regarding minors: temporarily allocate parental rights, visitations, support, counseling	Maximum 5 years, may be renewed; or upon court action for divorce	1st degree misdemeanor	Person, parent or adult household member on behalf of other family or household member	Yes	Copy to all law enforcement agencies with jurisdiction	Yes, contempt of court

Table 29: Protective Orders

Code Section	Activity Addressed by Order	Duration	Penalty for a Violation of Order	Who May Apply for Order	Fees Waived?	Transmission to Law Enforcement	Civil Liability
OKLAHOMA							
Tit. 22 §60.1, *et seq.*	Enjoin contact; exclude from dwelling; regarding minors: temporary custody, counseling; court costs and attorney fees	Temporary: until close of business on next day after order is issued. General: continues until modified or rescinded, or court-approved consent agreement	Misdemeanor: jail maximum 1 year and/or fine maximum $1,000. If 2nd or subsequent: misdemeanor: jail minimum 10 days, maximum 1 year and/or fine minimum $1,000 and maximum $5,000. If causes physical injury or impairment: misdemeanor: jail minimum 20 days, maximum 1 year and/or fine maximum $5,000. If minor child convicted: counseling and community service hours	Victim or any adult or emancipated minor household member on behalf of any other family or household member who is a minor or incompetent, or any minor who is 16 or 17	Yes, filing fee; court will assess fees at hearing	Within 24 hours of return of service, court will send copies to all appropriate law enforcement agencies designated by petitioner	
OREGON							
107.700, *et seq.*	Enjoin contact; exclude from dwelling; regarding minors: temporary custody, visitations, counseling	Temporary: 1 year restraining order, effective until expires or terminated by court	Contempt	Any person who has been the victim of abuse within preceding 180 days	Yes	Copy to county sheriff, and entered into Law Enforcement Data System	Yes, contempt of court

Table 29: Protective Orders

Code Section	Activity Addressed by Order	Duration	Penalty for a Violation of Order	Who May Apply for Order	Fees Waived?	Transmission to Law Enforcement	Civil Liability
			PENNSYLVANIA				
23 §6102, *et seq.*	Enjoin contact; exclude from dwelling, school, employment, or defendant provide suitable alternate housing; regarding minors: temporary custody, visitations, support; relinquish weapons; pay reasonbable losses suffered as a result of abuse	Temporary: effective until modified or terminated by court. General: maximum 1 year, may be extended indefinitely	Indirect criminal contempt: jail maximum 6 months and/or fine minimum $100 and maximum $1,000	Adult or emancipated minor or any parent, adult household member, or guardian ad litem on behalf of minor or incompetent	Yes, if petitioner prevails; if not, court decides whether petitioner able to pay	Petitioner may register order without cost or fee in any county or a copy may be sent to the Pennsylvania State Police registry. Copy to police department with proper jurisdiction and copy to county registry of protection order	Yes, civil contempt
			RHODE ISLAND				
15-15-1, *et seq.*	Enjoin contact; exclude from dwelling; regarding minors: temporary custody, support	Support payments: maximum 90 days. General: maximum 3 years, may be extended. Temporary: maximum 21 days, maybe extended	Contempt of court. If defendant has actual notice of protective order: misdemeanor: jail maximum 1 year and/or fine maximum $1,000 and counseling. If 2nd violation: jail minimum 10 days and maximum 1 year. If 3rd or subsequent: jail minimum 1 year and maximum 10 years	Any victim of domestic abuse		Copy forwarded immediately to law enforcement agency designated by petitioner	Yes, contempt of court

Table 29: Protective Orders

Code Section	Activity Addressed by Order	Duration	Penalty for a Violation of Order	Who May Apply for Order	Fees Waived?	Transmission to Law Enforcement	Civil Liability
			SOUTH CAROLINA				
20-4-10, *et seq.*	Enjoin contact; exclude from dwelling, employment or school; regarding minors: temporary custody, visitations, support; court costs and attorney fees	Minimum 6 months, maximum 1 year, may be extended. Regarding minor protective order: maximum 60 days or until divorce or support or maintenance hearing	If 1st offense: jail 30 days or fine maximum $200. If contempt of court: jail maximum 1 year and/or fine maximum $1,500	Any household member on behalf of self or minor household members	Yes	Copy to local law enforcement agencies with jurisdiction over area where petitioner resides	Yes, contempt of court
			SOUTH DAKOTA				
25-10-1, *et seq.*	Enjoin contact; exclude from dwelling; regarding minors: temporary custody, visitations, support, counseling	Protective order: maximum 3 years. Temporary: maximum 30 days	If knows of order: Class 1 misdemeanor. If assault occurs: Class 6 felony	Any family or household member	Yes, if affadavit filed	Copy to local law enforcement agency having jurisdiction over area where petitioner resides	Yes, contempt of court
			TENNESSEE				
36-3-601, *et seq.*	Enjoin contact; exclude from dwelling or provide suitable alternate housing; regarding minors: temporary custody, visitations, support; counseling	Protective order effective for 1 year, or court of divorce action modifies or dissolves it	Civil or criminal contempt: civil penalty of $50	Victim of abuse by present or former adult family or household member	Determined at hearing	Copy to local law enforcement agency with jurisdiction over area where petitioner resides	Yes, contempt of court

Table 29: Protective Orders

Code Section	Activity Addressed by Order	Duration	Penalty for a Violation of Order	Who May Apply for Order	Fees Waived?	Transmission to Law Enforcement	Civil Liability

TEXAS

Code Section	Activity Addressed by Order	Duration	Penalty for a Violation of Order	Who May Apply for Order	Fees Waived?	Transmission to Law Enforcement	Civil Liability
Family 71.01, *et seq. Repealed; now Family 71.001 et seq.*	Enjoin contact; exclude from dwelling, employment, school; regarding minors: enjoin contact, temporary custody, support; counseling; reasonable court costs and attorney fees	Temporary: maximum 20 days. General: maximum 1 year	Fine, maximum $4,000 and/or jail, maximum 1 year. If family violence occurs, can be prosecuted for a misdemeanor or felony, carry jail minimum 2 years. Temporary: maximum $500 fine or maximum 6 months jail.	Adult member of family; prosecuting attorney; department of protective and regulatory services	Yes; fees paid by respondent	Copy to chief of police where protected resides and to department of public safety	Yes, contempt of court

UTAH

Code Section	Activity Addressed by Order	Duration	Penalty for a Violation of Order	Who May Apply for Order	Fees Waived?	Transmission to Law Enforcement	Civil Liability
30-6-1, *et seq.*; 76-5-108	Enjoin contact; exclude from dwelling, school or employment; regarding minors: temporary custody, visitations; prohibit from purchasing, using, or possessing a firearm	Ex parte: Maximum 20 days unless modified. Civil provisions: 150 days	Class A misdemeanor	Any cohabitant or child residing with a cohabitant, or a cohabitant, department, or person or institution may apply for a minor	Yes	Copy by end of next business day to local law enforcement agencies designated by petitioner and copy to statewide domestic violations network	Yes, contempt of court

VERMONT

Code Section	Activity Addressed by Order	Duration	Penalty for a Violation of Order	Who May Apply for Order	Fees Waived?	Transmission to Law Enforcement	Civil Liability
Tit. 15 §1101, *et seq.*	Enjoin contact; exclude from residence or other locations; regarding minors: temporary custody, support (maximum 3 months)	A fixed period at the expiration of which time the court may extend order	Criminal contempt: jail maximum 6 months and/or fine maximum $1,000	Any family or household member on behalf of self or their children	Yes	Copy to department of public safety relief from abuse database	

VIRGINIA

Code Section	Activity Addressed by Order	Duration	Penalty for a Violation of Order	Who May Apply for Order	Fees Waived?	Transmission to Law Enforcement	Civil Liability
16.1-253.1, *et seq.*	Enjoin contact; exclude from dwelling or provide alternative housing; regarding minors: visitations	Emergency: expires by 5 p.m. on next business day	Contempt of court and Class 1 misdemeanor; no suspension of term	Any person or the court.		Copy to local police department or sheriff's office	Yes, contempt of court

Table 29: Protective Orders

Code Section	Activity Addressed by Order	Duration	Penalty for a Violation of Order	Who May Apply for Order	Fees Waived?	Transmission to Law Enforcement	Civil Liability
			WASHINGTON				
26.50.01, *et seq.*	Enjoin contact; exclude from dwelling, employment, school and day care; regarding minors: temporary custody; counseling; electronic monitoring; court costs and attorney fees	Restraining order to protect minors: maximum 1 year, may be extended. Ex parte temporary order: maximum 14 or 24 days, may be reissued	Gross misdemeanor: contempt of court. If assault less than 1st or 2nd degree occurs: Class C felony. If reckless or substantial risk of death or serious injury: Class C felony. If at least 2 prior protective order violations: Class C felony	Any person on behalf of self, or minor family or household member	Yes	Entered into statewide judicial information system within one judicial day; copy on or before next judicial day to appropriate law enforcement agency	Yes, contempt of court
			WEST VIRGINIA				
48-2A-1, *et seq.*	Enjoin contact; exclude from dwelling, employment; counseling; regarding minors: temporary custody, visitations, support; prohibition from possession of a firearm; reimburse for reasonable expenses	Final protective order: maximum 90 days; may be extended	Misdemeanor: jail minimum 1 day and maximum 1 year and fine, minimum $250 and maximum $2,000	Person or adult family or household member on behalf of minor or incapacitated	Yes	Copy within 24 hours to any law enforcement agency having jurisdiction including city police, county sheriff's office or local division of public safety	Yes, civil contempt
			WISCONSIN				
813.12; 813.122	Enjoin contact; exclude from dwelling; regarding minors: reasonable visitation; surrender of firearms, unless respondent is a peace officer	Injunction: maximum 2 years or until child victim is 18 years, whichever is first	If knowingly violates, jail maximum 9 months and/or fine maximum $1,000	Any person, or parent, stepparent or guardian of child victim		Copy to law enforcement agency with jurisdiction; made available to other agencies through a verification system	

Table 29: Protective Orders

Code Section	Activity Addressed by Order	Duration	Penalty for a Violation of Order	Who May Apply for Order	Fees Waived?	Transmission to Law Enforcement	Civil Liability
			WYOMING				
35-21-101, *et seq.*; 6-4-404	Enjoin contact; exclude from dwelling; regarding minors: temporary custody, support, counseling, (maximum 90 days)	Protective order: maximum 3 months, may be extended for additional 3 month periods	If willful violation: misdemeanor: jail maximum 90 days and/or fine maximum $500	Any victim of domestic abuse	Yes	Copy to county sheriff who notifies local law enforcement agency in petitioner's county	Yes

VI. GENERAL CIVIL LAWS

30. CIVIL RIGHTS

Civil rights laws are among the most volatile and controversial in the American legal system. The force behind these laws is that certain groups of individuals in our society need protection from infringement on certain basic rights that are recognized under our legal system and are inherent in our form of government.

Civil rights are considered fundamental to all citizens under the Constitution of the United States. These rights include freedom of speech and association, freedom to seek employment, and freedom from discrimination on the basis of religious belief, race, or national origin. When certain groups have historically been denied any of these civil rights, the government has stepped in to make it illegal to interfere in that group's exercise of their rights. For example, African Americans historically have been excluded from certain types of activities in pursuit of their livelihoods. Thus civil rights laws have been enacted at both the federal and state levels to both guarantee African Americans their rights to freely seek employment in the workplace and to obtain an education in the institution of their choice without fear of discrimination on the basis of race and to provide a legal remedy for individuals who are discriminated against. Under civil rights law, acts by certain classes of people that deny others their civil rights can be either criminal in nature or actionable in civil court.

Federal civil rights laws may be enforced by the Justice Department. Usually, violations of the laws are punished by fines and/or injunctions. They may also serve as the basis for private lawsuits by individuals. Civil rights laws usually specify limits to the amount of recovery available in lawsuits filed under them. Also, they often require that a civil rights suit be filed under the available statute, rather than under general common law. This is called the doctrine of preemption, where civil rights laws preempt ordinary tort actions. Preemption is important because it caps the amount of damages for which a defendant may be liable.

Many states have gone even further than the federal laws in protecting civil rights. In those states that have established their own civil rights laws, most have authorized either the creation of new state agencies or have authorized existing agencies to handle the enforcement, administration, and/or investigation of violations of the laws. In some cases, the jurisdiction of the agencies is preemptive. For example, if a worker is fired because of his or her age, the firing may violate civil rights laws against age discrimination. If the state laws preempt private actions, the employee may only bring the complaint against the employer through the state agency or under the state law. In this case, the employee is bound by any restrictions regarding the type or size of the remedy. If the state law is not preemptive, or if the state law permits separate rights of action by the employee, the employee will be free to pursue his or her own course of action against the employer in court. The potential recovery for individual acts of discrimination or other civil rights infringements can be virtually limitless.

In many states civil rights laws may be very specifically divided in coverage and in agencies within state government. Housing and employment are the most frequent specific types of discrimination covered by state laws.

Table 30: Civil Rights

State	Code Section	Agency	Administrative Preemption	Private Action Permitted?	Attorney Fees	Statute of Limitation
ALABAMA	No statutory provisions					
ALASKA	18.80.200, *et seq.*	Commission for Human Rights	No	Yes	Discretionary	41-1492.08: 1 yr.
ARIZONA	41-1401, *et seq.*	Civil Rights Advisory Board	No	§41-1492.08 (c): Yes	§41-1481 (J): Yes	2 yrs.; 180 days through the Civil Rights Division §41-1492.09
ARKANSAS	21-3-201(Public Employment); 4-87-101 (Credit); 11-4-601 (Employment)	None	No	21-3-201: No; 4-87-101:Yes; 11-4-611: Yes	4-87-105: Yes; 11-4-611: Yes	4-87-102: 1 yr.; 11-4-611: 2 yrs.
CALIFORNIA	Civ. §§51, *et seq.*; Civ. Proc. §338	Dept. of Fair Employment and Housing	No	Yes	Yes; §523-5	§338 Civ. Pro.: 3 yrs.
COLORADO	24-34-301, 306; 24-34-601 (Public accommodation)	Civil Rights Commission	24-34-301: Yes, with exception; 24-34-601: No	24-34-301: No, with exception for ill health; 24-34-601: Yes	Yes	24-34-604: 60 days
CONNECTICUT	46a-51, *et seq.*; 46a-98 (credit)	Commission on Human Rights and Opportunities	46a-52: Yes; 46a-98: No	Yes	Yes; 46a-98: Not specified	180 days, except violation of §46a-80a: 30 days; 46a-98: 1 yr.
DELAWARE	Tit. 6 §4601 (Housing); Tit. 19 §710 (Employment)	Tit. 6 §4601: Human Relations Commission; Tit. 19 §710: Dept. of Labor	Yes	Tit. 6 §4601: No; Tit. 19 §710: Yes	Tit. 6 §4601: No; Tit. 19 §712: Yes	Tit. 19 §710: 90/120 days; §6-4610: 1 yr.
DISTRICT OF COLUMBIA	1-2501 (Generally); 6-1701 (Handicapped)	Commission on Human Rights	No	Yes	Yes	§1-2544: 1 yr.
FLORIDA	760.01, *et seq.*	Commission on Human Relations	Yes	No	Yes	§760.10(10)1: 80 days
GEORGIA	7-6-1 (Credit); 34-1-2 (Employment); 34-1-3 (Discrimination)	None	No	7-6-2: Yes; 34-1-2: No	7-6-1: No; 34-1-2: Yes; 34-1-3: Yes	Not specified
HAWAII	378-1, *et seq.* (Employment); 515-3 (Realty)	378-1: Civil Rights Commission; 515-3: Dept. of Commerce and Consumer Affairs	Yes	No	Yes	90 days
IDAHO	67-5901	Commission on Human Rights	No	Yes	No	2 yrs.

Table 30: Civil Rights—Continued

State	Code Section	Agency	Administrative Preemption	Private Action Permitted?	Attorney Fees	Statute of Limitation
ILLINOIS	775 ILCS 5/1-101, *et seq.*	Human Rights Commission and Dept. of Human Rights	Yes	Yes, for temporary relief (775 ILCS 5/7A-104)	Yes	§775 ILCS 5/7A-102: 180 days
INDIANA	22-9-1-1, *et seq.*	Civil Rights Commission	No	Yes	No	Not specified
IOWA	601A.1, *et seq.*	Civil Rights Commission	Yes	Yes	Yes	180 days
KANSAS	44-1001 (Generally); 44-1015 (Housing); 44-1111 (Employment)	Commission on Human Rights	Yes	44-1001: No; 44-1015: Yes; 44-1111: No	No	44-1001: 6 months; 44-1015: 180 days; 44-1111: Not specified
KENTUCKY	344.010	Commission on Human Rights	Yes	Yes	Yes	180 days
LOUISIANA	46:2251 (Handicapped)	None	No	Yes	Yes	180 days to 1 yr.
MAINE	Tit. 5 §§4551, *et seq.*	Human Rights Commission	Yes	Yes	Yes, with conditions	6 months
MARYLAND	Art. 49B§1	Commission on Human Relations	Yes	No	No	Art. 49B§9A: 6 months
MASSACHUSETTS	Ch. 151B (Generally); Ch. 272 §§92A, 98 (Public Places)	Ch. 151B: Commission Against Discrimination; Ch. 272: None	151B: Yes; 272: No	151B: No; 272: Yes	151B: Yes; 272: No	151B: 6 months—agency, 272: 3 yrs.—civil action (Ch. 260 §5B)
MICHIGAN	MCL 37.2601, *et seq.*	Civil Rights Commission	No	Yes	Yes	Not specified
MINNESOTA	363.01, *et seq.*	Dept. of Human Rights	No	Yes	Yes	1 yr.
MISSISSIPPI	43-33-723, *et seq.* (Housing) NOTE: §25-9-149 prohibits discrimination in state service employment.	Home Corporation Oversight Committee	Yes	No	No	Not specified
MISSOURI	Ch. 213 (Human Rights); Ch. 408.550 (Credit)	Ch. 213: Commission on Human Rights; Ch. 408.550: None	213: Yes; 408.550: No	213: No; 408.550: Yes	Yes	213: 180 days with commission; 2 yrs. civil action; 408.550: 1 yr.

Table 30: Civil Rights—Continued

State	Code Section	Agency	Administrative Preemption	Private Action Permitted?	Attorney Fees	Statute of Limitation
MONTANA	49-2-101 (Generally); 49-4-101 (Handicapped)	49-2-101: Commission for Human Rights; 49-4-101: None	49-2-101: Yes; 49-4-101: No	49-2-101: No; 49-4-101: Yes	49-2-101: Separate action; 49-4-101: Yes	49-2-101: 180 to 300 days; 49-4-101: 2 yrs. (§27-2-211)
NEBRASKA	Ch. 20 (Generally); 48-1001 (Age)	Equal Opportunity Commission	Ch. 20: No; 48-1001: Yes	Yes	Ch. 20: Yes; 48-1001: No	180 days
NEVADA	613.310 (Employment); 651.050 (Public Housing); 598B.170 (Credit)	613.310: Equal Rights Commission or Labor Commission; 651.050: Equal Rights Commission; Ch. 598B.170: Banking Division	613.310: Yes; 651.050: No; Ch. 598B.170: No	Yes	613.310: No; 651.050: Yes; Ch. 598B.170: No	613.310: 180 days; 651.050: 1 yr.; Ch. 598B.170: 1 yr.
NEW HAMPSHIRE	Ch. 354A	Commission for Human Rights	No	Yes	No	180 days (Attorney General: 6 months)
NEW JERSEY	10:5-1	Division on Civil Rights	No	Yes	Yes	180 days
NEW MEXICO	Ch. 28-1-101	Human Rights Commission	Yes	Yes	Yes	180 days with commission/ 30 days for de novo appeal
NEW YORK	Exec. §290 (Generally); Exec. §296-a (Credit); Civ. Rights §§18a to 47c (Housing)	290: Division of Human Rights; 296-a: Banking Dept.; 18a-47c: State Human Rights Appeal Board	No	Yes	No	290: 1 yr.; 296-a: 1 yr.; 18a-47c: Not specified
NORTH CAROLINA	143-422.1	Human Relations Commission	No	No	No	None
NORTH DAKOTA	14-02.4-01	Department of Labor	No	Yes	Yes	180 days (Housing); 300 days 14-02.4-19 (Employment)

Table 30: Civil Rights—Continued

State	Code Section	Agency	Administrative Preemption	Private Action Permitted?	Attorney Fees	Statute of Limitation
OHIO	Ch. 4112 (Generally); 4112.02 (Housing); 4101.17 (Age); 4112.02.1 (Credit)	Civil Rights Commission	4112: Yes; 4112.02: No; 4101.17: No; 4112.02: No	4112: No; 4112.02: Yes; 4101.17: Yes; 4112.02: Yes	Yes	4112: 6 months with commission; 1 yr. with common pleas; 4101.17: Not specified; 4112.02: 1 yr. with commission; 1 yr. with common pleas
OKLAHOMA	Tit. 25 §1101, *et seq.*	Human Rights Commission	Yes	No	Yes	180 days
OREGON	659.010	Bureau of Labor and Industries	No	Yes	Yes	1 yr.
PENNSYLVANIA	Tit. 43 §951, *et seq.*	Human Relations Commission	No	Yes	No	180 days
RHODE ISLAND	34-37-1 (Housing); 28-5-1 (Employment); 28-6-18 (Sex); 42-87-1 (Handicapped)	42-87-1; 34-37-1; 28-5-1: Commission for Human Rights; 28-6-18: Department of Labor	42-87-1; 34-37-1; 28-6-18: No; 28-5-1: Yes	42-87-1: Yes; 34-27-1: Yes; 28-6-18: Yes; 28-5-1: Yes	No	34-37-1: 1 yr.; 28-5-1: 1 yr.; 28-6-18: Not specified; 42-87-1: Not specified
SOUTH CAROLINA	1-13-10	Human Affairs Commission	No	Yes	No	180 days
SOUTH DAKOTA	20-13-1; 60-12-15 (Sex)	20-13-1: Commission of Humanities; 60-12-15: None	20-13-1: Yes; 60-12-15: No	20-13-1: No; 60-12-15: Yes	20-13-1: No; 60-12-15: Yes	20-13-1: 180 days; 60-12-15: 2 yrs.
TENNESSEE	4-21-101	Human Rights Commission	No	Yes	Yes	180 days for filing with agency; 1 yr. for direct action (§28-3-104)
TEXAS	Hum. Res. §121.004	Department of Human Resources	No	Yes	No	Not specified
UTAH	13-7-3 (Public Places); 34-35-1 (Employment)	13-7-3: None; 34-35-1: Antidiscrimination Division	13-7-3: No; 34-35-1: Yes	13-7-3: Yes; 34-35-1: No	No	13-7-3: 3 yrs. (§78-12-26); 34-35-1: 180 days
VERMONT	Tit. 9 §4501 (Public Places and Housing); Tit. 21 §495 (Employment)	Tit. 9§4501 Human Rights Commission	No	Yes	Tit. 9 §4501: Yes; Tit. 21 §495: No	Tit. 9 §4501: Not specified; Tit. 21 §495: 6 yrs. (Tit. 12 §511)

Table 30: Civil Rights—Continued

State	Code Section	Agency	Administrative Preemption	Private Action Permitted?	Attorney Fees	Statute of Limitation
VIRGINIA	36-96.1, *et seq.* (Housing); 40.1-28.6 (Equal Pay)	36-86: Real Estate Board; 40.1-28.6: None	No	Yes	36-96.9: Yes; 40.1-28.6: No	Fair Housing, 36-96.9: 1 yrs.; 180 days after conclusion of administrative process, or within 2 years after occurence or termination of a discriminatory housing practice, whichever is later; Equal Pay, 40.1-28.6: 2 yrs.
WASHINGTON	49.60.010	Washington State Human Rights Commission	No	Yes	§49.60.230: Yes	6 months except real estate 1 yr.
WEST VIRGINIA	5-11-1	Human Rights Commission	No	Yes	Yes	180 days
WISCONSIN	101.22 (Housing and Public Places); 111.325 (Employment)	101.22; 111.325: Dept. of Industry, Labor, and Human Relations (Equal Rights Division)	101.22: No; 111.325: Yes	101.22:Yes; 111.325: No	101.22: Yes; 111.325: No	101.22: 1 yr.; 111.325: 300 days
WYOMING	27-9-101	Fair Employment Commission	Yes	No	No	§27-9-106: 90 days

31. CIVIL STATUTES OF LIMITATION

The idea behind statutes of limitation is mainly one of general practicability and fairness. It is never fair to let a legal matter hang unfinished over someone's head indefinitely. There needs to be a distinct end to each legal conflict in order to let the parties involved move on with their lives. Particular legal matters may cause parties to cease certain business transactions or personal activity as they await the outcome.

A similar dynamic is at work with respect to statutes of limitation. The offending party in any legal dispute knows that he or she committed or may be accused of committing some wrong against the other party. In such a case, the wronged party must decide whether to press a lawsuit in order to recover for his or her wrong. The law will not tolerate a procrastinative plaintiff, a plaintiff who delays for effect, or one who is negligent or forgetful. After a period of time has passed, the chance to sue disappears.

How Long?

The lengths of time for statutes of limitation correspond roughly to the amount of notice that both parties have regarding the underlying injury or wrong. The more notice both parties have that there is a problem and the more likely it is that the injured party will sue, the longer the statute of limitation. The less likely it is that the offending party will be aware of his wrong or the more inconsequential it is likely to be, the shorter the statute of limitation.

The longest statutes of limitation are generally those regarding the recovery of judgments after a lawsuit. Obviously, the parties are clearly on notice in this situation. If the losing party refuses to pay his judgment, it should come as no surprise that he will be sued, even if it is as many as ten years later. On the other hand, if one person is physically injured by another person but does not sue within a year or two, it is reasonable to expect that the plaintiff either forgot about the injury or it was not as serious as originally suspected. In this case, the potential defendant is protected from a lawsuit that he may not even be aware is pending, especially more than a year or two after the accident that caused the injury occurred.

Where no statute is listed on the following chart, it is probable that there is simply not a specific statute governing the situation. In these cases, a general civil statute of limitation most likely applies. For example, in cases of medical malpractice, the statute of limitation may just as easily be covered by the statute governing personal injury.

From When to When?

There are many interesting controversies about when statutes of limitation begin and end. In many cases, the injured party may not even know he was wronged until a great while after the wrong was committed. This is often true in the case of breach of contract or fraud, and it often arises, perhaps surprisingly, in cases of personal injury or medical malpractice. In the case of certain surgical procedures, the party may not know that, for example, a sponge was left in his abdomen or something else was done improperly—until years later. There has also been much controversy, now largely settled by statute, about whether the statute should begin to run when the wrong was committed or when it was discovered. Court decisions have largely gone in favor of the injured party, allowing the statute to start running upon discovery of the injury or when the injury or act of negligence should "reasonably have been discovered."

Most states "toll" or stop the statute of limitation upon the incapacity of the injured party. But there are a number of ways a person can be incapacitated. If the person has been committed to a mental hospital or is out of the country, these may toll the statute of limitation until they either regain their mental facilities or return from abroad.

Overall, the statutes of limitation are fair and reasonable limitations of potentially disruptive and always distracting legal action between parties. Dramatic stories about lawyers rushing to file papers before the statute runs out are almost always due to the injured party's (or the party's attorney's) procrastination or negligence.

Table 31:Civil Statutes of Limitation

Injury to Person	Libel/ Slander	Fraud	Injury to Personal Property	Professional Malpractice	Trespass	Collection of Rents	Contracts	Collection of Debt on Account	Judgments

ALABAMA

| Under a contract: 6 yrs. 6-2-34(1); In general 2 yrs 6-2-38(L) | 2 yrs. 6-2-38(K) | 2 yrs. from accrual of action (discovery) 6-2-3 | 6 yrs. §6-2-34(2) | Medical: 2 yrs. §6-5-482 | 6 yrs. §6-2-34(1, 2) | 6 yrs. §6-2-34(5) | Written: 10 yrs. if under seal; 6 yrs. if not §§6-2-33 to 6-2-34; Oral: 6 yrs. §6-2-34 | 6 yrs. stated liquidated account; 3 yrs. open unliqui-dated account §§6-2-34(5) and 6-2-37 | 20 yrs. §6-2-32 |

ALASKA

| 2 yrs. §09.10.070 | 2 yrs. §09.10.070 | | 6 yrs. §09.10.050 | Medical not under contract: 2 yrs. §09.10.070; under contract: 6 yrs. §09.10.050 | 6 yrs. §09.10.05 | | Written: 6 yrs. §09.10.050 Oral: 6 yrs. §09.10.050 | | |

ARIZONA

| False imprison-ment; 1 yr. §12-541; if not 2 yrs. §12-542 | 1 yr. §12-541 | 3 yrs. §12-543(3) | 2 yrs. §12-542 | Medical: 2 yrs. §12-542 | 2 yrs. §12-542(3) | | Written: 6 yrs. §12-548; Oral (for indebted-ness): 3 yrs. §12-543(1) | 3 yrs. §12-543(2) | 4 yrs. foreign judgment §12-544(3) |

ARKANSAS

| 1 yr. §16-56-104 | Libel: 3 yrs. Slander: 1 yr. §§16-56-104, 105 | | 3 yrs. §16-56-105 | | 3 yrs. §16-56-105 | 3 yrs. §16-56-112 | Written: 5 yrs. §16-56-111; Oral: 3 yrs. §16-56-105 | 3 yrs. if not written or under seal §16-56-105 | 10 yrs. §16-56-114 |

Table 31:Civil Statutes of Limitation—Continued

Injury to Person	Libel/ Slander	Fraud	Injury to Personal Property	Professional Malpractice	Trespass	Collection of Rents	Contracts	Collection of Debt on Account	Judgments
CALIFORNIA									
1 yr. CIV. PROC. §340(3)	1 yr. CIV. PROC. §340(3)	3 yrs. CIV. PROC. §338(d)	3 yrs. CIV. PROC. §338(b), (c)	Legal: 1 yr. from discovery, max. of 4 yrs. from the wrong; Vet.: 1 yr. for injury to animal CIV. PROC. §340.6	3 yrs. CIV. PROC. §338(b)	4 yrs. CIV. PROC. §337.2	Written: 4 yrs. §337; Oral: 2 yrs. CIV. PROC. §339	4 yrs. (book and stated accounts) CIV. PROC. §337	10 yrs. CIV. PROC. §337.5
COLORADO									
1 yr. §13-80-103(1)(a); 3 yrs. §13-80-101(n) if from use or operation of a motor vehicle	1 yr. §13-80-103(1)(a)	1 yr. for actions under §12-20-113 and 12-61-303 and 13-80-103(1)(f)(g)3 yrs. §13-80-101(1)(c)	3 yrs. §13-80-101(n) if from use or operation of a motor vehicle	Vet: 2 yrs. §13-80-102(1)(c)	2 yrs. §13-80-102	6 yrs. §13-80-103.5(1)(b)	Written: 3 yrs. §13-80-101; Oral: 3 yrs. §13-80-101; 2 yrs. §13-80-102 if tort action for tortious breach of contract	6 yrs. if contract §13-80-103.5	
CONNECTICUT									
3 yrs. §52-577	2 yrs. §52-597	3 yrs. §52-577	2 yrs. from discovery; max. of 3 from act §52-584	2 yrs. from discovery; max. of 3 from wrong §52-584	3 yrs. §52-577		Written: 6 yrs. §52-576; Oral: 3 yrs. §52-581	6 yrs. §52-576	20 yrs. (variations for small claims judgments) §52-598
DELAWARE									
2 yrs. Tit. 10 §8119	2 yrs. Tit. 10 §8119		2 yrs. Tit. 10 §8107	2 yrs. Tit. 10 §8119	3 yrs. Tit. 10 §8106		Written: 3 yrs. Tit. 10 §8106; Oral: 3 yrs. Tit. 10 §8106	3 yrs. Tit. 10 §8106	5 yrs. Tit. 10 §5072

Table 31:Civil Statutes of Limitation—Continued

Injury to Person	Libel/ Slander	Fraud	Injury to Personal Property	Professional Malpractice	Trespass	Collection of Rents	Contracts	Collection of Debt on Account	Judgments
				DISTRICT OF COLUMBIA					
1 yr. §12-301(4)	1 yr. §12-301(4)	3 yrs. §12-301(8)	3 yrs. §12-301(2, 3)	3 yrs. §12-301(8)	3 yrs. §12-301(3)	3 yrs. §12-301(8)	Written: 4 yrs. (sale contract); 3 yrs. (simple contract) §§28-2-725 and 12-301(7)	3 yrs. § 12-301(8)	12 yrs. §15-101; Foreign judgments according to law of foreign jurisdiction §12-307
				FLORIDA					
4 yrs. §95.11(3)(o)	2 yrs. §95.11(4)(g)	4 yrs. §95.11(3)(j)	4 yrs. §95.11(3)(h)	2 yrs.; Medical: 2-4 yrs. §95.11(4)(a) and (b)	4 yrs. §95.11(3)(g)		Written: 5 yrs. §95.11(2)(b), 1 yr. specific performance§95.11(5)(a)Oral: 4 yrs. §95.11(3)(k)		20 yrs. domestic §95.11(1); 5 yrs. foreign judgment §95.11(2)(a)
				GEORGIA					
2 yrs. §9-3-33	1 yr. §9-3-33	2 yrs. §9-3-33	4 yrs. §9-3-32	Medical: 2 yrs., max. of 5 from act §9-3-71	4 yrs. §9-3-30		Written: 6 yrs. §9-3-24; Oral: 4 yrs. §9-3-26	4 yrs. §9-3-25	5 yrs. foreign judgment §9-3-20
				HAWAII					
2 yrs. §657-7	2 yrs. §657-4	2 yrs. §657-7	2 yrs. §657-7	Medical: 2 yrs. from reasonable discovery to max. of 6 §657-7.3	2 yrs. §657-7	6 yrs. §657-1	Written: 6 yrs. §657-1; Oral: 6 yrs. §657-1	6 yrs. §657-1	10 yrs. from ct. of record §657-5; 6 yrs. if judgment from a court not of record §657-1

Table 31:Civil Statutes of Limitation—Continued

Injury to Person	Libel/ Slander	Fraud	Injury to Personal Property	Professional Malpractice	Trespass	Collection of Rents	Contracts	Collection of Debt on Account	Judgments
IDAHO									
2 yrs. §5-219(4 & 5)	2 yrs. §5-219(5)	3 yrs. §5-218(4)	3 yrs. §5-218(3)	2 yrs. §5-219(4)	3 yrs. §5-218(2)	5 yrs. §5-204	Written: 5 yrs. §5-216; Oral: 4 yrs. §5-217		6 yrs. §5-215(1)
ILLINOIS									
2 yrs. 735 ILCS 5/13-202	1 yr. 735 ILCS 5/13-201	For conceal-ment of a cause of action: 5 yrs. 735 ILCS 5/13-215; Fraud by decedent: 2 yrs. 735 ILCS 5/13-220	5 yrs. 735 ILCS 5/13-205	Medical: 2 yrs.-4 yrs. §735 ILCS 5/13-212; Legal: max. 6 yrs. 735 ILCS 5/13-214.3	5 yrs. 735 ILCS 5/13-205		Written: 10 yrs. 735 ILCS 5/13-206; Oral: 5 yrs. 735 ILCS 5/13-205		Judgment may be revived within 20 yrs., 735 ILCS 5/13-218
INDIANA									
2 yrs. §34-11-2-4(1)	2 yrs. §34-11-2-4(1)	6 yrs. §34-11-2-7(4)	2 yrs. §34-11-2-3	2 yrs. §34-11-2-3	6 yrs. §34-11-2-4	6 yrs. §34-11-2-4	Written: 10 yrs. §34-11-2-11; 6 yrs. for contract for payment of money §34-11-2-9; Oral: 6 yrs., 2 yrs. employ-ment agreements §§34-11-2-4 and 34-11-2-1	6 yrs. §34-11-2-4	20 yrs. §34-11-2-12

Table 31:Civil Statutes of Limitation—Continued

Injury to Person	Libel/ Slander	Fraud	Injury to Personal Property	Professional Malpractice	Trespass	Collection of Rents	Contracts	Collection of Debt on Account	Judgments
IOWA									
2 yrs. §614.1(2)	2 yrs. §614.1(2)	5 yrs. §614.1(4)	5 yrs. §614.1(4)	Medical: 2 yrs. from reasonable discovery; max. of 6 from act §614.1(9)	5 yrs. §614.1(4)		Written: 10 yrs. §614.1(5); Oral: 5 yrs. §614.1(4)		20 yrs.: judgment of court of record §614.1; (6); 10 yrs.: judgment of court not of record §614.1(5)
KANSAS									
1 yr. §60-514(b)	1 yr. §60-514(a)	2 yrs. §60-513 (a)(3)	2 yrs. §60-513 (a)(2)	2 yrs. from reasonable discovery, 4 max. §60-513(a)(7), 60-513(c)	2 yrs. §60-513(a)(1)		Written: 5 yrs. §60-511(1); Oral: 3 yrs. §60-512(1)		
KENTUCKY									
1 yr. §413.140 (1)(a)	1 yr. §413.140 (1)(d)	5 yrs. §413.120 (11)	5 yrs. §413.125	Professional service: 1 yr. §413.245; Medical: 1 yr. §413.140(e)	5 yrs. §413.120 (4)		Written: 15 yrs. §413.090 (2); Oral: 5 yrs. §413.120 (1)	5 yrs. §413.120	15 yrs. §413.090 (1)
LOUISIANA									
1 yr. Civ. Code Ann. §3492	1 yr. Civ. Code Ann. §3492	1 yr. Civ. Code Ann. §3492	1 yr. Civ. Code Ann. §3492	1 yr. Civ. Code Ann. §3492	1 yrs. Civ. Code Ann. §3492	3 yrs. Civ. Code Ann. §3494	Written: 10 yrs. Civ. Code Ann. §3499; Oral: 10 yrs. Civ. Code Ann. §3499	3 yrs. Civ. Code Ann. §3494(4)	Monetary judgments: 10 yrs. Civ. Code Ann. §3501

Table 31:Civil Statutes of Limitation—Continued

Injury to Person	Libel/ Slander	Fraud	Injury to Personal Property	Professional Malpractice	Trespass	Collection of Rents	Contracts	Collection of Debt on Account	Judgments
MAINE									
2 yrs. Tit. 14 §753	2 yrs. Tit. 14 §753	6 yrs. Tit. 14 §859		4 yrs. to 10 max. Tit. 14 §752-A; Attorneys: 2 yrs. §753-A			Written: 20 yrs. if under seal Tit. 14 §751		20 yrs. Tit. 14 §864
MARYLAND									
1 yr. CTS. & JUD. PROC. §5-105	1 yr. CTS. & JUD. PROC. §5-105	3 yr. general limit CTS. & JUD. PROC. §5-101	3 yrs. generally CTS. & JUD. PROC. §5-101	Medical: 5 yrs. from injury or 3 yrs. from discovery, whichever is shorter (max. 7) CTS. & JUD. PROC. §5-109			Written: 3 yrs.; 12 yrs. if under seal CTS. & JUD. PROC. §5-101; 5-102(a)(5)	3 yrs. CTS. & JUD. PROC. §5-101	12 yrs. CTS. & JUD. PROC. §5-102 (a)(3)
MASSACHUSETTS									
3 yrs. Ch. 260 §4	3 yrs. Ch. 260 §4		3 yrs. Ch. 260 §4	3 yrs., max. 7 yrs. (personal injury) Ch. 260 §4	3 yrs. Ch. 260 §2A		Written: 20 yrs. if under seal; 6 yrs. others Ch. 260 §§1, 2; Oral: 6 yrs. Ch. 260 §2	6 yrs. Ch. 260 §2	6 yrs. Ch. 260 §2
MICHIGAN									
2 yrs. §600.5805 (2)	1 yr. §600.5805 (7)	6 yrs. §600.5813	3 yrs. §600.5805 (8)	2 yrs. §600.5805 (4)	3 yrs. §600.5805 (8)		Written: 6 yrs. §600.5807 (8); Oral: 6 yrs. §600.5807 (8)		10 yrs. ct. of record; 6 yrs. ct. not of record §600.5809 (3)

Table 31:Civil Statutes of Limitation—Continued

Injury to Person	Libel/ Slander	Fraud	Injury to Personal Property	Professional Malpractice	Trespass	Collection of Rents	Contracts	Collection of Debt on Account	Judgments
MINNESOTA									
2 yrs. §541.07(1)	2 yrs. §541.07(1)	6 yrs. §541.05(6)	6 yrs. §541.05(4)	Medical and veterinary: 2 yrs. §541.07(1)	6 yrs. §541.05 (3)		Written: 6 yrs. §541.05(1); Oral: 6 yrs. §541.05(1)		10 yrs. §541.04
MISSISSIPPI									
1 yr. §15-1-35	1 yr. §15-1-35			2 yrs. from act or discovery §15-1-36			Oral: 3 yrs.; unwritten contract based on employ-ment: 1 yr. §15-1-29	3 yrs. §15-1-29	7 yrs. domestic and foreign judgments §§15-1-43, 45
MISSOURI									
2 yrs. §516.140	2 yrs. §516.140	10 yrs. §516.120 (5)	5 yrs. §516.120 (4)	Medical: 2 yrs. from discovery, max. 10. §516.105	5 yrs. §516.120 (3)		Written: 5 yrs; for payment of money or property, 10 yrs. §516.120 (1); 516.110; Oral: 5 yrs. §516.120 (1)	10 yrs. if in writing §516.110 (1)	10 yrs. §516.350
MONTANA									
2 yrs. §27-2-204(3)	2 yrs. §27-2-204(3)	2 yrs. §27-2-203	2 yrs. §27-2-207(2)	Legal: 3 yrs. from discovery, max. 10 yrs. §27-2-206; Medical: 3 yrs., max. 5 yrs. §27-2-205	2 yrs. §27-2-207		Written: 8 yrs. §27-2-202(1); Oral: 5 yrs. §27-2-202(2)	3 yrs. obligation or liability other than contract not in writing §27-2-202(3)	10 yrs. judgment of ct. of record; 5 yrs. otherwise §27-2-201(2)

Table 31:Civil Statutes of Limitation—Continued

Injury to Person	Libel/ Slander	Fraud	Injury to Personal Property	Professional Malpractice	Trespass	Collection of Rents	Contracts	Collection of Debt on Account	Judgments
NEBRASKA									
1 yr. §25-208	1 yr. §25-208	4 yrs. §25-207(4)	4 yrs. §25-207(2)	2 yrs. or 1 yr. from discovery §25-222; 2 yrs. §25-208	4 yrs. §25-207(1)		Written: 5 yrs. §25-205: Oral: 4 yrs. §25-206		5 yrs. (foreign) §25-205
NEVADA									
2 yrs. §11.190-(4)(c)	2 yrs. §11.190-(4)(c)	3 yrs. §11.190-(3)(d)	3 yrs. §11.190-(3)(c)	Accountant, Attorney, Veterinarian: 4 yrs.; Medical: 2 yrs. after discovery or 4 yrs. after act §11.207 and §41A.097	3 yrs. §11.190 (3)(b)		Written: 6 yrs. §11.190 (1)(b); Oral: 4 yrs. §11.190-2(c)	4 yrs. §11.190-(2)(a)	6 yrs. §11.190(1)(a)
NEW HAMPSHIRE									
3 yrs. §508:4	3 yrs. §508:4	3 yrs. §508:4	3 yrs. §508:4	3 yrs. §508:4	2 yrs. §539:8		Written: 20 yrs. under seal §508:5		20 yrs. §508:5
NEW JERSEY									
2 yrs. §2A:14-2	1 yr. §2A:14-3		6 yrs. §2A:14-1	2 yrs. §2A:14-2	6 yrs. §2A:14-1	16 yrs. §2A:14-4	Written: 6 yrs. §2A:14-1; Oral: 6 yrs. §2A:14-1	6 yrs. §2A:14-1	6 yrs. from court of record §2A:14-5
NEW MEXICO									
3 yrs. §37-1-8	3 yrs. §37-1-8	4 yrs. §37-1-4	4 yrs. §37-1-4		4 yrs. §37-1-4		Written: 6 yrs. §37-1-3; Oral: 4 yrs. §37-1-4	4 yrs.§37-1-4	14 yrs. from ct. of record; 6 yrs. otherwise §37-1-2, 3

Table 31:Civil Statutes of Limitation—Continued

Injury to Person	Libel/ Slander	Fraud	Injury to Personal Property	Professional Malpractice	Trespass	Collection of Rents	Contracts	Collection of Debt on Account	Judgments
NEW YORK									
1 yr. N.Y. CIV. PRAC. L. & R. §215	1 yr. N.Y. CIV. PRAC. L. & R. §215	6 yrs. N.Y. CIV. PRAC. L. & R. §213	3 yrs. N.Y. CIV. PRAC. L. & R. §214	3 yrs.; medical: 2 1/2 yrs.; foreign object in body of patient 1 yr. N.Y. CIV. PRAC. L. & R. §214(6) and §214-a	3 yrs. N.Y. CIV. PRAC. L. & R. §214		Written: 6 yrs. N.Y. CIV. PRAC. L. & R. §213; Oral: 6 yrs. N.Y. CIV. PRAC. L. & R. §213		20 yrs. N.Y. CIV. PRAC. L. & R. §211(b)
NORTH CAROLINA									
1 yr. §1-54	1 ys. §1-54	3 yrs. §1-52(9)	3 yrs. §1-52(4)		3 yrs. §1-52(3)		Written: 3 yrs. §1-52(1); Oral: 3 yrs. §1-52(1)		10 yrs. §1-47
NORTH DAKOTA									
2 yrs. §28-01-18	2 yrs. §28-01-18	6 yrs. §28-01-16(6)	6 yrs. §28-01-16(4)	2 yrs.; (Medical: max.6) §28-01-18	6 yrs. §28-01-16(3)		Written: 6 yrs. §28-01-16(1); Oral: 6 yrs. §28-01-16(1)		10 yrs. §28-01-15
OHIO									
1 yr. or 2 yrs. if bodily injury §§2305.11 (a); 2305.10	1 yr. §2305.11 (a)	4 yrs. §2305.09 (c)	2 yrs. §2305.10	1 yr.; Medical: 1 yr. to give notice which extends time 180 days after notice, max. 4 yrs. §2305.11(a)	4 yrs. §2305.09 (a)		Written: 15 yrs. §2305.06; Oral: 6 yrs. §2305.07	6 yrs. §2305.07	21 yrs. §2325.18

Table 31:Civil Statutes of Limitation—Continued

Injury to Person	Libel/ Slander	Fraud	Injury to Personal Property	Professional Malpractice	Trespass	Collection of Rents	Contracts	Collection of Debt on Account	Judgments
OKLAHOMA									
1 yr. Tit. 12 §95(4)	1 yr. Tit. 12 §95(4)	2 yrs. Tit. 12 §95(3)	2 yrs. Tit. 12 §95(3)		2 yrs. Tit. 12 §95(3)		Written: 5 yrs. Tit. 12§95(1); Oral: 3 yrs. Tit. 12 §95(2)		3 yrs. foreign judgment Tit. 12 §95(2)
OREGON									
2 yrs. §12.110	2 yrs. §12.110	2 yrs. from discovery §12.110	6 yrs. §12.080	Medical: 2 yrs. from act or reasonable discovery (max. 5 yrs.) §12.110(4)	6 yrs. §12.080 (3)	1 yr. §12.125	Written: 6 yrs. §12.080; Oral: 6 yrs. §12.080		10 yrs. §12.070
PENNSYLVANIA									
2 yrs. Tit. 42§5524(1)	1 yr. Tit. 42§5523(1)	2 yrs. Tit. 42§5524(7)	2 yrs. Tit. 42§5524(3)	2 yrs. Tit. 42 §5524(7)	2 yrs. Tit. 42 §5524(4)	21 yrs. Tit. 42§5530(2)	Written: 20 yrs. under seal; 4 years other Tit. 42 §5529(b); 5525(8); Oral: 4 yrs. Tit. 42§5525(3)		4 yrs. Tit. 42 §5525(5)
RHODE ISLAND									
3 yrs. §9-1-14	Slander: 1 yr. §9-1-14			Medical, Legal, Veterinarian, Accounting, Insurance, or Real Estate: 3 yrs. §9-1-14.1; 9-1-14.3			Written: 20 yrs. under seal; 4 yrs. sale of goods §§6A-2-725; 9-1-17		20 yrs. §9-1-17

Table 31:Civil Statutes of Limitation—Continued

Injury to Person	Libel/ Slander	Fraud	Injury to Personal Property	Professional Malpractice	Trespass	Collection of Rents	Contracts	Collection of Debt on Account	Judgments
SOUTH CAROLINA									
2 yrs. §15-3-550	2 yrs. §15-3-550	3 yrs. §15-3-530(7)	3 yrs. §15-3-530(3)	Medical: 3 yrs. from act or reasonable discovery (max. 6 yrs.); if foreign object in body: 2 yrs. §15-3-545	3 yrs. §15-3-530(3)		Written: 20 yrs. under seal; 3 yrs. others §§15-3-520, 530; Oral: 3 yrs. §15-3-530(1)		
SOUTH DAKOTA									
2 yrs. §15-2-15(1)	2 yrs. §15-2-15(1)	6 yrs. §15-2-13(6)	6 yrs. §15-2-13	Medical: 2 yrs. §15-2-14.1; Legal: 3 yrs. §15-2-14.2; CPA 4 yrs. §15-2-14.4	6 yrs. §15-2-13(3)		6 yrs. §§15-2-6, 13; Oral: 6 yrs. §15-2-13		20 yrs. domestic judgments; 10 yrs. foreign §§15-2-6, 8
TENNESSEE									
1 yr. §28-3-104(a)(1)	Libel: 1 yr.; Slander: 6 mos. §§28-3-103, 104		3 yrs. §28-3-105	Legal: 1 yr. CPA: 1 yr. §28-3-104	3 yrs. §28-3-105	6 yrs. §28-3-109(1)	Written: 6 yrs. §28-3-109(3); Oral: 6 yrs. §28-3-109		10 yrs. §28-3-110(2)
TEXAS									
2 yrs. Civ. Prac. & Rem. §16.003(a)	1 yr. Civ. Prac. & Rem. §16.002(a)		2 yrs. Civ. Prac. & Rem. §16.003(a)		2 yrs. Civ. Prac. & Rem. §16.003(a)		Written: 4 yrs. real property Civ. Prac. & Rem. §16.004(a)(1)	4 yrs. Civ. Prac. & Rem. §16.004(a)(3)	

Table 31:Civil Statutes of Limitation—Continued

Injury to Person	Libel/ Slander	Fraud	Injury to Personal Property	Professional Malpractice	Trespass	Collection of Rents	Contracts	Collection of Debt on Account	Judgments
UTAH									
1 yr. §78-12-29(4)	1 yr. §78-12-29(4)	3 yrs. §78-12-26(3)	3 yrs. §78-12-26(2)	Medical: 2 yrs. (max. 4 yrs.) §78-14-4	3 yrs. §78-12-26(1)	6 yrs. §78-12-23	Written: 6 yrs. §78-12-23; Oral: 4 yrs. §78-12-25(1)	4 yrs. §78-12-25(1)	8 yrs. §78-12-22
VERMONT									
3 yrs. Tit. 12 §512(1) §512(4)	3 yrs. Tit. 12 §512(3)	3 yrs. Tit. 12 §512	3 yrs. Tit. 12 §512(5)	Medical: 3 yrs. from incident or 2 from reasonable discovery (max. 7 yrs.) Tit. 12 §521			Written: 8 yrs. under seal; 6 yrs. others; 4 yrs. sales Tit. 12 §507; 9A §2-725; 12 §511; Oral: 6 yrs. Tit. 12§511	6 yrs., Tit. 12 §511	8 yrs. ct. of record; 6 yrs. not ct. of record Tit. 12 §506; Tit. 12 §511
VIRGINIA									
2 yrs. §8.01-243(a)	2 yrs. §8.01-243(a)	2 yrs. §8.01-243(a)	5 yrs. §8.01-243(b)	Health care providers: 1 to 2 yrs.; 10 max. §8.01-243.1	5 yrs. §8.01-243(b)		Written: 5 yrs. §8.01-246(2); Oral: 3 yrs. §8.01-246(4)		20 yrs.; 10 yrs. to enforce lien §8.01-251(a), (c)
WASHINGTON									
2 yrs. §4.16.100 (1)	2 yrs. §4.16.100 (1)	3 yrs. §4.16.080 (4)	3 yrs. §4.16.080 (2)		3 yrs. §4.16.080 (1)	6 yrs. §4.16.040 (2)	Written: 6 yrs. §4.16.040 (1); Oral: 3 yrs. §4.16.080 (3)	3 yrs. §4.16.040	10 yrs. §4.16.020 (2)

Table 31: Civil Statutes of Limitation—Continued

Injury to Person	Libel/ Slander	Fraud	Injury to Personal Property	Professional Malpractice	Trespass	Collection of Rents	Contracts	Collection of Debt on Account	Judgments
WEST VIRGINIA									
2 yrs. §55-2-12(b)	1 yr. §55-2-12(c)		2 yrs. §55-2-12(a)	2 yrs. §55-2-12(b)	2 yrs. §55-2-12	5 yrs. §55-4-21	Written: 10 yrs. §55-2-6; Oral: 5 yrs. §55-2-6		10 yrs. foreign judgment §55-2-13
WISCONSIN									
2 yrs. §893.57	2 yrs. §893.57	6 yrs. §893.93(1)(b)	6 yrs. §893.52	Medical: the later of 3 yrs. from incident or 1 yr. from discovery (max. 5 yrs.) §893.55(1), (2)	6 yrs. §893.52	6 yrs. §843.13(1)	Written: 6 yrs. §893.43; Oral: 6 yrs. §893.43		20 yrs.; 6 yrs. ct. not of record §§893.40, 893.42
WYOMING									
1 yr. §1-3-105(a)(v), (B)	1 yr. §1-3-105(a)(v)(A)	4 yrs. §1-3-105(a)(iv)(d)	4 yrs. §1-3-105(a)(iv)(b)		4 yrs. §1-3-105(a)(iv)(a)		Written: 10 yrs. §1-3-105(a)(i); Oral: 8 yrs. §1-3-105(a)(ii)(a)		5 yrs. foreign judgment §1-3-105(a)(iii)

32. GAMBLING

Gambling is an industry that is undergoing tremendous change. It was not too long ago that Nevada was the only state in the union that allowed casino gambling. Today, numerous states either are considering legalizing gambling, or have already done so. There are two factors that are driving the change. First, Native Americans have won the right to establish casinos on their lands regardless of the laws of the state in which they are located. The establishment of these casinos has softened the general public's attitudes toward casino gambling and has led to the introduction of legislative initiatives that permit it, or to voter referendums on the issue. Often, in each situation, the initiatives have resulted in outcomes favorable to gambling. The other factor that has led to legalization of gambling is the economic impact. Many of the regions where gambling has been legalized have realized untold economic benefits in terms of taxes, jobs and development of infrastructure, etc.

Despite the economic developments, the idea of legalizing gambling is not without controversy. Many argue that despite the economic benefits, there is also associated tragedy as people who are addicted to gambling have been known to gamble until they have lost everything and have wreaked havoc on their families and personal lives.

Casino gambling is not the only type of gambling that exists, nor is it the only kind of gambling addressed by state laws. As can be seen in the following chapter, there are many different ways to gamble. The most common subject of regulation is betting. Horses racing, dog racing or betting on sporting events are those most frequently and specifically banned. However regulation of regional events is common. Alaska lists about ten different events that are allowed, including many that would be unthinkable in the south: Deep Freeze Classic, Snow Machine Classic, and the Ice Classic are examples. Florida lists a number of legal gambling activities that relate specifically to the state's large number of retired citizens: penny-ante games with winnings not exceeding $10 .... including poker, pinochle, bridge, dominos, mahjong that are conducted by adults within a dwelling. One of the more unusual prohibitions is found in Massachusetts where gaming is not permitted within one mile of a cattle show or military muster.

Overall, the subject of legalized gambling as an industry is far from settled and is likely to change regularly in the coming years.

Table 32: Gambling

State/Code Section	Gambling	Horse Racing/ Off-Track Betting	Dog Racing/ Off-Track Betting	Casinos Allowed?	Other Kinds of Gambling-Related Activities Allowed or Banned
ALABAMA 13A-12-20 *et seq.*, 11-65-1	Staking or risking something of value upon the outcome of a contest of chance or future contingent event not under one's control.	Municipalities allowed to determine through referendum whether horse racing will be permitted.	Greyhound races allowed.	Casinos not specifically prohibited, but electronic gambling and other devices banned.	Pari-mutuel betting allowed in conjunction with horse and dog racing.
ALASKA 11.66.200, 43.35.140, 05.15.680 AK Gaming Reform Act	Staking or risking something of value upon the outcome of a contest of chance or future contingent event not under one's control or influence, upon an agreement or understanding that person will receive something of value in event of a certain outcome.		Dog mushers' contests allowed.	Gambling devices banned.	Several games of chance and/or skill allowed, including bingo, Canned Salmon Classic, Deep Freeze Classic, Fish Derby, Goose Classic, Ice Classic, King Slamon Classic, Mercury Classic, Mushing Sweepstakes, Race Classic, Rain Classic, Snow Machine Classic and numbers wheels.
ARIZONA 13-3301 *et seq.*; 5-101 *et seq.*	Risking or giving something of value for opportunity to obtain benefit from game, contest, or future contingent event.	Horse and harness racing permitted. Off-track betting prohibited.	Daytime dog racing not allowed on same day as daytime horse or harness races in same county.	Charitable organizations' casino night fundraisers allowed; casinos run for profit banned.	Gambling in which prizes are not offered as a lure to seperate players from their money allowed.
ARKANSAS 5-66-101 *et seq.*	Betting any money or any valuable thing on any game of hazard or skill.	Unlawful to bet on any horse race of any kind.	Franchised greyhound racing legal.	Gambling houses and deviced banned.	All wagering on all sports or games banned.
CALIFORNIA Penal code 330 *et seq.*; Bus and Prof Code 19400 *et seq.*, Horse Racing Law; Gov't Code 98001, *et seq.*, Tribal Government Gaming Act	Dealing, playing, or conducting, games of faro, monte, roulette, lansquenet, rouge et noir, rondo, tan, fan-tan, seven-and-a-half, twenty-one, hokey pokey.	Horse and harness racing permitted. Off-track betting prohibited.		Indian reservation casinos allowed.	"Razzle dazzle," card, dice games prohibited if played for money, credit, check, or anything of value. Draw poker banned only in counties of 4 million or more people.
COLORADO 18-10-101 *et seq.*; 12-60-101 *et seq.*; 12-47.1 CO Limited Gaming Act; 12-47.2 Tribal-State Gaming Compact	Risking money or any other thing of value for gain contingent in whole or part upon lot, chance, or the happening or outcome of an event over which the person taking a risk has no control.	Effective April 21, 2003, off-track simulcasts permitted. Out-of-state simulcasts permitted.	Greyhound races permitted; off-track simulcasts permitted. Special event greyhound race simulcasts from out of state permitted.	Limited: slot machines, poker and black jack with maximum single bet of $5. Only allowed in cities of Central, Black Hawk, and Cripple Creek. Indian reservation casinos allowed.	Election wagers banned; gaming for charitable organizations allowed.
CONNECTICUT 12-557 *et seq.*	Betting or wagering something of value for a chance of receiving something of value in return.	Daily double, exacta, quinella, trifecta, superfecta, twin trifecta, pick four, pick six, and other forms of parimutuel betting allowed	Off-track betting allowed. Wagering on out-of-state dog races allowed.	Bingo parlors allowed. Pequot and Mohegan tribes permitted to operate casinos per Tribal-State Compact.	Jai alai allowed. Any person licensed to conduct betting or wagering events must display informational materials for the prevention, treatment, and rehabilitation of compulsive gamblers. Charitable organizations' "Las Vegas Nights" allowed.

Table 32: Gambling—Continued

State/Code Section	Gambling	Horse Racing/ Off-Track Betting	Dog Racing/ Off-Track Betting	Casinos Allowed?	Other Kinds of Gambling-Related Activities Allowed or Banned
DELAWARE 3-10001 *et seq.;* 11-1401 *et seq.*	Recording or registering bets or wagers, or directly or indirectly betting or wagering, money or anything of value.	Horse and harness racing allowed; daily double allowed. Off-track betting on out-of-state races permitted.			Gambling in bowling alleys, craps games, and election wagering banned. Merchandising plans are not gambling.
DISTRICT OF COLUMBIA 22-1501 *et seq.*	Playing any game of chance for money or property.	All wagering on athletic contests, including horse racing, prohibited.		No house, vessel, or place on land or water, may be set up for gaming purposes. No gambling devices such as slot machines or roulette wheels permitted.	Bingo, raffles, and Monte Carlo night parties organized for educational and charitable purposes allowed. Three-card monte; confidence games; bookmaking; bucketing illegal.
FLORIDA 849.01 *et seq.*	Playing or engaging in any card game or game of chance, at any place, by any device, for money or another thing of value.	Pari-mutuel wagering meets of thoroughbred racing, quarter horse racing, or harness racing allowed with permit. Off-track and inter-track wagering allowed.	Pari-mutuel wagering on greyhound dog racing allowed with permit. Off-track and intertrack wagering allowed.	Pari-mutuel-style, not casino-style card rooms allowed. Tribal gaming pursuant to Indian Gaming Regulatory Act legal.	Penny-ante games with winnings not exceeding $10 permitted, including poker, pinochle, bridge, dominoes, and mahjongg, if conducted by adults in a dwelling. Cardrooms, bingo, gaming for charitable organizations allowed. Chain letters and pyramid schemes banned. Jai-alai allowed.
GEORGIA 16-12-20 *et seq.*	Betting upon the final result of any game or contest, or upon games played with cards, dice, or balls, in order to win money or other things of value, prohibited.	Prohibited.	Prohibited.	Maintenance of gambling places or equipment prohibited.	Election wagering, commercial gambling, dogfighting, chain letter and pyramid clubs banned. Raffles for charitable organizations allowed.
HAWAII 712-1220 *et seq.*	Staking or risking something of value upon outcome of a contest of chance or uncontrollable future contingent event in order to receive something of value banned.			Gambling aboard ships illegal. Possession of gambling devices, e.g. slot machines, illegal.	Possession of gambling records, promoting gambling, bookmaking, illegal. Social gambling, in which adult players in a private dwelling receive nothing of value or profit other than personal gambling winnings, permitted.
IDAHO 18-3801 *et seq.;* 54-2501 *et seq.* Idaho Racing Act	Risking any money, credit, deposit or other thing of value upon lot, chance, the operation of a gambling device or the happening or outcome of an event, including sporting events.	Live horse racing and sumulcasts legal.	Live in-state dog racing and pari-mutuel betting illegal.	Casino operations, including, but not limited to, blackjack, craps, roulette, poker, baccarat, or Keno. Antique slot machines may be displayed but not operated.	Bookmaking, possession of gambling records, pool selling prohibited. Bonafide contests of skill, speed, strength, or endurance in which awards are made only to entrants or owners of entrants; bona fide business transactions; games which award only additional play; and promotional contests allowed.

Table 32: Gambling—Continued

State/Code Section	Gambling	Horse Racing/ Off-Track Betting	Dog Racing/ Off-Track Betting	Casinos Allowed?	Other Kinds of Gambling-Related Activities Allowed or Banned
ILLINOIS 720 5/28-1 et seq.; 230 10/1 et seq. Riverboat Gambling Act; 230 5/1 et seq. Illinois Horse Racing Act	Playing games of chance or skill for money or other thing of value; wagering upon games, contests, or elections; owning or operating gambling devices; bookmaking; pool selling; contracting to buy or sell future commodities by payment only of differences in price; and transmitting wager information illegal.	Horse racing and pari-mutuel wagering allowed for licensees. Licensees must contribute to fund assisting persons residing or working on back stretch of racetracks. Licensees must provide information on assistance for compulsive gamblers.		Riverboat gambling allowed upon any navigable stream other than Lake Michigan, except within counties with population in excess of 3 million.	Compensation agreements; bona fide contests of skill, speed, strength, or endurance; manufacture of gambling devices; bingo; raffles; possession of antique slot machines; pull tab and jar games; and charitable games allowed.
INDIANA 35-45-5-1 et seq.; 4-33-1-1 et seq.	Risking money or other property for gain, contingent upon lot, chance, or the operation of a gambling device.	Horse racing and satellite facilities licensed for pari-mutuel wagering legal.		Riverboat gambling legal in counties contiguous to Lake Michigan, Ohio River, and Patoka Lake; gambling license can be suspended, revoked, or denied for failure to pay child support. Licensees encouraged to award contracts to women and minorities.	Bona fide contests of skill, speed, strength or endurance in which only entrants are awarded prizes; bona fide business transactions allowed. Bookmaking; pool-selling; maintenance of slot machines, dice tables, or roulette wheels; and conducting banking games banned.
IOWA 99.1 et seq.	Individuals may participate in card and parlor games, games of skill and chance, and wagers or bets if they are in the physical presence of each other as part of a bona fide social relationship. No person may win or lose more than $50 in a 24-hour period.	Horse racing legal. Licensees may simultaneously telecast out-of-state races within racetrack for purpose of pari-mutuel wagering.	Dog racing legal. Licensees may simultaneously telecast out-of-state races within racetrack for purpose of pari-mutuel wagering.	Excursion boat gambling, including coin-operated games legal. Gambling on land prohibited except for on Indian reservations.	Bookmaking; card counting; pyramid games illegal. Raffles not exceeding $200 in value; bingo legal. Any adult may hold an annual game night with a license, if no consideration is involved except goodwill.
KANSAS 21-4302–21-4308; 74-8801 et seq. Parimutuel Racing Act	Making a bet; entering or remaining in a gambling place with intent to bet; and playing a gambling device.	Nonprofit organizations may apply to state racing commission for license to construct or own racetrack facility and conduct horse races. No off-track betting.	Nonprofit organizations may apply to state racing commission for license to construct or own racetrack facility and conduct greyhound races. No off-track betting.	Commercial gambling illegal except in accordance with Indian tribal gaming statutes.	Bona fide business transactions; prizes to winners of bona fide contests of skill, speed, strength, or endurance; and bingo operated by bona fide nonprofit organizations.
KENTUCKY 528.010; 230.010 et seq.	Staking or risking something of value upon the outcome of a contest or game based upon an element of chance.	Horse running, trotting and pacing races; harness races; off-track interstate wagering legal.		Casinos and gambling establishments illegal.	Bookmaking; organizing or promoting gambling; possessing gambling records and devices banned. Charitable gaming allowed.

Table 32: Gambling—Continued

State/Code Section	Gambling	Horse Racing/ Off-Track Betting	Dog Racing/ Off-Track Betting	Casinos Allowed?	Other Kinds of Gambling-Related Activities Allowed or Banned
LOUISIANA 14:90 *et seq.*	Intentional conducting a game or contest in which a person risks the loss of anything of value in order to realize a profit.	Horse racing on licensed racetracks, interstate and international pari-mutuel wagering legal. Licensees must post information on services for compulsive gambling.	Dog racing prohibited.	Riverboat gambling allowed. Video draw poker legal in selected jurisdictions; information on services for compulsive gambling must be posted.	Gambling allowed on international commercial cruise ships sailing to ports in parishes with populations of 475,000 or more. Bona fide charitable raffles, bingo and Keno legal. Gambling via Internet illegal.
MAINE 17-A §951 *et seq.*	Staking or risking something of value upon the outcome of a contest of chance or a future contingent event, with intent to receive something of value in the event of a certain outcome.	Harness horse racing and off-track betting allowed.	Greyhound racing, and interstate simulcasts of greyhound racing, prohibited.	Gaming allowed only on Passamaquoddy tribal lands.	Bingo clubs for individuals 62 years of age or older; bona fide business contracts legal. Bookmaking; mutuel schemes; promoting gambling; possession of gambling records and/or devices illegal.
MARYLAND 27-240; 11-101 *et seq.* Horse Racing Act (expires July 1, 2001)	Wagering or betting in any manner to receive something of value dependent upon the result of any race, contest or contingency.	Thoroughbred and harness racing legal. Pari-mutuel betting; intertrack betting; and satellite simulcast betting allowed. All licensed thoroughbred owners must contribute to Jockey Injury Compensation Fund.		Occupying any house, building or vessel on land or water for the purpose of gambling prohibited. Slot machines legal.	Bookmaking; pool-making; jai alai illegal. Games of entertainment, e.g.bingo and raffles, including bona fide political committee raffles and raffles of real property by charitable organizations.
MASSACHUSETTS 271-1 *et seq.*; 128-1 *et seq.*	Winning $5 or more by gaming or betting on sides or hands of those playing, in a public place or while trespassing in a private place.	Licensed horse racing and on-track pari-mutuel or certificate wagering legal. Use of drugs to affect speed of horses prohibited.	Licensed dog racing and on-track pari-mutuel or certificate wagering legal. Use of drugs to affect speed of dogs prohibited.		Book making and pool making; betting in pool halls or bowling alleys; gaming within one mile of a cattle show, military muster or public gathering; using a telephone to place or accept a bet illegal.
MICHIGAN 750.301 *et seq.*; 432.201 *et seq.*	Accepting money or a valuable thing contingent upon result of contest or happening of uncertain event.	Live horse racing at licensed race tracks; on-track simulcasting; and on-track pari-mutuel wagering legal. Toll-free compulsive gaming helpline number must be posted at each entrance and exit of each licensed racetrack.		Gaming on Native American land governed by Indian Gaming Regulatory Act. Licensed casinos allowed. Compulsive gamblers may place themselves on a "disassociated persons" list which licensees use to bar them from entering casino facilities.	Pool selling; registering bets; gambling in stocks, bonds, grain or produce prohibited. Recreational card playing at senior citizen housing facility; league bowling at alleys not exceeding $1,000; redemption games; bingo; millionaire parties

Table 32: Gambling—Continued

State/Code Section	Gambling	Horse Racing/ Off-Track Betting	Dog Racing/ Off-Track Betting	Casinos Allowed?	Other Kinds of Gambling-Related Activities Allowed or Banned
MINNESOTA 349.11 *et seq.;* 609.75 *et seq.*	Lawful gambling regulated to prevent commercialization, insure integrity of operations, and provide for use of net profits only for lawful purposes. Making a bet; possessing a gambling device without a license; and allowing a structure under one's control to be used as a gambling place illegal.	Licensed on-track pari-mutuel system of wagering on horse races legal.		Gaming on tribal land governed by Indian Gaming Regulatory Act.	Pull-tabs; bingo; raffles; paddlewheels; tipboards all considered lawful gambling. Possession of a gambling device in one's dwelling for one's own amusement and social skill games with prizes not in excess of $200 legal.
MISSISSIPPI 97-33-1 *et seq.*	Encouraging any game, other than a dog fight, for money or other valuable thing.			Cruise vessels allowed on Mississippi River or waters within any county bordering river in which voters have approved gambling.	Cockfights; Indian ball play; duels; raffles; gambling devices; yacht races; shooting matches
MISSOURI 572.010 *et seq.;* 313.001 *et seq.*	Staking or risking something of value upon the outcome of a contest of chance or future contingent event.	Horse racing and pari-mutuel wagering on international or interstate horse race simulcasts legal. Off-track wagering illegal.		Licensed excursion gambling boats and floating facilities which house games of chance and skill, including poker, craps, blackjack, legal.	Bookmaking; possession of gambling records and devices illegal. Bingo sponsored by bona fide charitable organizations legal.
MONTANA 23-5-110 *et seq.*	Lawful gambling regulated to protect tourists, citizens, and government from unscrupulous players, proprietors, and activities, and to assist compulsive gamblers and their families.	Live or simulcast horse races at licensed racetracks or simulcast facilities legal. At least one race at each track each day must be limited to Montana-bred horses. Pari-mutuel, on-track wagering only.	Live or simulcast greyhound races at licensed race tracks or simulcast facilities legal. Pari-mutuel, on-track wagering only.	Video gambling devices legal.	Fishing derbies; wagering on natural occurrences; gambling activities sponsored by nonprofit organizations; possession of antique slot machines; shaking dice for a drink or music; Calcutta pools; bingo; Keno and raffles; sports pools and tab games; fantasy sports leagues authorized. Bookmaking, pool selling
NEBRASKA 28-1101 *et seq.;* 9-201 *et seq.*	Betting something of value upon the outcome of a future event which is determined by an element of chance.	Licensed horse racing; pari-mutuel wagering; off-track betting (including simulcasting and telephonic wagering); and exotic wagering such as daily double, exacta, quinella, trifecta, pick six legal. Sunday horse racing and drugging of horses illegal.		Tribal gaming legal, pursuant to Indian Gaming Regulatory Act.	Lawful business transactions; playing amusement devices; conducting prize contests; participating in bingo and raffles in accordance with state statutes legal.

Table 32: Gambling—Continued

State/Code Section	Gambling	Horse Racing/ Off-Track Betting	Dog Racing/ Off-Track Betting	Casinos Allowed?	Other Kinds of Gambling-Related Activities Allowed or Banned
NEVADA 463.160 *et seq.*	Dealing, operating, carrying on, or exposing for play any game, or operating inter-casino linked systems.	Licensed horse racing legal; off-track betting legal when conducted at licensed gaming facilities.	Licensed dog racing legal.	Licensed casino gambling legal.	Charitable lotteries legal. Manipulation of gaming equipment; use of unapproved wagering instruments illegal.
NEW HAMPSHIRE 647.2; 284.1 *et seq.*	Risking something of value upon a future contingent not under one's control or influence, upon an agreement or understanding that something of value will be received in the event of a certain outcome.	Licensed horse racing legal. On-track pari-mutuel wagering legal until 2009.	Licensed dog racing legal. On-track pari-mutuel wagering legal until 2009.	Cruise ships equipped with gambling machines whose primary purpose is touring may enter state for 48 hours, provided that all gambling machines are disabled while in state. Others prohibited.	Charitable organizations' raffles, bingo and games of chance; lucky 7; manufacture of gambling machines legal. Gambling on gas station premises; wagering on games or sports illegal.
NEW JERSEY 2C:37-1 *et seq.*; 5:5-1 *et seq.*	Unlicensed risking of something of value upon outcome of contest of chance or future contingent event not under actor's control, upon agreement that actor will receive something of value in event of a certain outcome.	Licensed horse racing legal. On-track pari-mutuel wagering; race simulcasts; licensed intertrack wagering; receipt of and wagering upon simulcast horse races held out of state legal. Influencing jockeys or owners; drugging horses; predetermining the winner of a horse race illegal. Each racetrack licensee may hold 3 charity racing days for the developmentally disabled and one charity racing day for backstretch benevolency programs per year.	Sled dog racing allowed for agricultural fairs and exhibitions only.	Licensed casino operation legal. All slot machines have minimum payout of 83%. Every casino licensee must establish goals for obtaining business contracts with minority and women's business enterprises.	Bookmaking; possession of gambling records; unlicensed maintenance of gambling resorts; possession of gambling devices not regulated by Casino Control Act; unlicensed conduct of games of chance on Sundays illegal. Raffles and bingo for charitable organiztions legal.
NEW MEXICO 30-19-1 *et seq.*	Making a bet; entering or remaining in a gambling place with intent to make a bet or play a gambling device.	Licensed horse racing; on-track pari-mutuel wagering; off-track race simulcasts without wagering legal until July 1, 2000.		Gambling places illegal, except as pursuant to Indian Gaming Compact.	Commercial gambling; permitting premises to be used for gambling; dealing in gambling devices; bookmaking; bribery of contest participants; accepting anything of value on the basis of results of a race, contest or game of skill or chance illegal. Manufacturing and exporting of gambling devices; senior citizen bingo.

Table 32: Gambling—Continued

State/Code Section	Gambling	Horse Racing/ Off-Track Betting	Dog Racing/ Off-Track Betting	Casinos Allowed?	Other Kinds of Gambling-Related Activities Allowed or Banned
NEW YORK 225.00 *et seq.;* 47A:101 *et seq.*	Staking or risking something of value upon the outcome of a contest of chance or a future contingent event not under person's control, upon an agreement that he/she will receive something of value, given a certain event.	Licensed horse and harness racing legal. Off-track pari-mutuel wagering at licensed facilities legal. Information must be posted regarding assistance for compulsive gamblers.			Promoting gambling; possession of gambling records; bookmaking; possession of gambling devices illegal. Games of chance sponsored by bona fide charitable organizations.
NORTH CAROLINA 14-289 *et seq.*	Operating a game of chance and playing at or betting on any game of chance at which money, property or other thing of value is bet, whether the same be in stake or not.	Horse racing prohibited.	Greyhound racing prohibited.		Pyramid and chain schemes; allowing gambling in houses of public entertainment; faro banks and tables; possession and operation of punchboards and slot machines illegal. Bingo games and raffles sponsored by nonprofit organizations legal.
NORTH DAKOTA 12.1-28-01 *et seq.*	Risking something of value for gain, contingent, wholly or partially, upon lot, chance, operation of gambling apparatus, or happening or outcome of an event, including elections or sporting events, over which person taking risk has no control.	Licensed horse racing; race simulcasts; pari-mutuel wagering, including place, show, quinella, and combination is legal. Prearranging the order of finish of a race is illegal.	Licensed dog racing; race simulcasts; pari-mutuel wagering, including place, show, quinella and combination.		Lawful contests of skill, speed, strength or endurance; lawful business transactions; bingo, twenty-one, pull tabs, poker, calcutta, paddlewheels, punchboards, sports pools and raffles sponsored by licensed charitable organizations legal. Bogus chips; marked cards; cheating devices; fraudulent schemes
OHIO 2915.01 *et seq.;* 3769.01 *et seq.*	Bookmaking; facilitating schemes or games of chance for profit; betting on schemes or games of chance for one's livelihood; possession of gambling devices; playing craps; roulette or slot machines for money.	Horse racing allowed with permit; on-track pari-mutuel wagering and wagering at fourteen satellite facilities legal. A portion of funds must be deposited into passport program for aged and disabled persons.		Operating a gambling house illegal except as pursuant to tribal-state compact.	Schemes of chance, such as bingo, conducted by charitable organizations, that are conducted four days or less not more than twice a year; licensed tag fishing tournaments are legal. Public gaming; cheating are illegal.
OKLAHOMA 21.941 *et seq.;* 3A.200 *et seq.* Horse Racing Act	Betting or bargaining that, dependent upon chance, one stands to lose or win something of value specified in an agreement between parties.	Licensed horse racing; pari-mutuel, off-track, interstate wagering legal. A portion of proceeds must be deposited into Equine Drug Testing Revolving Fund.		Tribal-State Compact governs casino gambling.	Bona fide business contracts; any charity game conducted pursuant to Oklahoma Charity Games Act; prizes offered to participants of public events such as rodeos, fairs, and athletic events legal. Pyramid schemes; dice games; three-card monte illegal.

Table 32: Gambling—Continued

State/Code Section	Gambling	Horse Racing/ Off-Track Betting	Dog Racing/ Off-Track Betting	Casinos Allowed?	Other Kinds of Gambling-Related Activities Allowed or Banned
OREGON 167.117 *et seq.*; 462.	Staking or risking something of value upon outcome of a contest of chance or future contingent event not under control of actor, upon agreement that actor would receive something of value in the event of a certain outcome.	Licensed horse racing and mutuel wagering legal. Off-track mutuel wagering authorized. Using drugs or electrical equipment to stimulate or depress horses prohibited.	Licensed dog racing and mutuel wagering legal. Off-track mutuel wagering authorized. Using drugs or electrical equipment to stimulate or depress dogs prohibited.	Only gambling places authorized at tribal gaming facilities.	Bona fide business contracts; contest of chance where players win prizes, not money, bingo, lotto, raffles, and Monte Carlo events sponsored by charitable organizations; social games are legal. Bookmaking; possession of gambling records; possession of gray machines; cheating illegal.
PENNSYLVANIA 18.5513	Elements of gambling are: consideration, element of chance, and reward.	Licensed horse and harness racing; interstate simulcasts; on- and off-track pari-mutuel wagering legal. Limit of six horse racing and five harness racing licenses available; corporations cannot conduct both horse and harness racing.			Pool selling and bookmaking; punch boards, drawing cards; private wire for gambling information; cockfighting; bullet play illegal. Bingo and local option small games of chance sponsored by charitable organizations; antique slot machines
RHODE ISLAND 11-19-1 *et seq ;* 41-3-1 *et seq.*	Directly or indirectly setting up, publicly or privately, any chance, game or device for the purpose of disposing of money, or assisting others in such actions.	Licensed horse racing, on-track pari-mutuel wagering legal. The majority of directors of a racetrack must be residents of Rhode Island.	Licensed dog racing, on-track pari-mutuel wagering legal in cities of Burrillville, Lincoln, and West Greenwich.	Operation of gambling places prohibited.	Bingo and raffles in senior citizen housing; bingo sponsored by charitable organizations; licensed jai alai within frontons in city of Newport are legal. Bookmaking, unlicensed horse races are illegal.
SOUTH CAROLINA 16-19-40 *et seq.*; 12-21-2770 *et seq.* Video Game Machines Act	Playing card or dice games; roley-poley; rouge et noir; faro; or at any gaming tables.	Horse racing at Springdale Course Track; used for Carolina Cup and Colonial Cup International Steeplechase only.		Establishments licensed to house video game machines must not receive primary gross income from machines. No more than eight machines in one establishment.	Card and dice games; lettered gaming tables; roley-poley tables; rouge et noir; faro banks; playing games in one's home on Sunday; betting on elections; pool selling; bookmaking; punchboards; gray machines are illegal.
SOUTH DAKOTA 22-25-1 *et seq.*	Wagering anything of value upon the outcome of game of chance; maintaining gambling place or equipment.	Licensed horse racing legal. Off-track pari-mutuel wagering authorized at satellite locations more than fifty miles away from any licensed horse track.	Licensed dog racing. Off-track pari-mutuel wagering authorized at satellite locations more than fifty miles away from any licensed dog track.	Limited card games and slot machines authorized within city of Deadwood. Governor must hold public hearings before entering into tribal gaming compacts.	Travel for sole purpose of gambling; persuading others to visit gambling places; and bookmaking are illegal. Ownership of antique slot machines and bingo sponsored by charitable organizations with no prize in excess of $2000 are legal.
TENNESSEE 4-36-101 *et seq.*	Risking anything of value for a profit whose return is to any degree contingent on chance, not including lawful business transactions.	Licensed horse racing; interstate simulcast wagering; and pari-mutuel wagering at licensed satellite teletheaters legal.			Promoting gambling; pyramid clubs; possessing gambling devices or records; customer referral rebates are illegal. Bingo and games of chance conducted by charitable organizations are legal.

Table 32: Gambling—Continued

State/Code Section	Gambling	Horse Racing/ Off-Track Betting	Dog Racing/ Off-Track Betting	Casinos Allowed?	Other Kinds of Gambling-Related Activities Allowed or Banned
TEXAS 10.47.01 et seq.; Civ. St. 179e Texas Racing Act	Agreement to win or lose something of value solely or partially by chance, not including insurance or offers of prizes to contestants in bona fide contests of skill, speed, strength, or endurance.	Licensed horse racing; simulcast races and on-track pari-mutuel wagering are legal.	Limit of three racetrack licenses for greyhound racing. Simulcast races and on-track pari-mutuel wagering are legal.	Keeping a gambling place is prohibited.	Promoting gambling; communicating gambling information; possessing gambling devices with intent to further gambling illegal. Social gambling; bingo and raffles sponsored by charitable organizations
UTAH 76-10-1101 et seq.; 4-38-1 et seq. Horse Regulation Act	Risking anything of value upon the outcome of a contest, game, scheme, or gaming device when the return or outcome is based upon an element of chance and is in accord with an agreement or understanding that someone will receive something of value in the event of a certain outcome.	Licensed horse racing and on-track pari-mutuel wagering legal. Use of any mechanical or electrical device or drugs in order to stimulate or retard horses prohibited.'			Lawful business transactions; playing amusement devices legal. Election wagering; possessing gambling records; confidence games illegal.
VERMONT 13-2133 et seq.	Winning or losing money or another valuable thing by play or hazard at any game.	Licensed horse racing legal except on Sundays before 1 PM. On-track pari-mutuel wagering allowed.		Gaming houses prohibited.	Games of chance sponsored by nonprofit organizations; contests or games of chance, including sweepstakes, provided that persons who enter are not required to venture money or other valuable things. Bookmaking; pool selling; touting gambling illegal.
VIRGINIA 18.2-325 et seq.; 59.1-364 et seq.	Making, placing or receiving any bet or wager of money or other thing of value, dependent upon the result of any game, contest, or event the outcome of which is uncertain or a matter of chance, whether such game, contest, or event, occurs or is to occur inside or outside Commonwealth limits.	Horse races, pari-mutuel wagering, and off-track betting at licensed satellite facilities legal.	Greyhound racing specifically prohibited.	Gambling devices and places illegal.	Bingo, raffles and duck races sponsored by nonprofit organizations; contests of skill or speed between men, animals, fowl or vehicles; games of chance in private residences legal. Winning by fraud illegal.
WASHINGTON 9.46.010 et seq.	Staking or risking something of value upon the outcome of a contest of chance or future contingent event not under the person's control or influence, upon an agreement that someone will receive something of value.	Licensed horse racing and pari-mutuel wagering allowed. Information on treatment for compulsive gamblers must be displayed at racing facilities.	Greyhound racing specifically prohibited.	Tribal gaming pursuant to Indian Gaming Regulatory Act and maintenance of licensed gambling facilities allowed.	Bucket shops; bunco steering; bookmaking; professional gambling illegal. Bingo, raffles, amusement games sponsored by charitable organizations; fishing derbies; sports pools; golfing and bowling sweepstakes; turkey shoots; social card games; promotional contests legal.

Table 32: Gambling—Continued

State/Code Section	Gambling	Horse Racing/ Off-Track Betting	Dog Racing/ Off-Track Betting	Casinos Allowed?	Other Kinds of Gambling-Related Activities Allowed or Banned
WEST VIRGINIA 61-10-1 *et seq.*; 29-22A-1 *et seq.*	Betting or wagering money or another thing of value on any game of chance, or knowingly furnishing money or another thing of value on any game of chance.	Licensed horse racing and pari-mutuel wagering allowed.	Licensed dog racing and pari-mutuel wagering allowed.	Video lottery games allowed at pari-mutuel racing facilities. Machines cannot use casino themes such as dice, roulette, or baccarat. May simulate classic slot machines.	Bucket shops; policy or numbers games; gambling at hotels illegal. Bingo, raffles, games of chance sponsored by charitable organizations legal.
WISCONSIN 945.01 *et seq.*; 562.001 *et seq.*	Bargain in which parties agree, dependent upon chance even though accompanied by some skill, one stands to win or lose something of value specified in the agreement.	Licensed horse racing and on-track pari-mutuel wagering legal. Off-track betting prohibited.	Licensed dog racing and on-track pari-mutuel wagering legal. Off-track betting prohibited.	Indian gaming legal. Commercial, i.e., casino gambling illegal.	Licensed bingo and raffles allowed. Crane games; snowmobile racing; bona fide business contracts; contests of skill, speed, strength and endurance legal. Bookmaking; dealing in gambling devices illegal.
WYOMING 6-7-101 *et seq.*; 11-25-101	Risking any property for gain contingent in whole or part upon lot, chance, or outcome of an event, including sporting event, over which person taking a risk has no control.	Licensed horse, harness, cutter, chariot, and chuckwagon racing and pari-mutuel wagering legal. Licensed off-track simulcast wagering legal.		Structures, boats or vehicels maintained for gambling purposes illegal.	Bona fide contests of skill, speed, strength, or endurance; bona fide business contracts; raffles, bingo and pulltabs sold by charitable organizations; bona fide social wagering; Calcutta wagering; display or private use of antique devices legal. Professional gambling; possessing gambling devices; gambling record keeping illegal.

33. LEGAL AGES

The law only recognizes as legal the acts of persons who possess the capacity to form the proper intent to perform the particular acts. Two aspects of "capacity" are recognized: the mental capacity to form the intent to commit an act, and maturity, or the roughly objective measure of the ability to form a legal intent. It is maintained that when a child reaches a certain age his or her capacity to form the proper intent matures. At this point a child can be held accountable for his or her actions.

The variation of age limits for different activities, such as marrying, voting, or consuming alcohol, illustrates the values a society places on certain types of activities and how a society values individual responsibility and accountability. For instance, when a minor intentionally injures another or damages property, he or she may be held liable for the act at age fourteen, and even earlier, in some instances, in certain courts. But he or she may not be allowed to drink or vote until age 21 or 18.

The limitations on a minor's ability to contract, however, are established to protect innocent third parties and ignorant or immature first parties. If a minor makes a foolish business decision out of immaturity or ignorance, the contract may be voided on the basis of a lack of capacity to contract.

Table 33: Legal Ages

State	Age of Majority	Emancipation	Contracts	Ability to Sue	Consent to Medical Treatment
ALABAMA	19 (§26-1-1)	18 (§26-13-1)	Minor 15 or more at nearest birthday may contract for life, health, accident, annuity insurance; however, not bound by any unperformed agreement to pay premium (§27-14-5)	May sue through personal representative, next friend, or guardian *ad litem;* if 14 or over has 30 days to choose guardian *ad litem* (ARCP 17)	
ALASKA	18 (§25.20.010)		May receive and give full discharge and acquittance for insurance payments up to $3000 if 16 or over (§21.42.290)		
ARIZONA	18 (§1-215); 21 years of age to consume alcohol	If veteran under Serviceman's Readjustment Act of 1944 (§44-131); marriage or military service Op. Atty. Gen. No. 69-27	Governed by common law (§47-1103); at 16 or over may contract for educational loans (§44-140.01) (Model Minor Student Capacity to Borrow Act)	By guardian or special administrator, guardian *ad litem*, next friend (§14-3614; §14-3615; Civ. 17(g))	Can contract for diagnosis and treatment of VD; hospital, medical, surgical care if emancipated, homeless, or married (§§44-132, *et seq.*); if under influence, consent assumed at 12 and over (§44-133.01)
ARKANSAS	18, except for sale of liquor (§9-25-101)	16 (§9-26-104)	Rescission by infant 18 or over permitted only upon full restitution; promise made after full age to pay debt contracted during infancy must be in writing (§§9-26-101; 4-59-101)	Next friend or guardian (§16-61-103, 104)	

Table 33: Legal Ages—Continued

State	Age of Majority	Emancipation	Contracts	Ability to Sue	Consent to Medical Treatment
CALIFORNIA	18 (Fam. Code §6500)	If has entered valid marriage, is on active duty in the armed forces, or has received declaration pursuant to Fam. Code §7002; if minor is 14 or over and is living apart from parent or guardian, managing own finances and minor's source of income isn't from an illegal activity, application for emancipation must be sustained unless contrary to minor's interests (§7120)	Yes (Fam. Code §6700) except he cannot give a delegation of power, made a contract relating to real property or personal property not in immediate possession or control of the minor (Fam. Code §6701)	Guardian Fam. Code §6601)	Parent or guardian may authorize (Fam. Code §6910); upon application by minor, courts may grant consent (§6911) or minor may consent if 15 years or older, living apart from parents, and managing own finances (§6922)
COLORADO	21, except as otherwise provided (2-4-401(6)	Occurs upon attainment of majority; *Koltay v. Koltay* 667 P.2d 1374 (Colo. 1983)	18 (§13-22-101(1)(a))	18 (§13-22-101(1)(c)); *Casa Bonita Restaurant v. Industrial Commission of the State of Colorado* 677 P.2d 344 (Colo. 1983)	18 (§13-22-101(1)(d))
CONNECTICUT	18; (§1-1d)	If veteran under Service Readjustment Act (§369-759)	Common law; at 15, individual may contract for life, health, accident insurance (§389-284)	§52-572(c) parent-child immunity abrogated in certain negligence action(§52-572(c)); if married, may sue only regarding marriage itself (§46b-43)	
DELAWARE	18, (Tit. 1 §701) Uniform Gifts to Minors Act; 18 to 21 (Tit. 12 §4501) and 21 re alcohol	18 (Tit. 1 §701)	18 (Tit. 6 §2705)	18 (Tit. 10 §3923)	
DISTRICT OF COLUMBIA	18, including minor married women (§30-401)		Common law; cannot be charged unless promise made in writing after age of majority (§28-3505)	When infant is a party in an action, the summons and complaint shall be served upon him personally and, when he is under 16 years, upon the person with whom he resides, if within the District §13-332	If connected to pregnancy, substance abuse, psychological disturbance, or sexually transmitted disease (22 DCMR §600.7)

Table 33: Legal Ages—Continued

State	Age of Majority	Emancipation	Contracts	Ability to Sue	Consent to Medical Treatment
FLORIDA	18; 21 re alcohol; if minor marries, disabilities removed (§743.01, 07)	If legal marriage occurs (§743.07); upon petition if 16 or older (§743.015)	May contract for higher education financing if 16 or over (§743.05); may contract generally if married (§743.01)	By next friend or court appointed guardian; can sue for injuries by neglect to natural or adopted parents (§768.0415; RCP §1.210(b))	If emergency (§743.064)
GEORGIA	18 (§39-1-1), except 14 to make a will (§53-2-22); 21 re alcohol (§3-3-23)	Marriage with or without parental consent	Generally voidable; however, if benefits continue after age of majority, contract is valid (§13-3-20)	Through guardian or guardian *ad litem* (§29-4-7); suit started by infant alone not void but guardian must be appointed before verdict (§9-2-28)	18 for treatment in general (§31-9-2); if treatment is for VD, minor may consent; female minor has valid consent for treatment in connection with pregnancy
HAWAII	18 (§577-1)	Legal marriage (§577-25); veteran or veteran's spouse (§577-2)	Disaffirmance must be made within reasonable time after reaching age of majority	Guardian *ad litem* (§551-2)	For counseling services for alcohol or drug abuse (§577-26); if for pregnancy, venereal disease or family planning services (§577A-2)
IDAHO	18 (§32-101)	Marriage (§32-101)	Cannot disaffirm otherwise valid contract to purchase necessities (§§32-101, *et seq.*); if 15 or over, may enter into insurance contract (§41-1807)	Through guardian, conservator, or like fiduciary, or infant may sue through guardian *ad litem* or next friend appointed by court (FRCP 17)	Age 14; treatment of infectious, contagious, communicable diseases (§39-3801)
ILLINOIS	18, except re alcohol (21)(235 ILCS 5/6-16); Uniform Transfers to Minors Act (21)(755 ILCS 5/11-1)	Minors between 16 and 18 may apply if no parental objection (§§750 ILCS 30/1, *et seq.*)	Voidable unless for necessities; executing contract binding only if ratified after 18; executed contract binding unless disaffirmed within reasonable time after age 18; minor may enter into contract for promissory note for attendance at Illinois college/university	Guardian *ad litem* must be appointed or can sue within 2 years of turning 18 (§735 ILCS 5/13-211)	18 or over; medical or surgical procedures

Table 33: Legal Ages—Continued

State	Age of Majority	Emancipation	Contracts	Ability to Sue	Consent to Medical Treatment
INDIANA	18; 21 re alcohol (§7.1-1-3-25)		If under 18, child is not able to contract except for necessities and higher education expenses (§20-12-21.3-1); minors 16 or older may contract for life, accident, sickness insurance and annuities (§27-1-12-15)	Through guardian *ad litem*, court has discretion as to whether to honor request for infant's choice (Trial Procedure Rule 17(C))	
IOWA	18, or through marriage or if a minor has been tried and convicted as an adult and been imprisoned, he is considered an adult for purposes of decisions regarding medical care and treatment during his incarceration (§599.1)	Veterans (§599.5)	For necessities; for other contracts, minor is bound unless disaffirmed after reasonable time of attaining majority and restoration made of money and property received (§599.2)	By minor's guardian or by next friend; court may substitute at its discretion (RCP 12)	
KANSAS	18, 16 if married (§38-101); 21 re alcohol (§§41-102, 175); 21 re Uniform Gifts to Minors Act (§38-1702)	At discretion of the court (§38-109)	Valid for necessities; also for other contracts unless disaffirmed in reasonable time after majority is obtained and money, property restored (§38-102); may consummate insurance contracts but must have consent of parents and cosignature of party over age 18 (§40-237)	Through infant's representative; if no representative, then through next friend or guardian *ad litem* (§§60-217(c); 59-2205)	Unmarried pregnant minor may consent to hospital, medical, and surgical care (§38-123); or any minor over 16 (§38-123b)
KENTUCKY	18 for all purposes except 21 for purchase of alcohol and 21 with respect to parent's obligation for care and treatment of handicapped children (§2.015)	Marriage does not remove infant disability	Valid for necessities; otherwise, common law generally governs; exception made for war veterans under §384.090 (18) and for borrowing for educational purpose with parental consent (§287.385)	May sue by guardian or next friend if unmarried (CR 17.03); if married, may sue on his or her own	

Table 33: Legal Ages—Continued

State	Age of Majority	Emancipation	Contracts	Ability to Sue	Consent to Medical Treatment
LOUISIANA	18 (CC §29); if mentally handicapped, minor status may be continued by court order (CC §§355, 358)	(1). Through notarial act by father or mother, if no father, at age 15; has right to full administration of estate but may not be bound to amount of money greater than 1 year's revenue (CC §§370-373) (2). through marriage, no specific age given; cannot be revoked; if under 16, minor may not deal in selling or affecting real property without court consent (CC §§379-384); (3). minor 16 or over may be judicially emancipated (CC §385)	Yes, if made with consent of tutors; if no tutor or one who neglects to supply necessaries, such contract for benefit of the minor is valid (CC §1922)	Through father, then mother or court appointed tutor if one or both parents are dead or parents divorced (CCP §683)	May consent without parental consent (R.S.40 §1095-6)
MAINE	18; 21 re alcohol (Tit. 22, §2)	Not by marriage; however, married person of any age may handle real or personal property. (19-A §801)	No, unless minor or authorized person ratified it at age of 18; exceptions are necessaries or real estate to which minor has title and retains benefit; contracts of minors re higher education are valid (Tit. 33 §52)	Through next friend or guardian *ad litem*, except in bastardy process	

Table 33: Legal Ages—Continued

State	Age of Majority	Emancipation	Contracts	Ability to Sue	Consent to Medical Treatment
MARYLAND	18 (Art. 1, §24); 21 re alcohol (Art. 2B §12-108); 21 re Uniform Transfers to Minors Act (Est. & Tr. Art. 13 §320)	Married minor may buy or sell property and to join in deed, mortgage, lease, notes if spouse is of age (Est. & Tr. Art. 13 §503(a)); age 15 re insurance and cannot repudiate on basis of minority (Est. & Tr. Art. 13 §503(c)); or if in military, can enter into real estate transactions (Est. & Tr. Art. 13-503 (b))	If not beneficial to minor, void *ab initio,* not ratifiable; if beneficial to minor or uncertain as to benefit or prejudice, voidable by infant, may be ratified at age 18; ratification may be express or through acceptance of benefits; voidable contract may be disaffirmed by minor during minority or reasonable time after age 18 (COML Art. 1 §103)	By guardian or next friend (R.P. 2-202[b][c])	If married or a parent or seeking help with drug use, alcoholism, VD, pregnancy, contraception falling short of sterilization, or if seeking consent would be life threatening (Health Gen. Art. 20 §§102, 104); minor 16 or older can consent to treatment for emotional disorder (Health Gen. Art. 20 §104); generally abortion cannot be performed on unmarried minor without notice to parents (Health Gen. Art. 20 §103)
MASSACHUSETTS	18 (Ch. 4 §7 cl. forty-eighth and cl. fifty-first; Ch. 231 §85P)	18 unless legally incapacitated for reason other than age (Ch. 231 §85P)	No, except for necessaries and education; 16 or over for motor vehicle liability insurance; 15 or over for life insurance (Ch. 175 §§113K, 128)	The district or juvenile court, when it appears necessary or convenient, appoint guardians of minors if the person who is the subject of the petition is a minor and there is a proceeding before such court. (Ch. 201 §1)	If 12 or over and certified to be drug dependent, may consent to appropriate medical care (Ch. 112 §12e); minor may also consent to emergency care when: married, widowed, divorced; is a parent; is a member of armed forces; lives separately from parents and manages own financial affairs; reasonably believes he has come into contact with dangerous public health disease; and reasonably believes she is pregnant (Ch. 112 §12F)

Table 33: Legal Ages—Continued

State	Age of Majority	Emancipation	Contracts	Ability to Sue	Consent to Medical Treatment
MICHIGAN	18 (MSA 772.52, *et seq.*	Through marriage (§551.251)	For necessities only; 16 for life/disability insurance contracts	By next friend or guardian of estate; if age 14 or over, can select own (Mich. Court Rules Rule 2.201 (E))	
MINNESOTA	18; 21 re Uniform Gifts to Minors Act (§645.451); if married may join in conveyance of realty prior to age 18 (§507.02)		For necessities only; other contracts voidable	At 14 by general guardian *ad litem* appointed by court; otherwise by general guardian, relative, or friend, by default (RCP §17.02)	
MISSISSIPPI	21	If married, treated as adult for divorce and custody claims (§§93-19-11; 93-5-9)	18 for personal property; ratification must be signed in writing (§15-3-11); married minors 18 or over can execute homestead agreements (§93-3-11)	18 to settle personal injury claims; married minor may file in marital matters; court appoints guardian *ad litem*	Family planning information
MISSOURI	18; 21 re Uniform Gifts to Minors Act (§§431.055; 442.040; 507.115)	If married, minor may convey or encumber real estate if spouse is of age (§442.040)	May be ratified after 18 (§431.060); for real property, may be disaffirmed within 2 years (§442.080)	By guardian, next friend, or court appointed (CR §52.02; §§507.110, *et* seq.)	
MONTANA	18 (§41-1-101); 21 re alcohol (§16-6-305)	Occurs upon marriage (§40-6-234)	Contracts subject to power to disaffirm (§41-1-302); disaffirm through consideration within reasonable time after age of majority (§41-1-304); for necessities which may not be disaffirmed (§41-1-305); contract to borrow money for higher education (§41-1-303); contracts authorized by statute; if granted emancipation (§41-1-306)	Through general guardian or guardian *ad* litem (§41-1-202)	Yes, if emancipated; separated from parents and self-supporting; pregnant; has a communicable disease; or addicted to alcohol or drugs; has had a child or graduated from high school; needs emergency care (§41-1-402)

Table 33: Legal Ages—Continued

State	Age of Majority	Emancipation	Contracts	Ability to Sue	Consent to Medical Treatment
NEBRASKA	19 (§43-2101); 21 re alcohol (§53-103[23])	Marriage (§43-2101)	Common law applies	Except as provided in Probate Code, actions by infant shall be commenced by guardian or next friend. (§25-307)	
NEVADA	18 (§129.010); 21 re alcohol (§202.020)	16 by court order (§129.080); if veteran or spouse of under Serviceman Readjustment Act of 1944 (§129.020)	Common law; valid if emancipated (§129.130)	General guardian or guardian *ad litem* (§12.050)	If emancipated (§129.130); or if living apart from parents, married, has a child, or has a health hazard (§129.030); or under influence of drugs (§129.050); or has a sexually transmitted disease (§129.060)
NEW HAMPSHIRE	18; 21 re alcohol and Uniform Gifts to Minors Act (Ch. 175 §1)		Bound with sureties by recognizances (Ch. 597 §14); can join with spouse in release of homestead interests (Ch. 460 §4)	Next friend; court may appoint guardian *ad litem*; settlement above a net amount of $10,000 must be court approved (Ch. 464-A §42)	
NEW JERSEY	18 (Tit. 9, Ch. 17B, §3); 21 re alcohol and Uniform Gifts to Minors Act (Tit. 46, Ch. 38 §14)		17, if minor spouse for sale of property (Tit. 37, Ch. 2 §30); 15 for insurance contracts (Tit. 17B, Ch. 24 §2)	By guardian or guardian *ad* litem (Rule 4:26-2)	
NEW MEXICO	28; 21 re alcohol (§28-6-1) 21 Uniform Gifts to Minors Act (§28-6-1)	Through marriage, death, adoption, majority of minor as well as death, resignation, or removal of guardian (§45-5-210)	Common law applies	By guardian, guardian *ad litem,* or next friend; married minor may sue in action against him or spouse without a guardian; infant may request guardian ad litem if 14 or over	

Table 33: Legal Ages—Continued

State	Age of Majority	Emancipation	Contracts	Ability to Sue	Consent to Medical Treatment
NEW YORK	18 (Dom. Rel. §2); 21 re alcohol (Alco. Bev. Cont. §65)		May disaffirm most contracts if disaffirmed within reasonable time after reaching majority; exceptions: (1). certain loans; (2). married infant buying home; (3). providing medical care for self/ child; (4). for performing athletic or arts services if court-approved; (5). life insurance if 15 or over; (6). or if veteran or veteran's spouse (Gen. Oblig. §§3-101, *et seq.*)	Through guardian or parent, adult spouse, guardian *ad litem* appointed by court or by infant if over 14 (Civ. Prac. L. & R. §1201)	
NORTH CAROLINA	18; 21 re alcohol, gift tax exemption; running for public office; Uniform Gifts to Minors Act §48A-1: The common-law definition of min or insofar as it pertains to the age of the minor is hereby repealed and abrogated. §48A-2:18	Upon marriage or becoming 18; may petition court if 16 or over (§§7A-717, *et seq.*)	Voidable subject to making restitution at common law; if 17 or over, may enter into contract to finance higher education; may be ratified by silence after 3 years subsequent to age of majority	By guardian, testamentary guardian, guardian *ad litem* (1A-1, R. 17(b)	VD, pregnancy, drug abuse, or emotional disturbance; any emancipated minor may consent to medical, dental, or health treatment for himself or child (§90-21.5)
NORTH DAKOTA	18; 21 re alcohol (§§14-10-01, *et seq.*)	Marriage; upon age 18, appointment of guardian or parent may relinquish to minor right of control and to earnings (§14-09-20)	May be disaffirmed upon age of majority or within 1 year thereafter; exception contract for reasonable value of necessary support or a statutory contract; cannot make contracts re personal or real property not in immediate possession or control, otherwise may contract subject to disaffirmance (14-10-09 to 10-13)	May sue or be sued, but court must appoint guardian *ad litem* (14-10-03, 04)	

Table 33: Legal Ages—Continued

State	Age of Majority	Emancipation	Contracts	Ability to Sue	Consent to Medical Treatment
OHIO	18; 21 re alcohol and Uniform Gift to Minors Act (§§3109.01; 2111.18.1)	Upon application to probate court (2111.18.1)	Voidable; may be disaffirmed at infancy or within reasonable time after age of majority; exception for necessaries (3109.01)	Through personal representative or otherwise may sue by next friend or defend by guardian *ad litem;* minor not represented must have court appoint guardian *ad litem* (2111.23, 2151.28.1)	
OKLAHOMA	18; 21 re alcohol and Uniform Gifts to Minors Act (58 §1201, *et seq.*)	Through court order; upon marriage (10 §10; 10 §91, *et seq.*)	Voidable when done within one year after age of majority; exception: contracts for necessaries and statutory obligations (15 §13, *et seq.*)	Guardian or next friend	Either parent may consent to medical treatment under certain circumstances; minor may consent to own treatment (63 §2601, *et seq.*)
OREGON	18; 21 re alcohol and Uniform Gifts to Minors Act (§109.510, *et seq.*)	By marriage, parent, or court decree (109.555; 109.510, *et seq.*)	Valid for necessaries and education; any others voidable upon attaining majority		No minimum for treatment of venereal disease (109.610 *et seq.*)
PENNSYLVANIA	21; 18 re matters under Probate, Estates, Fiduciary Code and Tit. 23, §5302	Marriage	Voidable except for necessaries until age 18; *Rivera v. Reading Housing Authority,* E.D. Pa. 1993, 819 F.Supp. 1323, Aff'n. 8F.2d 961	18 or older may sue or be sued as adult; infant may be represented by guardian, guardian ad litem, next friend (Tit. 23, §5101)	18, married or pregnant or upon graduation from high school
RHODE ISLAND	18; (§15-12-1); 21 re alcohol (3-8-1, *et seq.*); Uniform Transfers to Minors Act (18-7-1, *et seq.*)	Common law applies, *Pardey v. American Ship Windlass Co.* 34 A. 737 (1896)	Voidable except for necessaries, *Jacobs v. United Elec. Rys. Co.* 125 A. 286 (1924)	May sue through next friend; when sued, court-appointed guardian *ad litem, Keenan v. Aanagan* 147 A 617 (1929) *Vaughn v. Carr* 95 A 569 (1915)	
SOUTH CAROLINA	18; 21 re alcohol (§61-6-4080, 61-4-50, 61-4-580); Uniform Gifts to Minors Act (20-7-140, *et seq.*)		No, except for necessaries and if contract is signed in writing promising ratification after age 18 (20-7-250, *et seq.*)		Married minor or their spouse may consent to diagnostic, therapeutic, or post mortem (§20-7-27); or may consent if over 16 (20-7-280)

Table 33: Legal Ages—Continued

State	Age of Majority	Emancipation	Contracts	Ability to Sue	Consent to Medical Treatment
SOUTH DAKOTA	18 (§26-1-1); 21 re alcohol (35-9-1); Uniform Transfers to Minors Act (55-10A)	Upon marriage or age of majority; by express agreement if no longer dependent for support or active military duty (25-5-19; 25-5-24)	Contracts binding unless minor disaffirms as permitted; may make contract except re real property or personal property not under immediate control; may be disaffirmed if minor under 16 before age of majority or within one year afterwards; if 16 or older, can only disaffirm with restoration of consideration plus interest (26-2-1, *et seq.*)	Through a guardian or conservator or by a guardian ad litem (15-6-17(c))	
TENNESSEE	18; 21 re alcohol (1-3-113); Uniform Gifts to Minors Act (67-8-101)	No provision through marriage	May disaffirm within reasonable time after attaining age of majority; may also ratify expressly or by failure to disaffirm within reasonable time	May sue by guardian, next friend, or pauper's oath; defense by guardian *ad litem* (20-12-129; 21-1-701; 29-15-106)	
TEXAS	18 (Civ. Prac. & Rem. §129.01); Uniform Gifts to Minors Act (Prop. §141 *et seq.*)	If resident and 17 or 16 if living apart from guardian or parents and is self supporting or by marriage (Fam. §31.01)	Must disaffirm within reasonable time after reaching age of majority	Guardian, next friend, guardian *ad litem* (Tex. R. Civ. P. v. 44, 173)	Hospital, medical, surgical, and dental under certain circumstances or treatment for venereal disease, drug dependency, pregnancy with exception of abortion (Fam. §35.03)
UTAH	18 (§15-2-1) Uniform Transfers to Minors Act (75-5a-101 *et seq.*)	Marriage (15-2-1)	Bound for necessaries; otherwise, contracts valid unless disaffirmed within reasonable time after reaching age of majority and restoration of consideration (15-2-2, *et seq.*); minor 16 or over may contract for insurance (31A-21-103)	By guardian or guardian *ad litem* only (UT Rules of Civ. P. 17(b))	Informed consent of parent, guardian or authorized person must be obtained or female in connection with pregnancy or childbirth (78-14-5)

Table 33: Legal Ages—Continued

State	Age of Majority	Emancipation	Contracts	Ability to Sue	Consent to Medical Treatment
VERMONT	18 (§1-173); 21 re alcohol (7-2 (26)); Uniform Gifts to Minors Act (14-3201)		Voidable, subject to making restitution where possible	May sue by next friend; defendant infant represented by guardian *ad litem* (14-2657)	
VIRGINIA	18 (§1-13.42); 21 re alcohol (4.1-304); Uniform Transfers to Minors Act (31-37, *et seq.*)		Voidable as at Common Law subject to making restitution when possible with various exceptions for necessities	Next friend; defendant infant represented by guardian *ad litem* (8.01-8)	
WASHINGTON	18 (§26.28.010, *et seq.*); Uniform Transfers to Minors Act (11.114)		Bound for contracts for necessities; other contracts valid unless disaffirmed within reasonable time after reaching age of majority and restitution where possible of consideration (26.28.030, *et seq.*)	By guardian; if 14 or over may apply himself for court-appointed guardian; if under 14 application must be made to court through relative or friend (4.08.050)	
WEST VIRGINIA	21 (Ch. 60-3-22, Art. 3, §22); Uniform Transfers to Minors Act (Ch. 36-7-1)	By marriage, if under 16; if over 16 unmarried may apply to court; must show ability to support oneself and make decisions (Ch. 49-7-27)	Common law governs; ratification must be in writing and signed by charged party (Ch. 55-1-1)	In own name, next friend, or guardian; defends by guardian *ad litem* (Ch. 56-4-9)	
WISCONSIN	18 (§990.01(3)); Uniform Transfers to Minors Act (880.61)	By marriage unless incompetent (880.04(1))	Valid only for necessaries; necessaries contracts not valid if no implied or express provision for payment exists; contract made by infant may be ratified by acts or words after reaching age of majority, *Halbman v. Lemke* 298 NW2d 562 (1980); *Madison General Hosp. v. Haack,* 369 NW2d 663 (1985); *In re Kane's Estate,* 168 NW 402 (1918)	By guardian or guardian *ad litem* (803.01(3))	

Table 33: Legal Ages—Continued

State	Age of Majority	Emancipation	Contracts	Ability to Sue	Consent to Medical Treatment
WYOMING	18 (§14-1-101) Uniform Transfers to Minors Act (34-13-114, *et seq.*)	Through marriage, military service, or at age 17 if living separate, apart from parents; parents consent to living arrangement; minor deemed capable of handling financial affairs; and income is lawfully derived (14-1-201, *et seq.*)		General guardian, committee, conservator; otherwise by next friend or guardian *ad litem*, Wy Rule of Civil Proc. 17(c)	Yes if married, military, guardian can't be located, or living apart and self-supporting or is emancipated (14-1-101)

34. MEDICAL RECORDS

Federal, state, and local governments are responsible for protecting and safeguarding the public health and welfare. Accordingly, during terms of various epidemics the state has required the registration of infected persons in order to treat and/or quarantine them and to study the spread of the disease to ultimately control and eradicate it. Thus, although access to medical records is highly guarded, the reporting of diseases is widely practiced at all levels of government. The Center for Disease Control, for example, publishes *The Morbidity and Mortality Weekly Report,* containing a comprehensive list of all reported illnesses by both state and region that benefits the family practice doctor as well as the epidemiologist. The reports of cases that are reported, from the flu to various venereal diseases to AIDS (acquired immunodeficiency syndrome), are given in confidence, and access to the records is forbidden for most other purposes.

The outbreak of AIDS has sparked controversy over the confidentiality of medical records and diagnoses. Some employers and insurance companies have sought to have individuals tested for the HIV virus, which can lead to AIDS, before hiring in order to prevent considerable expenses in the future as the employee's health fails. Often these same parties argue for access to medical records for background checks as part of the interview process. The great tension regarding the rights of individuals with the HIV virus or AIDS, the public's interest in controlling and fighting the epidemic, and the interest of employers, insurers, and health officials in providing adequate and affordable medical care has created a very dynamic ethical and legal dilemma that will not soon be resolved.

The laws controlling and regulating access to medical records vary greatly from state to state, although the basic protection is always there: a person's medical records are personal and private. As is historically the case, the federal government has gotten increasingly involved in the area of individual rights and has enacted a number of pieces of privacy legislation. For example, the Federal Privacy Act of 1974 requires the release of information in federal files to the subject individual upon request, although some government agencies have established regulations allowing the release of information to a physician chosen by the requesting individual (5 U.S.C. 552a(f)(3)). Federally funded community mental health and mental retardation centers must maintain safeguards to preserve confidentiality and protect the rights of patients (52 U.S.C. 2689(d)(2)), and the Department of Defense may not use for any adverse personnel decision any personal information obtained in interviews with members of the service who are HIV positive (PL 49-661 §705(c)).

This chapter treats all statutes that could be found concerning privacy and medical records. It must be noted, however, that this emerging field is increasingly subject to revision and new legislative attention. In addition, in certain areas such as AIDS information, the courts may have construed other statutes as protecting or not protecting AIDS victims. In these cases the courts may be awaiting or inviting legislative action. Spaces on the chart that are left blank are those situations where specific laws cannot be found; this does not necessarily mean that an individual is without protection in these areas.

Table 34: Medical Records

State	Who Has Access	Privilege	Mandatory Reporting	Patient Waiver	Insurance Purposes	AIDS
ALABAMA	Notifiable disease records confidential (§22-11A-2)			Waiver of medical record of persons infected with sexually transmitted disease by written consent of patient (§22-11A-22)		An individual must be notified of a positive test result including face-to-face counseling, information on health care services and services related to locating and testing persons who have been in contact with infected individual. Otherwise confidentiality must be maintained §22-11A-53 & §22-11A-54
ALASKA	Any agent authorized by the principal, custodial, or non-custodial parent (§25.20.130; 13.26.344); Dept. of Social Services for financial records of medical assistance beneficiaries (§47.07.074)	In the case of emergency medical services, records of those treated may be disclosed to limited individuals for limited purposes (§18.08.087		Mental health records may be disclosed only with patient or an individual to whom the patient has given written consent to have information disclosed §47.30.845(2)		

Table 34: Medical Records—Continued

State	Who Has Access	Privilege	Mandatory Reporting	Patient Waiver	Insurance Purposes	AIDS
ARIZONA	Communicable disease related information confidential; release of information by consent or according to §36-664(A)(1)-(12)	Physicians and surgeons in most cases (§12-2235)	Nonaccidental injuries, malnourishment, physical neglect, sexual abuse, or other deprivation with intent to cause or allow injury or death of minor child and which cannot be attributed to other than medical history or accident must be reported to peace officer or child protective services. Such reports are confidential and may be used only in authorized judicial or administrative proceedings(§13-3620); reports and records about abused or incapacitated adult may only be used in authorized judicial or administrative proceedings (§46-454).			Any release of information must specifically authorize HIV-related information. Person with confidential HIV-related information may not be compelled to disclose information by subpoena, search warrant, or other judicial process, but may report if there is an identifiable third party at risk; no prohibition from listing in death certificate (§36-664)

Table 34: Medical Records—Continued

State	Who Has Access	Privilege	Mandatory Reporting	Patient Waiver	Insurance Purposes	AIDS
ARKANSAS	Not open to public (§25-19-105); patient (§23-76-129); or through patient's attorney (§16-46-106)	If a doctor believes the patient should be denied access to medical records, the doctor must provide patient (or patient's guardian/ attorney) a written determination that disclosure of such info would be detrimental to patient's health or well-bring (§16-46-106)		Express consent (§23-76-129)		Reporting required to Arkansas Dept. of Health by physicians and other medical and lab directors (§20-15-906); all information and reporting confidential (§20-15-904)
CALIFORNIA	§1795.12 Repealed by stats 1995, c. 415 (S.B. 1360), §104; §1795.14 Repealed by Stats 1995, c. 415 (S.B. 1360), §104	Doctors, including psychotherapists and psychiatrists (Ev. §1010); patient must waive doctor-patient confidentiality when plaintiff in civil suit (Ev. §1016)		Patient must waive doctor-patient confidentiality when plaintiff in civil suit (Ev. §1016); other: Civ. Code §56.	Insurer may obtain to the extent noted in (Civ. Code §56.10(c)(2)) Information disclosed to the extent necessary to allow responsibility for payment to be determined and made	Blood testing must be anonymous and test results may not disclose identities of persons tested even through subpoena (H&S 120975 and 121025)
COLORADO	Patient or designated representative with written authority, except for psychiatric records that would have significant negative psychological impact, in which case patient is entitled to summary (§25-1-801); both parents in joint custody (§14-10-123.5 repealed)		Certain diseases and conditions require reporting without patient consent			Confidential counseling and testing preferred; anonymous testing conducted for persons with high risk (§25-4-1405.5)

Table 34: Medical Records—Continued

State	Who Has Access	Privilege	Mandatory Reporting	Patient Waiver	Insurance Purposes	AIDS
CONNECTICUT	Patient may see and copy (§4-105); state law limits disclosure of mental health data about a patient by name or other identifier (§52-146h); state departments may receive information on patients only to the extent necessary to obtain support or payment for care of patient; all information is confidential (§17b-225)					Confidential HIV-related information disclosed only according to §19a-583
DELAWARE	All information and records of known or suspected cases of sexually transmitted disease (STD), including HIV infections, shall be strictly confidential; released only under certain circumstances:Tit.16 §711	No legally recognized privilege except attorney-client and priest-penitent shall apply in situations involving known or suspected child abuse, neglect, exploitation or abandonment (Tit. 16 §909)	Sexually transmitted diseases reported to division of Public Health, some reported in number and manner only (Tit. 16 §702)			Strictly confidential with exceptions made under certain circumstances (Tit. 16 §711)

Table 34: Medical Records—Continued

State	Who Has Access	Privilege	Mandatory Reporting	Patient Waiver	Insurance Purposes	AIDS
DISTRICT OF COLUMBIA	Person of record or his legal representative (§14-307); public mental health facility must make patient records available to patient's attorney or personal physician upon that person's written authorization (§21-562)	There is a physician or surgeon or mental health professsion-patient privilege. But the privilege is waived and professional must disclose confidential information in any court proceeding if judge determines that privilege should be waived in the interest of justice(§14-307) (§6-2511)				Information and records pertaining to persons with AIDS are confidential (§6-2805)
FLORIDA	Patient or his/her legal representative or health care provider except for psychological or psychiatric records which may be provided as a report instead of copies of records (§455.241); patient's guardian, curator, or personal representative, anyone authorized in writing (§395.3025)	Psychotherapist-patient (§455.241)		Medical records not disclosed unless patient gives written authorizations exceptions to the written authorization as provided in §455.241(2)		Confidential with exceptions to nondisclosure as provided in §381.004 (3)(e)
GEORGIA	Disclosure of medical records pursuant to laws requiring disclosure or to limited consent to disclosure does not destroy confidential or privileged nature (§24-9-42)	Psychiatrist (§24-9-21); physician (§24-9-40); pharmacist (§24-9-40)	Venereal disease and suspected child abuse (§§19-7-5; 31-17-2)	Patient must make written authorization or waiver (or parents/guardian in case of minor) except by subpoena or appropriate court order (§24-9-40)		All AIDS information confidential; may be disclosed to that person or in case of minor to parents or guardian and with notice, to reasonably believed spouse/partner (§24-9-47)

Table 34: Medical Records—Continued

State	Who Has Access	Privilege	Mandatory Reporting	Patient Waiver	Insurance Purposes	AIDS
HAWAII	Patient or his attorney, but doctor may require patient's authorization to make them available to attorney if detrimental to patient's health (§622-57)		Those with diseases or conditions declared to be communicable or dangerous to the public health (§325-2)	Medical research; sources of info protected in maternal and perinatal studies, in mental health and mental retardation studies and in cancer studies (§§324-1, *et seq.*)		All records of AIDS, HIV, or AIDS-related patients are confidential; release of information under circumstances in §325-101
IDAHO	Patient or agent by subpoena (§9-420); parent of minor child whether custodial or non (§32-717A); in some civil actions records may be open to discovery (§39-1392(e)); public medical records or records of those with reportable diseases exempt from disclosure (§9-340)	Physician (§9-203(4))	Child abuse cases within 24 hours (§16-1619); enumerated venereal diseases including AIDS and HIV (§39-602)	Patient or doctor or nurse responsible for entries in hospital record may request protective order to deny or limit access (§9-420)		Confidentiality of patient information maintained; use of information restricted to "public health requirements" and "those with a legitimate need to know" (§39-609)
ILLINOIS			Child abuse (325 ILCS 5/4); sexually transmissible diseases (410 ILCS §325/4)	Right to privacy and confidentiality in health care may be waived in writing by patient or patient's physician (410 ILCS 5013)		AIDS test information must be kept confidential (410 ILCS 305/1, *et seq.*) No disclosure of AIDS test information without consent, court order or as listed in 410 ILCS 305/9

Table 34: Medical Records—Continued

State	Who Has Access	Privilege	Mandatory Reporting	Patient Waiver	Insurance Purposes	AIDS
INDIANA	Patient, authorized representative, authorized health care worker 34-43-1-1, *et. seq.;* 16-41-8-1, *et seq.*	Doctor-patient communication not divulgible 34-46-3-1		Child abuse must be reported immediately by healthcare and non-healthcare workers to child protection agency or law enforcement 31-33-5-1	Insurance company may obtain records with written consent (§16-39-5-2)	All HIV cases must be reported (§16-41-2-3)
IOWA	Medical and psychiatric records held by Dept. of Human Services are confidential and may only be distributed to other agencies in course of official business or researchers so long as identity is not disclosed. (§217.30)		Confidential reports of venereal disease must be filed (§140.3 &. 4)			All reports and information related to HIV are strictly confidential medical information; released under circumstances in 141.10
KANSAS		Doctor-patient (with exceptions) (§§60-427); Psychologist-patient (74-5323)	Any physician or lab director with knowledge of AIDS sufferer must report to secretary of health and environment; information shall be confidential and disclosed as per §65-6002 (c)	Mental health records may not be disclosed except with patient's consent or court order or with consent of the head of the treatment facility (§59-2931)		Any physician or lab director with knowledge of AIDS sufferer must report to secretary of health and environment; information shall be confidential and disclosed as per §65-6002 (c)
KENTUCKY	Patient may make written request for medical record to hospital or provider (§422.317)	Psychiatrist-patient privilege (§422.330)		Patient or physician may ask to prohibit or limit use by protective order (§422.315)		Test results disclosed only to those listed in §214.181

Table 34: Medical Records—Continued

State	Who Has Access	Privilege	Mandatory Reporting	Patient Waiver	Insurance Purposes	AIDS
LOUISIANA	Healthcare providers must provide copies of records upon patient's request (unless injurious to health or welfare of patient) or subject to subpoena (§40:1299.96)	Healthcare provider-patient (usually waived in cases of child abuse or molestation) (Art. 510 Louisiana Code of Evidence)				Information related to HIV is confidential; disclosure according to §§1300.14 and 1300.15
MAINE	Patient unless doctor thinks it would be detrimental to his health, then to an authorized representative (22 §1711); attorney general in a criminal proceeding although still confidential (5 §200-E)	Doctor-patient; psychologist-patient (both abrogated in child protective activity) (22 §4015)				No person may disclose the results of an HIV test with exceptions in §19203
MARYLAND	Records of Secretary of Health & Mental Hygiene must be kept confidential. It is unlawful to disclose them except for research (Health-Gen §4-101, *et seq.*)	Psychologist/psychiatrist-patient (Cts. & Jud. Proc. §9-109)	Medical Advisory Board allowed to report to Motor Vehicle Administration on patients whose driving may be impaired for mental or physical reasons (Transp. §16-118)		When insurance company compiles medical file for health or life policies, they must permit claimant, agent or applicant to inspect file except information provided by doctor not available for 5 years unless doctor authorizes written release (Art. 48A §490c)	Test results confidential (Health Gen. §18-334) but if individual refuses to notify sexual or needle-sharing partners physician may inform local health officer (Health-Gen. §18-337)

465

Table 34: Medical Records—Continued

State	Who Has Access	Privilege	Mandatory Reporting	Patient Waiver	Insurance Purposes	AIDS
MASSACHUSETTS	Patient has right to confidentiality of all records and communications to extent provided by law and to inspect and receive copy of medical records (psychotherapist may give summary of record if it would adversely affect patient's well-being (Ch. 112 §12CC); employer requiring physical exam of any employee shall upon request furnish copy of medical report (Ch. 149 §19A); mental health records private except for court order, at patient's request, or if mental health commissioner allows for sake of best interest of patient and as required by section 178C-1780, inclusive of chapter (Ch. 123 §36)		Any injury from discharge of gun or a burn affecting over 5% of the body or a rape or sexual assault (victim's name not included in report) (Ch. 112 §12A and §12A½)			Labs and hospitals that conduct blood tests for AIDS must not disclose results without obtaining written informed consent of patients (Ch. 111 §70F)
MICHIGAN	Any review entity (331.531); Department of Health shall protect privileged communications and individual's expectation of privacy with regard to Department's activities (§333.2611)	Physician-patient privilege is recognized (§600.2157)	Serious communicable diseases (§333.5117)			All reports of HIV infection and AIDS are confidential; release subject to §333.5131

Table 34: Medical Records—Continued

State	Who Has Access	Privilege	Mandatory Reporting	Patient Waiver	Insurance Purposes	AIDS
MINNESOTA	Patient, patient's representative, or minor's parent or guardian has right to copy doctor's and hospital records about themselves (if provider determines that information is detrimental to physical or mental health of patient, may withhold information and supply to third party) (§144.335); mentally committed patients have access (§253B.03)	Physician, nurse, or psychologist may not disclose confidential information acquired in professional capacity without the consent of the patient (§595-02)				HIV prevention program–some reporting requirements (§214.19); victims can require HIV testing of sex offender and know results (§611A.07); commissioner may subpoena privileged medical information of those exposed by HIV infected dentist or physician in order to notify patients (§144.054 subdiv.2)
MISSISSIPPI	Medical or dental review committee for evaluation of quality of care; patient's identity not divulged (§41-63-1, and 3)	Physician, dentist, nurse, pharmacist and patient (§13-1-21)	Licensing boards may establish reporting requirements for Hepatitis B virus and HIV (§41-34-1, *et seq.*)	Patient waiver of doctor's privilege implied to comply with state and local health departments and for information regarding communicable diseases (§13-1-21)		Convicted sex offenders shall be tested for HIV; results reported to victims and spouses (§99-19-203)
MISSOURI		Attorney/ client physician, psychologies or dentist/ patient(§491. 060)				All information concerning one's HIV status is confidential; disclosure subject to §191.656

Table 34: Medical Records—Continued

State	Who Has Access	Privilege	Mandatory Reporting	Patient Waiver	Insurance Purposes	AIDS
MONTANA	Patient may authorize disclosure of healthcare information (50-16-526); without patient's authorization (50-16-530); all records of Department of Public Health and Human Services are confidential; disclosed according to §41-3-205 (3)	Doctor-patient (§26-1-805); Psychologist-client (§26-1-807)	Must report if conduct is such that might expose another to infection (50-18-106)			Person may not disclose or be compelled to disclose the identity of a subject of an HIV test or results (50-16-1009); HIV testing: 50-16-1007
NEBRASKA	Counsel for mentally ill patient (§83-1053); only patient, patient's guardian if patient is legally incompetent, mental health board, persons authorized by an order of a judge or court, persons authorized by written permission of the subject or Nebraska State Patrol or Dept of Health and Human Services pursuant to §09-2409.01 (§83-1068); medical review panel (§44-2843)		Reporting of patients with cancer to Dept. of Health upon its request for Cancer Registry (§81-642); brain injuries for Brain Injury Registry (§81.654); all "reportable diseases" (including sexually transmitted diseases) (§71.503.01)	Privileged communications waived by patient consent and court of record		
NEVADA	Patient has right to inspect and copy both doctor's and hospital's records; also authorized representative or investigator (§629.061); Required to forward record upon transfer to new medical facility (do not need patient's consent) (§§433.332; 449.705)	Privilege may be claimed by patient, his guardian or conservator or by the personal representative of a deceased patient. And doctor and Family therapist. (§49.235 and 49.248)	Communicable diseases (§441A.150)	Patient may refuse to disclose or forbid any other person (including family members) from disclosing medical information (§49.225); right does not extend to mental patient; other exceptions (§49.245)		

Table 34: Medical Records—Continued

State	Who Has Access	Privilege	Mandatory Reporting	Patient Waiver	Insurance Purposes	AIDS
NEW HAMPSHIRE	Records are deemed property of patient (§332:I-1); anyone with durable power of attorney for health care for patient (§137-J:7); patient and one with his written consent or with written certification of ombudsman (§161-F:14); no employee may be required to bear cost of any medical exam or furnish any records required by employer as condition of employment (§275:3)	Doctor-patient (§329:26)	Communicable diseases (141-C:7)			All records and information pertaining to person's HIV testing are confidential and protected from unwarranted intrusion (141-F:8) (Disclosures pursuant to 141-F:7 and F:8)
NEW JERSEY	§30:4-24.3 Confidential nature of certificates, applications, records and reports made pursuant to the provisions of Title 30 of the revised statutes and shall not be disclosed except as provided in §30:4-24.3. §2A:82-42: Injured person or his legal representative who has asserted (or is about to assert.) A claim for compensation or damages has right to examine hospital records.	Psychologist-patient (45:14B-28); Physician-patient (2A:84A-22.1, .2)	Child abuse (§9:6-8.30); pertussis vaccine (§26:2N-5); venereal disease (§26:4-41); AIDS (26:5C-6)			All records with identifying information are confidential (26:5C-6); disclosure per 26:5C-8, *et seq.*
NEW MEXICO	Office of state long-term care ombudsman for patient/resident/client (§28-17-13); confidential shall not be disclosed without authorization from patient. Authorization not required for disclosure of confidential information in certain circumstance. (§43-1-19); worker, employer, or employer's insurer, or the appropriate peer review organization, all records of any health care service provided the worker, upon written request (§52-10-1)	Physician/psychologist-patient (Rule 11-509)	Sexually transmitted diseases (§24-1-7)			Performance of test and results are confidential; disclosure subject to §24-2B-6

Table 34: Medical Records—Continued

State	Who Has Access	Privilege	Mandatory Reporting	Patient Waiver	Insurance Purposes	AIDS
NEW YORK	Medical director of prison in reference to inmate (Corrections §601); director of youth facility of a juvenile offender (Exec. §508); records access –no disclosures without patient consent; ombudsman (Exec §544); inspector of a mental facility –all information kept confidential (Men. Hyg. §16.11); physician or hospital must release medical file to another physician or hospital upon written request of parent, guardian, or patient; records concerning venereal disease treatment or abortion for minor may not be released, even to parent (NY Pub. Health §17)	Physician, dentist, podiatrist, chiropractor, and nurse. (Civ. Prac. §4504)				All HIV-related information is confidential and may only be disclosed according to §2782 N.Y. Pub. Health
NORTH CAROLINA	All privileged patient medical records possessed by Department of Health or local health department are confidential (§130A-12); pharmacists when necessary to provide services (§90-85.35)		Physicians, lab directors and local health directors must report communicable diseases; hospitals may report (§130A-133, *et seq.*)			All AIDS information and records are confidential; subject to release only according to §130A-143

Table 34: Medical Records—Continued

State	Who Has Access	Privilege	Mandatory Reporting	Patient Waiver	Insurance Purposes	AIDS
NORTH DAKOTA		Physician/psychotherapist-patient (§31-01-06) pursuant to North Dakota Rules of Ev., Rule 503	Sexually transmitted diseases, contagious, infectious, or chronic diseases which impact the public significantly and child abuse or neglect. The state department designates the diseases or conditions that must by reported. Such disease/conditions may include contagious, infection, sexually transmitted, or chronic diseases or any illness or injury which may have a significant impact on public health. (§§23-07-01; 50-25.1-01 to 03)			Information regarding HIV infection is strictly confidential; release subject to §23-07-02.2)
OHIO	Employee or designated representative may request records from employer, physician, health care professional, hospital, or lab when they are contracted by employer (§4113.23)	Doctor-patient (§2317-02(B))	Child abuse (§2151-421); occupational diseases (3701.25); cases of cancer for cancer registry (3701.262); contagious or infectious diseases (including AIDS) §3701.24			Disclosure of HIV or AIDS-related information subject to §3701.243

Table 34: Medical Records—Continued

State	Who Has Access	Privilege	Mandatory Reporting	Patient Waiver	Insurance Purposes	AIDS
OKLAHOMA	Patient has access to medical records in the cases of psychological/psychiatric records, patient has access if consented to by treating physician or court orders or upon finding that it is in the best interest of patient(Tit. 76 §19); health professional may inform parents of treatment needed or provided to minor; such disclosure does not breach right to privacy (Tit. 63 §2602; Tit. 43A §1-109)	Physician/psychotherapist-patient (Tit. 12 §2503; Tit. 43A §1-109))	Child abuse (physical, sexual and/or neglect); communicable or venereal disease (Tit. 10 §7103; Tit. 63 §1-528(b))			HIV tests or records upon written request of person affected, or in cases of certain crimes, test results released to victim (Tit. 63 §1-525)
OREGON	Institutions are encouraged to permit patient to copy doctor and hospital records and prevent unnecessary disclosure (§192.525)		Suspected violence: physical injury with knife, gun or other deadly weapon (in confidence)(§146-750)			HIV test results confidential (§433.075)
PENNSYLVANIA	Mental health records confidential and without a person's written consent may not be released/disclosed except as provided in §7111	Physician privilege limited to civil matters (Tit. 42 §5929)				All HIV-related information confidential; limited disclosure under Tit. 35 §7607
RHODE ISLAND	Patient (§5-37-22); holders of medical records must keep them confidential; patient's written consent generally required (§5-37.3-4)		Occupational diseases (§23-5-5); sexually transmitted and communicable diseases (§23-8-1; §23-11-5)			Disclosure of AIDS test result to third parties limited by §23-6-17

Table 34: Medical Records—Continued

State	Who Has Access	Privilege	Mandatory Reporting	Patient Waiver	Insurance Purposes	AIDS
SOUTH CAROLINA	Express written consent of patient (§44-115-40)	Mental health provider-patient (19-11-95)	Sexually transmitted diseases (z016744-29-70)			Information and records are strictly confidential except under circumstances in §44-29-135; in minor cases, if attending public school, superintendent and nurse must be notified; Court orders: §44-29-136
SOUTH DAKOTA		Physician-patient; waived for criminal proceedings or if physical or mental health of person is at issue (§19-2-3)	Venereal disease (34-23-2); child abuse or neglect (26-8A-3)			Victims of sexual assault may request testing and receive notification of results (23A-35B-1, *et seq.*)
TENNESSEE	Hospital records property of hospital, upon court order or written request of patient may see (§68-11-304); medical records of patients in state facilities and those whose care is paid for by state funds are confidential (§10-7-504)	Psychiatrists (§24-1-207); psychologists (§63-11-213)	Communicable diseases (68-5-101); sexually transmitted diseases (68-10-101)			No liability for real estate agent failing to disclose that occupant was HIV-infected (66-5-207); law enforcement officer may request arrested person be tested for Hepatitis B or HIV if exposed to blood (68-10-116); records strictly confidential; released as per 68-10-113

Table 34: Medical Records—Continued

State	Who Has Access	Privilege	Mandatory Reporting	Patient Waiver	Insurance Purposes	AIDS
TEXAS	Medical information identifiable as to individuals is to be kept confidential and information used for studies is privileged (Health & Safety §161.022)		Bullet or gunshot wounds (Health & Safety §161.041); certain occupational diseases (Health & Safety §84.003); certain communicable diseases (Health & Safety §81.041)			A person may require another person to undergo a medical prodedure or test designed to determine or help determine if a person has AIDS or HIV infection, antibodies to HIV, or infection with any other probable causative agent of AIDs unless as stipulated in §81.102. A test is confidential . May not be disclosed except as provided in §81.103; mandatory testing of person who may have infected law enforcement officials and certain other persons (Health & Safety §81.050)
UTAH	Patient's attorney with patient's written authorization (§78-25-25)	Doctor-patient (§78-24-8(4))	Suspected child abuse (§62A-4A-403); communicable and infectious diseases (including HIV and AIDS) (§26-6-3)			All reports regarding communicable diseases are confidential. May only be disclosed to authorized healthcare workers or researchers. 26-6-27

Table 34: Medical Records—Continued

State	Who Has Access	Privilege	Mandatory Reporting	Patient Waiver	Insurance Purposes	AIDS
VERMONT		Physician, chiropractor, dentist, nurse, or mental health professional not allowed to disclose information acquired in attending a patient in a professional capacity (Tit. 12 §1612)	Infectious venereal diseases (Tit. 18 §1093)			HIV-related testing and counseling information disclosed upon court order show-ing "compel-ling need" that can't be accommo-dated "by other means" (pseudonym substituted if possible) (Tit. 12 §1705)
VIRGINIA	Subject person can review his/her medical and mental records; however, mental records may not be personally reviewed in physician feels review would be injurious to persons physical or mental health or well-being (§2.1-342(B)(C)); patient or his attorney upon patient's written request to hospital or health care records except for records when doctor declares release would be injurious to patient's health or well-being (§8.01-413)	Duly licensed practitioner of any branch of the healing arts dealing with patient in professional capacity including clinical psychologist (§8.01-399)			Insurance company must provide medical information to individual or to medical professional designated by individual; must notify individual that information was released at time of disclosure (38.2-608)	All test results are confidential, released only to that per-son, his legal representa-tive, Depart-ment of Health, par-ents of minor, spouse, by court order, and others authorized by law (§32.1-36.1)
WASHINGTON	Patient may authorize disclosure (70.02.030); situations without patient's authorization: 70.02.050	Psychologist (18.83.110)	Child abuse or adult dependent or developmentally disabled (§26.44.030); tuberculosis (70.28.010); sexually transmitted diseases (70.24.105)			Disclosure of identity of person investigated, considered, or requested to test for HIV permitted to those under 70.24.105

Table 34: Medical Records—Continued

State	Who Has Access	Privilege	Mandatory Reporting	Patient Waiver	Insurance Purposes	AIDS
WEST VIRGINIA	Patient through written request; summary provided in case of psychiatric or psychological treatment (16-29-1)		Sexually transmitted diseases §16-4-6 and those diseases or conditions for which a report is requried by the state health director (§16-2A-5); suspected child abuse (§49-6A-2); gunshot and other wounds; burns (§§61-2-27 and 27A)	Physician-patient (except for W.V. Board of Medicine) (§30-3-9)		Disclosure of identity of person tested for HIV according to §16-3C-3
WISCONSIN	Patient may inspect and copy upon submitting statement of informed consent (§146.83); Patient health care records confidential. May be released to certain persons or to persons with the informed consent of the patient or of a person authorized by the patient. (§146.82)	Physician, registered nurse, chiropractor, psycholoigist, social worker, marriage and family therapist and professional counselor-patient (§905.04)	Sexually transmitted diseases (§252.11); tuberculosis (§252.07); abused or neglected children and abused unborn children (§48.981); communicable diseases (§252.05)			AIDS/HIV test results must remain confidential except as released per §252.15 (5)
WYOMING	Patient (with written authorization) §35-2-606; without authorization: §35-2-609	Doctor may testify only with patient's express consent or when patient voluntarily testifies himself on medical matters (§1-12-101)	Child abuse; sexually transmitted diseases; communicable disease (§§14-3-205; 35-4-130; 35-4-103)			

35. NEGLIGENCE

Negligence is an actionable tort. This means that if one person's carelessness causes another personal injury, the injured party may sue to recover damages (money) for his or her injuries. The idea that a person can sue for negligence is a relatively new phenomenon, only about a century old.

The reason for negligence's late recognition is because common law traditionally recognized only intentional torts; that is, it held parties responsible for injuries that were the result of intentional acts. It was irrelevant that the actor did not intend to injure anyone, much less the injured party, but it only needed to be shown that the actor intended the *action* that caused the injury. In these cases, evidence of who caused what injury was affirmative, direct, and fairly objective.

The concept of permitting someone to recover damages for injuries caused by someone's *lack of action* or *failure to do something* was a revolutionary concept. Since its recognition as an action in tort, negligence has become a major source of very large jury awards. It is the root of all product liability cases. When people complain about our legal system and the outrageous verdicts being awarded nowadays, they are speaking about negligence.

Originally, negligence was recognized by the courts as part of the common law. Over time, as causes of action became more numerous and as damages became larger, various efforts were undertaken to limit the appeal of negligence lawsuits.

Contributory Negligence

When contributory negligence first appeared in the repertoire of personal injury lawyers, the standards of proof needed to succeed were quite high and very severe. Originally, under the doctrine of contributory negligence if it were shown that the plaintiff contributed in any way to his injuries, he was barred from any recovery. This has been modified over time to permit the plaintiff to recover even if he contributed to his injuries, as long as his fault is under 50 percent. In these cases, recovery is relative to fault. For instance, if a jury finds a party's injuries worth $100,000 and holds that the party was 25 percent at fault,

the party's recovery would be $75,000. On the other hand, if the jury found the party 60 percent at fault, the party would be barred from any recovery.

Comparative Fault

The doctrine of contributory negligence eventually evolved, in some states, into a system of comparative fault that permitted recovery on a completely relative scale. Thus, in an accident one could be 90 percent at fault for one's own personal injury and still sue to recover the 10 percent of the damages suffered that were caused by the other party.

Contribution Among Tortfeasors

In the doctrine of contribution among tortfeasors, when there are multiple tortfeasors ("guilty" parties), all parties are equally liable for the damages caused to the injured party. This doctrine is quite harsh. For example, if the driver of a truck hits a pedestrian at night and the jury holds that the city is 15 percent responsible because it did not properly maintain the lighting at that portion of the road and the truck driver, who is 85 percent at fault, is uninsured, unemployed, and without assets, the city can be made to pay 100 percent of the damages. In most comparative fault states liability is the proportionate responsibility of each party.

The State of the Law

As can be seen by looking at the table of negligence laws, there is great diversity among the states as to how negligence is handled. As the law of negligence continues to mature and change, courts have led the way in defining the laws and legislatures have in may cases responded with statutes that both recognize the cause of action and often limit it as well.

There have been many attempts over the years to have Congress or state legislatures pass laws that would specifically limit the amount of recovery available to plaintiffs in negligence actions. So far, none has met with much success. Under the general term "tort reform," such acts promise to be proposed in the future.

Table 35: Negligence

State	Code Section	Uniform Act	Comparative Negligence	Contributory Negligence—Limit to Plaintiff's Recovery	Judicial Imposition of Comparative Negligence	Contribution Among Tortfeasors
ALABAMA	None	No		Plaintiff's negligence is a bar to recovery. Contributory negligence is an affirmative defense. ARCP, Rule 86)(c) *Jackson* v. *Waller*, 410 So.2d 98 (1982)	No.	No. *Gobble v. Bradford*, 147 So. 619 (1933); Con instrument with joint payees or indorsers, see §7-3-116
ALASKA	23.25.010 (Employer's liability for negligence)	No	Yes, §09.17.060 Contributory fault diminishes proportionately the award based on claimant's fault, but does not bar recovery ("Pure" comparative negligence)	See Comparative Negligence	*Kaatz v. Alaska*, 540 P.2d 1037 (1975); "Pure" form adopted and codified herein	Yes; §09.17.080(d)
ARIZONA	12-2505	Yes; §12-2501, *et seq.*	No right to comparative negligence if claimant intentionally, wilfully or wantonly caused/ contributed to injury or wrongful death §12-2505(A) in the pocket part			Yes; §12-2501, *et seq.*
ARKANSAS	16-64-122	Yes; 16-61-201 to 212	Liability determined by comparing claimant's fault w/ fault of party claimant seeks to recover damages §16-64-122	If Plaintiff's fault is of less degree than defendant's, he may recover amount diminished in proportion to degree of his own fault (§16-64-122); if plaintiff's fault is equal to or greater than defendant, he may not recover at all		Yes; §§16-61-201 to 212
CALIFORNIA	§1714	No	"Pure" form adopted by *Li v. Yellow Cab Co.,* 532 P.2d 1226 (1975).		*Li v. Yellow Cab Co.*, 119 Cal. Reptr. 858 (1975)	Yes; §1431.2 liability of each defendant per non-economic damages shall be several only and not joint.

Table 35: Negligence—Continued

State	Code Section	Uniform Act	Comparative Negligence	Contributory Negligence—Limit to Plaintiff's Recovery	Judicial Imposition of Comparative Negligence	Contribution Among Tortfeasors
COLORADO	13-21-111	Yes. §§13-50.5-101 to 13.50.5-106	Contributory negligence does not bar recovery if claimant's negligence is not greater than defendant's. But any damages allowed is diminished in proportion to claimant's attributed negligence	See Comparative Negligence		Yes; §§13-50.5-101 to 13.50.5-106
CONNECTICUT	52-572h		Comparative negligence does not bar recovery if claimant's negligence is not greater than combined negligence of defendant(s). However, damages are diminished in proportion to attributed negligence	See Comparative Negligence		Yes; §52-572(e); also §52-572(h). Must be brought within one year
DELAWARE	Tit. 10 §8132	Yes; Tit. 10 §§6301 to 6308	Claimant' contributory negligence does not bar recovery if such negligence is not greater than the defendant(s) negligence. But any awarded are diminished in proportion to claimant's attributed negligence	See Comparative Negligence		Yes; Tit. 10 §§6301 to 6308
DISTRICT OF COLUMBIA	None			Plaintiff's negligence is a bar to recovery except the liability of common carriers for injuries to employees, when plaintiff's negligence is slight and employer's is gross. See §44-402		No
FLORIDA	768.81, *et seq.*	Yes; §768.31	Any contributory fault chargeable to claimant diminishes proportionately the amount awarded as economic or uneconomic damages; §768.81	Percentage of own fault	*Hoffman v. Jones*, 280 So. 2d 431 (1973)	Yes; §768.31

Table 35: Negligence—Continued

State	Code Section	Uniform Act	Comparative Negligence	Contributory Negligence—Limit to Plaintiff's Recovery	Judicial Imposition of Comparative Negligence	Contribution Among Tortfeasors
GEORGIA	51-11-7	No	Claimant's contributory does not bar recovery provided his fault is less than defendant's and that by ordinary care claimant could not have avoided the consequences of defendant's negligence. However claimant's damages are diminished by amount in proportion to the amount of his fault.	If plaintiff by ordinary care could have avoided defendant's negligence, he is barred		Yes; §51-12-32
HAWAII	663-31	663-11 to 663-17	Contributory negligence or comparative responsibility does not bar recovery if claimant's negligence or comparative responsibility is not as great as defendants, but any damages are diminished in proportion to the negligence or comparative responsibility attributable to claimant	See comparative negligence.		§§663-11 to 663-17
IDAHO	6-801	No	Contributory negligence or comparative responsibility does not bar recovery if claimant's negligence or comparative responsibility is not as great as defendants, but any damages are diminished in proportion to the negligence or comparative responsibility attributable to claimant	See comparative negligence.		Yes; §6-803.
ILLINOIS	735 ILCS 5/ 2-1116	No	If plaintiff is more than 50% negligible, he is barred from recovery (735 ILCS 5/2-1116; passed 1986 in response to the "insurance crisis")	Over 50% negligence attributed to plaintiff; under 50% damages diminished in proportion to plaintiff's percentage of fault		Yes; 740 ILCS 100/0.01, *et seq.*

Table 35: Negligence—Continued

State	Code Section	Uniform Act	Comparative Negligence	Contributory Negligence—Limit to Plaintiff's Recovery	Judicial Imposition of Comparative Negligence	Contribution Among Tortfeasors
INDIANA	34-51-2-5, *et seq.*	No	Chargeable contributory fault diminishes proportion compensatory damages but does not bar recovery except as provided in 34-51-2-6.	Bar from recovery if contributory fault > fault of all persons whose fault proximatley contributed to clamant's damages.		No; §34-4-33-7, but section does not affect indemnity rights
IOWA	668.3; 668.5	No	Contributory fault does not bar recovery unless claimant's fault is greater than defendant's, but any damages diminished in proportion to attributable fault.	See comparative negligence.	*Goetzman v. Wichern,* 327 N.W. 2d 742 (1982)	Yes, §668.5
KANSAS	60-258a	No	Contributory negligence not a bar to recovery if claimant's negligence is less than causal negligence of defendants, but damages diminished in proportion to the amount of attributable negligence.	See comparative negligence.		Yes; 60-258a(a)
KENTUCKY	None	No	No; Failure to put child in safety restraint is statutorily not contributory negligence. (§189.125).	Employee not guilty of contributory negligence where violation by carrier of state/ federal safety statute contributed to injury or death. In the case were no safety statute has been violated, contributory negligence is not a bar to recovery, but damages diminished in proportion to the amount of attributable negligence. 277.320.	.	Yes; §412.030
LOUISIANA	La-Civ. Code Art 2323	No	Percentage of fault of all persons contributing is determined. If person who suffers as a result partly of his own negligence, the amount of damages reduced in proportion to% of attributable negligence.			No

Table 35: Negligence—Continued

State	Code Section	Uniform Act	Comparative Negligence	Contributory Negligence—Limit to Plaintiff's Recovery	Judicial Imposition of Comparative Negligence	Contribution Among Tortfeasors
MAINE	Tit. 14 §156	No.	Claim in respect of death or damage not defeated by reason of fault the person suffering the damage, but damages reduced to extent jury thinks just and equitable.	See comparative negligence.		No
MARYLAND	None	Art 50 repealed. Present provisions regarding joint Tort-feasors is in subtitle 14 of Title 3 of the courts and Judicial Proceedings Article.	Not using seatbelt is not contributory negligence (Transp. §§22-412.3 & 4)			Yes; §3-1401
MASSACHUSETTS	Ch. 231 §85	Ch. 231B §§1-4	Contributory negligence does not bar recovery if claimant's negligence is not greater than defendant's. But any damages allowed is diminished in proportion to claimant's attributed negligence	See comparative negligence.		Ch. 231B §§1-4
MICHIGAN	None		Allocation of liability in direct proportion to the person's percentage of fault. 600.2957.	Not a bar to recovery provided negligence is less than that of defendants. Further provisions applicable. 419.52 miscellaneous labor laws.	*Placek v. City of Sterling Heights*, 275 N.W.2d 511 (1979)	Yes; MCL 600.2925c
MINNESOTA	604.01, *et seq.*		Plaintiff's fault not greater than defendant's, but damages are diminished in proportion to fault	Plaintiff's fault greater than defendant's		No

Table 35: Negligence—Continued

State	Code Section	Uniform Act	Comparative Negligence	Contributory Negligence—Limit to Plaintiff's Recovery	Judicial Imposition of Comparative Negligence	Contribution Among Tortfeasors
MISSISSIPPI	11-7-15	No	Contributory negligence no bar to recovery, but damages diminished in proportion to the amount of attributable negligence.	See comparative negligence.		No.
MISSOURI	None		In products liability cases, comparative fault is an affirmative defense. Fault shall diminish damages proportionately but does not bar recovery. 537.765	Contributory fault as a compete bar to claimant's recovery in a products liability claim is abolished. doctrine of comparative fault to apply.	*Gustafson v. Benda*, 661 S.W. 2d 11 (1983)	Yes; §537.060
MONTANA	27-1-702	No	Claimant's negligence does not bar recovery if less than that of defendants. Damages diminished in proportion to the amount of negligence attributable.	See comparative negligence.		Yes; §27-1-703
NEBRASKA	25-21, 185.07 to 185.12		Plaintiff's award diminishes proportionally with negligence, but negligence equal to or greater than defendant's is a total bar.	See comparative negligence.		No; see §25-21, 185.10
NEVADA	41.141	17.225 to 17.305	Plaintiff's negligence not greater than defendant's	When claimant's negligence is greater than defendants, no recovery.		Yes; §§17.225 to 17.305
NEW HAMPSHIRE	507:7d	No	Contributory negligence does not bar recovery if claimant's negligence is not greater than defendant's. But any damages allowed is diminished in proportion to claimant's attributed negligence	See comparative negligence.		Yes; §507.7f

Table 35: Negligence—Continued

State	Code Section	Uniform Act	Comparative Negligence	Contributory Negligence—Limit to Plaintiff's Recovery	Judicial Imposition of Comparative Negligence	Contribution Among Tortfeasors
NEW JERSEY	2A:15-5.1, *et seq.*		Contributory negligence cannot be greater than the negligence of defendants. Damages diminished by the percentage sustained of negligence attributable to claimant	See comparative negligence.		Yes; 2A:15-5.3 & 2A:53A-2
NEW MEXICO	None	41-3-1 to 41-3-8	"Pure" comparative negligence		*Scott v. Rizzo,* 634 P.2d 1234 (1981)	Yes; §§41-3-1 to 41-3-8
NEW YORK	N.Y. Civ. Prac. L. & R. §§1411, *et seq.*		Contributory negligence does not bar recovery but damages are diminished in proportion to the attributable conduct.	See comparative negligence.		Yes; N.Y. Civ. Prac. L. & R. §§1401 *et seq.*
NORTH CAROLINA	None	§1B-1 to 1B-6	Defendant has burden of proving plaintiff was comparatively negligent (§1-139)			Yes; G.S. §§1B-1 to 1B-6
NORTH DAKOTA	None	32-38-01 to 04		Plaintiff's negligence as great as defendant's		Yes; §§32-38-01 to 04
OHIO	2315.19	2307.31, 2307.33	Contributory negligence not a bar recovery if negligence was not greater than combined negligence of persons claimant seeks recovery and all other persons claimant does not seek recovery. Damages diminished in proportion to claimant's fault.	See comparative negligence.		Yes; §§2307.31, 33
OKLAHOMA	Tit. 23 §13-14	Tit. 12 §832	Contributory negligence cannot be greater than negligence of defendants. Damages reduced in proportion to such person's contributory negligence.	See comparative negligence.		Yes; Tit. 12 §832

Table 35: Negligence—Continued

State	Code Section	Uniform Act	Comparative Negligence	Contributory Negligence—Limit to Plaintiff's Recovery	Judicial Imposition of Comparative Negligence	Contribution Among Tortfeasors
OREGON	18.470	No	Contributory negligence not a bar if fault attributable claimant is less than combined fault of defendants.	See comparative negligence.		Yes; §18.440
PENNSYLVANIA	Tit. 42 §7102	Tit. 42 §§8321-8327	Contributory negligence does not bar recovery if claimant's negligence is not greater than defendant's. But any damages allowed is diminished in proportion to claimant's attributed negligence	See comparative negligence.		Yes; Tit. 42 §§8321-8327
RHODE ISLAND	9-20-4	§§10-6-1 to 11	The fact that the claimant was not in the exercise of due care shall not bar recovery, but damages diminished in proportion to the amount of attributable negligence.	Only percentage of negligence attributable to plaintiff; award diminished proportionately (9-20-4)		Yes; §§10-6-1 to 11
SOUTH CAROLINA	None	§§15-38-10 to 70	Does not exist in South Carolina except by statute for railroad employer's liability	Plaintiff's negligence bar to recovery		Yes; §§15-38-10 to 70
SOUTH DAKOTA	20-9-2	15-8-11, *et seq.*	Plaintiff's negligence slight in comparison to defendant's; he may then recover in proportion to comparative fault (§20-9-2)	Plaintiff's negligence is found to be more than slight in comparison to defendant's negligence		Yes; SDCL §§15-8-11 to 22
TENNESSEE	None	29-11-101	Comparative negligence in reference to reviewing bank statements of accts. 47-4-406.	See comparative negligence.		Yes; TCA §§29-11-101 to 106
TEXAS	Civ. Prac. & Rem. §33.001	No	Plaintiff's negligence not greater than defendant's; award diminished in proportion to negligence (Civ. Prac. & Rem. §33.001)	See comparative negligence.		Yes; Civ. Prac. & Rem. §33.012

Table 35: Negligence—Continued

State	Code Section	Uniform Act	Comparative Negligence	Contributory Negligence—Limit to Plaintiff's Recovery	Judicial Imposition of Comparative Negligence	Contribution Among Tortfeasors
UTAH	78-27-37, *et. seq.*	No	Claimant's fault cannot exceed fault of person claimant seeks recovery combined W/. fault of those immune from suit.			18-27-40(2); A defendant is not entitled to contribution from any other person.
VERMONT	Tit. 12 §1036		Contributory negligence not a bar if negligence was not greater that causal total negligence but damages diminished in proportion to the amount of attributable negligence.	See comparative negligence.		No
VIRGINIA	8.01-58 (Contributory negligence is no bar to recovery in certain employee-railroad disputes.)	No	In an action against a common carrier, comparative negligence will not bar recovery and if carrier violated a safety code, the injured party won't be found comparatively negligent (8.01-58)			8.01-34; Contributory negligence may be applied when the wrong results from negligence and involves no moral turpitude
WASHINGTON	4.22.005 to 925	Yes; 4.22.005 to 925	Contributory fault diminishes proportionately the amount of damages, but does not bar recovery.	See comparative negligence.		Yes; §4.22.040
WEST VIRGINIA	None	No	Comparative negligence is reference to discovering and reporting unauthorized signature or alteration-bank statements. §46-4-406.	See comparative negligence.	*Bradley v. Appalachian Power Co.*, 256 S.E.2d 879 (1979), at 885.	Yes; §55-7-13
WISCONSIN	895.045	No	Contributory negligence is not a bar if claimant's negligence is not greater than defendants. Damages diminished in proportion to claimant' attributable negligence.	See comparative negligence.		Yes; common law right based on equitable principles (*State Farm Mutual Auto Ins. v. Continental Cas. Co.*, 59 N.W. 2d 425)

Table 35: Negligence—Continued

State	Code Section	Uniform Act	Comparative Negligence	Contributory Negligence—Limit to Plaintiff's Recovery	Judicial Imposition of Comparative Negligence	Contribution Among Tortfeasors
WYOMING	1-1-109	No	Contributory fault shall not bar recovery if fault is not more than 50% of the total fault of all actors. Damages diminished in proportion to the amount of fault attributable to claimant.	See comparative negligence.		No

36. RIGHT TO DIE

Euthanasia laws, living wills, and the durable power of attorney, often referred to as the "Right-to-Die" laws, are concerned with how an individual who has become incapacitated may exert some influence and control over certain decisions that will be made concerning his or her care. Living wills and the durable power of attorney permit individuals to instruct his or her survivors, guardians, or attending physicians to either administer or withhold life support if they are near death and unable to communicate, such as when in a coma.

The moral questions raised by the right-to-die laws are a direct result of developments in modern technology. From the earliest times, the primary goal of doctors has been to cure the sick and comfort the dying. However, modern technology has now allowed them to prolong life beyond the body's natural ability to maintain itself. Machines can artificially breathe for a person; intravenous feeding can artificially supply sustenance. Indeed, technology can keep a patient's body completely alive even when its brain is dead.

A major problem arises in situations such as these when the patient's desires are not known; it is then up to others to decide how long artificial life-sustaining procedures should be administered. Next of kin are nearly always the ones to whom this emotionally difficult decision falls, and the complexity of right-to-die laws reveals just how legally complicated the decision can be as well.

Next of kin are very often the persons most anxious to end their loved one's suffering. On the other hand, physicians, who are trained to prolong life, maintain an ethical and moral, as well as a legal, obligation to sustain life and are loathe to do anything that will end life unless they are protected from all liability stemming from charges of homicide or wrongful death or violations of codes of professional responsibility. In the past, every time the question of "pulling the plug" arose it was "taken care of quietly" or ended up in court, where a judge determined if the doctor should end life support. If the judge ruled that life support could be withheld, the attending physician and the health care provider were completely protected from liability.

Obviously, this was a very inefficient method of dealing with this situation. After one or two high-profile cases, the public generally accepted "pulling the plug" as an option for the terminally ill. Where once medical practitioners and the public looked upon the act as murder, many have come to see it as merciful. This change in attitude has manifested itself, in most states, in a body of rather dark statutes falling into three specific categories, living wills, durable power of attorney, and euthanasia.

Durable Power of Attorney

A durable power of attorney is an instrument that is similar to a living will except that it gives authority to a named individual to decide whether or not to begin or discontinue artificial life support. Any decision the holder of the durable power of attorney makes regarding life support is said to have the exact same legal effect as though the patient had made the decision himself or herself.

Euthanasia

No state sanctions euthanasia—also known as mercy killing—assisted suicide, or suicide. However, the terms of these right-to-die statutes are worded such that nearly all states include clauses explicitly stating that nothing in the statutes may be construed to condone suicide.

There is considerable diversity among states regarding the handling of the right-to-die issue, but the variance is entirely in the detail. While every state recognizes some form of durable power of attorney or living will, each has added its own character. Many states require state-sanctioned forms, while some allow as little as "some form of communication" to execute or revoke a durable power of attorney or living will.

Living Wills

A living will is a legal instrument that is executed by a person of sound mind and witnessed in much the same manner as a will. A living will expresses the individual's desires regarding life support should he or she become incapacitated as a result of a terminal illness: specifically, whether or not to administer artificial life-sustaining procedures in the event of an incurable or irreversible terminal condition that would otherwise result in death in a short time.

Note: Because laws governing the right to die are fast changing, all users of this book are advised to consult local statutes before acting on any information contained in this chapter.

Table 36a: Right to Die: Durable Power of Attorney

State/ Code Section	Specific Powers, Life- Prolonging Acts	Operative Facts	Revocation/Dura-tion	Reciprocity	Transfer of Patient if Physician Unwilling	Immunity for Attending Physician
ALABAMA No statutory provisions						
ALASKA 13.26.332, 335, *et seq.*	Consent or refusal to consent to medical care or relief for the principal from pain but agent may not authorize the termination of life-sustaining procedures; may include provision indicating whether a living will has been executed	(1) Must be set out in substantially the same form as found in statue §13.26.332; (2) designate health care decisions to agent	Revocable at any time		A third party shall honor the terms of a properly executed power of attorney, but physician may withdraw after services of another physician have been obtained	A third party who relies on reasonable representations of an attorney-in-fact does not incur a liability to the principal or principal's heirs, assigns, or estate
ARIZONA 36-3221, *et seq.* Health Care Power of Attorney	Power to give or refuse consent to all medical, surgical, hospital, and make health care decisions on that persons behalf	(1) Adult; (2) in writing; (3) language clearly indicating intent to create a health care power of attorney; (4) dated; (5) signed; (6) witnessed by at least one adult or a notary public and who is not related to principal by blood, marriage, or adoption & not entitled to any of principal's estate	Person may revoke health care directive or disqualify a surrogate by (1) written revocation; (2) orally notifying surrogate or health care provider; (3) making new health care directive; (4) any other act demonstrating specific intent to revoke	Health care directive prepared in another state is valid in this state if it was valid where and at the time it was adopted to the extent it does not conflict with the criminal laws of Arizona		Health care provider making good faith decisions in reliance on apparently genuine health care directive or decision of a surrogate is immune from civil, criminal, and professional discipline for that reliance
ARKANSAS 20-17-201, *et seq.* Arkansas Rights of the Terminally Ill & Permanently Unconscious Act	Any medical procedure or intervention that will serve only to prolong the dying process or to maintain the patient in a condition of permanent unconsciousness	The declaration may appoint a health care proxy who is at least 18 yrs. old as attorney-in-fact to make health care decisions including withholding or withdrawing of life-sustaining treatment	Revocable at any time in any manner by the declarant without regard to declarant's mental/physical condition. Effective upon communication to attending physician	A declaration executed in another state in compliance with the laws of that state or Arkansas law is validly executed	Physician shall as promptly as practicable take all reasonable steps to transfer care to another physician	Physician whose actions under this chapter are in accord with reasonable medical standards is not subject to criminal, civil, or professional liability with respect to them

Table 36a: Right to Die: Durable Power of Attorney—Continued

State/ Code Section	Specific Powers, Life- Prolonging Acts	Operative Facts	Revocation/Duration	Reciprocity	Transfer of Patient if Physician Unwilling	Immunity for Attending Physician
CALIFORNIA Probate §4650, §4700 *et seq.* Durable Powers of Attorney for Health Care	Decisions on any care, treatment, service, or procedure to maintain, diagnose, or treat an individual's physical or mental condition; including decision to begin, continue, increase, limit, discontinue or not begin any health care. Same right as principal to receive information and consent regarding health care decisions and records except to consent to commitment, convulsive treatment, or psychosurgery, sterilization or abortion.	Durable power of attorney must specifically authorize the attorney-in-fact to make health care decisions; dated; witnessed by 2 attesting to the principal's signature and signing statutory declaration (§4701) or by a notary public; prevails over declaration (§7185 *et seq.*); substantially same form as §4703 (statutory form)	No authority while principal can give informed consent to a health care decision. Anytime while principal has capacity to give a durable power of attorney, he may (1) revoke the appointment of the attorney-in-fact orally or in writing; (2) revoke the agent's authority by notifying the physician orally or in writing; (3) a subsequent durable power of attorney revokes prior one; (4) divorce revokes any designation of former spouse	Enforceable if executed in another state or jurisdiction in compliance with the laws of that state or jurisdiction or in substantial compliance with the laws of California		Subject to limitations, a physician acting in good faith on decision of attorney-in-fact is not subject to criminal, civil, or professional liability except to the same extent that would be the case if the principal, having had capacity to give informed consent, had made the health care decision on his/her own behalf under like circumstances
COLORADO 15-14-503, *et seq.* Colorado Patient Autonomy Act	Authority of an agent to act on behalf of principal who lacks decisional capacity in consenting to or refusing medical treatment including artificial nourishment and hydration; may include conditions or limitations of agent's authority		Divorce, dissolution, annulment, or legal separation revokes any designation of former spouse as agent; otherwise can be revoked at any time	A durable power of attorney executed in another state shall be presumed to comply with this law and may, in good faith, be relied on by a health care provider	Physician must provide for prompt transfer; physician must not provide care and comfort pending transfer	No criminal or civil liability or regulatory sanction for complying in good faith with medical treatment decision of agent acting in accordance with advanced medical directive

Table 36a: Right to Die: Durable Power of Attorney—Continued

State/ Code Section	Specific Powers, Life- Prolonging Acts	Operative Facts	Revocation/Dura-tion	Reciprocity	Transfer of Patient if Physician Unwilling	Immunity for Attending Physician
CONNECTICUT 1-54a; 19a-570, *et seq.*	Consent, refuse consent, or withdraw consent to any medical treatment other than that designed solely to maintain physical comfort, the withdrawal of life support systems, or of nutrition or hydration; does not apply to pregnant patient	See statutory form §1-43 for power of attorney or appointment of attorney-in-fact for health care decisions see form in §19a-575a—must be 18 yrs., signed, dated in presence of two adult witnesses	May be revoked at any time, in any manner; automatically revoked by divorce, legal separation, annulment, or dissolution of marriage if spouse is appointed as health care agent, unless principal specifies otherwise		Physician shall act as promptly as practicable and take all reasonable steps to transfer patient to complying physician	Physician withholding, removing life-support system of an incapacitated patient shall not be civilly or criminally liable if decision was based on physician's (1) best medical judgment; (2) physician deems patient in a terminal condition; (3) patient's wishes were considered according to an executed document
DELAWARE 16 §2501, *et seq.*	Grant, refuse, withdraw consent to provision of medical treatment, including right to refuse medical treatment which would extend appointer's life	(1) Adult; (2) written declaration; (3) attending physician judges appointer incapable due to condition resulting from illness or injury of making decision to accept or refuse medical treatment; (4) signed by appointer or another person at his express direction and in his presence; (5) dated; (6) 2 or more adult witnesses	Revocable at any time without regard to declarant's mental state or competency by (1) destruction of declaration with intent to revoke; (2) oral statement in presence of 2 persons 18 yrs. or older expressing intent to revoke; (3) written revocation signed and dated by declarant or (4) new declaration with contrary intent			Physicians or nurses acting in reliance on properly executed document are presumed to be acting in good faith and there is no civil or criminal liability unless negligent

Table 36a: Right to Die: Durable Power of Attorney—Continued

State/ Code Section	Specific Powers, Life- Prolonging Acts	Operative Facts	Revocation/Duration	Reciprocity	Transfer of Patient if Physician Unwilling	Immunity for Attending Physician
DISTRICT OF COLUMBIA 21-2201 Health Care Decisions	To grant, refuse, withdraw consent to the provision of any health-care service, treatment, or procedure if principal is incapable of making or communicating decisions himself	(1) Competent adult; (2) in writing; (3) must include language clearly communicating the intent for attorney-in-fact to have authority to make health-care decisions on behalf of the principal with language that power is effectuated upon principal's incapacity; (4) dated; (5) signed; (6) in presence of 2 adult witnesses; sample form §21-2207	Revocable at any time by notifying health care provider or attorney-in-fact orally or in writing. Divorce automatically revokes designation of former spouse			

Table 36a: Right to Die: Durable Power of Attorney—Continued

State/ Code Section	Specific Powers, Life- Prolonging Acts	Operative Facts	Revocation/Dura- tion	Reciprocity	Transfer of Patient if Physician Unwilling	Immunity for Attending Physician
FLORIDA 765.201, *et seq.* Health Care Surrogate Act	All health care decisions regarding principal's health care during principal's incapacity, including life-prolonging procedures: any medical procedure, treatment, or intervention which utilizes mechanical or other artificial means to sustain, restore, supplant a spontaneous vital function and serves only to prolong the dying process of a patient in terminal condition. Does not include medication or medical procedure to provide comfort care or to alleviate pain; cannot withhold or withdraw life prolonging procedures from pregnant patient prior to viability	(1) Competent adult (2)signed; (3) in presence of 2 adult witnesses	Revocable at any time by principal by (1) signed, dated writing; (2) destruction of declaration; (3) oral expression of intent to revoke; (4) subsequent advance health care directive materially different from the previously executed advance directive; (5) divorce revokes any designation of the former spouse as surrogate	An advance directive executed in another state in compliance with the laws of that state or Florida is validly executed	Physician should make reasonable efforts to transfer to a willing health care provider. Physician unwilling to carry out the patient's wishes because of moral or ethical beliefs must within 7 days: (1) transfer the patient and pay the cost of transporting the patient to another health care provider or (2) carry out the wishes of the patient unless provisions of judicial intervention	Health care facility, provider, or other person acting under their direction is not subject to criminal, civil, or professional liability for carrying out health care decision
GEORGIA 31-36-1, *et seq.* Durable Power of Attorney for Health Care	All powers the individual may have to be informed about and to consent or refuse to consent to any type of health care for the individual including withholding or withdrawal of life-sustaining or death-delaying procedures or after death, anatomical gifts, autopsies or disposition of remains	(1) In writing; (2) signed by principal; (3) attested and subscribed by 2 or more competent adult witnesses; (4) statutory form §31-36-10 may be used	Revocable at any time by principal without regard to physical or mental condition by (1) destruction of the document; (2) written revocation signed and dated by the principal; (3) by oral or any other expression of intent to revoke in presence of an adult witness who within 30 days must sign and date in writing confirming the expression of such intent; (4) divorce revokes agency in former spouse		Physician should promptly inform the agent who is responsible to make the transfer, but physician will continue to afford consultation and care in connection with the pending transfer	No health care provider subject to any civil, criminal, or professional liability solely for complying with decision of agent

Table 36a: Right to Die: Durable Power of Attorney—Continued

State/ Code Section	Specific Powers, Life- Prolonging Acts	Operative Facts	Revocation/Dura-tion	Reciprocity	Transfer of Patient if Physician Unwilling	Immunity for Attending Physician
HAWAII 551D-1, *et seq.* Uniform Durable Power of Attorney Act	Agent authorized to make any lawful health care decisions that could have been made by principal at time of election. Agent may decide that principal's life should not be prolonged through surgery, resuscitation, life-sustaining medicine, or procedures for provision of nutrition or hydration if explicitly appointed	(1) Competent adult; (2) in writing and signed by principal or another in his or her presence at expressed direction; (3) dated; (4) in presence of 2 or more adult witnesses; (5) signature notarized; (6) with words such as "This power of attorney shall not be affected by the disability (or become effective upon disability) of principal." (Sample form §551D-2.6)	Effective only during period of incapacity of principal as determined by licensed physician. Not revoked until notice of actual death or disability of principal is given to attorney-in-fact (durable or otherwise).			
IDAHO 39-4505, *et seq.* Natural Death Act	Health care decisions for principal, meaning consent, refusal of consent, or withdrawal of consent to any care, treatment, services, or procedure to maintain, diagnose, or treat an individual's physical condition. Also includes life-prolonging care decisions (see Living Wills for description of life-prolonging measures)	(1) Signed by principal; (2) dated; (3) signed by 2 witnesses; (4) person must be adult; (5) may list alternative holders of power (sample form §39-4505)	Effective only when competent person is unable to communicate rationally. Revocable at any time by the maker without regard to competence by (1) destruction of the document; (2) by written, signed revocation; (3) by verbal expression of intent to revoke.		Physician may withdraw without civil or criminal liability provided physician makes a good faith effort to assist patient in transferring before his/her withdrawal	No civil or criminal liability for physician acting in accordance with wishes of patient as expressed by statutory procedure

Table 36a: Right to Die: Durable Power of Attorney—Continued

State/ Code Section	Specific Powers, Life- Prolonging Acts	Operative Facts	Revocation/Dura-tion	Reciprocity	Transfer of Patient if Physician Unwilling	Immunity for Attending Physician
ILLINOIS 755 ILCS 45/ 4-1 Powers of Attorney for Health Care Law (If no power of attorney for health care or no living will, see Health Care Surrogate Act, 755 ILCS 40/ 1 *et seq.*)	Health care powers may be delegated to an agent and include consent or refusal or withdrawal of any type of health care for individual. May extend beyond principal's death if necessary to permit anatomical gift, autopsy, or disposition of remains	Neither attending physician nor health care provider may act as agent (statutory short form at 45/4-10). Living will not operative as long as properly authorized agent is available.	Revocable at any time by principal without regard to mental or physical condition by (1) written revocation signed and dated; (2) oral expression in presence of witness who signs and dates a written confirmation; (3) destruction of power of attorney in manner indicating intent to revoke		Agent responsible for transfer after being promptly informed by attending physician of his refusal or failure to comply, but attending physician must afford all reasonably necessary consultation and care in connection with transfer	No civil, criminal, or professional liability if good faith reliance on any decision or direction by agent not clearly contrary to terms of a health care agency
INDIANA 16-36-1-1, *et seq.* Health Care Consent	Appoint a representative to act in matters affecting the appointer's health care: any care, treatment, service, or procedure to maintain, diagnose, or treat an individual's physical or mental condition including admission to a health care facility and disclosure of medical records to health care provide; this appointment does not affect individual's authorization re: life-prolonging measures (i.e. a living will)	(1) In writing; (2) signed by appointer; (3) witnessed by adult; (4) may specify conditions and terms of the authority delegated; (5) begins when appointer becomes incapable of consenting	Individual capable of consenting to health care may revoke appointment at any time by notifying representative or health care provider orally or in writing. Individual who may consent to his own health care may disqualify others from consenting or revoking appointment for the individual (disqualification must be in writing)			No criminal, civil, or professional liability for a physician acting in good faith in reliance on the agent's direction

Table 36a: Right to Die: Durable Power of Attorney—Continued

State/ Code Section	Specific Powers, Life- Prolonging Acts	Operative Facts	Revocation/Dura-tion	Reciprocity	Transfer of Patient if Physician Unwilling	Immunity for Attending Physician
IOWA 144B.1, *et seq.* Durable Power of Attorney for Health Care	Consent, refusal of consent, or withdrawal of consent to health care. Attorney-in-fact has priority over court-appointed guardian to make health care decisions; does not include provision of nutrition or hydration except when required parenterally through intubation	(1) Explicitly authorizes attorney-in-fact to make health care decisions; (2) 2 adult witnesses signing in the presence of each other and the principal; (3) notarized; (4) substantially complies with requirements (sample form 1448.5)	May be revoked at any time in any manner by which principal is able to communicate intent to revoke. Power revoked in case of divorce where spouse designated durable power of attorney for health care.	Similar document executed in another state in compliance with the laws of that state is valid and enforceable in Iowa; to the extent the document is consistent with Iowa law.	Unwilling physician must make provisions to transfer patient to willing health care provider	Health care provider not subject to civil or criminal liability or professional disciplinary action if acting in good faith on decision of attorney-in-fact
KANSAS 58-625 *et seq.* Durable Power of Attorney for Health Care Decisions	Consent, refuse consent, or withdraw consent to any care, treatment, service, or procedure to maintain, diagnose, or treat a physical or mental condition and make decisions about organ donation, autopsy, and disposition of body; make all necessary arrangements for principal at any hospital/facility and employ health care personnel; request and review and execute any information regarding principal's affairs, including medical and hospital records.	(1) Writing must have words of intent that principal conferred authority to be exercised not-withstanding principal's subsequent incapacity; (2) dated; (3) signed; (4) in presence of 2 adult witnesses or notarized; (5) substantially in statutory form of §58-632 (6) effective upon occurrence of principal's disability or incapacity	By an instrument in writing witnessed as required for power of attorney or "set out another manner of revocation, if desired."	Any durable power of attorney for health care decisions which is valid under the laws of the state of the principal's residence at the time it was signed is valid under the act.		

Table 36a: Right to Die: Durable Power of Attorney—Continued

State/ Code Section	Specific Powers, Life- Prolonging Acts	Operative Facts	Revocation/Dura- tion	Reciprocity	Transfer of Patient if Physician Unwilling	Immunity for Attending Physician
KENTUCKY 311.621 *et seq.* Kentucky Living Will Directive Act.	Surrogate may make health care decisions grantor could make if he or she had decisional capacity, provided all decisions are in accordance with granter's wishes and surrogate has considered recommendations of attending physician; these decisions include withholding or withdrawal of artificial nutrition or hydration if (1) death is imminent (i.e. death is expected within a few days); (2) provision of nutrition cannot be physically assimilated; (3) burden or provision of such nutrition and hydration outweighs benefit. (Artificial nutrition or hydration not to be withdrawn if needed for comfort or relief of pain.); (4) When patient is in permanently unconscious state and advanced directive has authorized withdrawal or withholding of such nutrition and hydration. Life sustaining treatment and artificially provided nutrition and hydration shall be provided to pregnant woman unless attending physician and one other physician determine such treatment will not permit continuing development and live birth of unborn child or will be physically harmful to woman or prolong severe pain which cannot be alleviated by medication	(1) Grantor with decisional capability; (2) may designate 1 or 2 adults as surrogates; (3) if 2 or more, any decisions must be unanimous; (4) in writing, dated and signed by grantor; (5) 2 adult witnesses, signed in presence of grantor and in presence of each other or notarized; (6) surrogate may not make decisions when physician has determined in good faith that grantor has decisional capability	(1) May be revoked in whole or in part or surrogate's powers reduced or limited at any time if grantor has decisional capacity; (2) oral statement of intent to revoke in presence of 2 adults, one of whom is a health care provider; (3) destruction of declaration with intent to revoke; (4) effective immediately for attending physician once revocation received; (5) oral statement by grantor with decisional capacity to revoke overrides previous written directive	Directives made outside the provisions of this act does not restrict health care providers from following such directives if they are consistent with accepted medical practice.	Physician must immediately inform patient and family or guardian and shall not impede transfer to complying physician or health care facility; patient's medical records and information shall be supplied to receiving physician or facility	Unlawful for any health care facility or licensing agency to discriminate against health care professional that is unwilling to comply with advanced directive of patient as long as he or she complies with notification and transfer provisions of act. Not subject to criminal prosecution or civil liability or deemed to have engaged in unprofessional conduct as a result of withholding or withdrawing life prolonging treatment in accordance with directive unless shown by preponderance of evidence that there was bad faith

Table 36a: Right to Die: Durable Power of Attorney—Continued

State/ Code Section	Specific Powers, Life- Prolonging Acts	Operative Facts	Revocation/Dura-tion	Reciprocity	Transfer of Patient if Physician Unwilling	Immunity for Attending Physician
LOUISIANA 40:1299.58.1 (c) *et seq.* Declarations Concerning Life-sustaining Procedures	Any medical procedure or intervention, including but not limited to invasive administration of nutrition and hydration, which would serve only to prolong the dying process for a person diagnosed as having a terminal and irreversible condition. Does not include any measure necessary for comfort care	The declaration made under statutory "Declarations Concerning Life-sustaining Procedures" may include designation of another person to make treatment decision for the declarant should s/he be diagnosed with terminal or irreversible condition and be comatose, incompetent or otherwise mentally or physically incapable of communication (sample form §1299.58.3 (c))	Revocable at any time by declarant without regard to mental state or competency by (1) destruction of document; (2) written revocation signed and dated by declarant; (3) oral or nonverbal expression by declarant of intent to revoke. Effective upon communication to physician	Declaration properly executed in and under the laws of another states is deemed to be validly executed.	Physician shall make reasonable effort to transfer patient to another physician	Any health care facility, physician or other person acting under their direction shall not be criminally, civilly, or professionally liable for withholding life-sustaining procedures in accordance with the provisions of this chapter
MAINE 18A §5-501, *et seq.* Durable Power of Attorney; §5-701 *et seq.*	Consent or withhold consent or approval relating to any medical or other health care treatment of the principal including life-sustaining treatment when principal is in terminal condition or persistent vegetative state	(1) Signed by principal or another at principal's direction; (2) 2 witnesses other than designated attorney-in-fact (unless prior to effective date of statute); (3) contains words to the effect that authority is exercisable not withstanding incapacity or disability (sample form §5-702(c))	May be revoked or terminated by a fiduciary of principal only with prior approval of court upon petition by any interested person	Declaration executed in another state in compliance with laws of that state and Maine is valid	Attending physician or other health care provider who is unwilling shall take all reasonable steps as promptly as practicable to transfer to another physician willing to comply. Willful failure to transfer is a Class E crime	Physician or other health care provider whose action is in accord with reasonable medical standards and in good faith is not subject to criminal or civil liability or discipline for unprofessional conduct

Table 36a: Right to Die: Durable Power of Attorney—Continued

State/ Code Section	Specific Powers, Life- Prolonging Acts	Operative Facts	Revocation/Dura-tion	Reciprocity	Transfer of Patient if Physician Unwilling	Immunity for Attending Physician
MARYLAND 5-601 et seq. Health Care Decisions Act	Appointment by declarant under advance directive to make health care decisions for declarant under circumstances stated in directive based on wishes of declarant; decision regarding the provision, withholding of life-sustaining procedures should be based, in whole or in part, on the patients pre-existing, long-term mental or physical disability or a patient's economic disadvantage; can't authorize sterilization or treatment for mental disorder	(1) Voluntary; (2) dated and in writing; (3) signed by declarant or at express direction of declarant; (4) subscribed by 2 witnesses; (5) effective when attending physician and second physician certify in writing that patient is incapable of making an informed decision on basis of physical examination within 2 hours of certification (if patient is unconscious, second physician is not required); (6) communicated to physician who shall made it part of declarant's medical records	Revocable at any time by (1) signed and dated writing; oral statement to health care practitioner; (3) execution of subsequent directive	Declaration executed out-of-state by nonresident is effective if declaration is in compliance with the laws of Maryland or the laws of the state where executed (to the extent permitted by the laws of Maryland)	Attending physician shall make every reasonable effort to transfer declarant to another healthcare provider; assist in transfer; and pending transfer comply with competent individual or healthcare agent/ surrogate for person incapable of making a decision if failure to comply would likely result in death of individual	Any healthcare provider who withholds or withdraws health care or life-sustaining procedures in accordance with this subtitle and in good faith, is not subject to civil or criminal liability and may not be found to have committed professional misconduct

Table 36a: Right to Die: Durable Power of Attorney—Continued

State/ Code Section	Specific Powers, Life- Prolonging Acts	Operative Facts	Revocation/Dura-tion	Reciprocity	Transfer of Patient if Physician Unwilling	Immunity for Attending Physician
MASSACHUSETTS Ch. 201D §1, *et seq.* Health Care Proxies	Any and all health care decisions on principal's behalf that principal could make including decisions about life-sustaining treatment (which do not include those procedures to provide comfort care or pain alleviation), subject to any express limitations of health care proxy's authority (proxy has priority over other persons, including one with durable power of attorney unless limited by principal or court order)	(1) Competent adult; (2) in writing; (3) signed; (4) in presence and subscribed by 2 adult witnesses, that the principal appeared to be 18, of sound mind and under no constraint or undue influence; (5) Health care proxy must contain identities of principal and health care agent and indicate principal intends agent to have authority to make health care decisions on his behalf and describe any limitations and indicate agent's authority effective if it is determined that principal lacks decisional capacity	Revocable by (1) notification of agent or health care provider orally or in writing or by any other act evidencing specific intent to revoke the proxy; (2) execution of subsequent health care proxy; (3) divorce or legal separation where spouse was principal's agent under health care proxy	Effective if executed in another state or jurisdiction if in compliance with laws of that state or jurisdiction provided §14 and §15 of Chap. 201D are not violated (re: refusal to honor proxy)	Physician should arrange for transfer of patient to equivalent facility "reasonably accessible" to patient's family; if unable to do so, physician shall seek judicial relief or honor agent's decision	No civil, criminal, or professional liability for carrying out in good faith a health care decision by an agent pursuant to a health care proxy

Table 36a: Right to Die: Durable Power of Attorney—Continued

State/ Code Section	Specific Powers, Life- Prolonging Acts	Operative Facts	Revocation/Duration	Reciprocity	Transfer of Patient if Physician Unwilling	Immunity for Attending Physician
MICHIGAN §700.496 *et seq.* Uniform Durable Power of Attorney Act	Designation may include statement of patient's desires on care, custody, and medical treatment decisions (effective only when patient is unable to participate in medical treatment decisions); may authorize patient advocate to exercise 1 or more powers concerning patient's care, custody, and medical treatment that patient could have exercised on own behalf. Patient advocate may make decision to withhold or withdraw treatment which would allow patient to die only if patient has expressed in a clear and convincing manner that patient advocate is allowed to do so and that patient acknowledges that such a decision would allow death	(1) 18 yrs.; (2) sound mind; (3) signed in writing; (4) in the presence of and signed by 2 witnesses; (5) proposed patient advocate must sign acceptance; (6) executed voluntarily; (7) made part of patient's medical record before implementation; (8) exercisable only when patient is unable to participate in decisions; (9) cannot be used for pregnant patient	(1) Revocable at any time and in any manner sufficient to communicate intent by patient to revoke; (2) resignation or removal of patient advocate; (3) subsequent designation that revokes prior designation, either expressly or by inconsistency; (4) divorce revokes designation of patient advocate in former spouse; (5) death of patient; (6) order of probate court; (7) occurrence of provision for revocation contained in designation; (8) any current desires of patient are binding on patient advocate		Physician or health care provider is bound by sound medical practice and instructions of patient advocate if patient advocate complies with law	Person providing, performing, withholding, withdrawing medical treatment reasonably relying on decisions of patient advocate is liable in same manner and to same extent as if patient had made decision on his or her own behalf

Table 36a: Right to Die: Durable Power of Attorney—Continued

State/ Code Section	Specific Powers, Life- Prolonging Acts	Operative Facts	Revocation/Dura- tion	Reciprocity	Transfer of Patient if Physician Unwilling	Immunity for Attending Physician
MINNESOTA 145C.01, *et seq.* Durable Power of Attorney for Health Care (see also designation of proxy under §145B.01 *et seq.*	Power to consent, refuse to consent, withdraw consent to any care, treatment, procedure or health care decision to maintain, diagnose, or treat mental or physical condition of principal including food and water by artificial means	(1) signed by principal; (2) dated; (3) signed by 2 adult witnesses or acknowledged by principal before a notary public; (4) when inconsistencies arise between proxy, living will, or agent, most recently executed document takes precedence (suggested statutory form §145C.05)	Divorce revokes any designation of former spouse as agent to make health care decisions. Revocable at any time by (1) destroying; (2) written statement expressing intent to revoke; (3) verbally expressing intent to revoke in presence of 2 witnesses; (4) executing subsequent instrument	Power of attorney document, when executed in another state in compliance with that state's law is valid and enforceable in Minnesota to the extent it is consistent with Minnesota law	Provider who has legal and actual capability of providing transfer and who is unwilling to provide directed health care may transfer patient to complying provider but must take all reasonable steps to provide directed health care until patient is transferred	Health care provider not subject to criminal prosecution, civil liability or professional disciplinary action who relies in good faith on health care decision made by agent; no criminal, civil, or professional liability for health care provider who administers health care to keep patient alive (despite agent's decision) if all reasonable steps were promptly taken to transfer patient to complying provider

Table 36a: Right to Die: Durable Power of Attorney—Continued

State/ Code Section	Specific Powers, Life- Prolonging Acts	Operative Facts	Revocation/Dura-tion	Reciprocity	Transfer of Patient if Physician Unwilling	Immunity for Attending Physician
MISSISSIPPI 41-41-151 to 183 Durable Power of Attorney for Health Care Act	Consent, refuse consent, or withdraw consent to any care, treatment, service, or procedure to maintain, diagnose, or treat an individual's physical or mental condition; may include decisions after death such as anatomical gift, autopsy, etc. Does not affect health care treatment in an emergency	(1) Durable power of attorney must specifically authorize the attorney-in-fact to make health care decisions; (2) dated; (3) witnessed by 2 individuals or notarized according to form set out in §41-41-159(b); (4) should follow substantially statutory form (§41-41-163)	Unless the document provides a shorter time, it shall be effective until revoked by principal. Durable power of attorney revocable at any time the principal has capacity to give a durable power of attorney for health care by notifying the attorney-in-fact in writing or notifying the health care provider in writing or by executing subsequent valid durable power of attorney for health care (revokes prior durable power of attorney for health care)			No civil, criminal, or professional responsibility if health care provider relies in good faith on health care decision
MISSOURI 404.800, *et seq.* Durable Power of Attorney-Health Care	May make health care decisions, but no agent may authorize withdrawal of artificially supplied nutrition and hydration which the patient may ingest through natural means	(1) Signed; (2) dated; (3) includes provision that durable power shall not terminate if principal becomes disabled or incapacitated; (4) powers generally commence upon certification by 2 licensed physicians that patient is incapacitated	Revocable at any time in any manner by which patient is able to communicate the intent to revoke. Effective upon communication to agent or to physician		Physician may not impede the attorney-in-fact from transferring patient to another physician or facility	Any third party acting in good faith may rely on the instructions of the attorney-in-fact without liability to the patient or the patient's successors-in-interest

Table 36a: Right to Die: Durable Power of Attorney—Continued

State/ Code Section	Specific Powers, Life- Prolonging Acts	Operative Facts	Revocation/Dura- tion	Reciprocity	Transfer of Patient if Physician Unwilling	Immunity for Attending Physician
MONTANA 50-9-101 *et seq.* Rights of the Terminally Ill Act	Withholding or withdrawal of life-sustaining treatment, defined as any medical procedure or intervention that will serve only to prolong the dying process. Qualified patient may designate another individual to make decisions governing withholding or withdrawal of life-sustaining treatment. Life-sustaining procedures may not be withdrawn when qualified patient is known to be pregnant and when it is likely fetus will result in live birth	(1) 18 yrs. and of sound mind; (2) signed by declarant or another at his request; (3) 2 witnesses; (4) communicated to physician and made part of patient's medical record; (5) declared to be terminal and no longer able to make decisions regarding life-sustaining treatment; (7) declarant may designate another individual, 18 yrs. old and of sound mind, to make decisions regarding life-sustaining treatment (sample form §50-9-103)	Revocable at any time in any manner without regard to physical or mental condition. Effective upon notice	Declaration made in another state in compliance with that state's laws executed in a substantially similar manner to laws of Montana is effective	Unwilling physician shall take all reasonable steps as promptly as practicable to transfer to another who is willing	Individual appointed under this section not criminally or civilly liable for decisions made pursuant to executed declaration; attending physician or health care provider not subject to civil or criminal liability or guilty of unprofessional conduct if acting in accordance with reasonable medical standards and in good faith.

Table 36a: Right to Die: Durable Power of Attorney—Continued

State/ Code Section	Specific Powers, Life- Prolonging Acts	Operative Facts	Revocation/Dura-tion	Reciprocity	Transfer of Patient if Physician Unwilling	Immunity for Attending Physician
NEBRASKA 30-3401*et seq.* Health Care Power of Attorney	Consent, refusal of consent, withdrawal of consent to health care. Shall not include (1) withdrawal of routine comfort care; (2) withdrawal of usual and typical provision of nutrition and hydration; (3) withdrawal or withholding of life-sustaining procedures or artificially administered nutrition or hydration except if declarant gives that authority. (Note that an attempted suicide by the principal shall not be construed as indicating the principal's wishes with regard to health care.)	(1) In writing; (2) identify parties; (3) specifically authorize attorney-in-fact to make decisions when principal is incapable (this must be documented by physician indicating cause and nature of incapacity); (4) signed and witnessed by 2 adults; (5) show date of execution; (6) substantially in form of §30-3408; (7) not operative when principal is known to be pregnant and live birth is probable	Revocable at any time by competent principal in any manner he/she is able to communicate an intent to revoke; withdrawal at any time by attorney-in-fact. Otherwise, effective until death of principal; divorce or legal separation, unless otherwise noted in divorce decree, shall be deemed to revoke power of attorney for health care in spouse.	Declaration executed in another state is valid according to its terms if valid under the laws of that state	Unwilling physician shall inform attorney-in-fact and promptly assist in transferring principal to willing physician	No criminal, civil, or professional liability if acting in good faith. Does not limit liability for negligence (no physician required to accept decision from attorney-in-fact until provider has received original or copy of signed power of attorney for health care)
NEVADA 449-800 et seq. Durable Power of Attorney for Health Care	Attorney-in-fact has power to make health care decisions before or after death for disabled principal including consent, refusal of consent, or withdrawal of consent to any care, treatment, service, or procedure to maintain, diagnose, or treat physical or mental condition except treatment specifically stated: commitment to mental facility, convulsive treatment, psychosurgery, sterilization, or abortion or any other specifically designated treatments.	(1) Signed; (2) notarized or 2 witnesses; (3) sample form: §449-613 to designate person to make decision re: life-sustaining treatment; §449-830 mandatory form to create durable power of attorney.	Divorce revokes designation of former spouse. Power of attorney remains valid indefinitely unless principal designates shorter period or it is revoked or another power of attorney is executed subsequently.			

Table 36a: Right to Die: Durable Power of Attorney—Continued

State/ Code Section	Specific Powers, Life- Prolonging Acts	Operative Facts	Revocation/Duration	Reciprocity	Transfer of Patient if Physician Unwilling	Immunity for Attending Physician
NEW HAMPSHIRE 137-J:1 *et seq.* Durable Power of Attorney for Health Care	Document delegating health care decisions to agent; includes consent, refusal to consent or withdrawal of consent to any care, treatment, admission to a health care facility, any service or procedure to maintain, diagnose or treat an individual's physical or mental condition. Artificial nutrition and hydration may not be withdrawn or withheld unless clear expression of such power in document. Does not include power to consent to voluntary admission to state institution, voluntary sterilization or consent to withholding of life-sustaining treatment for pregnant patient unless treatment will not permit continuing development and live birth of unborn child.	(1) In writing; (2) substantially statutory form; (3) 2 subscribing witnesses who affirm that principal appeared to be of sound mind and free from duress and that he was aware of the nature of the document and signed it voluntarily; (4) include disclosure statement in substantially same form as §137-J:14 prior to execution	Revocable by (1) notifying attorney-in-fact or health care provider orally or in writing or in any other way communicating specific intent to revoke; (2) execution of subsequent durable power of attorney; (3) filing of action of divorce if spouse is agent. Revocation effective upon notice to health care provider or to attorney-in-fact. Person who is directly interested or related to patient may file an action to revoke durable power of attorney on grounds that principal was not of sound mind or under duress, fraud, or undue influence.	Documents executed in another state are enforceable if they are in compliance with the law of that state or jurisdiction; foreign instruments are restricted to and must be in compliance with the laws of New Hampshire.	Unwilling physician or health care provider must inform attorney-in-fact and allow for transfer of patient to another facility	No person acting in good faith pursuant to durable power of attorney terms shall be subject to criminal or civil liability or unprofessional conduct. No liability for facility which refuses to carry out terms of agent's direction provided they informed agent of their refusal.

Table 36a: Right to Die: Durable Power of Attorney—Continued

State/ Code Section	Specific Powers, Life- Prolonging Acts	Operative Facts	Revocation/Dura-tion	Reciprocity	Transfer of Patient if Physician Unwilling	Immunity for Attending Physician
NEW JERSEY 26:2H-53, *et seq.* Advanced Directives for Health Care	Decisions to accept or refuse treatment, service, or procedure used to diagnose, treat, or care for a patient's physical or mental condition including life-sustaining treatment. Includes decisions on acceptance or rejection of services of particular physician or health care provider or transfer of care; on the use of any medical device or procedure, artificially provided fluids and nutrition, drugs, surgery or therapy that uses mechanical or other artificial means to sustain, restore, or supplant a vital bodily function and thereby increase the expected life span of a patient; does not include provision of comfort care or alleviation of pain	(1) Competent adult; (2) signed; (3) dated; (4) 2 witnesses who shall attest that declarant is of sound mind and free of duress and undue influence or notarized or other person authorized to administer oaths. May be supplemented by video or audio tape recording; (5) directive implemented when determination of lack of decision-making capacity is documented and confirmed by physicians	Revocable by (1) oral or written notification; (2) execution of subsequent directive; (3) divorce revokes former spouse's designation as representative. Patient's clearly expressed wishes take precedent over any patient's decision or proxy directive	Effective if executed in compliance with New Jersey law or the laws of that state. Effective if executed in a foreign country in compliance with that country's laws or the laws of New Jersey and is not contrary to public policy of New Jersey	Unwilling physician should act as soon as practicable to effect an appropriate, respectful and timely transfer of care and to assure patient is not abandoned or treated disrespectfully	No civil, criminal, or professional liability for any physician acting in good faith and pursuant to this act

Table 36a: Right to Die: Durable Power of Attorney—Continued

State/ Code Section	Specific Powers, Life- Prolonging Acts	Operative Facts	Revocation/Dura-tion	Reciprocity	Transfer of Patient if Physician Unwilling	Immunity for Attending Physician
NEW MEXICO 24-7A-1 *et seq.* Uniform Health Care Decisions Act	Agent has power of attorney for health care to make health care decisions including selection and discharge of health care providers, approval and disapproval of diagnostic tests, surgical procedures, programs of medication, orders not to resuscitate, and directions to provide, withhold or withdraw artificial nutrition and hydration and all others forms of treatment or health care which maintains, diagnoses, or otherwise affects an individual's mental or physical condition.	(1) Adult or emancipated minor having capacity; (2) in writing; (3) signed by principal; (4) may include individual instructions; (5) effective upon determination that principal lacks capacity	Individual with capacity may revoke by (1) signed writing; (2) personally informing supervising health care provider; (3) in any manner that communicates intent to revoke; (4) filing for divorce or legal separation revokes designation of spouse as agent (revived by remarriage); (5) conflicting earlier health care directive (to the extent of the conflict)	Valid if it complies with provisions of Uniform Health Care Decisions Act regardless of where it was executed or communi-cated.	Physicians or health care provider who declines to comply with health care decision must inform patient or agent; provide continuing care until a transfer can be effected, and make reasonable efforts to assist in transfer to willing health care provider or physician.	No civil or criminal liability or discipline for unprofessional conduct if health care provider acting in good faith and in accordance with generally accepted health care standards in complying with provisions of this act.

Table 36a: Right to Die: Durable Power of Attorney—Continued

State/ Code Section	Specific Powers, Life- Prolonging Acts	Operative Facts	Revocation/Dura-tion	Reciprocity	Transfer of Patient if Physician Unwilling	Immunity for Attending Physician
NEW YORK Pub. Health Law §2980, *et seq.* Health Care Agent and Proxies	Any decision to consent or refuse consent of any treatment, service, or procedure to diagnose or treat an individual's physical or mental condition	(1) Competent adult; (2) signed; (3) dated; (4) 2 adult witnesses who shall sign proxy and state that principal appeared to execute proxy willingly and free from duress; (5) indicate that principal wants agent to make health care decisions for him; (6) agent's authority begins when it is determined that principal lacks capacity to make health care decisions (made by attending physician to a reasonable degree of medical certainty and in writing; in case of decision to withhold or withdraw life-sustaining treatment another physician must confirm determination; (7) sample form §2981 (5) (d)	Proxy may provide that it expires on a specified date or occurrence of condition; otherwise in effect until revoked. Revocable by (1) notifying agent or health care provider orally, in writing, or any other act evidencing intent to revoke; (2) divorce if former spouse was agent; (3) upon execution of a subsequent health care proxy	Effective if executed in another state in compliance with laws of that state	If agent's health care decision can not be honored, agent must be informed prior to admission if possible and transferred promptly to another hospital that is reasonably accessible under the circumstances and willing to honor agent's decision. Health care provider shall cooperate in facilitating such transfer.	No criminal, civil, or professional liability for acting in good faith pursuant to statute

Table 36a: Right to Die: Durable Power of Attorney—Continued

State/ Code Section	Specific Powers, Life- Prolonging Acts	Operative Facts	Revocation/Dura- tion	Reciprocity	Transfer of Patient if Physician Unwilling	Immunity for Attending Physician
NORTH CAROLINA §32A-15 *et seq.* Health Care Powers of Attorney	Decisions regarding life-sustaining procedures, including those which serve to artificially prolong the dying process and may include mechanical ventilation, dialysis, antibiotics, artificial nutrition and hydration and other forms of treatment which sustain, restore, or supplant vital bodily functions but do not include care necessary to provide comfort or alleviate pain	(1) 18 yrs. old; (2) understanding and capacity to make and communicate health care decisions; (3) in writing; (4) signed in presence of 2 witnesses and acknowledged before a notary (suggested form §32A-25)	May be revoked at anytime by principal capable of making and communicating health care decisions or by death of principal or by execution of a subsequent instrument or written instrument of revocation or any other method where intent to revoke is communicated (effective upon communication). Revoked on decree of divorce if spouse is agent, except if alternate has been appointed. If all health care attorneys-in-fact are unwilling or unable to act, the health care power of attorney will cease to be effective			No person acting on the authority of the health care attorney shall be liable for actions taken pursuant to decision of health care attorney. Withholding or discontinuing life-sustaining procedures shall not be considered suicide or cause of death for criminal or civil purpose.

Table 36a: Right to Die: Durable Power of Attorney—Continued

State/ Code Section	Specific Powers, Life- Prolonging Acts	Operative Facts	Revocation/Dura-tion	Reciprocity	Transfer of Patient if Physician Unwilling	Immunity for Attending Physician
NORTH DAKOTA 23-06.5-01 *et seq.* Durable Power of Attorney for Health Care	Agent has power to make any health care decisions principal could if he did not lack capacity (lack of capacity must be certified in writing by principal's attending physician), decisions including consent, refusal to consent or withdrawal of consent or request any care, treatment, service, or procedure to maintain, diagnose, or treat individual's physical or mental condition; does not include admission to mental health facility, psychosurgery, abortion, or sterilization.	(1) Signed; (2) 2 witnesses who affirm principal was of sound mind and signed it freely and voluntarily; (3) agent must accept appointment in writing; (4) statutory form of durable power of attorney (§23-06.5-17) is preferred format	Revocable by (1) notification of agent orally, in writing, or any other act evidencing specific intent to revoke; (2) execution of subsequent durable power of attorney; (3) divorce where spouse was principal's agent	Effective if executed in another state in compliance with the law of that state	Physician has duty to inform principal or agent and take all reasonable steps to transfer care to another who is willing to honor agent's directive	No civil, criminal, or professional liability if acting in good faith and with ordinary care pursuant to directives of durable power of attorney
OHIO 1337.11, *et seq.* Durable Power of Attorney for Health Care	Medical procedure, treatment, intervention, or other measure that will serve to prolong the process of dying, including right to give informed consent and make other decisions principal could if s/he had capacity	(1) Adult; (2) sound mind; (3) signed; (4) dated; (5) signed in presence of 2 adult witnesses or notarized (including attestation that principal is of sound mind and free from duress)	Does not expire unless principal specifies an expiration date in the instrument. Revocable at any time in any manner; effective when expressed, but if physician had knowledge of the durable power of attorney, revocation is effective on communication to physician. Valid Durable Power of Attorney for health care revokes prior instrument	Effective if document complies with the laws of the state where executed and that substantially complies with Ohio law	Physician may not prevent or delay patient's transfer to another physician	No civil, criminal, or professional liability for good faith reliance which is in accordance with reasonable medical standards on agent's health care decisions

Table 36a: Right to Die: Durable Power of Attorney—Continued

State/ Code Section	Specific Powers, Life- Prolonging Acts	Operative Facts	Revocation/Dura-tion	Reciprocity	Transfer of Patient if Physician Unwilling	Immunity for Attending Physician
OKLAHOMA Tit. 58 §1071, *et seq.;* Tit. 63 §3101.1 *et seq.*	Under Uniform Durable Power of Attorney Act, agent may grant complete or limited authority to make health and medical care decisions but not life-sustaining treatment decisions unless the power complies with requirements for a "health care proxy" under Oklahoma Rights of Terminally Ill or Persistently Unconscious Act, Tit. 63 §3101 *et seq.*	(1) Signed; (2) 2 adult witnesses who sign in the presence of the principal and each other; (3) substantially the same form as Tit. 58 §1072.2 (4)(3)	Revocable in whole or in part in any manner at any time without regard to declarant's mental or physical condition. Effective upon communication to physician	Effective if executed in another state if substantially complies with the Uniform Durable Power of Attorney Act	Physician shall take all reasonable steps to arrange for care by another physician	No civil, criminal, or professional liability for carrying out the directives of durable power of attorney in good faith and in accordance with reasonable medical standards
OREGON 127.505 *et seq.* Advanced Directives for Health Care	Power to make health care decisions for principal regarding life-sustaining procedures including any medical procedure or intervention that uses mechanical or other artificial means to sustain, restore, or supplant a vital function only when authorized or when principal is terminally ill and such treatment only serves to artificially prolong the moment of death; does not include procedures to sustain patient cleanliness and comfort	(1) In writing; (2) signed by two witnesses who make written declarations; (3) mandatory statutory form §127.531 ORS; (4) agent must accept appointment	Agent may withdraw up to time of principal's incapacity. Principal may revoke (1) in any manner by which s/he is able to communicate to health care provider or attorney-in-fact intent to revoke; (2) by execution of subsequent durable power of attorney; (3) upon divorce if spouse is agent	Valid execution in compliance with formalities of that state where principal is resident or is located or with state of Oregon	Physician must promptly notify health care representative if unable or unwilling to comply with durable power of attorney and representative shall make a reasonable effort to transfer the principal to a complying physician	Health care provider acting on a durable power of attorney or health care agent in good faith is not liable for criminal, civil, or professional disciplinary actions
PENNSYLVANIA 20 Pa CSA §5601-5604 Powers of Attorney	Authorize admission to medical facility and enter into agreements for principal's care and to consent, arrange, and authorize medical and surgical procedures including administration of drugs	(1) In writing; (2) signed; (3) in the presence of 2 witnesses; (4) presumed durable	Durable power of attorney not affected by subsequent disability or incapacity. Agent must have actual notice of revocation for it to be effective. Divorce revokes power of attorney for spouse.			Person acting in good faith reliance on power of attorney shall incur no liability as a result.

Table 36a: Right to Die: Durable Power of Attorney—Continued

State/ Code Section	Specific Powers, Life- Prolonging Acts	Operative Facts	Revocation/Dura- tion	Reciprocity	Transfer of Patient if Physician Unwilling	Immunity for Attending Physician
RHODE ISLAND 23-4.10-1, *et seq.* Health Care Power of Attorney	Any medical procedure or intervention that will only prolong the dying process; it shall not include intervention necessary to alleviate pain or provide comfort	(1) 18 yrs.; (2) resident of Rhode Island; (3) 2 adult witnesses; (4) only in statutory form set forth in §23-4.10-2; (5) no effect or force to document if patient is pregnant and live birth is probable with continued application of treatment	Revocable at any time in any manner declarant is able to communicate intent to revoke, without regard to physical or mental condition. Effective upon communication to physician. Controls over living will executed by same person for any inconsistent provisions	Durable power of attorney executed in another state in compliance with laws of that state is valid	Unwilling physician must make necessary arrangements to effect transfer to complying physician	No civil, criminal, or professional liability when acting in accordance with the statute and in accordance with reasonable medical standards.
SOUTH CAROLINA 62-5-501, *et seq.* Powers of Attorney (see also §44-77-85. Agent may be appointed to effectuate declaration.)	Medical procedure or intervention serving only to prolong the dying process, not including medication or treatment for pain alleviation or comfort care. Principal should indicate whether provision of nutrition and hydration through surgically implanted tubes is desired	(1) Substantially in statutory form §62-5-504 (D); (2) signed; (3) dated; (4) 2 witnesses; (5) state name and address of adult agent; (6) can't withhold or withdraw life-sustaining procedures during pregnancy	Revocable by (1) written or oral statement or other act constituting notification to agent or health care provider of specific intent to revoke; (2) principal's execution of subsequent health care power of attorney	Effective if executed in compliance with South Carolina law or laws of another state and recorded as required by §62-5-501 (c)	Physician must make reasonable effort to locate a physician who will follow directive and has a duty to transfer patient to that physician.	No civil, criminal, or professional liability for relying in good faith on agent's health care decisions
SOUTH DAKOTA 59-7-2.1, *et seq.*	Any health care decisions for principal which principal could have made if s/he had decisional capacity including rejection or withdrawal of consent for medical procedures, treatment, or intervention. Agent may not authorize withholding artificial nutrition and hydration for comfort care or pain relief. Artificial nutrition or hydration may be withheld under certain circumstances or if specifically authorized.	Specific intent must be included in document for durable power of attorney to extend even when principal is disabled but life-sustaining treatment must be given to a pregnant woman unless live birth unlikely to a reasonable degree of medical certainty.	Revocation must be recorded with register of deeds			No civil, criminal, or professional liability for physician acting in good faith on a health care decision by agent or attorney-in-fact

515

Table 36a: Right to Die: Durable Power of Attorney—Continued

State/ Code Section	Specific Powers, Life- Prolonging Acts	Operative Facts	Revocation/Dura-tion	Reciprocity	Transfer of Patient if Physician Unwilling	Immunity for Attending Physician
TENNESSEE 34-6-201, *et seq.* Durable Power of Attorney for Health Care Act	Any procedure, treatment to diagnose, assess, or treat a disease, illness, or injury, including surgery, drugs, transfusions, mechanical ventilation, dialysis, CPR, artificial nourishment, hydration or other nutrients, radiation. Death by starvation or dehydration allowed only if specifically directed with statutory phrase.	Signed before 2 witnesses and notary public and specifically authorizes health care decisions	Revocable by (1) notifying the attorney-in-fact orally or in writing; (2) notifying health care giver orally or in writing; (3) executing subsequent durable power of attorney; (4) divorce if former spouse was designated; (5) principal's current wishes supersede durable power of attorney	Effective if document complies with laws of Tennessee or laws of the state of principal's residence	Prompt and orderly transfer required	No criminal, civil, or professional liability for physician acting in good faith
TEXAS Civ. Prac. & Rem. Code 135.001, *et seq.* Durable Power of Attorney for Health Care	Decisions regarding consent to health care, treatment, service, or procedure to maintain, diagnose, or treat individual's physical or mental condition. Agent may not consent to voluntary in-patient mental health services, convulsive treatment, psychosurgery, abortion, or neglect of principal through omission of care primarily intended to provide for comfort of principal	(1) Signed; (2) in presence of 2 or more subscribing witnesses; (3) substantially statutory to form (§135.015 and .016) and accompanied by disclosure statement. Principal may designate alternative agents	Effective indefinitely upon execution and delivery of document unless revoked. Revocable orally or in writing with specific intent to revoke or execution of subsequent power of attorney; divorce if spouse is agent. Effective upon receipt and notice to agent and health care provider. Treatment may not be given or withheld from principal regardless of his capacity or the existence of a durable power of attorney if principal objects	Durable power of attorney executed in another state valid if it complies with the law of that state or jurisdiction	Physician must notify agent immediately to arrange for transfer	Agent not liable for health care decision made in good faith. Physician not liable for acts or decisions made under durable power of attorney if done in good faith and does not constitute a failure to exercise due care in the provision of health care services

Table 36a: Right to Die: Durable Power of Attorney—Continued

State/Code Section	Specific Powers, Life- Prolonging Acts	Operative Facts	Revocation/Duration	Reciprocity	Transfer of Patient if Physician Unwilling	Immunity for Attending Physician
UTAH 75-2-1106 Special Power of Attorney; 75-2-1101 *et seq.* for proxy/agent by directive	Any medical procedure or intervention that would serve only to prolong the dying process including artificial nutrition and hydration unless declaration specifically excludes; does not include medication, sustenance, or any procedure to alleviate pain; separate procedure for "do not resuscitate" directive.	Agent/proxy:(1) 18 yrs.; (2) in writing; (3) dated and signed; (4)suggested form §75-2-1105. For power of attorney: must be before notary public and the suggested form is §75-2-1106; power of attorney takes precedent over earlier signed directives	Current wishes of declarant take precedent over any directive. Revocable at any time by (1) signed revocation; (2) destruction of document; (3) oral expression of intent to revoke in presence of witness. Effective on receipt by physician	A similar instrument executed in another state is presumed to comply with Utah law and may be relied upon in good faith.	Unwilling physician required to transfer patient promptly	No civil, criminal, or professional liability for good faith compliance with directive
VERMONT Tit. 14 §3451, *et seq.* Durable Power of Attorney for Health Care	To make health care decisions for principal during periods of incapacity as certified in writing by principal's attending physician including withdrawal of consent to any care, treatment, service, or procedure or to maintain, diagnose, or treat an individual's physical or mental condition; does not include consent to sterilization or admission to state institution	(1) Signed; (2) 2 witnesses; (3) signed statement that principal understands a disclosure statement on durable powers of attorney; (4) substantially same form as §3466	Principal's current wishes supersede directives at all times. Revocable by (1) notifying agent or health care provider orally or in writing or any other act evidencing specific intent to revoke; (2) executing a subsequent durable power of attorney; (3) divorce, if former spouse was principal's agent	Effective if in compliance with the law of the state in which it was executed	Unwilling physician must inform agent and principal if possible and assist in selecting another physician willing to honor agent's directive	No civil, criminal, or professional liability if physician acts in good faith; no immunity for failure to exercise due care in provision of services

Table 36a: Right to Die: Durable Power of Attorney—Continued

State/ Code Section	Specific Powers, Life- Prolonging Acts	Operative Facts	Revocation/Dura-tion	Reciprocity	Transfer of Patient if Physician Unwilling	Immunity for Attending Physician
VIRGINIA 54.1-2981 Health Care Decisions Act	Any medical procedure, treatment, intervention, utilizing mechanical or other artificial means to sustain, restore, or supplant a vital function, or is of a nature to afford patient no reasonable expectation of recovery from a terminal condition and when applied to a patient in terminal condition, would serve only to prolong the dying process. Includes artificially administered hydration and nutrition and CPR by emergency medical services personnel, but does not include any medication or procedure to alleviate pain or provide comfort care	(1) Competent adult; (2) written advance directive; (3) signed in presence of 2 subscribing witnesses; (4) oral declaration in presence of physician and 2 witnesses for those in terminal condition; (5) responsibility of declarant to provide notification of advance directive to attending physician. (suggested form §54.1-2984))	Revocable at any time by (1) signed, dated writing; (2) physical cancellation or destruction; (3) oral expression of intent to revoke. Effective upon communication to attending physician	Directive executed in another state valid if in compliance with Virginia law or law of state where executed. Such directives shall be construed in accordance with Virginia laws	If physician thinks treatment is medically or ethically inappropriate or is contrary to terms of advanced directive, unwilling physician must make reasonable effort to transfer patient to another physician	No civil, criminal, or professional liability if acting in good faith. It would have to be shown by preponderance of the evidence that the person authorizing life-prolonging procedures acted in bad faith
WASHINGTON 11.94.010, *et seq.* Power of Attorney	Appointed attorney-in-fact may make health care decisions on principal's behalf or provide informed consent	(1) In writing; (2) principal designates another as his attorney-in-fact; must include words showing intent of principal that authority be conferred notwithstanding principal's disability	Continues until revoked or terminated by principal, court-appointed guardian or court order			Anyone acting in good faith and without negligence shall incur no liability

Table 36a: Right to Die: Durable Power of Attorney—Continued

State/ Code Section	Specific Powers, Life- Prolonging Acts	Operative Facts	Revocation/Dura-tion	Reciprocity	Transfer of Patient if Physician Unwilling	Immunity for Attending Physician
WEST VIRGINIA 16-30A-1, *et seq.* Medical Power of Attorney	To affect a patient's decision to accept or reject medical or surgical treatments which prolong the dying process artificially	(1) 18 yrs.; (2) in writing; (3) signed by declarant or someone at his or her directive; (4) dated; (5) 2 witnesses; (6) notarized; (7) with words indicating effective upon patient's incapacity; substantially same form as §16-30A-18	Desires of principal at all times supersede effect of medical power of attorney. Revocable at any time by (1) destruction of document; (2) written revocation signed and dated; (3) verbal expression with witness present; (4) divorce if former spouse was designated	Valid if in compliance with laws of West Virginia or state where executed and expressly delegates health care decisions	Unwilling physician shall cause the transfer of principal to a complying physician	No criminal civil liability for good faith compliance with directions of medical power of attorney or representative
WISCONSIN 155.01 et seq. Power of Attorney for Health Care	Designation of another for purpose of making informed decisions in the exercise of the right to accept, maintain, discontinue, or refuse any care, treatment, service or procedure to diagnose, maintain, or treat physical or mental condition. Feeding tube may be withheld or withdrawn unless it would cause pain. Agent may not consent to withholding or withdrawing of orally ingested nutrition or hydration unless provision is medically contra-indicated	(1) 18 yrs. and sound mind; (2) in writing; (3) signed; (4) dated; (5) 2 witnesses; (6) voluntarily executed; (7) takes effect upon finding of incapacity by 2 physicians; (8) substantially same form as §155.30; (9) may file with register in probate	Revocable at any time by (1) canceling or destroying document; (2) revocation in writing signed and dated; (3) verbal revocation in presence of 2 witnesses; (4) executing a subsequent power of attorney; (5) divorce if former spouse was attorney-in-fact. Power of principal who does not have incapacity supersedes power of attorney at all times		Must make good faith attempt to transfer principal to complying physician.	No civil, criminal, or professional liability if acting in good faith

Table 36a: Right to Die: Durable Power of Attorney—Continued

State/ Code Section	Specific Powers, Life- Prolonging Acts	Operative Facts	Revocation/Duration	Reciprocity	Transfer of Patient if Physician Unwilling	Immunity for Attending Physician
WYOMING 3-5-201, *et seq.* Durable Power of Attorney for Health Care	Consent, refusal of consent, or withdrawal of consent to any medical procedure, care, treatment, intervention, or nourishment by artificial means in the event of a terminal condition except for alleviation of pain and comfort care and consent to convulsive treatment, psychosurgery, or commitment to mental facility; does not affect health care treatment in an emergency	(1) Signed; (2) dated; (3) 2 witnesses; (4) notarized; (5) attorney-in-fact authorized to make health care decisions	Principal's wishes if able to give informed consent take precedent over durable power of attorney. Revocable by (1) notifying attorney-in-fact in writing; (2) notifying health care provider in writing; (3) divorce if former spouse was attorney-in-fact; (4) a subsequent valid durable power of attorney for health care			No criminal, civil, or professional liability if acting in good faith

Table 36b: Right to Die: Euthanasia

State	Code Section	Mercy Killing Condoned	Operative Facts
ALABAMA	22-8A-10; 22-8A-9(a)	Euthanasia not condoned or authorized nor is allowed any affirmative act or omission to end life other than to permit the natural process of dying	Withholding or withdrawal of life-sustaining procedures in accordance with chapter 22-8A shall not constitute assisting suicide.
ALASKA	18.12.080(a) and (f)	Euthanasia or mercy killing not condoned, authorized, or approved by Alaska law.	Withholding or withdrawing any life-sustaining procedures under an order, protocol, or a declaration does not constitute a suicide or homicide
ARIZONA	36-3201, *et seq.* (Chapter 32)	Euthanasia, suicide, or assisted suicide is not authorized, or approved by Arizona law.	Authorized surrogate or health care provider complying with provisions of chapter are immune from liability.
ARKANSAS	20-17-210(a), (g)	Euthanasia or mercy killing not condoned, authorized, or approved by Arkansas law.	Death resulting from withholding or withdrawal of life-sustaining treatment pursuant to declaration and in accordance with this section does not constitute suicide or homicide.
CALIFORNIA	Probate §4723; H&S §7191.5	Nothing condones, authorizes, or approves mercy killing or permits an affirmative act or omission to end life other than the withholding of health care pursuant to a durable power of attorney so as to permit the natural process of dying. In making health care decisions under a durable power of attorney, an attempted suicide shall not be construed to indicate a decision of the principal that health care treatment be restricted or inhibited.	Death resulting from withholding or withdrawing life-sustaining treatment in accordance with the Natural Death Act does not constitute for any purposes suicide or homicide.
COLORADO	15-14-504; 15-18-111, 112; 15-18.5-101(3); 15-18.6-108	Nothing condones, authorizes, or approves euthanasia or mercy killing or shall be construed as permitting any affirmative or deliberate act to end a person's life except to permit natural death.	Withholding or withdrawing life-sustaining procedures pursuant to a declaration or the law shall not constitute a suicide or homicide.
CONNECTICUT	No statutory provisions		
DELAWARE	16 §2512, 63 §386, 70 §392	§3 of Delaware Laws C.386: nothing in this act condones, authorizes, or approves of mercy killing; permits any affirmative act or omission to end life other than to permit the natural process of dying	Neither execution of declaration nor fact that maintenance medical treatment is withheld from patient in accordance with the declaration shall constitute suicide.
DISTRICT OF COLUMBIA	6-2430; 21-2212; 6-2428	Euthanasia not condoned, authorized, or approved nor is any affirmative or deliberate act or omission to end a human life other than to permit the natural process of dying.	Withholding or withdrawing life-sustaining procedures in accordance with the Natural Death chapter shall not constitute the crime of assisting suicide.
FLORIDA	765.309	Nothing construed to condone, authorize, or approve mercy killing or euthanasia or to permit any affirmative or deliberate act or omission to end life other than to permit the natural process of dying.	The withdrawing of life-prolonging procedures from a patient in accordance with any provision of this chapter does not for any purpose constitute a suicide.

Table 36b: Right to Die: Euthanasia—Continued

State	Code Section	Mercy Killing Condoned	Operative Facts
GEORGIA	31-32-9; 31-32-11	Mercy killing is not condoned, authorized, or approved nor is any affirmative or deliberate act or omission permitted to end life other than to permit the process of dying.	The making of a living will pursuant to this chapter shall not for any purpose constitute a suicide.
HAWAII	327D-13, 14	Mercy killing or euthanasia not condoned, authorized, or approved by Hawaii law.	Death resulting from withholding or withdrawal of life sustaining procedures does not constitute suicide. Execution of declaration does not constitute attempted suicide
IDAHO	39-152	Does not make legal or condone mercy killing, euthanasia, or assisted suicide	
ILLINOIS	755 ILCS 35/9 and 45/ 4-8e and 40/50	Nothing in this Act shall be construed to condone mercy killing or to permit any affirmative or deliberate act or omission to end life other than to permit natural process of dying.	Withholding or withdrawal of death delaying procedures from a qualified patient or in accordance with terms of this Act or a health care agency shall not constitute suicide or homicide or murder.
INDIANA	16-36-1-13, 16-36-4-19	Euthanasia not condoned or authorized by Indiana law. This chapter does not authorize euthanasia or any affirmative or deliberate act or omission to end life other than to permit the natural process of dying, including the withholding or withdrawing of life prolonging procedures under this chapter	
IOWA	144A.11.6 and 144B.12	This chapter should not be construed to condone, authorize, or approve mercy killing or euthanasia or any affirmative or deliberate act or omission to end life other than to permit the natural process of dying.	Death resulting from withholding or withdrawal of life-sustaining procedures pursuant to a declaration and in accordance with this chapter does not, for any purpose, constitute a suicide or homicide
KANSAS	65-28.108(a); 65-28.109	Nothing in this act shall be construed to condone, authorize, or approve mercy killing or to permit any affirmative or deliberate act or omission to end life other than to permit the natural process of dying.	Acting in accordance with the Natural Death Act shall not for any purpose constitute a suicide or the crime of assisting suicide.
KENTUCKY	311.637 and 311.639	Nothing in KRS §§311.621-311.643 shall be construed to condone mercy killing or euthanasia or to permit any affirmative or deliberate act to end life other than to permit natural process of dying.	Withholding or withdrawal of life prolonging treatment or artificially provided nutrition and hydration shall not constitute suicide.
LOUISIANA	40:1299.58.10(A), (B)(1)	Nothing in this section shall be construed to condone, authorize, or approve mercy killing or euthanasia or to permit any affirmative or deliberate act or omission to end life other than to permit the natural process of dying.	The withholding of life-sustaining procedures in accordance with this part shall not for any purpose constitute suicide.

Table 36b: Right to Die: Euthanasia—Continued

State	Code Section	Mercy Killing Condoned	Operative Facts
MAINE	5-711	This part does not condone, authorize, or approve of mercy killing, euthanasia, or suicide	Neither the decision to withhold or withdraw or actual withholding or withdrawal of life sustaining treatment which results in death shall be deemed a suicide or homicide.
MARYLAND	Health-Gen. §§5-611 and 5-614	Nothing in this subtitle should be construed to condone, authorize, or approve of mercy killing or euthanasia or to permit any affirmative or deliberate act or omission to end life other than to permit the natural process of dying.	Withdrawal or withholding of life-sustaining procedures in accordance with this subtitle shall not for any purpose be considered to be a suicide.
MASSACHUSETTS	Ch. 201D §12	Nothing in this chapter shall be construed to constitute, condone, authorize, or approve suicide or mercy killing or to permit any affirmative or deliberate act to end one's own life other than to permit the natural process of dying.	
MICHIGAN	§700.496; *333.5660*	Designation of a patient advocate shall not be construed to condone, allow, permit, authorize, or approve suicide or homicide. The Michigan Commission on Death and Dying was created and commissioned to develop and submit to the legislature recommendations concerning the voluntary self-termination of life. Designation of a person to withdraw or withhold life-sustaining treatment shall not be construed to condone, allow, permit, authorize, or approve suicide or homicide. (As of this writing, this section has been repealed under the provision contained in it, and prosecutors in the state are currently prosecuting persons accused of assisting in a suicide under common law rules.)	
MINNESOTA	145B:14; 145C:14	Euthanasia, mercy killing, suicide, or assisted suicide is not condoned or authorized or approved by Minnesota law.	
MISSISSIPPI	4-41-227	The Uniform Health-Care Decisions Act does not authorize mercy killing, assisted suicide, euthanasia, or the provision, withholding, or withdrawal of health care.	Death resulting from the withholding of health care does not for any purpose constitute a suicide or homicide.
MISSOURI	404.845; 459.055	Euthanasia or mercy killing is not condoned or authorized by Missouri law, nor does it permit any affirmative or deliberate act or omission to shorten or end life.	When patient's death results from withholding or withdrawing life-sustaining treatment in accordance with a durable power of attorney, the death shall not constitute a suicide or homicide for any purpose.

Table 36b: Right to Die: Euthanasia—Continued

State	Code Section	Mercy Killing Condoned	Operative Facts
MONTANA	50-9-205; 50-10-104	Montana's Right of the Terminally Ill Act does not condone, authorize, or approve mercy killing or euthanasia.	Under §§50-10-101, *et seq.*, an individual may register and wear a Health & Safety Board certified identification that signifies the possessor has executed a declaration under §50-9-103 or has qualified so that his or her attending physician has issued a Do Not Resuscitate Order and has documented grounds for the order in the possessor's medical file; death resulting from the withholding or withdrawal of life-sustaining procedures pursuant to such an order is not, for any purpose, suicide or homicide.
NEBRASKA	20-412; 28-307; 30-3401	This Act does not confer any new rights regarding provision or rejection of specific medical care and does not alter laws regarding homicide, suicide, or assisted suicide. Nor does it approve, authorize, or condone homicide, suicide, or assisted suicide. Assisting suicide is a Class IV felony.	Death from withholding or withdrawal of life-sustaining treatment in accordance with this Act shall not constitute, for any purpose, homicide or suicide
NEVADA	449.650; 449.670; 450B.400-450B.590	Euthanasia or mercy killing not condoned or authorized or approved by Nevada law.	Death resulting from withholding or withdrawal of life-sustaining treatment in accordance with Nevada law does not for any purpose constitute suicide or homicide.
NEW HAMPSHIRE	137-H:10, 13	Euthanasia, mercy killing, or assisted suicide are not condoned or authorized by New Hampshire law. Nor does New Hampshire law permit any affirmative or deliberate act or omission to end life other than to permit the natural process of dying of those in a terminal or permanently unconscious condition.	Withdrawing or withholding life-sustaining procedures from a patient according to living will or consistent with 137-H:3 shall not be construed as suicide for any legal purpose.
NEW JERSEY	26:2H-77; 26:2H-54	No one has the right to or is authorized to practice active euthanasia.	Withholding or withdrawing of life-sustaining treatment pursuant to an advanced directive for health care when performed in good faith shall not constitute homicide, suicide, assisted suicide, or active euthanasia.
NEW MEXICO	24-7A-13	Uniform Health Care Decisions Act does not authorize mercy killing, assisted suicide, euthanasia, or the provision, withholding or withdrawal of health care to the extent prohibited by other statutes	Withholding of medical treatment pursuant to Right to Die Act shall not for any purpose constitute suicide.
NEW YORK	Pub. Health Law §2989	Statute not intended to promote or permit suicide, assisted suicide, or euthanasia; nor to be construed to permit agent to consent to any act or omission to which the principal could not consent under law.	

Table 36b: Right to Die: Euthanasia—Continued

State	Code Section	Mercy Killing Condoned	Operative Facts
NORTH CAROLINA	90-320(b); §32A-24	Provisions in the act do not authorize any affirmative or deliberate act or omission to end life other than to permit natural process of dying.	Withholding life support is not considered suicide or cause of death for civil or criminal purposes.
NORTH DAKOTA	23-06.4-01 and 11; 23-06.5-01	Euthanasia, mercy killing, or assisted suicide is not condoned or authorized by North Dakota law, nor is any other act or omission other than to allow the natural process of dying.	Death resulting from withholding or withdrawal of life-prolonging treatment does not constitute for any purpose, suicide or homicide.
OHIO	2133.12(A), (D)	Euthanasia, mercy killing, or assisted suicide is not condoned or authorized by Ohio law.	Death of any patient resulting from withholding life-sustaining treatment does not constitute suicide, murder or any homicide offense for any purpose.
OKLAHOMA	Tit. 63 §§3101.2, 3101.12	Euthanasia, mercy killing, or assisted suicide is not condoned or authorized by Oklahoma law.	Death from withdrawing life-sustaining treatment shall not constitute homicide or suicide.
OREGON	127.570	Nothing in statute is intended to condone, authorize, or approve mercy killing or permit affirmative or deliberate act or omission to end life, other than to allow the natural process of dying.	Withholding or withdrawal of life-sustaining procedures or artificially administered nutrition and hydration does not constitute suicide, assisted suicide, homicide, or mercy killing.
PENNSYLVANIA	20 §5402; §5410	Mercy killing, euthanasia, aided suicide is not condoned, authorized, or approved; nor is any affirmative or deliberate act to end life other than defined by this Act.	Withholding or withdrawal of life-sustaining treatment in accordance with this chapter shall not constitute suicide or homicide.
RHODE ISLAND	23-4.10-9; 23-4.11-10	Euthanasia or mercy killing is not condoned or authorized by Rhode Island law.	Death resulting from withdrawal or withholding of life-sustaining procedures does not constitute suicide or homicide.
SOUTH CAROLINA	44-77-110, 130; 62-5-504(M), (O); 44-78-50	Euthanasia or mercy killing is not condoned or authorized by South Carolina law, nor is any act or omission other than to allow the natural process of dying.	Effectuation of health care power of attorney or execution of declaration does not constitute suicide for any purpose.
SOUTH DAKOTA	34-12D-14, 20	Euthanasia, mercy killing, or assisted suicide is not condoned or authorized by South Dakota law.	Death by withdrawing or withholding life-sustaining treatment does not constitute suicide or homicide.
TENNESSEE	32-11-110		Withdrawal or withholding of medical care in accordance with provisions of this Act does not constitute suicide, euthanasia, or homicide.
TEXAS	Health & Safety §672.017; §672.020; 674.021	Mercy killing or euthanasia is not condoned or authorized by Texas law, nor is any act or omission other than to allow the natural process of dying.	Withdrawal or withholding of life-sustaining procedures does not constitute offense of Aiding Suicide
UTAH	75-2-1116, 1118	Euthanasia, mercy killing, or suicide is not condoned or authorized by Utah law.	Withholding or withdrawal of life-sustaining procedures does not constitute suicide or assisting suicide

Table 36b: Right to Die: Euthanasia—Continued

State	Code Section	Mercy Killing Condoned	Operative Facts
VERMONT	Tit. 18, §5260		Acting pursuant to terminal care document in withholding or withdrawal of life-sustaining procedures from patient is not suicide.
VIRGINIA	§§54.1-2990, 2991	Mercy killing or euthanasia is not condoned, approved, or authorized by Virginia law, nor is any affirmative or deliberate act or omission other than to allow the natural process of dying permitted.	Acting in accordance with Health Care Decisions Act in withholding or withdrawing life-prolonging procedures does not constitute suicide.
WASHINGTON	70.122.100 and .070	Euthanasia or physician-assisted suicide is not condoned or authorized by Washington law, nor is any act or omission other than to allow the natural process of dying.	Withholding or withdrawal of life-sustaining treatment shall not constitute suicide or homicide
WEST VIRGINIA	16-30A-16	Euthanasia or mercy killing is not condoned or authorized by West Virginia law, nor is any act or omission other than to allow the natural process of dying.	
WISCONSIN	154.11; 155.70	Euthanasia is not condoned or authorized by Wisconsin law, nor is any affirmative or deliberate act or omission other than to allow the natural process of dying.	Withholding or withdrawal of life-sustaining procedures or feeding tubes does not constitute suicide. Execution of declaration does not constitute attempted suicide.
WYOMING	35-22-108, 109; 3-5-2, 211	Euthanasia or mercy killing is not condoned or authorized by Wyoming law, nor is any affirmative or deliberate act or omission other than to allow the natural process of dying.	Withholding or withdrawal of life-sustaining procedures from a qualified patient in accordance with this chapter does not constitute a crime.

Table 36c: Right to Die: Living Wills

State/Code Section	Specific Powers, Life- Prolonging Acts	Operative Facts	Revocation/ Duration	Reciprocity	Transfer of Patient if Physician Unwilling	Immunity for Attending Physician
ALABAMA 22-8A Natural Death Act	Any medical procedure or intervention serving only to prolong the dying process and where death will occur whether or not such intervention is utilized; does not include medication or any medical procedure deemed necessary to provide comfort care or pain alleviation	(1) Competent adult; (2) in writing; (3) signed by declarant; (4) dated; (5) signed in presence of 2 or more witnesses over 19; (6) declaration should be substantially in statutory format	Revocable at any time by (1) destruction of document in manner intending to cancel; (2) execution of written revocation by declarant; (3) oral revocation in presence of adult witness (over 19)		Physician shall permit the patient to be transferred	No criminal, civil, or professional liability for physician acting in good faith pursuant to reasonable medical standards and pursuant to a declaration
ALASKA 18.12 Living Wills and Do Not Resuscitate Orders	Withholding or withdrawal of procedures that merely prolong the dying process and are not necessary for comfort or to alleviate pain; includes the administration of food and water by gastric tube or IV; declaration may provide declarant does not want nutrition and hydration administered intravenously or by gastric tube	(1) Competent; (2) 18 yrs.; (3) signed; (4) witnessed by 2 persons over 18 and unrelated to declarant or acknowledged by a person qualified to take acknowledgments; (5) may be in statutory form	Revocable at any time and in any manner declarant is able to communicate intent to revoke without regard to physical/mental condition; effective upon communication; becomes part of declarant's medical record	Declaration executed in another state in compliance with the law of that jurisdiction is effective	Physician may withdraw after services of another physician have been obtained	Physician causing the withholding or withdrawal of life-sustaining procedures from a qualified patient not subject to civil, criminal, or professional liability. Attending doctor has no right to compensation for services after withholding should have been effective and may be liable to patient and heirs for a civil penalty of less than $1000 plus costs associated with failure to comply with order or declaration; this is exclusive remedy at law for damages.

Table 36c: Right to Die: Living Wills—Continued

State/Code Section	Specific Powers, Life- Prolonging Acts	Operative Facts	Revocation/ Duration	Reciprocity	Transfer of Patient if Physician Unwilling	Immunity for Attending Physician
ARIZONA 36-3201 *et seq.* Living Wills and Health Care Directives	Does not include comfort care or alleviation of pain but may include life-sustaining treatment artificially delaying the moment of death, CPR, drugs, electric shock, artificial breathing, artificially administered food and fluids	(1) Adult; (2) in writing; (3) language clearly indicating intent to create a living will; (4) dated; (5) signed; (6) witnessed by at least one adult or a notary public	Person may revoke health care directive or disqualify a surrogate by (1) written revocation; (2) orally notifying surrogate or health care provider; (3) making new health care directive; (4) any other act demonstrating specific intent to revoke	Health care directive prepared in another state is valid in this state if it was valid where and at the time it was adopted to the extent it does not conflict with the criminal laws of Arizona	Physician must effect prompt transfer to a physician willing to comply	Health care provider making good faith decisions in reliance on apparently genuine health care directive or decision of a surrogate or living will is immune from criminal, civil, and professional discipline for that reliance (unless negligent)
ARKANSAS 20-17-201, *et seq.*	Any medical procedure or intervention that will serve only to prolong the dying process or to maintain the patient in a condition of permanent unconsciousness	(1) Sound mind; (2) 18 yrs.; (3) signed by declarant; (4) witnessed by 2 individuals	Revocable at any time, in any manner by the declarant without regard to the declarant's mental/physical condition; effective upon communication to attending physician	A declaration executed in another state in compliance with the laws of that state or Arkansas law is validly executed	Physician shall as promptly as practicable take all reasonable steps to transfer care to another physician	Physician whose actions under this chapter are in accord with reasonable medical standards is not subject to criminal, civil, or professional liability with respect to them
CALIFORNIA H&S §7185 *et seq.* Natural Death Act	Any medical procedure or intervention that will serve only to prolong the process of dying or an irreversible coma or persistent negative state; does not include treatment to alleviate pain or provide comfort care	(1) Sound mind; (2) over 18; (3) signed by declarant; (4) witnessed by 2; (5) declaration shall contain substantially same information in §7186.5; (6) operative when declarant in terminal condition as certified in writing by 2 physicians; (7) not effective while patient is pregnant	Revocable at any time in any manner without regard to declarant's mental/physical condition; revocation is effective upon its communication to the attending physician	Declaration executed in another state in compliance with the laws of that state or California law is valid	Physician shall take all reasonable steps as promptly as practicable to transfer the patient to a physician who is willing to comply	Physician is not subject to civil, criminal, or professional liability for acting in good faith pursuant to declaration

Table 36c: Right to Die: Living Wills—Continued

State/Code Section	Specific Powers, Life- Prolonging Acts	Operative Facts	Revocation/ Duration	Reciprocity	Transfer of Patient if Physician Unwilling	Immunity for Attending Physician
COLORADO 15-18-102, *et seq.* Colorado Medical Treatment Decision Act; 15-18.6-101, Directive Relating to Cardiopulmonary Resuscitation; 15-14-503 Colorado Patient Autonomy Act	Any medical procedure or intervention that would serve only to prolong the dying process; it shall not include any medical procedure for nourishment or considered by attending physician to provide comfort or alleviate pain; however, artificial nourishment may be withdrawn pursuant to declaration that artificial nutrition (1) not be provided or continued when it is the only procedure being provided; (2) be continued for a specified period when it is the only procedure being provided	(1) Competent; (2) adult; (3) executed before 2 competent witnesses	Revocable by declarant orally, in writing, or by burning, tearing, cancelling; obliterating, or destroying the declaration			No hospital or physician acting under direction of physician and participating in the withholding or withdrawal of life-sustaining procedures in compliance with a declaration shall be subject to any civil or criminal liability or licensing sanction in the absence of revocation, fraud, misrepresentation, or improper execution.
CONNECTICUT 19a-570, *et seq.* Removal of Life Support Systems	Any medical procedure or intervention serving only to postpone the moment of death or maintain individual in a state of permanent unconsciousness including artificial means of nutrition/ hydration, artificial respiration, CPR, but does not include comfort care and pain alleviation	(1) 18 yrs.; (2) signed; (3) dated; (4) presence of 2 witnesses; (5) in substantially form of §19a-575a	May be revoked at any time in any manner		Physician shall act as promptly as practicable and take all reasonable steps to transfer patient to complying physician.	Physician withholding, removing life-support system of an incapacitated patient shall not be civilly or criminally liable if decision was based on physician's (1) best medical judgment; (2) physician deems patient in a terminal condition; (3) patient's wishes were considered according to an executed document

Table 36c: Right to Die: Living Wills—Continued

State/Code Section	Specific Powers, Life- Prolonging Acts	Operative Facts	Revocation/ Duration	Reciprocity	Transfer of Patient if Physician Unwilling	Immunity for Attending Physician
DELAWARE 16 §2501, *et seq.* Health Care Decisions	Right to refuse medical or surgical treatment via written declaration instructing any physician to cease or refrain from medical or surgical treatment	(1) Legally adult, competent, of sound mind; (2) written declaration; (3) declarant in terminal condition confirmed in writing by 2 physicians; (4) signed by declarant or another person in declarant's presence and at his express direction; (5) dated; (6) 2 or more adult witnesses who state in writing that they are not prohibited from being a witness; (7) not pregnant	Revocable at any time without regard to declarant's mental state or competency by (1) destruction of declaration with intent to revoke; (2) oral statement in presence of 2 persons 18 years or older expressing intent to revoke; (3) written revocation signed and dated by declarant or; (4) new declaration with contrary intent; (5) receipt of emergency treatment			Physicians or nurses acting in reliance on properly executed document are presumed to be acting in good faith and there is no civil or criminal liability or discipline for unprofessional conduct.
DISTRICT OF COLUMBIA 6-2421, *et seq.* Natural Death Act	Any medical procedure or intervention which would serve only to artificially prolong the dying process and where death will occur whether or not such procedures are utilized; does not include medication or any medical procedure necessary to alleviate pain or provide comfort care	(1) 18 yrs.; (2) in writing; (3) dated; (4) signed; (5) in presence of 2 or more witnesses over 18; (6) declaration should be in substantially the statutory form of §6-2422	Revocable at any time by declarant without regard to declarant's mental state by (1) destruction of documents; (2) written revocation signed and dated; (3) verbal expression of intent to revoke in presence of an 18 year old witness; desires of qualified patient at all times supersede the effect of the declaration		Physician must effect a transfer and failure to do so shall constitute unprofessional conduct	No civil, criminal, professional liability for physician who acts in good faith pursuant to reasonable medical standard and to a declaration made

Table 36c: Right to Die: Living Wills—Continued

State/Code Section	Specific Powers, Life- Prolonging Acts	Operative Facts	Revocation/ Duration	Reciprocity	Transfer of Patient if Physician Unwilling	Immunity for Attending Physician
FLORIDA 765.101, *et seq.* Health Care Advance Directives	Any medical procedure, treatment, or intervention which utilizes mechanical or other artificial means to sustain, restore, supplant a spontaneous vital function and serves only to prolong the dying process of a patient in terminal condition; does not include medication or a medical procedure to provide comfort care or to alleviate pain	(1) Competent; (2) adult; (3) signed by principal; (4) in presence of 2 subscribing witnesses (suggested form in 765.302) one of whom is neither a spouse nor a blood relative	Revocable at any time by principal by (1) signed, dated writing; (2) destruction of the declaration; (3) oral expression of intent to revoke; (4) subsequent advance directive materially different from the previously executed advance directive; (5) divorce revokes the designation of former spouse as surrogate. Revocation effective when properly communicated.	An advanced directive executed in another state in compliance with the laws of that state or Florida is validly executed	Physician should make reasonable efforts to transfer to a health care provider who will comply with the declaration; a physician unwilling to carry out the patient's wishes because of moral or ethical beliefs must within 7 days: (1) transfer the patient and pay the cost of transporting the patient to another health care provider or (2) carry out the wishes of the patient unless provisions of judicial intervention apply	Health care facility, provider or other person who acts under the direction of a health care facility, or provider is not subject to criminal prosecution or civil or professional liability for carrying out a health care decision

Table 36c: Right to Die: Living Wills—Continued

State/Code Section	Specific Powers, Life- Prolonging Acts	Operative Facts	Revocation/ Duration	Reciprocity	Transfer of Patient if Physician Unwilling	Immunity for Attending Physician
GEORGIA 31-32-1, *et seq.*	Any medical procedures or interventions which would serve only to prolong the dying process for a patient in a terminal condition, a coma, or persistent vegetative state with no reasonable expectation of regaining consciousness or cognitive function; may include the provision of nourishment and hydration but shall not include medication or any medical procedure to alleviate pain	(1) Competent; (2) adult; (3) signed by declarant; (4) in presence of 2 competent adults not related to declarant; (5) any declaration constituting declarant's intent shall be honored regardless of the form or when executed	Revocable at any time by declarant without regard to mental state or competency by (1) destruction of document; (2) declarant signs and dates a written revocation expressing intent to revoke; (3) any verbal or nonverbal expression by declarant of intent to revoke which clearly revokes the living will as opposed to a will relating to the disposition of property after death	Any declaration regardless of form which constitutes declarant's intent shall be honored	Advise promptly the next of kin or guardian and at their election make a good faith attempt to effect a transfer or permit the next of kin or guardian to obtain complying physician	No physician acting in good faith in accordance with the requirements of this chapter shall be subject to any civil liability, guilty of any criminal act, or unprofessional conduct
HAWAII 327D-1, *et seq.* Medical Treatment Decisions	Execute declaration directing provision, continuation, withholding, or withdrawal of any medical procedure or intervention including artificial provisions of fluids, nourishment, medication that when administered to patient will only serve to prolong dying process; does not include procedure necessary for patient comfort or relief	(1) Competent person, age of majority; (2) in writing; (3) signed by declarant or another person in his presence and at his expressed direction; (4) dated; (5) signed in presence of 2 or more adult witnesses; (6) all signatures notarized; (7) not pregnant; (8) in terminal condition or permanent loss of ability to communicate concerning medical treatment (sample form §327D-4)	Revocable at any time by various methods including: (1) in writing signed and dated by declarant; (2) unambiguous verbal expression by declarant in front of 2 witnesses; (3) canceling, destroying declaration in declarant's presence and at his direction; (4) unambiguous verbal expression to attending physician	Document executed in another state is valid if it substantially complies with requirements of this chapter	Physician shall without delay make necessary arrangements to transfer patient and medical records to another physician; transfer without unreasonable delay or with good faith attempt to transfer is not abandonment and not subject to liability	No criminal prosecution or civil liability or deemed to have engaged in unprofessional conduct as result of withholding or withdrawal of life sustaining procedures unless absence of actual notice of revocation is result of negligence of health care provider, physician, or other person. Failure to transfer is professional misconduct

Table 36c: Right to Die: Living Wills—Continued

State/Code Section	Specific Powers, Life- Prolonging Acts	Operative Facts	Revocation/ Duration	Reciprocity	Transfer of Patient if Physician Unwilling	Immunity for Attending Physician
IDAHO 39-4501. *et seq.* Natural Death Act	Any medical procedure or intervention which utilizes mechanical means to sustain or supplant a vital function serving only to artificially prolong the moment of death and where death is imminent whether or not procedures are utilized; does not include the administration of medication or a medical procedure to alleviate pain	(1) Of sound mind; (2) emancipated minor or 18 yrs. or older; (3) voluntarily made; (4) 2 witnesses must sign; (5) not enforced during course of pregnancy	Revocable at any time by declarant without regard to competence by (1) destruction of the document; (2) by written, signed revocation; (3) by verbal expression of intent to revoke		Physician may withdraw without civil or criminal liability provided the physician makes a good faith effort to assist the patient in transferring before his/her withdrawal	No civil or criminal liability for a physician acting in accordance with the wishes of the patient as expressed by statutory procedure
ILLINOIS 755 ILCS 35/1, *et seq.* Illinois Living Will Act (If no living will or power of attorney for health care, see health care Surrogate Act, 755 ILCS 40/1 *et seq.*)	Individual may execute document directing that if he is suffering from a terminal condition and no longer able to participate actively in decisions about himself, then death–delaying procedure shall not be utilized for the prolongation of his life. These procedures include any which serve to postpone the moment of death and specifically include, but are not limited to, assisted ventilation, artificial kidney treatment, intravenous feeding/medication, blood transfusions and tube feedings, but does not include procedures providing for patient's comfort care or alleviation of pain	(1) Sound mind and age of majority or status of emancipated person (sample form at 35/3e); (2) signed by declarant or another at declarant's direction; (3) 2 witnesses over 18; (4) not pregnant (or at point where could develop to point of live birth with continued application of death delaying procedures); (5) notify attending physician	Revocable by declarant at any time without regard to mental or physical condition (1) in writing signed and dated by declarant or person acting at his/her direction; (2) by oral expression in presence of witness who signs and dates a written confirmation; (3) by destroying declaration in manner indicating intent to cancel; revocation is effective upon communication to attending physician	Declaration executed in another state in compliance with law of that state or Illinois is valid	Patient is responsible to initiate transfer; if patient not able to initiate transfer then attending physician shall without delay notify person with highest priority who is available, able, and willing to make arrangements for transfer for effectuation of patient's declaration	No physician, health care provider, or health care expert who in good faith and pursuant to reasonable medical standards causes or participates in withholding or withdrawal of death delaying procedure from qualified patient per declaration shall be subject to criminal or civil liability or be found to have committed an act of unprofessional conduct

Table 36c: Right to Die: Living Wills—Continued

State/Code Section	Specific Powers, Life- Prolonging Acts	Operative Facts	Revocation/ Duration	Reciprocity	Transfer of Patient if Physician Unwilling	Immunity for Attending Physician
INDIANA §16-36-4-1 *et seq.* Living Wills and Life Prolonging Procedures Act	Living will declarant may ask that life prolonging procedures that would sustain, restore, or supplant a vital function or that would serve to prolong the dying process not be used in case of terminal diagnosis and incapacity; this does not include any medical procedure or medication necessary to provide comfort care or alleviate pain.	(1) Person of sound mind, 18 yrs. old; (2) voluntary; (3) in writing; (4) dated; (5) signed in presence of 2 adult witnesses; (6) notice to declarant's attending physician; (7) is presumptive evidence of declarant's intent; (8) not enforced if pregnant (sample form §16-36-4-10). Witnesses must not be related to declarant. Destroying or falsifying a Living Will Declaration or a Life-Prolonging Declaration is a Class D felony. Destroying, falsifying, or concealing a revocation of a Declaration is a Class C felony.	Living will declaration is presumed valid. Revocable at any time by (1) signed and dated in writing; (2) physical destruction by declarant or at declarant's direction; (3) oral expression of revocation		Physician who refuses to comply shall transfer to another physician who will comply unless (1) physician believes declaration is not validly executed and (2) patient is unable to validate declaration. If patient not transferred for above reason, physician should try and ascertain patient's intent and declaration's validity from persons listed in §16-36-4-13 (g)(1-7).	Act of withdrawing or withholding life-prolonging procedures for qualified patient is lawful, and physician is not subject to criminal or civil liability or unprofessional conduct if done in good faith and in accordance with reasonable medical standards. Violation of any provisions of act subjects physician to disciplinary sanctions by medical licensing board.

Table 36c: Right to Die: Living Wills—Continued

State/Code Section	Specific Powers, Life- Prolonging Acts	Operative Facts	Revocation/ Duration	Reciprocity	Transfer of Patient if Physician Unwilling	Immunity for Attending Physician
IOWA 144A.2 Life-Sustaining Procedures Act	Declarant may declare desire to not have life-sustaining procedures employed to prolong life; life sustaining procedures are those that utilize mechanical or artificial means to sustain, restore, or supplant a spontaneous vital function and/or when applied to a patient in a terminal condition would only serve to prolong the dying process, does not include provision of nutrition or hydration except when required parenterally or though intubation or the administration of medication or performance of medical procedures which provide comfort care or alleviate pain; declaration shall not be in effect when declarant is pregnant as long as fetus can develop to point of live birth	(1) Declarant competent adult; (2) signed in presence of 2 witnesses and in the presence of each other; (3) physician may presume declaration is valid; (4) actual notice of declaration to attending physician; (5) declaration given effect when declarant's condition is terminal and he is unable to make treatment decisions. (sample form 144A.3(5)) At least one witness must not be related to declarant.	Revocable at any time in any manner that declarant can communicate intent, without regard to mental or physical condition. Physician shall make revocation part of medical records	Similar document executed in another state in compliance with the laws of that state is valid and enforceable in Iowa, to the extent the document is consistent with Iowa law.	Physician shall take reasonable steps to transfer patient to another physician or facility	Individual or health care provider is not liable civilly or criminally or guilty of unprofessional conduct for complying in good faith with provisions in declaration indicating withholding or withdrawal of life-sustaining procedures. Persons complying with provisions in executed declaration may assert statutory provisions as absolute defense

Table 36c: Right to Die: Living Wills—Continued

State/Code Section	Specific Powers, Life- Prolonging Acts	Operative Facts	Revocation/ Duration	Reciprocity	Transfer of Patient if Physician Unwilling	Immunity for Attending Physician
KANSAS 68-28, 101 *et seq.* Natural Death Act	Any medical procedure or intervention which would serve only to prolong the dying process and where death will occur whether or not such procedure is utilized. Does not include medication or any medical procedures necessary to alleviate pain or provide comfort care Declaration not in effect during declarant's pregnancy.	(1) Any adult; (2) in writing; (3) signed by declarant; (4) dated; (5) in presence of 2 or more adult witnesses; (6) no effect during course of pregnancy; (7) responsibility of declarant to notify attending physician; (8) substantially same form as 65-28, 103(c). No witness can be related to declarant.	Revocable at any time by declarant by (1) destruction of document; (2) written revocation signed and dated by principal; (3) verbal expression in presence of adult witnesses who signs and dates a written confirmation. Effective upon receipt by physician. Desires of patient at all times supersede the declaration		Physician shall effect the transfer— failure to do so constitutes unprofessional conduct	No criminal, civil, or professional liability for acting in good faith and pursuant to reasonable medical standards when acting pursuant to a declaration
KENTUCKY 311.621, *et seq.* Kentucky Living Will Directive Act	Any medical procedure, treatment, or intervention which utilizes mechanical or other artificial means to sustain prolong, restore, or supplant a spontaneous vital function or when administered would only prolong dying process. Does not include medication or procedure to alleviate pain.	(1) Adult with decisional capacity; (2) in writing; (3) dated; (4) either witnessed by 2 or more adults in presence of grantor and in presence of each other or acknowledged before notary; (5) in substantially the same form as §311.625(1). No witness can be related to grantor.	Revocable by (1) written declaration signed and dated by declarant; (2) oral statement of intent to revoke in presence of 2 adults, one of which is a health care provider; (3) destruction of declaration with intent to revoke; (4) effective immediately for attending physician once revocation received; (5) oral statement by grantor with decisional capacity to revoke overrides previous written directive	Directives made outside the provisions of this act does not restrict health care providers from following such directives if they are consistent with accepted medical practice.	Physician must immediately inform patient and family or guardian and shall not impede transfer to complying physician or health care facility; patient's medical records and information shall be supplied to receiving physician or facility	Not subject to criminal prosecution or civil liability or deemed to have engaged in unprofessional conduct as a result of withholding or withdrawing life prolonging treatment in accordance with directive unless shown by preponderance of evidence that there was bad faith

Table 36c: Right to Die: Living Wills—Continued

State/Code Section	Specific Powers, Life- Prolonging Acts	Operative Facts	Revocation/ Duration	Reciprocity	Transfer of Patient if Physician Unwilling	Immunity for Attending Physician
LOUISIANA 40:1299.58.1, *et seq*. Declarations Concerning Life-Sustaining Procedures	Any medical procedure or intervention, including but not limited to invasive administration of nutrition and hydration, which would serve only to prolong the dying process for a person diagnosed as having a terminal and irreversible condition. Does not include any measure necessary for comfort care	(1) Any adult; (2) written declaration; (3) signed by declarant; (4) in presence of 2 adult witnesses; (5) oral or nonverbal declaration may be made in presence of 2 adult witnesses by any nonwritten means of communication at any time subsequent to the diagnosis of a terminal and irreversible condition (sample form §1299.58.3(c))	Revocable at any time by declarant without regard to mental state or competency by (1) destruction of document; (2) written revocation signed and dated by declarant; (3) oral or nonverbal expression by the declarant of the intent to revoke. Effective upon communication to physician	Declaration properly executed in and under the laws of another state is deemed to be validly executed	Physician shall make a reasonable effort to transfer the patient to another physician	Any health care facility, physician, or other person acting under the direction of a physician shall not be civilly, criminally, or professionally liable for withholding life-sustaining procedures in accordance with the provisions of this chapter
MAINE 18-A§§5-801, *et seq*. Uniform Health-Care Decision Act.	Any medical procedure or intervention administered only to prolong process of dying. May include artificially administered nutrition and hydration	(1) In writing and signed of sound mind and over 18; (2) signed by declarant or another at his direction; (3) witnessed by 2 people; (4) communicated to attending physician; (5) effective upon determination that principal lacks capacity (6) physician records terms of declaration and determination of terminal condition	Revocable at any time and in any manner without regard to declarant's mental or physical condition. Revocation effective upon communication to attending physician or health care provider by declarant or witness to revocation	Declaration executed in another state in compliance with laws of that state and Maine is valid	Attending physician or other health care provider who is unwilling shall take all reasonable steps as promptly as practicable to transfer to another physician willing to comply and provide continuing care until transfer is effected. Willful failure to transfer is Class E crime	Physician or other health care provider whose action is in accord with reasonable medical standards and in good faith is not subject to criminal or civil liability or discipline for unprofessional conduct

Table 36c: Right to Die: Living Wills—Continued

State/Code Section	Specific Powers, Life- Prolonging Acts	Operative Facts	Revocation/ Duration	Reciprocity	Transfer of Patient if Physician Unwilling	Immunity for Attending Physician
MARYLAND 5-601, *et seq.* Health Care Decisions Act	Any medical procedure, treatment, or intervention which uses mechanical or other artificial means to maintain, restore a spontaneous vital function or of such a nature as to afford patient no reasonable expectation of recovery from a terminal condition, persistent vegetative state, or end-stage condition; includes artificially administered hydration, nutrition, and CPR. Does not include medication or procedure necessary to alleviate pain or provide comfort care; may include an anatomical gift directive	(1) Voluntary; (2) dated and in writing; (3) signed by declarant or at express direction of declarant; (4) subscribed by 2 witnesses; (5) effective when attending physician and second physician certify in writing that patient is incapable of making an informed decision on basis of physical examination within 2 hrs. of certification (if patient is unconscious, 2nd physician not required); (6) oral directives must be made in presence of attending physician and one witness; physician must sign and date documentation in patient's medical record. (suggested forms §5-603)	Revocable at any time by (1) signed and dated in writing; (2) oral statement to health care practitioner; (3) execution of subsequent directive; (4) destruction of directive.	Declaration executed out-of-state by nonresident is effective if declaration is in compliance with the laws of Maryland or the laws of the state where executed (to the extent permitted by the laws of Maryland)	Attending physician shall make every reasonable effort to transfer declarant to another health care provider; assist in transfer; and pending transfer, comply with competent individual or health care agent/ surrogate for person incapable of making a decision if failure to comply would likely result in death of individual.	Any health care provider who withholds or withdraws health care or life-sustaining procedures in accordance with this subtitle and in good faith, is not subject to civil or criminal liability and may not be found to have committed professional misconduct
MASSACHUSETTS No statutory provisions (But see Health Care Proxies Chap. 201D et seq.)						
MICHIGAN No statutory provisions (But see Uniform Durable Power of Attorney Act §700.496)						

Table 36c: Right to Die: Living Wills—Continued

State/Code Section	Specific Powers, Life- Prolonging Acts	Operative Facts	Revocation/ Duration	Reciprocity	Transfer of Patient if Physician Unwilling	Immunity for Attending Physician
MINNESOTA 145B.01, *et seq.* Living Will Act	Decisions on whether to administer, withhold, or withdraw medical treatment, services, or procedures to maintain, diagnose, or treat an individual's physical condition when the individual is in a terminal condition. Decisions must be based on reasonable medical practice including (1) continuation of appropriate care to maintain comfort, hygiene, human dignity, and to alleviate pain; (2) oral administration of food and water to a patient who accepts it, except for clearly documented medical reasons	(1) Competent adult; (2) signed by declarant; (3) signed by 2 witnesses or notary public; (4) must state preference regarding artificial administration of nutrition and hydration or give decision to proxy; (5) must be in substantially the statutory form of §145B.04; (6) operative when delivered to physician or health care provider; (7) not given effect if patient is pregnant and it is possible that fetus could develop to live birth with continued treatment	Revocable at any time in any manner in whole or in part by declarant without regard to declarant's physical or mental condition. Effective upon communication to physician. Divorce revokes any designation of the former spouse as a proxy to make health care decisions	Effective when executed in another state if it substantially complies with Minnesota law	Physician must notify competent declarant of unwillingness but has no duty to transfer. If physician received living will from competent patient and did not notify declarant of unwillingness to comply and declarant subsequently becomes incompetent, physician must take all reasonable steps to transfer to complying physician	
MISSISSIPPI 41-41-201, *et seq.* Uniform Health-Care Decisions Act	May authorize the withdrawal of life-sustaining mechanisms defined as cessation of use of extraordinary techniques and applications including mechanical devises which prolong life through artificial means	(1) Adult or emancipated minor; (2) in writing; (3) dated; (4) signed by principal; (5) signed by 2 adult witnesses, at least one of whom is not related to principal; (6) acknowledged by notary public.	Revocable at any time in any manner that comunicates an intent ot revoke. Designation of agent revoked only by signed writing or by personally informing physician.		Physician must promptly inform patient; provide continuing care until transfer can be effectuated; make all reasonable efforts to assist in transfer.	Physician acting in good faith and in accordance with provisions of this Act, who causes withdrawal of life-sustaining mechanisms is not guilty of a criminal offense, or civil or professional liability

Table 36c: Right to Die: Living Wills—Continued

State/Code Section	Specific Powers, Life- Prolonging Acts	Operative Facts	Revocation/ Duration	Reciprocity	Transfer of Patient if Physician Unwilling	Immunity for Attending Physician
MISSOURI 459.010, *et seq.* Declaration; Life Support	Any medical procedure or intervention which would serve only to prolong artificially the dying process where death will occur within a short time whether or not such procedure or intervention is utilized. Does not include medication or procedure to provide comfort care or alleviate pain or any procedure to provide nutrition or hydration	(1) Competent person; (2) in writing; (3) signed by declarant; (4) dated; (5) if not wholly in declarant's handwriting, signed in presence of 2 adult witnesses (sample form §459.015(3)); (6) operative only when declarant's condition is determined to be terminal or declarant is unable to make treatment decisions; (7) declaration shall have no effect during course of declarant's pregnancy	Revocable at any time in any manner declarant is able to communicate intent to revoke, without regard for mental or physical condition. Directions of declarant shall at all times supersede declaration		Physician must take all reasonable steps to effect the transfer of a declarant	No criminal, civil, or professional liability for acting in good faith pursuant to usual and customary medical standards who withholds or withdraws death-prolonging procedures from patient pursuant to a declaration

Table 36c: Right to Die: Living Wills—Continued

State/Code Section	Specific Powers, Life- Prolonging Acts	Operative Facts	Revocation/ Duration	Reciprocity	Transfer of Patient if Physician Unwilling	Immunity for Attending Physician
MONTANA 50-9-101 *et seq.* Rights of the Terminally Ill Act	Withholding or withdrawal of life-sustaining treatment, defined as any medical procedure or intervention that will serve only to prolong the dying process. Qualified patient may designate another individual to make decisions governing withholding or withdrawal of life-sustaining treatment. Life-sustaining procedures may not be withdrawn when qualified patient is known to be pregnant and when it is likely fctus will result in live birth	(1) 18 years or more and of sound mind; (2) signed by declarant or another at declarant's direction; (3) witnessed by 2 individuals; (4) communicated to physician and made part of patient's medical record; (5) declared to be terminal and no longer able to make decisions regarding life-sustaining treatment; (6) absent contrary actual notice, physician or health care provider may presume that declaration is valid (sample form §50-9-103)	Revocable at any time in any manner without regard to physical or mental condition. Effective upon communication to attending physician or health care provider. Health care provider or emergency medical services personnel in receipt of such communication shall act upon revocation an communicate it to attending physician at earliest opportunity. Revocation shall become part of declarant's medical record	Declaration made in another state in compliance with that state's laws executed in a substantially similar manner to laws of Montana is effective	Attending physician or health care provider who is unable or unwilling to comply shall take all reasonable steps as promptly as practicable to transfer to another who is willing	Attending physician or health care provider not subject to civil or criminal liability or guilty of unprofessional conduct as long as acting in accordance with reasonable medical standards and in good faith

Table 36c: Right to Die: Living Wills—Continued

State/Code Section	Specific Powers, Life- Prolonging Acts	Operative Facts	Revocation/ Duration	Reciprocity	Transfer of Patient if Physician Unwilling	Immunity for Attending Physician
NEBRASKA 20-401, *et seq.* Rights of the Terminally Ill Act	Any medical procedure or intervention that will serve only to prolong the process of dying or maintain the patient in a persistent vegetative act, meaning that to a reasonable degree of medical certainty one has a total and irreversible loss of consciousness and capacity for cognitive interaction with the environment with no reasonable hope of improvement. Does not affect physician's responsibility to provide treatment, including nutrition and hydration for patient's comfort care or alleviation of pain. Life-sustaining treatment shall be provided if declarant is pregnant and fetus is likely to develop to the point of live birth with continued application of life-sustaining treatment	(1) Adult of sound mind; (2) signed by declarant or another at declarant's direction; (3) witnessed by 2 adults or notary public (adult is one who is over 19 yrs. or is or has been married); (4) communicated to attending physician; (5) patient in terminal condition, persistent vegetative state, or unable to make decisions regarding administration of life-sustaining treatment (sample form §20-404)	Revocable at any time in any manner without regard to declarant's mental or physical condition effective upon communication to physician or other health care provider. Revocation shall become part of declarant's medical record.	Declaration executed in another state in compliance with that state or Nebraska is valid	Physician shall take all prompt and reasonable steps to transfer to a willing physician	Not subject to civil, criminal, or professional discipline in the absence of knowledge of revocation or whose action under this Act is in accord with reasonable medical standards. Unjustifiable violation of patient's directions shall be a civil cause of action maintainable by patient or patient's next officer

Table 36c: Right to Die: Living Wills—Continued

State/Code Section	Specific Powers, Life- Prolonging Acts	Operative Facts	Revocation/ Duration	Reciprocity	Transfer of Patient if Physician Unwilling	Immunity for Attending Physician
NEVADA 449.535, *et seq.* Uniform Act on Rights of the Terminally Ill	Any medical procedure which utilizes mechanical or other artificial methods to sustain, restore, or supplant a vital function; does not include medication or procedures necessary to alleviate pain. Artificial nutrition and hydration by way of gastro-intestinal tract is considered medical procedure or life sustaining treatment and must be withheld unless different desire is expressed in writing or agent has authority to withhold consent.	(1) 18 yrs. or older; (2) may designate another to make decisions governing withholding or withdrawing; (3) signed by declarant or another at declarant's direction; (4) 2 witnesses; (5) sample form §449-610 and 449-613; (6) not operative if patient is known to be pregnant and live birth is probable (7) declaration part of medical record	Revocable at any time and in any manner. Effective upon communication to the attending physician or other provider of health care	Declaration executed in another state in compliance with the law of that state or of this state is valid	Physician shall take all reasonable steps as promptly as possible to transfer care of declarant to another physician	Not subject to civil, criminal liability or professional discipline if acted in good faith and in accordance with reasonable medical standards. No liability for failure to follow patient's directions; physician may consider "other factors" in determining whether the circumstances warrant following the directions

Table 36c: Right to Die: Living Wills—Continued

State/Code Section	Specific Powers, Life- Prolonging Acts	Operative Facts	Revocation/ Duration	Reciprocity	Transfer of Patient if Physician Unwilling	Immunity for Attending Physician
NEW HAMPSHIRE 137-H:1 *et seq.* Living Wills	Qualified patient may instruct physician not to use life-sustaining procedures in the event the person is in a terminal condition or is permanently unconscious. "Life-sustaining procedures" means any medical procedure or intervention which utilizes mechanical or artificial means to sustain, restore, or supplant a vital function which would only serve to artificially postpone the moment of death where in the written judgement of the attending and consulting physician, the patient is in a terminal condition or permanently unconscious; does not include medication, sustenance, or performance of any medical procedure to alleviate pain or provide comfort. There must be a clear expression of one's intent to withdraw or withhold artificial nutrition and hydration.	(1) Person of sound mind, 18 yrs. or older; (2) document signed voluntarily by declarant (3) 2 subscribing witnesses not a spouse or heir at law; (4) upon request, physician shall made document part of medical record; (5) effective if person is permanently incapable of participating in decisions about his care; (6) suggested form §137-H:3; (7) not permitted when physician has knowledge that patient is pregnant	Revocable by (1) destroying document; (2) oral or written revocation before 2 witnesses. Revocation effective upon communication to attending physician	Documents executed in another state are enforceable if in compliance with the law of that state or jurisdiction; foreign living wills are restricted by, and must be in compliance with laws and requirements of New Hampshire	Physician unwilling or unable to comply shall notify and inform the patient and/or patient's family. Patient or his family may then request transfer to another physician. Physician shall make necessary arrangements without delay to effect transfer to chosen physician	Physician or health care professional is immune from civil or criminal liability for good faith actions in keeping with reasonable medical standards pursuant to the living will and in accordance with New Hampshire Law

Table 36c: Right to Die: Living Wills—Continued

State/Code Section	Specific Powers, Life- Prolonging Acts	Operative Facts	Revocation/ Duration	Reciprocity	Transfer of Patient if Physician Unwilling	Immunity for Attending Physician
NEW JERSEY 26:2H-53, *et seq.* Advanced Directives for Health Care	Decisions to accept or refuse any treatment, service, or procedure used to diagnose, treat, or care for a patient's physical or mental condition including life-sustaining treatment; includes decisions to accept or refuse services of a particular physician or health care provider or a transfer of care; or use of any medical device or procedure, artificially provided fluids and nutrition drugs, surgery, or therapy that uses mechanical or other artificial means to sustain, restore, or supplant a vital bodily function and thereby increase the expected life span of a patient; does not include providing comfort care or to alleviate pain.	(1) Competent; (2) adult; (3) signed; (4) dated; (5) in presence of 2 witnesses who shall attest that declarant is of sound mind and free of duress and undue influence or in front of a notary public, attorney, or another person authorized to administer oaths. May be supplemented by video or audio tape recording; (6) directive implemented when determination of lack of decision-making capacity is documented and confirmed by physicians	Revocable by oral or written notification or execution of subsequent directive. Divorce revokes former spouse's designation as the health care representative. Patient's clearly expressed wishes take precedent over any patient's decision or instruction directive	Effective if executed in compliance with New Jersey law or the laws of that state. Effective if executed in a foreign country in compliance with that country's laws or the laws of New Jersey and is not contrary to the public policy of New Jersey	Physician should act as soon as practicable to effect an appropriate, respectful, and timely transfer of care and to assure that patient is not abandoned or treated disrespectfully	No civil, criminal, or professional liability for any physician acting in good faith and pursuant to this act
NEW MEXICO 24-7A-1, *et seq.* Uniform Health-Care Decisions Act	Any medical treatment or procedure without which the individual is likely to die within a short time	(1) Of sound mind; (2) age of majority; (3) written or oral; (4) dated; (5) 2 adult witnesses; (6) effective when patient no longer able to make own health-care decisions.	Revocable at any time in any way tha communicates an intent to revoke.	Document Uniformly applied and construed among states enacting Uniform Health-Care Decisions Act.	Physician must take appropriate steps to transfer the patient to another qualified physician and provice continuing care to patient until transfer.	No civil or criminal liability or professional discipline for acting pursuant to statute in good faith

Table 36c: Right to Die: Living Wills—Continued

State/Code Section	Specific Powers, Life- Prolonging Acts	Operative Facts	Revocation/ Duration	Reciprocity	Transfer of Patient if Physician Unwilling	Immunity for Attending Physician
NEW YORK No statutory provisions (But see Health Care Agents and Proxies Public Health Art.29-C §2980 *et seq.*)						
NORTH CAROLINA 90-320, *et seq.* Right to Natural Death	Declarant may instruct attending physicians to withhold extraordinary means to keep declarant alive whose condition is either terminal and incurable or who is in a persistent vegetative state as confirmed in writing by second physician which would only serve to postpone artificially the moment of death by sustaining, restoring, or supplanting a vital function	(1) Signed; (2) in the presence of 2 witnesses who believe declarant is of sound mind; (3) dated; (4) notarized or proved before a clerk; (5) specific form §90-321(a)	Revocable in any manner by which declarant is able to communicate his intent to revoke without regard for mental or physical state— effective upon communication to physician			Withholding or discontinuing of extraordinary means shall not be considered cause of death for civil or criminal purposes. These provisions may be asserted as a defense to any civil or criminal suits or charges filed against a health care provider

Table 36c: Right to Die: Living Wills—Continued

State/Code Section	Specific Powers, Life- Prolonging Acts	Operative Facts	Revocation/ Duration	Reciprocity	Transfer of Patient if Physician Unwilling	Immunity for Attending Physician
NORTH DAKOTA 23.06.4-01, *et seq.* Uniform Rights of Terminally Ill Act	Any medical procedure, treatment, or intervention that serves only to prolong the process of dying. Does not include the provision of the appropriate nutrition and hydration (presumed to be in the best interests of the patient) or any medical procedure necessary to provide comfort care or to alleviate pain or procedures performed in emergency, pre-hospital situations; medical treatment must be provided to a pregnant patient—unless to a reasonable degree of certainty, such treatment won't maintain patient to ensure live birth or is physically harmful	(1) Sound mind; (2) 18 yrs.; (3) signed by declarant; (4) witnessed by 2 persons; (5) substantially same form as §23-06.4-03 (3) (may add specific directives)	Revocable at any time in any manner as long as declarant is competent, including (1) by signed, dated writing; (2) destruction of document; (3) oral expression of intent to revoke. Effective upon communication to physician or other health care provider	Effective if executed in another state by a resident of that state in compliance with the laws of that state or the laws of North Dakota	Physician must take all reasonable steps to transfer patient as promptly as practical to physician willing to comply with statute	No civil, criminal, or professional liability for actions authorized by statute unless done in a grossly negligent manner
OHIO 2133.01, *et seq.* Modified Uniform Rights of the Terminally Ill Act	Any medical procedure, treatment, intervention, or other measure that will serve principally to prolong the process of dying. Declarant may authorize withholding hydration and nutrition; cannot withdraw or withhold life-sustaining treatment from pregnant patient, unless it is believed to a reasonable degree of certainty, that the fetus would not be born alive.	(1) Adult; (2) of sound mind; (3) signed by declarant; (4) dated; (5) in presence of 2 witnesses or a notary public who attests that principal is of sound mind and free from duress	Revocable at any time and in any manner; effective when expressed and communicated to a witness or physician	Effective if executed in another state in compliance with that law or in substantial compliance with Ohio law	Physician may not prevent or unreasonably delay a transfer	No civil, criminal, or professional liability for physician acting in good faith within the scope of their authority

Table 36c: Right to Die: Living Wills—Continued

State/Code Section	Specific Powers, Life- Prolonging Acts	Operative Facts	Revocation/ Duration	Reciprocity	Transfer of Patient if Physician Unwilling	Immunity for Attending Physician
OKLAHOMA Tit. 63 §3101.1 *et seq.*; §3080 *et seq.* Rights of the Terminally Ill or Persistently Unconscious Act	Any medical procedure or intervention that will serve only to prolong the dying process including artificial administration of nutrition and hydration but only if declarant has specifically authorized its withdrawal. Does not include treatment to alleviate pain or the normal consumption of food and water	(1) 18 yrs.; (2) of sound mind; (3) signed by declarant; (4) witnessed by 2 adults; (5) in substantially the same form as §3103.4(B); (6) operative when communicated to attending physician and when declarant can no longer make decisions regarding the administration of life-sustaining treatment; not operative during course of pregnancy	Revocable in whole or in part in any manner at any time without regard to declarant's mental or physical condition. Effective upon communication to physician	Effective if complies with Oklahoma law or in compliance with law of that state so long as it does not exceed authorizations allowed under Oklahoma law	Physician shall take all reasonable steps to arrange for care by another physician; must comply with decision until transfer.	No civil, criminal, or professional liability for carrying out the advance directive pursuant to statute in good faith and in accord with reasonable medical standards
OREGON 127.505, *et seq.* Advance Directives for Health Care	Life-sustaining acts means mechanical or other artificial means to sustain, restore, or supplant a vital function that is used to maintain life of a person suffering from a terminal condition and serves only to prolong artificially the moment of death; does not include procedures to sustain patient cleanliness and comfort	(1) In writing; (2) signed by two witnesses who make written declaration; (3) mandatory statutory form §127.531 ORS; (4) at least one witness must not be related to declarant	Agent may withdraw up to time of principal's incapacity. Principal may revoke (1) in any manner by which s/he is able to communicate to health care provider or attorney-in-fact, intent to revoke; (2) by execution of subsequent durable power of attorney; (3) upon divorce if spouse is agent	Valid subject to laws of Oregon if executed in compliance with the laws of the state where principal is located or resides or with the laws of the state of Oregon.	Physician shall notify any representative or discharge patient (without abandoning) or make a reasonable effort to locate and transfer to a willing physician.	No liability, if in good faith has acted on fully executed directive, for criminal or civil liability or professional disciplinary action

Table 36c: Right to Die: Living Wills—Continued

State/Code Section	Specific Powers, Life- Prolonging Acts	Operative Facts	Revocation/ Duration	Reciprocity	Transfer of Patient if Physician Unwilling	Immunity for Attending Physician
PENNSYLVANIA 20§5401 *et seq.* Advanced Directive for Health Care Act	Any medical procedure or intervention that serves only to prolong the process of dying or maintain the patient in a state of permanent unconsciousness; includes artificially or invasively administered nutrition and hydration if specifically provided for in declaration. Does not apply to emergency medical services.	(1) sound mind; (2) 18 yrs. or graduated from high school or married; (3) signed by declarant; (4) 2 adult witnesses; (5) suggested form 20§5404(b); (6) operative when declarant determined to be incompetent by attending physician as certified in writing; (7) not operative during pregnancy unless it will not maintain woman so as to permit live birth	Revoked at any time in any manner without regard to declarant's mental or physical condition. Effective upon communication to physician.		Unwilling physician must inform declarant, surrogate, or family, and make every reasonable effort to assist in the transfer of declarant to complying physician	No civil, criminal, or professional liability in following wishes of declarant pursuant to declaration executed according to statute.
RHODE ISLAND 23-4.11-1, *et seq.* Rights of Terminally Ill Act	Any medical procedure or intervention serving only to prolong the dying process. Does not include anything necessary to alleviate pain or provide comfort and care; must wear DNR bracelet in order to effectuate "do not resuscitate" order.	(1) 18 yrs.; (2) signed; (3) in presence of 2 witnesses (suggested form §23-4.11-3(a)); (4) given no force or effect as long as live birth is probable for pregnant patient; neither witness related to declarant.	Revocable at any time in any manner by which declarant is able to communicate the intent to revoke without regard to physical or mental condition. Only effective upon communication to physician by declarant or one witnessing the revocation	Declaration executed in another state in compliance with the laws of that state is valid.	Physician shall make necessary arrangements to effect a transfer	No civil, criminal, or professional liability for acting in accordance with requirements of the statute and in accordance with reasonable medical standards

Table 36c: Right to Die: Living Wills—Continued

State/Code Section	Specific Powers, Life- Prolonging Acts	Operative Facts	Revocation/ Duration	Reciprocity	Transfer of Patient if Physician Unwilling	Immunity for Attending Physician
SOUTH CAROLINA 44-77-10, *et seq.* Death with Dignity Act	Medical procedures or intervention serving only to prolong the dying process; does not include treatment for comfort care or pain alleviation; declarant should indicate whether nutrition and hydration through surgically implanted tubes is desired; if declarant fails to do so, nutrition and hydration necessary for comfort care and pain alleviation will be provided.	(1) Declaration must set out intent for no life-sustaining procedures; (2) signed; (3) dated; (4) in presence of officer authorized to administer oaths; (5) presence of 2 witnesses; (6) substantially same as §44-77-50; (7) not effective during course of declarant's pregnancy; (8) terminal condition must be certified by 2 examining physicians (permanent unconsciousness must be at least for 90 days; or with high degree of medical certainty and must be given active treatment for at least 6 hrs. following diagnosis before physician can give effect to declaration).	(1) Destruction of document when communicated to physician; (2) written revocation signed and dated upon communication to physician; oral expression of intent to revoke when communicated to physician; (3) communication of oral revocation may be made by someone present when revocation made, if communicated within reasonable time and declarant is physically or mentally able to confirm or by designee if declarant is incompetent; (4) execution of subsequent declaration	For patients in terminal condition, document with same intent as this chapter and in compliance with the laws of that state is effective.	Physician must make a reasonable effort to locate a physician who will effectuate patient's declaration and has a duty to transfer patient to such physician	No criminal or civil liability for acting in good faith and in accordance with the standards of reasonable medical care pursuant to the statute

Table 36c: Right to Die: Living Wills—Continued

State/Code Section	Specific Powers, Life- Prolonging Acts	Operative Facts	Revocation/ Duration	Reciprocity	Transfer of Patient if Physician Unwilling	Immunity for Attending Physician
SOUTH DAKOTA 34-12D-1, *et seq.* Living Wills	Any medical procedure or intervention that will serve only to postpone death or maintain person in state of permanent unconsciousness. Does not include comfort care, hygiene and human dignity, oral administration of food and water, or medical procedure to alleviate pain	(1) Competent adult; (2) signed by declarant; (3) witnessed by 2 adults; (4) may be in presence of notary public (suggested form §34-12D.3); (5) not operative for pregnant woman unless live birth unlikely to a reasonable degree of medical certainty	Revocable at any time in any manner without regard to declarant's physical or mental condition. Effective upon communication to physician or other health care provider	Document is valid if it meets execution requirements of place where executed, place where declarant was a resident, or requirements of the state of South Dakota	Unwilling physician must make a reasonable effort to locate and transfer a patient to a physician who will honor the declaration; must continue treatment or care until transfer is effectuated	No civil, criminal, or professional liability for giving effect to a declaration
TENNESSEE 32-11-101, *et seq.* Right to Natural Death Act	Any procedure, treatment to diagnose, assess, or treat a disease, illness, or injury. Includes surgery, drugs, transfusions, mechanical ventilation, dialysis, CPR, artificial nourishment, hydration or other nutrients, radiation. Death by starvation or dehydration allowed only if specifically directed by using statutory phrase.	(1) Competent adult; (2) signed; (3) in presence of 2 witnesses; (4) substantially in form of §32-11-105. Witnesses must not be related to declarant.	Revocable at any time by declarant regardless of mental state if effectively communicated to the physician by written revocation dated and signed or oral statement made to physician	Effective if in compliance with Tennessee law or the law of the state of declarant's residence	Unwilling physician must make every reasonable effort to assist in a transfer. Failure to do so will subject him to civil and professional liability	No civil, criminal, or professional liability if acting in accord with reasonable medical standards

Table 36c: Right to Die: Living Wills—Continued

State/Code Section	Specific Powers, Life- Prolonging Acts	Operative Facts	Revocation/ Duration	Reciprocity	Transfer of Patient if Physician Unwilling	Immunity for Attending Physician
TEXAS Health & Safety Code §672.001, *et seq.* Natural Death Act	Medical procedure or intervention that uses mechanical or other artificial means to sustain, restore, or supplant a vital function and artificially postpone the moment of death of a patient in terminal condition whose death is imminent within a relatively short time without the procedure. Does not include administration of medication or performance of procedure to provide comfort or alleviate pain. May designate a person to make treatment decisions in the event declarant becomes comatose or otherwise incompetent.	(1) Competent adult; (2) 2 witnesses; (3) may be oral with 2 witnesses and attending physician; (4) directive shall become a part of medical record of declarant (if oral, witnesses must sign medical records) (suggested form: §672.004); (5) not operative for pregnant patients	Revocable at any time without regard to declarant's mental state or competency. May be revoked by declarant or someone in presence destroying document; by signed and dated written revocation; orally stating intent to revoke. Effective when delivered or mailed to attending physician, or when physician notified of oral revocation. Directive effective until revoked. Desire of qualified competent patient supersedes directive		Unwilling physician must make reasonable effort to transfer patient to another physician	Immune from effects of revocation if not adequately notified. No criminal or civil liability for failing to effectuate a directive if there is no knowledge of it. By complying with legal directive, one does not commit act of criminally aiding suicide. It is Class A misdemeanor to destroy or conceal directive without declarant's consent. A person is guilty of criminal homicide if they procure directive by forgery or deception. No civil, criminal, or professional liability for acting in accordance with this Act unless negligent.

Table 36c: Right to Die: Living Wills—Continued

State/Code Section	Specific Powers, Life- Prolonging Acts	Operative Facts	Revocation/ Duration	Reciprocity	Transfer of Patient if Physician Unwilling	Immunity for Attending Physician
UTAH 75-2-1101; Personal Choice and Living Will Act	Any medical procedure or intervention that would serve only to prolong the dying process including artificial nutrition and hydration unless declaration specifically excludes; does not include medication, sustenance, or any procedure to alleviate pain or provide comfort care. Separate procedure for do not resuscitate directive	(1) 18 yrs.; (2) in writing; (3) signed by declarant or at his directive; (4) dated; (5) signed in presence of 2 or more adult witnesses; (6) substantially same form as §75-2-1104(4); (7) no force during course of declarant's pregnancy	Current wishes of declarant take precedent over any directive. Revocable at any time by signed revocation or destruction of document or oral expression of intent to revoke in presence of adult witness. Effective on receipt by physician	Similar instrument executed in another state is presumed to comply with Utah law and may be relied upon in good faith	Unwilling physician required to transfer patient promptly	No civil, criminal, or professional liability for good faith compliance with a directive
VERMONT Tit. 18 §§5251, *et seq.* Terminal Care Document	Any medical procedure or intervention utilizing mechanical or other artificial means to sustain, restore, supplant a vital function serving only to postpone the moment of death and where patient is in a terminal state according to judgment of physician	(1) 18 yrs.; (2) of sound mind; (3) in presence of 2 or more witnesses; (4) suggested form: §5253	Revocable only orally in presence of 2 or more witnesses or by destroying the document		Unwilling physician must actively assist in selecting another physician willing to honor patient's directive	No civil or criminal liability for physician acting pursuant to the terminal care document

Table 36c: Right to Die: Living Wills—Continued

State/Code Section	Specific Powers, Life- Prolonging Acts	Operative Facts	Revocation/ Duration	Reciprocity	Transfer of Patient if Physician Unwilling	Immunity for Attending Physician
VIRGINIA 54.1-2981, *et seq.* Health Care Decision Act	Any medical procedure, treatment, intervention, utilizing mechanical or other artificial means to sustain, restore, or supplant a vital function, or is of a nature to afford a patient no reasonable expectation of recovery from a terminal condition, and when applied to a patient in terminal condition, would serve only to prolong the dying process. Includes artificially administered hydration and nutrition and CPR by emergency medical services personnel but does not include any medication or procedure to alleviate pain or provide comfort care.	(1) Competent adult; (2) written advance directive; (3) signed in presence of 2 subscribing witnesses; (4) oral declaration in presence of physician and 2 witnesses for those in terminal condition; (5) responsibility of declarant to provide notification of advanced directive to attending physician (suggested form §54.1-2984)	Revocable at any time by (1) signed, dated writing; (2) physical cancellation or destruction of declaration; (3) oral expression of intent to revoke. Effective upon communication to attending physician	Directive executed in another state valid if in compliance with Virginia law or law of state where executed. Such directives shall be construed in accordance with Virginia laws.	If physician thinks treatment is medically or ethically inappropriate or contrary to terms of advanced directive, unwilling physician shall make reasonable effort to transfer patient to another physician.	No civil, criminal, or professional liability if acting in good faith. It would have to be shown by preponderance of the evidence that the person authorizing life-prolonging procedures acted in bad faith
WASHINGTON 70.122.010, *et seq.* Natural Death Act	Withdrawal or withholding of any medical or surgical intervention which utilizes mechanical or other artificial means including artificially provided nutrition and hydration to sustain, restore, or supplant a vital function which would serve only to artificially prolong life. Shall not include administration of medication to alleviate pain	(1) Any adult; (2) signed by declarant; (3) presence of 2 witnesses; (4) suggested form: §70.122.030. Witnesses must not be related to declarer.	Revocable at any time without regard to declarer's mental state or competency by defacing or destroying document; written revocation signed and dated and communicated to attending physician; oral revocation to physician by declarant or one acting on behalf of declarant	Valid to the extent permitted by Washington law and federal constitution law	Attending physician must inform patient or agent of any policy that would preclude the honoring of patient's directive. If patient chooses to retain that physician, a written plan is filed showing physician's intended actions should directive become operative.	No civil, criminal, or professional liability if acting in good faith unless otherwise negligent

Table 36c: Right to Die: Living Wills—Continued

State/Code Section	Specific Powers, Life- Prolonging Acts	Operative Facts	Revocation/ Duration	Reciprocity	Transfer of Patient if Physician Unwilling	Immunity for Attending Physician
WEST VIRGINIA 16-30-1, *et seq.* West Virginia Natural Death Act	Any medical procedure or intervention which should serve solely to artificially prolong the dying process or maintain the person in a persistent vegetative state; does not include medication or other medical procedure necessary for comfort or to alleviate pain	(1) 18 yrs.; (2) in writing; (3) executed by declarant or at his direction; (4) dated; (5) in presence of 2 witnesses; (6) in front of notary public; (7) suggested form: §16-30-3(e)	Revocable at any time without regard to declarant's mental state by destruction of document, written revocation effective on delivery or verbal expression in presence of a witness; desires of capable declarant always supersede effect-of-living will	Valid in West Virginia if executed in compliance with West Virginia law or the law of state where executed and expressly provides for withholding or withdrawal of life-prolonging intervention or termination of life-sustaining procedure	Unwilling physician must effect a transfer to physician willing to honor the living will	No criminal or civil liability if acting in good faith and pursuant to reasonable medical standards
WISCONSIN 154.01, *et seq.* Natural Death	Any medical procedure or intervention that would serve to prolong the dying process but not avert death; includes assistance in respiration, artificial maintenance of blood pressure and heart rate, blood transfusion, kidney dialysis, and similar procedures but does not include pain alleviation or provision of nutrition or hydration	(1) 18 yrs. and of sound mind; (2) signed; (3) in presence of 2 witnesses; (4) notify physician; (5) form: §154.03; (6) no effect during pregnancy; (7) may file with register in probate. Witnesses must not be related to declarant.	Revocable at any time by destruction of document, written revocation signed and dated, or verbal expression of revocation effective upon notifying physician. Desires of qualified patient supersede declaration at all times			No criminal, civil, or professional liability when acting in good faith

Table 36c: Right to Die: Living Wills—Continued

State/Code Section	Specific Powers, Life- Prolonging Acts	Operative Facts	Revocation/ Duration	Reciprocity	Transfer of Patient if Physician Unwilling	Immunity for Attending Physician
WYOMING 35-22-101 *et seq.* Living Will	Any medical procedure, intervention, or nourishment by artificial means which would serve only to prolong the dying process of a qualified patient; does not include medication or procedure necessary for comfort care or alleviation of pain	(1) Adult; (2) in writing; (3) signed and dated; (4) in presence of 2 or more adult witnesses; (5) substantially same form as §35-22-102(d); (6) no effect during course of qualified patient's pregnancy; (7) terminal condition must be certified in writing by 2 physicians. Witnesses must not be related to declarant.	Revocable by destruction of document, written revocation, verbal expression of intent to revoke in presence of adult witness. Patient's immediate desires at all times supersede the document		Unwilling physician must attempt to effect transfer of patient	No criminal or civil liability for physician acting in good faith and pursuant to reasonable medical standards

37. STALKING

Stalking is a relatively new crime now on the books in every state. It is generally defined as the intentional, repeated following of a person for the purpose of harassing the person with express or implied threats of violence or death. The definitions vary only slightly from state to state with some states adding things like lying in wait, surveillance, or warnings from police officers. Stalking statutes have become very important legal devices that, with protective orders, can help shield people from the threatening or harassing behavior of others in a variety of circumstances.

Most notably, celebrities have been the victims of stalking activity, when fans become obsessed with the object of their attention. Stalking may also occur when a jilted lover becomes obsessed with his or her ex-lover or spouse, or even when a person becomes obsessed with a complete stranger or co-worker. The crime can turn every day life into a nightmare for the victim of this crime. Consequently states have been quick to enact laws that specifically protect victims from harassing or stalking activity, even if the victim has not yet actually been physically injured by the defendant.

Several states have particular requirements in order for enhanced penalties to apply. The enhanced stalking crimes are usually distinguished by their designations as either first and second degree, or felony and misde-

meanor stalking. Most often, enhancements are if the victim is below a certain age, or if the defendant has violated a court order or protective order, or if a deadly weapon was used.

Minnesota has a very broad stalker statute that exemplifies the variety of situations in which the law is used. Under this law, a person can be found guilty of stalking by harassment, or by intent to injure person, property or rights of another. A stalker may stalk using telephone calls, letters, telegraphs, delivery of packages or engaging in any conduct which interferes or intrudes on another's privacy or liberty. These acts are considered "gross misdemeanors." They are various situations where the crime of stalking in Minnesota is increased to a felony if the harassing activity is based on race, color, religion, sex, sexual orientation, disability or national origin, if stalking is accomplished by falsely impersonating another or using a dangerous weapon, if the victim is under 18 or if stalker is more than 36 months older than the victim. Although Minnesota's state is unusual in terms of the breadth and detailed listing of activities covered, nearly every element contained in it can be found in some form in the provisions of some other state. A few states have added to the stalker's penalties liability for the victim's counseling for emotional trauma caused by the stress of the stalking experience.

Table 37: Stalking

State/Code Section	Defined As	Punishment/ Classification	Repeat Offense	Arrest or Restraining Order Specifically Authorized by Statute?	Constitutionally Protected Activities Exempted?
ALABAMA 13A-6-90, *et seq.*	A person who intentionally and repeatedly follows or harasses another and who makes a credible threat, express or implied, with intent to place person in reasonable fear of death or serious bodily harm	The crime of stalking is a Class C felony. Aggravated stalking if stalking and also violates any court order or injunction. Aggravated stalking is a Class B felony.			Yes
ALASKA 11.41.260 & 41.270	Knowingly engage in course of conduct that recklessly places another in fear of death or physical injury or in fear of death or physical injury of a family member	Stalking in the 1st degree (Class C felony) requires stalking plus violation of an order, probation, parole; under 16 years old, use of a deadly weapon, or previous conviction. Stalking in the 2nd degree is a Class A misdemeanor			
ARIZONA 13-2923	Intentionally or knowingly engages in course of conduct that is directed toward another and causes fear	Class 5 felony unless fear imminent physical injury or death then Class 4 felony;			
ARKANSAS 5-71-229	Stalking in 1st degree: purposely engages in course of conduct that harasses another person and makes a terroristic threat with intent of placing in imminent fear and (A) violates protective order or a no contact order or (B) has been convicted in previous 10 years of stalking or (C) is armed with a deadly weapon or represents that they are so armed. 2nd degree stalking: purposely engages in course of conduct that harasses another person and makes a terroristic threat with intent of placing in imminent fear	Stalking in 1st degree: Class B felony; Stalking in 2nd degree: Class C felony [Language of statute does not state this. However, the "degrees" of stalking imply repeat offense.]	If within 10 years: Stalking in 1st degree: Class B felony		Yes

Table 37: Stalking—Continued

State/Code Section	Defined As	Punishment/ Classification	Repeat Offense	Arrest or Restraining Order Specifically Authorized by Statute?	Constitutionally Protected Activities Exempted?
CALIFORNIA Penal 646.9	Willfully, maliciously, and repeatedly follows or harasses another and makes credible threat with intent to place another in reasonable fear of death or great bodily injury or to place [in fear of] the death or great bodily injury of his/her immediate family, 646.9(a) as amended by 1992 amendments/ 1993 amendments	1 year in county jail and/or $1,000; if probation granted or sentenced suspended, counseling required. However, court, upon showing of good cause, may find that counseling shall not be imposed. 646.9(j)	If stalks when there is a temporary restraining order, injunction, court order, is punishable by imprisonment in a county jail for not more than 1 year and/or $1,000 fine. 646.9(b) as amended by 1993 amendment. Every person who, having been convicted of a felony under this section, commits second/subsequent violation of section against the same victim and involving an act of violence or credible threat of violence is punishable in state prison for 16 months, two or three years and $10,000 fine. 646.9(c) as amended by 1993 amendment	Restraining order may be valid for up to 10 years. 646.9(k)	Constitutionally protected activity is not included within the meaning of "course of conduct" 646.9 (f). Section does not apply to labor picketing. 646.9(i)
COLORADO 18-9-111 4(a)(I)(II)	If directly or indirectly through another person knowingly (1) makes a credible threat to another person and, in connection with such threat, repeatedly follows person or person's immediate family or (2) makes credible threat to another person and, in connection with such threat, repeatedly makes any form of communication with that person or person's immediate family, whether or not a conversation ensues	Class 3 misdemeanor. If person knowingly makes threats and follows party or their family or makes any form of communication with party or their family: Class 6 felony if 1st offense. If at time of offense there is a temporary restraining order, injunction, or other court order: Class 6 felony	If within 7 years of a Class 6 felony: Class 5 felony 18-9-111 5(a)(9.5)		No

Table 37: Stalking—Continued

State/Code Section	Defined As	Punishment/ Classification	Repeat Offense	Arrest or Restraining Order Specifically Authorized by Statute?	Constitutionally Protected Activities Exempted?
CONNECTICUT 53a-181 (c)(d)(c)	Stalking in 1st degree 53a-181(c): Commission of stalking in the 2nd degree and (1) has been previously convicted of this section or 53a-181(d) or (2) such conduct violates a court order in effect at the time of the offense or (3) person is under 16 Stalking in the 2nd degree 53a-181(d): When, with intent to cause another person to fear for his physical safety, he wilfully and repeatedly follows or lies in wait for person and causes person to reasonably fear for physical safety Stalking in the 3rd degree 53a-181(e): When recklessly causes another person to reasonably fear for physical safety by wilfully and repeatedly following or lying in wait for such person	Stalking 1st degree: Class D felony; Stalking 2nd degree: Class A misdemeanor; Stalking 3rd degree: Class B misdemeanor	See 1st degree.		No

Table 37: Stalking—Continued

State/Code Section	Defined As	Punishment/ Classification	Repeat Offense	Arrest or Restraining Order Specifically Authorized by Statute?	Constitutionally Protected Activities Exempted?
DELAWARE Tit. 11 §1312A	Any person who intentionally engages in a course of conduct directed at specific person which would cause a reasonable person to fear physical injury to himself, to a friend/associate, to family member or to third person and whose conduct induces such fear. (1998 supp.) 1312A(a)	If commit the crime of stalking by engaging in a course of conduct which includes any act(s) prohibited by a then-existing court order or sentence, shall be sentenced minimum of 6 months. (1998 supp.). 1312A(f) Stalking is a Class F felony. If course of conduct includes threat of death/serious physical injury to victim, immediate family or third person, it is a Class D felony. If perpetrator possesses deadly weapon during act comprising course of conduct, it is a Class C felony. (1998 supp.). 1312A(e)	If convicted of stalking within 5 years of prior conviction, shall receive minimum 1 year sentence (1998 supp.). 1312A(g)	No	No. Lawful picketing is an affirmative defense; also conduct that occurs in furtherance of law enforcement activities or to private investigators, security officers or private detectives. (1998 supp.). 1312A(c) and (d)
DISTRICT OF COLUMBIA 22-504	Intent to cause emotional distress or place in reasonable fear by repeated following or harassing; or willfully or maliciously and repeatedly follows or harasses. 22-504(b)	Fined maximum $500 and/or imprisonment maximum 1 year. If court order pending: must give bond for maximum 1 year. 22-504(b)	If within 2 years of 1st conviction: fine up to 1.5 times maximum fine authorized and imprisonment up to 1.5 times maximum term authorized. 22-504(d). If convicted more than once: fine up to 3 times maximum fine authorized and imprisonment up to 3 times maximum term		Yes. 22-504(b); conduct by a party to a labor dispute in furtherance of labor or management objectives in that dispute . . .

Table 37: Stalking—Continued

State/Code Section	Defined As	Punishment/ Classification	Repeat Offense	Arrest or Restraining Order Specifically Authorized by Statute?	Constitutionally Protected Activities Exempted?
FLORIDA 784.048	Willful, malicious, and repeated following or harassing. 704.048(2)	Sentencing/fines: apply 775.082, 083,084 Stalking misdemeanor is 1st degree Aggravated stalking is felony of the 3rd degree 784.048(3), (4) and (5) Aggravated stalking: wilful, malicious and repeated following or harassing another with credible threats with the intent to place person in reasonable fear of death or bodily injury; or wilfully, maliciously, repeatedly follows or harasses minor under 16; or after injunction for protection or any court-imposed prohibition of conduct, knowingly, wilfully, maliciously and repeatedly follows or harasses another person.	In violation of injunction or domestic violence protective order: felony in 3rd degree	Arrest without warrant if probable cause to believe statute is violated. 784.048(6)	Yes. 784.048(1)(b); includes picketing and organized protests
GEORGIA 16-5-90, *et seq.* [1998: changes in 1996 supplement]	Following, surveillance, or contact with another to harass and intimidate. Aggravated stalking: stalking in violation of court order, bond, injunction or probation 16-5-90(a) 16-5-91(a)	Misdemeanor. Aggravated stalking: felony; imprisonment minimum 1 year and maximum 10 years and fine maximum $10,000 16-5-90(b) 16-5-91(b)	For 2nd and subsequent convictions: felony; imprisonment minimum 1 year and maximum 5 years 16-5-90(c)		Yes. 16-5-92
HAWAII 711.1106, *et seq.*	Pursuit or surveillance with intent to harass, annoy, or alarm or in reckless disregard of risk thereof without legitimate purpose and which causes other to reasonably believe actor intends to cause bodily injury or property damage	Petty misdemeanor. Aggravated stalking: if stalking and previously convicted of stalking same person and actions in violation of court order or action violates probation or pretrial release: Class C felony	If person harasses another by stalking on one occasion for same/similar purpose, becomes misdemeanor. 711-1106.5(2). See also definition of aggravated stalking		

Table 37: Stalking—Continued

State/Code Section	Defined As	Punishment/ Classification	Repeat Offense	Arrest or Restraining Order Specifically Authorized by Statute?	Constitutionally Protected Activities Exempted?
IDAHO 18-7905	Willful, malicious and repeated following or harassing of person or their immediate family. 18-7905(a)	Jail maximum 1 year and/or fine maximum $1,000. If violates temporary restraining order or injunction against same person: jail maximum 1 year and/or fine maximum $1,000	If within 7 years of prior convictions against same person: felony		
ILLINOIS Ch. 720 §5/12-7.3	Knowingly and without lawful justification follows or surveils another on at least 2 separate occasions and threatens or places in reasonable apprehension	Aggravated stalking is stalking in conjunction with causing bodily harm, confining or restraining victim or violating court order or injunction. Aggravated stalking: Class 3 felony	2nd or subsequent conviction: Class 2 felony		Picketing or exercise of the right of free speech or assembly that is otherwise lawful
INDIANA 35-45-10, *et seq.*	Knowing or intentional conduct with repeated acts that would cause reasonable person to feel terrorized, frightened or threatened and that actually causes such feelings. 35-45-10-1	Class D felony. Class C felony if at least one of the following applies: (1) a person stalks and makes threat with intent to place victim in reasonable fear; or (2) court issued order to protect same victim(s) and perpetrator has actual notice of order; or (3) a criminal complaint of stalking pending in court and perpetrator has actual notice of complaint. Class B felony if: the act(s) were committed with deadly weapon or perpetrator has unrelated conviction for an offense against same victim(s)	See Class C felony classification.		Yes

Table 37: Stalking—Continued

State/Code Section	Defined As	Punishment/ Classification	Repeat Offense	Arrest or Restraining Order Specifically Authorized by Statute?	Constitutionally Protected Activities Exempted?
IOWA 708.11	Purposefully engages in course of conduct that would cause reasonable person to fear bodily injury or death to himself or immediate family; perpetrator knows or should have known that person would be fearful and course of conduct actually induces fear. 708.11	Aggravated misdemeanor	Class D felony: if stalking in violation of protective order or with dangerous weapon or stalks a person under 18 years or it is 2nd offense. Class C felony for 3rd or subsequent offense	Upon filing and a finding of probable cause or after filing of indictment, court shall issue an arrest warrant	
KANSAS 21-3438	Intentional, malicious and repeated following or harassment of another person and making a credible threat with the intent to place such person in reasonable fear for such person's safety. 21-3438(a)	Severity level 10 person felony. If restraining order or injunction from same victim: severity level 9 person felony. 21-3438(b)	If within 7 years and same victim: level 8 person felony. 21-3438(c)		Yes. 21-3438(a)
KENTUCKY 508.130 to .150	Intentional course of conduct directed at specific person(s) which seriously annoys, intimidates, or harasses and which serves no legitimate purpose. 508.130(1)(a)	Stalking in 1st degree: intentional stalking with explicit or implicit threat of sexual contact, injury, or death and protective order for same victim; or criminal complaint; or convicted of felony or Class A misdemeanor; or within previous 5 years; or stalking with deadly weapon. Stalking in 1st degree is a Class D felony. Stalking in 2nd degree: stalking with explicit or implicit threat of sexual contact, injury, or death: Class A misdemeanor. 508.140			Yes. 2508.130(2)

Table 37: Stalking—Continued

State/Code Section	Defined As	Punishment/ Classification	Repeat Offense	Arrest or Restraining Order Specifically Authorized by Statute?	Constitutionally Protected Activities Exempted?
LOUISIANA 14.40.2	Willful, malicious, and repeated following or harassing with intent to place in fear of death or bodily injury. §40.2 A	Maximum 1 year jail and/or fine $2,000 maximum. If had dangerous weapon: fine $1,000 and/or jail 1 year. If stalking and protective order for same victim, or criminal proceeding for stalking victim or injunction: jail 90 days minimum and 2 years maximum and/ or fined maximum $5,000. Note: anyone over 13 who stalks a child 12 and under and is found to have placed child in reasonable fear of death or bodily injury of family member shall be punished by 1 year minimum, 3 years maximum in jail and/ or $1,500 minimum, $5,000 maximum fine	If 2nd within 7 years: jail minimum 180 days and maximum 3 years and/or fined maximum $5,000. If 3rd or subsequent within 7 years: jail minimum 2 years and maximum 5 years and/or fined maximum $5,000		Yes. §40.2 C(2)
MAINE 17A§506-A	Without reasonable cause, engages in course of conduct with the intent to harass, torment or threaten another person after forbidden by law or court. §506-A1	Class E crime §506-A2	If 2 or more prior convictions within 5 years involving same victim or member of victim's family: Class C crime §506-A2		
MARYLAND Art. 27 §123.	Malicious course of conduct of approaching or pursuing with intent to place in reasonable fear of bodily injury or death	Misdemeanor: jail maximum 5 years and/or fine maximum $5,000			Yes. Does not apply to any peaceable activity intended to express political views or provide information to others. §123(b)

Table 37: Stalking—Continued

State/Code Section	Defined As	Punishment/ Classification	Repeat Offense	Arrest or Restraining Order Specifically Authorized by Statute?	Constitutionally Protected Activities Exempted?
MASSACHUSETTS 265 §43	Wilfully and maliciously engages in conduct which seriously alarms or annoys a specific person and would cause reasonable person to suffer substantial emotional distress and makes threat with intent to place person in fear of death or bodily injury. §43(a)(1)	Imprisonment in state prison no more than 5 years or fined no more than $1,000, or imprisonment in house of correction no more than 25 years or both. §43(a)(2). If stalking and in violation of protective order: jail or state prison minimum 1 year and maximum 5 years	Jail or state prison minimum 2 years or maximum 10 years. §43(c)		
MICHIGAN 750.411(h); 750.411(i); 600.2954.	Willful course of conduct involving repeated or continuing harassment that would cause reasonable person to feel terrorized, frightened, intimidated, threatened, harassed, or molested and that actually causes victim to feel such. Aggravated stalking: stalking and violation of restraining order or injunction, violation of probation, pretrial release or bond release, or threats against victim, victim's family or an individual living with victim; or previous stalking conviction	Misdemeanor: punishable by imprisonment no more than 1 year and/ or maximum fine of $1,000; if victim is under 18 and perpetrator is 5 years older than victim, a felony punishable by imprisonment no more than 5 years and/or fine no more than $10,000; perpetrator/stalker may also be placed on probation no more than 5 years. Aggravated stalking: felony punishable by imprisonment no more than 5 years and/or fine no more than $10,000; if victim is under 18 and stalker is 5 years older than victim, by imprisonment maximum 10 years and/or fine maximum $15,000; probation no more than 5 years may be imposed	Aggravated stalking: felony		Yes.

Table 37: Stalking—Continued

State/Code Section	Defined As	Punishment/ Classification	Repeat Offense	Arrest or Restraining Order Specifically Authorized by Statute?	Constitutionally Protected Activities Exempted?
MINNESOTA 609.749	Harassment: engage in intentional conduct which the actor knows/ has reason to know victim would feel frightened, threatened, oppressed, persecuted, or intimidated and causes such reaction(s)	Gross misdemeanor. Felony: stalking based on race, color, religion, sex, sexual orientation, disability, or national origin; or stalking by falsely impersonating another or with a dangerous weapon; or stalks a victim under 18 and actor is more than 36 months older than victim. Note: if person stalked and used a firearm, court may order that person not possess any firearm between 3 years and life.	Felony: if repeat or has certain prior convictions within 10 years of discharge		Yes, includes speech, handbilling, and picketing
MISSISSIPPI 97-3-107	Willful, malicious, and repeated following or harassing or threatening with intent to place in reasonable fear of death or bodily injury. 97-3-107(1)	Jail maximum 1 year and/or fine maximum $1,000. If violates protective order or restraining order: jail maximum 1 year and/ or fine maximum $1,000	If within 7 years and against same victim and involving act of violence or a credible threat: jail maximum 3 years and/or fine maximum $2,000		Yes. 97-3-107(4)
MISSOURI 455.01, *et seq.*	Purposely and repeatedly harasses or follows with intent of harassing another adult	Class A misdemeanor	If within 5 years: Class D felony		Yes.
MONTANA 45-5-220	Purposely and knowingly causes another distress or apprehension by repeatedly following or harassing, threatening, or intimidating	Jail maximum 1 year and/or fine maximum $1,000. If victim under protection of a restraining order: jail maximum 5 years and/or fine maximum $10,000 and medical costs, counseling, and other costs incurred by the victim. Note: perpetrator may have to pay medical, counseling and other costs.	Jail maximum 5 years and/or fine maximum $10,000		Yes
NEBRASKA 28.311.02 to 311.05	Willful harassing with intent to injure, terrify, threaten, or intimidate	Class I misdemeanor	If prior conviction against same victim within 7 years: class IV felony		Labor picketing

Table 37: Stalking—Continued

State/Code Section	Defined As	Punishment/ Classification	Repeat Offense	Arrest or Restraining Order Specifically Authorized by Statute?	Constitutionally Protected Activities Exempted?
NEVADA 200.575-597	Willful or malicious conduct that causes reasonable person to feel terrorized, frightened, intimidated, or harassed and actually causes victim to feel such. 200.575(1)	Misdemeanor. Aggravated stalking: (A) stalking with threats of death or bodily harm: Class B felony, jail minimum 1 year or maximum 6 years and fine maximum $5,000; or (B) stalking spouse during dissolution of marriage; or (C) stalking the other parent of his child during custody battle. If (B) or (C): 1st offense: gross misdemeanor; if 2nd or subsequent offense Class B felony, jail minimum 1 year and maximum 6 years and maximum $500 fine	Gross misdemeanor	Yes, if reasonable cause to believe there is a protective order issue, person has received a copy, and he is acting in violation of that order. 200.597	Yes, including picketing; activities of reporters, photographers, and cameramen; free speech and assembly
NEW HAMPSHIRE 633:3-a	Any of the following: (A) following from place to place on more than one occasion for no legitimate purpose with intent to place person in fear of safety or under circumstances that would cause reasonable person to fear; (B) appearing on more than one occasion for no legitimate purpose in proximity to residence, place of employment or other place with intent to place person in fear of safety or under circumstances that would cause reasonable person to fear; (C) if there is an order, follows or appears in proximity to any other place	Class A misdemeanor	If 2nd or subsequent within 7 years: Class B felony	May arrest without warrant if has probable cause to believe suspect's acts violate statute within 6 hours	Yes.

Table 37: Stalking—Continued

State/Code Section	Defined As	Punishment/ Classification	Repeat Offense	Arrest or Restraining Order Specifically Authorized by Statute?	Constitutionally Protected Activities Exempted?
NEW JERSEY 2C:12-10	Purposeful conduct directed at specific person that would cause a reasonable person to fear bodily injury or death to himself or family member and knowingly, recklessly, or negligently places person in reasonable fear of bodily injury or death to himself or family member. 2C:12-10(b)(1)(2)	Crime of the 4th degree. If court order prohibiting the behavior: crime in the 3rd degree	If 2nd or subsequent against same victim: crime in the 3rd degree		Organized group picketing
NEW MEXICO 30:3A-3	Knowingly pursuing a pattern of conduct that would cause reasonable person to feel frightened, intimidated, or threatened. Stalker must intend to cause reasonable apprehension. Stalker must follow, surveil, or harass. 30:3A-3 A (1), (2) and (3).	Misdemeanor. Must also complete professional counseling.	Upon 2nd or subsequent conviction, guilty of 4th degree felony. Must also complete professional counseling.		
NEW YORK Penal 120.13 & 14; 240.26, .31	Menacing in the 2nd degree: repeatedly follows over a period of time, intentionally placing another in reasonable fear. Harassment in the 2nd degree: with intent to harass, annoy, or alarm another, subjects or threatens to subject person to physical contact or follows in public place or alarms or seriously annoys person which serves no legitimate purpose.	Menacing in 1st degree (committing crime of menacing in 2nd degree within 10 years of prior conviction): Class E misdemeanor. Harassment in 1st degree: Class B misdemeanor; Harassment in 2nd degree: violation	If convicted of menacing in 2nd degree within 10 years and commits menacing in 2nd degree: menacing in 1st degree which is a Class E felony. Harassment in 1st degree is a Class B misdemeanor. Aggravated harassment in the 2nd degree is a Class A misdemeanor		Yes; for harassment does not apply to activities regulated by National Labor Relations Act, Railway Labor Act, or Federal Employment Labor Management Act.
NORTH CAROLINA §14.277.3	Willfully following with intent to place in reasonable fear, after reasonable warning or request to desist; conduct over time evidences continuity of purpose	Class 2 misdemeanor. If court order: Class 1 misdemeanor	If within 5 years and prior conviction: Class I felony		

Table 37: Stalking—Continued

State/Code Section	Defined As	Punishment/ Classification	Repeat Offense	Arrest or Restraining Order Specifically Authorized by Statute?	Constitutionally Protected Activities Exempted?
NORTH DAKOTA 12.1-17-07.1	Intentional conduct directed at specific person which frightens, intimidates, or harasses and serves no legitimate purpose	Class A misdemeanor. Class C felony if previous conviction of assault, terrorizing, menacing, or harassing same victim, or violation of court order or previous stalking conviction.	Class C felony: repeat offense or violation by assault, terrorizing, menacing, or harassment		Yes
OHIO 2903.211 (menacing by stalking)	Knowingly causing another fear of physical harm or mental distress	Misdemeanor in 1st degree	Felony of 4th degree	2935.03	
OKLAHOMA Tit. 21 §1173 [Text effective July 1, 1999]	Wilfully, maliciously, and repeatedly follows or harasses another in a manner that causes person to feel frightened, intimidated, threatened, etc., and actually causes such feelings	Misdemeanor: punishable by maximum 1 year jail sentence and/or maximum $1,000 fine. If there is a court order, injunction, probation/ parole conditions or preceding violation within 10 years: felony with a maximum fine of $2,500	Second act of stalking within 10 years: felony with a maximum fine of $2,500. If stalker commits an act of stalking in violation of §§(B) and (C): felony with fine between $2,500 and $10,000		Yes.
OREGON 163.732	Knowingly alarms or coerces another person or person's family member/household by engaging in repeated and unwanted contact. The contact causes victim(s) reasonable apprehension regarding personal safety. 163.732(a)(b) and (c).	Class A misdemeanor. Class C felony if perpetrator has prior conviction for stalking or violates court order	Class C felony		
PENNSYLVANIA 18-§2709	Course of conduct or repeated acts without authorization with intent to place in reasonable fear or cause substantial emotional distress	Misdemeanor of the 1st degree. If previously convicted of crime of violence against victim, family or household member: felony of the 3rd degree	Felony of the 3rd degree		Yes, labor disputes or any constitutionally protected activity

Table 37: Stalking—Continued

State/Code Section	Defined As	Punishment/ Classification	Repeat Offense	Arrest or Restraining Order Specifically Authorized by Statute?	Constitutionally Protected Activities Exempted?
RHODE ISLAND 11-59-2	Harassment or willful, malicious and repeated following with intent to place in reasonable fear	Jail maximum 1 year and/or fine maximum $1,000	Felony: jail maximum 5 years and/or fine maximum $10,000		
SOUTH CAROLINA 16-3-1700. et. seq.	Pattern of words or conduct that causes fear of death, assault, bodily injury, criminal sexual contact, kidnapping, or property damage to victim or victim's family member. Aggravated stalking is stalking accompanied by an act of violence	Misdemeanor punishable by maximum fine of $1,000 and/or maximum prison term of 1 year. If injunction or order: misdemeanor punishable by maximum fine of $2,000 and/or maximum prison term of 2 years. Aggravated stalking is a felony punishable by maximum fine of $5,000 and/or maximum prison term of 5 years. Engaging in aggravated stalking when there is an injunction or order: felony with maximum fine of $7,000 and/or maximum prison term of 10 years	Stalking: If within 7 years, considered felony with maximum fine of $5,000 and/or maximum prison term of 5 years. Aggravated stalking: If within 7 years, considered felony with maximum fine of $10,000 and/or maximum prison term of 10 years	Restraining order authorized	Constitutionally protected activity is not included within the meaning of "course of conduct"
SOUTH DAKOTA 22-19A-1, *et seq.*	Willful, malicious and repeated following or harassing or making credible threats with intent of placing in reasonable fear	Class 1 misdemeanor. If violates protective order or injunction, Class 6 felony. If victim is 12 years or younger, Class 1 misdemeanor	If within 7 years and against same victim and involving acts of violence or credible threat: Class 5 felony		
TENNESSEE 39-17-315	Intentionally and repeatedly follows or harasses in a manner that causes fear	Class A misdemeanor	If within 7 years: Class E felony. If within 7 years and the same victim: Class C felony		Yes, following another during course of a lawful business activity

Table 37: Stalking—Continued

State/Code Section	Defined As	Punishment/ Classification	Repeat Offense	Arrest or Restraining Order Specifically Authorized by Statute?	Constitutionally Protected Activities Exempted?
TEXAS 42.072	A person commits an offense if on more than one occasion and pursuant to scheme or course of conduct directed at specific person, knowingly engages in conduct that: (1) stalker knows/ reasonably believes victim will view as threatening, (2) causes fear, and (3) would cause a reasonable person to fear	Class A misdemeanor	Felony of 3rd degree		
UTAH 76-5-106.5	Intentionally or knowingly causes a reasonable person fear 76-5-106.5 (a)(b)(c)	Class B misdemeanor. Class A misdemeanor if: (1) previous conviction of stalking, (2) conviction in another jurisdiction to an offense similar to stalking, or (3) convicted of felony offense in which victim or victim's family was victim. Felony of the 3rd degree if: (1) used deadly weapon or other means of force, (2) previously convicted 2 or more times of stalking, (3) convicted 2 or more times in another jurisdiction of offenses similar to stalking, (4) convicted 2 or more times in any combination of (2) and (3), (5) convicted 2 or more times of felonies in which victim was also a victim of felonies	Class A misdemeanor. If 2 or more convictions: felony of the 3rd degree 76-5-106.5(5)		

Table 37: Stalking—Continued

State/Code Section	Defined As	Punishment/ Classification	Repeat Offense	Arrest or Restraining Order Specifically Authorized by Statute?	Constitutionally Protected Activities Exempted?
VERMONT Tit. 13 §1061, *et seq.*	Intentionally follows, lies in wait, or harasses and causes fear without legitimate purpose	Stalking: imprisoned no more than 2 years and/or maximum fine $5,000. Aggravated stalking: intentionally stalks and (1) such conduct violates court order, or (2) previous conviction of stalking or aggravated stalking, or (3) convicted of offense an element of which involves an act of violence against same person, or (4) victim under 16. Aggravated stalking punishable by maximum prison term of 5 years and/or maximum fine of $25,000	See aggravated stalking		Constitutionally protected activity not included within the meaning of "course of conduct"
VIRGINIA 18.2-60.3	Intent or knowledge that repeated acts cause reasonable fear	Class 1 misdemeanor	3rd or subsequent conviction within 5 years: Class 6 felony	Yes	
WASHINGTON 9A.46.110	Intentionally and repeatedly harasses or follows and causes reasonable fear and s/ he intends to frighten, intimidate, or harass or knows or reasonably knows acts cause fear or harassment and without lawful authority and doesn't amount to a felony attempt of another crime	Gross misdemeanor. If previously convicted of harassing same victim or violating protective order of victim; or armed with deadly weapon; or victim was a public officer stalked in retaliation; or victim is/was a witness stalked in retaliation: Class C felony	Class C felony		

Table 37: Stalking—Continued

State/Code Section	Defined As	Punishment/ Classification	Repeat Offense	Arrest or Restraining Order Specifically Authorized by Statute?	Constitutionally Protected Activities Exempted?
WEST VIRGINIA 61-2-9a	(1) knowingly, willfully and repeatedly follows and harasses, or (2) knowingly, willfully and repeatedly follows and makes credible threat, or (3) knowingly, willfully and repeatedly harasses and makes credible threat against a person with whom he or she has had a past relationship or would like to have a relationship	Misdemeanor: jail for maximum of 6 months and/or maximum fine of $1,000. Misdemeanor if stalks in violation of court order entered pursuant to §48-2-13 or §48-2-15 or §48-2A-5 or §48-2A-6: county jail between 90 days and 1 year and/or fine between $2,000 and $5,000	If 2nd conviction within 5 years of prior conviction: county jail between 90 days and 1 year and/or fine between $2,000 and $5,000. If 3rd or subsequent within 5 years: felony; locked up in penitentiary between 1 and 5 years and/or fine between $3,000 and $10,000. If there is restraining order and convicted of 2nd or subsequent offense: county jail for 6 months to 1 year and/or fine between $2,000 and $5,000	Upon conviction, court may issue restraining order for period not to exceed 10 years	Yes, assembly and petitions for redress of grievances
WISCONSIN 940.32	Actor knows or should know that his intentional conduct causes reasonable person to fear bodily injury to or death of himself or of his immediate family. Acts actually induce such fear	Class A misdemeanor. Class D felony: if stalker intentionally gains access to record in electronic format that contains personally identifiable information. Class E felony: stalker inflicts bodily harm or stalker has previous conviction against same victim within 7 years. Guilty of a Class D felony also when guilty of Class E and had prior conviction and gains access to record	If within 7 years and against same victim: Class E felony. If prior conviction and gains access to electronic record: Class D felony		Yes, freedom of speech and peaceable assembly

Table 37: Stalking—Continued

State/Code Section	Defined As	Punishment/ Classification	Repeat Offense	Arrest or Restraining Order Specifically Authorized by Statute?	Constitutionally Protected Activities Exempted?
WYOMING 6-2-506	With intent to harass, conduct was likely to harass by communication, following, placing under surveillance, or otherwise harassing 6-2-506 b(i)(ii)(iii)(iv)	Misdemeanor: jail maximum 6 months and/or fine maximum $750. If caused serious bodily harm or violates probation, parole or bail or violates temporary or permanent protective order: felony stalking: jail maximum 10 years. If acts occurred within 5 years of prior conviction, and if caused serious bodily harm or violates probation, parole or bail or violates temporary or permanent protective order: felony stalking: jail maximum 10 years	If within 5 years: felony stalking: jail maximum 10 years		Yes, lawful demonstration, assembly or picketing

38. STATE LOTTERIES

State lotteries have become nearly ubiquitous as state government activity. Thirty-eight states permit lotteries. In virtually all states with lotteries, the stated purpose is to raise revenue. However, there is wide diversity in how the money raised is distributed. Most states (about 16) designate lottery profits for schools and education, about thirteen states distribute profit to the general fund, or a fund for economic development, such as highway construction, in support of stadium authorities. A few states designate lottery revenues to fund various general environmental activities.

Many states apply the revenues to more than one purpose. A few states are quite unique. For example, Pennsylvania uses its revenue for programs designed to help the elderly with rent rebates and property tax assistance. Massachusetts uses its revenue in support of the arts. Maryland and Washington use substantial portions of their lottery revenue to raise money for sports stadium construction and operation.

A number of states have enacted provisions designed to help problem gamblers. Louisiana, for example, requires all lottery tickets to be printed with a toll-free gambler's assistance hotline phone number. At least four other states also have various provisions designed to assist problem gambles, the establishment of funds for the assistance of problem gamblers.

One interesting provision in many state lottery laws provides for the garnishment of prizes to collect various debts, ranging from unpaid taxes to outstanding child support obligations. Usually, only prizes over a certain amount may be garnished. One state specifies that only prizes over $100 may be garnished, another sets the limit at $2,500. Texas permits garnishment of prizes won by persons who have defaulted on guaranteed student loans.

Interestingly, there are some unusual circumstances in various states. Maine, New Hampshire and Vermont each authorize two lotteries: their own and a Tri-State Lotto that is authorized under a tri-state compact. The proceeds are distributed equally among the three states. Finally, it is interesting to note that Nevada does not permit a state lottery. Perhaps this would be seen as competing with one of the states major industries.

Overall, the matter of state lotteries is only one category, albeit a big one, of the laws relating to gambling. The law of gambling is a very complex and varied area of state regulation. Of late, gambling itself has been subject to many political pressures, both for and against legalization. Although gambling is not treated in this chapter, one interested in the subject may use statute citations provided to locate the general gambling laws for each state.

Table 38: State Lotteries

State	Code Section	Distribution of Revenue	Additional Purpose	Prize Subject to Garnishment	Time Limit to Claim Prize/ Disposition	Prohibited Related Activities
ALABAMA	Prohibited: Art. N §65 AL Constitution					
ALASKA	Prohibited: 05.15.10, *et seq.*					
ARIZONA	5-501, *et seq.*	18.5% state lottery fund (for administrative and advertising expenses); 31.5% commerce and economic development commission fund and local transportation assistance fund; 50% payment of prizes		On prizes over $600, a set-off is allowed for any debts over $100 owed to the state, including overdue support	180 days/70% to state lottery prize fund and 30% to special advocate fund	Sale to minor; alteration of ticket; sale by unauthorized person; sale at unauthorized price
ARKANSAS	Prohibited: Art. 19 §14. AR Constitution					
CALIFORNIA	Gov. §8880, *et seq.*	50% prizes; 34% benefit public education; 16% expenses	For the preservation of the rights, liberties, and welfare of the people to benefit education without additional or increased taxes, money should supplement, not be substituted for, public education funds	Payment of prize may be assigned such as to a trust, conservator, or as collateral to secure a loan.	180 days; to benefit public purpose of education	Sales to minors; counterfeit/ altered tickets
COLORADO	24-35-201, *et seq.*	Of net proceeds: 40% conservation trust fund with 10% going to Division of Parks and Outdoor Recreation for acquisition and development; 50% of total revenue for disbursements of prizes	Acquisition of state correctional facilities	Offset for those who owe child support debt or arrearages up to full amount of prize	180 days	Sell ticket at greater price; unauthorized sale; sale to minor

Table 38: State Lotteries—Continued

State	Code Section	Distribution of Revenue	Additional Purpose	Prize Subject to Garnishment	Time Limit to Claim Prize/ Disposition	Prohibited Related Activities
CONNECTICUT	12-568, *et seq.*	70% interdistrict cooperative grant program; 30% pilot program to assist educational paraprofessionals				Forgery/ counterfeiting tickets; sale of out-of-state lottery tickets; unlicensed sale; at greater price §12-568 repealed 7/1/96
DELAWARE	29-4801, *et seq.*	At least 30% to the General Fund of the state from the "State Lottery Fund"; 45% payment of prizes; 20% administration and expenses	To produce the greatest income for the state; for "video lottery"—to provide nonstate supported assistance to the harness and thoroughbred racing industries		1 year/State Lottery Fund	Sales to minors; at greater price; alteration/ forgery
DISTRICT OF COLUMBIA	2-2501, *et seq.*	1st pay operation, administration and capital expenses (including payment of prizes); remainder to General Fund of District of Columbia as general purpose revenue funds Lottery and charitable gamess fund pays for operation §2-2512			1 year/General Fund of District of Columbia	Unauthorized sales; forged/ counterfeited/ altered tickets; sale to minor
FLORIDA	24.101, *et seq.*	50% payment of prizes; 38% Educational Enhancement Trust Fund; remaining revenue to pay administrative expenses of lottery department	To support improvements in public education and not as a substitute for educational funds	On prizes over $600; offset by outstanding obligation to any state agency or owing child support through a court	180 days/added to "pool from which future prizes are awarded or for special prize promotions"	Unlawful assignment/ transfer; unauthorized sale as retailer; sale to minor; counterfeited/ altered ticket; at greater price; extension offered to purchase ticket

Table 38: State Lotteries—Continued

State	Code Section	Distribution of Revenue	Additional Purpose	Prize Subject to Garnishment	Time Limit to Claim Prize/ Disposition	Prohibited Related Activities
GEORGIA	50-27-1, *et seq.*	45% prize money; 35% of net proceeds to go to Lottery for Education Account (with 10% as a scholarship shortfall reserve account)	To support improvements and enhancements for educational purposes and programs; funds used as supplement, not substitute	On prizes over $5,000, set-off for all debts over $100 owed to any state agency including taxes, child support, and judgments or liens	180 days/up to $200,000 to Department of Human Resources to treat compulsive gambling disorders with the rest added to a pool for future prizes or special prize promotions	Sale only at set price by authorized retailer; sale to minors; stolen, forged, or counterfeited tickets
HAWAII	Offense of gambling is prohibited. 712-1220. *et seq.*					
IDAHO	67-7401, *et seq.*	45% prize expense; 15% administrative costs; 3¾% advertising and promotional costs. Of rest of net income: 1/2 to permanent building account; 1/2 to school district building account with a one-time allotment to permanent building fund advisory council for Vietnam Veterans Memorial	To benefit public purposes consonant with the public good	Subject to garnishment for unpaid taxes, child or spousal support; or public assistance benefits	180 days/added to future prize pools	Sales to minors; counterfeited, altered, or forged tickets
ILLINOIS	20 ILCS 1605\1 *et seq.*	Set by department; all revenue to go to "State Lottery Fund"	To support the state's Common School Fund	Withheld for past due support	Set by department/added to prize pool for special drawings	At greater price; to charge a fee to redeem a prize; from unlicensed sales agent; altering ticket; sale to minors

Table 38: State Lotteries—Continued

State	Code Section	Distribution of Revenue	Additional Purpose	Prize Subject to Garnishment	Time Limit to Claim Prize/ Disposition	Prohibited Related Activities
INDIANA	4-30-1-1, *et seq.*	Administrative trust fund for prizes and expenses; any surplus revenue (where roughly $30 million goes to state teachers' retirement fund and $10 million to pension relief fund with remaining surplus to the "Build Indiana Fund" for highway construction, job creation, economic development and state and local capital projects)	To enable the people of Indiana to benefit from significant money for capital improvements	For prizes over $599, if owes (1)outstanding debt to state agency, (2) delinquent state taxes, or (3) child support paid through a court [if multiple obligations, 1st to child support, 2nd to judgments owed, 3rd to tax liens, and 4th to unsecured debts owed by prize winner]	180 days/added to pool for future prizes or used for special prize promotions	Sale to minors; stolen/ counterfeited/ altered tickets; at different price; by unauthorized retailer or agent; sale on credit
IOWA	99E.1, *et seq.*	50% payment of prizes; 3/10% of gross lottery revenue to gambler's assistance fund; 4% expenses for marketing, educational and informational material for lottery plus reasonable expenses of conducting lottery; remaining funds to CLEAN fund (Committing the Lottery to Environment, Agriculture and Natural Resources)		State tax deducted from prize payment	Period deemed appropriate by commissioner/ added to future prize pools and given to holders of winning tickets or shares in addition to amounts already allocated	Sale at greater price; sale to minor (under 21); unauthorized sale; forged/ altered ticket

Table 38: State Lotteries—Continued

State	Code Section	Distribution of Revenue	Additional Purpose	Prize Subject to Garnishment	Time Limit to Claim Prize/ Disposition	Prohibited Related Activities
KANSAS	74-8701, *et seq.*; 79-4801, *et seq.*	30% lottery operating fund for expenses; 45% prizes; rest to state gaming revenues fund and state general fund for state economic development, correctional institution buildings, county reappraisal fund	Lottery shall be abolished July 1, 2002.		Within period established by rules and regulations/addcd to prize pools of subsequent lottery games	Forgery; unauthorized sale. Sale at greater price sale to minor (under 18)
KENTUCKY	154A.010. et seq.	35% general fund; rest for expenses and prizes			180 days/ added to pool for future prizes or special prize promotions	Sale to minor; alter or forge tickets; attempt to win through fraud or deception or tampering with lottery equipment
LOUISIANA	47:9000, *et seq.*	Corporate operating fund for expenses and prizes; with at least 35% to Lottery Proceeds Fund with $250,000 allocated to Compulsive and Problem Gaming Fund	"Enable the people of the state to benefit from the profits"; tickets must include toll-free phone number for mental health services for compulsive arrearages or problem gambling	Outstanding child support arrearages	180 days/ added to pool for future prizes or special prize promotions	Sale to minor; false or altered tickets; influence winning or tampering with lottery equipment; illegal lottery devices; skimming lottery proceeds; bulk sale
MAINE	Tit. 8 §371, *et seq.;* and "Tri-State Lotto" with New Hampshire and Vermont Tit. 8 §401, *et seq.*	45% distributed as prizes; rest divided between expenses, General Fund, and Maine Outdoor Heritage Fund			1 year/transferred to General Fund as undedicated revenue	Sale at greater price; sale to minor

Table 38: State Lotteries—Continued

State	Code Section	Distribution of Revenue	Additional Purpose	Prize Subject to Garnishment	Time Limit to Claim Prize/ Disposition	Prohibited Related Activities
MARYLAND	State Gov't. §9-101, *et seq.*; Family Law §10-113.1; Art. 27 §640B	Pro rata basis for prizes and administrative expenses; for sports lotteries, proceeds go to Maryland Stadium Authority; for other lotteries, into General Fund of the state		Under appropriate court order, prize may be paid to person other than winner; any child support arrearage over $150; or any unpaid state or municipal tax	182 days/ added to unclaimed prize fund or nondaily/weekly lottery drawing	Sale to minor; forged/altered tickets; unauthorized sale, §9-124 state gov't
MASSACHUSETTS	Ch. 10 §24, *et seq.*	45% payment of prizes; 15% administration and operating expenses; balance State Lottery Fund	Authorized to conduct lottery for the benefit of the arts; provide property tax relief and continue services at the local level	For past due child support on any prizes over $600	1 year/allocated in same manner as other lottery revenue	Forged/altered tickets; sale to minor; sale at greater price
MICHIGAN	MCL 432.41 10% of yearly state lottery addvertising budget not to exceed $1 mil. goes to compulsive gaming prevention fund	After payment of prizes (approximately 45%) and expenses, net revenue to state school aid fund		For prizes over $1,000, for liabilities to state or support arrearages	1 year/deposited in state school aid fund and distributed pursuant to law	Sales to minors; sale at greater price; unauthorized sale; forged/ altered ticket
MINNESOTA	349A.0, *et seq.*	14.5% lottery operations; 2.75% advertising; 60% prizes; rest to lottery fund/ special revenue fund with 40% of these net proceeds going to Minnesota Environment and Natural Resources Trust Fund		For delinquent state taxes; child support; court ordered restitution; or amount due any other claimant agency	1 year/30% of unclaimed prize money is added to prize pools of subsequent lottery games; 70% of unclaimed money is distributed as follows: 60% to the general fund and 40% to the Minnesota environment and natural resources trust fund	Sale to or purchase by minors; sale at greater price; unauthorized sale
MISSISSIPPI	Prohibited 97-33-31					

Table 38: State Lotteries—Continued

State	Code Section	Distribution of Revenue	Additional Purpose	Prize Subject to Garnishment	Time Limit to Claim Prize/ Disposition	Prohibited Related Activities
MISSOURI	313.200, *et seq.*	After expenses and prizes paid, remaining moncys to general revenue fund		Only pursuant to an appropriate judicial order; set-offs for delinquent child support	1 year/revert to state lottery fund	Sale to minors; sale at greater price; forged/ altered ticket; unauthorized sale
MONTANA	23-7-101	45% prize money; after expenses, net revenue transferred to state lottery fund (9.1% to board of crime control) Net revenue transferred to state general fund effective 7/1/99		For prizes over $600. those owing child support through state child support enforcement agency	6 months/paid into state lottery fund	Sale to minor; purchase only with cash or check; no credit
NEBRASKA	9-801, *et seq.*	After payment of expenses and prizes, at least 25% to the following funds: 49¾% to Education Innovation Fund; 24¾% Solid Waste Landfill Closure Assistance Fund (until 1997); 25% Nebraska Environmental Trust Fund (until 1997–then 49¾%); 1% to Compulsive Gamblers' Assistance Fund	Education Fund to encourage and fund high performance learning innovations, pilot projects, and model programs	On prizes over $500, any outstanding state tax liability or child or spousal support	Period of time set by regulation/ used at discretion of tax commissioner for purposes set out in lottery statutes	Sale to person under 19 years of age; at price other than proscribed; unauthorized sale; alter ticket; no phone; mail or credit sales
NEVADA	Prohibited. Art. 4 §24 Nevada Constitution					
NEW HAMPSHIRE	287F:1, *et seq.*: "Tri-State Lotto" with Maine and Vermont	50% common prize pool; operating costs charged proportionally to each state	For raising additional revenue		1 year/credited to prize pool	Sale at greater price; sale to minor; unauthorized sale

Table 38: State Lotteries—Continued

State	Code Section	Distribution of Revenue	Additional Purpose	Prize Subject to Garnishment	Time Limit to Claim Prize/ Disposition	Prohibited Related Activities
NEW JERSEY	5:9-1, *et seq.*	Payment of prizes and expenses with appropriations to state institutions and state aid for education (these appropriations and total lottery revenue shall be published twice yearly in 10 newspapers throughout the state)	Entire net proceeds to be used for state institutions and state aid for education including higher education and senior citizen education	For arrears of court-ordered child support obligations, and former recipients of Aid to Families with Dependent Children (AFDC), food stamps, or low income home energy assistance who were overpaid	1 year/allocated in same manner as lottery revenue is allocated by state	Forged/altered tickets; sale above fixed price; unauthorized sale
NEW MEXICO	6-24-1, *et seq.*	50% to prizes minus operating expenses with net remaining revenues: 60% to Public School Capital Outlay Fund and 40% to lottery tuition fund	To benefit state residents by funding critical capital outlay needs of public schools and provide tuition assistance to resident undergraduates at New Mexico post-secondary schools	On prizes over $600, those owing debt to or collected by human services department for child support enforcement	Time period established by authority/paid into prize fund	Sale at greater price; sale to minors; unauthorized sale; no sales on credit; forged/ altered tickets; influencing winning of prize through fraud or deception
NEW YORK	Tax §1600, *et seq.*	40–60% for prizes depending on the game; 45–25% to state lottery fund	Supplemental aid to all school children; signs must be posted to assist compulsive gamblers; special instant game in New York City to benefit anti-crime division	On prizes over $600, applied against past-due support (including alimony, child or spousal support or maintenance) and against any public assistance benefits given an individual within the last 10 years (not to exceed 50% of prize)	1 year/retained in lottery prize account to be used for special lotto or supplemental lotto prizes or for promotion purposes to supplement other games on an occasional basis	Sale to minors (under 21)
NORTH CAROLINA	Prohibited. §14-289, *et seq.*					
NORTH DAKOTA	Prohibited. Art. XI §25, North Dakota Constitution					

Table 38: State Lotteries—Continued

State	Code Section	Distribution of Revenue	Additional Purpose	Prize Subject to Garnishment	Time Limit to Claim Prize/ Disposition	Prohibited Related Activities
OHIO	3770.01, *et seq.*	50% prize payment less operation expenses; then at least 30% Lottery Profits Education Fund	Lottery Profits Education Fund used to support elementary, secondary, vocational, and special education programs in appropriations made by the general assembly	On prizes over $600, for default of support payment under support order	180 days/returned to state lottery fund in unclaimcd lottery prizes fund	Sale at greater price; unauthorized sale; sale to minor; influence lottery sales agent; on Ohio fairgrounds at annual exhibition
OKLAHOMA	Prohibited. Tit. 21 §§105, *et seq.*					
OREGON	461.010, *et seq.*; Art. XV §4 Oregon Constitution	50% prizes; 16% expenses; 34% benefit public purpose (state lottery fund for jobs and economic development in Oregon)	To provide additional moneys for public purpose of creating jobs and furthering economic development in Oregon without additional or increased taxes	On prizes in excess of $600, garnishment for person in arrears on child support obligation	1 year/remain property of lottery commission and be allocated to the benefit of the public purpose (may be exempt from 1 year redemption period if in active military service with evidence of possession of winning—then have 1 year after discharge to redeem	Sale at greater price; sale to minors; altered/ forged tickets
PENNSYLVANIA	Tit. 72 §§3761, *et seq.*; 22 §4308	40% to pay prizes; after expenses, rest pursuant to "Senior Citizens Property Tax or Rent Rebate and Older Persons Inflation Needs Act"	For purpose of providing property tax relief to the elderly and to provide free or reduced fare transit service for the elderly; also to curb illegal gambling operations in Pennsylvania	For prizes over $2,500, for delinquent support obligor, arrearages are deducted	1 year/ paid to state lottery fund for statutorily prescribed purposes	Sales in excess of fixed price; unauthorized sales; sales to minors
RHODE ISLAND	42-61-1, *et seq.*	45–55% prize fund (keno 45–65%) less expenses; 30% (20% for keno) to general revenue fund (different percentages for video lottery games)		For prizes over $600, set-off for unpaid child support arrearages over $500	1 year/reverts to lottery fund	Sales above fixed price; sales to minors; altered /forged tickets

Table 38: State Lotteries—Continued

State	Code Section	Distribution of Revenue	Additional Purpose	Prize Subject to Garnishment	Time Limit to Claim Prize/ Disposition	Prohibited Related Activities
SOUTH CAROLINA	Prohibited. 16-19-10, *et seq.*					
SOUTH DAKOTA	42-7A-1, *et seq.*	Expenses and prizes (approx. 50%) from lottery operating fund; net proceeds to state general fund; state corrections facility construction fund, and state capital construction fund (lottery expenses may not exceed amount of net proceeds to these funds) Video lottery income directly deposited in state property tax reduction fund. SDCL§42-7A-24		For prizes in excess of $100, liability setoff program to satisfy debts owed or collected through state agencies (child support payments have priority)	1 year or period deemed appropriate by executive director/added to prize pools of subsequent lottery games	Counterfeiting lottery tickets; sale at greater price; sales to minors
TENNESSEE	Prohibited. Art. XI, §5 Tennessee Constitution					
TEXAS	Establish-ment of pooled bond fund; lottery prize reserve fund; unclaimed prize fund and prize payment account; and foundation school fund. TX Gov. §§466.355	Payment of prizes, cost and expenses not to exceed 15%; rest to state lottery account in general revenue fund (but not to be considered "revenue")		Delinquent tax, child support payments, or default in student guaranteed loan shall be deducted	180 days/ provides additional money to state lottery account	Sales to minors; sales by phone; stolen, forged or altered tickets; sale at greater price; sale on credit; unauthorized sale; sale for food stamps or with AFDC check; influencing selection of winner; fraud
UTAH	Prohibited. Art. VI, §27 Utah Constitution					

Table 38: State Lotteries—Continued

State	Code Section	Distribution of Revenue	Additional Purpose	Prize Subject to Garnishment	Time Limit to Claim Prize/ Disposition	Prohibited Related Activities
VERMONT	T.31 §651, *et seq.;* and "Tri-State Lotto," T.31 §671, *et seq.*	After payment of prizes and expenses, proceeds go to state lottery fund, which after expenses, goes to general fund to be used solely for capital expenses and debt service. Not less than 50% to be paid in prizes			After one year, unclaimed prizes revert to state lottery fund	Sale to minors; sale at greater price; no license to convicted felons.
VIRGINIA	58.1-4000, *et seq.*	Operating costs and administration not to exceed 10% (with special reserve fund); rest to general fund solely for purpose of public education		Unpaid child support obligations and payment of public assistance owed by individual	180 days/paid into Literary Fund (prizes of less than $25 go into state lottery fund)	Sale over fixed price; sales to minors; altered/ forged tickets
WASHINGTON	67.70.010, *et seq.*	State lottery fund used for: payment of prizes and lottery administration; deposits to housing trust fund; distribution to county for payment of baseball stadium bonds (for no more than 20 years)		On prizes over $600, any debts to state agency or political subdivision may be setoff	180 days/retained in state lottery fund for further use as prizes	Sale to minors; sale at greater price; altered/ forged tickets

Table 38: State Lotteries—Continued

State	Code Section	Distribution of Revenue	Additional Purpose	Prize Subject to Garnishment	Time Limit to Claim Prize/ Disposition	Prohibited Related Activities
WEST VIRGINIA	29-22-1	45% disbursement as prizes; 15% operation and administration expenses; excess is net profit: goes to school building debt service fund (up to $18 million); lottery education fund; school construction fund; lottery senior citizens fund; commerce division of tourism and parks		For delinquent payment of child or spousal support	180 days/reverts to state lottery fund for the purpose of awarding additional prizes	Altered/forged tickets; unauthorized sales; sale at greater price; sales to minors
WISCONSIN	Prohibited. Art. 4 §24, Constitution of Wisconsin					
WYOMING	Prohibited. 6-7-101, *et seq.*					

39. WILLS

The purpose of a will is to permit the living to provide for those who come after him or her. By "willing" their estates, individuals can control the way their property is distributed after their deaths. If an individual dies without a will and without heirs or relatives, however, the estate escheats to the state. A will is thus a way to keep the estate in the hands of family and/or loved ones, and out of the hands of the state.

Over the years, the law of wills developed into a very mechanical, strict set of rules generally uniform among states that safeguard against unscrupulous heirs who may forge or tamper with wills for financial gain. Virtually all states require the testator (the person making the will) to be over eighteen or "an adult," the will must be typed or printed, and the only writing permitted on the document is the signature of the testator and witnesses.

Some noteworthy types of wills are nuncupative and holographic. Nuncupative wills are oral testaments with a very special, very limited purpose. Typically, the oral will has the power to dispose of only a limited amount of personal property. The original purpose of this type of will was to permit mortally injured soldiers or sailors to give gifts of personal property to their comrades-in-arms. This provision is still reflected in many of the nuncupative statutes; it permits a dying individual to grant specific bequests to friends who may have cared for him during his last injury.

Holographic wills are testaments that are entirely handwritten instead of being typed or printed. They are generally not as formal as typed wills and are therefore more suspect by law, for a greedy heir may more easily be able to persuade the testator to hastily write out a will without the proper amount of counsel or reflection. It is for these reasons that holographic wills are looked upon with general disfavor, are subject to closer scrutiny, and are less commonly recognized than other wills.

Table 39: Wills

State	Code Section	Age of Testator	Number of Witnesses	Nuncupative (Oral Wills)	Holographic Wills
ALABAMA	43-8-130, *et seq.*	18 years or older and of sound mind	Signed by at least two persons, each of whom witnessed either the signing or testator's acknowledgment of signature or of will	Not recognized	Not recognized because of statutory requirement that every will must be witnessed and attested by at least two people; will in handwriting of testator and attested to by two witnesses is not considered holographic will
ALASKA	13.11-150, *et seq.* Chapter 11 repealed, §18 Ch. 75 SLA 1996	18 years or older and of sound mind. 13.12.501	Signed by at least 2 individuals, each of whom signs within a reasonable time after the witness witnesses either the signing of the will as described in (2) or the testator's acknowledgment of signature or the will. 13.12.502(a)(3)	Valid for mariner at sea or soldier in the military service for personal property as he would have done by common law or by reducing the same to writing; proof must be made within 6 months of words spoken or reduced to writing within 30 days	Recognized as valid if signature and material provisions are in handwriting of testator; does not need to be witnessed. 13.12.502(b)
ARIZONA	14-2501, *et seq.*	18 years or older and of sound mind	Signed by at least two persons, each of whom signed within a reasonable time after that person witnessed testator's acknowledgment of signature or of will. 14-2502A(3)	Not recognized	Valid if signature and material provisions are in handwriting of testator; does not need to be witnessed (portions not in testator's handwriting may not be established as testator's will by extrinsic evidence of intent). 14-2503
ARKANSAS	28-25-101, *et seq.*	18 years or older and of sound mind	Two or more attesting witnesses must sign at the request and in the presence of the testator. Testator shall declare to the attesting witnesses that instrument is his will. 28-25-103(c)	Not mentioned	Valid if entire body and signature is in handwriting of testator and evidence of three credible disinterested witnesses to handwriting
CALIFORNIA	Prob. §§6100, *et seq.*	18 years or older and of sound mind	At least 2 persons present at the same time, witnessing either signing of will or testator's acknowledgment and must understand that it is testator's will. 6110(c)	Not recognized	Valid if signature and material provisions are in handwriting of testator; does not need witnesses; must show testamentary intent which can be shown by extrinsic evidence. 6111

Table 39: Wills—Continued

State	Code Section	Age of Testator	Number of Witnesses	Nuncupative (Oral Wills)	Holographic Wills
COLORADO	15-11-501, *et seq.*	18 years or older and of sound mind	Signed by at least two "generally competent" persons, either before or after the testator's death, each of whom signed within a reasonable time after he or she witnessed, in the conscious presence of the testator, either the signing or testator's acknowledgment of signature or of will. 15-11-502(1)(c)	Not recognized	Valid whether or not there are witnesses if signature and material provisions are in handwriting of testator. 15-11-502(2)
CONNECTICUT	45a-250, *et seq.*	18 years or older and of sound mind	Attested by two witnesses, each of them subscribing in presence of testator. 45a-251	Invalid if executed in Connecticut. 45a-251	Executed in Connecticut is not admissible but valid if properly made outside the state according to the laws of that state. 45a-251
DELAWARE	12-201, et seq.	18 years or older and of sound and deposing mind and memory	Attested and subscribed in testator's presence by two or more credible, generally competent witnesses; need not be signed in presence of witnesses or that witnesses sign in the presence of each other. 12-202	Not mentioned	Must meet requirements of all wills. 12-202. Any will not complying with subsection (a) shall be void
DISTRICT OF COLUMBIA	18-102, *et seq.*	18 years or older and of sound and disposing mind and capable of executing a valid deed or contract	Attested and subscribed in presence of testator by two credible witnesses. 18-103(2)	Oral will made after 1/1/1902 is not valid except that person in actual military or naval service or mariner at sea may create oral will if (a) oral will is proved by at least 2 individuals present at the making and were requested by the testator to bear witness that oral disposition was the last will and (b) will made during time of last illness of deceased and (c) substance of will reduced to writing 10 days after it was made	Attested and subscribed in the presence of testator by 2 witnesses, although they need not sign in each other's presence or physically observe each other's signature.

Table 39: Wills—Continued

State	Code Section	Age of Testator	Number of Witnesses	Nuncupative (Oral Wills)	Holographic Wills
FLORIDA	§§732.501, *et seq.*	18 years and of sound mind	Signed in presence of two attesting witnesses; witnesses must sign in presence of each other and testator. 732.502(1)(c)	Not recognized	Not recognized; properly executed will in testator's handwriting is not considered holographic will. 732.502(2)
GEORGIA	§§53-2-20, *et seq.*	14 years and not "laboring under some legal disability arising from a want of capacity or from a want of perfect liberty of action.". 53-2-22	Must be subscribed and attested in testator's presence by two or more competent witnesses; testator must sign/ acknowledge signature in presence of two witnesses. 53-2-40	Can be made only in time of last illness and must be proved by oath of at least two witnesses present at making testator must have told those present to bear witness that such was his will; must be reduced to writing within 30 days of speaking. 53-2-48	Not recognized
HAWAII	§§560:2-501, *et seq.*	18 years or older and of sound mind	Signed by at least two individuals, each of whom signed within a reasonable time after the individual witnessed either the signing of the will or the testator's acknowledgment of that signature or acknowledgment of will. 560:2-502(a)(3)	Must be in writing	A will that does not comply with subsection (a) is valid as a holographic will, whether or not witnessed, if the signature and material portions of document are in the testator's handwriting. 560:2-502(b)
IDAHO	§§15-2-501, *et seq.*	18 years or older or any emancipated minor and of sound mind	Signed by two or more persons 18 yrs. or older, each of whom witnessed either the signing or testator's acknowledgment of the signature or of the will. 15-2-502	Not recognized	Valid if signature and material provisions are in handwriting of testator; does not need witnesses. 15-2-503
ILLINOIS	755 ILCS 5/4-1, *et seq.*	18 years or older and of sound mind and memory	Attested in presence of testator by two or more credible witnesses (not necessarily in each other's presence). 755 ILCS 5/4-3	Not valid	Not valid

Table 39: Wills—Continued

State	Code Section	Age of Testator	Number of Witnesses	Nuncupative (Oral Wills)	Holographic Wills
INDIANA	§§29-1-5-1, *et seq.*	Any person of sound mind over 18 or who is younger and a member of the armed forces or merchant marine or its allies	Must be signed and acknowledged in presence of two or more witnesses; witnesses must sign in presence of testator and each other. 29-1-5-3	Valid only if made in imminent peril of death and testator dies from such peril; need two disinterested witnesses; one witness needs to reduce to writing within 30 days after declaration; and must be submitted to probate within 6 months after death; may only dispose of personal property not exceeding $1,000 in value; except persons in active military service in time of war can dispose of personal property not exceeding $10,000 in value; does not revoke existing written will—only changed so as to give effect to the nuncupative will. 29-1-5-4	No statutory provisions
IOWA	§§633.264, *et seq.*	Any person of full age and sound mind	Witnessed, at his request, by two competent (at least 16 yrs. old) witnesses who must sign in presence of testator and each other. 633.279	Not authorized	Not valid unless executed as stated in §633.279
KANSAS	§§59-601, *et seq.*	Anyone of sound mind and possessing rights of majority	Must be attested and subscribed in presence of testator by two or more competent witnesses who saw testator subscribe or heard him acknowledge same. 59-606	Made in last sickness, oral will is valid in respect to personal property if reduced to writing and subscribed by two competent, disinterested witnesses within 30 days after speaking the testamentary words (cannot alter or revoke prior written will 138 P.2d 497). 59-608	Not recognized

Table 39: Wills—Continued

State	Code Section	Age of Testator	Number of Witnesses	Nuncupative (Oral Wills)	Holographic Wills
KENTUCKY	§§394.020, *et seq.*	18 years or older and of sound mind (persons under 18 may obtain power "specially given to that effect"). However a parent, though under 18, may by will appoint a guardian for his child. 394.030	If will is not wholly written by testator, subscription must be made or will acknowledged by testator in presence of at least two credible witnesses; witnesses must sign in presence of testator and each other. 394.040	Provisions recognizing validity for personal property for soldiers in actual service or marines at sea repealed effective June 16, 1972. 394.050	Recognized if "wholly written by the testator"
LOUISIANA	Civ. Code §§1476, *et seq.*	To have the capacity to make a donation inter vivos or mortis causa, a person must also be able to comprehend generally the nature and consequences of the disposition that he is making. Minor over 16 can dispose only mortis causa (in prospect of death).	Different numbers of witnesses required for different classifications of wills. Civ. Code 1591, *et. seq.*	Valid by: (1) Public Act: must be received by notary public in presence of 3 witnesses residing in place of execution or 5 not residing in place; must be written by notary as dictated and read to testator in presence of witnesses; must be signed by testator or expressly mentioned why he cannot and signed by at least one witness; (2) Act Under Private Signature: written by testator or another from his dictation and presented in front of 5 witnesses who reside in place of execution or 7 who do not (3 and 5 consecutively, if in the country and no other witnesses can be had). Arts. 1578, 1579, 1581	Valid if entirely written, dated, and signed by testator; it is not subject to any other formality and may be made anywhere (even out-of-state). Art. 1588
MAINE	Tit. 18A §§2-501, *et seq.*	18 years or older and of sound mind	Signed by at least two persons, each of whom witnessed either the signing or testator's acknowledgment of signature or of will. 18A 2-502	Not recognized	Valid if signature and material provisions are in handwriting of testator; does not need to be witnessed. 18A 2-503

Table 39: Wills—Continued

State	Code Section	Age of Testator	Number of Witnesses	Nuncupative (Oral Wills)	Holographic Wills
MARYLAND	Estates & Trusts §§4-101, *et seq.*	18 years or older and legally competent	Must be attested and signed in presence of testator by two or more credible witnesses. 4-102	Not mentioned	Valid if made outside U.S. by person serving in U.S. Armed Forces (no attesting witnesses necessary) but is void after one year after testator's discharge unless testator has died or does not then possess testamentary capacity. 4-103; 4-104
MASSACHUSETTS	Ch. 191-1, *et seq.*	18 years or older and sound mind	Attested and subscribed in testator's presence by two or more competent witnesses	Soldiers in actual service or mariner at sea may make nuncupative will of personal property. 191-6	Not recognized
MICHIGAN	MCL §§700.121, *et seq.*	18 years or older and sound mind	Signed by at least two competent persons, each of whom witnessed either the signing or testator's acknowledgment of signature or of will. 700.122	Not recognized	Valid if dated and testator's signature appears at end of will and material provisions are in testator's handwriting; does not need witnesses. 700.123
MINNESOTA	§§524.2-501, *et seq.*	18 years or older and of sound mind	Signed by at least two persons, each of whom signed within a reasonable time after witnessing either the signing or testator's acknowledgment of signature or of will. 524.2-502	Not recognized	Not recognized

Table 39: Wills—Continued

State	Code Section	Age of Testator	Number of Witnesses	Nuncupative (Oral Wills)	Holographic Wills
MISSISSIPPI	91-5-1, *et seq.*	18 years or older and of sound and disposing mind	Attested to by two or more credible witnesses in testator's presence	Must be made in time of last illness of the deceased at his habitation or where he resided for 10 days prior to death (except when taken sick and dies from home before return to habitation). Value bequeathed cannot exceed $100 unless it be proved by two witnesses that testator(trix) called on some person present to take notice or bear testimony that such is his/her will. Will not received to probate after 6 months unless reduced to writing within 6 days after speaking the same. 91-5-19	Must be testamentary in character, wholly written, dated, and signed by testator(trix).
MISSOURI	474.310, *et seq.*	18 years or older and of sound mind	Must be attested by two or more competent witnesses subscribing their names to the will in presence of testator. 474.320	Valid only if made in imminent peril of death and death results, declared to be his will before two disinterested witnesses, reduced to writing under direction of one of witnesses within 30 days and submitted for probate within 6 months of death; can only dispose of personal property of no more than $500 and does not change or revoke existing will; may be revoked by another nuncupative will. 474-340	No statutory or judicial pronouncement of validity
MONTANA	72-2-521, *et seq.*; (UPC adopted)	18 years or older and of sound mind	Signed by at least two persons, each of whom signed within a reasonable time after having witnessed either the signing or testator's acknowledgment of signature or of will. 72-2-522(1)(c)	Not recognized	Valid, whether or not witnessed, if signature and material provisions are in testator's handwriting. 72-2-522(2)

Table 39: Wills—Continued

State	Code Section	Age of Testator	Number of Witnesses	Nuncupative (Oral Wills)	Holographic Wills
NEBRASKA	UPC adopted as NPC at §§30-2326, *et seq.*	18 years or older or anyone not a minor and of sound mind	Signed by at least two individuals, each of whom witnessed either the signing or testator's acknowledgment of signature or of the will. 30-2327	Not recognized	Valid, whether or not witnessed, if signature, material provisions, and an indication of the date of signing are in handwriting of testator; in absence of such indication of date, if instrument is the only such instrument or contains no inconsistency with any like instrument or if date is determinable from contents, from extrinsic circumstances, or from any other evidence. 30-2328
NEVADA	133.020, *et seq.*	Every person of sound mind over 18. Any married woman may dispose of all her separate estate by will, absolutely, without consent of husband. A married woman may dispose of community property by will as provided by law. 133.030	Attested by at least two competent witnesses subscribing their names to the will in presence of testator. 133.040	Valid if estate up to the extent of $1000 in value, if proved by two witnesses present at making, and made during last sickness. 133.100	Valid if entirely written, dated, and signed in handwriting of testator. Can be made in or out of state and need not be witnessed; may dispose of all or part of estate, real or personal. 133.090

Table 39: Wills—Continued

State	Code Section	Age of Testator	Number of Witnesses	Nuncupative (Oral Wills)	Holographic Wills
NEW HAMPSHIRE	551-1, *et seq.*	18 years or older or married and of sound mind	Attested and subscribed in testator's presence and at request of testator by two or more credible witnesses. 551-2	Not valid where property exceeds in value $100, unless declared in presence of three witnesses, in last sickness, and in his usual dwelling (except where taken sick away from home and died before his return), or unless memo was reduced to writing within 6 days and presented to probate court within 6 months after making; also valid for soldier in actual military service or mariner or seaman at sea; may dispose of movables and personal estate. 551-15; 16	Not recognized
NEW JERSEY	3B:3-1, *et seq.*	18 years or older and of sound mind	Signed by at least two people who witnessed signing or testator's acknowledgment of the signature or of the will. 3B:3-2	Not recognized	Valid whether or not witnessed if signature and material provisions are in testator's handwriting. 3B:3-3
NEW MEXICO	Chap. 45 §§2-501, *et seq.*	Anyone who is 18 yrs. of age or older and of sound mind	Must be signed by at least two individuals each of whom must sign in presence of testator and each other after each witnessed the signing of the will. 45-2-502	Not recognized	Not recognized
NEW YORK	Estates, Powers & Trusts §§3-1.1, *et seq.*	18 years or older. and of sound mind and memory	Signed at the end by testator or acknowledged in presence of two attesting witnesses; witnesses must attest to testator's signature within 30 days, and at testator's request, sign their names and residence addresses at the end of the will. 3-2.1(a)(4)	Valid only if made by members of armed forces while in actual military or naval service during a war or other armed conflict, person who serves with or accompanies an armed force engaged in such activity, or mariner at sea	Same provisions as for nuncupative wills and written entirely in testator's handwriting. 3-2.2(a)(2), b(1)(2)(3)

Table 39: Wills—Continued

State	Code Section	Age of Testator	Number of Witnesses	Nuncupative (Oral Wills)	Holographic Wills
NORTH CAROLINA	§ 31-1, *et seq.*	18 years or older and of sound mind	Attested by at least two competent witnesses, each of whom must sign will in presence of testator but need not sign in presence of each other. 31-3.3	Made by person in his last sickness or in such imminent peril of death and who does not survive such sickness or peril and declared to be his will before two competent witnesses simultaneously present and specially requested by him to bear witness thereto. 31-3.5	Written entirely in testator's handwriting and subscribed by testator and found after testator's death among his valuable papers or in safe deposit box or other safe place or with some person under his authority for safekeeping; no witness required. 31-3.4
NORTH DAKOTA	30.1-08-01, *et seq.*	Any adult who is of sound mind	Signed by at least two persons, each of whom signed within a reasonable time after witnessing either the signing of the will or the testator's acknowledgment of signature or of will. 30.1-08-02	Not recognized	30.1-08002(2): a will that does not comply with subsection 1 is valid as a holographic will, whether or not witnessed, if the signature and material portions of the document are in the testator's handwriting. 30.1-08-03: holographic will.
OHIO	2107.02, *et seq.*	18 or over of sound mind and memory and not under restraint	Attested and subscribed in presence of testator by two or more competent witnesses who saw testator subscribe or heard him acknowledge his signature. 2107.03	Valid if made in last sickness as to personal estate if reduced to writing and subscribed by two competent disinterested witnesses within 10 days after speaking; witnesses must prove that testator is of sound mind, memory, and not under restraint and he called upon some person present at the time the testamentary words were spoken to bear testimony that it is his will; must be offered to probate within 6 months after death. 2107.60	Not recognized

Table 39: Wills—Continued

State	Code Section	Age of Testator	Number of Witnesses	Nuncupative (Oral Wills)	Holographic Wills
OKLAHOMA	Tit. 84. 41, *et seq.*	18 years or older and of sound mind	Two attesting witnesses signed in presence of testator at end of the will. 84.55	Valid with following requirements: (1) no more than $1000; (2) must be proved by two witnesses present at making, one of whom was asked by testator to bear witness as such; (3) testator must have been in actual military service in field or duty at sea and in actual contemplation, fear, or peril of death or testator must have been in expectation of immediate death from injury received same day. 84.46	Must be entirely written, dated, and signed by testator's hand; need not be witnessed. 84.54
OREGON	112.225, *et seq.*	18 years or older or lawfully married and of sound mind	At least two witnesses who see testator sign will or hear him acknowledge signature and attest by signing their names to it. 112.235	Not recognized	Not recognized
PENNSYLVANIA	20-2501, *et seq.*	18 years or older and of sound mind	Two witnesses signing will in presence of testator; testator must declare instrument to be his will in presence of witnesses. 20-2502	Not valid; provisions of §20-2503 repealed effective July 1, 1972. 20-2504	Not recognized
RHODE ISLAND	33-5-2, *et seq.*	18 years or older and of sane mind	Must be signed or acknowledged by testator in front of two or more witnesses present at same time who must attest and subscribe will in presence of testator. 33-5-5	Not recognized except any soldier or airman in actual military service or any mariner or seaman at sea can dispose of his personal estate as he might have done under common law. 33-5-6	Not recognized except any soldier or airman in actual military service or any mariner or seaman at sea can dispose of his personal estate as he might have done under common law. 33-5-6
SOUTH CAROLINA	62-2-501, *et seq.*	18 years or older and of sound mind	Signed by at least two persons each of whom witnessed either the signing or testator's acknowledgment of signature or of will. 62-2-502	No statutory recognition of soldiers' and mariners' wills of personalty nor nuncupative wills of personalty.	Impliedly forbidden by statute unless specifically recognized by valid out-of-state execution or out-of-state probate. 62-2-505

Table 39: Wills—Continued

State	Code Section	Age of Testator	Number of Witnesses	Nuncupative (Oral Wills)	Holographic Wills
SOUTH DAKOTA	29A-2-501, *et seq.* (U.P.C.)	18 years or older and of sound mind	Signed in conscious presence of testator by two or more individuals who, in the conscious presence of testator, witnessed either the signing of the will or the testator's acknowledgment of that signature. 29A-2-502(b)(3)	Not recognized	Valid if signature and material portions are in testator's handwriting; need not be witnessed. 20A-2-502(A)
TENNESSEE	32-1-102, *et seq.*	18 years or older and of sound mind	Two or more attesting witnesses must sign in presence of testator and each other after testator signifies to the attesting witnesses that the instrument is his will and he signs or acknowledges his signature, or at his direction and in his presence have someone else sign his name. 32-1-104	Must be made only by person in imminent peril of death and valid only if testator dies as result of peril; must be declared to be his will before two disinterested witnesses, reduced to writing by or under direction of one of the witnesses within 30 days and submitted to probate within 6 months after death of testator; only valid for personal property not exceeding $1000 unless person is in active military, air, or naval service in time of war, then $10,000; neither revokes nor changes existing written will. 32-1-106	Signature and material provisions must be in handwriting of testator and handwriting must be proved by two witnesses (no witnesses necessary to the will). 32-1-105
TEXAS	Probate §§57, *et seq.*	18 years or older or lawfully married or member of U.S. Armed Forces or auxiliaries or of the maritime service and of sound mind	Attested by two or more credible witnesses above age of 14 subscribing names in presence of testator §59	Must have been made during last sickness, at residence or where he has resided for at least 10 days or more before date of will unless taken sick and dies away from home; when value is more than $30, must be proved by three credible witnesses that testator called upon someone to bear testimony that such is his will. §65	Will wholly written in handwriting of testator needs no attesting witnesses and may be self-proved by testator attaching affidavit that it is his last will. §60

Table 39: Wills—Continued

State	Code Section	Age of Testator	Number of Witnesses	Nuncupative (Oral Wills)	Holographic Wills
UTAH	Tit. 75-2-501, *et seq.*	18 years or older and of sound mind	Signed by at least 2 individuals, each of whom signed within a reasonable time after he witnessed either the signing, testator's acknowledgment of that signature, or testator's acknowledgment of the will	Not recognized	Valid whether or not witnessed if signature and material provisions are in handwriting of testator; last executed holographic will controls; if not dated, consistent provisions are valid; inconsistent provisions are invalid. 75-2-503; 75-2-502
VERMONT	14-1, *et seq.*	"Of age" (18 years) and of sound mind	Attested and subscribed by three or more credible witnesses in presence of testator and in presence of each other. §14-5	Shall not pass personal estate over $200; not proved unless memo made in writing (by person present at making) within 6 days from making of will and presented for probate within 6 months from death of testator; soldier in actual military service or seaman at sea may dispose of wages and personal estate as he would at common law. §14-6, 7	Not recognized unless statutory formalities are satisfied. §14-5
VIRGINIA	64.1-46, *et seq.*	18 years or older and of sound mind. 64.1-47	Two or more competent witnesses present at same time who must subscribe will in presence of testator (no form of attestation necessary). 64.1-49	Valid for soldier in actual military service or mariner or seaman at sea to dispose of personal property. 64.1-53	If will is wholly in handwriting of testator and signed by him, neither acknowledgment nor witnesses are necessary; proof of handwriting must be by at least two disinterested witnesses. 64.1-49

Table 39: Wills—Continued

State	Code Section	Age of Testator	Number of Witnesses	Nuncupative (Oral Wills)	Holographic Wills
WASHINGTON	11.12.010, *et seq.*	18 years or older and of sound mind	Attested by two or more competent witnesses by subscribing their names to the will or by signing an affidavit that complies with §11.20.020(2) while in the presence of and at the direction of the testator. 11.12.020	No real estate; personal property not more than $1000; members of U.S. Armed Forces and persons employed on U.S. Merchant Marine vessels may dispose of wages and personal property; must be made with two witnesses present at time of making that testator requested person to bear witness to will and that it was made at time of last sickness; must be reduced to writing, proof offered within 6 months of words spoken, and citation issued to widows and heirs-at-law that they might contest. 11.12.025	Not valid
WEST VIRGINIA	41-1-1, *et seq.*	18 years or older and of sound mind. 41-1-2	Two witnesses present at same time when will is signed or acknowledged by testator must sign in presence of testator and each other. 41-1-3	Soldiers in actual military service and mariners or seamen at sea may dispose of personal estate as he would at common law. 41-1-5	If will is wholly in handwriting of testator and signed by him, does not need acknowledgment or witnesses
WISCONSIN	853.01, *et seq.*	18 years or older and of sound mind	Signed by two or more competent witnesses in presence of testator and each other. 853.03(2)	Not valid	Without witnesses, not recognized under Wisconsin law unless executed in accordance with law of place where executed or law of state of domicile at time of execution. 853.05
WYOMING	2-6-101, *et. seq.*	Any person of legal age and sound mind	Two competent witnesses and signed by testator or by some person in his presence and by his express direction. 2-6-112	Not recognized	Valid if entirely written and signed in hand of testator himself; need not be witnessed. 2-6-113

VII. REAL ESTATE LAWS

40. ADVERSE POSSESSION

The doctrine of "adverse possession" is one of the most interesting in the field of real property law. The character of the law reflects the pioneer spirit of a growing world in both North America and Europe over the last few centuries.

If a person moves into possession of property, improves it and possesses it in a public manner, then after a certain amount of time he will acquire title to the property even though it is actually owned by someone else. The idea for adverse possession has at its root that land should not lie idle. If it does, it is wasted to the community. Therefore, if someone moves onto the land and makes it productive, that person may earn the right to claim it as his or her own. It is also reflective of the imprecise nature of ancient land sales: a person who believes he owns land, establishes himself on it in public, and is not hindered after a period of time, that person is entitled to own the land.

Requirements

The basic requirement for adverse possession is that the claiming party must take exclusive possession of the property. This type of possession is called "open and notorious" or proactive and absolutely not secretive possession. Some states require that the possession be "under color of title," or that the person must believe that he has the *right* to possess it *and* has some form of document or is relying on some fact that while not actually *conveying* title, appears to do so. In addition, many states require concurrent the payment of property taxes for a specified period of time, and a few states also require that improvements be made upon the land. Eventually, the possessor is required to file for title with the county recorder. The actual owner then has a limited amount of time in which to challenge the newcomer's title. Essentially, the owner's only argument is to claim some sort of disability; such as age, mental instability, or imprisonment. The owner is not required to do much in order to stop the possessor from acquiring title; merely sending the possessor a note granting permission to be there will usually suffice. Various rules exist regarding the continuousness of the possession and the ability to "tack" various periods of possession together in order to satisfy the time of possession requirement; see your state codes or the code of the state in which you are interested for more detailed information.

Table 40: Adverse Possession

State	Code Section	Prescriptive Period	Occupation	Time to Challenge	Improve-ments	Payment of Taxes	Title from Tax Assessor
ALABAMA	6-5-200	20 yrs. *Bradely* v. *Demos* 599 So.2d 1148	and Color of Title: 10 yrs. and Payment of Taxes: 10 yrs.			10 yrs. required	
ALASKA	09.45.052		and Color of Title: 7 yrs.			Not required but is considered proof 559 P. 2d 1049	
ARIZONA	12-523 to 528	2 yrs. (if occupied with no claim to title)	and Color of Title: 3 yrs. or 5 yrs. if city lot		Taxes plus cultivation: 5 yrs.; Cultivation only: 10 yrs.	5 consecutive yrs. before suit to recover	
ARKANSAS	18-61-101, 18-11-101 et seq.	7 yrs.	Can't eject after 5 yrs.	After disability lifted: 3 yrs.		7 successive years	
CALIFORNIA	Civ. Proc. §§318, 325, 328		and Payment of Taxes: 5 yrs.	With disability: 20 yrs.; After disability lifted: 5 yrs.		5 years required	
COLORADO	38-41-101, *et seq.*	18 yrs.	and Color of Title/ Payment of Taxes: 7 yrs.	After disability lifted: 2 yrs.		7 years	
CONNECTICUT	52-575	15 yrs.		After disability lifted: 5 yrs.			
DELAWARE	Tit. 10 §§7901, *et seq.*	20 yrs.		After disability lifted: 10 yrs.			
DISTRICT OF COLUMBIA	12-301; 16-1113, 16-3301	15 yrs.		With disability: max. 22 yrs.; After disability lifted: 2 yrs.			
FLORIDA	95.16, 18, 191, 192		and Color of Title: 7 yrs. and Payment of Taxes: 7 yrs.				4 yrs.
GEORGIA	170, 171, 44-5-161, et seq.	20 yrs.	and Color of Title: 7 yrs.	Prescriptive period does not run until disability removed.			
HAWAII	657-31.5, 34; 669-1	20 yrs.		After disability lifted: 5 yrs.			
IDAHO	5-203 to 213		and Color of Title: 5 yrs. and Payment of Taxes: 5 yrs.	After disability lifted: 5 yrs.	Taxes plus cultivation 5 years	Required	

Table 40: Adverse Possession—Continued

State	Code Section	Prescriptive Period	Occupation	Time to Challenge	Improve-ments	Payment of Taxes	Title from Tax Assessor
ILLINOIS	735 ILCS 5/13-101, *et seq.*	20 yrs.	and Color of Title: 7 yrs. and Payment of Taxes: 7 yrs.	After disability lifted: 2 yrs.			7 yrs.
INDIANA	32-1-20-1 et seq. 34-11-1-2	10 yrs. (15 yrs. if cause of action arose before Sept. 1, 1982)		After disability lifted: 2 yrs.		Required	
IOWA	614.8, 17, 560.2	Within 1 year (after 7/1/80)	and Color of Title/Payment of taxes; 1 yr.	After disability lifted: 1 yr.			
KANSAS	60-503, 507, 508	15 yrs.		With disability: max. 23 yrs.; After disability lifted: 2 yrs.			
KENTUCKY	413.010, 060	15 yrs.	and Color of Title: 7 yrs.	After disability lifted: 7 yrs.			
LOUISIANA	C.C. Art. 3473, *et seq.*	30 yrs.	and Color of Title: 10 yrs.				
MAINE	Tit. 14 §§801, *et seq.*	20 yrs.	and Color of Title/payment of taxes: 20 years	After disability lifted: 10 yrs. notwithstanding 20 yrs. have expired		Required on uncultivated lands in unincorpo-rated areas	
MARYLAND	Cts. & Jud. Proc. §5-103, 201	20 yrs.		After disability lifted: 3 yrs.			
MASSACHUSETTS	260§21	20 yrs.					
MICHIGAN	MCL §600.5801, 5851	15 yrs.		After disability lifted: 1 yr.			10 years
MINNESOTA	541.02, 15	15 yrs.	and payment of taxes for 5 consecutive years	With disability: 5 yrs. (except for infancy); After disability lifted: 1 yr.			
MISSISSIPPI	15-1-7, 13, 15	10 yrs.	and Color of Title: 10 years and Payment of Taxes: 2 years	With disability: 31 yrs.; After disability lifted: 10 yrs.			3 yrs. after 2 yrs. from day of sale by tax collector
MISSOURI	516.010, 030	10 yrs.		After disability lifted: 3 yrs., max. 21 yrs.			

Table 40: Adverse Possession—Continued

State	Code Section	Prescriptive Period	Occupation	Time to Challenge	Improvements	Payment of Taxes	Title from Tax Assessor
MONTANA	70-19-401, 411, 413	5 yrs.	and Color of Title: 5 yrs. and Color of Title/Payment of Taxes: 5 yrs.	After disability lifted: 5 yrs.		Required	
NEBRASKA	25-202, 213	10 yrs.		With disability: 20 yrs.; After disability lifted: 10 yrs.			
NEVADA	11.070, 110, 150, 180	5 yrs.	and Color of Title: 5 yrs. and Color of Title/Payment of Taxes: 5 yrs.	After disability lifted: 2 yrs.		Required	
NEW HAMPSHIRE	508:2, 3	20 yrs.		After disability lifted: 5 yrs.			
NEW JERSEY	2A:14-30 to 32; 2A:62-2	30 yrs. or 60 yrs. if woodland	and Color of Title: 30 yrs. and Payment of Taxes: 5 yrs.	After disability lifted: 5 yrs.			
NEW MEXICO	37-1-22	10 yrs.	and Color of Title/ Payment of Taxes: 10 yrs.	After disability lifted: 1 yr.		Required	
NEW YORK	Real Prop. Acts & Procedures 501, *et seq.*	10 yrs.	and Color of Title: 10 yrs.				
NORTH CAROLINA	1-38, 40, 1-17	20 yrs.	and Color of Title: 7 yrs.	After disability lifted: 3 yrs.			
NORTH DAKOTA	28-01-04, 08, 14; 47-06-03	20 yrs.	and Color of Title: 20 yrs. and Color of Title/Payment of Taxes: 10 yrs.	After disability lifted: 10 yrs.			
OHIO	2305.04	21 yrs.		With disability: 21 yrs.; After disability lifted: 10 yrs.			
OKLAHOMA	12§93, 94	15 yrs.		After disability lifted: 2 yrs.			5 yrs.
OREGON	12.050, 160	10 yrs.		With disability: 5 yrs.; After disability lifted: 1 yr.			
PENNSYLVANIA	Tit. 42§5530	21 yrs.					
RHODE ISLAND	34-7-1	10 yrs.		After disability lifted: 10 yrs.			
SOUTH CAROLINA	15-67-210	10 yrs.	and Color of Title: 10 yrs.				

Table 40: Adverse Possession—Continued

State	Code Section	Prescriptive Period	Occupation	Time to Challenge	Improve-ments	Payment of Taxes	Title from Tax Assessor
SOUTH DAKOTA	15-3-1, 2, 14 to 16	20 yrs.	and Color of Title: 20 yrs. and Color of Title/Payment of Taxes: 10 yrs.	With disability: 20 yrs.; After disability lifted: 10 yrs.			
TENNESSEE	28-2-101, 102, 106, 109, 110	7 yrs.	and Payment of Taxes: 20 yrs.	After disability lifted: 3 yrs.			
TEXAS	Civ. Prac. & Rem. §16.024, *et seq.*	5 yrs.	and Color of Title: 3 yrs. and Color of Title/Payment of taxes: 5 yrs	With disability: 25 yrs.	Taxes plus cultivation: 5 yrs.; Cultivation only: 10 yrs.	Required	
UTAH	78-12-7, 12	7 yrs.	and Color of Title/ Payment of Taxes: 7 yrs.		Cultivation only: 7 yrs.	Required	
VERMONT	Tit. 12 §501	15 yrs.					
VIRGINIA	8.01-236, 237	15 yrs.	and Color of Title: 15 yrs	With disability: 25 yrs. max.			
WASHINGTON	7.28.050, 070, 090		and Color of Title: 7 yrs. and Color of Title/Payment of Taxes: 7 yrs.	Without disability: 3 yrs.		Required	
WEST VIRGINIA	55-2-1, 3	10 yrs.		After disability lifted: 5 yrs.			
WISCONSIN	893.16, 25 to 27	20 yrs.	and Color of Title: 10 yrs. and Color of Title/Payment of Taxes: 7 yrs.	With disability: 5 yrs., except when due to insanity or imprisonment. After disability lifted: 2 yrs.			
WYOMING	1-3-103, 104	10 yrs.		After disability lifted: 10 yrs.			

41. HOMESTEAD

Homestead laws are designed to protect small individual property owners and ordinary folks from the ravages of economic climates and conditions that are often harsh and out of their control. Homestead laws allow an individual to register a portion of his real and personal property as "homestead," thereby making that portion of the individual's estate off-limits to most creditors. The idea behind these homestead laws is the preservation of the family farm, home, or other assets in the face of severe economic conditions.

The items and amounts of money that can be set aside as a homestead are varied. The rules governing which property can be registered in this fashion seem to adhere to regional patterns. Real property that may be subject to the homestead exemptions vary in value from a $300 exemption from judgments in Pennsylvania to a $200,000 exemption for persons over age sixty-two in Massachusetts. They vary in character from the District of Columbia's allowable homestead of $200 worth of tools, and, if a professional, $300 worth of furniture, and $300 in clothes per person, to Colorado's unlimited acreage or Texas's 200 acres. In each case, the property that may be homesteaded is designed to perpetuate the family's estate and improve its chances for survival in hard times.

Limitations

The homestead is a back-up and a type of insurance against unexpected catastrophe; it will not ordinarily protect you from a bad business deal or from ordinary bankruptcy. Nonetheless, because an unscrupulous person could manipulate the homestead protections as a shield from living up to his legal obligations, there is much case law on homesteads. Indeed, ordinary business and commercial creditors ordinarily may penetrate property set aside as homestead.

Table 41: Homestead

State	Code Section	Maximum Value Of Property	Maximum Acreage (Urban)	Maximum Acreage (Rural)
ALABAMA	§6-10-2; Const. Art. X, §205	Const.: $2,000; Stat.: $5,000	Const.: Lot Stat.: Lot or track *Tyler* v. *Jewett* 82 Ala. 93	Const.: 80 acres; Stat.: 160 acres
ALASKA	09.38.010	$54,000		
ARIZONA	33-1101	$100,000		
ARKANSAS	16-66-210; Const. Art. IX, §4, §5	$2,500. All homesteads less than $1,000 assessed valuation are exempt from all state taxes referred to in art. XVI, §18 of Ark. Constitution. If homestead's value exceeds $1,000, exemption shall apply to first $1,000 of valuation (CONST. amend. XXII §1).	1 acre but not less than ¼ acre (without regard to valuation)	160 acres but not less than 80 acres (without regard to valuation)
CALIFORNIA	Civ. Proc. §704.710, *et seq.* For money judgments	$125,000 if either spouse is over 65 or disabled and unable to engage in substantial employment; $125,000 if person is 55 or older with gross income of not more than $15,000 or if married not more than $20,000 and sale is involuntary; $75,000 if debtor or spouse resides in house with at least one member of the family with no interest in the homestead; $50,000 for all others		
COLORADO	38-41-201	$30,000	No limits to acreage	No limits to acreage
CONNECTICUT	12-81(21)	$10,000 if disabled veteran; only $5,000 exemtion if loss the use of one arm or one leg ; $3,000 maximum income if unmarried and over 65; $5,000 maximum income if married and over 65; $6,000 maximum income for all others--combined adjusted gross income and tax exempt interest		
DELAWARE	Tit. 10 §4902 (personal property); Tit. 22 §1002	$75 trade, business in New Castle, Sussex County; $50 trade, business in Kent County; homestead exemption for persons 65 and older to be determined by local ordinance		
DISTRICT OF COLUMBIA	15-501 (personal property)	$200 for tools, $300 if professional or artist for furniture, $300 for clothes per person in value		
FLORIDA	§196.031; Const. Art. X, §4	$10,000 if person is over 65; $9,500 if totally disabled and is a permanent resident for 5 consecutive years prior to claim; $25,000 for taxes levied by governing bodies of school districts; $5,000 for all others	½ acre (Art. X, §4)	160 acres (§222.03; Art. X, §4)
GEORGIA	44-13-1	$5,000		

Table 41: Homestead—Continued

State	Code Section	Maximum Value Of Property	Maximum Acreage (Urban)	Maximum Acreage (Rural)
HAWAII	651-92	$30,000 if head of family or 65 years old; $20,000 for all others		
IDAHO	55-1001, 1003	Lesser of $50,000 or total net value of lands, mobile home, or improvements. Net value means market value minus all liens and encumbrances.		
ILLINOIS	735 ILCS 5/12-901	$7,500, if 2 or more own property, value of each proportional exemption can't exceed a total of $15,000		
INDIANA	34-55-10-2	$7,500 for residential; $4,000 for other real estate or tangible personal property; $100 for intangible personal property; total value of property may not exceed $10,000		
IOWA	561.1, *et seq.*	$500	½ acre	40 acres
KANSAS	60-2301		1 acre	160 acres
KENTUCKY	427.010, .080	$5,000 plus $3,000 in any personal property		
LOUISIANA	Const. Art. VII, §20	$7,500	160 acres	160 acres
MAINE	Tit. 14 §4422	$60,000 if debtor or dependent is either 60 or older, disabled, or unable to engage in gainful employment; Aggregate interest not to exceed $12,500 (or $25,000 if have minor dependents) including exemptions for car, clothing, furniture, jewelry, and tools of the trade		
MARYLAND	Cts. & Jud. PROC. §11-504	$3,000 plus an additional $2,500 in a Title 11 bankruptcy in value, in real property, or personal property		
MASSACHUSETTS	Ch. 188 §1, 1A	$200,000 if 62 or over or disabled, meeting the federal requirements of SSI; $100,000 for all others		
MICHIGAN	600.6023	$3,500	Lot	40 acres
MINNESOTA	510.01, *et seq.*	$200,000, or if primarily agricultural, $500,000	½ acre	160 acres
MISSISSIPPI	85-3-21	$75,000		160 acres
MISSOURI	513.475	$8,000		
MONTANA	70-32-101, 104	$40,000		
NEBRASKA	77-3502; 40-101	$10,000	1 acre (77-3502); 2 lots (40-101)	160 acres
NEVADA	115.010	$95,000		
NEW HAMPSHIRE	480: 1	$30,000		

Table 41: Homestead—Continued

State	Code Section	Maximum Value Of Property	Maximum Acreage (Urban)	Maximum Acreage (Rural)
NEW JERSEY	54: 4-8.57, *et seq.*; 2A: 17-19 personal property	$1,000 personal property; Homeowner, $150 min. rebate if income is less than $70,000; min. is $100 if income is between $70,000 and $100,000 Renter, $65 min. rebate if income is less than $70,000; min. is $35 if income is between $70,000 and $100,000	None	None
NEW MEXICO	42-10-1, 9, 10	$30,000 or in lieu thereof, $2,000 in any property; $500 for personal property		
NEW YORK	N.Y. Civ. Prac. L. & R. §5206	$10,000		
NORTH CAROLINA	Const. Art. X, §2	$1,000		
NORTH DAKOTA	47-18-01	$80,000		
OHIO	2329.66	$5,000		
OKLAHOMA	Tit. 31 §2		1 acre or maximum value of $5,000, but not less than ¼ acre without regard to valuation	160 acres
OREGON	23.240, 23.250	$25,000 or $33,000 if more than one debtor is subject to liability	1 block	160 acres
PENNSYLVANIA	Tit. 42 §8123; Tit. 72 §4751-3	$300 monetary exemption from judgment only; for senior citizens, a formula based on a sliding scale of income up to $15,000		
RHODE ISLAND	9-26-4	$500 for tools $1,000 for furniture	Allows for real property to be exempted but no limitation given in acreage	Allows for real property to be exempted but no limitation given in acreage
SOUTH CAROLINA	15-41-30	$5,000 up to a maximum of $10,000 if there are multiple exemptions on same living unit		
SOUTH DAKOTA	43-31-4		1 acre; mineral lands: 1 acre	160 acres; mineral lands: 40 acres placer claim; 5 acres lode mining
TENNESSEE	26-2-301	$5,000 or $7,500 if more than one debtor is subject to liability		
TEXAS	Const. Art. XVI, §51		1 acre	200 acres
UTAH	78-23-3	$8,000 if head of family; $2,000 for spouse; $500 for each dependent		
VERMONT	Tit. 27 §101	$30,000		
VIRGINIA	34-4	$5,000 plus if support dependent, then $500 for each dependent		

Table 41: Homestead—Continued

State	Code Section	Maximum Value Of Property	Maximum Acreage (Urban)	Maximum Acreage (Rural)
WASHINGTON	6.13.010, 030	$30,000		
WEST VIRGINIA	§38-9-1; Const. Art. VI, §43	$5,000		
WISCONSIN	815.20; 990.01 (14)	$40,000	Not less than ¼ acre or more than 40 acres	
WYOMING	1-20-101	$10,000		

42. LEASES AND RENTAL AGREEMENTS

When an individual agrees to rent or lease real estate property, he, the tenant, signs either a lease or a rental agreement with the owner of the property outlining the terms of the agreement. The difference between rentals and leases is that the terms of leases are generally for at least one year, though lease payments are usually paid by the month. Terms for rentals are generally month-to-month, although they are occasionally paid on a weekly term. Virtually all states recognize that at the end of a lease, the term converts to a month-to-month rental unless a new lease is signed and the landlord continues to accept monthly payments.

Many states have imposed limits on the size of security deposits safeguarding against damage to the property that may be collected by landlords. The highest deposit stated in a statute is three months' rent for a furnished property, but generally the limit is one month's rent. A number of states require landlords holding deposits to add interest when it is returned. Landlords are also required by most states to itemize any deductions taken from deposits and return them within set time periods after the lease is terminated.

Most states have statutes limiting discrimination by landlords. Under these statutes, landlords are prohibited from not renting to certain classes of people, for example, those with young children and pets. New classes are also finding their way into the law books. Since 1993 seven states have added sexual orientation, familial status, and national origin to the list of prohibited bases for discrimination by landlords. State legislatures generally ensure equal access to housing to the broadest range of citizens.

Table 42: Leases and Rental Agreements

State	Code Section	Terms of Leases	Deposits	Discrimination	Uniform Residential Landlord & Tenant Act Adopted?
ALABAMA	24-8-4; 24-8-7; 35-9-4	Renting for an unspecified term is presumed to be for the length of time used to estimate the rental amount, in absence of agreement respecting length of time for rent, renting is presumed to be monthly		No discrimination on basis of race, color, religion, sex, familial status, national origin; municipal corporations may zone/regulate as to different classes of inhabitants, but not to discriminate against or favor any class of inhabitants; housing for older persons exempted	No
ALASKA	18.80.210; 34.03.020, 070, 290	Unless otherwise agreed, rent is payable monthly and shall be term of month-to-month	Limit of 2 months rent (unless rent exceeds $2,000/month), interest on deposit not required; deposit must be returned within 14 days of termination if terminate under §§34.03.290, otherwise 30 days	No discrimination on basis of sex, physical/mental disability, marital status, changes in marital status, pregnancy, parenthood, race, religion, color, national origin	Yes
ARIZONA	9-462.01(11); 33-303, 342, 1321; 41-1491.14	Lease does not automatically renew but is converted into a tenancy from month-to-month	Limit 1½ months' rent; interest on deposit not required; deposit must be returned within 14 days of termination	No discrimination on basis of race, color, religion, sex, familial status, national origin; any municipality may establish age-specific community zoning and may restrict residency to head of household or spouse of specific age or older and prohibit minors; housing for older persons exempted	Yes
ARKANSAS	18-16-304, 305	When rent accepted by a landlord of a holding-over tenant, the term becomes a tenancy from year-to-year. (*Jonesboro Trust Co.* v. *Harbough,* 244 S.W. 455, 456 (Ark. 1922))	Limit of 2 months' rent; interest on deposit not required; deposit must be returned within 30 days of termination		No

Table 42: Leases and Rental Agreements—Continued

State	Code Section	Terms of Leases	Deposits	Discrimination	Uniform Residential Landlord & Tenant Act Adopted?
CALIFORNIA	C.C. §51.2, 1945, 1950.5; Govt. Code §§12920, 12955	If tenant remains in possession and landlord accepts rent, parties are presumed to have renewed lease on same terms and for same time, not to exceed 1 year	Limit 2 months rent for unfurnished, 3 months rent for furnished; interest on deposit not required; deposit must be refunded within 2 weeks of termination	No discrimination based on race, color, religion, sex, marital status, national origin, ancestry, familial status or disability; special accommodations for senior citizen housing, familial status or disability	No
COLORADO	13-40-104; 24-34-502; 38-12-102, *et seq.*		Interest on deposit not required; damages subtracted must be itemized and balance returned within 1 month of termination unless otherwise agreed, but never over 60 days.	No discrimination on basis of age, sex, marital status, handicap, race, religion, creed, color, national origin, but does not prohibit compliance with local zoning ordinance provisions concerning residential restrictions on marital status	No
CONNECTICUT	46a-64c; 47a-3d; 47a-21	Holdover not evidence of a new lease; converts to month-to-month	Tenant under 62: limit 2 months rent; tenant over 62: limit 1 month rent; interest on deposit required; deposit must be refunded within 30 days or within 15 days of receiving tenant's forwarding address	No discrimination on basis of race, creed, color, national origin, ancestry, sex, marital status, age, lawful source of income, familial status; may refuse to rent to people not blood related who are not married; public or private programs allowed to assist persons over 64 as long as there is no discrimination on basis of age among those eligible	No

Table 42: Leases and Rental Agreements—Continued

State	Code Section	Terms of Leases	Deposits	Discrimination	Uniform Residential Landlord & Tenant Act Adopted?
DELAWARE	Tit. 6 §4602; 25 §5511, 6503; 25§§6303-6304	Tenant remains in possession and landlord accepts rent, creation of new tenancy from year-to-year is inferred (*Makin* v. *Mack*, 336 A.2d 230 (1975)	Limit 1 month rent; interest on deposit not required; deposit must be returned within 15 days of termination; if deposit not returned within 30 days, tenant entitled to double the amount of security deposit	No discrimination on basis of race, age, marital status, creed, color, sex, handicap, national origin; landlord may reserve 10 or more units exclusively for rent by senior citizens (anyone over 62). Refusal to rent because of children in family, increase in rent, penalty, reservation of rental units for use by senior citizens, tenant may obtain summary of landlord-tenant code, use ignorance of law defense.	No
DISTRICT OF COLUMBIA	1-2515; 45-2555; Security Deposit Act 2/20/76, D.C. Law 1-48	Receipt of rent for new term or part thereof amounts to waiver of landlord's right to demand possession) *Shapiro* v. *Christopher*, 195 F.2d 785 (D.C. Cir. 1952); *Byrne* v. *Morrison*, 25 App. D.C. 72 (1905))	Interest on deposit required at 5% annually for all deposits after 2/20/76, only for deposit on tenancy for 12 months or more; deposit returned within 45 days of termination	No discrimination on basis of race, color, religion, national origin, sex, age, marital status, personal appearance, sexual orientation, family responsibilities, physical handicap, matriculation, political affiliation, source of income, place of residence or business; also illegal to discriminate against families receiving or eligible to receive Tenant Assistance Program assistance	No

Table 42: Leases and Rental Agreements—Continued

State	Code Section	Terms of Leases	Deposits	Discrimination	Uniform Residential Landlord & Tenant Act Adopted?
FLORIDA	83.04, 49; 760.23	Mere payment of rent is not construed as a renewal for the term; but if tenant holding over does so with written consent of landlord then it becomes a tenancy at will	No limits on deposits; landlord may elect to (1) put deposit in non-interest bearing account; (2) hold in interest bearing account at either 75% of average rate or 5%; or (3) post a surety bond and pay tenant interest at 5%; landlord must tell tenant in 30 days which he's doing; must return deposit within 15 days	No discrimination on basis of race, color, national origin, sex, handicap, or religion; same as Fair Housing Act	Yes
GEORGIA	8-3-201, 202; 44-7-31	Rent accepted after expiration of 1 year lease implies renewal of lease for another year (*Allen v. Montgomery,* 105 S.E. 33)	Deposit must be deposited in escrow account and held in trust for tenant; any damages subtracted must be itemized and deposit must be returned within 30 days of termination	No discrimination on basis of race, color, religion, sex, handicap, familial status, or national origin; allowable housing for "older people" included in statutes	No
HAWAII	515-3, 4; 521-44, 71	Landlord accepting rent in advance after First month of holdover creates a month-to-month tenancy absent contrary agreement; absence of any agreement makes term equal to that at which the rent is computed; notice to quit must give 25 days	Limit 1 month rent; no interest on deposit required; deposit must be returned within 14 days of termination	No discrimination on basis of HIV infection, race, sex, color, marital status, parental status, ancestry, handicapped status; section regarding parental status does not apply to housing for older persons as defined in 42 USC §2607(b)(2)	Yes

Table 42: Leases and Rental Agreements—Continued

State	Code Section	Terms of Leases	Deposits	Discrimination	Uniform Residential Landlord & Tenant Act Adopted?
IDAHO	6-321; 67-5909	Whether landlord waives right to give notice to quit the tenancy is question of intent; intent to waive must clearly appear; each case to be judged on case-by-case basis (*Riverside Dev. Co. v. Ritchie*, 650 P.2d 657, 663)	No limit on deposit; no interest on deposit required; deposit must be returned within max. of 21 days or within 30 days after surrender of possession by tenant	No discrimination on basis of race, color, religion, sex, national origin, with exceptions	No
ILLINOIS	65 ILCS 5/11-11.1-1; 775 ILCS 5/3-105, 106; 765 ILCS 715/1	Tenant holds over and landlord receives rent, presumed that new year-to-year tenancy created, absent express intent otherwise. (*Demerath v. Schennum*, 59 N.E.2d 348)	No limits on deposit; interest required on deposit at minimum deposit passbook savings account interest rate paid by largest commercial bank in the state if held for over 6 months and if lessor owns 25 units or more in one building or complex of buildings	No discrimination on basis of race, color, religion, sex, creed, ancestry, national origin, physical/mental handicap; statute repealed prohibiting discrimination against children; provisions for senior citizen housing	No
INDIANA	22-9.5-3-4; 22-9.5-5-1; 32-7-5-12	Holding over from a year tenancy and paying rent creates year-to-year tenancy (*Alleman v. Vink*, 62 N.E. 461)	No limits on deposit; interest on deposit not required; any damages subtracted must be itemized and returned within 45 days of termination	No discrimination on basis of race, color, religion, sex, familial status, handicap, or national origin; housing for older persons exempted	No
IOWA	562A.9(4); 562A.12; 601A; 216.8	Holding over converts to month-to-month tenancy	Limit 2 months rent; any interest earned on deposit for first 5 years of tenancy is landlord's property; deposit must be returned within 30 days if given forwarding address	No discrimination on basis of race, color, creed, sex, religion, origin, disability, or family status; housing for older persons exempted	Yes

Table 42: Leases and Rental Agreements—Continued

State	Code Section	Terms of Leases	Deposits	Discrimination	Uniform Residential Landlord & Tenant Act Adopted?
KANSAS	44-1016; 58-2545; 58-2550	Holdover converts to month-to-month tenancy	Limit 1 month rent; special rules for pets and furnishings; interest on deposit not required unless renting from municipal housing authority; deposit must be returned within 14 days and not to exceed 30 days along with itemized deductions	No discrimination on basis of race, religion, color, sex, disability, familial status, national origin or ancestry, or an intention to make any such preference, limitation, specification or discrimanation; housing for older persons exempted	Yes
KENTUCKY	344.360, 362; 383.565(3), 580	Holdover converts to month-to-month tenancy	No limit on deposit; interest on deposit not required; landlord must send notice to last known/ determinable address that tenant has a refund due; if tenant does not respond within 60 days, it becomes landlord's property	No discrimination on basis of race, color, religion, national origin, sex, familial status, disability; housing for older persons exempted; landlord may refuse to rent to unmarried couple	Yes
LOUISIANA	9:3251; 51:2602, 2605, 2606	Landlord's right to eject is waived when he accepts rent from holdover tenant (*Canal Realty & Improvement Co.* v. *Pailet,* 46 So.2d 303 (1950))	No limit on deposit; interest on deposit not required; deposit must be returned within one month of termination along with an itemized statement	No discrimination on basis of race, color, religion, sex, handicap, familial status, national origin; housing for older persons exempted	No
MAINE	Tit. 5§4552; 14§6031, *et seq.*		Limit 2 months rent; interest on deposit not required; deposit must be returned within 30 days if tenancy at will 21 days	No discrimination on basis of race, color, sex, physical or mental disability, religion, ancestry, national origin, familial status; housing for older persons exempted.	No

Table 42: Leases and Rental Agreements—Continued

State	Code Section	Terms of Leases	Deposits	Discrimination	Uniform Residential Landlord & Tenant Act Adopted?
MARYLAND	Real Prop. 8-203, 402; MD Code (1957) Art 49B §20, *et seq.*	Holdover tenancy becomes week-to-week if weekly before and month-to-month in all other cases	Limit greater of $50 or 2 months rent; interest on deposit required at 4% simple interest per year; landlord must return deposit within 45 days of termination	No discrimination on basis of race, religion, color, sex, national origin, marital status, handicap. If owner maintains personal residence in dwelling which has 5 or less units, owner may discriminate on sex or marital status. May rent to elderly exclusively only if dwelling planned specifically for specified age group	No
MASSACHUSETTS	Ch. 151B §4; Ch. 186 §15B	Payment and acceptance of rent create tenancy at will (*Staples* v. *Collins,* 73 N.E.2d 729 (1947)); certain acts/conduct may negate this presumption (*Corcoran Management Co., Ins.* v. *Withers,* 513 N.E.2d 218)	Limit 1 month rent; interest on deposit required at 5% from first day of tenancy if landlord has held deposit for one year; deposit must be returned within 30 days	No discrimination on basis of race, religious creed, color, national origin, sex, sexual orientation (unless orientation is for minor child), age, ancestry, marital status, member of armed forces, handicapped in any multiple dwelling, contiguously located housing accommodations or publicly assisted dwellings	

Table 42: Leases and Rental Agreements—Continued

State	Code Section	Terms of Leases	Deposits	Discrimination	Uniform Residential Landlord & Tenant Act Adopted?
MICHIGAN	37.2102; 37.2502; 37.2503; 554.601, *et seq.*	Holdover converts to year-to-year tenancy (*Faraci* v. *Fassvio,* 212 Mich. 216)	Limit 1 ½ months rent; interest on deposit not required	No discrimination on basis of religion, race, color, national origin, age, sex, height, weight, marital status. Housing programs for elderly exempted; children may be restricted to certain areas of complex (*Dept. of Civil Rights* v. *Beznos Co.,* 421 Mich. 110)) Represent to a person that real property is not available or deny real property to a person, for inspection, sale, rental, or lease when in fact it is so "available" Discriminate against a person in the brokering or appraising of real property. A person may not be denied access to, or membership or participate in, a multiple listing to do business of selling or renting because of race, religion, color, national origin, age, sex, familial status, or marital status.	No
MINNESOTA	363.02, 03; 504.07, 20	Period of the shortest interval between times of payment of rent under expired lease shall be implied	No limit on deposit; interest on deposit required at 4% until May 1, 1997, then 5.5% simple interest thereafter	No discrimination on basis of race, color, creed, religion, national origin, sex, marital status, disability, sexual orientation, familial status; housing for older persons exempted; landlords may advertise "adults only"	No
MISSISSIPPI	89-8-19, 21; 43-33-723	Holdover converts to month-to-month tenancy unless tenant pays weekly	No limit on deposit; interest on deposit not required; deposit must be returned within 45 days of termination	No discrimination on basis of race, religious principles, color, sex, national origin, ancestry, handicap, age, families because of children; housing for older persons exempted	No

Table 42: Leases and Rental Agreements—Continued

State	Code Section	Terms of Leases	Deposits	Discrimination	Uniform Residential Landlord & Tenant Act Adopted?
MISSOURI	108.470; 213.040; 441.060; 535.300	All tenancies not made in writing and signed by parties shall be held as month-to-month	Limit 2 months rent; interest on deposit not required; deposit must be must be returned within 30 days of termination	No discrimination on basis of race, color, religion, national origin, ancestry, sex, handicap; may not discriminate on marital status for housing loans	No
MONTANA	49-2-305; 70-24-201(2), 429; 70-25-201, *et seq.*	Holdover converts to month-to-month tenancy unless tenant pays weekly, then week-to-week	No limit on deposit; interest on deposit not required; before any damages are subtracted from deposit, landlord must give tenant an itemized list and provide an opportunity for tenant to clean or fix the problem; deposit must be returned within 10 days of termination	No discrimination on basis of sex, marital status, race, creed, religion, age, familial status, physical/mental handicap, color, national origin; housing for older persons exempted; landlord may discriminate against children in duplex in which owner resides in half	Yes
NEBRASKA	18-1724; 76-1414, 76-1416	Holdover converts to month-to-month tenancy unless tenant pays weekly, then week-to-week	Limit 1 month rent plus ¼ of 1 month rent pet deposit; deposit must be returned within 14 days after demand and designation of location to be mailed	No discrimination on basis of race, color, creed, religion, ancestry, sex, marital status, national origin, familial status, handicap or disability	Yes
NEVADA	118.010, *et seq.*; 118A.240; 118A.470; 207.300	Holdover converts to month-to month tenancy unless tenant pays weekly, then week-to-week	Limit 3 months rent; interest on deposit not required; deposit must be returned within 30 days of termination	No discrimination on basis of race, religious creed, color, national origin, disability, ancestry, familial status, sex	No

Table 42: Leases and Rental Agreements—Continued

State	Code Section	Terms of Leases	Deposits	Discrimination	Uniform Residential Landlord & Tenant Act Adopted?
NEW HAMPSHIRE	354-A:1; 540:1; 540-A:6, 7	Every tenancy shall be deemed to be at-will and rent payable on demand absent contrary contract shown	Limit 1 month rent or $100, whichever is greater. Interest on deposit required and must be returned to tenant if he holds the deposit for one year or longer; deposit must be retuned within 30 days	No discrimination on basis of age, sex, race, creed, color, marital status, physical/mental disability, national origin, familial status; retirement communities exempted	No
NEW JERSEY	2A:42-101; 10:5-4; 46:8-10; 46:8-21.1, 2	Holdover converts to month-to-month tenancy absent agreement to the contrary	Limit 1 ½ months rent; interest on deposit required; any damages subtracted from deposit must be itemized and balance of deposit must be returned within 30 days of termination	No discrimination on basis of race, creed, color, national origin, ancestry, age, marital status, affectionate or sexual orientation, familial status, or sex, subject only to conditions and limitations applicable alike to all persons; retirement communities exempted; landlord may discriminate against children in owner-occupied house with 2 dwelling units; housing opportunity declared to be a civil righ. No discrimination against buyer or renter because of the handicap of a person residing in or intending to reside in a dwelling after it is sold, rented or made available or because of any person associated with the buyer or renter	No

Table 42: Leases and Rental Agreements—Continued

State	Code Section	Terms of Leases	Deposits	Discrimination	Uniform Residential Landlord & Tenant Act Adopted?
NEW MEXICO	28-1-7(G); 47-8-15, 18, 37	Holdover converts to month-to-month tenancy unless tenant pays weekly, then week-to-week	If term is under one year, then limit is 1 month rent; interest on deposit required if landlord demands deposit in excess of 1 month rent; deposit must be returned within 30 days of termination or departure, whichever is later	No discrimination on basis of race, religion, color, national origin, ancestry, sex, or physical or mental handicap	Yes
NEW YORK	Real Prop. §§232-G 236-237; Exec. §296(5)(A); Rent & Evict. Regs. §2105.5; Gen. Oblig. §§7-103, 105	Holdover converts to month-to-month tenancy absent agreement otherwise	Limit 1 month rent; interest on deposit required	No discrimination on basis of race, creed, color, national origin, sex, age, disability, marital status, familial status; exception for housing accommodations exclusively for those 55 and older or same sex; landlord may discriminate against children in senior citizen housing, 1 or 2 family homes, mobile homes parks for those 55 or older	No

Table 42: Leases and Rental Agreements—Continued

State	Code Section	Terms of Leases	Deposits	Discrimination	Uniform Residential Landlord & Tenant Act Adopted?
NORTH CAROLINA	41A-4; 41A-6(e); 42-26; 42-50, *et seq.*	Landlord may treat tenant as trespasser and eject or may recognize him as tenant with presumption of year-to-year tenancy. (*Murrill* v. *Palmer,* 80 S.E. 55); this presumption is rebuttable and will yield to the actual intention of the parties (*Gurtis* v. *City of Sanford,* 197 S.E. 2d 584 (1973)	Limits: week-to-week, 2 weeks rent; month-to-month, 1 ½ months rent; over month-to-month, 2 months rent; interest on deposits not required; deposit must be returned within 30 days of termination	No discrimination on basis of race, religion, color, sex, national origin, handicap, or familial status; housing for older persons exempted. Exemptions to §41A-6 Not more than four (4) families living independently of each other within the same building. Rental of room or rooms in private house, not boarding house provided lesson or member of family live there also. Single sex dorminatories; private clubs not open to public; religious institutions , charitable organizaitons, etc. operated and owned by religious institutions.	No
NORTH DAKOTA	14-02.4-12; 47-16-06, 07.1	Lease renews on holdover for same time and terms as previous one but not exceeding one year	Limit 1 month rent; interest on deposit required unless occupancy less than 9 months; deposit must be returned within 30 days	No discrimination on basis of race, color, religion, sex, national origin, age, physical or mental handicap, or status in marriage or public assistance	No
OHIO	4112.02(H); 5321, *et seq.*	Presumption that holdover converts to year-to-year term but it is rebuttable (*Bumiller* v. *Walker,* 116 N.E. 797 (1917))	Limit greater of $50 or 1 month rent. Interest on deposit required at 5% per year if tenant remains in possession 6 months or more; deposit must be returned within 30 days of termination	No discrimination on basis of race, color, religion, sex, ancestry, handicap, national origin, familial status	No
OKLAHOMA	41 §§35, 115; 25 §1452, 1453	Parties presumed to have renewed lease for same terms and time, not exceeding 1 year	No limit on deposit; interest on deposit not required; deposit must be returned within 30 days of termination	No discrimination on basis of race, color, religion, gender, national origin, age, familial status, handicap; housing for older persons exempted	No

Table 42: Leases and Rental Agreements—Continued

State	Code Section	Terms of Leases	Deposits	Discrimination	Uniform Residential Landlord & Tenant Act Adopted?
OREGON	90.240(4), 300, 900; 659.033	Holdover converts to month-to-month tenancy	No limit on deposit; interest on deposit not required; deposit must be returned within 30 days after termination	No discrimination on basis of race, color, sex, marital status, familial status, religion, source of income or national origin; housing for older persons exempted	Yes
PENNSYLVANIA	Tit. 43 §955; Tit. 68 §250.511	Holdover converts to same term as original lease if it was for 1 year or less	Limit 2 months rent; interest on deposit required if deposit held over 2 years	No discrimination on basis of race, color, familial status, age, religious creed, ancestry, sex, national origin, handicap, disability; housing for older persons exempted	No
RHODE ISLAND	34-37-2; 34-18-19, 39	Parties may agree to a term, otherwise month-to-month unless tenant pays weekly, then week-to-week	Limit 1 month rent; interest on deposit not required; deposit must be returned within 20 days of termination	No discrimination on basis of race, color, religion, sex, sexual orientation, marital status, ancestral origin, handicap, age or familial status. Right to equal housing opportunities for all individuals in the state declared a civil right; housing specifically for older persons exempted; landlord may discriminate against children if house is 2 units, one of which is occupied by owner, or 4 units and one unit is owner-occupied and one occupied by senior citizen/infirm person for whom children would be a hardship	Yes
SOUTH CAROLINA	27-40-10, *et seq.*; 27-40-310, 27-40-410, 27-40-770; 31-21-10	Holdover converts to month-to-month tenancy unless tenant pays weekly, then week-to-week	No limit on deposit; interest on deposit not required; deposit must be returned within 30 days of termination	No discrimination on basis of race, color, religion, sex, familial status, or national origin; housing for older persons exempted; landlord may discriminate against children in single family dwellings and certain other small unit buildings	Yes

Table 42: Leases and Rental Agreements—Continued

State	Code Section	Terms of Leases	Deposits	Discrimination	Uniform Residential Landlord & Tenant Act Adopted?
SOUTH DAKOTA	20-13-20, *et seq.*; 43-32-6.1, 14, 24	Holdover converts to rental on same terms and same time as original lease	Limit 1 month rent, unless otherwise agreed because special conditions pose a danger to premises maintenance; interest on deposit not required; deposit must be returned within 2 weeks of termination	No discrimination on basis of race, color, creed, religion, sex, ancestry, disability, familial status or national origin; housing for older persons exempted; landlord may discriminate against children in duplexes where one unit is owner-occupied	No
TENNESSEE	4-21-601; 66-28-201, 301, 512	Holdover converts to month-to-month tenancy or upon agreement, apportionable day-to-day	No limit on deposit; interest on deposit not required	No discrimination on basis of race, color, creed, religion, sex, handicap, familial status, or national origin; housing for older persons exempted	Yes
TEXAS	Prop. §§92.101, *et seq.*; Tex. Rev. Civ. Stat. Ann. Art. 1f §1.01, *et seq.*	Holdover implies an agreement between landlord and tenant; normally lease for 1 year will be implied absent express or implied contrary agreement (*Barragan* v. *Munoz,* 525 S.W. 2d 559 (1975))	No limit on deposit; interest on deposit required; deposit must be returned within 30 days of termination	No discrimination on basis of race, color, religion, sex, familial status, national origin; housing for older persons exempted	No
UTAH	57-17-1, *et seq.*; 57-21-1, *et seq.*	Holdover tenant is bound to covenants previously agreed to and binding in first term (*Cottonwood Mall Co.* v. *Sine,* 767 P.2d 499, 503.)	No limit on deposit; interest on deposit not required; deposit must be returned within 15 days of termination or 30 days if there is damage to the rented premise	No discrimination on basis of race, color, religion, sex, national origin, familial status, source of income, disability; housing for older persons exempted; no discrimination against children unless in adults-only apartment complex, condo, or other housing not violating federal law	No

Table 42: Leases and Rental Agreements—Continued

State	Code Section	Terms of Leases	Deposits	Discrimination	Uniform Residential Landlord & Tenant Act Adopted?
VERMONT	Tit. 9 §4461, 4503	Holdover may convert into year-to-year tenancy; result of legal consequence of conduct of parties and does not depend on tenant's intention (*Malaitty* v. *Carroll Co.,* 41 A.2d 144 (Vt. 1945))	No limit on deposit; interest on deposit not required; deposit must be returned within 14 days of termination or landlord forfeits right to withhold any of it.	No discrimination on basis of race, sex, age, marital status, religious creed, color, national origin, handicap, recipient of public assistance, or because person intends to occupy with children; housing for older persons exempted	No
VIRGINIA	36-96, *et seq.*; 55-248	Holdover converts to month-to-month or any lesser term	Limit 2 months rent; interest on deposit held longer than 13 months required at rate equal to the Federal Reserve Board discount rate accrued every 6 months; deposit must be returned within 30 days of termination	No discrimination on basis of race, color, religion, national origin, sex, elderliness, or familial status; special provisions for housing for elderly	Yes
WASHINGTON	49.60.010; 59.04.010, 020; 59.18.260, *et seq.*	When term of tenancy is indefinite, period becomes that on which rent is payable	No limit on deposit, but no deposit may be collected unless rental agreement is in writing; interest on deposit not required; deposit must be returned within 14 days of termination	No discrimination on basis of race, creed, color, national origin, sex, marital status, age, or any sensory, mental, or physical handicap	No
WEST VIRGINIA	5-11A-5, 9; 37-6-5	Holdover converts to year-to-year tenancy upon terms of original lease (*Allen* v. *Bartlett,* 20 W. Va. 46)		No discrimination on basis of race, color, religion, ancestry, familial status, blindness, handicap, or national origin; housing for older persons exempted	No

Table 42: Leases and Rental Agreements—Continued

State	Code Section	Terms of Leases	Deposits	Discrimination	Uniform Residential Landlord & Tenant Act Adopted?
WISCONSIN	101.22; 704.25	Landlord may elect to hold tenant to month-to-month basis on holdover, unless the lease for weekly or daily rent		No discrimination on basis of race, sex, color, sexual orientation, disability, religion, national origin, marital status, family status, income source (lawful), age, ancestry; housing for older persons exempted	No
WYOMING	6-9-102; 34-2-128, 129	Accepting rent on holdover does not imply renewal, constitutes only tenancy by sufferance		No discrimination based on race, color, sex, creed, or national origin	No

VIII.   TAX LAWS

43. CONSUMER TAXES

The taxation system in the United States is very complicated due, in part, to the attempt by governing bodies to make taxation, across the board, appear reasonable and invisible.

Overall, there are two types of consumer taxes. Some are meant merely to raise revenues while others are designed to inhibit certain behavior. (In the income tax arena, however, which is significantly in the domain of the federal government, taxes and deductions and exemptions are used to actually promote certain behavior, such as saving money or buying a house.) In many cases, the behavioral control aspect of the tax has outweighed the particular tax's revenue-raising function. For example, tobacco-producing states do not have cigarette taxes (Kentucky, 3¢, North Carolina, 5¢, and Virginia, 2.5¢) that are as high as those in states that, for various reasons, attempt to inhibit smoking (Washington, 82.5¢, Michigan, 75¢ and New Jersey 80¢).

Market forces also influence consumer taxes. For example, the tax on wines produced in California is low compared to taxes on wines produced in other states. If California taxes were close to the national average, then California wines sold in other states would have artificially inflated prices, thus hurting its marketability.

The taxes treated in this chapter are not exhaustive. Rather, they are representative of the most common and significant consumer taxes levied by states.

Table 43: Consumer Taxes

State	Sales Tax	Cigarette Tax	Gasoline Tax	Use Tax	Liquor Tax	Gambling Tax
ALABAMA	4% §40-23-2	16.5¢ §40-25-2	12¢ §§40-17-31, 220	4% §§40-23-61, 63	Liquor monopoly state; Beer 5.0¢/12 oz. + 1.625¢/4 oz. (§§28-3-184, 190); Wine and spirits 10% wholesale price (§28-3-200) + 46% (§§28-3-201 to 205); Table wine 45¢/liter (§28-7-16) Native Farm wines 5.0¢/gallon	NA
ALASKA	None	29¢ §43.50.190, §43.50.090	8¢ §43.40.010	None	Beer 35¢/gal.; Wine and spirits ≤21% alcohol 85¢/gal., >21% $5.60/gal. §43.60.010	NA
ARIZONA	5% §42-1317	58¢ §§42-1204, 1231	18¢ §28-1501	Same as sales for same type of activity §42-1408	Beer 16¢/gal.; Wine <24% 84¢/gal., >24% 25¢/gal.; Spirits $3.00/gal. §42-1204	NA
ARKANSAS	4.5% §§26-52-301, 302	31.5¢ §26-57-208	18.5¢ §§26-55-205, 1002	4.5% §§26-52-302; 26-53-106, 107	Beer 20¢/gal.; Light wine 25¢/gal.; Wine 75¢/gal.; Spirits $2.50/gal. §3-7-104; Premixed spirits $1.00/gal.; Light spirits 50¢/gal.	NA
CALIFORNIA	6% Rev. & Tax §§6051 to 6051.4	37¢ Rev. & Tax §§30101, 30123	18¢ Rev. & Tax §7351	6% Rev. & Tax §§6201 to 6201.4	Beer $6.20/barrel; Still wines 20¢/gal.; Sparkling wine 30¢/gal.; Spirits $3.30/gal. Rev. & Tax §§32151, 32201, 32220	NA
COLORADO	3% §39-26-106	20¢ §39-28-103	22¢ §39-27-102	3% §39-26-202	Beer 8¢/gal.; Wine 7.33¢/liter (12.33¢/liter Colorado wines); Spirits 60.26¢/liter §§12-46-111, 127	Not to exceed 40% of adjusted gross profits §12-47.1-601
CONNECTICUT	6% §§12-408, 411	50¢ §12-296	36¢ 7/96; 37¢ 10/96; 38¢ 1/97; §12-458 35¢ 7/97 32¢ 7/98	6% §§12-408, 411	Beer $6.00/barrel; Still wine <21% 60¢/gal., >21% and sparkling wine $1.50/gal.; Spirits $4.50/gal. §12-435	NA

Table 43: Consumer Taxes—Continued

State	Sales Tax	Cigarette Tax	Gasoline Tax	Use Tax	Liquor Tax	Gambling Tax
DELAWARE	None	24¢ Tit. 30 §5305	23¢ Tit. 30 §5110	2% Tit. 30 §4302	Beer $4.85/barrel; Wine 97¢/gal.; Spirits <25% $2.50/gal., >25% $3.75/gal. Tit. 4 §§581, 709	NA
DISTRICT OF COLUMBIA	5.75% §47-2002	65¢ §47-2402	20¢ §47-2301	5.75% §47-2202	Beer $2.79/barrel; Wine <14% 30¢/gal, >14% 40¢/gal.; Sparkling wine 45¢/gal.; Spirits $1.50/gal. §§25-124, 138	NA
FLORIDA	6% §§212.03, *et. seq.*	33.9¢ §210.02	4¢ §206.41	6% §§212.03, *et seq.*	Beer 48¢/gal.; Wine <17.259% $2.25/gal., >17.259% $3.00/gal.; Sparkling wine $3.50/gal.; Spirits 17.259% to 55.78% $6.50/gal., >55.78% $9.53/gal. §§563.05; 564.06; 565.12	NA
GEORGIA	4% §48-8-30	12¢ §48-11-2	7.5¢ + 3% of retail sale price §48-9-3	4% §48-8-30	Beer $10/barrel, in bottles or cans 4.5¢/12 oz.; Wine 40¢/liter + 27¢ excise tax on dessert wine; Spirits 50¢/liter, $1.20/liter imported §§3-5-60; 3-6-50; 3-4-60, 3-5-80	NA
HAWAII	4% §237-13	60¢ §245-3	16¢ + additional county rates §243-4, 5	4% §238-2	Draft beer 53¢/gal.; Bottle beer 92¢/gal.; Still wine $1.36/gal.; Sparkling wine $2.09/gal.; Spirits $5.92/gal. §244D-4; rates adjusted semiannually	NA
IDAHO	5% §§63-3619, 3621	28¢ §63-2506	25¢ §§63-2402, 2405, 2416, 2417	5% §§63-3619, 3621	Liquor monopoly state; Beer $4.65/barrel; Wine 45¢/gal.; 15% of price per unit on all goods sold in state dispensary 23-217, 1319, 1008	

Table 43: Consumer Taxes—Continued

State	Sales Tax	Cigarette Tax	Gasoline Tax	Use Tax	Liquor Tax	Gambling Tax
ILLINOIS	6.25% 35 ILCS 120/2-10	44¢ 35 ILCS 130/2	19¢ 35 ILCS 505/2	6.25% 35 ILCS 105/3-10	Beer 7¢/gal.; Wine <14% 23¢/gal., >14% 60¢/gal.; Spirits $2.00/gal. 235 ILCS 5/8-1	Riverboat gambling tax $2 per person admitted; wagering tax 20% adjusted gross receipts 230 ILCS 10/ 12, 230 ILCS 10/13
INDIANA	5% §§6-2.5-2-2, 6-2.5-3-3	15.5¢ §6-7-1-12	15¢ §6-6-1.1-201	5% §§6-2.5-2-2, 6-2.5-3-3	Beer 11.5¢/gal.; Wine <21% 47¢/gal., >21% $2.68/gal.; Spirits $2.68/gal. §§7.1-4-2-1; 7.1-4-3-1; 7.1-4-5-1	NA
IOWA	5% §422.43	36¢ §453A.6	20¢ §452A.3	5% §423.2	Liquor monopoly state; Beer $5.89/barrel; Wine $1.75/gal. §§123, 123.22, 136, 183	Excursion boat gambling tax: 5% on first $1 million; 10% next $2 million; 20% over $3 million (after 12/31/96, over $3 million: 22%, increasing 2%/yr. to a maximum of 36%§99F.11
KANSAS	4.9% §79-3603	24¢ §79-3310	18¢ §§79-34, 141	4.9% §79-3703	Beer 18¢/gal.; Wine <14% 30¢/gal., >14% 75¢/gal.; Spirits $2.50/gal. §§41-501(b); 79-3818, 4101, 41a02	NA
KENTUCKY	6% §§139.200, 310	3¢ §138.140	15¢ (9% of average wholesale price plus supplementary highway user motor fuel tax, computed quarterly) §138.220	6% §§139.200, 310	Beer $2.50/barrel; Wine 50¢/gal.; Spirits $1.92/gal. §§243.720	NA
LOUISIANA	4% §§; 47:302, 331	20¢ §47:841	20¢ §§47:711, 820.1	4% §§; 47:302, 331	Beer $10/barrel; Still wine <14% 3¢/liter, 14-24% 6¢/liter, >24% 42¢/liter; Sparkling wine 42¢/liter; Spirits 66¢/liter §§26:341, 342	NA

Table 43: Consumer Taxes—Continued

State	Sales Tax	Cigarette Tax	Gasoline Tax	Use Tax	Liquor Tax	Gambling Tax
MAINE	6% Tit. 36 §§1811, 1861	37¢ Tit. 36§4365	19¢ Tit. 36 §2903	6% Tit. 36 §§1811, 1861	Liquor monopoly state; Beer 35¢/gal.; Wine 60¢/gal.; Sparkling wine $1.24/ gal.; Spirits: Commission must sell at price that will produce state liquor tax of at least 65% of delivered case cost plus $1.25/ proof gal. Tit. 28-A §§1651, 1652, 1703	NA
MARYLAND	5% Tax-Gen. §11-104	36¢ Tax-Gen. §12-105	23.5¢ Tax-Gen. §9-305	5% Tax-Gen. §11-104	Beer 9¢/gal.; Wine 40¢/gal.; Spirits $1.50 gal.; Tax-Gen. §5-201.105	NA
MASSACHUSETTS	5% Ch. 64H §2	51¢ Ch. 64C §6	21¢ (19.1% of average price, but minimum cannot be less than 21¢/gal.) Ch. 62C§3A; Ch. 64A§1; Ch. 64E§4; Ch. 64F§3	5% Ch. 64I §2	Beer $3.30/barrel; Still wine 55¢/gal.; Sparkling wine 70¢/ gal.; Spirits <15% $1.10/ proof gal., 15-50% $4.05/proof gal., >50% $4.05/proof gal. Ch. 138 §21	NA
MICHIGAN	6% §205.52	75¢ §§205.427	19¢ §§207.102; 259.203	6% §205.93	Liquor monopoly state; Beer $6.30/gal.; Wine <16% 13.5¢/ liter, >16% 20¢/liter; Spirits offsale 13.85% of retail selling price, onsale 12% of retail selling price §§436.16, 40, 101, 121	NA
MINNESOTA	6.59% + 1.5% state-imposed local use tax§§297A.02, 14	48¢ §297F.05	20¢ §296A.07	65% + 1.5% state-imposed local use tax §§297A.02, 14	Beer 3.2% $2.40/ barrel, >3.2% $4.60/ barrel; Wine 14% 30¢/gal., 14-21% 95¢/gal., 21-24% $1.82/gal., >24% $3.52/gal.; Sparkling wine $1.82/ gal.; Spirits $5.03/gal. §297G.03, 297G.04	Horseracing 6% of net receipts plus 1% of gross bets §240.15; Gambling 9.5% other than pull tabs and tip boards §297E.02

Table 43: Consumer Taxes—Continued

State	Sales Tax	Cigarette Tax	Gasoline Tax	Use Tax	Liquor Tax	Gambling Tax
MISSISSIPPI	7% §§27-65-15, *et seq.*	18¢ §27-69-13	18¢ §27-55-11	Same rate as sales tax 27-67-5	Liquor monopoly state; Beer, light wine 42.68¢/gal.; Wine 35¢/gal.; Sparkling wine $1/gal.; Spirits $2.50/gal. A 27.5% markup is imposed on all alcoholic beverages sold by the Alcoholic Beverage Control Division §§27-71-7, 5, 201, 307, 335; 67-1-41	4% <$50,000/mo., 6% $50,000-134,000/mo.; 8% over $134,000/mo. §75-76-177
MISSOURI	4% + 1.5% state-imposed local use tax §144.020; Mo. Const. Art. IV §§43(a) and 47(c)	17¢ §149.015	17¢ §142.025	Same rate as sales tax §144.610	Beer $1.86/barrel; Wine 30¢/gal.; Spirits $2/gal. §§311.550; 312.320, 520	Riverboat gambling tax: $2.00 per person admitted, 20% on adjusted gross receipts §313.820
MONTANA	None	18¢ §16-11-111	27¢ §15-70-204	None	Liquor monopoly state; Beer $4.30/barrel; Wine 28¢/liter; Spirits 22.4% retail selling price for companies <200,000 gal./year nationwide, 26% for >200,000 gal./year §§16-1-401, 404, 406, 411; 16-2-301	NA
NEBRASKA	4.5% (Legislature is required to set rate each year) §§77-2701.02, 2715.01 July 1, 1999 5%	34¢ §77-2602	24.8¢ §§66-4, 105; 66-4,144; 66-4,145; 66-4,146; 66-489	§§77-2701.02, 2715.01 4.5% July 1, 1999 5%	Beer 23¢/gal.; Wine <14% 75¢/gal., >14% $1.35/gal.; Spirits $3.00/gal.; Wine from farm wineries 5¢/gal. §53-160	NA
NEVADA	6.5% §§372.105, 185; 374.110, 190; 377.040	35¢ §370.165	23.9¢ §§365.170, 180, 190, 192	6.5% §§372.105, 185; 374.110, 190; 377.040	Beer 9¢/gal.; Wine <14% 40¢/gal., 14-22% 75¢/gal., >22% $2.05/gal. §369.330	Gross revenues <$50,000/mo. 3%; $50,000-134,000 4%; >$134,000 6.25% §§463.320,370

Table 43: Consumer Taxes—Continued

State	Sales Tax	Cigarette Tax	Gasoline Tax	Use Tax	Liquor Tax	Gambling Tax
NEW HAMPSHIRE	None	37¢ §78:7	18¢ §260:32	None	Liquor monopoly state; 30¢/gal. on all beverages sold at retail; Domestic wine 5% of gross sales §§177:1; 178:6, 28, 30	NA
NEW JERSEY	6% §54:32B-3	80¢ §54:40A-8	10.5¢ §54:39-27	6% §54:32B-6	Beer 12¢/gal.; Wine 70¢/gal.; Spirits $4.40/gal. §54:43-1	8% of gross revenues §5:12-144
NEW MEXICO	5% §7-9-4	21¢ §7-12-3	17¢ §7-13-3	5% §7-9-7	Beer 41¢/gal.; Wine 45¢/liter; Spirits $1.60/liter §7-17-5	NA
NEW YORK	4% Tax §§1105, 1110	56¢ §471	8¢ §§284, *et seq.*	4% §§1105, 1110	Beer 21¢/gal.; Still and sparkling wine 18.93¢/liter/gal. (natural); Spirits <24% 67¢/gal.; other $1.70/liter Tax Ch. 60 §424	NA
NORTH CAROLINA	4% §105-164.4	5¢ §105-113.5	17.5¢ §105-449.80	4% §105-164.4	Liquor monopoly state; Beer 48.387¢/gal. in barrels, 53.376¢/gal. in containers <7.75 gal.; Wine 21¢/liter unfortified, 24¢/liter fortified; Spirits 28% retail §§105-113.80; 18A-15(3)(c)	NA
NORTH DAKOTA	5% §§57-39.2-02.1, 03.2	44¢ §§57-36-06, 27	20¢ §57-43.1-02	5% §§57-40.2-02.1, 57-40.2-03.2	Beer 8¢/gal. in barrels, 16¢/gal. in bottles; Wine <17% 50¢/gal.; 17-24% 60¢/gal.; Sparkling wine $1.00/gal.; Spirits $2.50/gal. §5-03-07	NA

Table 43: Consumer Taxes—Continued

State	Sales Tax	Cigarette Tax	Gasoline Tax	Use Tax	Liquor Tax	Gambling Tax
OHIO	5% §5739.025	24¢ §§5743.02, 023, 32, 322	.02¢ §§5735.25; 5735.05	Same rate as sales tax §5741.02	Liquor monopoly state; Beer $5.58/barrel; bottled: .14¢/oz. <12 oz.; .84¢/6oz. in containers >12 oz.; Wine 4-14% 32¢/gal., 14-21% $1.00/gal.; Vermouth $1.10/gal.; Sparkling wine $1.50/gal.; Spirits $1.20/gal. §§4301.10, 12, 42, 43, 4305.01, 09; 4307.02; 4309.04	NA
OKLAHOMA	4.5% Tit. 68 §§1354; 1362	.08¢ Tit. 68 §§302	16¢ + 1¢ if sold by distributor Tit. 68 §§500.4	4.5% §1402	Beer <3.2% $11.25/barrel, >3.2% $12.50/barrel; Wine <14% 19¢/liter, >14% 37¢/liter; Sparkling wine 55¢/liter; Spirits $1.47/liter Tit. 37 §§163.3; 553; 576	NA
OREGON	None	58¢ §323.030	24¢ §319.020	None	Liquor monopoly state; Beer $2.60/barrel; Alcoholic beverages <14% 67¢/gal., 14-21% 77¢/gal.; Oregon Liquor Control Commission fixes prices §§471.725, 730; 473.030	NA
PENNSYLVANIA	6% Tit. 72 §§7202, 7210	31¢ Tit. 72 §8206	12.5¢ Tit. 72 §§2611d, 2612.1; Tit. 75 §9511.1	6% Tit. 72 §§7202; 7210	Liquor monopoly state; Beer 8¢/gal.; Wine.5-24%.005/unit proof/gal.; Spirits $1.00/gal. Tit. 47 §§301, 746, 747, 795	NA

Table 43: Consumer Taxes—Continued

State	Sales Tax	Cigarette Tax	Gasoline Tax	Use Tax	Liquor Tax	Gambling Tax
RHODE ISLAND	7% §§44-18-18, 20	71¢ §44-20-12	28¢ §31-36-7	7% §44-18-20	Made in state: Beer .097¢/gal., $3.00/barrel; Still wine 60¢/gal. (from Rhode Island grapes 30¢); Sparkling wine 75¢/gal.; Spirits $3.75/gal. Imported into state: Beer .065¢/gal., $2.00/barrel; Still wine 40¢/gal.; Sparkling wine 50¢/gal.; Spirits $2.50/gal. §3-10-1	NA
SOUTH CAROLINA	5% §§12-36-910, 2620	7¢ §12-21-620	16¢ §§12-28-310, 320, 330	5% §§12-36-1310, 2620	Beer <5% .006¢/gal.; Wine <21% 90¢/gal.; All other alcoholic beverages 12¢/8oz. or 50.7¢/liter; Wholesalers are subject to additional tax; Additional excise tax on sale of wine §§12-21-1020, 1030, 1040, 1310; 12-33-230, 240, 410, 425, 460	NA
SOUTH DAKOTA	4% §10-45-2	33¢ §§10-50-3; 10-50-10	18¢ §10-47B-4	Same general rates as sales tax §§10-46-2	Beer $8.50/barrel; Wine 3.2-14% 93¢/gal., 14-20% $1.45/gal., 21-24% (except sparkling) $2.07/gal.; All other $3.93/gal.; Additional 2% imposed on all but malt beverages by wholesaler from distiller, manufacturer, or supplier §§35-5-3; 35-5-6.1	8% of adjusted gross proceeds; May be decreased or increased by Commission on Gaming from 5-15% §42-7B-28
TENNESSEE	6% 67-6-202, 205, 209, 221	13¢ + 5¢ for dealers or distributors §§67-4-1004, 1005	20¢ 67-3-1301	6% 67-6-202, 205, 209, 221	Beer <5% $3.90/barrel; Wine <21% $1.10/gal.; Spirits $4/gal., <7% $1.10/gal. §§57-3-302, 303; 57-5-201	NA

Table 43: Consumer Taxes—Continued

State	Sales Tax	Cigarette Tax	Gasoline Tax	Use Tax	Liquor Tax	Gambling Tax
TEXAS	6.25% Tax §§151.051, 101	41¢ Tax §154.021	20¢ Tax §153.102	6.25% Tax §§151.051, 101	Beer $6.00/barrel; Malt liquor >4% 19.8¢/gal.; Still wine <14% 20.4¢/gal., >14% 40.8¢/gal.; Sparkling wine 51.6¢/gal.; Spirits $2.40/gal. (minimum tax 5¢/pkg. <2 oz., 12.2¢/pkg 8 oz.) Tax §§201.01, *et seq.*	Bingo Enabling Act 5% gross receipts (state); 2% gross receipts (local); 3% facility rental; 3% prize Civ. Stat. Art. 179d
UTAH	4.75% §59-12-103	26.5¢ §§59-14-204, 302	19.5¢ §59-13-201	4.75% §59-12-103	Liquor monopoly state; Beer $11/barrel; 13% retail purchase price all other §§32A-2-101; 59-15-101; 59-16-100	NA
VERMONT	5% Tit. 32 §9771	44¢ §7771	15¢ Tit. 10 §1942, Tit. 32 §9773	4% Tit. §9773	Liquor monopoly state; Beer 26.5¢/gal. if <6% and 55¢/gal. if 6-8%; Wine 55¢/gal.; Spirits and fortified wine 25% of gross revenues Tit. 7 §§421, 422	NA
VIRGINIA	3.5% §§58.1-603, 604	2.5¢ §§58.1-1001, 1018	17.5¢ §58.1-2105	3.5% §§58.1-603, 604	Liquor monopoly state; Beer $25.65/barrel, 2¢/bottle <7 oz., 2.65¢/bottle 7-12 oz., 2.22 mills/oz./bottle >12 oz.; Wine 40¢/liter §§4-128; 4-22.1	NA
WASHINGTON	6.5% §82.08.020	81.5¢; 82.5¢ after 6/96 §§82.24.020, 027	23¢ §82.36.025	6.5% §82.12.020	Liquor monopoly state; Beer $2.60/barrel + $2.00/barrel, $20.50/liter; Wine <14% 21.50¢/liter, >14% 43.94¢/liter + 1¢/liter on all other wine; Additional tax on sales of wine and beer at 7% of basic tax rates §§66.08.050; 66.24.210, 220, 290; 82.02.030	NA

Table 43: Consumer Taxes—Continued

State	Sales Tax	Cigarette Tax	Gasoline Tax	Use Tax	Liquor Tax	Gambling Tax
WEST VIRGINIA	6% §11-15-9	17¢ §11-17-3	20.5¢ §11-14-3	6% §11-15A-2	Nonintoxicating beer $5.50/barrel; Intoxicating liquor 5% of purchase price §11-16-13 60-3A-21	NA
WISCONSIN	5% §§77.52, 53	59¢ §139.31(1)	23.4¢ §§78.01, 015, 40, 405, 017, 407	5% §77.52, 53	Beer $2/barrel; Wine <14% 6.605¢/liter, 14-21% 11.89¢/liter; All other 85.86¢/liter; administrative fee on all beverages >21% 3¢/gal.; Other intoxicating liquor 85.86¢/liter §§139.02, 03, 06	NA
WYOMING	4% §39-15-104	12¢ §39-18-104	14¢ §39-17-104	4% §39-16-104	Liquor monopoly state; Beer .5¢/liter; Wine .75¢/ml.; Spirits 2.5¢/100 ml. §12-3-101	NA

44. PERSONAL INCOME TAX

If you live in Alaska, Florida, Nevada, South Dakota, Texas, Washington, or Wyoming, you may not be aware that most of the rest of the country has to file two tax returns every April. Every other state, aside from these lucky seven, requires income tax—over and above federal taxes—from its citizens.

Deductions and exemptions available to the taxpayer can be very detailed and vary greatly from state to state. Because of their number, no attempt has been made here to list them. As an example, Tennessee claims one of the more interesting exemptions: the income of a prisoner of war is not taxed. There is also a provision to exempt all income of estates of individuals who perished in Operations Desert Storm and Desert Shield. Wisconsin has a "recycling tax surcharge" for all people or entities filing returns; the only exemption is for entities engaged in farming. The surcharge lasts until 1999 and carries a maximum of $9,800 per year.

North Dakota has the highest percentage tax rate at 12 percent of taxable income over $50,000. Massachusetts taxes interest, capital gains, and dividends at 12 percent. California and Montana are next with 11 percent rates. Hawaii has a 10 percent rate, and after that states tend to group together. Most rates in the higher brackets are in the 5 percent to 8 percent range. However, Rhode Island and Vermont tax at rates of up to 32% and 25%, respectively, but the percentages are applied to the total federal tax liability and are not applied directly to the taxpayer's income.

Arizona and Ohio have the highest income brackets: $300,000 and over, and $200,000 and over respectively. The intent here is clearly to have the rich pay taxes at higher rates and shoulder more of the load for maintaining the revenue base; a pragmatic view, however, is that higher brackets protect those in the middle from the higher rates at the top. New Jersey is the only other state with an income tax bracket over $150,000. Most states have an upper bracket that is below $60,000.

Six states (and the District of Columbia) have had their income tax schemes challenged in court: Delaware, Illinois, Michigan, Nebraska, Ohio, and Oklahoma. All of these tax codes have been "certified" constitutional by federal courts.

The chart in this chapter deals only with the general principles of state personal income tax. The tax tables are accurate but are very much consolidated and generalized in order to give the reader a broad basis for comparison. The rates listed are, for the most part, for married couples filing jointly or for heads of households. Where this is not the case, the rate is noted. Slightly different rates and tables will apply in most states for couples filing separately or for single individuals. Also, there are countless deductions and exemptions available to the taxpayer that are similar to those available in the federal income tax code. Included here are only the general deductions and exemptions for determining state taxable income. See your state codes or the code of the state in which you are interested for detailed information.

Table 44: Personal Income Tax

State	Code Section	Who is Required to File	Rate	Federal Income Tax Deductible	Federal Income Used as Basis
ALABAMA	40-18-1, *et seq.*	Resident natural persons, fiduciaries, estates and trusts, and nonresidents receiving income from property owned or business transacted in the state	First $1,000, 2%; Next $5,000, 4%; Over $6,000, 5%	Yes	Yes
ALASKA	Income tax repealed 1/1/79, Alaska Laws 1980, 2d Sp. Sess. §9, ch. 2	Individual may file at his or her option to obtain certain tax credits for political donations or expenses for household and child care necessary for employment. Credit allowed only if legislature appropriates money.			
ARIZONA	43-1011, *et seq.*	All Arizona residents and nonresidents that derive income from activity or ownership of property within the state; Partnerships are not taxable	First $20,000, 2.90%; Next $30,000, 3.3%; Next $50,000, 3.90%; Next $200,000, 4.80%; $300,001 and over, 5.17%	No	Yes
ARKANSAS	26-51-201, *et seq.*	Resident individuals, estates and trusts, and nonresidents deriving income from local property or activity; Partnerships are not taxable	First $2,999, 1%; Next $3,000, 2.5%; Next $3,000, 3.5%; Next $6,000, 4.5%; Next $10,000, 6%; $25,000 or over, 7%; general rate for all taxpayers; special reduced rates available for low income	No	No
CALIFORNIA	REV. & TAX CODE §§17041, *et seq.*	Resident persons, including estates and trusts; nonresidents and part-year residents are liable for pro-rata share	$0 to $7,300 = 1%; $7,301 to $17,300 = $73 plus 2% of the excess over $7,301; $17,301 to $22,300 = $273 plus 4% of the excess over $17,301; $22,301 to $27,600 = $473 plus 6% of the excess over $22,301; $27,601 to $32,600 = $791 plus 8% of the excess over $27,601; over $32,600 = $1,191 plus 9.3% of the excess over $32,600;	No	Yes

Table 44: Personal Income Tax—Continued

State	Code Section	Who is Required to File	Rate	Federal Income Tax Deductible	Federal Income Used as Basis
COLORADO	39-22-104, *et seq.*	Every individual, estate, and trust that is required to file federal return; non- and part-year residents are liable for pro-rata share; Partnerships are not subject to tax	5% of federal taxable income; general rate for all taxpayers; alternative rates may apply	No	Yes
CONNECTICUT	51, *et seq.*, act 3, Laws (1991), 1st sp. sess. Act 160, Law 1995 §12-700, *et seq.*	Each resident individual, trust, and estate with Connecticut taxable income; Nonresident individuals, estates, and trusts on Connecticut income	$0 to $3,500 = 3.0% $3,501 and over = $105 plus 4.5% of the excess over $3,501	No	Yes
DELAWARE	Tit .30 §1102, *et seq.*	Individuals, estates, and trusts with Delaware taxable income; Residents and nonresidents of Wilmington are subject to an additional tax of 1.25% on all wages, salaries, commissions, and net profit	First $9,000, 3%; over $9,000, $180 plus 4.5% excess	No	Yes; $2,000 to $5,000, 2.6%; $5,001 to $10,000, 4.3%; $10,001 to $20,000, 5.2%; $20,001 to $25,000, 5.60%; $25,001 to $60,000, 5.95%; Over $60,001, 6.40%
DISTRICT OF COLUMBIA	47-1806, *et seq.*	Any individual domiciled in the district, any resident of 183 days or more, and estates and trusts	First $10,000, 6%; $10,001 to $20,000 = $600 plus 8% of excess over $10,000; Over $20,000 = $1,400 plus 10% of excess over $20,000; general rate for all resident taxpayers	No	Yes
FLORIDA	No personal income tax				

Table 44: Personal Income Tax—Continued

State	Code Section	Who is Required to File	Rate	Federal Income Tax Deductible	Federal Income Used as Basis
GEORGIA	48-7-1, *et seq.* Act 912 Law 1994	Resident and non-resident individuals with taxable net income and estates and trusts; Partnerships are not taxable; Counties and municipalities may levy a 1% tax on an entire taxable net income	First $1,000 = 1%; $1,000 to $3,000 = $10 plus 2% of amount over $1,000; $3,000 to $5,000 = $50 plus 3% of amount over $3,000; $5,000 to $7,000 = $110 plus 4% of amount over $5,000; $7,000 to $10,000 = $190 plus 5% of amount over $7,000; Over $10,000 = $340 plus 6% of amount over $10,000	No	Yes
HAWAII	235, *et seq.*	Resident individual, estate or trust, and nonresident individual estates or trusts on income derived from Hawaii sources	First $4,000 = 1.6%; $4,000 to $8,000 = $64 plus 3.9% of excess over $4,000; $8,000 to $16,000 = $220 plus 6.8% of excess over $8,000; $16,000 to $24,000 = $764 plus 7.2% of excess over $16,000; $24,000 to $32,000 = $1,340 plus 7.5% of excess over $24,000; $32,000 to $40,000 = $1,940 plus 7.8% of excess over $32,000; $40,000 to $60,000 = $2,564 plus 8.2% of excess over $40,000; $60,000 to $80,000 = $4,204 plus 8.5% of excess over $60,000 Over 80,000 = $5,904 plus 8.75% of excess over $80,000	No	Yes

Table 44: Personal Income Tax—Continued

State	Code Section	Who is Required to File	Rate	Federal Income Tax Deductible	Federal Income Used as Basis
IDAHO	63-3024, *et seq.* Ch. 111 Law 1995	Resident individuals, estates and trusts with taxable income and nonresident or part-year resident individuals, estates and trusts from Idaho sources; Partnerships are not taxable	Under $1,000 = 2% $1,000 but less than $2,000 = $20 plus 4% of excess over $1,000; $2,000 but less than $3,000 = $60 plus 4.5% of excess over $2,000; $3,000 but less than $4,000 = $105 plus 5.5% of excess over $3,000; $4,000 but less than $5,000 = $160 plus 6.5% of excess over $4,000; $5,000 but less than $7,500 = $225 plus 7.5% of excess over $5,000; $7,500 but less than $20,000 = $412.50 plus 7.8% of excess over $7,500; Over $20,000 = $1,387.50 plus 8.2% of excess over $20,000; for married couples filing joint return, tax is twice tax imposed on half of aggregate Idaho taxable income	No	Yes
ILLINOIS	35 ILCS 5/201, *et seq.*	Individuals, estates, and trusts; Partnerships are not taxable	3% of taxable net income imposed on all taxpayers; An additional personal property replacement tax of 1.5% of net income is imposed on partnerships, trusts, and S corporations.	No	Yes
INDIANA	6-3-2-1, *et seq.*	Resident individuals, estates and trusts, and nonresidents on adjusted gross income derived from Indiana sources; Partnerships are not taxable	3.4% of adjusted gross income; general rate for all resident taxpayers; additional local taxes may be required	No	Yes

Table 44: Personal Income Tax—Continued

State	Code Section	Who is Required to File	Rate	Federal Income Tax Deductible	Federal Income Used as Basis
IOWA	422, *et seq.*	Residents, part-year residents, nonresidents, estates and trusts	$0 to $1,060 = .4%; $1,060 to $2,120 = $4.24 plus 0.8% of excess over $1,060; $2,120 to $4,240 = $12.72 plus 2.7% of excess over $2,120; $4,240 to $9,540 = $69.96 plus 5% of excess over $4,240; $9,540 to $15,900 = $334.96 plus 6.8% of excess over $9,540; $15,900 to $21,200 = $767.44 plus 7.2% of excess over $15,900; $21,200 to $31,800 = $1,149.04 plus 7.55% of excess over $21,200; $31,800 to $47,700 = $1,949.34 plus 8.8% of excess over $31,800; Over $47,700 = $3,348.54 plus 9.98% of excess over $47,700; general rate for all taxpayers; an alternative minimum tax is imposed equal to 75% of the maximum state individual income tax rate for the tax year of the state alternative minimum taxable income; no tax for residents or nonresidents who make less than $9,000 in net income; local taxes may also be required	Yes	Yes
KANSAS	79-32, 110, *et seq.*	Resident and nonresidents, estates, trusts and fiduciaries; Partnerships and S corporations are not taxable	First $30,000 = 3.5%; $30,000 to $60,000 = $1,050 plus 6.25% of excess over $30,000; Over $60,000 = $2,925 plus 6.45% of excess over $60,000	No	Yes
KENTUCKY	141.020, *et seq.*	Residents, nonresidents on net income from businesses, trade, professions or other activities carried on in the state or tangible or intangible property located in the state	First $3,000, 2%; Next $1,000, 3%; Next $1,000, 4%; Next $3,000, 5%; $8,000 and over 6%; general rate for all taxpayers; local taxes may also be required	No	Yes

Table 44: Personal Income Tax—Continued

State	Code Section	Who is Required to File	Rate	Federal Income Tax Deductible	Federal Income Used as Basis
LOUISIANA	47:200, *et seq.*	Residents and nonresidents on Louisiana income; Individuals permanently domiciled in the state are taxed on all income from whatever source; All others are taxed on Louisiana income; Partnerships are not taxable	First $10,000, 2%; Next $40,000, 4%; Over $50,000, 6%; (Maximum tax rates for individuals); Joint returns: tax is determined as if net income and personal exemption credits were reduced by half	No	Yes
MAINE	Title 36 §§5111, *et seq.*	Every resident: entire taxable income and nonresidents: adjusted gross income, estates, and trusts: entire taxable income; Partnerships and LLC's are not taxable	Less than $6,100 = 2%; $6,100 to $12,150 = $122 plus 4.5% of the excess over $6,100; $12,150 to $24,300 = $394 plus 7% of the excess over $12,150; $24,300 or more = $1,245 plus 8.5% of the excess over $24,300; Beginning in 1997-98 married couples filing joint returns with less than $60,000 will get lower tax rates if their preceding fiscal year tax revenue exceeds a target amount	No	Yes
MARYLAND	Tax-Gen. Art. 10-102, *et seq.*	Residents and nonresidents on taxable net income. Partnerships are not taxed.	First $1,000, 2%; Second $1,000, 3%; Third $1,000, 4%; Over $3,000, 5%; local taxes may be required	No	Yes
MASSACHUSETTS	Ch. 62, generally	Individuals, including fiduciaries, estates of deceased Massachusetts inhabitants, and nonresidents earning income in Massachusetts; Partnerships and S corporations are not taxed; A "corporate trust" engaged in business in Massachusetts is taxed	Interest, dividends, net capital gains, 12%; All other income 5.95%; plus after 1995 various rates for net capital gains and losses; no tax can exceed 10% Massachusetts AGI in excess over specified threshold unless AGI exceeds 1.75 times the threshold	No	Yes
MICHIGAN	206.51	Individuals, estates, and trusts; Each person with business activity in Michigan allocated or apportioned to Michigan is subject to the single business tax; Partnerships and S corporations are not taxable	4.4% of taxable income; local taxes may be required	No	Yes

Table 44: Personal Income Tax—Continued

State	Code Section	Who is Required to File	Rate	Federal Income Tax Deductible	Federal Income Used as Basis
MINNESOTA	290.01, *et seq.*	Resident and nonresident individuals, estates and trusts	$0 to $19,910, 6%; $19,911 to $79,120, 8%; Over $79,120, 8.5% (married individuals filing jointly and surviving spouses)	No	Yes
MISSISSIPPI	27-7-5, *et seq.*	Resident individuals, trusts and estates on entire net income from property owned or sold and business trade or occupation carried on in Mississippi by nonresident individuals, partnerships, trusts and estates; Partnerships and S corporations are not taxable	First $5,000, 3%; Next $5,000, 4%; Over $10,000, 5%	No	No
MISSOURI	143.011, *et seq.*	Resident individuals, nonresidents with income derived from Missouri sources, and estates and trusts; Partnerships are not taxable; local taxes may be required	First $1,000 = 1.5%; Next $1,000 = $15 plus 2% of excess over $1,000; Next $1,000 = $35 plus 2.5% of excess over $2,000; Next $1,000 = $60 plus 3% of excess over $3,000; Next $1,000 = $90 plus 3.5% of excess over $4,000; Next $1,000 = $125 plus 4% of excess over $5,000; Next $1,000 = $165 plus 4.5% of excess over $6,000; Next $1,000 = $210 plus 5% of excess over $7,000; Next $1,000 = $260 plus 5.5% of excess over $8,000; Next $1,000 = $315 plus 6% of excess over $9,000	Yes	Yes

Table 44: Personal Income Tax—Continued

State	Code Section	Who is Required to File	Rate	Federal Income Tax Deductible	Federal Income Used as Basis
MONTANA	15-30-101, *et seq.*	Residents on entire net income; Nonresidents on net income from property owned and business carried on in Montana; Estates and trusts are taxed during administration except if for educational, charitable, or religious purposes; Partnerships and S corporations are not taxed	First $1,800 = 2%; $1,801 to $3,600 = 3% less $18; $3,601 to $7,200 = 4% less $54; $7,201 to $10,700 = 5% less $126; $10,701 to $14,300 = 6% less $233; $14,301 to $17,900 = 7% less $376; $17,901 to $25,100 = 8% less $555; $25,101 to $35,800 = 9% less $806; $35,801 to $62,700 = 10% less $1,164; Over $62,700 = 11% less $1,791	Yes	Yes
NEBRASKA	77-2701, *et seq.*	Residents on entire income and nonresidents on income derived from Nebraska sources; Estates and trusts are taxable; Partnerships and S corporations are not taxable	First $4,000, 2.62%; Next $26,000, 3.65%; Next $16,750, 5.24%; Over $46,750, 6.99%	No	Yes
NEVADA	No personal income tax				
NEW HAMPSHIRE	77:1-1, *et seq.*	Inhabitants and part-year residents, partnerships, associations and trusts, and fiduciaries with income of more than $2,400 per year	5%, limited to interest and dividends	No	No
NEW JERSEY	54A:1, *et seq.*	Individuals, estates and trusts, residents and nonresident taxed on gross income; Nonresidents are only taxed on income derived from New Jersey sources; Partnerships and associations are not taxable; Local taxes may be required	First $20,000 = 1.4%; $20,001 to $50,000 = $280 plus 1.75% of excess over $20,000; $50,001 to $70,000 = $805 plus 2.45% of excess over $50,000; $70,001 to $80,000 = $1,295 plus 3.5% of excess over $70,000; $80,001 to $150,000 = $1,645 plus 5.525% of excess over $80,000; Over $150,000 = $5,512.50 plus 6.37% of excess over $150,000	No	No

Table 44: Personal Income Tax—Continued

State	Code Section	Who is Required to File	Rate	Federal Income Tax Deductible	Federal Income Used as Basis
NEW MEXICO	7-2-7, *et seq.*	Residents on net income and nonresidents deriving income from business, employment, or property in New Mexico, including estates and trusts	First $7,000 = 1.7%; $7,001 to $14,000 = $119 plus 3.2% of excess over $7,001; $14,001 to $20,000 = $343 plus 4.7% of excess over $14,001; $20,001 to $33,000 = $625 plus 6.0% of excess over $20,001; $33,001 to $53,000 = $1,405 plus 7.1% of excess over $33,001; $53,001 to $83,000 = $2,825 plus 7.9% of excess over $53,001; Over $83,000 = $5,195 plus 8.2% of excess over $83,000	No	Yes
NEW YORK	Tax 601, *et seq.* Ch. 60 §601	Individuals, estates and trusts, and nonresidents on income derived from New York sources; Partnerships are not taxable; New York City taxes resident individuals, estates, and trusts on their city taxable income; Partnerships are not taxable (§§11-1701, *et seq.*); A city income tax surcharge of 15% of net state tax is imposed on resident individuals, estates, and trusts of Yonkers	First $16,000 = 4%; $16,001 to $22,000 = $640 plus 4.5% of excess over $16,001; $22,001 to $26,000 = $910 plus 5.25% of excess over $22,001; $26,001 to $40,000 = $1,120 plus 5.9% of excess over $26,001; Over $40,000 = $1,946 plus 6.85% of excess over $40,000	No	Yes
NORTH CAROLINA	105-134, *et seq.*	Every individual on North Carolina taxable income, and income of estates and trusts; Partnerships are not taxable	Up to $21,250, 6%; Next $78,750, 7%; Over $100,000, 7.75%	No	Yes
NORTH DAKOTA	57-38-02, *et seq.*	Residents and nonresidents on property owned, employment, or business carried on in North Dakota; Individuals, estates, and trusts have optional tax available (§57-38-30.3); Partnerships are not taxed	First $3,000, 2.67%; Next $2,000, 4%; Next $3,000, 5.33%; Next $7,000, 6.67%; Next $10,000, 8%; Next $10,000, 9.33%; Next $15,000, 10.67%; Over $50,000, 12%	Yes	Yes

Table 44: Personal Income Tax—Continued

State	Code Section	Who is Required to File	Rate	Federal Income Tax Deductible	Federal Income Used as Basis
OHIO	5747.01, *et seq.*	Every individual and estate residing in or earning or receiving income in Ohio; Partnerships are not taxable; Local taxes may be required	First $5,000 = 0.743%; $5,000 to $10,000 = $37.15 plus 1.486% of excess over $5,000; $10,000 to $15,000 = $111.45 plus 2.972% of excess over $10,000; $15,000 to $20,000 = $260.05 plus 3.715% of excess over $15,000; $20,000 to $40,000 = $445.80 plus 4.457% of excess over $20,000; $40,000 to $80,000 = $1,337.20 plus 5.201% of excess over $40,000; $80,000 to $100,000 = $3,417.60 plus 5.943% of excess over $80,000; $100,000 to $200,000 = $4,606.20 plus 6.9% of excess over $100,000; Over $200,000 = $11,506.20 plus 7.5% of excess over $200,000	No	Yes
OKLAHOMA	Title 68 §2355, *et seq.*	Resident and nonresident individuals, estates, and trusts on taxable Oklahoma income; Partnerships are not taxable	First $2,000, 0.5%; Next $3,000, 1%; Next $2,500, 2%; Next $2,300, 3%; Next $2,400, 4%; Next $2,800, 5%; Next $6,000, 6%; Remainder 7%	Yes	Yes
OREGON	316.037, *et seq.*	Every Oregon resident on entire taxable income and every nonresident or part-year resident on a prorated amount of their entire taxable income; Estates and trusts are taxable; Partnerships are not taxable; Local taxes may be required	First $2,000 = 5%; $2,001 to $5,000 = $100 plus 7% of the excess over $2,000; Over 5,000 =$310 plus 9% of the excess over $5,000	Yes	Yes
PENNSYLVANIA	Tit. 72 §§7301, *et seq.*	Resident and nonresident individuals, estates, or trusts; Nonresidents only pay for portion of income derived from Pennsylvania sources; Partnerships and associations are not taxable; Local taxes may be required	2.8%	No	No

Table 44: Personal Income Tax—Continued

State	Code Section	Who is Required to File	Rate	Federal Income Tax Deductible	Federal Income Used as Basis
RHODE ISLAND	44-30-1, *et seq.*	Resident and nonresident individuals, estates, and trusts on Rhode Island income; Partnerships are not taxed	If federal income tax liability is greater than $15,000: 27.5% of federal income tax liability up to $15,000 and 32% of federal income tax liability over $15,000	No	Yes
SOUTH CAROLINA	12-6-510, *et seq.*	Individuals, estates, and trusts; Partnerships are not subject to tax; Part-year and nonresidents are subject to special tax	First $2,220 = 2.5%; $2,221 to $4,440 = $56 plus 3% of excess; $4,441 to $6,660 = $123 plus 4% of excess; $6,661 to $8,880 = $212 plus 5% of excess; $8,881 to $11,100 = $323 plus 6% of excess; Over $11,100 = $456 plus 7% of excess	No	Yes
SOUTH DAKOTA	No personal income tax				
TENNESSEE	67-2-101, *et seq.*	Resident persons, partnerships, associations, trusts, estates, and corporations	6%, limited to interest and dividends, not including ordinary commercial paper, trade acceptances and CD's, and certificates of deposit	No	No
TEXAS	No personal income tax				
UTAH	59-10-104, *et seq.*	Resident individuals, estates and trusts, and nonresidents on state taxable income derived from Utah sources; Partnerships are not taxable	First $1,500 = 2.3%; $1,500 to $3,000 = $35.00 plus 3.3% of excess over $1,500; $3,000 to $4,500 = $84.00 plus 4.2% of excess over $3,000; $4,500 to $6,000 = $147.00 plus 5.2% of excess over $4,500; $6,000 to $7,500 = $225.00 plus 6% of excess over $6,000; Over $7,500 = $315.00 plus 7% of excess over $7,500	Yes, but only half	Yes
VERMONT	Tit. 32 §§5822, *et seq.*	Residents, nonresidents, estates, and trusts on Vermont income	28% of federal income tax	No	Yes

Table 44: Personal Income Tax—Continued

State	Code Section	Who is Required to File	Rate	Federal Income Tax Deductible	Federal Income Used as Basis
VIRGINIA	58.1-320, *et seq.*	Individuals, estates, and trusts; Partnerships are not taxable; Estates and trusts are subject to tax on their Virginia taxable income; Local taxes may be required	First $3,000, 2%; Next $2,000, 3%; Next $12,000, 5%; Over $17,000, 5.75%	No	Yes
WASHINGTON	No personal income tax				
WEST VIRGINIA	11-21-4e	Every individual, estate, and trust; Special tax on nonresidents with West Virginia income; Partnerships are not taxable	First $10,000 = 3%; $10,000 to $25,000 = $300 plus 4% of excess over $10,000; $25,000 to $40,000 = $900 plus 4.5% of excess over $25,000; $40,000 to $60,000 = $1,575 plus 6% of excess over $40,000; Over $60,000 = $2,775 plus 6.5% of excess over $60,000	No	Yes
WISCONSIN	71.02, *et seq.*	Individuals, fiduciaries (except fiduciaries of nuclear decomposing trust or reserve fund), and trusts on net income; nonresident individuals and trusts on income derived from Wisconsin sources; nonresident's and part-year resident's tax liability is prorated according to amount of income derived from Wisconsin sources; Special "recycling surcharges" apply to all Wisconsin individuals, estates, trusts, businesses, and partnerships except those engaged solely in farming	$0 to $10,000, 4.9%; $10,001 to $20,000, 6.55%; $20,001 and over 6.93%	No	Yes
WYOMING	No personal income tax				

APPENDIX
STATUTORY COMPILATIONS USED IN THIS BOOK

The code section numbers used in this book refer to sections within the statutory compilations listed below. In those states where multiple compilations are available, the one preferred by **The Blue Book, A Uniform System of Citation,** 15th ed., 1991 (Harvard Law Review Association: Cambridge, Mass.) is used. Occasionally the preferred code was not available; every effort, however, was then made to verify the accuracy of the citations and/or convert section numbers to the preferred system.

Some states do not use a universal system of numeration but separately number individually named codes. For these states the individual code names and the abbreviations used in the book are listed.

Table 45: Statutory Compilations

State	Statutory Compilation	Abbreviation
ALABAMA	Code of Alabama	
ALASKA	Alaska Statutes	
ARIZONA	Arizone Revised Statues Annotated	
ARKANSAS	Arkansas Code of 1987 Annotated	
CALIFORNIA	West's Annotated California Code	
	The following are the named codes in the California codification:	
	Business & Professions	Bus. & Prof.
	Civil	Civ.
	Civil Procedure	Civ. Proc.
	Commercial	Com.
	Corporations	Corp.
	Education	Educ.
	Election	Elec.
	Evidence	Evid.
	Financial	Fin.
	Fish and Game	Fish & Game
	Food and Agricultural	Food & Agric.
	Government	Gov't
	Harbors and Navigation	Harb. & Nav.
	Health and Safety	Health & Safety
	Insurance	Ins.
	Labor	Lab.

(Continued)

667

Table 45: Statutory Compilations—Continued

State	Statutory Compilation	Abbrevation
	Military and Veterans	Mil. & Vt.
	Penal	Pen.
	Probate	Prob.
	Public Contract	Pub. Cont.
	Public Resources	Pub. Res.
	Public Utilities	Pub. Util.
	Revenue and Taxation	Rev. & Tax
	Streets and Highways	Sts. & High.
	Unemployment Insurance	Unemp. Ins.
	Vehicle	Veh.
	Water	Wat.
	Welfare and Institutions	Welf. & Inst.
COLORADO	West's Colorado Revised Statutes Annotated	
CONNECTICUT	Connecticut General Statutes Annotated (West)	
DELAWARE	Delaware Code Annotated	
DISTRICT OF COLUMBIA	District of Columbia Code Annotated	
FLORIDA	Florida Statutes Annotated (West)	
GEORGIA	Code of Georgia Annotated (Harrison)	
HAWAII	Hawaii Revised Statutes	
IDAHO	Idaho Code	
ILLINOIS	West's Smith-Hurd Illinois Compiled Statues Annotated	
INDIANA	Burns Indiana Statutes Annotated Code Edition	
IOWA	Code of Iowa (1991); Iowa Code Annotated (West)	
KANSAS	Kansas Statutes Annotated	
KENTUCKY	Kentucky Revised Statues Annotated, Official Edition (Michie/Bobbs-Merrill)	
LOUISIANA	West's Louisiana Revised Statutes Annotated	
	West's Louisiana Civil Code Annotated	
MAINE	Maine Revised Statutes Annotated (West)	
MARYLAND	Annotated Code of Maryland	
	The following are the named codes in the Maryland codification:	
	Agriculture	Agric.
	Alcoholic Beverages	Alco. Bev.
	Business Occupations and Professions	Bus. Occ. & Prof.
	Commercial Law I	Com. Law I
	Commercial Law II	Com. Law II
	Constitutions	Const.

(Continued)

Table 45: Statutory Compilations—Continued

State	Statutory Compilation	Abbrevation
	Corporations and Associations	Corps. & Ass'ns.
	Courts and Judicial Proceedings	Cts. & Jud. Proc.
	Criminal Law	Crim. Law
	Economic Development	Econ. Dev.
	Education	Educ.
	Elections	Elec.
	Environment	Envir.
	Estates and Trusts	Est. & Trusts
	Family Law	Fam. Law
	Financial Institutions	Fin. Inst.
	General Provisions	Gen. Prov.
	Health-Environmental	Health-Envtl.
	Health-General	Health-Gen.
	Health Occupations	Health Occ.
	Insurance	Ins.
	Local Government	Local Gov't
	Natural Resources	Nat. Res.
	Public Safety	Pub. Safety
	Real Property	Real Prop.
	Social Services	Soc. Serv.
	State Finance and Procurement	State Fin. & Proc.
	State Government	State Gov't
	State Personnel	State Pers.
	Tax-General	Tax-Gen.
	Tax-Property	Tax-Prop.
	Transportation	Transp.
	Annotation Code of Maryland (1957)	__§__
MASSACHUSETTS	Annotated Laws of Massachusetts	
MICHIGAN	Michigan Statutes Annotated (Callaghan)	
MINNESOTA	Minnesota Statues Annotated (West)	
MISSISSIPPI	Mississippi Code Annotated	
MISSOURI	Vernon's Annotated Missouri Statutes	
MONTANA	Montana Code Annotated	
NEBRASKA	Revised Statutes of Nebraska	
NEVADA	Nevada Revised Statutes	
NEW HAMPSHIRE	New Hampshire Revised Statutes Annotated	
NEW JERSEY	New Jersey Statutes Annotated (West)	

(Continued)

Table 45: Statutory Compilations—Continued

State	Statutory Compilation	Abbreviation
NEW MEXICO	New Mexico Statutes Annotated	
NEW YORK	McKinney's Consolidated Laws of New York Annotated	
	Consolidated Laws Service.	
	The following are the named codes in the New York codification:	
	Abandoned Property	Aband. Prop.
	Agricultural Conservation and Adjustment	Agric. Conserv. & Adj.
	Agriculture and Markets	Agric. & Mkts
	Alcoholic Beverage Control	Alco. Bev Cont
	Alternative County Government	Alt County Gov't
	Arts and Cultural Government	Arts & Cult.
	Aff.	
	Banking	Banking
	Benevolent Orders	Ben. Ord.
	Business Corporations	Bus. Corp.
	Canal	Canal
	Civil Practice Law and Rules	N.Y. Civ. Prac. L.&R.
	Civil Rights	Civ. Rights
	Civil Service	Civ. Serv.
	Commerce	Com.
	Cooperative Corporations	Coop. Corp.
	Correction	Correct.
	County	County
	Criminal Procedure	Crim. Proc.
	Debtor and Creditor	Debt. & Cred.
	Domestic Relations	Dom. Rel.
	Education	Educ.
	Election	Elec.
	Eminent Domain Procedure Law	Em. Dom. Proc.
	Employers' Liability	Empl'rs Liab.
	Energy	Energy
	Environmental Conservation	Envtl. Conserv.
	Estates, Powers and Trusts	Est. Powers & Trusts
	Executive	Exec.
	General Association	Gen. Ass'ns
	General Business	Gen. Bus.
	General City	Gen. City
	General Construction	Gen.Constr.

(Continued)

Table 45: Statutory Compilations—Continued

State	Statutory Compilation	Abbrevation
	General Municipal	Gen. Mun.
	General Obligations	Gen. Oblig.
	Highway	High.
	Indian	Indian
	Insurance	Ins.
	Judiciary	Jud.
	Labor	Lab.
	Legislative	Leg.
	Lien	Lien
	Local Finance	Local Fin.
	Mental Hygiene	Mental Hyg.
	Military	Mil.
	Multiple Dwelling	Mult. Dwell.
	Multiple Residence	Mult. Res.
	Municipal Home Rule	Mun. Home Rule
	Navigation	Nav.
	Not-for-Profit Corporation	Not-for-Profit Corp.
	Optional County Government	Opt. County Govt.
	Parks, Recreation and Historic Preservation	Parks, Rec. & Hist. Preserv.
	Partnership	Partnership
	Penal	Penal
	Personal Property	Pers. Prop.
	Private Housing Finance	Priv. Hous. Fin.
	Public Authorities	Pub. Auth.
	Public Buildings	Pub. Bldgs.
	Public Health	Pub. Health
	Public Housing	Pub. Hous.
	Public Lands	Pub. Lands
	Public Officers	Pub. Off.
	Public Service	Pub. Serv.
	Racing, Pari-Mutuel Wagering and Breeding	Rac. Pari-Mut. Wag. & Breed.
	Railroad	R.R.
	Rapid Transit	Rapid Trans.
	Real Property	Real Prop.
	Real Property Actions and Proceedings	Real Prop. Acts.
	Real Property Tax	Real Prop. Tax
	Religious Corporations	Rel. Corp.

(Continued)

Table 45: Statutory Compilations—Continued

State	Statutory Compilation	Abbrevation
	Retirement and Social Security	Ret. & Soc. Sec.
	Rural Electric Cooperative	Rural Elec. Coop.
	Second Class Cities	Second Class Cities
	Social Services	Soc. Serv.
	Soil and Water Conservation Districts	Soil & Water Conserv. Dist.
	State Administrative Procedure Act	A.P.A.
	State Finance	State Fin.
	State Law	State L.
	State Printing and Public Documents	State Print. & Pub. Doc.
	Statute of Local Governments	Stat. Local Gov'ts
	Surrogate's Court Procedure Act	Surr. Ct. Proc. Act
	Tax	Tax
	Town	Town
	Transportation	Transp.
	Transportation Corporations	Transp. Corp.
	Uniform Commercial Code	U.C.C.
	Uniform Commercial Code Appendix	U.C.C. App.
	Unconsolidated	Unconsol.
	Vehicle and Traffic	Veh. & Traf.
	Village	Vill.
	Volunteer Firefighters' Benefit	Vol. Fire. Ben.
	Workers' Compensation	Work. Comp.
NORTH CAROLINA	General Statues of North Carolina	
NORTH DAKOTA	North Dakota Century Code	
OHIO	Ohio Revised Code Annotated (Anderson)	
OREGON	Oregon Revised Statutes	
PENNSYLVANIA	Purdon's Pennsylvania Consolidated Statutes Annotated (by title)	
RHODE ISLAND	General Laws of Rhode Island	
SOUTH CAROLINA	Code of Laws of South Carolina 1976 Annotated (Law. Co-op.)	
SOUTH DAKOTA	South Dakota Codified Laws Annotated	
TENNESSEE	Tennessee Code Annotated	
TEXAS	Vernon's Texas Codes Annotated	
	The following are the named codes found in the Texas codification:	
	Agriculture	Agric.
	Alcoholic Beverage	Alco. Bev.
	Business and Commerce	Bus. & Com.

(Continued)

Table 45: Statutory Compilations—Continued

State	Statutory Compilation	Abbrevation
	Civil Practice and Remedies	Civ. Prac. & Rem.
	Corporations and Associations	Corps. & Ass'ns
	Criminal Procedure	Crim. Proc.
	Education	Educ.
	Election	Elec.
	Family	Fam.
	Financial	Fin.
	Government	Gov't
	Health and Safety	Health & Safety
	Highway	High.
	Human Resources	Hum. Res.
	Insurance	Ins.
	Labor	Lab.
	Local Government	Local Gov't
	Natural Resources	Nat. Res.
	Occupations	Occ.
	Parks and Wildlife	Parks & Wild.
	Penal	Penal
	Probate	Prob.
	Property	Prop.
	Resources	Res.
	Tax	Tax
	Utilities	Util.
	Vehicles	Veh.
	Water	Water
	Welfare	Welf.
	Vernon's Texas Revised Civil Statues Annotated	
	Vernon's Texas Code of Criminal Procedure Annotated	
UTAH	Utah Code Annotated	
VERMONT	Vermont Statues Annotated	
VIRGINIA	Code of Virginia Annotated	
WASHINGTON	Revised Code of Washington Annotated	
WEST VIRGINIA	West Virginia Code	
WISCONSIN	West's Wisconsin Statues Annotated	
WYOMING	Wyoming Statutes Annotated (Michie)	